CW00552481

# BRITISH RAILWAYS
# LOCOMOTIVES &
# COACHING STOCK
# 2014

The Complete Guide to all
Locomotives & Coaching Stock which
operate on the National Rail network and
Eurotunnel

Robert Pritchard & Peter Hall

Published by Platform 5 Publishing Ltd,
3 Wyvern House, Sark Road, Sheffield S2 4HG, England.

Printed in England by Berforts Information Press, Eynsham, Oxford.

ISBN 978 1 909431 09 6

# CONTENTS

# CONTENTS

## SECTION 4 – ELECTRIC MULTIPLE UNITS

## SECTION 5 – ON-TRACK MACHINES

## SECTION 6 – UK LIGHT RAIL & METRO SYSTEMS

## SECTION 7 – CODES

## COVER PHOTOGRAPHS

**Front Cover:** DB Schenker-liveried 60010 passes Longport with 6F58 15.26 Ratcliffe–Liverpool coal empties on 7 June 2013.     **Cliff Beeton**

**Back Cover:** Converted from Class 460s for South West Trains, a pair of newly outshopped Class 458/5 EMUs, 458 531 and 458 534, are illustrated shortly after passing through Bracknell with a test run from Staines to Reading on 6 December 2013.     **Ken Brunt**

# BRITAIN'S RAILWAY SYSTEM

## INFRASTRUCTURE & OPERATION

Britain's national railway infrastructure is owned by a "not for dividend" company, Network Rail (NR). Many stations and maintenance depots are leased to and operated by Train Operating Companies (TOCs), but some larger stations remain under NR control. The only exception is the infrastructure on the Isle of Wight, which is nationally owned and leased to South West Trains.

Trains are operated by TOCs over Network Rail, regulated by access agreements between the parties involved. In general, TOCs are responsible for the provision and maintenance of the locomotives, rolling stock and staff necessary for the direct operation of services, whilst NR is responsible for the provision and maintenance of the infrastructure and also for staff to regulate the operation of services.

During 2012 the letting of new franchises was suspended pending a review of the franchise system following the cancelling of the award of the West Coast franchise to First Group. The process was restarted in 2013 but it is going to take a number of years to catch-up and several franchises are to receive short-term extensions in the meantime. At the time of writing extensions had been agreed with First for First Capital Connect and Great Western, whilst Invitations to Tender had been issued for two new franchises – Essex Thameside and the combined Thameslink, Southern & Great Northern franchise.

## DOMESTIC PASSENGER TRAIN OPERATORS

The large majority of passenger trains are operated by the TOCs on fixed-term franchises. Franchise expiry dates are shown in the list of franchisees below:

| *Franchise* | *Franchisee* | *Trading Name* |
|---|---|---|
| **Chiltern** | Deutsche Bahn (Arriva)<br>(until 31 December 2021) | **Chiltern Railways** |

Chiltern Railways operates a frequent service between London Marylebone, Banbury and Birmingham Snow Hill, with some peak trains extending to Kidderminster. There are also regular services from Marylebone to Stratford-upon-Avon and to Aylesbury Vale Parkway via Amersham (along the London Underground Metropolitan Line). The fleet consists of DMUs of Classes 121 (used on the Princes Risborough–Aylesbury route), 165, 168 and 172 plus a number of loco-hauled rakes used on some of the Birmingham trains, worked by Class 67s hired from DB Schenker.

| **Cross-Country** | Deutsche Bahn (Arriva)<br>(until 31 March 2016)* | **CrossCountry** |
|---|---|---|

*Franchise extension to be negotiated to November 2019.*

CrossCountry operates a network of long distance services between Scotland, North-East England and Manchester to the South-West of England, Reading, Southampton, Bournemouth and Guildford, centred on Birmingham New Street. These trains are mainly formed of diesel Class 220/221 Voyagers, supplemented by a small number of HSTs on the NE–SW route. Inter-urban services also link Nottingham, Leicester and Stansted Airport with Birmingham and Cardiff. These use Class 170 DMUs.

**East Midlands**  Stagecoach Group plc  **East Midlands Trains**
(until 31 March 2015)*
*Franchise extension to be negotiated to October 2017.*

EMT operates a mix of long distance high speed services on the Midland Main Line (MML), from London St Pancras to Sheffield (Leeds at peak times and some extensions to York/Scarborough) and Nottingham, and local and regional services ranging from the Norwich–Liverpool route to Nottingham–Skegness, Nottingham–Mansfield–Worksop, Nottingham–Matlock and Derby–Crewe. It also operates local services in Lincolnshire. Trains on the MML are worked by a fleet of Class 222 DMUs and ten HSTs, whilst the local and regional fleet consists of DMU Classes 153, 156 and 158.

**Essex Thameside**  National Express Group plc  **c2c**
(until 13 September 2014)
*Franchise may be extended to 2 May 2015 if required.*

c2c operates an intensive, principally commuter, service from London Fenchurch Street to Southend and Shoeburyness via both Upminster and Tilbury. The fleet consists entirely of Class 357 EMUs.

**Greater Western**  First Group plc  **First Great Western**
(until 20 September 2015)
First Great Western operates long distance trains from London Paddington to South Wales, the West Country and Worcester and Hereford. In addition there are frequent trains along the Thames Valley corridor to Newbury and Oxford, plus local and regional trains throughout the South-West including the Cornish, Devon and Thames Valley branches, the Reading–Gatwick North Downs line and Cardiff–Portsmouth Harbour and Bristol–Weymouth regional routes. A fleet of 53 HSTs is used on the long-distance trains, with DMUs of Classes 165, 166 used on the North Downs and Thames Valley routes and Class 180s used alongside HSTs on the Cotswold Line to Worcester and Hereford. Classes 143, 150, 153 and 158 are used on local and regional trains in the South-West. A small fleet of four Class 57s is maintained to work the overnight "Cornish Riviera" Sleeper service between London and Penzance.

**Greater Anglia**  Abellio (NS) (until 19 July 2014)  **Greater Anglia**
*Franchise extension to be negotiated to October 2016.*

Greater Anglia operates main line trains between London Liverpool Street, Ipswich and Norwich and local trains across Norfolk, Suffolk and parts of Cambridgeshire. It also runs local and commuter services into Liverpool Street from the Great Eastern (including Southend, Braintree and Clacton) and West Anglia (including Cambridge and Stansted Airport) routes. It operates a very varied fleet of Class 90s with loco-hauled Mark 3 sets, DMUs of Classes 153, 156 and 170 and EMUs of Classes 315, 317, 321, 360 and 379.

**Integrated Kent**  Govia Ltd (Go-Ahead/Keolis)  **Southeastern**
(until 12 October 2014)
*Franchise extension to be negotiated to June 2018.*

Southeastern operates all services in the South-East London suburbs, the whole of Kent and part of Sussex, which are primarily commuter services to London. It also operates domestic high speed trains on HS1 from St Pancras to Ashford, Ramsgate, Dover and Faversham with additional peak services on other routes. EMUs of Classes 375, 376, 465 and 466 are used, along with Class 395s on the High Speed trains.

**InterCity East Coast**     Directly Operated Railways     **East Coast**
(until February 2015)

*Currently run on an interim basis by DfT management company Directly Operated Railways (trading as East Coast). This arrangement is due to continue until a new franchise is let to the private sector in 2015.*

East Coast operates frequent long distance trains on the East Coast Main Line between London King's Cross, Leeds, York, Newcastle and Edinburgh, with less frequent services to Bradford, Harrogate, Skipton, Hull, Lincoln, Glasgow, Aberdeen and Inverness. A mixed fleet of Class 91s and 30 Mark 4 sets, and 14 HST sets, are used on these trains.

**InterCity West Coast**     Virgin Rail Group Ltd     **Virgin Trains**
(until 9 November 2014)

*Franchise extension to be negotiated to April 2017.*

Virgin operates long distance services along the West Coast Main Line from London Euston to Birmingham/Wolverhampton, Manchester, Liverpool and Glasgow using Class 390 Pendolino EMUs. It also operates Class 221 Voyagers on the Euston–Chester–Holyhead route, whilst a mixture of 221s and 390s are used on the Euston–Birmingham–Glasgow/Edinburgh route. One rake of Mark 3 loco-hauled stock is also leased, and normally used on Thursdays and Fridays.

**London Rail**     MTR/Deutsche Bahn     **London Overground**
(until 12 November 2016)

*This is a Concession and is different from other rail franchises, as fares and service levels are set by Transport for London instead of the DfT.*

London Overground operates services on the Richmond–Stratford North London Line and the Willesden Junction–Clapham Junction West London Line, plus the new East London Line from Highbury & Islington to New Cross and New Cross Gate, with extensions to Clapham Jn (via Denmark Hill), Crystal Palace and West Croydon. It also runs services from London Euston to Watford Junction. All these use Class 378 EMUs whilst Class 172 DMUs are used on the Gospel Oak–Barking route.

**Merseyrail Electrics**     Serco/Abellio (NS)     **Merseyrail**
(until 19 July 2028)

*Under the control of Merseytravel PTE instead of the DfT. Franchise reviewed every five years to fit in with the Merseyside Local Transport Plan.*

Merseyrail operates services between Liverpool and Southport, Ormskirk, Kirkby, Hunts Cross, New Brighton, West Kirby, Chester and Ellesmere Port, all worked by EMUs of Classes 507 and 508.

**Northern Rail**     Serco/Abellio (NS)     **Northern**
(until 1 April 2014)*

*Franchise extension to be negotiated to April 2017.*

Northern operates a range of inter-urban, commuter and rural services throughout the North of England, including those around the cities of Leeds, Manchester, Sheffield, Liverpool and Newcastle. The network extends from Chathill in the north to Nottingham in the south, and Cleethorpes in the east to St Bees in the west. Long distance services include Leeds–Carlisle, Middlesbrough–Carlisle, Leeds–Nottingham and York–Blackpool North. The operator uses a large fleet of DMUs of Classes 142, 144, 150, 153, 155, 156 and 158 and EMUs of Classes 321, 322, 323 and 333.

| **ScotRail** | First Group plc | **ScotRail** |
| | (until 31 March 2015) | |

ScotRail provides almost all passenger services within Scotland and also trains from Glasgow to Carlisle via Dumfries, some of which extend to Newcastle (jointly operated with Northern). The company also operates the overnight Caledonian Sleeper services between London and Glasgow, Edinburgh, Inverness, Aberdeen and Fort William. In addition to the Sleeper loco-hauled stock (hauled by Class 67s and 90s hired from DB Schenker), the company operates a large fleet of DMUs of Classes 156, 158 and 170 and EMU Classes 314, 318, 320, 334 and 380. One loco-hauled rake is also used on a Fife Circle commuter train, hauled by a Class 67.

| **South Central** | Govia Ltd (Go-Ahead/Keolis) | **Southern** |
| | (until 25 July 2015)* | |

*Upon termination of the Southern franchise in July 2015 it is to be combined with the existing First Capital Connect franchise to form a new Thameslink, Southern & Great Northern franchise.*

Southern operates predominantly commuter services between London, Surrey and Sussex, as well as services along the South Coast between Southampton, Brighton, Hastings and Ashford, and also the cross-London service linking South Croydon and Milton Keynes. It also operates metro services in South London and Gatwick Express, which is a premium non-stop service between London Victoria and Gatwick Airport. Class 171 DMUs are used on Brighton–Ashford and London Bridge–Uckfield services, whilst all other services are in the hands of EMUs of Classes 313, 377, 442 and 455.

| **South Western** | Stagecoach Group plc | **South West Trains** |
| | (until 3 February 2017)* | |

*Franchise extension to be negotiated to April 2019.*

South West Trains operates trains from London Waterloo to destinations across the South and South-West including Woking, Basingstoke, Southampton, Portsmouth, Salisbury, Exeter, Reading and Weymouth as well as suburban services from Waterloo. SWT also runs services between Ryde and Shanklin on the Isle of Wight, using former London Underground 1938 stock (Class 483). The rest of the fleet consists of DMU Classes 158 and 159 and EMU Classes 444, 450, 455 and 458. The fleet of Class 456s transferred from Southern to SWT at the end of 2013 (although they won't enter traffic until spring 2014) and the fleet of 30 4-car 458s is currently being augmented to 36 5-car units with the addition of the former Gatwick Express Class 460 vehicles.

| **Thameslink & Great Northern** | First Group plc | **First Capital Connect** |
| | (until 13 September 2014) | |

*A new Thameslink, Southern & Great Northern franchise is planned to start in September 2014. In July 2015 this will be combined with the Southern franchise.*

First Capital Connect operates trains on the Thameslink route between Bedford and Brighton via central London and also on the Sutton and Wimbledon loops. A joint service with Southeastern is also operated to Sevenoaks, Orpington and Ashford. FCC also runs services on the Great Northern route between London King's Cross and Moorgate to Welwyn Garden City, Hertford North, Peterborough, Cambridge and Kings Lynn. The fleet consists of EMU Classes 319 and 377 for the Thameslink route services and Classes 313, 317, 321 and 365 for the Great Northern route services.

| **Trans-Pennine Express** | First Group/Keolis (until 1 April 2015) | **TransPennine Express** |

*Franchise extension to be negotiated to February 2016.*

TransPennine Express operates predominantly long distance inter-urban services linking major cities across the North of England, along with Edinburgh and Glasgow in Scotland. The main services are Manchester Airport/Manchester Piccadilly–Newcastle/Middlesbrough/Hull plus Liverpool–Scarborough and Liverpool–Newcastle (from May 2014) along the North Trans-Pennine route via Huddersfield, Leeds and York, and Manchester Airport–Cleethorpes along the South Trans-Pennine route via Sheffield. TPE also operates Manchester Airport–Blackpool/Barrow/Windermere/Edinburgh/Glasgow. The fleet consists of DMU Classes 170 (used on the Hull and Cleethorpes routes) and 185. Between December 2013 and May 2014 Class 350 EMUs are being introduced onto the Manchester Airport–Scotland services.

| **Wales & Borders** | Deutsche Bahn (Arriva) (until 14 October 2018)* | **Arriva Trains Wales** |

*The franchise agreement includes the provision for the term to be further extended by mutual agreement by up to five years beyond October 2018. Management of the franchise is devolved to the Welsh Government, but DfT is still the procuring authority.*

Arriva Trains Wales operates a mix of long distance, regional and local services throughout Wales, including the Valley Lines network of lines around Cardiff, and also through services to the English border counties and to Manchester and Birmingham. The fleet consists of DMUs of Classes 142, 143, 150, 158 and 175 and one loco-hauled rake used on a premium Welsh Government sponsored service on the Cardiff–Holyhead route, hauled by a Class 67.

| **West Midlands** | Govia Ltd (Go-Ahead/Keolis) (until 19 September 2015)* | **London Midland** |

*Franchise extension to be negotiated to June 2017.*

London Midland operates long distance and regional services from London Euston to Northampton and Birmingham/Crewe and also between Birmingham and Liverpool as well as local and regional services around Birmingham, including to Stratford-upon-Avon, Worcester, Hereford, Redditch and Shrewsbury. It also operates the Bedford–Bletchley and Watford Jn–St Albans Abbey branches. The fleet consists of DMU Classes 150, 153, 170 and 172 and EMU Classes 321, 323 and 350.

* Franchise agreement includes provision for an extension of up to seven 4-week reporting periods.

The following operators run non-franchised services (* special summer services only):

| Operator | Trading Name | Route |
|---|---|---|
| BAA | Heathrow Express | London Paddington–Heathrow Airport |
| First Hull Trains | First Hull Trains | London King's Cross–Hull |
| Grand Central | Grand Central | London King's Cross–Sunderland/ Bradford Interchange |
| North Yorkshire Moors Railway Enterprises | North Yorkshire Moors Railway | Pickering–Grosmont–Whitby/ Battersby |
| West Coast Railway Company | West Coast Railway Company | Birmingham–Stratford-upon-Avon* Fort William–Mallaig* York–Wakefield–York–Scarborough* |

# INTERNATIONAL PASSENGER OPERATIONS

Eurostar (UK) operates passenger services between the UK and mainland Europe, jointly with the national operators of France (SNCF) and Belgium (SNCB/NMBS). Eurostar International is owned by three shareholders: SNCF (55%), London & Continental Railways (40%) and SNCB (5%).

In addition, a service for the conveyance of accompanied road vehicles through the Channel Tunnel is provided by the tunnel operating company, Eurotunnel.

# FREIGHT TRAIN OPERATIONS

The following operators operate freight services or empty passenger stock workings under "Open Access" arrangements:

**Colas Rail:** In addition to its On-Track Machines and infrastructure activities, Colas Rail operates a number of freight flows, principally steel traffic to Boston using its Class 56s and coal from Portbury to Ratcliffe plus timber from Carlisle, Ribblehead and Baglan Bay to Chirk using its Class 56s or 66s. The small fleet of three Class 47s are used as required whilst the operator was also due to take delivery of a new fleet of Class 70s in 2014.

**DB Schenker Rail (UK):** Still the biggest freight operator in the country, DBS (formerly EWS before being bought by DB) has seen some of its core traffic lost to competitors in recent years. It still provides a large number of infrastructure trains to Network Rail and operates coal, steel, intermodal and aggregate trains nationwide. The core fleet is Class 66s. Of the original 250 ordered 176 are still used in the UK, with the remainder having moved to DB's French and Polish operations, although some of the French locos do return to the UK when major maintenance is required. A fleet of between 20 and 25 Class 60s are also used on the heavier trains.

DBS's six Class 59/2s are used alongside the Mendip Rail 59/0s and 59/1s on stone traffic from the Mendip quarries and around the South-East. DBS's fleet of Class 67s are mainly used on passenger or standby duties for Arriva Trains Wales, Chiltern Railways, East Coast and ScotRail. Class 90s are hired to ScotRail for use on the Sleeper services but see little use on freight, whilst the fleet of Class 92s are mainly used on intermodal duties, including a limited number of overnight trains on High Speed 1.

DBS also operates a number of charter trains.

**Devon & Cornwall Railways** (a subsidiary of British American Railway Services): DCRail mainly operates scrap, spoil and coal trains using its fleet of 56s and also provides locos from its fleet of 31s or 56s for stock moves.

**Direct Rail Services:** DRS has built on its original nuclear flask traffic to operate a number of different services. The main flows are intermodal (mostly Anglo-Scottish) plus the provision of crews and locos to Network Rail for autumn Railhead Treatment Trains. Its Class 47s are also used on charter work. DRS has the most varied fleet of locomotives of all the operators, with Class 20s, 37s, 47s, 57s and 66s. It has also ordered 15 new Vossloh diesels (Class 68s) and 10 new Vossloh electric locos (Class 88s), that will also feature a diesel engine.

**Freightliner:** Freightliner has two divisions: Intermodal operates container trains from the main Ports at Southampton, Felixstowe, Tilbury and Thamesport to major cities including London, Manchester, Leeds and Birmingham. The Heavy Haul division covers the movement of coal, cement, infrastructure and aggregates nationwide. Most services are worked by Class 66s, with new Class 70s used on some of the heavier intermodal trains and some Heavy Haul flows, principally coal, cement and ballast trains. A small fleet of Class 86 and 90 electrics is used on intermodal trains on the Great Eastern and West Coast Main Lines, the Class 86s mainly being used in pairs on the WCML between Crewe and Coatbridge.

**GB Railfreight:** GBRf, owned by Eurotunnel, operates a mixture of traffic types, mainly using Class 66s together with a small fleet of Class 73s on infrastructure duties in the South-East. A growing fleet of Class 92s is also used on some intermodal flows to/from Dollands Moor and on an Ipswich–Trafford Park train. Traffic includes coal, intermodal, biomass and gypsum as well as infrastructure services for Network Rail and London Underground.

**West Coast Railway Company:** WCRC has a freight licence but doesn't operate any freight as such – only empty stock movements. Its fleet of 47s, supplemented by a smaller number of 33s, 37s and 57s, is used on charter work nationwide, including the prestigious Royal Scotsman.

# MAINTENANCE OF LOCOMOTIVES

Depot allocation codes for all locomotives are shown in this book (apart from shunters where the actual location of each is shown). It should be noted that today much locomotive maintenance is undertaken away from these depots. This may be undertaken at fuelling points, berthing sidings or similar, or by mobile maintenance teams. Therefore locomotives in particular may not return to their "home" depots as often as in the past.

# PROVISION OF INFORMATION

This book has been compiled with care to be as accurate as possible, but in some cases information is not officially available and the publisher cannot be held responsible for any errors or omissions. The author would like to thank all Train Operating Companies, Freight Companies, Rolling Stock Leasing Companies, spot-hire companies and the Rolling Stock Library that have helped with the compilation of this book. Thanks are also due to those who sent reports of changes observed during 2013 for the **Today's Railways UK** magazine "Stock Changes" column.

The authors of this book will be pleased to receive notification of any inaccuracies readers may find in the series, and also any additional information to supplement our records and thus enhance future editions. Please send comments to:

Robert Pritchard, Platform 5 Publishing Ltd, 3 Wyvern House, Sark Road, Sheffield, S24HG, England.

**Tel:** 0114 255 2625    **e-mail:** robert@platform5.com.

This book is updated to January 2014.

# 1. LOCOMOTIVES

# INTRODUCTION

## SCOPE

This section contains details of all locomotives which can run on Britain's national railway network, plus those of Eurotunnel. Locomotives which are owned by, for example, DB Schenker and Freightliner which have been withdrawn from service and awaiting disposal are listed in the main part of the book. Locos which are awaiting disposal at scrapyards are listed in the "Locomotives Awaiting Disposal" section.

Only preserved locomotives which are currently used on the National Rail network are included. Others, which may still be Network Rail registered but not at present certified for use, are not included, but will be found in the Platform 5 book, "Preserved Locomotives and Multiple Units".

## LOCOMOTIVE CLASSES

Locomotive classes are listed in numerical order of class. Principal details and dimensions are quoted for each class in metric and/or imperial units as considered appropriate bearing in mind common UK usage.

**Builders:** These are shown in class headings. Abbreviations used are found in section 7.6.

All dimensions and weights are quoted for locomotives in an "as new" condition with all necessary supplies (eg oil, water and sand) on board. Dimensions are quoted in the order length x width. Lengths quoted are over buffers or couplers as appropriate. All widths quoted are maxima. Where two different wheel diameter dimensions are shown, the first refers to powered wheels and the second refers to non-powered wheels. All weights are shown as metric tonnes (t = tonnes).

## NUMERICAL LISTINGS

Locomotives are listed in numerical order. Where numbers actually carried are different from those officially allocated, these are noted in class headings where appropriate. Where locomotives have been recently renumbered, the most immediate previous number is shown in parentheses. Each locomotive entry is laid out as in the following example:

| RSL No. | Detail | Livery | Owner | Pool | Allocn. | Name |
|---------|--------|--------|-------|------|---------|------|
| 60007 +* | **DB** | DB | WCBT | TO | The Spirit of Tom Kendell |

**Detail Differences.** Only detail differences which currently affect the areas and types of train which locomotives may work are shown. All other detail differences are excluded. Where such differences occur within a class or part class, they are shown in the "Detail" column alongside the individual locomotive number.

Standard abbreviations used for the locomotives section are:

| | |
|---|---|
| a | Train air brake equipment only. |
| b | Drophead buckeye couplers. |
| c | Scharfenberg couplers. |
| d | Fitted with retractable Dellner couplers. |
| e | European Railway Traffic Management System (ERTMS) signalling equipment fitted. |
| i | Fitted with Tightlock couplers |
| k | Fitted with Swinghead Automatic "buckeye" combination couplers. |
| p | Train air, vacuum and electro-pneumatic brakes. |
| r | Radio Electric Token Block signalling equipment fitted. |
| s | Slow Speed Control equipment. |
| v | Train vacuum brake only. |
| x | Train air and vacuum brakes ("Dual brakes"). |
| + | Additional fuel tank capacity. |
| § | Sandite laying equipment. |

In all cases use of the above abbreviations indicates the equipment indicated is normally operable. Meaning of non-standard abbreviations and symbols is detailed in individual class headings.

**Codes:** Codes are used to denote the livery, owner, pool and depot of each locomotive. Details of these will be found in section 7 of this book.
(S) denotes that the locomotive is currently stored.

**Names:** Only names carried with official sanction are listed. Names are shown in UPPER/lower case characters as actually shown on the name carried on the locomotive.

# GENERAL INFORMATION

## CLASSIFICATION AND NUMBERING

All locomotives are classified and allocated numbers by the Rolling Stock Library under the TOPS numbering system, introduced in 1972. This comprises a two-digit class number followed by a three-digit serial number. Where the actual number carried by a locomotive differs from the allocated number, or where an additional number is carried to the allocated number, this is shown by a note in the class heading.

For diesel locomotives, class numbers offer an indication of engine horsepower as shown in the table below.

| Class No. Range | Engine hp |
|---|---|
| 01–14 | 0–799 |
| 15–20 | 800–1000 |
| 21–31 | 1001–1499 |
| 32–39 | 1500–1999 |
| 40–54, 57 | 2000–2999 |
| 55–56, 58–70 | 3000+ |

For electric locomotives class numbers are allocated in ascending numerical order under the following scheme:

Class 71–80       Direct current and DC/diesel dual system locomotives.
Class 81 onwards  Alternating current and AC/DC dual system locos.

Numbers in the 89xxx series are allocated by the Rolling Stock Library to locomotives which have been deregistered but subsequently re-registered for use on the Network Rail network and whose original number has already been reused. 89xxx numbers are normally only carried inside locomotive cabs and are not carried externally in normal circumstances.

## WHEEL ARRANGEMENT

For main line locomotives the number of driven axles on a bogie or frame is denoted by a letter (A = 1, B = 2, C = 3 etc) and the number of non-powered axles is denoted by a number. The use of the letter "o" after a letter indicates each axle is individually powered, whilst the "+" symbol indicates bogies are inter-coupled.

For shunting locomotives, the Whyte notation is used. In this notation the number of leading wheels are given, followed by the number of driving wheels and then the trailing wheels.

# HAULAGE CAPABILITY OF DIESEL LOCOMOTIVES

The haulage capability of a diesel locomotive depends upon three basic factors:

1. Adhesive weight. The greater the weight on the driving wheels, the greater the adhesion and more tractive power can be applied before wheelslip occurs.

2. The characteristics of its transmission. To start a train the locomotive has to exert a pull at standstill. A direct drive diesel engine cannot do this, hence the need for transmission. This may be mechanical, hydraulic or electric. The present British Standard for locomotives is electric transmission. Here the diesel engine drives a generator or alternator and the current produced is fed to the traction motors. The force produced by each driven wheel depends on the current in its traction motor. In other words, the larger the current, the harder it pulls. As the locomotive speed increases, the current in the traction motor falls, hence the *Maximum Tractive Effort* is the maximum force at its wheels the locomotive can exert at a standstill. The electrical equipment cannot take such high currents for long without overheating. Hence the *Continuous Tractive Effort* is quoted which represents the current which the equipment can take continuously.

3. The power of its engine. Not all power reaches the rail, as electrical machines are approximately 90% efficient. As the electrical energy passes through two such machines (the generator or alternator and the traction motors), the *Power at Rail* is approximately 81% (90% of 90%) of the engine power, less a further amount used for auxiliary equipment such as radiator fans, traction motor blowers, air compressors, battery charging, cab heating, Electric Train Supply (ETS) etc. The power of the locomotive is proportional to the tractive effort times the speed. Hence when on full power there is a speed corresponding to the continuous tractive effort.

# HAULAGE CAPABILITY OF ELECTRIC LOCOMOTIVES

Unlike a diesel locomotive, an electric locomotive does not develop its power on board and its performance is determined only by two factors, namely its weight and the characteristics of its electrical equipment. Whereas a diesel locomotive tends to be a constant power machine, the power of an electric locomotive varies considerably. Up to a certain speed it can produce virtually a constant tractive effort. Hence power rises with speed according to the formula given in section three above, until a maximum speed is reached at which tractive effort falls, such that the power also falls. Hence the power at the speed corresponding to the maximum tractive effort is lower than the maximum speed.

# BRAKE FORCE

The brake force is a measure of the braking power of a locomotive. This is shown on the locomotive data panels so operating staff can ensure sufficient brake power is available on freight trains.

## ELECTRIC TRAIN SUPPLY (ETS)

A number of locomotives are equipped to provide a supply of electricity to the train being hauled to power auxiliaries such as heating, cooling fans, air conditioning and kitchen equipment. ETS is provided from the locomotive by means of a separate alternator (except Class 33 locomotives, which have a DC generator). The ETS index of a locomotive is a measure of the electrical power available for train supply.

Similarly, most loco-hauled coaches also have an ETS index, which in this case is a measure of the power required to operate equipment mounted in the coach. The sum of the ETS indices of all the hauled vehicles in a train must not exceed the ETS index of the locomotive.

ETS is commonly (but incorrectly) known as ETH (Electric Train Heating), which is a throwback to the days before loco-hauled coaches were equipped with electrically powered auxiliary equipment other than for train heating.

## ROUTE AVAILABILITY (RA)

This is a measure of a railway vehicle's axle load. The higher the axle load of a vehicle, the higher the RA number on a scale from 1 to 10. Each Network Rail route has a RA number and in general no vehicle with a higher RA number may travel on that route without special clearance.

## MULTIPLE & PUSH-PULL WORKING

Multiple working between vehicles (ie two or more powered vehicles being driven from one cab) is facilitated by jumper cables connecting the vehicles. However, not all types are compatible with each other, and a number of different systems are in use, each system being incompatible with any other.

**Association of American Railroads (AAR) System:** Classes 59, 66, 67 and 70.
**Blue Star Coupling Code:** Classes 20, 25, 31, 33, 37 40 and 73.
**DRS System:** Classes 20/3, 37, 47 and 57.
**Green Circle Coupling Code:** Class 47 (not all equipped).
**Orange Square Coupling Code:** Class 50.
**Red Diamond Coupling Code:** Classes 56 and 58.
**SR System:** Classes 33/1, 73 and various electric multiple units.
**Within Own Class only:** Classes 43 and 60.

Many locomotives use a time-division multiplex (TDM) system for push-pull and multiple working which utilises the existing RCH jumper cables fitted to coaching stock vehicles. Previously these cables had only been used to control train lighting and public address systems.

Class 47 locos 47701–47717 were equipped with an older non-standard TDM system.

# 1.1. DIESEL LOCOMOTIVES

## CLASS 08          BR/ENGLISH ELECTRIC          0-6-0

**Built:** 1955–62 by BR at Crewe, Darlington, Derby Locomotive, Doncaster or Horwich Works.
**Engine:** English Electric 6KT of 298 kW (400 hp) at 680 rpm.
**Main Generator:** English Electric 801.
**Traction Motors:** Two English Electric 506.
**Maximum Tractive Effort:** 156 kN (35000 lbf).
**Continuous Tractive Effort:** 49 kN (11100 lbf) at 8.8 mph.
**Power At Rail:** 194 kW (260 hp).        **Train Brakes:** Air & vacuum.
**Brake Force:** 19 t.                     **Dimensions:** 8.92 x 2.59 m.
**Weight:** 49.6–50.4 t.                   **Wheel Diameter:** 1372 mm.
**Design Speed:** 20 mph.                  **Maximum Speed:** 15 mph.
**Fuel Capacity:** 3037 litres.            **RA:** 5.
**Train Supply:** Not equipped.
**Multiple Working:** m Equipped for multiple working. All others not equipped.

† – Fitted with remote control equipment.

For shunting locomotives, instead of the two-letter depot code, actual locations at the time of publication are given.

Class 08s that don't have current Network Rail engineering acceptance are considered to be "in industrial service" and can be found in section 1.4 of this book.

08850 has acceptance for use between Battersby and Whitby only, for rescue purposes.

**Non-standard liveries/numbering:**

08480   Yellow with a red bodyside band. Carries number "TOTON No 1".
08616   Carries number 3783.
08696   Carries no number.
08701   Carries number "Tyne 100".
08721   As **B**, but with a black roof & "Express parcels" branding with red & yellow stripe.
08824   Carries number "IEMD01".

Originally numbered in series D3000–D4192.

**Class 08/0. Standard Design.**

| 08077 | **FL** | P | DHLT | LH Group, Barton-under-Needwood (S) |
|---|---|---|---|---|
| 08405 | a† | **E** | DB | WSGC | Dagenham Yard |
| 08410 | a | **FB** | FW | EFSH | Penzance Long Rock Depot |
| 08428 | ak | **E** | DB | WSSC | Bescot Yards |
| 08451 | | **B** | AM | ATLO | Manchester Longsight Depot |
| 08454 | | **K** | AM | ATLO | Manchester Longsight Depot |
| 08472 | a | **WA** | WA | RFSH | Edinburgh Craigentinny Depot |
| 08480 | a | **0** | DB | WSXX | Toton Depot |

| | | | | |
|---|---|---|---|---|
| 08483 a | **GL** | FW | EFSH | Old Oak Common HST Depot |
| 08495 † | **E** | DB | WQBA | Crewe International Depot (S) |
| 08500 | **E** | DB | WQBA | Tees Yard (S) |
| 08523 | **RS** | RL | MRSO | Inverness Depot |
| 08525 | **ST** | EM | EMSL | Leeds Neville Hill Depot |
| 08530 | **FL** | P | DFLS | Southampton Maritime FLT |
| 08531 a | **FL** | P | DFLS | LH Group, Barton-under-Needwood |
| 08567 † | **E** | DB | WQBA | Crewe International Depot (S) |
| 08571 a | **WA** | WA | HBSH | Bounds Green Depot |
| 08575 | **FL** | P | DHLT | Southampton Maritime FLT (S) |
| 08578 † | **E** | DB | WQBA | Toton Depot (S) |
| 08580 | **E** | DB | WQCA | Bescot Yards (S) |
| 08585 | **FL** | P | DFLS | Felixstowe FLT |
| 08593 | **E** | DB | WQCA | Crewe International Depot (S) |
| 08596 a† | **WA** | WA | HBSH | Bounds Green Depot |
| 08605 † | **E** | DB | WSRC | Carlisle Yards |
| 08611 | **V** | AM | ATLO | Manchester Longsight Depot |
| 08615 | **WA** | WA | RFSH | Edinburgh Craigentinny Depot |
| 08616 | **LM** | LM | EJLO | Birmingham Tyseley Depot |
| 08617 | **K** | AM | ATLO | Wembley Depot |
| 08623 | **DB** | DB | WSSC | Bescot Yards |
| 08624 | **FL** | P | DFLS | Trafford Park FLT |
| 08630 | **E** | DB | WQCA | Toton Yards (S) |
| 08632 † | **E** | DB | WSRC | Hoo Junction Yards |
| 08633 † | **E** | DB | WSSC | Margam Yard |
| 08641 | **FB** | FW | EFSH | Plymouth Laira Depot |
| 08644 | **FB** | FW | EFSH | Plymouth Laira Depot |
| 08645 | **FB** | FW | EFSH | Plymouth Laira Depot |
| 08653 | **E** | DB | WQCA | Toton Yards (S) |
| 08663 a | **FB** | FW | EFSH | Bristol St Philip's Marsh Depot |
| 08669 a | **WA** | WA | RFSH | Wabtec Rail, Doncaster Works |
| 08676 † | **E** | DB | WSRC | Mossend Yard |
| 08690 | **ST** | EM | EMSL | Leeds Neville Hill Depot |
| 08691 | **FL** | FL | DFLS | LH Group, Barton-under-Needwood |
| 08696 a | **G** | AM | ATLO | Glasgow Polmadie Depot |
| 08701 a† | **RX** | DB | WQCA | Toton Yards (S) |
| 08703 a | **E** | DB | WSSC | Doncaster Yards |
| 08706 † | **E** | DB | WQBA | Crewe International Depot (S) |
| 08709 | **E** | DB | WQCA | Bescot Yards (S) |
| 08711 k | **RX** | DB | WQCA | Tees Yard (S) |
| 08714 | **E** | DB | WSXX | Axiom Rail, Stoke-on-Trent Works |
| 08721 | **0** | AM | ATLO | Liverpool Edge Hill Depot |
| 08724 | **WA** | WA | HBSH | Wabtec Rail, Doncaster Works |
| 08735 † | **E** | DB | WQBA | Eastleigh Yards (S) |
| 08737 a† | **E** | DB | WQBA | Crewe International Depot (S) |
| 08738 m | **ECR** | DB | WQBA | Toton Yards (S) |
| 08742 † | **RX** | DB | WSSC | Mossend Yard |
| 08752 † | **E** | DB | WSSC | Westbury Yards |
| 08754 | **B** | RL | MRSO | Norwich Crown Point Depot |
| 08757 † | **RG** | DB | WQBA | Crewe International Depot (S) |
| 08782 a† | **CU** | DB | WSSC | Doncaster Yards |

| | | | | |
|---|---|---|---|---|
| 08784 † | **E** | DB | WQBA | Toton Depot (S) |
| 08785 a | **FL** | P | DFLS | Southampton Maritime FLT |
| 08788 | **K** | RL | MRSO | Inverness Depot |
| 08790 | **B** | AM | ATLO | Wolverhampton Oxley Depot |
| 08795 | **K** | FW | EFSH | Swansea Landore Depot |
| 08799 a | **E** | DB | WSSC | Hoo Junction Yards |
| 08802 † | **E** | DB | WQBA | Doncaster Yards (S) |
| 08804 † | **E** | DB | WQBA | Crewe International Depot (S) |
| 08805 | **B** | LM | EJLO | Birmingham Soho Depot |
| 08822 | **FB** | FW | EFSH | Bristol St Philip's Marsh Depot |
| 08824 ak | **K** | DB | WSXX | Crewe International Depot |
| 08836 | **FB** | FW | EFSH | Old Oak Common HST Depot |
| 08847 | **CD** | RL | MRSO | Allely's Heavy Haulage, Studley, Warks |
| 08850 | **B** | NY | MBDL | Grosmont Depot |
| 08853 a | **WA** | WA | RFSH | Wabtec Rail, Doncaster Works |
| 08865 | **E** | DB | WQBA | Crewe International Depot (S) |
| 08874 | **SL** | RL | MRSO | Norwich Crown Point Depot |
| 08877 | **DG** | DB | WQCA | Wigan Springs Branch Depot |
| 08879 † | **E** | DB | WSRC | Hinksey Yard |
| 08886 | **E** | DB | WQCA | Crewe International Depot (S) |
| 08887 a | **B** | AM | ATLO | Wembley Depot |
| 08888 † | **E** | DB | WSRC | Didcot Yards |
| 08891 | **FL** | P | DHLT | LH Group, Barton-under-Needwood (S) |
| 08899 | **MA** | EM | EMSL | Derby Etches Park Depot |
| 08904 | **E** | DB | WSGC | Eastleigh Yards |
| 08907 | **DB** | DB | WSSC | Bescot Yards |
| 08908 | **ST** | EM | EMSL | Leeds Neville Hill Depot |
| 08922 | **DG** | DB | WQBA | Toton Depot (S) |
| 08925 | **G** | GB | GBWM | March Whitemoor Yard |
| 08934 a | **VP** | GB | GBWM | Cardiff Tidal Steelworks |
| 08939 m | **ECR** | DB | WQBA | Toton Yards (S) |
| 08948 c | **EP** | EU | GPSS | Temple Mills Depot |
| 08950 | **ST** | EM | EMSL | Leeds Neville Hill Depot |

**Class 08/9. Reduced height cab.** Converted 1985–87 by BR at Landore.

| | | | | |
|---|---|---|---|---|
| 08993 | **E** | DB | WQBA | Doncaster Depot (S) |
| 08994 a | **E** | DB | WQBA | Toton Depot (S) |
| 08995 a | **E** | DB | WQBA | Crewe International Depot (S) |

# CLASS 09    BR/ENGLISH ELECTRIC    0-6-0

**Built:** 1959–62 by BR at Darlington or Horwich Works.
**Engine:** English Electric 6KT of 298 kW (400 hp) at 680 rpm.
**Main Generator:** English Electric 801.
**Traction Motors:** English Electric 506.
**Maximum Tractive Effort:** 111 kN (25000 lbf).
**Continuous Tractive Effort:** 39 kN (8800 lbf) at 11.6 mph.
**Power At Rail:** 201 kW (269 hp).      **Train Brakes:** Air & vacuum.
**Brake Force:** 19 t.                   **Dimensions:** 8.92 x 2.59 m.
**Weight:** 49 t.                        **Wheel Diameter:** 1372 mm.
**Design Speed:** 27 mph.                **Maximum Speed:** 27 mph.
**Fuel Capacity:** 3037 litres.          **RA:** 5.
**Train Supply:** Not equipped.          **Multiple Working:** Not equipped.

Class 09s that don't have current Network Rail engineering acceptance are considered to be "in industrial service" and can be found in section 1.4 of this book.

Class 09/0 were originally numbered D3665–D3671, D3719–D3721, D4099–D4114.

**Class 09/0. Built as Class 09.**

| 09002 | **G** | GB | GBWM | March Whitemoor Yard |
| 09006 | **E** | DB | WQCA | Doncaster Depot (S) |
| 09009 | **G** | GB | GBWM | Trafford Park FLT |
| 09026 a | **G** | SN | HWSU | Brighton Lovers Walk Depot |

**Class 09/1. Converted from Class 08. 110 V electrical equipment.**
**Converted:** 1992–1993 by RFS Industries, Kilnhurst.

| 09106 (08759) | **DB** | DB | WSSC | Warrington Yards |

**Class 09/2. Converted from Class 08. 90 V electrical equipment.**
**Converted:** 1992 by RFS Industries, Kilnhurst.

| 09201 (08421) ak† | **DG** | DB | WSGC | Knottingley Depot |

**Class 08 and Class 09 names:**

| 08451 | M.A. SMITH | 08691 | Terri |
| 08483 | DUSTY Driver David Miller | 08721 | DOWNHILL C.S. |
| 08495 | NOEL KIRTON OBE | 08782 | CASTLETON WORKS |
| 08525 | DUNCAN BEDFORD | 08790 | Steve Purser |
| 08585 | Vicky | 08799 | FRED |
| 08616 | TYSELEY 100 | 08805 | CONCORDE |
| 08630 | BOB BROWN | 08822 | John |
| 08645 | Mike Baggott | 08874 | Catherine |
| 08663 | Jack | 08908 | IVAN STEPHENSON |
| 08669 | Bob Machin | 08950 | DAVID LIGHTFOOT |
| 08690 | DAVID THIRKILL | 09026 | Cedric Wares |

# CLASS 20    ENGLISH ELECTRIC    Bo-Bo

**Built:** 1957–68 by English Electric at Vulcan Foundry, Newton-le-Willows or by Robert Stephenson & Hawthorns at Darlington.
**Engine:** English Electric 8SVT Mk II of 746 kW (1000 hp) at 850 rpm.
**Main Generator:** English Electric 819/3C.
**Traction Motors:** English Electric 526/5D or 526/8D.
**Maximum Tractive Effort:** 187 kN (42000 lbf).
**Continuous Tractive Effort:** 111 kN (25000 lbf) at 11 mph.
**Power At Rail:** 574 kW (770 hp).     **Train Brakes:** Air & vacuum.
**Brake Force:** 35 t.                  **Dimensions:** 14.25 x 2.67 m.
**Weight:** 73.4–73.5 t.                **Wheel Diameter:** 1092 mm.
**Design Speed:** 75 mph.               **Maximum Speed:** 75 mph.
**Fuel Capacity:** 1727 litres.         **RA:** 5.
**Train Supply:** Not equipped.         **Multiple Working:** Blue Star.

Originally numbered in series D8007–D8190, D8315–D8325.

**Non-standard liveries/numbering:**

20088 RFS grey (carries No. 2017).
20189 London Underground red. Also carries No. L189.
20227 White, red & blue with London Underground roundels.

**Class 20/0. Standard Design.**

| | | | | |
|---|---|---|---|---|
| 20016 | B | HN | HNRS | LM (S) |
| 20081 | B | HN | HNRS | LM (S) |
| 20088 | 0 | HN | HNRS | LM (S) |
| 20092 | U | HN | HNRS | LM (S) |
| 20096 | B | HN | GBEE | BH |
| 20107 | B | HN | GBEE | BH |
| 20118 | F0 | HN | GBEE | BH | Saltburn-by-the-Sea |
| 20132 | F0 | HN | GBEE | BH |
| 20142 | B | 20 | GBEE | SK |
| 20189 | 0 | 20 | GBEE | SK |
| 20227 | 0 | 2L | GBEE | SK |

**Class 20/3. Direct Rail Services refurbished locos.** Details as Class 20/0 except:

**Refurbished:** 15 locomotives were refurbished 1995–96 by Brush Traction at Loughborough (20301–305) or 1997–98 by RFS(E) at Doncaster (20306–315). Disc indicators or headcode panels removed.
**Train Brakes:** Air.                  **Maximum Speed:** 60 mph (+ 75 mph).
**Weight:** 73 t (+ 76 t).              **Fuel Capacity:** 2909 (+ 4909) litres.
**Brake Force:** 35 t (+ 31 t).         **RA:** 5 (+ 6).
**Multiple Working:** DRS system.

| | | | | | |
|---|---|---|---|---|---|
| 20301 | (20047) r | DS | DR | XHNC | KM | Max Joule 1958–1999 |
| 20302 | (20084) r | DS | DR | XHNC | KM |
| 20303 | (20127) r | DS | DR | XHNC | KM |
| 20304 | (20120) r | DS | DR | XHNC | KM |
| 20305 | (20095) r | DS | DR | XHNC | KM | Gresty Bridge |
| 20308 | (20187) r+ | DS | DR | XHNC | KM |
| 20309 | (20075) r+ | DS | DR | XHNC | KM |

| 20311 (20102) r+ | **HN** HN | GBEE | BH |
| 20312 (20042) r+ | **DS** DR | XHNC | KM |
| 20314 (20117) r+ | **HN** HN | GBEE | BH |

**Class 20/9. Harry Needle Railroad Company (former Hunslet-Barclay/ DRS) locos.** Details as Class 20/0 except:

**Refurbished:** 1989 by Hunslet-Barclay at Kilmarnock.
**Train Brakes:** Air.                    **Fuel Capacity:** 1727 (+ 4727) litres.
**RA:** 5 (+ 6).

| 20901 (20101) | **GB** HN | GBEE | BH |
| 20903 (20083) + | **DR** HN | HNRS | BO (S) |
| 20904 (20041) + | **DR** HN | HNRS | BO (S) |
| 20905 (20225) + | **GB** HN | GBEE | BH |

# CLASS 25    BR/BEYER PEACOCK/SULZER    Bo-Bo

**Built:** 1965 by Beyer Peacock at Gorton.
**Engine:** Sulzer 6LDA28-B of 930 kW (1250 hp) at 750 rpm.
**Main Generator:** AEI RTB15656.          **Traction Motors:** AEI 253AY.
**Maximum Tractive Effort:** 200 kN (45000 lbf).
**Continuous Tractive Effort:** 93 kN (20800 lbf) at 17.1 mph.
**Power At Rail:** 708 kW (949 hp).      **Train Brakes:** Air & vacuum.
**Brake Force:** 38 t.                    **Dimensions:** 15.39 x 2.73 m.
**Weight:** 71.5 t.                       **Wheel Diameter:** 1143 mm.
**Design Speed:** 90 mph.                 **Maximum Speed:** 60 mph.
**Fuel Capacity:** 2270 litres.           **RA:** 5.
**Train Supply:** Not equipped.           **Multiple Working:** Blue Star.

Original number is D7628, which the loco currently carries.

Only certified for use on Network Rail metals between Whitby and Battersby, as an extension of North Yorkshire Moors Railway services.

| 25278 | **GG** NY | MBDL | NY | SYBILLA |

# CLASS 31    BRUSH/ENGLISH ELECTRIC    A1A-A1A

**Built:** 1958–62 by Brush Traction at Loughborough.
**Engine:** English Electric 12SVT of 1100 kW (1470 hp) at 850 rpm.
**Main Generator:** Brush TG160-48.       **Traction Motors:** Brush TM73-68.
**Maximum Tractive Effort:** 160 kN (35900 lbf).
**Continuous Tractive Effort:** 83 kN (18700 lbf) at 23.5 mph.
**Power At Rail:** 872 kW (1170 hp).      **Train Brakes:** Air & vacuum.
**Brake Force:** 49 t.                    **Dimensions:** 17.30 x 2.67 m.
**Weight:** 106.7–111 t.                  **Wheel Diameter:** 1092/1003 mm.
**Design Speed:** 90 mph.                 **Maximum Speed:** 90 mph.
**Fuel Capacity:** 2409 litres.           **RA:** 5 or 6.
**Train Supply:** Not equipped.           **Multiple Working:** Blue Star.

Originally numbered D5520–D5699, D5800–D5862 (not in order).

**Non-standard numbering:** 31190 Also carries number D5613.

**Class 31/1. Standard Design.** RA: 5.

| | | | | | |
|---|---|---|---|---|---|
| 31105 | Y | NR | QADD | ZA | |
| 31106 a | B | HJ | RVLO | ZA | |
| 31128 | B | NS | NRLO | NY | CHARYBDIS |
| 31190 | G | BA | HTLX | WH | |
| 31233 a | Y | NR | QADD | ZA | |
| 31285 | Y | NR | QADD | ZA | |

**Class 31/4. Electric Train Supply equipment.** RA: 6.
**Train Supply:** Electric, index 66.

| | | | | | |
|---|---|---|---|---|---|
| 31452 | DC | BA | HTLX | ZA | |
| 31454 | IC | BA | HTLX | WH (S) | |
| 31459 | K | BA | RVLO | ZA | CERBERUS |
| 31465 | Y | NR | QADD | ZA | |
| 31468 | FR | BA | RVLO | WO (S) HYDRA | |

**Class 31/6. ETS through wiring and controls.** RA: 5.

| | | | | | |
|---|---|---|---|---|---|
| 31601 | (31186) | DC | BA | HTLX | WH |
| 31602 | (31191) | Y | BA | HTLX | WO (S) |

# CLASS 33       BRCW/SULZER       Bo-Bo

**Built:** 1960–62 by the Birmingham Railway Carriage & Wagon Company at Smethwick.
**Engine:** Sulzer 8LDA28 of 1160 kW (1550 hp) at 750 rpm.
**Main Generator:** Crompton Parkinson CG391B1.
**Traction Motors:** Crompton Parkinson C171C2.
**Maximum Tractive Effort:** 200 kN (45000 lbf).
**Continuous Tractive Effort:** 116 kN (26000 lbf) at 17.5 mph.
**Power At Rail:** 906 kW (1215 hp).       **Train Brakes:** Air & vacuum.
**Brake Force:** 35 t.                             **Dimensions:** 15.47 x 2.82 (2.64 m 33/2).
**Weight:** 76-78 t.                               **Wheel Diameter:** 1092 mm.
**Design Speed:** 85 mph.                     **Maximum Speed:** 85 mph.
**Fuel Capacity:** 3410 litres.               **RA:** 6.
**Train Supply:** Electric, index 48 (750 V DC only).
**Multiple Working:** Blue Star.

Originally numbered in series D6500–D6597 but not in order.

**Non-standard numbering:** 33012 Carries number D6515.

**Class 33/0. Standard Design.**

| | | | | | |
|---|---|---|---|---|---|
| 33012 | G | 71 | MBDL | Swanage Rly | |
| 33025 | WC | WC | AWCX | SH (S) | Glen Falloch |
| 33029 | WC | WC | AWCA | CS | Glen Loy |
| 33030 | DR | WC | AWCX | CS (S) | |

**Class 33/2. Built to former Loading Gauge of Tonbridge–Battle Line.**
Equipped with slow speed control.

| | | | | | |
|---|---|---|---|---|---|
| 33207 | WC | WC | AWCA | CS | Jim Martin |

# CLASS 37     ENGLISH ELECTRIC     Co-Co

**Built:** 1960–66 by English Electric at Vulcan Foundry, Newton-le-Willows or by Robert Stephenson & Hawthorns at Darlington.
**Engine:** English Electric 12CSVT of 1300 kW (1750 hp) at 850 rpm.
**Main Generator:** English Electric 822/10G.
**Traction Motors:** English Electric 538/A.
**Maximum Tractive Effort:** 245 kN (55500 lbf).
**Continuous Tractive Effort:** 156 kN (35000 lbf) at 13.6 mph.
**Power At Rail:** 932 kW (1250 hp).     **Train Brakes:** Air & vacuum.
**Brake Force:** 50 t.     **Dimensions:** 18.75 x 2.74 m.
**Weight:** 102.8–108.4 t.     **Wheel Diameter:** 1092 mm.
**Design Speed:** 90 mph.     **Maximum Speed:** 80 mph.
**Fuel Capacity:** 4046 (+ 7683) litres.     **RA:** 5 (§ 6).
**Train Supply:** Not equipped.
**Multiple Working:** Blue Star († DRS system).

Originally numbered D6600–D6608, D6700–D6999 (not in order).

**Class 37/0. Standard Design.** Details as above.

| | | | | | |
|---|---|---|---|---|---|
| 37038 | a† | **DR** | DR | XHNC | KM |
| 37059 | ar+†**DS** | | DR | XHSS | CR (S) |
| 37069 | ar+†**DS** | | DR | XHSS | Daventry |
| 37116 | + | **B** | CS | MBDL | Chinnor (S) |
| 37165 | a+ | **CE** | WC | AWCX | CS (S) |
| 37175 | a | **BL** | CS | MBDL | Bo'ness (S) |
| 37194 | a+† **DS** | | DR | XHNC | KM |
| 37198 | + | **Y** | NR | MBDL | GCR (S) |
| 37214 | | **WC** | WC | AWCX | CS (S) |
| 37218 | ar+†**DS** | | DR | XHNC | KM |
| 37219 | | **ML** | CS | MBDL | WH (S) |
| 37259 | ar† | **DS** | DR | XHNC | KM |
| 37261 | a+ | **DS** | DR | XHSS | CR (S) |

**Class 37/4. Refurbished with electric train supply equipment.** Main generator replaced by alternator. Regeared (CP7) bogies. Details as Class 37/0 except:
**Main Alternator:** Brush BA1005A.     **Power At Rail:** 935 kW (1254 hp).
**Traction Motors:** English Electric 538/5A.
**Maximum Tractive Effort:** 256 kN (57440 lbf).
**Continuous Tractive Effort:** 184 kN (41250 lbf) at 11.4 mph.
**Weight:** 107 t.     **Design Speed:** 80 mph.
**Fuel Capacity:** 7683 litres.
**Train Supply:** Electric, index 30.

| | | | | | | |
|---|---|---|---|---|---|---|
| 37401 | ar | **BL** | DR | XHHP | Bo'ness | Mary Queen of Scots |
| 37402 | a | **DS** | DR | XHAC | KM | Stephen Middlemore 23.12.1954–8.6.2013 |
| 37405 | ar | **DS** | DR | XHAC | KM | |
| 37409 | ar† | **DS** | DR | XHAC | KM | Lord Hinton |
| 37419 | ar | **DS** | DR | XHAC | KM | Carl Haviland 1954–2012 |
| 37421 | | **RR** | CS | MBDL | RU (S) | |
| 37422 | ar | **DS** | DR | XHHP | KM (S) | |
| 37423 | ar† | **DS** | DR | XHAC | KM | Spirit of the Lakes |

| 37425 ar | **DS** | DR | XHAC | | KM | Sir Robert McAlpine/Concrete Bob |

**Class 37/5. Refurbished without train supply equipment. Main generator replaced by alternator. Regeared (CP7) bogies.** Details as Class 37/4 except:
**Maximum Tractive Effort:** 248 kN (55590 lbf).
**Weight:** 106.1–110.0 t.

| 37503 r§ | **E** | DR | XHSS | BH (S) | |
| 37510 a | **DS** | DR | XHSS | BH (S) | |
| 37516 s | **WC** | WC | AWCA | CS | Loch Laidon |
| 37517 as | **LH** | WC | AWCX | CS (S) | |
| 37518 ar | **IC** | WC | AWCA | CS | Fort William/An Gearasdan |
| 37521 r§ | **E** | DR | XHSS | BH (S) | English China Clays |

**Class 37/6. Originally refurbished for Nightstar services. Main generator replaced by alternator. UIC jumpers.** Details as Class 37/5 except:
**Maximum Speed:** 90 mph.        **Train Brake:** Air.
**Train Supply:** Not equipped, but electric through wired.
**Multiple Working:** DRS system.

| 37601 a | **DS** | DR | XHNC | KM | Class 37-'Fifty' |
| 37602 ar | **DS** | DR | XHNC | KM | |
| 37603 a | **DS** | DR | XHNC | KM | |
| 37604 a | **DS** | DR | XHNC | KM | |
| 37605 ar | **DS** | DR | XHNC | KM | |
| 37606 a | **DS** | DR | XHNC | KM | |
| 37607 ar | **DS** | DR | XHNC | KM | |
| 37608 ar | **DS** | DR | XHNC | KM | |
| 37609 a | **DS** | DR | XHNC | KM | |
| 37610 a | **DS** | DR | XHNC | KM | |
| 37611 a | **DS** | DR | XHNC | KM | |
| 37612 a | **DS** | DR | XHNC | KM | |

**Class 37/5 continued.**

| 37667 ars† | **DS** | DR | XHNC | KM | |
| 37668 s | **E** | WC | AWCX | CS (S) | |
| 37669 r | **WC** | WC | AWCX | BH (S) | |
| 37670 r | **DB** | DR | XHSS | ZA (S) | |
| 37676 a | **WC** | WC | AWCA | CS | Loch Rannoch |
| 37682 ar | **DS** | DR | XHNC | KM | |
| 37685 a | **WC** | WC | AWCA | CS | Loch Arkaig |
| 37688 ar† | **DS** | DR | XHNC | KM | Kingmoor TMD |
| 37696 as | **F** | DR | XHSS | ZA (S) | |

**Class 37/7. Refurbished locos. Main generator replaced by alternator. Regeared (CP7) bogies. Ballast weights added.** Details as Class 37/5 except:
**Main Alternator:** GEC G564AZ (37796–803) Brush BA1005A (others).
**Maximum Tractive Effort:** 276 kN (62000 lbf).
**Weight:** 120 t.         **RA:** 7.

| 37703 | **DS** | DR | XHHP | Daventry | |
| 37706 | **WC** | WC | AWCA | CS | |
| 37710 | **LH** | WC | AWCX | CS (S) | |
| 37712 a | **WC** | WC | AWCX | CS (S) | |

| 37714 | **DS** | DR | XHHP | Daventry |
| 37716 | **GIF** | DR | XHHP | ZA (S) |
| 37718 | **GIF** | DR | XHHP | ZA (S) |
| 37800 | **GIF** | EP | EPUK | WH (S) |
| 37884 | **GIF** | EP | EPUK | WH (S) |

**Class 97/3. Class 37s refurbished for Network Rail for use on the Cambrian Lines** which are signalled by ERTMS. Details as Class 37/0.

| 97301 | (37100) | e | **Y** | NR | QETS | ZA | |
| 97302 | (37170) | e | **Y** | NR | QETS | ZA | |
| 97303 | (37178) | e | **Y** | NR | QETS | ZA | |
| 97304 | (37217) | e | **Y** | NR | QETS | ZA | John Tiley |

# CLASS 40     ENGLISH ELECTRIC     1Co-Co1

**Built:** 1958–62 by English Electric at Vulcan Foundry, Newton-le-Willows.
**Engine:** English Electric 16SVT Mk2 of 1490 kW (2000 hp) at 850 rpm.
**Main Generator:** English Electric 822/4C.
**Traction Motors:** English Electric 526/5D or EE526/7D.
**Maximum Tractive Effort:** 231 kN (52000 lbf).
**Continuous Tractive Effort:** 137 kN (30900 lbf) at 18.8 mph.

| | |
|---|---|
| **Power At Rail:** 1160 kW (1550 hp). | **Train Brakes:** Air & vacuum. |
| **Brake Force:** 51 t. | **Dimensions:** 21.18 x 2.78 m. |
| **Weight:** 132 t. | **Wheel Diameter:** 914/1143 mm. |
| **Design Speed:** 90 mph. | **Maximum Speed:** 90 mph. |
| **Fuel Capacity:** 3250 litres. | **RA:** 6. |
| **Train Supply:** Steam. | **Multiple Working:** Blue Star. |

Originally numbered D345. Currently carries No. 345.

| 40145 | **B** | 40 | ELRD | BQ |

# CLASS 43     BREL/PAXMAN     Bo-Bo

**Built:** 1975–82 by BREL at Crewe Works.
**Engine:** MTU 16V4000R41R of 1680kW (2250 hp) at 1500 rpm.
(* Paxman 12VP185 of 1565 kW (2100 hp) at 1500 rpm.)
**Main Alternator:** Brush BA1001B.
**Traction Motors:** Brush TMH68–46 or GEC G417AZ, frame mounted.
**Maximum Tractive Effort:** 80 kN (17980 lbf).
**Continuous Tractive Effort:** 46 kN (10340 lbf) at 64.5 mph.

| | |
|---|---|
| **Power At Rail:** 1320 kW (1770 hp). | **Train Brakes:** Air. |
| **Brake Force:** 35 t. | **Dimensions:** 17.79 x 2.74 m. |
| **Weight:** 70.25 t. | **Wheel Diameter:** 1020 mm. |
| **Design Speed:** 125 mph. | **Maximum Speed:** 125 mph. |
| **Fuel Capacity:** 4500 litres. | **RA:** 5. |
| **Train Supply:** Three-phase electric. | |

**Multiple Working:** Within class, jumpers at non-driving end only.

† Buffer fitted.

43013, 43014 & 43062 are fitted with measuring apparatus & front-end cameras.

| 43002 | **FB** | A | EFPC | LA | |
|---|---|---|---|---|---|
| 43003 | **FB** | A | EFPC | LA | ISAMBARD KINGDOM BRUNEL |
| 43004 | **FB** | A | EFPC | LA | First for the future/ |
| | | | | | First ar gyfer y dyfodol |
| 43005 | **FB** | A | EFPC | LA | |
| 43009 | **FB** | A | EFPC | LA | First transforming travel |
| 43010 | **FB** | A | EFPC | LA | |
| 43012 | **FB** | A | EFPC | LA | |
| 43013 † | **Y** | P | QCAR | EC | |
| 43014 † | **Y** | P | QCAR | EC | |
| 43015 | **FB** | A | EFPC | LA | |
| 43016 | **FB** | A | EFPC | LA | |
| 43017 | **FB** | A | EFPC | LA | |
| 43018 | **FB** | A | EFPC | LA | |
| 43020 | **FB** | A | EFPC | LA | MTU Power. Passion. Partnership |
| 43021 | **FB** | A | EFPC | LA | David Austin – Cartoonist |
| 43022 | **FB** | A | EFPC | LA | |
| 43023 | **FB** | A | EFPC | LA | |
| 43024 | **FB** | A | EFPC | LA | Great Western Society 1961–2011 |
| | | | | | Didcot Railway Centre |
| 43025 | **FB** | A | EFPC | LA | IRO The Institution of Railway Operators |
| | | | | | 2000–2010 TEN YEARS |
| | | | | | PROMOTING OPERATIONAL EXCELLENCE |
| 43026 | **FB** | A | EFPC | LA | |
| 43027 | **FB** | A | EFPC | LA | Glorious Devon |
| 43028 | **FB** | A | EFPC | LA | |
| 43029 | **FB** | A | EFPC | LA | |
| 43030 | **FB** | A | EFPC | LA | Christian Lewis Trust |
| 43031 | **FB** | A | EFPC | LA | |
| 43032 | **FB** | A | EFPC | LA | |
| 43033 | **FB** | A | EFPC | LA | Driver Brian Cooper |
| | | | | | 15 June 1947–5 October 1999 |
| 43034 | **FB** | A | EFPC | LA | TravelWatch SouthWest |
| 43035 | **FB** | A | EFPC | LA | |
| 43036 | **FB** | A | EFPC | LA | |
| 43037 | **FB** | A | EFPC | LA | PENYDARREN |
| 43040 | **FB** | A | EFPC | LA | Bristol St. Philip's Marsh |
| 43041 | **FB** | A | EFPC | OO | Meningitis Trust Support for Life |
| 43042 | **FB** | A | EFPC | OO | |
| 43043 * | **ST** | P | EMPC | NL | |
| 43044 * | **ST** | P | EMPC | NL | |
| 43045 * | **ST** | P | EMPC | NL | |
| 43046 * | **ST** | P | EMPC | NL | |
| 43047 * | **ST** | P | EMPC | NL | |
| 43048 * | **ST** | P | EMPC | NL | T.C.B. Miller MBE |
| 43049 * | **ST** | P | EMPC | NL | Neville Hill |
| 43050 * | **ST** | P | EMPC | NL | |
| 43052 * | **ST** | P | EMPC | NL | |
| 43053 | **FB** | P | EFPC | LE | University of Worcester |

| 43054 | * | **ST** | P | EMPC | NL | |
| 43055 | * | **ST** | P | EMPC | NL | The Sheffield Star 125 Years |
| 43056 | | **FB** | P | EFPC | LE | The Royal British Legion |
| 43058 | * | **ST** | P | EMPC | NL | |
| 43059 | * | **ST** | P | EMPC | NL | |
| 43060 | * | **ST** | P | EMPC | NL | |
| 43061 | * | **ST** | P | EMPC | NL | |
| 43062 | | **Y** | P | QCAR | EC | John Armitt |
| 43063 | | **FB** | P | EFPC | OO | |
| 43064 | * | **ST** | P | EMPC | NL | |
| 43066 | * | **ST** | P | EMPC | NL | |
| 43069 | | **FB** | P | EFPC | OO | |
| 43070 | | **FB** | P | EFPC | OO | The Corps of Royal Electrical and Mechanical Engineers |
| 43071 | | **FB** | P | EFPC | OO | |
| 43073 | * | **ST** | P | EMPC | NL | |
| 43075 | * | **ST** | P | EMPC | NL | |
| 43076 | * | **ST** | P | EMPC | NL | IN SUPPORT OF HELP for HEROES |
| 43078 | | **FB** | P | EFPC | OO | |
| 43079 | | **FB** | P | EFPC | OO | |
| 43081 | * | **ST** | P | EMPC | NL | |
| 43082 | * | **ST** | P | EMPC | NL | RAILWAY children – THE VOICE FOR STREET CHILDREN WORLDWIDE |
| 43083 | * | **ST** | P | EMPC | NL | |
| 43086 | | **FB** | P | EFPC | OO | |
| 43087 | | **FB** | P | EFPC | OO | 11 Explosive Ordnance Disposal Regiment Royal Logistic Corps |
| 43088 | | **FB** | P | EFPC | OO | |
| 43089 | * | **ST** | P | EMPC | NL | |
| 43091 | | **FB** | P | EFPC | OO | |
| 43092 | | **FB** | FG | EFPC | OO | |
| 43093 | | **FB** | FG | EFPC | OO | |
| 43094 | | **FB** | FG | EFPC | OO | |
| 43097 | | **FB** | FG | EFPC | OO | Environment Agency |
| 43098 | | **FB** | FG | EFPC | OO | |
| 43122 | | **FB** | FG | EFPC | OO | |
| 43124 | | **FB** | A | EFPC | LE | |
| 43125 | | **FB** | A | EFPC | LE | |
| 43126 | | **FB** | A | EFPC | LE | |
| 43127 | | **FB** | A | EFPC | LE | Sir Peter Parker 1924–2002 Cotswold Line 150 |
| 43128 | | **FB** | A | EFPC | LE | |
| 43129 | | **FB** | A | EFPC | LE | |
| 43130 | | **FB** | A | EFPC | LE | |
| 43131 | | **FB** | A | EFPC | LE | |
| 43132 | | **FB** | A | EFPC | LE | We Save the Children – Will You? |
| 43133 | | **FB** | A | EFPC | LE | |
| 43134 | | **FB** | A | EFPC | LE | |
| 43135 | | **FB** | A | EFPC | LE | |
| 43136 | | **FB** | A | EFPC | LE | |
| 43137 | | **FB** | A | EFPC | LE | Newton Abbot 150 |

| 43138 | **FB** | A  | EFPC | LE | |
| 43139 | **FB** | A  | EFPC | LE | Driver Stan Martin |
|       |        |    |      |    | 25 June 1950 – 6 November 2004 |
| 43140 | **FB** | A  | EFPC | LE | Landore Diesel Depot |
|       |        |    |      |    | 1963 Celebrating 50 years 2013/ |
|       |        |    |      |    | Depo Diesel Glandŵr |
|       |        |    |      |    | 1963 Dathlu 50 Mlynedd 2013 |
| 43141 | **FB** | A  | EFPC | LE | |
| 43142 | **FB** | A  | EFPC | LE | Reading Panel Signal Box 1965–2010 |
| 43143 | **FB** | A  | EFPC | LE | Stroud 700 |
| 43144 | **FB** | A  | EFPC | LE | |
| 43145 | **FB** | A  | EFPC | LE | |
| 43146 | **FB** | A  | EFPC | LE | |
| 43147 | **FB** | A  | EFPC | LE | |
| 43148 | **FB** | A  | EFPC | LE | |
| 43149 | **FB** | A  | EFPC | LE | University of Plymouth |
| 43150 | **FB** | A  | EFPC | LE | |
| 43151 | **FB** | A  | EFPC | LE | |
| 43152 | **FB** | A  | EFPC | LE | |
| 43153 | **FB** | FG | EFPC | OO | |
| 43154 | **FB** | FG | EFPC | OO | |
| 43155 | **FB** | FG | EFPC | OO | |
| 43156 | **FB** | P  | EFPC | OO | Dartington International Summer School |
| 43158 | **FB** | FG | EFPC | OO | |
| 43159 | **FB** | P  | EFPC | OO | |
| 43160 | **FB** | P  | EFPC | OO | Sir Moir Lockhead OBE |
| 43161 | **FB** | P  | EFPC | OO | |
| 43162 | **FB** | P  | EFPC | OO | |
| 43163 | **FB** | A  | EFPC | OO | Exeter Panel Signal Box |
|       |        |    |      |    | 21st Anniversary 2009 |
| 43164 | **FB** | A  | EFPC | OO | |
| 43165 | **FB** | A  | EFPC | OO | Prince Michael of Kent |
| 43168 | **FB** | A  | EFPC | OO | |
| 43169 | **FB** | A  | EFPC | OO | THE NATIONAL TRUST |
| 43170 | **FB** | A  | EFPC | OO | |
| 43171 | **FB** | A  | EFPC | OO | |
| 43172 | **FB** | A  | EFPC | OO | |
| 43174 | **FB** | A  | EFPC | OO | |
| 43175 | **FB** | A  | EFPC | OO | GWR 175TH ANNIVERSARY |
| 43176 | **FB** | A  | EFPC | OO | |
| 43177 | **FB** | A  | EFPC | OO | |
| 43179 | **FB** | A  | EFPC | OO | Pride of Laira |
| 43180 | **FB** | P  | EFPC | OO | |
| 43181 | **FB** | A  | EFPC | OO | |
| 43182 | **FB** | A  | EFPC | OO | |
| 43183 | **FB** | A  | EFPC | OO | |
| 43185 | **FB** | A  | EFPC | OO | Great Western |
| 43186 | **FB** | A  | EFPC | OO | |
| 43187 | **FB** | A  | EFPC | OO | |
| 43188 | **FB** | A  | EFPC | OO | |
| 43189 | **FB** | A  | EFPC | OO | RAILWAY HERITAGE TRUST |

| | | | | | |
|---|---|---|---|---|---|
| 43190 | **FB** | A  | EFPC | OO | |
| 43191 | **FB** | A  | EFPC | OO | |
| 43192 | **FB** | A  | EFPC | OO | |
| 43193 | **FB** | P  | EFPC | OO | |
| 43194 | **FB** | FG | EFPC | OO | |
| 43195 | **FB** | P  | EFPC | OO | |
| 43196 | **FB** | P  | EFPC | OO | |
| 43197 | **FB** | P  | EFPC | OO | |
| 43198 | **FB** | FG | EFPC | OO | Oxfordshire 2007 |

**Class 43/2. Rebuilt East Coast, CrossCountry and Grand Central power cars**. Power cars have been renumbered by adding 200 to their original number or 400 to their original number (Grand Central) except 43123 which became 43423.

| | | | | | |
|---|---|---|---|---|---|
| 43206 (43006) | **EC** | A | IECP | EC | |
| 43207 (43007) | **XC** | A | EHPC | EC | |
| 43208 (43008) | **NX** | A | IECP | EC | Lincolnshire Echo |
| 43238 (43038) | **EC** | A | IECP | EC | |
| 43239 (43039) | **EC** | A | IECP | EC | |
| 43251 (43051) | **EC** | P | IECP | EC | |
| 43257 (43057) | **EC** | P | IECP | EC | |
| 43272 (43072) | **EC** | P | IECP | EC | |
| 43274 (43074) | **EC** | P | IECP | EC | |
| 43277 (43077) | **EC** | P | IECP | EC | |
| 43285 (43085) | **XC** | P | EHPC | EC | |
| 43290 (43090) | **EC** | P | IECP | EC | mtu fascination of power |
| 43295 (43095) | **EC** | A | IECP | EC | |
| 43296 (43096) | **EC** | A | IECP | EC | |
| 43299 (43099) | **EC** | P | IECP | EC | |
| 43300 (43100) | **EC** | P | IECP | EC | Craigentinny |
| 43301 (43101) | **XC** | P | EHPC | EC | |
| 43302 (43102) | **EC** | P | IECP | EC | |
| 43303 (43103) | **XC** | P | EHPC | EC | |
| 43304 (43104) | **XC** | A | EHPC | EC | |
| 43305 (43105) | **NX** | A | IECP | EC | |
| 43306 (43106) | **EC** | A | IECP | EC | |
| 43307 (43107) | **EC** | A | IECP | EC | |
| 43308 (43108) | **EC** | A | IECP | EC | |
| 43309 (43109) | **EC** | A | IECP | EC | |
| 43310 (43110) | **NX** | A | IECP | EC | |
| 43311 (43111) | **EC** | A | IECP | EC | |
| 43312 (43112) | **NX** | A | IECP | EC | |
| 43313 (43113) | **NX** | A | IECP | EC | |
| 43314 (43114) | **EC** | A | IECP | EC | |
| 43315 (43115) | **EC** | A | IECP | EC | |
| 43316 (43116) | **EC** | A | IECP | EC | |
| 43317 (43117) | **EC** | A | IECP | EC | |
| 43318 (43118) | **NX** | A | IECP | EC | |
| 43319 (43119) | **EC** | A | IECP | EC | |
| 43320 (43120) | **NX** | A | IECP | EC | |
| 43321 (43121) | **XC** | P | EHPC | EC | |

| | | | | | | |
|---|---|---|---|---|---|---|
| 43357 | (43157) | **XC** | P | EHPC | EC | |
| 43366 | (43166) | **XC** | A | EHPC | EC | |
| 43367 | (43167) | **EC** | A | IECP | EC | DELTIC 50 1955–2005 |
| 43378 | (43178) | **XC** | A | EHPC | EC | |
| 43384 | (43184) | **XC** | A | EHPC | EC | |
| 43423 | (43123) † | **GC** | A | GCHP | HT | 'VALENTA' 1972–2010 |
| 43465 | (43065) † | **GC** | A | GCHP | HT | |
| 43467 | (43067) † | **GC** | A | GCHP | HT | |
| 43468 | (43068) † | **GC** | A | GCHP | HT | |
| 43480 | (43080) † | **GC** | A | GCHP | HT | |
| 43484 | (43084) † | **GC** | A | GCHP | HT | PETER FOX 1942–2011 PLATFORM 5 |

# CLASS 47     BR/BRUSH/SULZER     Co-Co

**Built:** 1963–67 by Brush Traction, at Loughborough or by BR at Crewe Works.
**Engine:** Sulzer 12LDA28C of 1920 kW (2580 hp) at 750 rpm.
**Main Generator:** Brush TG160-60 Mk4 or TM172-50 Mk1.
**Traction Motors:** Brush TM64-68 Mk1 or Mk1A.
**Maximum Tractive Effort:** 267 kN (60000 lbf).
**Continuous Tractive Effort:** 133 kN (30000 lbf) at 26 mph.
**Power At Rail:** 1550 kW (2080 hp).     **Train Brakes:** Air.
**Brake Force:** 61 t.     **Dimensions:** 19.38 x 2.79 m.
**Weight:** 111.5–120.6 t.     **Wheel Diameter:** 1143 mm.
**Design Speed:** 95 mph.
**Maximum Speed:** 95 mph (* 75 mph).
**Fuel Capacity:** 3273 (+ 5887).     **RA:** 6 or 7.
**Train Supply:** Not equipped.
**Multiple Working:** m Green Circle (operational locos only).

Originally numbered in series D1100–D1111, D1500–D1999 but not in order.

**Non-standard liveries/numbering:**

| | |
|---|---|
| 47270 | Also carries the number 1971. |
| 47773 | Also carries the number D1755. |
| 47812 | Also carries the number D1916. |
| 47815 | Also carries the number D1748. |

**Class 47/0 (Dual-braked locos) or Class 47/2 (Air-braked locos). Standard Design.** Details as above.

| | | | | | | |
|---|---|---|---|---|---|---|
| 47194 | a+ | **F** | WC | AWCX | CS (S) | |
| 47236 | + | **FE** | WC | AWCX | CS (S) | |
| 47237 | x+ | **WC** | WC | AWCA | CS | |
| 47245 | x+m | **WC** | WC | AWCA | CS | |
| 47270 | a+ | **B** | PO | AWCA | CS | SWIFT |

**Class 47/3 (Dual-braked locos) or Class 47/2 (Air-braked locos).**
Details as Class 47/0 except: **Weight:** 113.7 t.

| | | | | | | |
|---|---|---|---|---|---|---|
| 47355 | am+ | **K** | WC | AWCX | CS (S) | |
| 47368 | x | **F** | WC | AWCX | CS (S) | |
| 47375 | +m | **B** | NS | NRLO | BO | TINSLEY TRACTION DEPOT |

**Class 47/4. Electric Train Supply equipment.**
Details as Class 47/0 except:

**Weight:** 120.4–125.1 t.                    **Fuel Capacity:** 3273 (+ 5537) litres.
**Train Supply:** Electric. ETH 66.          **RA:** 7.

| | | | | | |
|---|---|---|---|---|---|
| 47492 | x | **RX** | WC | AWCX | CS (S) |
| 47500 | x | **WC** | WC | AWCX | CS (S) |
| 47501 | xm+ | **DS** | DR | XHNB | KM | Craftsman |
| 47526 | x | **BL** | WC | AWCX | CS (S) |
| 47580 | x | **BL** | 47 | MBDL | TM | County of Essex |

**Class 47/7. Former Railnet dedicated locos.** All have twin fuel tanks.

| | | | | | |
|---|---|---|---|---|---|
| 47727 | m | **CS** | CS | COLO | WH | Rebecca |
| 47739 | m | **CS** | CS | COLO | WH | Robin of Templecombe 1938–2013 |
| 47746 | x | **WC** | WC | AWCA | CS | |
| 47749 | m | **CS** | CS | COLO | WH | Demelza |
| 47760 | x | **WC** | WC | AWCA | CS | |
| 47768 | | **RX** | WC | AWCX | CS (S) | |
| 47769 | | **V** | HN | HNRL | Dartmoor Rly | Resolve |
| 47772 | x | **RX** | WC | AWCX | CS (S) | |
| 47773 | x | **GG** | 70 | MBDL | TM | |
| 47776 | x | **RX** | WC | AWCX | CS (S) | |
| 47786 | | **WC** | WC | AWCA | CS | Roy Castle OBE |
| 47787 | | **WC** | WC | AWCX | CS (S) | Windsor Castle |
| 47790 | m | **VN** | DR | XHNB | KM | Galloway Princess |

**Class 47/4 continued.** RA6. Most fitted with extended-range fuel tanks (+).

| | | | | | |
|---|---|---|---|---|---|
| 47798 | x | **RP** | NM | MBDL | YK | Prince William |
| 47802 | +m | **DS** | DR | XHAC | KM | Pride of Cumbria |
| 47804 | | **WC** | WC | AWCA | CS | |
| 47805 | +m | **DS** | DR | XHAC | KM | John Scott 12.5.45–22.5.12 |
| 47810 | +m | **DS** | DR | XHAC | KM | Peter Bath MBE 1927–2006 |
| 47811 | + | **GL** | FL | DFLH | BA (S) | |
| 47812 | +m | **GG** | RV | RTLO | CD | |
| 47813 | +m | **DS** | DR | XHNB | KM | Solent |
| 47815 | +m | **GG** | RV | RTLO | CD | GREAT WESTERN |
| 47816 | + | **GL** | FL | DFLH | BA (S) | |
| 47818 | +m | **DS** | DR | XHAC | KM | |
| 47826 | + | **WC** | WC | AWCA | CS | |
| 47828 | +m | **DS** | DR | XHAC | KM | |
| 47830 | + | **GL** | FL | DFLH | BH (S) | |
| 47832 | +m | **VN** | DR | XHNB | KM | Solway Princess |
| 47841 | +m | **DS** | DR | XHAC | KM | |
| 47843 | +m | **RV** | RV | RTLO | CD | VULCAN |
| 47847 | +m | **BL** | RV | RTLO | CD (S) | |
| 47848 | +m | **RV** | RV | RTLO | CD | TITAN STAR |
| 47851 | + | **WC** | WC | AWCA | CS | |
| 47853 | +m | **DS** | DR | XHAC | KM | RAIL EXPRESS |
| 47854 | + | **WC** | WC | AWCA | CS | Diamond Jubilee |

## CLASS 50     ENGLISH ELECTRIC     Co-Co

**Built:** 1967–68 by English Electric at Vulcan Foundry, Newton-le-Willows.
**Engine:** English Electric 16CVST of 2010 kW (2700 hp) at 850 rpm.
**Main Generator:** English Electric 840/4B.
**Traction Motors:** English Electric 538/5A.
**Maximum Tractive Effort:** 216 kN (48500 lbf).
**Continuous Tractive Effort:** 147 kN (33000 lbf) at 23.5 mph.

| | |
|---|---|
| **Power At Rail:** 1540 kW (2070 hp). | **Train Brakes:** Air & vacuum. |
| **Brake Force:** 59 t. | **Dimensions:** 20.88 x 2.78 m. |
| **Weight:** 116.9 t. | **Wheel Diameter:** 1092 mm. |
| **Design Speed:** 105 mph. | **Maximum Speed:** 90 mph. |
| **Fuel Capacity:** 4796 litres. | **RA:** 6. |
| **Train Supply:** Electric, index 61. | **Multiple Working:** Orange Square. |

Originally numbered D444 & D449.

| 50044 | **B** | 50 | CFOL | KR | Exeter |
|---|---|---|---|---|---|
| 50049 | **BL** | 50 | CFOL | KR | Defiance |

## CLASS 52     BR/MAYBACH     C-C

**Built:** 1961–64 by BR at Swindon Works.
**Engine:** Two Maybach MD655 of 1007 kW (1350 hp) at 1500 rpm.
**Transmission:** Hydraulic. Voith L630rV.
**Maximum Tractive Effort:** 297 kN (66700 lbf).
**Continuous Tractive Effort:** 201 kN (45200 lbf) at 14.5 mph.

| | |
|---|---|
| **Power At Rail:** 1490 kW (2000 hp). | **Train Brakes:** Air & vacuum. |
| **Brake Force:** 83 t. | **Dimensions:** 20.7 m x 2.78 m. |
| **Weight:** 110 t. | **Wheel Diameter:** 1092 mm. |
| **Design Speed:** 90 mph. | **Maximum Speed:** 90 mph. |
| **Fuel Capacity:** 3900 litres. | **RA:** 6. |
| **Train Supply:** Steam. | **Multiple Working:** Not equipped. |

Never allocated a number in the 1972 number series.

Registered on TOPS as No. 89416.

| D1015 | **M** | DT | MBDL | | TM | WESTERN CHAMPION |
|---|---|---|---|---|---|---|

## CLASS 55     ENGLISH ELECTRIC     Co-Co

**Built:** 1961 by English Electric at Vulcan Foundry, Newton-le-Willows.
**Engine:** Two Napier-Deltic D18-25 of 1230 kW (1650 hp) each at 1500 rpm.
**Main Generators:** Two English Electric 829/1A.
**Traction Motors:** English Electric 538/A.
**Maximum Tractive Effort:** 222 kN (50000 lbf).
**Continuous Tractive Effort:** 136 kN (30500 hp) at 32.5 mph.

| | |
|---|---|
| **Power At Rail:** 1969 kW (2640 hp). | **Train Brakes:** Air & vacuum. |
| **Brake Force:** 51 t. | **Dimensions:** 21.18 x 2.68 m. |
| **Weight:** 100 t. | **Wheel Diameter:** 1092 mm. |
| **Design Speed:** 105 mph. | **Maximum Speed:** 100 mph. |

**Fuel Capacity**: 3755 litres.       **RA**: 5.
**Train Supply**: Electric, index 66.  **Multiple Working**: Not equipped.

Originally numbered D9002, D9009 & D9000.

55022 registered on TOPS as No. 89500.

| 55002 | **B** | NM | MBDL | YK | THE KING'S OWN YORKSHIRE LIGHT INFANTRY |
| 55009 | **GG** | DP | MBDL | BQ | ALYCIDON |
| 55022 | **B** | MW | ELRD | BQ | ROYAL SCOTS GREY |

# CLASS 56   BRUSH/BR/RUSTON   Co-Co

**Built**: 1976–84 by Electroputere at Craiova, Romania (as sub contractors for Brush) or BREL at Doncaster or Crewe Works.
**Engine**: Ruston Paxman 16RK3CT of 2460 kW (3250 hp) at 900 rpm.
**Main Alternator**: Brush BA1101A.
**Traction Motors**: Brush TM73-62.
**Maximum Tractive Effort**: 275 kN (61800 lbf).
**Continuous Tractive Effort**: 240 kN (53950 lbf) at 16.8 mph.
**Power At Rail**: 1790 kW (2400 hp).  **Train Brakes**: Air.
**Brake Force**: 60 t.                **Dimensions**: 19.36 x 2.79 m.
**Weight**: 126 t.                    **Wheel Diameter**: 1143 mm.
**Design Speed**: 80 mph.             **Maximum Speed**: 80 mph.
**Fuel Capacity**: 5228 litres.       **RA**: 7.
**Train Supply**: Not equipped.       **Multiple Working**: Red Diamond.

All equipped with Slow Speed Control.

Class 56s exported for use abroad are listed in section 1.6 of this book.

**Non-standard liveries**: 56009 All over blue.

56303 All over dark green.

56311 Light grey with yellow cabsides.

| 56007 | **FER** | UR | MBDL | LR (S) |
| 56009 | **O** | UR | MBDL | BL (S) |
| 56018 | **FER** | UR | MBDL | WH (S) |
| 56031 | **FER** | UR | MBDL | LR (S) |
| 56032 | **FER** | UR | MBDL | WH (S) |
| 56037 | **E** | UR | MBDL | BL (S) |
| 56038 | **FER** | UR | MBDL | BO (S) |
| 56049 | **FER** | CS | COLS | WH (S) |
| 56051 | **FER** | CS | COLS | WH (S) |
| 56060 | **FER** | UR | MBDL | WH (S) |
| 56065 | **FER** | UR | MBDL | BO (S) |
| 56069 | **FER** | UR | MBDL | LR (S) |
| 56074 | **FER** | CS | COLS | WH (S) |
| 56077 | **LH** | UR | MBDL | BL (S) |
| 56078 | **CS** | CS | COFS | WH |
| 56081 | **FER** | UR | MBDL | LR (S) |
| 56087 | **CS** | CS | COFS | WH |

| | | | | | |
|---|---|---|---|---|---|
| 56090 | **FER** | CS | COLS | WH (S) | |
| 56091 | **FER** | BA | HTLX | WH | |
| 56094 | **CS** | CS | COFS | WH | |
| 56096 | **FER** | CS | COLS | WH (S) | |
| 56098 | **LH** | UR | MBDL | BH (S) | |
| 56103 | **FER** | BA | HTLX | WH (S) | |
| 56104 | **FER** | UR | MBDL | WH (S) | |
| 56105 | **CS** | CS | COFS | WH | |
| 56106 | **FER** | UR | MBDL | LR (S) | |
| 56113 | **CS** | CS | COFS | WH | |
| 56128 | **F** | BA | HTLX | WH (S) | |

| | | | | | |
|---|---|---|---|---|---|
| 56301 (56045) | **FA** | 56 | HTLX | WH | |
| 56302 (56124) | **CS** | CS | COFS | WH | |
| 56303 (56125) | **O** | BA | HTLX | WH | |
| 56311 (56057) | **O** | BA | HTLX | WH | |
| 56312 (56003) | **DC** | BA | HTLX | WH | Jeremiah Dixon Son of County Durham Surveyor of the Mason-Dixon Line U.S.A. |

# CLASS 57                     BRUSH/GM                        Co-Co

**Built:** 1964–65 by Brush Traction at Loughborough or BR at Crewe Works as Class 47. Rebuilt 1997–2004 by Brush Traction at Loughborough.
**Engine:** General Motors 12 645 E3 of 1860 kW (2500 hp) at 904 rpm.
**Main Alternator:** Brush BA1101D.
**Traction Motors:** Brush TM64-68 Mark 1 or Mark 1a.
**Maximum Tractive Effort:** 244.5 kN (55000 lbf).
**Continuous Tractive Effort:** 140 kN (31500 lbf) at ?? mph.

| | |
|---|---|
| **Power at Rail:** 1507 kW (2025 hp). | **Train Brakes:** Air. |
| **Brake Force:** 80 t. | **Dimensions:** 19.38 x 2.79 m. |
| **Weight:** 120.6 t. | **Wheel Diameter:** 1143 mm. |
| **Design Speed:** 75 mph. | **Maximum Speed:** 75 mph. |
| **Fuel Capacity:** 5550 litres. | **RA:** 6 |
| **Train Supply:** Not equipped. | **Multiple Working:** † DRS system. |

**Class 57/0. No Train Supply Equipment. Rebuilt 1997–2000.**

| | | | | |
|---|---|---|---|---|
| 57001 (47356) | **WC** | WC | AWCA | CS |
| 57002 (47322) † | **DS** | P | XHCK | KM |
| 57003 (47317) † | **DS** | P | XHCK | KM |
| 57004 (47347) † | **DS** | DR | XHCK | KM |
| 57005 (47350) | **AZ** | WC | AWCX | CS (S) |
| 57006 (47187) | **WC** | WC | AWCA | CS |
| 57007 (47332) † | **DS** | P | XHCK | KM |
| 57008 (47060) † | **DS** | P | XHCK | KM |
| 57009 (47079) † | **DS** | P | XHCK | KM |
| 57010 (47231) † | **DS** | P | XHCK | KM |
| 57011 (47329) † | **DS** | P | XHCK | KM |
| 57012 (47204) † | **DS** | P | XHCK | KM |

**Class 57/3. Electric Train Supply Equipment. Former Virgin Trains locos. Rebuilt 2002–04.** Details as Class 57/0 except:

**Engine:** General Motors 12645F3B of 2050 kW (2750 hp) at 954 rpm.
**Main Alternator:** Brush BA1101F (recovered from a Class 56) or Brush BA1101G.
**Fuel Capacity:** 5887 litres.                    **Train Supply:** Electric, index 100.
**Design Speed:** 95 mph.                          **Maximum Speed:** 95 mph.
**Brake Force:** 60 t.                             **Weight:** 117 t.

| | | | | | |
|---|---|---|---|---|---|
| 57301 | (47845) i | **Y** | P | QADD | ZG |
| 57302 | (47827) d | **DS** | P | XHVT | KM | Chad Varah |
| 57303 | (47705) d | **Y** | P | QADD | ZG |
| 57304 | (47807) d | **DS** | P | XHVT | KM | Pride of Cheshire |
| 57305 | (47822) d | **Y** | P | QADD | ZG |
| 57306 | (47814) i | **Y** | P | QADD | ZG |
| 57307 | (47225) d | **DR** | P | XHVT | KM | LADY PENELOPE |
| 57308 | (47846) d | **DS** | P | XHVT | KM | County of Staffordshire |
| 57309 | (47806) d | **DS** | P | XHVT | KM | Pride of Crewe |
| 57310 | (47831) d | **Y** | P | QADD | ZG |
| 57311 | (47817) d | **DS** | P | XHVT | KM | Thunderbird |
| 57312 | (47330) d | **Y** | P | QADD | ZG | Peter Henderson |
| 57313 | (47371) | **AB** | WC | AWCA | CS |
| 57314 | (47372) | **WC** | WC | AWCA | CS |
| 57315 | (47234) | **WC** | WC | AWCA | CS |
| 57316 | (47290) | **AB** | WC | AWCA | CS |

**Class 57/6. Electric Train Supply Equipment. Prototype ETS loco. Rebuilt 2001.** Details as Class 57/0 except:

**Main Alternator:** Brush BA1101E.                **Fuel Capacity:** 3273 litres.
**Train Supply:** Electric, index 95.              **Weight:** 113 t.
**Design Speed:** 95 mph.                          **Maximum Speed:** 95 mph.
**Brake Force:** 60 t.

| | | | | | |
|---|---|---|---|---|---|
| 57601 | (47825) | **WC** | WC | AWCA | CS |

**Class 57/6. Electric Train Supply Equipment. First Great Western locos. Rebuilt 2004.** Details as Class 57/3.

| | | | | | |
|---|---|---|---|---|---|
| 57602 | (47337) | **FB** | P | EFOO | OO | Restormel Castle |
| 57603 | (47349) | **FB** | P | EFOO | OO | Tintagel Castle |
| 57604 | (47209) | **GW** | P | EFOO | OO | PENDENNIS CASTLE |
| 57605 | (47206) | **FB** | P | EFOO | OO | Totnes Castle |

# CLASS 58                    BREL/RUSTON                    Co-Co

**Built:** 1983–87 by BREL at Doncaster Works.
**Engine:** Ruston Paxman 12RK3ACT of 2460 kW (3300 hp) at 1000 rpm.
**Main Alternator:** Brush BA1101B.      **Traction Motors:** Brush TM73-62.
**Maximum Tractive Effort:** 275 kN (61800 lbf).
**Continuous Tractive Effort:** 240 kN (53950 lbf) at 17.4 mph.
**Power At Rail:** 1780 kW (2387 hp).    **Train Brakes:** Air.
**Brake Force:** 60 t.                   **Dimensions:** 19.13 x 2.72 m.
**Weight:** 130 t.                       **Wheel Diameter:** 1120 mm.

**Design Speed:** 80 mph.
**Fuel Capacity:** 4214 litres.
**Train Supply:** Not equipped.

**Maximum Speed:** 80 mph.
**RA:** 7.
**Multiple Working:** Red Diamond.

All equipped with Slow Speed Control.

Class 58s exported for use abroad are listed in section 1.6 of this book.

| | | | | | |
|---|---|---|---|---|---|
| 58008 | **ML** | DB | WQDA | EH (S) | |
| 58012 | **F** | DB | WQCA | TO (S) | |
| 58022 | **F** | DB | WQCA | CD (S) | |
| 58023 | **ML** | DB | WQCA | TO (S) | |
| 58048 | **E** | DB | WQCA | CE (S) | |

# CLASS 59      GENERAL MOTORS      Co-Co

**Built:** 1985 (59001/002/004) or 1989 (59005) by General Motors, La Grange, Illinois, USA or 1990 (59101–104), 1994 (59201) and 1995 (59202–206) by General Motors, London, Ontario, Canada.
**Engine:** General Motors 16-645E3C two stroke of 2460 kW (3300 hp) at 904 rpm.
**Main Alternator:** General Motors AR11 MLD-D14A.
**Traction Motors:** General Motors D77B.
**Maximum Tractive Effort:** 506 kN (113 550 lbf).
**Continuous Tractive Effort:** 291 kN (65 300 lbf) at 14.3 mph.
**Power At Rail:** 1889 kW (2533 hp).  **Train Brakes:** Air.
**Brake Force:** 69 t.  **Dimensions:** 21.35 x 2.65 m.
**Weight:** 121 t.  **Wheel Diameter:** 1067 mm.
**Design Speed:** 60 (* 75) mph.  **Maximum Speed:** 60 (* 75) mph.
**Fuel Capacity:** 4546 litres.  **RA:** 7.
**Train Supply:** Not equipped.  **Multiple Working:** AAR System.

**Class 59/0. Owned by Aggregate Industries.**

| | | | | | |
|---|---|---|---|---|---|
| 59001 | **AI** | AI | XYPO | MD | YEOMAN ENDEAVOUR |
| 59002 | **FY** | AI | XYPO | MD | ALAN J DAY |
| 59004 | **FY** | AI | XYPO | MD | PAUL A HAMMOND |
| 59005 | **AI** | AI | XYPO | MD | KENNETH J PAINTER |

**Class 59/1. Owned by Hanson Quarry Products.**

| | | | | | |
|---|---|---|---|---|---|
| 59101 | **HA** | HA | XYPA | MD | Village of Whatley |
| 59102 | **HA** | HA | XYPA | MD | Village of Chantry |
| 59103 | **HA** | HA | XYPA | MD | Village of Mells |
| 59104 | **HA** | HA | XYPA | MD | Village of Great Elm |

**Class 59/2. Owned by DB Schenker.**

| | | | | | |
|---|---|---|---|---|---|
| 59201 | * | **DB** | DB | WDAM | MD |
| 59202 | * | **DB** | DB | WDAM | MD | Alan Meddows Taylor MD Mendip Rail Limited |
| 59203 | * | **DB** | DB | WDAM | MD |
| 59204 | * | **DB** | DB | WDAM | MD |
| 59205 | *b | **DB** | DB | WDAM | MD |
| 59206 | *b | **DB** | DB | WDAM | MD | John F. Yeoman Rail Pioneer |

# CLASS 60          BRUSH/MIRRLEES          Co-Co

**Built:** 1989–93 by Brush Traction at Loughborough.
**Engine:** Mirrlees 8MB275T of 2310 kW (3100 hp) at 1000 rpm.
**Main Alternator:** Brush BA1006A.
**Traction Motors:** Brush TM2161A.
**Maximum Tractive Effort:** 500 kN (106500 lbf).
**Continuous Tractive Effort:** 336 kN (71570 lbf) at 17.4 mph.
**Power At Rail:** 1800 kW (2415 hp).      **Train Brakes:** Air.
**Brake Force:** 74 (+ 62) t.              **Dimensions:** 21.34 x 2.64 m.
**Weight:** 129 (+ 131) t.                 **Wheel Diameter:** 1118 mm.
**Design Speed:** 62 mph.                  **Maximum Speed:** 60 mph.
**Fuel Capacity:** 4546 (+ 5225) litres.   **RA:** 8.
**Train Supply:** Not equipped.            **Multiple Working:** Within class.

All equipped with Slow Speed Control.

\* Refurbished locos.

60034, 60064, 60072, 60073, 60077, 60082, 60084 and 60090 carry their
names on one side only.

60500 originally carried the number 60016.

**Advertising/promotional liveries:** 60066 Powering Drax (silver).

60074  Teenage Cancer Trust (light blue).

60099  Tata Steel (silver).

| | | | | | |
|---|---|---|---|---|---|
| 60001 | \* | **DB** | DB | WCAT | TO |
| 60002 | + | **E** | DB | WQDA | CD (S) High Peak |
| 60003 | + | **E** | DB | WQBA | TO (S) FREIGHT TRANSPORT ASSOCIATION |
| 60004 | + | **E** | DB | WQBA | TO (S) |
| 60005 | + | **E** | DB | WQBA | TO (S) |
| 60006 | | **CU** | DB | WQBA | TO (S) |
| 60007 | +\* | **DB** | DB | WCBT | TO    The Spirit of Tom Kendell |
| 60008 | | **E** | DB | WQBA | TO (S) Sir William McAlpine |
| 60009 | + | **E** | DB | WQBA | TO (S) |
| 60010 | +\* | **DB** | DB | WCBT | TO |
| 60011 | + | **DB** | DB | WCBT | TO |
| 60012 | + | **E** | DB | WQBA | TO (S) |
| 60013 | | **EG** | DB | WQDA | TO (S) Robert Boyle |
| 60014 | | **EG** | DB | WQBA | TO (S) |
| 60015 | +\* | **DB** | DB | WCBT | TO |
| 60017 | +\* | **DB** | DB | WCBT | TO |
| 60018 | | **E** | DB | WQBA | TO (S) |
| 60019 | \* | **DB** | DB | WCAT | TO    Port of Grimsby & Immingham |
| 60020 | +\* | **DB** | DB | WCBT | TO |
| 60021 | + | **E** | DB | WQDA | TO (S) |
| 60022 | + | **E** | DB | WQBA | TO (S) |
| 60023 | + | **E** | DB | WQBA | TO (S) |
| 60024 | \* | **DB** | DB | WCAT | TO |
| 60025 | + | **E** | DB | WQBA | TO (S) |

| | | | | | |
|---|---|---|---|---|---|
| 60026 + | E | DB | WQDA | TO (S) | |
| 60027 + | E | DB | WQBA | TO (S) | |
| 60028 + | EG | DB | WQDA | CD (S) | John Flamsteed |
| 60029 | E | DB | WQDA | CD (S) | Clitheroe Castle |
| 60030 + | E | DB | WQDA | TO (S) | |
| 60031 | E | DB | WQBA | TO (S) | |
| 60032 | F | DB | WQBA | TO (S) | |
| 60033 + | CU | DB | WQBA | TO (S) | Tees Steel Express |
| 60034 | EG | DB | WQBA | TO (S) | Carnedd Llewelyn |
| 60035 | E | DB | WCAT | TO | |
| 60036 | E | DB | WQBA | TO (S) | GEFCO |
| 60037 + | E | DB | WQBA | TO (S) | |
| 60038 + | E | DB | WQDA | CD (S) | AvestaPolarit |
| 60039 * | DB | DB | WCAT | TO | |
| 60040 * | DB | DB | WCAT | TO | The Territorial Army Centenary |
| 60041 + | E | DB | WQDA | TO (S) | |
| 60042 | E | DB | WQBA | TO (S) | |
| 60043 | E | DB | WQBA | TO (S) | |
| 60044 | DB | DB | WCAT | TO | |
| 60045 | E | DB | WCAT | TO | The Permanent Way Institution |
| 60046 + | EG | DB | WQDA | CD (S) | William Wilberforce |
| 60047 | E | DB | WQDA | CD (S) | |
| 60048 | E | DB | WQDA | TO (S) | |
| 60049 | E | DB | WQAA | TO (S) | |
| 60050 | E | DB | WQBA | TO (S) | |
| 60051 + | E | DB | WQBA | TO (S) | |
| 60052 + | E | DB | WQBA | TO (S) | Glofa Twr – The last deep mine in Wales – Tower Colliery |
| 60053 | E | DB | WQBA | TO (S) | |
| 60054 +* | DB | DB | WCBT | TO | |
| 60055 + | EG | DB | WQDA | CD (S) | Thomas Barnardo |
| 60056 + | EG | DB | WQDA | CD (S) | William Beveridge |
| 60057 | EG | DB | WQBA | TO (S) | Adam Smith |
| 60058 + | E | DB | WQBA | TO (S) | |
| 60059 +* | DB | DB | WCBT | TO | Swinden Dalesman |
| 60060 | EG | DB | WQBA | TO (S) | |
| 60061 | F | DB | WQDA | TO (S) | |
| 60062 * | DB | DB | WCAT | TO | Stainless Pioneer |
| 60063 * | DB | DB | WCAT | TO | |
| 60064 + | EG | DB | WQBA | TO (S) | Back Tor |
| 60065 | E | DB | WCAT | TO | Spirit of JAGUAR |
| 60066 | AL | DB | WCAT | TO | |
| 60067 | EG | DB | WQBA | TO (S) | |
| 60068 | EG | DB | WQBA | TO (S) | |
| 60069 | E | DB | WQBA | TO (S) | Slioch |
| 60070 + | F | DB | WQBA | TO (S) | John Loudon McAdam |
| 60071 + | E | DB | WCBT | TO | Ribblehead Viaduct |
| 60072 | EG | DB | WQBA | TO (S) | Cairn Toul |
| 60073 | EG | DB | WQBA | TO (S) | Cairn Gorm |
| 60074 * | AL | DB | WCAT | TO | Teenage Spirit |
| 60075 | E | DB | WQBA | TO (S) | |

| | | | | | |
|---|---|---|---|---|---|
| 60076 | **EG** | DB | WQDA | CD (S) | |
| 60077 + | **EG** | DB | WQBA | TO (S) | Canisp |
| 60078 | **ML** | DB | WQBA | TO (S) | |
| 60079 * | **DB** | DB | WCAT | TO | |
| 60080 + | **E** | DB | WQBA | TO (S) | |
| 60081 + | **GW** | DB | WQBA | TO (S) | |
| 60082 | **EG** | DB | WQBA | CD (S) | Mam Tor |
| 60083 | **E** | DB | WQBA | TO (S) | |
| 60084 | **EG** | DB | WQBA | TO (S) | Cross Fell |
| 60085 | **E** | DB | WQDA | TO (S) | MINI Pride of Oxford |
| 60086 | **EG** | DB | WQBA | TO (S) | |
| 60087 | **E** | DB | WQDA | TO (S) | |
| 60088 | **F** | DB | WQBA | TO (S) | |
| 60089 + | **E** | DB | WQBA | TO (S) | |
| 60090 + | **EG** | DB | WQBA | TO (S) | Quinag |
| 60091 +* | **DB** | DB | WCBT | TO | |
| 60092 +* | **DB** | DB | WCBT | TO | |
| 60093 | **E** | DB | WQBA | TO (S) | |
| 60094 | **E** | DB | WQBA | TO (S) | Rugby Flyer |
| 60095 | **EG** | DB | WQDA | CD (S) | |
| 60096 + | **E** | DB | WQDA | BZ (S) | |
| 60097 + | **E** | DB | WQBA | TO (S) | |
| 60098 + | **E** | DB | WQBA | TO (S) | |
| 60099 | **AL** | DB | WCAT | TO | |
| 60100 * | **DB** | DB | WCAT | TO | |
| 60500 | **E** | DB | WQBA | TO (S) | |

# CLASS 66          GENERAL MOTORS/EMD          Co-Co

**Built:** 1998–2008 by General Motors/EMD, London, Ontario, Canada (Model JT42CWR (low emission locos Model JT42CWRM)) or 2013–14 by EMD/Progress Rail, Muncie, Indiana (66752–759).
**Engine:** General Motors 12N-710G3B-EC two stroke of 2385 kW (3200 hp) at 904 rpm (low emission locos General Motors 12N-710G3B-T2).
**Main Alternator:** General Motors AR8/CA6.
**Traction Motors:** General Motors D43TR.
**Maximum Tractive Effort:** 409 kN (92000 lbf).
**Continuous Tractive Effort:** 260 kN (58390 lbf) at 15.9 mph.

| | |
|---|---|
| **Power At Rail:** 1850 kW (2480 hp). | **Train Brakes:** Air. |
| **Brake Force:** 68 t. | **Dimensions:** 21.35 x 2.64 m. |
| **Weight:** 127 t. | **Wheel Diameter:** 1120 mm. |
| **Design Speed:** 87.5 mph. | **Maximum Speed:** 75 mph (unless stated). |
| **Fuel Capacity:** 6550 litres. | **RA:** 7. |
| **Train Supply:** Not equipped. | **Multiple Working:** AAR System. |

All equipped with Slow Speed Control.

Class 66s previously used in the UK but now in use abroad are listed in section 1.6 of this book. Some of the 60 DBS 66s moved to France return to Great Britain from time to time for maintenance or operational requirements.

**Advertising livery:** 66048 Stobart Rail (two tone blue & white).

**Class 66 delivery dates.** The Class 66 design has evolved over a 15-year -plus period, with over 400 locomotives delivered. For clarity the delivery dates (by year) for each batch of locos is as follows:

| | |
|---|---|
| 66001–250 | EWS (now DB Schenker). 1998–2000 (some now in use in France or Poland). |
| 66301–305 | Fastline. 2008. Now used by DRS. |
| 66401–410 | DRS. 2003. Now in use with GB Railfreight or Colas Rail and renumbered 66733–737 and 66742–746 (66734 since scrapped). |
| 66411–420 | DRS. 2006. Now leased by Freightliner (66411/412/417 exported to Poland). |
| 66421–430 | DRS. 2007 |
| 66431–434 | DRS. 2008 |
| 66501–505 | Freightliner. 1999 |
| 66506–520 | Freightliner. 2000 |
| 66521–525 | Freightliner. 2000 (66521 since scrapped). |
| 66526–531 | Freightliner. 2001 |
| 66532–537 | Freightliner. 2001 |
| 66538–543 | Freightliner. 2001 |
| 66544–553 | Freightliner. 2001 |
| 66554 | Freightliner. 2002† |
| 66555–566 | Freightliner. 2002 |
| 66567–574 | Freightliner. 2003. 66573–574 now used by Colas Rail and renumbered 66846–847. |
| 66575–577 | Freightliner. 2004. Now used by Colas Rail and renumbered 66848–850. |
| 66578–581 | Freightliner. 2005. Now used by GBRf and renumbered 66738–741. |
| 66582–594 | Freightliner. 2007 (66582/583/584/586 exported to Poland). |
| 66595–599 | Freightliner. 2008 |
| 66601–606 | Freightliner. 2000 |
| 66607–612 | Freightliner. 2002 (66607/609/611/612 exported to Poland) |
| 66613–618 | Freightliner. 2003 |
| 66619–622 | Freightliner. 2005 |
| 66623–625 | Freightliner. 2007 (66624/625 exported to Poland). |
| 66701–707 | GB Railfreight. 2001 |
| 66708–712 | GB Railfreight. 2002 |
| 66713–717 | GB Railfreight. 2003 |
| 66718–722 | GB Railfreight. 2006 |
| 66723–727 | GB Railfreight. 2006 |
| 66728–732 | GB Railfreight. 2008 |
| 66747–749 | Built in 2008 as 20078968-004/006/007 (DE 6313/15/16) for Crossrail AG in the Netherlands but never used. Sold to GB Railfreight in 2012. |
| 66750–751 | Built in 2003 as 20038513-01/04 and have worked in the Netherlands, Germany and Poland. GBRf secured these two locomotives on lease in 2013. |
| 66752–759 | On order for GBRf and due for delivery 2014. |
| 66951–952 | Freightliner. 2004 |
| 66953–957 | Freightliner. 2008 |

† Replacement for 66521, written off in the Great Heck accident in 2001.

**Class 66/0. DB Schenker-operated locos.**

All fitted with Swinghead Automatic "Buckeye" Combination Couplers except 66001 and 66002.

† Fitted with additional lights and drawgear for Lickey banking duties.

t Fitted with tripcocks for working over London Underground tracks between Harrow-on-the-Hill and Amersham.

| | | | | | |
|---|---|---|---|---|---|
| 66001 t | **DB** | A | WBAT | TO | |
| 66002 | **E** | A | WBAT | TO | Lafarge Quorn |
| 66003 | **E** | A | WBAT | TO | |
| 66004 | **E** | A | WBAT | TO | |
| 66005 | **E** | A | WBAT | TO | |
| 66006 | **E** | A | WBAT | TO | |
| 66007 | **E** | A | WBAT | TO | |
| 66008 | **E** | A | WBAT | TO | |
| 66009 | **E** | A | WBAT | TO | |
| 66011 | **E** | A | WBAT | TO | |
| 66012 | **E** | A | WBAT | TO | |
| 66013 | **E** | A | WBAT | TO | |
| 66014 | **E** | A | WBAT | TO | |
| 66015 | **E** | A | WBAT | TO | |
| 66016 | **E** | A | WBAT | TO | |
| 66017 t | **E** | A | WBAT | TO | |
| 66018 | **E** | A | WBAT | TO | |
| 66019 t | **E** | A | WBAT | TO | |
| 66020 | **E** | A | WBAT | TO | |
| 66021 | **E** | A | WBAT | TO | |
| 66023 | **E** | A | WBAT | TO | |
| 66024 | **E** | A | WBAT | TO | |
| 66025 | **E** | A | WBAT | TO | |
| 66027 | **E** | A | WBAT | TO | |
| 66030 | **E** | A | WBAT | TO | |
| 66031 | **E** | A | WBAT | TO | |
| 66034 | **E** | A | WBAT | TO | |
| 66035 | **E** | A | WBAT | TO | |
| 66037 | **E** | A | WBAT | TO | |
| 66039 | **E** | A | WBAT | TO | |
| 66040 | **E** | A | WBAT | TO | |
| 66041 | **E** | A | WBAT | TO | |
| 66043 | **E** | A | WBAT | TO | |
| 66044 | **E** | A | WBAT | TO | |
| 66046 | **E** | A | WBAT | TO | |
| 66047 | **E** | A | WBAT | TO | |
| 66048 | **AL** | A | WQDA | TO (S) | James the Engine |
| 66050 | **E** | A | WBAT | TO | EWS Energy |
| 66051 | **E** | A | WBAT | TO | |
| 66053 | **E** | A | WBAT | TO | |
| 66054 | **E** | A | WBAT | TO | |
| 66055 † | **E** | A | WBLT | TO | |
| 66056 † | **E** | A | WBLT | TO | |

| | | | | | |
|---|---|---|---|---|---|
| 66057 † | **E** | A | WBLT | TO | |
| 66058 † | **E** | A | WBLT | TO | |
| 66059 † | **E** | A | WBLT | TO | |
| 66060 | **E** | A | WBAT | TO | |
| 66061 | **E** | A | WBAT | TO | |
| 66063 | **E** | A | WBAT | TO | |
| 66065 | **E** | A | WBAT | TO | |
| 66066 | **E** | A | WBAT | TO | |
| 66067 | **E** | A | WBAT | TO | |
| 66068 | **E** | A | WBAT | TO | |
| 66069 | **E** | A | WBAT | TO | |
| 66070 | **E** | A | WBAT | TO | |
| 66074 | **E** | A | WBAT | TO | |
| 66075 | **E** | A | WBAT | TO | |
| 66076 | **E** | A | WBAT | TO | |
| 66077 | **E** | A | WBAT | TO | Benjamin Gimbert G.C. |
| 66078 | **E** | A | WBAT | TO | |
| 66079 | **E** | A | WBAT | TO | James Nightall G.C. |
| 66080 | **E** | A | WBAT | TO | |
| 66081 | **E** | A | WBAT | TO | |
| 66082 | **E** | A | WBAT | TO | |
| 66083 | **E** | A | WBAT | TO | |
| 66084 | **E** | A | WBAT | TO | |
| 66085 | **E** | A | WBAT | TO | |
| 66086 | **E** | A | WBAT | TO | |
| 66087 | **E** | A | WBAT | TO | |
| 66088 | **E** | A | WBAT | TO | |
| 66089 | **E** | A | WBAT | TO | |
| 66090 | **E** | A | WBAT | TO | |
| 66091 | **E** | A | WBAT | TO | |
| 66092 | **E** | A | WBAT | TO | |
| 66093 | **E** | A | WBAT | TO | |
| 66094 | **E** | A | WBAT | TO | |
| 66095 | **E** | A | WBAT | TO | |
| 66096 | **E** | A | WBAT | TO | |
| 66097 | **DB** | A | WBAT | TO | |
| 66098 | **E** | A | WBAT | TO | |
| 66099 r | **E** | A | WBBT | TO | |
| 66100 r | **E** | A | WBBT | TO | |
| 66101 r | **DB** | A | WBBT | TO | |
| 66102 r | **E** | A | WBBT | TO | |
| 66103 r | **E** | A | WBBT | TO | |
| 66104 r | **E** | A | WBBT | TO | |
| 66105 r | **E** | A | WBBT | TO | |
| 66106 r | **E** | A | WBBT | TO | |
| 66107 r | **E** | A | WBBT | TO | |
| 66108 r | **E** | A | WBBT | TO | |
| 66109 | **E** | A | WBAT | TO | |
| 66110 r | **E** | A | WBBT | TO | |
| 66111 r | **E** | A | WBBT | TO | |
| 66112 r | **E** | A | WBBT | TO | |

| | | | | | |
|---|---|---|---|---|---|
| 66113 r | **E** | A | WBBT | TO | |
| 66114 r | **E** | A | WBBT | TO | |
| 66115 | **E** | A | WBAT | TO | |
| 66116 | **E** | A | WBAT | TO | |
| 66117 | **E** | A | WBAT | TO | |
| 66118 | **DB** | A | WBAT | TO | |
| 66119 | **E** | A | WBAT | TO | |
| 66120 | **E** | A | WBAT | TO | |
| 66121 | **E** | A | WBAT | TO | |
| 66122 | **E** | A | WBAT | TO | |
| 66124 | **E** | A | WBAT | TO | |
| 66125 | **E** | A | WBAT | TO | |
| 66126 | **E** | A | WBAT | TO | |
| 66127 | **E** | A | WBAT | TO | |
| 66128 | **E** | A | WBAT | TO | |
| 66129 | **E** | A | WBAT | TO | |
| 66130 | **E** | A | WBAT | TO | |
| 66131 | **E** | A | WBAT | TO | |
| 66132 | **E** | A | WBAT | TO | |
| 66133 | **E** | A | WBAT | TO | |
| 66134 | **E** | A | WBAT | TO | |
| 66135 | **E** | A | WBAT | TO | |
| 66136 | **E** | A | WBAT | TO | |
| 66137 | **E** | A | WBAT | TO | |
| 66138 | **E** | A | WBAT | TO | |
| 66139 | **E** | A | WBAT | TO | |
| 66140 | **E** | A | WBAT | TO | |
| 66141 | **E** | A | WBAT | TO | |
| 66142 | **E** | A | WBAT | TO | |
| 66143 | **E** | A | WBAT | TO | |
| 66144 | **E** | A | WBAT | TO | |
| 66145 | **E** | A | WBAT | TO | |
| 66147 | **E** | A | WBAT | TO | |
| 66148 | **E** | A | WBAT | TO | |
| 66149 | **E** | A | WBAT | TO | |
| 66150 | **E** | A | WBAT | TO | |
| 66151 | **E** | A | WBAT | TO | |
| 66152 | **DB** | A | WBAT | TO | Derek Holmes Railway Operator |
| 66154 | **E** | A | WBAT | TO | |
| 66155 | **E** | A | WBAT | TO | |
| 66156 | **E** | A | WBAT | TO | |
| 66158 | **E** | A | WBAT | TO | |
| 66160 | **E** | A | WBAT | TO | |
| 66161 | **E** | A | WBAT | TO | |
| 66162 | **E** | A | WBAT | TO | |
| 66164 | **E** | A | WBAT | TO | |
| 66165 | **E** | A | WBAT | TO | |
| 66167 | **E** | A | WBAT | TO | |
| 66168 | **E** | A | WBAT | TO | |
| 66169 | **E** | A | WBAT | TO | |
| 66170 | **E** | A | WBAT | TO | |

| 66171 | E | A | WBAT | TO | |
|-------|---|---|------|----|-|
| 66172 | E | A | WBAT | TO | PAUL MELLENEY |
| 66174 | E | A | WBAT | TO | |
| 66175 | E | A | WBAT | TO | |
| 66176 | E | A | WBAT | TO | |
| 66177 | E | A | WBAT | TO | |
| 66181 | E | A | WBAT | TO | |
| 66182 | E | A | WBAT | TO | |
| 66183 | E | A | WBAT | TO | |
| 66184 | E | A | WBAT | TO | |
| 66185 | DB | A | WBAT | TO | DP WORLD London Gateway |
| 66186 | E | A | WBAT | TO | |
| 66187 | E | A | WBAT | TO | |
| 66188 | E | A | WBAT | TO | |
| 66192 | E | A | WBAT | TO | |
| 66193 | E | A | WBAT | TO | |
| 66194 | E | A | WBAT | TO | |
| 66197 | E | A | WBAT | TO | |
| 66198 | E | A | WBAT | TO | |
| 66199 | E | A | WBAT | TO | |
| 66200 | E | A | WBAT | TO | RAILWAY HERITAGE COMMITTEE |
| 66201 | E | A | WBAT | TO | |
| 66204 | E | A | WBAT | TO | |
| 66206 | E | A | WBAT | TO | |
| 66207 | E | A | WBAT | TO | |
| 66213 | E | A | WBAT | TO | |
| 66221 | E | A | WBAT | TO | |
| 66230 | E | A | WBAT | TO | |
| 66232 | E | A | WBAT | TO | |
| 66238 | E | A | WBAT | TO | |
| 66250 | E | A | WBAT | TO | |

**Class 66/3. Former Fastline-operated loco now operated by DRS. Low emission**. Details as Class 66/0 except:

**Engine:** EMD 12N-710G3B-U2 two stroke of 2420 kW (3245 hp) at 904 rpm.
**Traction Motors:** General Motors D43TRC.
**Fuel Capacity:** 5150 litres.

| 66301 | DS | BN | XHIM | KM |
|-------|----|----|------|----|
| 66302 | DS | BN | XHIM | KM |
| 66303 | DS | BN | XHIM | KM |
| 66304 | DS | BN | XHIM | KM |
| 66305 | DS | BN | XHIM | KM |

**66413–434. Low emission. Macquarie Group-owned.** Details as Class 66/0 except:

**Engine:** EMD 12N-710G3B-U2 two stroke of 2420 kW (3245 hp) at 904 rpm.
**Traction Motors:** General Motors D43TRC.
**Fuel Capacity:** 5150 litres.

**Non-standard/Advertising liveries:** 66414 Two tone blue & white (formerly Stobart Rail).

66434 Malcolm Rail (blue).

| | | | | |
|---|---|---|---|---|
| 66413 | **DS** | MQ | DFHG | LD |
| 66414 | **O** | MQ | DFIN | LD |
| 66415 | **DS** | MQ | DFHG | LD |
| 66416 | **DS** | MQ | DFIN | LD |
| 66418 | **DS** | MQ | DFIN | LD |
| 66419 | **DS** | MQ | DFHG | LD |
| 66420 | **DS** | MQ | DFIN | LD |
| 66421 | **DS** | MQ | XHIM | KM |
| 66422 | **DS** | MQ | XHIM | KM |
| 66423 | **DS** | MQ | XHIM | KM |
| 66424 | **DS** | MQ | XHIM | KM |
| 66425 | **DS** | MQ | XHIM | KM |
| 66426 | **DS** | MQ | XHIM | KM |
| 66427 | **DS** | MQ | XHIM | KM |
| 66428 | **DS** | MQ | XHIM | KM |
| 66429 | **DS** | MQ | XHIM | KM |
| 66430 | **DS** | MQ | XHIM | KM |
| 66431 | **DS** | MQ | XHIM | KM |
| 66432 | **DS** | MQ | XHIM | KM |
| 66433 | **DS** | MQ | XHIM | KM |
| 66434 | **AL** | MQ | XHIM | KM |

**Class 66/5. Freightliner-operated locos.** Details as Class 66/0.

**Advertising livery:** 66522 Shanks Waste (one half of loco Freightliner green and one half Shanks' Waste light green).

| | | | | | |
|---|---|---|---|---|---|
| 66501 | **FL** | P | DFGM | LD | Japan 2001 |
| 66502 | **FL** | P | DFGM | LD | Basford Hall Centenary 2001 |
| 66503 | **FL** | P | DFGM | LD | The RAILWAY MAGAZINE |
| 66504 | **FH** | P | DFGM | LD | |
| 66505 | **FL** | P | DFGM | LD | |
| 66506 | **FL** | E | DFHH | LD | Crewe Regeneration |
| 66507 | **FL** | E | DFHH | LD | |
| 66508 | **FL** | E | DFHH | LD | |
| 66509 | **FL** | E | DFHH | LD | |
| 66510 | **FL** | E | DFHH | LD | |
| 66511 | **FL** | E | DFHH | LD | |
| 66512 | **FL** | E | DFHH | LD | |
| 66513 | **FL** | E | DFHH | LD | |
| 66514 | **FL** | E | DFHH | LD | |
| 66515 | **FL** | E | DFHH | LD | |

| 66516 | FL | E | DFGM | LD | |
|---|---|---|---|---|---|
| 66517 | FL | E | DFGM | LD | |
| 66518 | FL | E | DFHH | LD | |
| 66519 | FL | E | DFHH | LD | |
| 66520 | FL | E | DFHH | LD | |
| 66522 | AL | E | DFHH | LD | |
| 66523 | FL | E | DFHH | LD | |
| 66524 | FL | E | DFHH | LD | |
| 66525 | FL | E | DFHH | LD | |
| 66526 | FL | P | DFHH | LD | Driver Steve Dunn (George) |
| 66527 | FL | P | DFHH | LD | Don Raider |
| 66528 | FL | P | DFHH | LD | |
| 66529 | FL | P | DFHH | LD | |
| 66530 | FL | P | DFHH | LD | |
| 66531 | FL | P | DFHH | LD | |
| 66532 | FL | P | DFGM | LD | P&O Nedlloyd Atlas |
| 66533 | FL | P | DFGM | LD | Hanjin Express/Senator Express |
| 66534 | FL | P | DFGM | LD | OOCL Express |
| 66535 | FL | P | DFHH | LD | |
| 66536 | FL | P | DFHH | LD | |
| 66537 | FL | P | DFGM | LD | |
| 66538 | FL | E | DFIM | LD | |
| 66539 | FL | E | DFHH | LD | |
| 66540 | FL | E | DFIM | LD | Ruby |
| 66541 | FL | E | DFIM | LD | |
| 66542 | FL | E | DFIM | LD | |
| 66543 | FL | E | DFIM | LD | |
| 66544 | FL | P | DFHH | LD | |
| 66545 | FL | P | DFHH | LD | |
| 66546 | FL | P | DFHH | LD | |
| 66547 | FL | P | DFHH | LD | |
| 66548 | FL | P | DFHH | LD | |
| 66549 | FL | P | DFHH | LD | |
| 66550 | FL | P | DFHH | LD | |
| 66551 | FL | P | DFHH | LD | |
| 66552 | FL | P | DFHH | LD | Maltby Raider |
| 66553 | FL | P | DFHH | LD | |
| 66554 | FL | E | DFHH | LD | |
| 66555 | FL | E | DFHH | LD | |
| 66556 | FL | E | DFIM | LD | |
| 66557 | FL | E | DFHH | LD | |
| 66558 | FL | E | DFIM | LD | |
| 66559 | FL | E | DFHH | LD | |
| 66560 | FL | E | DFHH | LD | |
| 66561 | FL | E | DFHH | LD | |
| 66562 | FL | E | DFHH | LD | |
| 66563 | FL | E | DFHH | LD | |
| 66564 | FL | E | DFIM | LD | |
| 66565 | FL | E | DFIM | LD | |
| 66566 | FL | E | DFIM | LD | |
| 66567 | FL | E | DFIM | LD | |

| 66568 | FL | E | DFIM | LD |
| 66569 | FL | E | DFIM | LD |
| 66570 | FL | E | DFIM | LD |
| 66571 | FL | E | DFIM | LD |
| 66572 | FL | E | DFIM | LD |

**Class 66/5. Freightliner-operated low emission locos.** Details as Class 66/0 except:

**Engine:** EMD 12N-710G3B-U2 two stroke of 2420 kW (3245 hp) at 904 rpm.
**Traction Motors:** General Motors D43TRC.
**Fuel Capacity:** 5150 litres.

| 66585 | FL | MQ | DFHG | LD | The Drax Flyer |
| 66587 | FL | MQ | DFIN | LD | |
| 66588 | FL | MQ | DFIN | LD | |
| 66589 | FL | MQ | DFIN | LD | |
| 66590 | FL | MQ | DFIN | LD | |
| 66591 | FL | MQ | DFIN | LD | |
| 66592 | FL | MQ | DFIN | LD | Johnson Stevens Agencies |
| 66593 | FL | MQ | DFIN | LD | 3MG MERSEY MULTIMODAL GATEWAY |
| 66594 | FL | MQ | DFIN | LD | NYK Spirit of Kyoto |
| 66595 | FL | BN | DFHG | LD | |
| 66596 | FL | BN | DFHG | LD | |
| 66597 | FL | BN | DFHG | LD | Viridor |
| 66598 | FL | BN | DFHG | LD | |
| 66599 | FL | BN | DFHG | LD | |

**Class 66/6. Freightliner-operated locomotives with modified gear ratios.** Details as Class 66/0 except:

**Maximum Tractive Effort:** 467 kN (105080 lbf).
**Continuous Tractive Effort:** 296 kN (66630 lbf) at 14.0 mph.
**Design Speed:** 65 mph.                    **Maximum Speed:** 65 mph.

| 66601 | FL | P | DFHH | LD | The Hope Valley |
| 66602 | FL | P | DFHH | LD | |
| 66603 | FL | P | DFHH | LD | |
| 66604 | FL | P | DFHH | LD | |
| 66605 | FL | P | DFHH | LD | |
| 66606 | FL | P | DFHH | LD | |
| 66607 | FL | P | DFHH | LD | |
| 66610 | FL | P | DFHH | LD | |
| 66613 | FL | E | DFHH | LD | |
| 66614 | FL | E | DFHH | LD | |
| 66615 | FL | E | DFHH | LD | |
| 66616 | FL | E | DFHH | LD | |
| 66617 | FL | E | DFHH | LD | |
| 66618 | FL | E | DFHH | LD | Railways Illustrated Annual Photographic Awards Alan Barnes |
| 66619 | FL | E | DFHH | LD | Derek W. Johnson MBE |
| 66620 | FL | E | DFHH | LD | |
| 66621 | FL | E | DFHH | LD | |
| 66622 | FL | E | DFHH | LD | |

**Class 66/6. Freightliner-operated low emission loco with modified gear ratios.**
**Fuel Capacity:** 5150 litres.

**Advertising livery:** 66623 Bardon Aggregates (blue).

| 66623 | **AL** | MQ | DFHG | LD | Bill Bolsover |
|-------|--------|-----|------|-----|---------------|

**Class 66/7. GB Railfreight-operated locos.** Details as Class 66/0.

**Non-standard/Advertising liveries:**

66705 **GB** livery but with the addition of "Union Jack" bodyside vinyls.

66709 MSC – blue with images of a container ship.

66718 London Underground 150, black).

66720 Day and night (various colours, different on each side).

66721 London Underground 150, white with tube map images).

66750/751 Rush Rail all over blue.

| 66701 | **GB** | E | GBCM | PG | |
|-------|--------|---|------|-----|---|
| 66702 | **GB** | E | GBCM | PG | Blue Lightning |
| 66703 | **GB** | E | GBCM | PG | Doncaster PSB 1981–2002 |
| 66704 | **GB** | E | GBCM | PG | Colchester Power Signalbox |
| 66705 | **GB** | E | GBCM | PG | Golden Jubilee |
| 66706 | **GB** | E | GBCM | PG | Nene Valley |
| 66707 | **GB** | E | GBCM | PG | Sir Sam Fay GREAT CENTRAL RAILWAY |
| 66708 | **GB** | E | GBCM | PG | Jayne |
| 66709 | **AL** | E | GBCM | PG | Sorrento |
| 66710 | **GB** | E | GBCM | PG | Phil Packer BRIT |
| 66711 | **GB** | E | GBCM | PG | |
| 66712 | **GB** | E | GBCM | PG | Peterborough Power Signalbox |
| 66713 | **GB** | E | GBCM | PG | Forest City |
| 66714 | **GB** | E | GBCM | PG | Cromer Lifeboat |
| 66715 | **GB** | E | GBCM | PG | VALOUR – IN MEMORY OF ALL RAILWAY EMPLOYEES WHO GAVE THEIR LIVES FOR THEIR COUNTRY |
| 66716 | **GB** | E | GBCM | PG | LOCOMOTIVE & CARRIAGE INSTITUTION CENTENARY 1911–2011 |
| 66717 | **GB** | E | GBCM | PG | Good Old Boy |

**66718–746. Low emission. GB Railfreight locos.** 66733–737 renumbered from former DRS locos 66401–405. 66738–741 renumbered from former Freightliner locos 66578–581. 66742–746 renumbered from former DRS/Colas Rail locos 66406–410/841–845.

All details as Class 66/0 except 66718–732/747–749 as below:

**Engine:** EMD 12N-710G3B-U2 two stroke of 2420 kW (3245 hp) at 904 rpm.
**Traction Motors:** General Motors D43TRC.
**Fuel Capacity:** 5546 litres (66718–722) or 5150 litres (66723–732/747–749).

66747–749 were built for Crossrail AG in the Netherlands and purchased by GBRf in 2012.

66750/751 were built for mainland Europe in 2003. They were leased by GBRf in 2013.

| | | | | | | |
|---|---|---|---|---|---|---|
| 66718 | **AL** | E | GBCM | | PG | Sir Peter Hendy CBE |
| 66719 | **MT** | E | GBCM | | PG | METRO-LAND |
| 66720 | **0** | E | GBCM | | PG | |
| 66721 | **AL** | E | GBCM | | PG | Harry Beck |
| 66722 | **MT** | E | GBCM | | PG | Sir Edward Watkin |
| 66723 | **FS** | E | GBSD | | PG | Chinook |
| 66724 | **FS** | E | GBSD | | PG | Drax Power Station |
| 66725 | **FS** | E | GBSD | | PG | SUNDERLAND |
| 66726 | **FS** | E | GBSD | | PG | SHEFFIELD WEDNESDAY |
| 66727 | **FS** | E | GBSD | | PG | Andrew Scott CBE |
| 66728 | **GB** | P | GBCM | | PG | Institution of Railway Operators |
| 66729 | **GB** | P | GBCM | | PG | DERBY COUNTY |
| 66730 | **GB** | P | GBCM | | PG | Whitemoor |
| 66731 | **GB** | P | GBCM | | PG | interhub GB |
| 66732 | **GB** | P | GBCM | | PG | GBRf The First Decade 1999–2009 |
| | | | | | | John Smith – MD |

| | | | | | | | |
|---|---|---|---|---|---|---|---|
| 66733 | (66401) r | **GB** | P | GBFM | PG | | |
| 66735 | (66403) r | **GB** | P | GBFM | PG | | |
| 66736 | (66404) r | **GB** | P | GBFM | PG | | WOLVERHAMPTON WANDERERS |
| 66737 | (66405) r | **GB** | P | GBFM | PG | | Lesia |
| 66738 | (66578) | **GB** | GB | GBCM | PG | | |
| 66739 | (66579) | **GB** | GB | GBCM | PG | | Bluebell Railway |
| 66740 | (66580) | **GB** | GB | GBCM | PG | | |
| 66741 | (66581) | **GB** | GB | GBCM | PG | | |
| 66742 | (66406, 66841) | **GB** | GB | GBRT | | PG | ABP Port of Immingham |
| | | | | | | | Centenary 1912–2012 |
| 66743 | (66407, 66842) | **GB** | GB | GBRT | | PG | |
| 66744 | (66408, 66843) | **GB** | GB | GBRT | | PG | Crossrail |
| 66745 | (66409, 66844) | **GB** | GB | GBRT | | PG | Modern Railways |
| | | | | | | | The first 50 Years |
| 66746 | (66410, 66845) | **GB** | GB | GBRT | | PG | |
| 66747 | (20078968-004) | **U** | GB | GBNL | | PG | |
| 66748 | (20078968-006) | **U** | GB | GBNL | | PG | |
| 66749 | (20078968-007) | **U** | GB | GBNL | | PG | |
| 66750 | (20038513-01) | **0** | BN | GBDR | | PG | |
| 66751 | (20038513-04) | **0** | BN | GBDR | | PG | |

**66752–759. Low emission.** On order for GB Railfreight and due for delivery 2014. Full details awaited.

| | |
|---|---|
| 66752 | GB |
| 66753 | GB |
| 66754 | GB |
| 66755 | GB |
| 66756 | GB |
| 66757 | GB |
| 66758 | GB |
| 66759 | GB |

**Class 66/8. Colas Rail locos.** Renumbered from former Freightliner locos 66573–577. Details as Class 66/0.

| | | | | | |
|---|---|---|---|---|---|
| 66846 | (66573) | **CS** | CS | COLO | RU |
| 66847 | (66574) | **CS** | CS | COLO | RU |
| 66848 | (66575) | **CS** | CS | COLO | RU |
| 66849 | (66576) | **CS** | CS | COLO | RU | Wylam Dilly |
| 66850 | (66577) | **CS** | CS | COLO | RU | David Maidment OBE |

**Class 66/9. Freightliner locos. Low emission "demonstrator" locos.** Details as Class 66/0 except:

**Engine:** EMD 12N-710G3B-U2 two stroke of 2420 kW (3245 hp) at 904 rpm.
**Traction Motors:** General Motors D43TRC.
**Fuel Capacity:** 5905/5150 litres.

| | | | | |
|---|---|---|---|---|
| 66951 | **FL** | E | DFHG | LD |
| 66952 | **FL** | E | DFHG | LD |

**Class 66/9. Freightliner-operated low emission locos.** Owing to the 665xx number range being full, subsequent deliveries of 66/5s were numbered from 66953 onwards. Details as Class 66/5 (low emission).

| | | | | | |
|---|---|---|---|---|---|
| 66953 | **FL** | BN | DFHG | LD | |
| 66954 | **FL** | BN | DFIN | LD | |
| 66955 | **FL** | BN | DFIN | LD | |
| 66956 | **FL** | BN | DFHG | LD | |
| 66957 | **FL** | BN | DFHG | LD | Stephenson Locomotive Society 1909–2009 |

# CLASS 67    ALSTOM/GENERAL MOTORS EMD Bo-Bo

**Built:** 1999–2000 by Alstom at Valencia, Spain, as sub-contractors for General Motors (General Motors model JT42 HW-HS).
**Engine:** GM 12N-710G3B-EC two stroke of 2385 kW (3200 hp) at 904 rpm.
**Main Alternator:** General Motors AR9A/HEP7/CA6C.
**Traction Motors:** General Motors D43FM.
**Maximum Tractive Effort:** 141 kN (31770 lbf).
**Continuous Tractive Effort:** 90 kN (20200 lbf) at 46.5 mph.

| | |
|---|---|
| **Power At Rail:** 1860 kW. | **Train Brakes:** Air. |
| **Brake Force:** 78 t. | **Dimensions:** 19.74 x 2.72 m. |
| **Weight:** 90 t. | **Wheel Diameter:** 965 mm. |
| **Design Speed:** 125 mph. | **Maximum Speed:** 125 mph. |
| **Fuel Capacity:** 4927 litres. | **RA:** 8. |
| **Train Supply:** Electric, index 66. | **Multiple Working:** AAR System. |

All equipped with Slow Speed Control and Swinghead Automatic "Buckeye" Combination Couplers.

67001/002/029 have been modified to operate in push-pull mode on the Arriva Trains Wales loco-hauled set.

67004, 67007, 67009 and 67011 are fitted with cast iron brake blocks for working the Fort William Sleeper. **Maximum Speed:** 80 mph.

67008/010/012–015/017/018/025 have been modified to operate in push-pull mode of the Chiltern Railways loco-hauled sets.

67027 carries its name on one side only.

**Non-standard liveries:**

67026 Diamond Jubilee silver.

67029 All over silver with DB logos.

| | | | | | |
|---|---|---|---|---|---|
| 67001 | **AB** | A | WAWC | CE | |
| 67002 | **AB** | A | WAWC | CE | |
| 67003 | **AB** | A | WAAC | CE | |
| 67004 r | **E** | A | WABC | CE | |
| 67005 | **RZ** | A | WAAC | CE | Queen's Messenger |
| 67006 | **RZ** | A | WAAC | CE | Royal Sovereign |
| 67007 r | **E** | A | WABC | CE | |
| 67008 | **E** | A | WACC | CE | |
| 67009 r | **E** | A | WABC | CE | |
| 67010 | **CM** | A | WACC | CE | |
| 67011 r | **E** | A | WABC | CE | |
| 67012 | **CM** | A | WACC | CE | A Shropshire Lad |
| 67013 | **CM** | A | WACC | CE | Dyfrbont Pontcysyllte |
| 67014 | **CM** | A | WACC | CE | Thomas Telford |
| 67015 | **CM** | A | WAAC | CE | David J. Lloyd |
| 67016 | **E** | A | WAAC | CE | |
| 67017 | **E** | A | WACC | CE | Arrow |
| 67018 | **DB** | A | WACC | CE | Keith Heller |
| 67019 | **E** | A | WAAC | CE | |
| 67020 | **E** | A | WAAC | CE | |
| 67021 | **E** | A | WAAC | CE | |
| 67022 | **E** | A | WAAC | CE | |
| 67023 | **E** | A | WACC | CE | |
| 67024 | **E** | A | WAAC | CE | |
| 67025 | **E** | A | WACC | CE | Western Star |
| 67026 | **O** | A | WAAC | CE | Diamond Jubilee |
| 67027 | **E** | A | WAAC | CE | Rising Star |
| 67028 | **E** | A | WAAC | CE | |
| 67029 | **O** | A | WAWC | CE | Royal Diamond |
| 67030 r | **E** | A | WABC | CE | |

## CLASS 68     VOSSLOH     Bo-Bo

New Vossloh "UKLight" locomotives under construction for DRS. The first locomotive was due to be delivered in early 2014. Full details awaited.

**Built:** 2012–14 by Vossloh, Valencia, Spain.
**Engine:** Caterpillar C175-16 of 2800 kW (3750 hp) at 1740 rpm.
**Main Alternator:**
**Traction Motors:**
**Maximum Tractive Effort:** 317 kN (71 260 lbf).
**Continuous Tractive Effort:**
**Power At Rail:**     **Train Brakes:** Air.
**Brake Force:** 65.2 t.     **Dimensions:**
**Weight:** 86 t.     **Wheel Diameter:**
**Design Speed:** 100 mph.     **Maximum Speed:** 100 mph.
**Fuel Capacity:** 6000 litres.     **RA:**
**Train Supply:** Electric, index 60.
**Multiple Working:** Within class and with Class 88.

| | |
|---|---|
| 68001 | BN |
| 68002 | BN |
| 68003 | BN |
| 68004 | BN |
| 68005 | BN |
| 68006 | BN |
| 68007 | BN |
| 68008 | BN |
| 68009 | BN |
| 68010 | BN |
| 68011 | BN |
| 68012 | BN |
| 68013 | BN |
| 68014 | BN |
| 68015 | BN |

## CLASS 70     GENERAL ELECTRIC     Co-Co

New GE "PowerHaul" locomotives. 70012 was badly damaged whilst being unloaded in 2011 and was returned to Pennsylvania.

70801 (originally 70099) is a Turkish-built demonstrator that arrived in Britain in October 2012. Colas Rail has now leased this locomotive and in 2013 ordered a further nine locomotives (70802–810) that are due for delivery during 2014.

**Built:** 2009–11 by General Electric, Erie, Pennsylvania, USA or by TÜLOMSAS, Eskişehir, Turkey (70801).
**Engine:** General Electric PowerHaul P616LDA1 of 2848 kW (3820 hp) at 1500 rpm.
**Main Alternator:** General Electric GTA series.
**Traction Motors:** AC-GE 5GEB30.

**Maximum Tractive Effort**: 544 kN (122 000 lbf).
**Continuous Tractive Effort**: 427 kN (96 000 lbf) at ?? m.p.h.

| | |
|---|---|
| **Power At Rail**: | **Train Brakes**: Air. |
| **Brake Force**: 96.7 t. | **Dimensions**: 21.71 x 2.64 m. |
| **Weight**: 129 t. | **Wheel Diameter**: 1066 mm. |
| **Design Speed**: 75 mph. | **Maximum Speed**: 75 mph. |
| **Fuel Capacity**: 6000 litres. | **RA**: 7. |
| **Train Supply**: Not equipped. | **Multiple Working**: AAR System. |

| | | | | | |
|---|---|---|---|---|---|
| 70001 | **FH** | MQ | DFGI | LD | PowerHaul |
| 70002 | **FH** | MQ | DFGH | LD | |
| 70003 | **FH** | MQ | DFGH | LD | |
| 70004 | **FH** | MQ | DFGH | LD | The Coal Industry Society |
| 70005 | **FH** | MQ | DFGH | LD | |
| 70006 | **FH** | MQ | DFGH | LD | |
| 70007 | **FH** | MQ | DFGI | LD | |
| 70008 | **FH** | MQ | DFGI | LD | |
| 70009 | **FH** | MQ | DFGI | LD | |
| 70010 | **FH** | MQ | DFGH | LD | |
| 70011 | **FH** | MQ | DFGH | LD | |
| 70013 | **FH** | MQ | DFGH | LD | |
| 70014 | **FH** | MQ | DFGH | LD | |
| 70015 | **FH** | MQ | DFGI | LD | |
| 70016 | **FH** | MQ | DFGI | LD | |
| 70017 | **FH** | MQ | DFGI | LD | |
| 70018 | **FH** | MQ | DFGI | LD | |
| 70019 | **FH** | MQ | DFGI | LD | |
| 70020 | **FH** | MQ | DFGI | LD | |
| | | | | | |
| 70801 | (70099) | **CS** | GL | MBDL | CF (S) |
| | | | | | |
| 70802 | **CS** | | | | |
| 70803 | **CS** | | | | |
| 70804 | **CS** | | | | |
| 70805 | **CS** | | | | |
| 70806 | | | | | |
| 70807 | | | | | |
| 70808 | | | | | |
| 70809 | | | | | |
| 70810 | | | | | |

# 1.2. ELECTRO-DIESEL & ELECTRIC LOCOMOTIVES

## CLASS 73          BR/ENGLISH ELECTRIC          Bo-Bo

Electro-diesel locomotives which can operate either from a DC supply or using power from a diesel engine.

**Built:** 1965–67 by English Electric Co. at Vulcan Foundry, Newton-le-Willows.
**Engine:** English Electric 4SRKT of 447 kW (600 hp) at 850 rpm.
**Main Generator:** English Electric 824/5D.
**Electric Supply System:** 750 V DC from third rail.
**Traction Motors:** English Electric 546/1B.
**Maximum Tractive Effort (Electric):** 179 kN (40000 lbf).
**Maximum Tractive Effort (Diesel):** 160 kN (36000 lbf).
**Continuous Rating (Electric):** 1060 kW (1420 hp) giving a tractive effort of 35 kN (7800 lbf) at 68 mph.
**Continuous Tractive Effort (Diesel):** 60 kN (13600 lbf) at 11.5 mph.
**Maximum Rail Power (Electric):** 2350 kW (3150 hp) at 42 mph.
**Train Brakes:** Air, vacuum & electro-pneumatic († Air & electro-pneumatic).
**Brake Force:** 31 t.                **Dimensions:** 16.36 x 2.64 m.
**Weight:** 77 t.                      **Wheel Diameter:** 1016 mm.
**Design Speed:** 90 mph.              **Maximum Speed:** 90 mph.
**Fuel Capacity:** 1409 litres.        **RA:** 6.
**Train Supply:** Electric, index 66 (on electric power only).
**Multiple Working:** SR 27-way System & Blue Star.

Formerly numbered E6001–E6020/E6022–E6026/E6028–E6049 (not in order).

Locomotives numbered in the 732xx series are classed as 73/2 and were originally dedicated to Gatwick Express services.

Two separate rebuilt projects are underway. For GBRf 73204/206/209 are being rebuilt at Brush, Loughborough with an MTU R43 4000 V7 1500 hp engine (these will be renumbered 73901–903). For Network Rail 73104/211 are being rebuilt at RVEL, Derby with a pair of QSK19 750 hp engines (these will become 73951–952).

**Non-standard liveries:**

73107  Two-tone grey.
73109  Mid blue.
73139  Weardale Railway Brown & cream.

| | | | | | |
|---|---|---|---|---|---|
| 73101 | **PC** | RE | RVLO | ZA (S) | |
| 73107 | **O** | 20 | MBED | SE | Redhill 1844–1994 |
| 73109 | **O** | GB | GBED | SE | |
| 73119 | **B** | GB | GBED | SE | Borough of Eastleigh |
| 73133 | **TT** | TT | MBED | BM | |
| 73136 | **GB** | GB | GBED | SE | |
| 73138 | **Y** | NR | QADD | ZA | |

| 73139 | **0** | RE | RVLO | ZA (S) | |
| 73141 | **GB** | GB | GBED | SE | Charlotte |
| 73201 † | **B** | 20 | MBED | SE | Broadlands |
| 73202 † | **SN** | P | MBED | SL | |
| 73205 † | **IC** | GB | GBED | SE | Jeanette |
| 73207 † | **BL** | GB | GBED | SE | |
| 73208 † | **B** | GB | GBED | SE | |
| 73212 † | **GB** | GB | GBED | SE | Fiona |
| 73213 † | **GB** | GB | GBED | SE | Rhodalyn |
| 73235 † | **SD** | P | HYWD | BM | |

The 7390x number series reserved for rebuilt GBRf locomotives:

| 73901 | (73209) | GB | GBBR | LB (S) |
| 73902 | (73204) | GB | GBBR | LB (S) |
| 73903 | (73206) | GB | GBBR | LB (S) |

The 7395x number series reserved for rebuilt Network Rail locomotives:

| 73951 | (73104) | RE | RVLO | ZA (S) |
| 73952 | (73211) | RE | RVLO | ZA (S) |

## CLASS 86    BR/ENGLISH ELECTRIC    Bo-Bo

**Built:** 1965–66 by English Electric Co at Vulcan Foundry, Newton-le-Willows or by BR at Doncaster Works.
**Electric Supply System:** 25 kV AC 50 Hz overhead.
**Train Brakes:** Air.                    **Brake Force:** 40 t.
**Dimensions:** 17.83 x 2.65 m.       **Weight:** 83–86.8 t.
**RA:** 6.                                **Multiple Working:** TDM system.
**Train Supply:** Electric, index 66.

Formerly numbered E3101–E3200 (not in order).

Class 86s exported for use abroad are listed in section 1.6 of this book.

**Class 86/1. Class 87-type bogies & motors.**

Details as above except:
**Traction Motors:** GEC 412AZ frame mounted.
**Maximum Tractive Effort:** 258 kN (58000 lbf).
**Continuous Rating:** 3730 kW (5000 hp) giving a tractive effort of 95 kN (21300 lbf) at 87 mph.
**Maximum Rail Power:** 5860 kW (7860 hp) at 50.8 mph.
**Wheel Diameter:** 1150 mm.          **Weight:** 86.8 t.
**Design Speed:** 110 mph.            **Maximum Speed:** 110 mph.

| 86101 | **B** | EL | ACAC | WN | Sir William A Stanier FRS |

**Class 86/2. Standard design rebuilt with resilient wheels & Flexicoil suspension.**

**Traction Motors:** AEI 282BZ axle hung.
**Maximum Tractive Effort:** 207 kN (46500 lbf).
**Continuous Rating:** 3010 kW (4040 hp) giving a tractive effort of 85 kN (19200 lbf) at 77.5 mph.

**Maximum Rail Power:** 4550 kW (6100 hp) at 49.5 mph.
**Wheel Diameter:** 1156 mm.          **Weight:** 85–86.2 t.
**Design Speed:** 125 mph.            **Maximum Speed:** 100 mph.

**Non-standard livery:** 86259 BR "Electric blue".

| | | | | | |
|---|---|---|---|---|---|
| 86229 | **V** | EP | EPEX | LM (S) | |
| 86231 | **V** | EP | EPEX | LM (S) | |
| 86234 | **AR** | EP | EPEX | LM (S) | |
| 86235 | **AR** | EP | EPUK | LM (S) | |
| 86246 | **AR** | EP | EPEX | LM (S) | |
| 86247 | **EX** | P | DHLT | CP (S) | |
| 86251 | **V** | EP | EPEX | LM (S) | |
| 86259 x | **0** | PP | MBEL | WN | Les Ross |

**Class 86/4.**

**Traction Motors:** AEI 282AZ axle hung.
**Maximum Tractive Effort:** 258 kN (58000 lbf).
**Continuous Rating:** 2680 kW (3600 hp) giving a tractive effort of 89 kN (20000 lbf) at 67 mph.
**Maximum Rail Power:** 4400 kW (5900 hp) at 38 mph.
**Wheel Diameter:** 1156 mm.          **Weight:** 83–83.9 t.
**Design Speed:** 100 mph.            **Maximum Speed:** 100 mph.

| | | | | |
|---|---|---|---|---|
| 86401 | **N** | EL | ACXX | WN (S) Northampton Town |

**Class 86/5. Regeared locomotive operated by Freightliner.**

Details as Class 86/4 except:

**Continuous Rating:** 2680 kW (3600 hp) giving a tractive effort of 117 kN (26300 lbf) at 67 mph.
**Maximum Speed:** 75 mph.            **Train Supply:** Electric, isolated.

| | | | | |
|---|---|---|---|---|
| 86501 (86608) | **FL** | FL | DFGC | CP |

**Class 86/6. Freightliner-operated locomotives.**

Details as Class 86/4 except:

**Maximum Speed:** 75 mph.            **Train Supply:** Electric, isolated.

| | | | | |
|---|---|---|---|---|
| 86604 | **FL** | FL | DFNC | CP |
| 86605 | **FL** | FL | DFNC | CP |
| 86607 | **FL** | FL | DFNC | CP |
| 86609 | **FL** | FL | DFNC | CP |
| 86610 | **FL** | FL | DFNC | CP |
| 86612 | **FL** | P | DFNC | CP |
| 86613 | **FL** | P | DFNC | CP |
| 86614 | **FL** | P | DFNC | CP |
| 86622 | **FH** | P | DFNC | CP |
| 86627 | **FL** | P | DFNC | CP |
| 86628 | **FL** | P | DFNC | CP |
| 86632 | **FL** | P | DFNC | CP |
| 86637 | **FH** | P | DFNC | CP |
| 86638 | **FL** | P | DFNC | CP |
| 86639 | **FL** | P | DFNC | CP |

**Class 86/7. Europhoenix-owned locomotives.** Refurbished Class 86/2s for the UK spot-hire market. Details as Class 86/2 unless stated.

**Maximum Speed:** 110 mph.      **Weight:** 85t.
**Train Supply:** Electric, index 74.

| | | | | | |
|---|---|---|---|---|---|
| 86701 | (86205) | **CS** EP | EPUK | BH (S) | Orion |
| 86702 | (86260) | **EL** EP | EPUK | BH (S) | Cassiopeia |

**Class 86/9. Network Rail-owned locomotives.** Rebuilt from Class 86/2s for use as Mobile Load Bank test locos to test Overhead Line Equipment, initially on the WCML. No. 1 end Traction Motors isolated.

**Maximum Speed:** 60 mph.      **Train Supply:** Electric, isolated.

| | | | | |
|---|---|---|---|---|
| 86901 | (86253) | **Y** EP | EPEX | LM (S) |
| 86902 | (86210) | **Y** EP | EPEX | LM (S) |

# CLASS 87      BREL/GEC      Bo-Bo

**Built:** 1973–75 by BREL at Crewe Works.
**Electric Supply System:** 25 kV AC 50 Hz overhead.
**Traction Motors:** GEC G412AZ frame mounted.
**Maximum Tractive Effort:** 258 kN (58000 lbf).
**Continuous Rating:** 3730 kW (5000 hp) giving a tractive effort of 95 kN (21300 lbf) at 87 mph.
**Maximum Rail Power:** 5860 kW (7860 hp) at 50.8 mph.
**Train Brakes:** Air.      **Brake Force:** 40 t.
**Dimensions:** 17.83 x 2.65 m.      **Weight:** 83.3 t.
**Wheel Diameter:** 1150 mm.      **Design Speed:** 110 mph.
**Maximum Speed:** 110 mph.      **Train Supply:** Electric, index 95.
**RA:** 6.      **Multiple Working:** TDM system.

Class 87s exported for use abroad are listed in section 1.6 of this book.

| | | | | | |
|---|---|---|---|---|---|
| 87002 | **B** | EL | ETLO | WN | Royal Sovereign |

# CLASS 88      VOSSLOH      Bo-Bo

Ten new Vossloh bi-mode locomotives on order for DRS and due for delivery 2015. Full details awaited.
**Built:** 2014–15 by Vossloh, Valencia, Spain.
**Electric Supply System:** 25 kV AC 50 Hz overhead.
**Engine:** Caterpillar 12-cylinder 700 kW (940 hp) at 1800 rpm.
**Traction Motors:** ABB.
**Maximum Tractive Effort (Electric):**
**Maximum Tractive Effort (Diesel):**
**Continuous Rating:** 4000 kW (5360 hp).
**Maximum Rail Power:**      **Dimensions:**
**Train Brakes:** Air.      **Brake Force:**
**Weight:**      **Wheel Diameter:**
**Fuel capacity:**      **Train Supply:**
**Design Speed:** 100 mph.      **Maximum Speed:** 100 mph.
**RA:**

**Multiple Working:** Within class and with Class 68.

| | |
|---|---|
| 88001 | BN |
| 88002 | BN |
| 88003 | BN |
| 88004 | BN |
| 88005 | BN |
| 88006 | BN |
| 88007 | BN |
| 88008 | BN |
| 88009 | BN |
| 88010 | BN |

# CLASS 90            GEC                              Bo-Bo

**Built:** 1987–90 by BREL at Crewe Works (as sub contractors for GEC).
**Electric Supply System:** 25 kV AC 50 Hz overhead.
**Traction Motors:** GEC G412CY frame mounted.
**Maximum Tractive Effort:** 258 kN (58000 lbf).
**Continuous Rating:** 3730 kW (5000 hp) giving a tractive effort of 95 kN (21300 lbf) at 87 mph.
**Maximum Rail Power:** 5860 kW (7860 hp) at 68.3 mph.
**Train Brakes:** Air.

| | |
|---|---|
| **Brake Force:** 40 t. | **Dimensions:** 18.80 x 2.74 m. |
| **Weight:** 84.5 t. | **Wheel Diameter:** 1150 mm. |
| **Design Speed:** 110 mph. | **Maximum Speed:** 110 mph. |
| **Train Supply:** Electric, index 95. | **RA:** 7. |

**Multiple Working:** TDM system.

| | | | | | |
|---|---|---|---|---|---|
| 90001 | b | **1** | P | IANA | NC |
| 90002 | b | **1** | P | IANA | NC | Eastern Daily Press 1870–2010 SERVING NORFOLK FOR 140 YEARS |
| 90003 | b | **NX** | P | IANA | NC | Rædwald of East Anglia |
| 90004 | b | **1** | P | IANA | NC | City of Chelmsford |
| 90005 | b | **GA** | P | IANA | NC | Vice-Admiral Lord Nelson |
| 90006 | b | **1** | P | IANA | NC | Modern Railways Magazine/ Roger Ford |
| 90007 | b | **1** | P | IANA | NC | Sir John Betjeman |
| 90008 | b | **NX** | P | IANA | NC | The East Anglian |
| 90009 | b | **1** | P | IANA | NC | Diamond Jubilee |
| 90010 | b | **1** | P | IANA | NC | BRESSINGHAM STEAM & GARDENS |
| 90011 | b | **1** | P | IANA | NC | Let's Go East of England |
| 90012 | b | **1** | P | IANA | NC | Royal Anglian Regiment |
| 90013 | b | **1** | P | IANA | NC | The Evening Star PRIDE OF IPSWICH 1885–2010 125 YEARS OF SERVING SUFFOLK |
| 90014 | b | **GA** | P | IANA | NC | Norfolk and Norwich Festival |
| 90015 | b | **NX** | P | IANA | NC | Colchester Castle |
| 90016 | b | **FL** | P | DFLC | CP | |
| 90017 | b | **E** | DB | WQBA | CE (S) | |
| 90018 | b | **DB** | DB | WEAC | CE | |

| 90019 b | **FS** | DB | WEAC | CE | |
| 90020 b | **E** | DB | WEDC | CE | Collingwood |
| 90021 | **FS** | DB | WEAC | CE | |
| 90022 | **EG** | DB | WQBA | CE (S) | Freightconnection |
| 90023 | **E** | DB | WQBA | CE (S) | |
| 90024 | **FS** | DB | WEAC | CE | |
| 90025 | **F** | DB | WQBA | CE (S) | |
| 90026 | **E** | DB | WEAC | CE | |
| 90027 | **F** | DB | WQBA | CE (S) | Allerton T&RS Depot |
| 90028 | **E** | DB | WEDC | CE | |
| 90029 | **DB** | DB | WEAC | CE | |
| 90030 | **E** | DB | WQBA | CE (S) | |
| 90031 | **E** | DB | WQBA | CE (S) | The Railway Children Partnership Working For Street Children Worldwide |
| 90032 | **E** | DB | WQBA | CE (S) | |
| 90033 | **FE** | DB | WQBA | CE (S) | |
| 90034 | **E** | DB | WEAC | CE | |
| 90035 | **E** | DB | WEAC | CE | |
| 90036 | **DB** | DB | WEAC | CE | |
| 90037 | **E** | DB | WQBA | CE (S) | Spirit of Dagenham |
| 90038 | **FE** | DB | WQBA | CE (S) | |
| 90039 | **E** | DB | WEAC | CE | |
| 90040 | **E** | DB | WQBA | CE (S) | The Railway Mission |
| 90041 | **FL** | P | DFLC | CP | |
| 90042 | **FF** | P | DFLC | CP (S) | |
| 90043 | **FF** | P | DFLC | CP | Freightliner Coatbridge |
| 90044 | **FF** | P | DFLC | CP | |
| 90045 | **FH** | P | DFLC | CP | |
| 90046 | **FL** | P | DFLC | CP | |
| 90047 | **FF** | P | DFLC | CP | |
| 90048 | **FF** | P | DFLC | CP | |
| 90049 | **FH** | P | DFLC | CP | |
| 90050 | **FF** | AV | MBEL | CP (S) | |

# CLASS 91                    GEC                               Bo-Bo

**Built:** 1988–91 by BREL at Crewe Works (as sub contractors for GEC).
**Electric Supply System:** 25 kV AC 50 Hz overhead.
**Traction Motors:** GEC G426AZ.
**Maximum Tractive Effort:** 190 kN (43 000 lbf).
**Continuous Rating:** 4540 kW (6090 hp) giving a tractive effort of 170 kN at 96 mph.
**Maximum Rail Power:** 4700 kW (6300 hp) at ?? mph.
**Train Brakes:** Air.
**Brake Force:** 45 t.
**Weight:** 84 t.
**Design Speed:** 140 mph.
**Train Supply:** Electric, index 95.
**Multiple Working:** TDM system.

**Dimensions:** 19.41 x 2.74 m.
**Wheel Diameter:** 1000 mm.
**Maximum Speed:** 125 mph.
**RA:** 7.

Locomotives originally numbered in the 910xx series, but renumbered upon completion of overhauls at Bombardier, Doncaster by the addition of 100 to their original number. The exception to this rule was 91023 which was renumbered 91132.

91114 has been fitted with a second pantograph for evaluation purposes.

**Non-standard/advertising liveries:** 91101 Flying Scotsman (purple).

91110 Battle of Britain (black and grey).

91125 Sky 1 (blue).

| | | | | | |
|---|---|---|---|---|---|
| 91101 | **AL** | E | IECA | BN | |
| 91102 | **EC** | E | IECA | BN | City of York |
| 91103 | **EC** | E | IECA | BN | |
| 91104 | **EC** | E | IECA | BN | |
| 91105 | **EC** | E | IECA | BN | |
| 91106 | **EC** | E | IECA | BN | |
| 91107 | **EC** | E | IECA | BN | SKYFALL |
| 91108 | **EC** | E | IECA | BN | |
| 91109 | **EC** | E | IECA | BN | Sir Bobby Robson |
| 91110 | **AL** | E | IECA | BN | BATTLE OF BRITAIN MEMORIAL FLIGHT |
| 91111 | **EC** | E | IECA | BN | |
| 91112 | **EC** | E | IECA | BN | |
| 91113 | **EC** | E | IECA | BN | |
| 91114 | **EC** | E | IECA | BN | Durham Cathedral |
| 91115 | **EC** | E | IECA | BN | Blaydon Races |
| 91116 | **EC** | E | IECA | BN | |
| 91117 | **EC** | E | IECA | BN | WEST RIDING LIMITED |
| 91118 | **GN** | E | IECA | BN | |
| 91119 | **EC** | E | IECA | BN | |
| 91120 | **EC** | E | IECA | BN | |
| 91121 | **EC** | E | IECA | BN | |
| 91122 | **EC** | E | IECA | BN | |
| 91124 | **EC** | E | IECA | BN | |
| 91125 | **AL** | E | IECA | BN | |
| 91126 | **EC** | E | IECA | BN | |
| 91127 | **EC** | E | IECA | BN | |
| 91128 | **EC** | E | IECA | BN | |
| 91129 | **EC** | E | IECA | BN | |
| 91130 | **EC** | E | IECA | BN | |
| 91131 | **EC** | E | IECA | BN | |
| 91132 | **EC** | E | IECA | BN | |

## CLASS 92 BRUSH Co-Co

**Built:** 1993–96 by Brush Traction at Loughborough.
**Electric Supply System:** 25 kV AC 50 Hz overhead or 750 V DC third rail.
**Traction Motors:** Asea Brown Boveri design. Model 6FRA 7059B (Asynchronous 3-phase induction motors).
**Maximum Tractive Effort:** 400 kN (90 000 lbf).
**Continuous Rating:** 5040 kW (6760 hp) on AC, 4000 kW (5360 hp) on DC.

**Maximum Rail Power:**
**Brake Force:** 63 t.
**Weight:** 126 t.
**Design Speed:** 140 km/h (87 mph).
**Train Supply:** Electric, index 108 (AC), 70 (DC).
**RA:** 7.

**Train Brakes:** Air.
**Dimensions:** 21.34 x 2.67 m.
**Wheel Diameter:** 1070 mm.
**Maximum Speed:** 145 km/h (90 mph).

\* Modified to operate freight trains on High Speed 1.

Class 92s exported for use abroad are listed in section 1.6 of this book.

**Advertising livery:** 92017 Stobart Rail (two-tone blue & white).

| | | | | | |
|---|---|---|---|---|---|
| 92002 | **EG** | HB | WFCC | CE | H.G. Wells |
| 92003 | \* **EG** | HB | WFDC | CE | Beethoven |
| 92004 | **EG** | HB | WQBA | CE (S) | Jane Austen |
| 92005 | **EG** | HB | WFAC | CE | Mozart |
| 92006 | **EP** | ET | PTXX | CO (S) | Louis Armand |
| 92007 | **EG** | HB | WQAA | CE (S) | Schubert |
| 92008 | **EG** | HB | WQAB | CE (S) | Jules Verne |
| 92009 | \* **DB** | HB | WQBA | CE (S) | Marco Polo |
| 92010 | **EP** | ET | GBET | CO | Molière |
| 92011 | **EG** | HB | WFAC | CE | Handel |
| 92013 | **EG** | HB | WQAA | CE | Puccini |
| 92014 | **EP** | ET | PTXX | CO (S) | Emile Zola |
| 92015 | \* **DB** | HB | WFBC | CE | |
| 92016 | \* **DB** | HB | WFBC | CE | |
| 92017 | **AL** | HB | WQAA | CE (S) | Bart the Engine |
| 92018 | **EP** | ET | PTXX | CO (S) | Stendhal |
| 92019 | **EG** | HB | WQAB | CE (S) | Wagner |
| 92020 | **EP** | ET | PTXX | CO (S) | Milton |
| 92021 | **EP** | ET | PTXX | CO (S) | Purcell |
| 92022 | **EG** | HB | WQAA | CE (S) | Charles Dickens |
| 92023 | **EP** | ET | PTXX | CO (S) | Ravel |
| 92024 | **EG** | HB | WFAC | CE | J.S. Bach |
| 92026 | **EG** | HB | WQAA | CE (S) | Britten |
| 92028 | **EP** | ET | GBET | CO | Saint Saëns |
| 92029 | **EG** | HB | WFAC | CE | Dante |
| 92030 | **EG** | HB | WFCC | CE | Ashford |
| 92031 | \* **DB** | HB | WFBC | CE | |
| 92032 | **GB** | ET | GBET | CO | IMechE Railway Division |
| 92033 | **EP** | ET | PTXX | CO (S) | Berlioz |
| 92035 | **EP** | HB | WQBA | CE (S) | Mendelssohn |
| 92036 | \* **EG** | HB | WFBC | CE | Bertolt Brecht |
| 92037 | **EG** | HB | WFAC | CE | Sullivan |
| 92038 | **EP** | ET | GBET | CO | Voltaire |
| 92039 | **EG** | HB | WFAC | CE | Johann Strauss |
| 92040 | **EP** | ET | PTXX | CO (S) | Goethe |
| 92041 | **EG** | HB | WFAC | CE | Vaughan Williams |
| 92042 | \* **DB** | HB | WFBC | CE | |
| 92043 | **EP** | ET | GBET | CO | Debussy |
| 92044 | **EP** | ET | GBET | CO | Couperin |
| 92045 | **EP** | ET | PTXX | LB (S) | Chaucer |
| 92046 | **EP** | ET | PTXX | LB (S) | Sweelinck |

▲ EWS-liveried 08633 (which is remote-control fitted) waits its next turn at Westbury on 04/07/12. **Tony Christie**

▼ One of two 08s based at Inverness, 08788, turns one of the ScotRail Caledonian Sleeper coaches in the station on 31/07/13. **Alexander Colley**

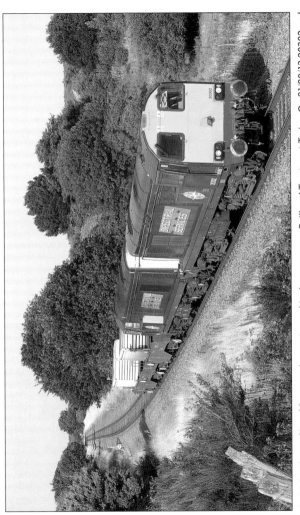

▲ DRS still uses Class 20s on nuclear trains and in the autumn on Railhead Treatment Trains. On 21/08/13 20302 and 20312 trundle along the East Suffolk Line at Eyke, between Saxmundham and Melton, with 6M69 15.42 Sizewell–Willesden nuclear flasks. **Aubrey Evans**

▲ BR Blue-liveried 20107 and 20096 top-and-tail two tanks used as barrier vehicles with 20905/901 at East Goscote, between Syston and Melton Mowbray, on 26/07/13. The train was a 7Z23 17.21 Old Dalby–Barrow Hill.　**Paul Biggs**

▼ Network Rail still uses Class 31s on test trains. On 26/08/13 31233 works a 3Z01 Derby–Westbury at Charfield, Gloucestershire.　**Jamie Squibbs**

▲ West Coast Railway Company-liveried 33207 "Jim Martin" pilots GWR 5029 "Nunney Castle" on the 08.20 Bristol Temple Meads–Weymouth "Seaside Express" railtour at Hawkeridge Junction near Westbury on 28/07/13. **Mark Few**

▼ DRS-liveried 37402 and 37608 work a lightweight 6K73 08.50 Sellafield–Crewe nuclear flask train at Kirkhead Wood near Kents Bank on 06/04/13. **Tom McAtee**

▲ Network Rail-yellow-liveried 97304 "John Tiley" slowly heads along the Roxby Gullet branch from Scunthorpe with the Radio Survey Train from Derby on 29/09/13. 97303 was on the rear. **Andrew Mason**

▲ CrossCountry-liveried 43321 heads away from Plymouth with the 12.23 Plymouth–Glasgow Central on 05/04/13. **Robert Pritchard**

▼ Grand Central-liveried 43467 brings up the rear of the 17.31 Sunderland–London King's Cross at York on 06/08/12. **Robert Pritchard**

▲ Colas Rail-liveried 47749 "Demelza" approaches Teignmouth with 6Z29 12.42 Newton Abbot–Westbury engineers train on 10/09/13. **David Hunt**

▼ D1015 "Western Champion" returned to the main line in summer 2013. On 07/09/13 it approaches Weymouth with the 05.53 Leicester–Weymouth "Western Wessexman" railtour. **David Hunt**

▲ Carrying the new Devon & Cornwall Railways metallic grey livery, 56312 passes Dudley, near Cramlington, with 6Z17 15.00 Butterwell–York Holgate Sidings loaded coal on 01/10/13.
**Jimmy Wilson**

▲ First Great Western's four Class 57s are usually only used on the overnight Sleeper trains and opportunities for daylight photos are limited. On 15/07/13 57605 "Totnes Castle" works an 07.55 Penzance–Old Oak Common empty stock at Totnes after the loco had failed the previous night. **David Hunt**

▼ West Coast Railway Company-liveried 57315 leads the 06.05 Sheffield–Bristol Temple Meads Statesman railtour past Isham, south of Kettering on the Midland Main Line, on 04/09/13. **John Coleman**

▲ Two freights were captured heading north on the Midland Main Line on the evening of 19/07/13 – DB Schenker-liveried 60010 works 6E38 13.54 Colnbrook–Lindsey empty bogie tanks as Freightliner 66615 works 6D45 15.53 Luton–Mountsorrel.

**Paul Biggs**

▲ Hanson Quarry Products-liveried 59101 "Village of Whatley" works 6C80 Machen Quarry–Westbury Yard stone train at Somerton on 03/08/13. **Jamie Squibbs**

▼ Carrying the new Freightliner PowerHaul livery, 66504 passes Slitting Mill crossing, north of Barrow Hill, with 4E01 03.32 Southampton–Leeds intermodal on 19/08/13. **Andrew Wills**

▲ DBS-liveried 66101 approaches Syston Junction with 4M86 15.51 Ely–Peak Forest empty stone train on 19/07/13. **Joshua Day**

▼ GBRf-liveried 66731 "interhub GB" is seen near Stenson Junction with 6K50 15.12 Toton–Crewe departmental train on 26/08/13. **Paul Biggs**

▲ In the former Wrexham & Shropshire two-tone grey/silver livery now adopted by Chiltern as its Mainline livery, 67012 "A Shropshire Lad" passes Kings Sutton with the 18.15 London Marylebone–Kidderminster on 26/07/13.     **Nigel Gibbs**

▼ Freightliner-liveried 70013 passes East Goscote with 6M90 07.00 West Thurrock–Tunstead empty cement tanks on 26/09/13.     **Paul Biggs**

▲ Non-standard two-tone grey-liveried 73107 "Redhill 1844–1994" top-and-tails a Cricklewood–Derby test train with 73109 at Cossington on 02/06/13.

**Ben Wheeler**

▼ Owned by Les Ross, original BR electric blue-liveried 86259 sees regular main line charter work. On 03/08/13 it passes Cromwell (between Retford and Newark) with an 07.18 Edinburgh–London King's Cross private charter. **Lindsay Atkinson**

▲ In a special Battle of Britain livery, East Coast 91110 "Battle of Britain Memorial Flight" crosses Relly Mill Viaduct, just south of Durham, with the 08.00 London King's Cross–Edinburgh on 12/07/13.
**Phil Wright**

▲ DB Schenker-liveried 90036 passes Hitchin with the diverted southbound ScotRail Highland Sleeper on 17/07/13. **Alisdair Anderson**

▼ DBS Class 92s 92042 and 92016 (dead in train) haul 4O68 03.30 Hams Hall–Dollands Moor intermodal south at Hemel Hempstead on 09/01/13.
**Alisdair Anderson**

# 1.3. EUROTUNNEL LOCOMOTIVES

## DIESEL LOCOMOTIVES

### 0001–0007          MaK                                    Bo-Bo

**Built:** 1991–92 by MaK at Kiel, Germany (Model DE1004).
**Engine:** MTU 12V 396 TC13 of 940 kW (1260 hp) at 1800 rpm.
**Main Alternator:** ABB.                 **Traction Motors:** ABB.
**Maximum Tractive Effort:** 305 kN (68600 lbf).
**Continuous Tractive Effort:** 140 kN (31500 lbf) at 20 mph.
**Power At Rail:** 750 kW (1012 hp).     **Dimensions:** 14.40 x ?? m.
**Brake Force:** 120 kN.                  **Wheel Diameter:** 1000 mm.
**Weight:** 82 t.                         **Maximum Speed:** 100 km/h.
**Design Speed:** 120 km/h.               **Train Brakes:** Air.
**Fuel Capacity:** 3500 litres.           **Multiple Working:** Within class.
**Train Supply:** Not equipped.           **Signalling System:** TVM430 cab signalling.

Registered on TOPS as 21901–907.

| | | | |
|---|---|---|---|
| 0001 | **GY** | ET | CO |
| 0002 | **GY** | ET | CO |
| 0003 | **GY** | ET | CO |
| 0004 | **GY** | ET | CO |
| 0005 | **GY** | ET | CO |

The following two locos were rebuilt from NS 6400 Class 6456 and 6457 (built 1991) and added to the Eurotunnel fleet in 2011.

| | | | |
|---|---|---|---|
| 0006 | **GY** | ET | CO |
| 0007 | **GY** | ET | CO |

### 0031–0042          HUNSLET/SCHÖMA                         0-4-0

**Built:** 1989–90 by Hunslet Engine Company at Leeds as 900 mm gauge.
**Rebuilt:** 1993–94 by Schöma in Germany to 1435 mm gauge.
**Engine:** Deutz FL10L 413FW of 170 kW (230 hp) at 2300 rpm.
**Transmission:** Mechanical Clark 5000 series.
**Maximum Tractive Effort:**
**Continuous Tractive Effort:**
**Power At Rail:**
**Brake Force:**                          **Dimensions:** 6.63 x 2.69 m.
**Weight:** 26–28 t.                      **Wheel Diameter:**
**Design Speed:** 48 km/h.                **Maximum Speed:** 50 km/h.
**Fuel Capacity:**                        **Train Brakes:** Air.
**Train Supply:** Not equipped.           **Multiple Working:** Not equipped.

* Rebuilt with inspection platforms to check overhead catenary.

| | | | | |
|---|---|---|---|---|
| 0031 | **GY** | ET | CO | FRANCES |

| 0032 |   | **GY** | ET | CO | ELISABETH |
|------|---|--------|----|----|-----------|
| 0033 |   | **GY** | ET | CO | SILKE |
| 0034 |   | **GY** | ET | CO | AMANDA |
| 0035 |   | **GY** | ET | CO | MARY |
| 0036 |   | **GY** | ET | CO | LAURENCE |
| 0037 |   | **GY** | ET | CO | LYDIE |
| 0038 |   | **GY** | ET | CO | JENNY |
| 0039 | * | **GY** | ET | CO | PACITA |
| 0040 |   | **GY** | ET | CO | JILL |
| 0041 | * | **GY** | ET | CO | KIM |
| 0042 |   | **GY** | ET | CO | NICOLE |

# ELECTRIC LOCOMOTIVES

## 9005–9840          BRUSH/ABB          Bo-Bo-Bo

**Built:** 1993–2002 by Brush Traction at Loughborough.
**Supply System:** 25 kV AC 50 Hz overhead.
**Traction Motors:** Asea Brown Boveri design. Asynchronous 3-phase motors.
Model 6FHA 7059 (as built). Model 6FHA 7059C (7000 kW rated locos).
**Maximum Tractive Effort:** 400kN (90 000 lbf).
**Continuous Rating:** Class 9/0 and 9/1: 5760 kW (7725 hp). Class 9/7 and 9/8:
7000 kW (9387 hp).

| | |
|---|---|
| **Maximum Rail Power:** | **Multiple Working:** TDM system. |
| **Brake Force:** 50 t. | **Dimensions:** 22.01 x 2.97 x 4.20 m. |
| **Weight:** 136 t. | **Wheel Diameter:** 1250 mm. |
| **Design Speed:** 100 mph. | **Maximum Speed:** 100 mph. |
| **Train Supply:** Electric. | **Train Brakes:** Air. |

**Class 9/0 Original build locos.** Built 1993–94.

| 9005 | **EB** | ET | CO | JESSYE NORMAN |
|------|--------|----|----|---------------|
| 9007 | **EB** | ET | CO | DAME JOAN SUTHERLAND |
| 9011 | **EB** | ET | CO | JOSÉ VAN DAM |
| 9013 | **EB** | ET | CO | MARIA CALLAS |
| 9015 | **EB** | ET | CO | LÖTSCHBERG 1913 |
| 9018 | **EB** | ET | CO | WILHELMENIA FERNANDEZ |
| 9022 | **EB** | ET | CO | DAME JANET BAKER |
| 9024 | **EB** | ET | CO | GOTTHARD 1882 |
| 9026 | **EB** | ET | CO | FURKATUNNEL 1982 |
| 9029 | **EB** | ET | CO | THOMAS ALLEN |
| 9033 | **EB** | ET | CO | MONTSERRAT CABALLE |
| 9036 | **EB** | ET | CO | ALAIN FONDARY |
| 9037 | **EB** | ET | CO | GABRIEL BACQUIER |

**Class 9/7. Increased power freight shuttle locos.** Built 2001–02 (9711–23
built 1998–2001 as 9101–13 and rebuilt as 9711–23 2010–12).

| 9701 | **EB** | ET | CO |
|------|--------|----|----|
| 9702 | **EB** | ET | CO |
| 9703 | **EB** | ET | CO |

```
9704    EB  ET  CO
9705    EB  ET  CO
9706    EB  ET  CO
9707    EB  ET  CO

9711  (9101)  EB  ET  CO
9712  (9102)  EB  ET  CO
9713  (9103)  EB  ET  CO
9714  (9104)  EB  ET  CO
9715  (9105)  EB  ET  CO
9716  (9106)  EB  ET  CO
9717  (9107)  EB  ET  CO
9718  (9108)  EB  ET  CO
9719  (9109)  EB  ET  CO
9720  (9110)  EB  ET  CO
9721  (9111)  EB  ET  CO
9722  (9112)  EB  ET  CO
9723  (9113)  EB  ET  CO
```

**Class 9/8 Locos rebuilt from Class 9/0 by adding 800 to the loco number.
Uprated to 7000 kW.**

```
9801    EB  ET  CO         LESLEY GARRETT
9802    EB  ET  CO         STUART BURROWS
9803    EB  ET  CO         BENJAMIN LUXON
9804    EB  ET  CO         VICTORIA DE LOS ANGELES
9806    EB  ET  CO         REGINE CRESPIN
9808    EB  ET  CO         ELISABETH SODERSTROM
9809    EB  ET  CO         FRANÇOISE POLLET
9810    EB  ET  CO         JEAN-PHILIPPE COURTIS
9812    EB  ET  CO         LUCIANO PAVAROTTI
9814    EB  ET  CO         LUCIA POPP
9816    EB  ET  CO         WILLARD WHITE
9817    EB  ET  CO (S)     JOSÉ CARRERAS
9819    EB  ET  CO         MARIA EWING
9820    EB  ET  CO         NICOLAI GHIAROV
9821    EB  ET  CO         TERESA BERGANZA
9823    EB  ET  CO         DAME ELISABETH LEGGE-SCHWARZKOPF
9825    EB  ET  CO
9827    EB  ET  CO         BARBARA HENDRICKS
9828    EB  ET  CO         DAME KIRI TE KANAWA
9831    EB  ET  CO
9832    EB  ET  CO         RENATA TEBALDI
9834    EB  ET  CO         MIRELLA FRENI
9835    EB  ET  CO         NICOLAI GEDDA
9838    EB  ET  CO         HILDEGARD BEHRENS
9840    EB  ET  CO
```

# 1.4. FORMER BR MAIN LINE LOCOS IN INDUSTRIAL SERVICE

Former British Rail main line locomotives considered to be in "industrial use" are listed here. These locomotives do not currently have Network Rail engineering acceptance for operation on the national railway network.

*Number Other no./name    Location*

## Class 03

| | | |
|---|---|---|
| 03084 | HELEN-LOUISE | West Coast Railway Company, Carnforth |
| 03179 | CLIVE | First Capital Connect, Hornsey Depot, London |
| 03196 | JOYCE/GLYNIS | West Coast Railway Company, Carnforth |
| D2381 | | West Coast Railway Company, Carnforth |

## Class 07

| | | |
|---|---|---|
| D2991 | 07007 | Arlington Fleet Services, Eastleigh Works, Hampshire |

## Class 08

| | | |
|---|---|---|
| 08202 | CHUFFER | The Potter Group, Queen Adelaide, Ely |
| 08308 | | Weardale Railway, Wolsingham, County Durham |
| 08331 | | Midland Railway-Butterley, Derbyshire |
| 08375 | 21 | Hanson Cement, Ketton Cement Works, nr Stamford |
| 08389 | | Nemesis Rail, Burton-upon-Trent, Staffordshire |
| 08393 | | LH Group, Barton-under-Needwood, Staffordshire |
| 08401 | | Celsa Steel (UK), Castle Works, Cardiff |
| 08411 | | Colne Valley Railway, Halstead, Essex |
| 08417 | | RVEL, RTC Business Park, Derby |
| 08418 | | West Coast Railway Company, Carnforth |
| 08423 | H011  14 | PD Ports, Teesport, Grangetown, Middlesbrough |
| 08441 | | Felixstowe Dock & Railway Company, Felixstowe |
| 08442 | RICHARD J. WENHAM EASTLEIGH DEPOT | LNWR, Eastleigh Depot, Hampshire |
| 08445 | | Daventry International Railfreight Terminal, Crick |
| 08447 | | John G Russell (Transport), Hillington, Glasgow |
| 08460 | | Colne Valley Railway, Halstead, Essex |
| 08484 | CAPTAIN NATHANIEL DARELL | Felixstowe Dock & Railway Company, Felixstowe |
| 08485 | | West Coast Railway Company, Carnforth |
| 08499 | | Colas Rail, Canton Depot, Cardiff |
| 08502 | | Flixborough Wharf, Flixborough, Scunthorpe |
| 08503 | | Barry Island Railway, Vale of Glamorgan |
| 08507 | | Riviera Trains, Crewe Diesel Depot/Down Holding Sdgs |
| 08511 | | Tilbury Freightliner Terminal, Tilbury, Essex |
| 08516 | | LNWR, Barton Hill Depot, Bristol |
| 08527 | | Barrow Hill Roundhouse, Chesterfield, Derbyshire |
| 08536 | | RVEL, RTC Business Park, Derby |
| 08568 | St. Rollox | Knorr-Bremse Rail Systems, Springburn Depot, Glasgow |
| 08573 | | Bombardier Transportation, Ilford Works, London |

| | | |
|---|---|---|
| 08588 | | Cemex UK, Washwood Heath, Birmingham |
| 08598 | H016 HERCULES | Chasewater Light Railway, Brownhills, Staffordshire |
| 08600 | | AV Dawson, Ayrton Rail Terminal, Middlesbrough |
| 08602 | 004  BOMBER | Bombardier Transportation, Derby Works |
| 08613 | H064 | Celtic Energy, Onllwyn Coal & Distribution Centre, West Glamorgan |
| 08622 | H028 19 | Hanson Cement, Ketton Cement Works, nr Stamford |
| 08629 | Wolverton | Knorr-Bremse Rail Systems, Wolverton Works, Milton Keynes |
| 08643 | | Aggregate Industries, Merehead Rail Terminal |
| 08648 | OLD GEOFF  20 | PD Ports, Teesport, Grangetown, Middlesbrough |
| 08649 | Bradwell | Knorr-Bremse Rail Systems, Wolverton Works, Milton Keynes |
| 08650 | ISLE OF GRAIN | Bardon Aggregates, Isle of Grain, Kent |
| 08652 | | Hanson Aggregates, Whatley Quarry, near Frome |
| 08670 | | Colas Rail, Canton Depot, Cardiff |
| 08678 | ARTILA | West Coast Railway Company, Carnforth |
| 08682 | Lionheart | Bombardier Transportation, Derby Works |
| 08683 | | EMD, Longport Works, Stoke-on-Trent |
| 08685 | | Barrow Hill Roundhouse, Chesterfield, Derbyshire |
| 08697 | | RVEL, RTC Business Park, Derby |
| 08699 | | Weardale Railway, Wolsingham, County Durham |
| 08704 | D3871 | Riviera Trains, Crewe Diesel Depot/Down Holding Sdgs |
| 08730 | The Caley | Knorr-Bremse Rail Systems, Springburn Depot, Glasgow |
| 08743 | Bryan Turner | SembCorp Utilities Teesside, Wilton, Middlesbrough |
| 08750 | | Weardale Railway, Wolsingham, County Durham |
| 08756 | | Tata Steel, Shotton Works, Deeside, Flintshire |
| 08762 | | Cemex UK, Washwood Heath, Birmingham |
| 08764 | | Maritime Transport, Tilbury Railport, Tilbury, Essex |
| 08765 | | Nemesis Rail, Burton-upon-Trent, Staffordshire |
| 08774 | ARTHUR VERNON DAWSON | AV Dawson, Ayrton Rail Terminal, Middlesbrough |
| 08786 | | Barrow Hill Roundhouse, Chesterfield, Derbyshire |
| 08787 | 08296 | Hanson Aggregates, Machen Quarry, nr Newport |
| 08807 | | AV Dawson, Ayrton Rail Terminal, Middlesbrough |
| 08809 | | Weardale Railway, Wolsingham, County Durham |
| 08810 | | Northern, Heaton Depot, Newcastle |
| 08818 | MOLLY | Flixborough Wharf, Flixborough, Scunthorpe |
| 08823 | LIBBIE | Daventry International Railfreight Terminal, Crick |
| 08834 | | Bombardier Transportation, Old Dalby Test Centre, Asfordby |
| 08846 | 003 | Bombardier Transportation, Derby Works |
| 08868 | | LNWR, Crewe Carriage Depot, Crewe, Cheshire |
| 08870 | H024 | Weardale Railway, Wolsingham, County Durham |
| 08871 | 22 | PD Ports, Teesport, Grangetown, Middlesbrough |
| 08873 | | Hams Hall Distribution Park, Coleshill, Warwickshire |
| 08885 | H042  18 | Weardale Railway, Wolsingham, County Durham |
| 08892 | | First Capital Connect, Hornsey Depot, London |
| 08903 | JOHN W. ANTILL | SembCorp Utilities Teesside, Wilton, Middlesbrough |
| 08905 | | Hope Construction Materials, Hope Cement Works, Derbyshire |
| 08912 | | AV Dawson, Ayrton Rail Terminal, Middlesbrough |
| 08913 | | LH Group, Barton-under-Needwood, Staffordshire |
| 08918 | | Nemesis Rail, Burton-upon-Trent, Staffordshire |
| 08924 | 1 | Hope Construction Materials, Hope Cement Works, Derbyshire |

| 08927 | D4157 | EMD, Roberts Road Depot, Doncaster |
| 08933 | | Aggregate Industries, Merehead Rail Terminal |
| 08936 | | Tata Steel, Shotton Works, Deeside, Flintshire |
| 08937 | D4167 | |
| | BLUEBELL MEL | Bardon Aggregates, Meldon Quarry, near Okehampton |
| 08943 | | Bombardier Transportation, Central Rivers Depot, Barton-under-Needwood |
| 08947 | HOWIE | Arlington Fleet Services, Eastleigh Works, Hampshire |
| 08954 | | Alstom, Longsight Depot, Manchester |
| 08956 | | Bombardier Transportation, Old Dalby Test Centre, Asfordby |

### Class 09

| 09007 | D3671 | London Overground, Willesden Depot, London |
| 09014 | | Nemesis Rail, Burton-upon-Trent, Staffordshire |
| 09022 | | Victoria Group, Port of Boston, Boston |
| 09204 | | LNWR, Crewe Carriage Depot, Crewe, Cheshire |

### Class 14

| D9504 | | Kent & East Sussex Railway |
| D9529 | 14029 | Nene Valley Railway |

### Class 20

| 20056 | 81 | Tata Steel, Appleby-Frodingham Works, Scunthorpe |
| 20066 | 82 | Barrow Hill Roundhouse, Chesterfield, Derbyshire |
| 20168 | 2 SIR GEORGE EARLE | Hope Construction Materials, Hope Cement Works, Derbyshire |
| 20906 | 3 | Hope Construction Materials, Hope Cement Works, Derbyshire |

### Class 47

| 47714 | | Bombardier Transportation, Old Dalby Test Centre, Asfordby |

# 1.5. LOCOMOTIVES AWAITING DISPOSAL

Locomotives that are still extant but at scrapyards are listed here.

### Class 08

| 08646 | F | European Metal Recycling, Kingsbury |
| 08783 | E | European Metal Recycling, Kingsbury |
| 08798 | E | European Metal Recycling, Attercliffe |
| 08872 | E | European Metal Recycling, Attercliffe |
| 08921 | E | European Metal Recycling, Kingsbury |

### Class 09

| 09023 | E | European Metal Recycling, Kingsbury |
| 09107 | E | European Metal Recycling, Kingsbury |

### Class 31

| 31422 | IC | CF Booth, Rotherham |

# 1.6. LOCOMOTIVES EXPORTED FOR USE ABROAD

This section details former BR (plus privatisation era) diesel and electric locomotives that have been exported from the UK for use in industrial locations or by a main line operator abroad. Not included are locos that are "preserved" abroad, which are included in our "Preserved Locomotives" publication.

*Number  Other no./name     Location*

**Class 04**

| | | |
|---|---|---|
| D2289 | | Lonato SpA, Lonato Steelworks, Lonato, Brescia, Italy |

**Class 56**

| | | |
|---|---|---|
| 56101 | 0659 001-5 | FLOYD, Hungary |
| 56115 | 0659 002-3 | FLOYD, Hungary |
| 56117 | 0659 003-1 | FLOYD, Hungary |

**Class 58**

| | | |
|---|---|---|
| 58001 | | Axiom Rail, France, (S) Alizay |
| 58004 | | Axiom Rail, France, (S) Alizay |
| 58005 | | Axiom Rail, France, (S) Alizay |
| 58006 | | Axiom Rail, France, (S) Alizay |
| 58007 | | Axiom Rail, France, (S) Alizay |
| 58009 | | Axiom Rail, France, (S) Alizay |
| 58010 | | Axiom Rail, France, (S) Alizay |
| 58011 | | Axiom Rail, France, (S) Alizay |
| 58013 | | Axiom Rail, France, (S) Alizay |
| 58015 | | Transfesa, Spain, (S) Monforte del Cid, Alicante |
| 58018 | | Axiom Rail, France, (S) Alizay |
| 58020 | L43 | Transfesa, Spain, (S) Monforte del Cid, Alicante |
| 58021 | | Axiom Rail, France, (S) Alizay |
| 58024 | L42 | Transfesa, Spain, (S) Monforte del Cid, Alicante |
| 58025 | | DB Schenker, Spain, (S) Albacete |
| 58026 | | Axiom Rail, France, (S) Alizay |
| 58027 | L52 | DB Schenker, Spain, (S) Albacete |
| 58029 | L44 | Transfesa, Spain, (S) Monforte del Cid, Alicante |
| 58030 | L46 | Transfesa, Spain, (S) Monforte del Cid, Alicante |
| 58031 | L45 | Transfesa, Spain, (S) Monforte del Cid, Alicante |
| 58032 | | Axiom Rail, France, (S) Alizay |
| 58033 | | Axiom Rail, France, (S) Alizay |
| 58034 | | Axiom Rail, France, (S) Alizay |
| 58035 | | Axiom Rail, France, (S) Alizay |
| 58036 | | Axiom Rail, France, (S) Alizay |
| 58038 | | Axiom Rail, France, (S) Alizay |
| 58039 | | Axiom Rail, France, (S) Alizay |
| 58040 | | Axiom Rail, France, (S) Alizay |
| 58041 | L36 | Transfesa, Spain, (S) Albacete |

| 58042 |     | Axiom Rail, France, (S) Alizay |
| 58043 | L37 | Transfesa, Spain, (S) Monforte del Cid, Alicante |
| 58044 |     | Axiom Rail, France, (S) Woippy, Metz |
| 58046 |     | Axiom Rail, France, (S) Alizay |
| 58047 | L51 | Transfesa, Spain, (S) Monforte del Cid, Alicante |
| 58049 |     | Axiom Rail, France, (S) Alizay |
| 58050 | L53 | DB Schenker, Spain, (S) Albacete |

**Class 59**

| 59003 | YEOMAN HIGHLANDER | |
|       | 259 003-2 | Heavy Haul Power International, Germany |

**Class 66**

| 66010 | Euro Cargo Rail, France |
| 66022 | Euro Cargo Rail, France |
| 66026 | Euro Cargo Rail, France |
| 66028 | Euro Cargo Rail, France |
| 66029 | Euro Cargo Rail, France |
| 66032 | Euro Cargo Rail, France |
| 66033 | Euro Cargo Rail, France |
| 66036 | Euro Cargo Rail, France |
| 66038 | Euro Cargo Rail, France |
| 66042 | Euro Cargo Rail, France |
| 66045 | Euro Cargo Rail, France |
| 66049 | Euro Cargo Rail, France |
| 66052 | Euro Cargo Rail, France |
| 66062 | Euro Cargo Rail, France |
| 66064 | Euro Cargo Rail, France |
| 66071 | Euro Cargo Rail, France |
| 66072 | Euro Cargo Rail, France |
| 66073 | Euro Cargo Rail, France |
| 66123 | Euro Cargo Rail, France |
| 66146 | DB Schenker Rail Polska, Poland |
| 66153 | DB Schenker Rail Polska, Poland |
| 66157 | DB Schenker Rail Polska, Poland |
| 66159 | DB Schenker Rail Polska, Poland |
| 66163 | DB Schenker Rail Polska, Poland |
| 66166 | DB Schenker Rail Polska, Poland |
| 66173 | DB Schenker Rail Polska, Poland |
| 66178 | DB Schenker Rail Polska, Poland |
| 66179 | Euro Cargo Rail, France |
| 66180 | DB Schenker Rail Polska, Poland |
| 66189 | DB Schenker Rail Polska, Poland |
| 66190 | Euro Cargo Rail, France |
| 66191 | Euro Cargo Rail, France |
| 66195 | Euro Cargo Rail, France |
| 66196 | DB Schenker Rail Polska, Poland |
| 66202 | Euro Cargo Rail, France |
| 66203 | Euro Cargo Rail, France |
| 66205 | Euro Cargo Rail, France |
| 66208 | Euro Cargo Rail, France |

| | | |
|---|---|---|
| 66209 | | Euro Cargo Rail, France |
| 66210 | | Euro Cargo Rail, France |
| 66211 | | Euro Cargo Rail, France |
| 66212 | | Euro Cargo Rail, France |
| 66214 | | Euro Cargo Rail, France |
| 66215 | | Euro Cargo Rail, France |
| 66216 | | Euro Cargo Rail, France |
| 66217 | | Euro Cargo Rail, France |
| 66218 | | Euro Cargo Rail, France |
| 66219 | | Euro Cargo Rail, France |
| 66220 | | DB Schenker Rail Polska, Poland |
| 66222 | | Euro Cargo Rail, France |
| 66223 | | Euro Cargo Rail, France |
| 66224 | | Euro Cargo Rail, France |
| 66225 | | Euro Cargo Rail, France |
| 66226 | | Euro Cargo Rail, France |
| 66227 | | DB Schenker Rail Polska, Poland |
| 66228 | | Euro Cargo Rail, France |
| 66229 | | Euro Cargo Rail, France |
| 66231 | | Euro Cargo Rail, France |
| 66233 | | Euro Cargo Rail, France |
| 66234 | | Euro Cargo Rail, France |
| 66235 | | Euro Cargo Rail, France |
| 66236 | | Euro Cargo Rail, France |
| 66237 | | DB Schenker Rail Polska, Poland |
| 66239 | | Euro Cargo Rail, France |
| 66240 | | Euro Cargo Rail, France |
| 66241 | | Euro Cargo Rail, France |
| 66242 | | Euro Cargo Rail, France |
| 66243 | | Euro Cargo Rail, France |
| 66244 | | Euro Cargo Rail, France |
| 66245 | | Euro Cargo Rail, France |
| 66246 | | Euro Cargo Rail, France |
| 66247 | | Euro Cargo Rail, France |
| 66248 | | DB Schenker Rail Polska, Poland |
| 66249 | | Euro Cargo Rail, France |
| 66411 | 66013 | Freightliner, Poland |
| 66412 | 66015 | Freightliner, Poland |
| 66417 | 66014 | Freightliner, Poland |
| 66582 | 66009 | Freightliner, Poland |
| 66583 | 66010 | Freightliner, Poland |
| 66584 | 66011 | Freightliner, Poland |
| 66586 | 66008 | Freightliner, Poland |
| 66608 | 66603 | Freightliner, Poland |
| 66609 | 66604 | Freightliner, Poland |
| 66611 | 66605 | Freightliner, Poland |
| 66612 | 66606 | Freightliner, Poland |
| 66624 | 66602 | Freightliner, Poland |
| 66625 | 66601 | Freightliner, Poland |

## Class 86

| | | |
|---|---|---|
| 86215 | 91 55 0450 005-8 | FLOYD, Hungary |
| 86217 | 91 55 0450 006-6 | FLOYD, Hungary |
| 86218 | 91 55 0450 004-1 | FLOYD, Hungary |
| 86228 | 91 55 0450 007-4 | FLOYD, Hungary |
| 86232 | 91 55 0450 003-3 | FLOYD, Hungary |
| 86233 | | Bulmarket, Bulgaria (S) |
| 86242 | 91 55 0450 008-2 | FLOYD, Hungary |
| 86248 | 91 55 0450 001-7 | FLOYD, Hungary |
| 86250 | 91 55 0450 002-5 | FLOYD, Hungary |
| 86424 | 91 55 0450 009-0 | FLOYD, Hungary (S) |

## Class 87

| | | |
|---|---|---|
| 87003 | 87003-0 | BZK, Bulgaria |
| 87004 | 87004-8 Britannia | BZK, Bulgaria |
| 87006 | 87006-3 | BZK, Bulgaria |
| 87007 | 87007-1 | BZK, Bulgaria |
| 87008 | 87008-9 | BZK, Bulgaria (S) |
| 87009 | | Bulmarket, Bulgaria |
| 87010 | 87010-5 | BZK, Bulgaria |
| 87012 | 87012-1 | BZK, Bulgaria |
| 87013 | 87013-9 | BZK, Bulgaria |
| 87014 | 87014-7 | BZK, Bulgaria (S) |
| 87017 | Iron Duke | Bulmarket, Bulgaria |
| 87019 | 87019-6 | BZK, Bulgaria |
| 87020 | 87020-4 | BZK, Bulgaria |
| 87022 | 87022-0 | BZK, Bulgaria |
| 87023 | Velocity | Bulmarket, Bulgaria |
| 87025 | | Bulmarket, Bulgaria |
| 87026 | 87026-1 | BZK, Bulgaria |
| 87028 | 87028-7 | BZK, Bulgaria |
| 87029 | 87029-5 | BZK, Bulgaria |
| 87033 | 87033-7 | BZK, Bulgaria |
| 87034 | 87034-5 | BZK, Bulgaria |

## Class 92

| | | |
|---|---|---|
| 92001 | 91 53 0472 002-1 Mircea Eliade | DB Schenker, Romania |
| 92012 | 91 53 0472 001-3 Mihai Eminescu | DB Schenker, Romania |
| 92025 | Oscar Wilde | DB Schenker, Bulgaria |
| 92027 | George Eliot | DB Schenker, Bulgaria |
| 92034 | Kipling | DB Schenker, Bulgaria |

# 2. LOCO-HAULED COACHING STOCK

# INTRODUCTION

## NUMBERING SYSTEMS

Seven different numbering systems were in use on British Rail. These were the British Rail series, the four pre-nationalisation companies' series', the Pullman Car Company's series and the UIC (International Union of Railways) series. In this book BR number series coaches and former Pullman Car Company series are listed separately. There is also a separate listing of "Saloon" type vehicles, that includes pre-nationalisation survivors, which are registered to run on the national railway system, Locomotive Support Coaches and Service Stock. Please note the Mark 2 Pullman vehicles were ordered after the Pullman Car Company had been nationalised and are therefore numbered in the British Rail series.

Also listed separately are the British Rail and Pullman Car Company number series coaches used on North Yorkshire Moors Railway services on the national railway system. This is due to their very restricted sphere of operation.

The BR number series grouped vehicles of a particular type together in chronological order. Major modifications affecting type of accommodation resulted in renumbering into a more appropriate or new number series. Since privatisation such renumbering has not always taken place resulting in renumbering which has been more haphazard and greater variations within numbering groups.

## LAYOUT OF INFORMATION

Coaches are listed in numerical order of painted number in batches according to type.

Each coach entry is laid out as in the following example (previous number(s) column may be omitted where not applicable):

| No. | Prev. No. | Notes | Livery | Owner | Operator | Depot/Location |
|---|---|---|---|---|---|---|
| 42346 | (41053) | *h | **FD** | A | GW | LA |

**Notes:**

The owner is the responsible custodian of the coach and this may not always be the legal owner.

The operator is the organisation which facilitates the use of the coach and may not be the actual train operating company which runs the train. If no operator is shown the coach is considered to be not in use.

The depot is the facility primarily responsible for the coaches maintenance. Light maintenance and heavy overhauls may be carried out elsewhere.

The location is where coaches not in use are currently being kept/stored.

# DETAILED INFORMATION & CODES

Under each type heading, the following details are shown:

- "Mark" of coach (see below).
- Descriptive text.
- Number of First Class seats, Standard Class seats, lavatory compartments and wheelchair spaces shown as F/S nT nW respectively.
- Bogie type (see below).
- Additional features.
- ETH Index.
- Weight: All weights are shown as metric tonnes (t = tonnes).

# BOGIE TYPES

**BR Mark 1 (BR1).** Double bolster leaf spring bogie. Generally 90 mph, but Mark 1 bogies may be permitted to run at 100 mph with special maintenance. Weight: 6.1 t.

**BR Mark 2 (BR2).** Single bolster leaf-spring bogie used on certain types of non-passenger stock and suburban stock (all now withdrawn). Weight: 5.3 t.

**COMMONWEALTH (C).** Heavy, cast steel coil spring bogie. 100 mph. Weight: 6.75 t.

**B4.** Coil spring fabricated bogie. Generally 100 mph, but B4 bogies may be permitted to run at 110 mph with special maintenance. Weight: 5.2 t.

**B5.** Heavy duty version of B4. 100 mph. Weight: 5.3 t.

**B5 (SR).** A bogie originally used on Southern Region EMUs, similar in design to B5. Now also used on locomotive-hauled coaches. 100 mph.

**BT10.** A fabricated bogie designed for 125 mph. Air suspension.

**T4.** A 125 mph bogie designed by BREL (now Bombardier Transportation).

**BT41.** Fitted to Mark 4 vehicles, designed by SIG in Switzerland. At present limited to 125 mph, but designed for 140 mph.

# BRAKES

Air braking is now standard on British main line trains. Vehicles with other equipment are denoted:

b    Air braked, through vacuum pipe.
v    Vacuum braked.
x    Dual braked (air and vacuum).

## HEATING & VENTILATION

Electric heating and ventilation is now standard on British main-line trains. Certain coaches for use on charter services may also have steam heating facilities, or be steam heated only.

## PUBLIC ADDRESS

It is assumed all coaches are now fitted with public address equipment, although certain stored vehicles may not have this feature. In addition, it is assumed all vehicles with a conductor's compartment have public address transmission facilities, as have catering vehicles.

## COOKING EQUIPMENT

It is assumed that Mark 1 catering vehicles have gas powered cooking equipment, whilst Mark 2, 3 and 4 catering vehicles have electric powered cooking equipment unless stated otherwise.

## ADDITIONAL FEATURE CODES

| | |
|---|---|
| d | Central door locking. |
| dg | Driver–Guard communication equipment. |
| f | Facelifted or fluorescent lighting. |
| h | "High density" seating. |
| k | Composition brake blocks (instead of cast iron). |
| n | Day/night lighting. |
| pg | Public address transmission and driver-guard communication. |
| pt | Public address transmission facility. |
| q | Catering staff to shore telephone. |
| W | Wheelchair space. |
| ★ | Blue star multiple working cables fitted. |

## NOTES ON ETH INDICES

The sum of ETH indices in a train must not be more than the ETH index of the locomotive. The normal voltage on British trains is 1000 V. Suffix "X" denotes 600 amp wiring instead of 400 amp. Trains whose ETH index is higher than 66 must be formed completely of 600 amp wired stock. Class 33 and 73 locomotives cannot provide a suitable electric train supply for Mark 2D, Mark 2E, Mark 2F, Mark 3, Mark 3A, Mark 3B or Mark 4 coaches. Class 55 locomotives provide an ets directly from one of their traction generators into the train line. Consequently voltage fluctuations can result in motor-alternator flashover. Thus these locomotives are not suitable for use with Mark 2D, Mark 2E, Mark 2F, Mark 3, Mark 3A, Mark 3B or Mark 4 coaches unless modified motor-alternators are fitted. Such motor alternators were fitted to Mark 2D and 2F coaches used on the East Coast Main Line, but few remain fitted.

# BUILD DETAILS

**Lot Numbers**
Vehicles ordered under the auspices of BR were allocated a lot (batch) number when ordered and these are quoted in class headings and sub-headings.

**Builders**
These are shown for each lot. Abbreviations used are shown in Section 7.6.

Information on sub-contracting works which built parts of vehicles eg the underframes etc is not shown.

In addition to the above, certain vintage Pullman cars were built or rebuilt at the following works:

Metropolitan Carriage & Wagon Company, Birmingham (later Alstom).
Midland Carriage & Wagon Company, Birmingham.
Pullman Car Company, Preston Park, Brighton.
Conversions have also been carried out at the Railway Technical Centre, Derby, LNWR Crewe and Blakes Fabrications, Edinburgh.

# VEHICLE NUMBERS

Where a coach has been renumbered, the former number is shown in parentheses. If a coach has been renumbered more than once, the original number is shown first in parentheses, followed by the most recent previous number.

# THE DEVELOPMENT OF BR STANDARD COACHES

## Mark 1

The standard BR coach built from 1951 to 1963 was the Mark 1. This type features a separate underframe and body. The underframe is normally 64 ft 6 in long, but certain vehicles were built on shorter (57 ft) frames. Tungsten lighting was standard and until 1961, BR Mark 1 bogies were generally provided. In 1959 Lot No. 30525 (Open Standard) appeared with fluorescent lighting and melamine interior panels, and from 1961 onwards Commonwealth bogies were fitted in an attempt to improve the quality of ride which became very poor when the tyre profiles on the wheels of the BR1 bogies became worn. Later batches of Open Standard and Open Brake Standard retained the features of Lot No. 30525, but compartment vehicles – whilst utilising melamine panelling in Standard Class – still retained tungsten lighting. Wooden interior finish was retained in First Class vehicles where the only change was to fluorescent lighting in open vehicles (except Lot No. 30648, which had tungsten lighting). In later years many Mark 1 coaches had BR 1 bogies replaced by B4.

## XP64

In 1964, a new prototype train was introduced. Known as "XP64", it featured new seat designs, pressure heating & ventilation, aluminium compartment doors and corridor partitions, foot pedal operated toilets and B4 bogies. The vehicles were built on standard Mark 1 underframes. Folding exterior doors were fitted, but these proved troublesome and were later replaced with hinged doors. All XP64 coaches have been withdrawn, but some have been preserved.

## Mark 2

The prototype Mark 2 vehicle (W 13252) was produced in 1963. This was a Corridor First of semi-integral construction and had pressure heating & ventilation, tungsten lighting, and was mounted on B4 bogies. This vehicle has now been preserved at the Mid Norfolk Railway. The production build was similar, but wider windows were used. The Open Standard vehicles used a new seat design similar to that in the XP64 and fluorescent lighting was provided. Interior finish reverted to wood. Mark 2 vehicles were built from 1964–66.

## Mark 2A–2C

The Mark 2A design, built 1967–68, incorporated the remainder of the features first used in the XP64 coaches, ie foot pedal operated toilets (except Open Brake Standard), new First Class seat design, aluminium compartment doors and partitions together with fluorescent lighting in first class compartments. Folding gangway doors (lime green coloured) were used instead of the traditional one-piece variety.

Mark 2B coaches had wide wrap around doors at vehicle ends, no centre doors and a slightly longer body. In Standard Class there was one toilet at each end instead of two at one end as previously. The folding gangway doors were red.

Mark 2C coaches had a lowered ceiling with twin strips of fluorescent lighting and ducting for air conditioning, but air conditioning was never fitted.

### Mark 2D–2F

These vehicles were fitted with air conditioning. They had no opening top-lights in saloon windows, which were shallower than previous ones.

Mark 2E vehicles had smaller toilets with luggage racks opposite. The folding gangway doors were fawn coloured.

Mark 2F vehicles had a modified air conditioning system, plastic interior panels and InterCity 70 type seats.

### Mark 3

The Mark 3 design has BT10 bogies, is 75 ft (23 m) long and is of fully integral construction with InterCity 70 type seats. Gangway doors were yellow (red in Kitchen Buffet First) when new, although these were changed on refurbishment. Loco-hauled coaches are classified Mark 3A, Mark 3 being reserved for HST trailers. A new batch of Open First and Open Brake First, classified Mark 3B, was built in 1985 with Advanced Passenger Train-style seating and revised lighting. The last vehicles in the Mark 3 series were the driving brake vans ("Driving Van Trailers") built for West Coast Main Line services but now used elsewhere.

A number of Mark 3 vehicles have recently been converted for use as HST trailers with Grand Central, CrossCountry and First Great Western.

### Mark 4

The Mark 4 design was built by Metro-Cammell for use on the East Coast Main Line after electrification and featured a body profile suitable for tilting trains, although tilt is not fitted, and is not intended to be. This design is suitable for 140 mph running, although is restricted to 125 mph because the signalling system on the route is not suitable for the higher speed. The bogies for these coaches were built by SIG in Switzerland and are designated BT41. Power operated sliding plug exterior doors are standard. All Mark 4s were rebuilt with completely new interiors in 2003–05 for GNER and referred to as "Mallard" stock. These rakes generally run in fixed formations and are now operated by East Coast.

# 2.1. BR NUMBER SERIES COACHING STOCK

## KITCHEN FIRST

Mark 1. Spent most of its life as a Royal Train vehicle and was numbered 2907 for a time. 24/–. Built with Commonwealth bogies, but B5 bogies substituted. ETH 2.

Lot No. 30633 Swindon 1961. 41 t.

| 325 | **VN** | OE | *NB* | CP | DUART |
|-----|--------|-----|------|-----|-------|

## PULLMAN KITCHEN

Mark 2. Pressure Ventilated. Built with First Class seating but this has been replaced with a servery area. 2T. B5 bogies. ETH 6.

Lot No. 30755 Derby 1966. 40 t.

| 504 | **PC** | WC | *WC* | CS | ULLSWATER |
|-----|--------|-----|------|-----|-----------|
| 506 | **PC** | WC | *WC* | CS | WINDERMERE |

## PULLMAN OPEN FIRST

Mark 2. Pressure Ventilated. 36/– 2T. B4 bogies. ETH 5.

Lot No. 30754 Derby 1966. 35 t.

**Non-standard livery:** 546 Maroon & beige.

| 546 | **O** | WC | | CS | CITY OF MANCHESTER |
|-----|--------|-----|------|-----|--------------------|
| 548 | **PC** | WC | *WC* | CS | GRASMERE |
| 549 | **PC** | WC | *WC* | CS | BASSENTHWAITE |
| 550 | **PC** | WC | *WC* | CS | RYDAL WATER |
| 551 | **PC** | WC | *WC* | CS | BUTTERMERE |
| 552 | **PC** | WC | *WC* | CS | ENNERDALE WATER |
| 553 | **PC** | WC | *WC* | CS | CRUMMOCK WATER |

## PULLMAN OPEN BRAKE FIRST

Mark 2. Pressure Ventilated. 30/– 2T. B4 bogies. ETH 4.

Lot No. 30753 Derby 1966. 35 t.

| 586 | **PC** | WC | *WC* | CS | DERWENTWATER |
|-----|--------|-----|------|-----|--------------|

## BUFFET FIRST

Mark 2F. Air conditioned. Converted 1988–89/91 at BREL, Derby from Mark 2F Open Firsts. 1200/01/03/11/20/21/50 have Stones equipment, others have Temperature Ltd. 25/– 1T 1W. B4 bogies. d. ETH 6X.

**1200/03/11/20**. Lot No. 30845 Derby 1973. 33 t.
**1201/07/10/12/21/50/54**. Lot No. 30859 Derby 1973–74. 33 t.

| | | | | | |
|------|---------------|-----|-----|-----|-------|
| 1200 | (3287, 6459) | **RV** | RV | *RV* | EH | AMBER |
| 1201 | (3361, 6445) | **CH** | VT | *WC* | CS |
| 1203 | (3291) | **IC** | RV | *RV* | EH |
| 1207 | (3328, 6422) | **V** | OE | | ZG |
| 1210 | (3405, 6462) | **FS** | E | *SR* | IS |
| 1211 | (3305) | **PC** | RA | *ST* | CS |
| 1212 | (3427, 6453) | **V** | RV | *RV* | EH |
| 1220 | (3315, 6432) | **FS** | E | *SR* | IS |
| 1221 | (3371) | **IC** | OE | | ZG |
| 1250 | (3372) | **V** | RV | | EH |
| 1254 | (3391) | **BG** | DR | | BH |

## KITCHEN WITH BAR

Mark 1. Built with no seats but three Pullman-style seats now fitted in bar area. B5 bogies. ETH 1.

Lot No. 30624 Cravens 1960–61. 41 t.

| | | | | |
|------|----|-----|-----|----|
| 1566 | | **VN** | OE | *NB* | CP |

## KITCHEN BUFFET UNCLASSIFIED

Mark 1. Built with 23 loose chairs. All remaining vehicles refurbished with 23 fixed polypropylene chairs and fluorescent lighting. 1683/91/92/99 were further refurbished with 21 chairs, wheelchair space and carpets. ETH 2 (* 2X).

Now used on charter trains with the seating area adapted to various uses including servery and food preparation areas, with some or all seating removed.

**1651–99**. Lot No. 30628 Pressed Steel 1960–61. Commonwealth bogies. 39 t.
**1730**. Lot No. 30512 BRCW 1960–61. B5 bogies. 37 t.

**Non-standard liveries:** 1683 and 1699 Oxford Blue.

| | | | | | | | | | | | |
|------|-----|-----|----|-----|-----|------|-----|----|-----|-----|----|
| 1651 | | **CC** | RV | *RV* | EH | | 1683 | | **O** | RV | *RV* | EH |
| 1657 | | **CH** | RV | | ZG | | 1691 | | **CC** | RV | *RV* | EH |
| 1659 | | **PC** | RA | *ST* | CS | | 1692 | | **CH** | RV | *RV* | EH |
| 1666 | x | **M** | RP | *BK* | BT | | 1699 | | **O** | RV | *RV* | EH |
| 1671 | x* | **CH** | RV | *RV* | EH | | 1730 | x | **M** | BK | *BK* | BT |

# BUFFET STANDARD

Mark 2F. Air conditioned. Temperature Ltd equipment. InterCity 70 seats. Converted 1974 from Mark 2F Open Standard 5970 as a prototype self-service buffet for APT-P. Sold to Northern Ireland Railways 1983, regauged to 5'3" and numbered 546. Since withdrawn, repatriated to Great Britain and converted back to standard gauge. Gas cooking. –/19. B5 bogies. ETH 12X.

Lot No. 30860 Derby 1973–74. 33 t.

| 1800 | | **M** | WC | | CS |
|------|--|-------|----|--|----|

# BUFFET STANDARD

Mark 1. These vehicles are basically an open standard with two full window spaces removed to accommodate a buffet counter, and four seats removed to allow for a stock cupboard. All remaining vehicles now have fluorescent lighting. –/44 2T. Commonwealth bogies. ETH 3.

1842 was refurbished and fitted with a microwave oven in 1988.

1861 has had its toilets replaced with store cupboards.

**1813–32.** Lot No. 30520 Wolverton 1960. 38 t.
**1840–42.** Lot No. 30507 Wolverton 1960. 37 t.
**1859–63.** Lot No. 30670 Wolverton 1961–62. 38 t.
**1882.** Lot No. 30702 Wolverton 1962. 38 t.

| 1813 | x | **CH** | RV | *RV* | EH | | 1860 | x | **M** | WC | *WC* | CS |
|------|---|--------|----|------|----|--|------|---|-------|----|------|----|
| 1832 | x | **CC** | RV | *RV* | EH | | 1861 | x | **M** | WC | *WC* | CS |
| 1840 | v | **M** | WC | *WC* | CS | | 1863 | x | **CH** | RV | | CM |
| 1842 | | **CH** | RV | *RV* | EH | | 1882 | x | **M** | WC | *WC* | CS |
| 1859 | x | **M** | BK | *BK* | BT | | | | | | | |

# KITCHEN BUFFET UNCLASSIFIED

Mark 1. These vehicles were built as Unclassified Restaurants. They were rebuilt with buffet counters and 23 fixed polypropylene chairs, then further refurbished by fitting fluorescent lighting. ETH 2X.

s   Modified for use as servery vehicle with seating removed.

**1953.** Lot No. 30575 Swindon 1960. B4/B5 bogies. 36.5 t.
**1961.** Lot No. 30632 Swindon 1961. Commonwealth bogies. 39 t.

| 1953 | s | **VN** | OE | *NB* | CP | | 1961 | x | **G** | WC | *WC* | CS |
|------|---|--------|----|------|----|--|------|---|-------|----|------|----|

# CHARTER TRAIN STAFF COACHES

Mark 1. Converted from Corridor Brake Composites in 1988. Commonwealth bogies. ETH 2.

Lot No. 30732 Derby 1964. 37 t.

| | | | | |
|---|---|---|---|---|
| 2833 | (21270) | **M** | WC *WC* | CS |
| 2834 | (21267) | **M** | RV | EH |

# HM THE QUEEN'S SALOON

Mark 3. Converted from an Open First built 1972. Consists of a lounge, bedroom and bathroom for HM The Queen, and a combined bedroom and bathroom for the Queen's dresser. One entrance vestibule has double doors. Air conditioned. BT10 bogies. ETH 9X.

Lot No. 30886 Wolverton 1977. 36 t.

| | | | | |
|---|---|---|---|---|
| 2903 | (11001) | **RP** | NR *RP* | ZN |

# HRH THE DUKE OF EDINBURGH'S SALOON

Mark 3. Converted from an Open Standard built 1972. Consists of a combined lounge/dining room, a bedroom and a shower room for the Duke, a kitchen and a valet's bedroom and bathroom. Air conditioned. BT10 bogies. ETH 15X.

Lot No. 30887 Wolverton 1977. 36 t.

| | | | | |
|---|---|---|---|---|
| 2904 | (12001) | **RP** | NR *RP* | ZN |

# ROYAL HOUSEHOLD SLEEPING CAR

Mark 3A. Built to similar specification as Sleeping Cars 10647–729. 12 sleeping compartments for use of Royal Household with a fixed lower berth and a hinged upper berth. 2T plus shower room. Air conditioned. BT10 bogies. ETH 11X.

Lot No. 31002 Derby/Wolverton 1985. 44 t.

| | | | |
|---|---|---|---|
| 2915 | **RP** | NR *RP* | ZN |

# HRH THE PRINCE OF WALES'S DINING CAR

Mark 3. Converted from HST TRUK built 1976. Large kitchen retained, but dining area modified for Royal use seating up to 14 at central table(s). Air conditioned. BT10 bogies. ETH 13X.

Lot No. 31059 Wolverton 1988. 43 t.

| | | | | |
|---|---|---|---|---|
| 2916 | (40512) | **RP** | NR *RP* | ZN |

# ROYAL KITCHEN/HOUSEHOLD DINING CAR

Mark 3. Converted from HST TRUK built 1977. Large kitchen retained and dining area slightly modified with seating for 22 Royal Household members. Air conditioned. BT10 bogies. ETH 13X.

Lot No. 31084 Wolverton 1990. 43 t.

2917   (40514)      **RP**  NR  *RP*            ZN

# ROYAL HOUSEHOLD CARS

Mark 3. Converted from HST TRUKs built 1976/77. Air conditioned. BT10 bogies. ETH 10X.

Lot Nos. 31083 (* 31085) Wolverton 1989. 41.05 t.

2918   (40515)      **RP**  NR              ZN
2919   (40518) *    **RP**  NR              ZN

# ROYAL HOUSEHOLD COUCHETTES

Mark 2B. Converted from Corridor Brake First built 1969. Consists of luggage accommodation, guard's compartment, workshop area, 350 kW diesel generator and staff sleeping accommodation. B5 bogies. ETH 2X.

Lot No. 31044 Wolverton 1986. 48 t.

2920   (14109, 17109)   **RP**  NR  *RP*        ZN

Mark 2B. Converted from Corridor Brake First built 1969. Consists of luggage accommodation, kitchen, brake control equipment and staff accommodation. B5 bogies. ETH 7X.

Lot No. 31086 Wolverton 1990. 41.5 t.

2921   (14107, 17107)   **RP**  NR  *RP*        ZN

# HRH THE PRINCE OF WALES'S SLEEPING CAR

Mark 3B. Air conditioned. BT10 bogies. ETH 7X.

Lot No. 31035 Derby/Wolverton 1987.

2922                 **RP**  NR  *RP*            ZN

# ROYAL SALOON

Mark 3B. Air conditioned. BT10 bogies. ETH 6X.

Lot No. 31036 Derby/Wolverton 1987.

2923                 **RP**  NR  *RP*            ZN

# OPEN FIRST

Mark 1. 42/– 2T. ETH 3. Many now fitted with table lamps.

3058 was numbered DB 975313, 3068 was numbered DB 975606 and 3093 was numbered DB 977594 for a time when in departmental service for BR.

**3058–69.** Lot No. 30169 Doncaster 1955. B4 bogies. 33 t (* Commonwealth bogies 35 t).
**3093.** Lot No. 30472 BRCW 1959. B4 bogies. 33 t.
**3096–3100.** Lot No. 30576 BRCW 1959. B4 bogies. 33 t.

| | | | | | | |
|---|---|---|---|---|---|---|
| 3058 | *x **M** | WC *WC* | CS | FLORENCE | | |
| 3066 | **CC** | RV *RV* | EH | | | |
| 3068 | **CC** | RV *RV* | EH | | | |
| 3069 | **CC** | RV *RV* | EH | | | |
| 3093 | x **M** | WC *WC* | CS | FLORENCE | | |

| | | | |
|---|---|---|---|
| 3096 | x **M** | BK *BK* | BT |
| 3097 | **CC** | RV *RV* | EH |
| 3098 | x **CH** | RV *RV* | EH |
| 3100 | x **CH** | RV *RV* | EH |

Later design with fluorescent lighting, aluminium window frames and Commonwealth bogies.

3128/36/41/43/44/46/47/48 were renumbered 1058/60/63/65/66/68/69/70 when reclassified Restaurant Open First, then 3600/05/08/09/02/06/04/10 when declassified to Open Standard, but have since regained their original numbers. 3136 was numbered DB 977970 for a time when in use with Serco Railtest as a Brake Force Runner.

3105 has had its luggage racks removed and has tungsten lighting.

**3105–28.** Lot No. 30697 Swindon 1962–63. 36 t.
**3130–50.** Lot No. 30717 Swindon 1963. 36 t.

| | | | | | | | | | |
|---|---|---|---|---|---|---|---|---|---|
| 3105 | x | **M** | WC *WC* | CS | 3125 | x | **CH** | JH *RV* | EH |
| 3106 | x | **M** | WC *WC* | CS | 3127 | | **G** | RV | EH |
| 3107 | x | **CH** | RV *RV* | EH | 3128 | x | **M** | WC *WC* | CS |
| 3110 | x | **CH** | RV *RV* | EH | 3130 | x | **M** | WC *WC* | CS |
| 3112 | x | **CH** | RV *RV* | EH | 3133 | x | **M** | RV | EH |
| 3113 | x | **M** | WC *WC* | CS | 3136 | x | **M** | WC *WC* | CS |
| 3114 | | **G** | RV | EH | 3140 | x | **CH** | RV *RV* | EH |
| 3115 | x | **M** | BK *BK* | BT | 3141 | | **M** | RV *RV* | EH |
| 3117 | x | **M** | WC *WC* | CS | 3143 | x | **M** | WC *WC* | CS |
| 3119 | | **CC** | RV *RV* | EH | 3144 | x | **M** | RV *RV* | EH |
| 3120 | | **CC** | RV *RV* | EH | 3146 | | **M** | RV *RV* | EH |
| 3121 | | **CH** | RV *RV* | EH | 3147 | | **CH** | RV *RV* | EH |
| 3122 | x | **CH** | RV *RV* | EH | 3148 | | **M** | JH *RV* | EH |
| 3123 | | **CC** | RV *RV* | EH | 3149 | | **CC** | RV *RV* | EH |
| 3124 | | **G** | RV | EH | 3150 | | **M** | BK *BK* | BT |

**Names:**

| | | | |
|---|---|---|---|
| 3105 | JULIA | 3128 | VICTORIA |
| 3106 | ALEXANDRA | 3130 | PAMELA |
| 3113 | JESSICA | 3136 | DIANA |
| 3117 | CHRISTINA | 3143 | PATRICIA |

## OPEN FIRST

Mark 2D. Air conditioned. Stones equipment. 42/– 2T. B4 bogies. ETH 5.

† Interior modified to Pullman Car standards with new seating, new
  panelling, tungsten lighting and table lights for the "Northern Belle".

Lot No. 30821 Derby 1971–72. 34 t.

| | | | | | |
|---|---|---|---|---|---|
| 3174 | † | **VN** | OE | *NB* | CP | GLAMIS |
| 3182 | † | **VN** | OE | *NB* | CP | WARWICK |
| 3188 | | **PC** | RA | *ST* | CS | CADAIR IDRIS |

## OPEN FIRST

Mark 2E. Air conditioned. Stones equipment. 42/– 2T (p 36/– 2T). B4 bogies.
ETH 5.

r  Refurbished with new seats.
† Interior modified to Pullman Car standards with new seating, new
  panelling, tungsten lighting and table lights for the "Northern Belle".

Lot No. 30843 Derby 1972–73. 32.5 t. († 35.8 t).

| | | | | | | |
|---|---|---|---|---|---|---|
| 3223 | | **RV** | RA | | BO | DIAMOND |
| 3231 | p | **PC** | RA | *ST* | CS | BEN CRUACHAN |
| 3232 | dr | **BG** | OE | | CD | |
| 3240 | | **RV** | RA | | BO | SAPPHIRE |
| 3247 | † | **VN** | OE | *NB* | CP | CHATSWORTH |
| 3267 | † | **VN** | OE | *NB* | CP | BELVOIR |
| 3273 | † | **VN** | OE | *NB* | CP | ALNWICK |
| 3275 | † | **VN** | OE | *NB* | CP | HARLECH |

## OPEN FIRST

Mark 2F. Air conditioned. 3277–3318/58–79 have Stones equipment, others
have Temperature Ltd. All refurbished in the 1980s with power-operated
vestibule doors, new panels and new seat trim. 42/– 2T. B4 bogies. d. ETH 5X.

r  Further refurbished with table lamps and modified seats with burgundy
   seat trim.
u Fitted with power supply for Mark 1 Kitchen Buffet Unclassified.

**3277–3318**. Lot No. 30845 Derby 1973. 33.5 t.
**3325–3426**. Lot No. 30859 Derby 1973–74. 33.5 t.
**3431–38**. Lot No. 30873 Derby 1974–75. 33.5 t.

| | | | | | | | | | | | | |
|---|---|---|---|---|---|---|---|---|---|---|---|---|
| 3277 | | **AR** | RV | *RV* | EH | | 3313 | r | **M** | WC | *WC* | CS |
| 3278 | r | **BP** | RV | *RV* | EH | | 3314 | r | **V** | RV | *RV* | EH |
| 3279 | u | **M** | DB | *SR* | TO | | 3318 | | **M** | DB | *SR* | TO |
| 3292 | | **M** | DB | *SR* | TO | | 3325 | r | **V** | RV | *RV* | EH |
| 3295 | | **AR** | RV | *RV* | EH | | 3326 | r | **M** | WC | *WC* | CS |
| 3304 | r | **V** | RV | *RV* | EH | | 3330 | r | **RV** | RV | *RV* | EH |
| 3312 | | **PC** | RA | *ST* | CS | | 3331 | | **M** | DB | *SR* | TO |

| | | | | | | | | | | | |
|---|---|---|---|---|---|---|---|---|---|---|---|
| 3333 | r | **V** | RV | *RV* | EH | | 3374 | | **BG** | DR | | BH |
| 3334 | | **AR** | RV | *RV* | EH | | 3379 | u | **AR** | RV | *RV* | EH |
| 3336 | u | **AR** | RV | *RV* | EH | | 3384 | r | **RV** | RV | *RV* | EH |
| 3340 | r | **V** | RV | *RV* | EH | | 3386 | r | **V** | RV | *RV* | EH |
| 3344 | r | **V** | RV | *RV* | EH | | 3388 | | **M** | DB | Eastleigh East Yd | |
| 3345 | r | **V** | RV | *RV* | EH | | 3390 | r | **RV** | RV | *RV* | EH |
| 3348 | r | **RV** | RV | *RV* | EH | | 3392 | r | **M** | WC | *WC* | CS |
| 3350 | r | **M** | WC | *WC* | CS | | 3395 | r | **M** | WC | *WC* | CS |
| 3351 | | **CH** | VT | *WC* | CS | | 3397 | r | **RV** | RV | *RV* | EH |
| 3352 | r | **M** | WC | *WC* | CS | | 3399 | u | **M** | DB | Eastleigh East Yd | |
| 3356 | r | **RV** | RV | *RV* | EH | | 3400 | | **M** | DB | *SR* | TO |
| 3358 | | **M** | DB | *SR* | TO | | 3417 | | **AR** | RV | *RV* | EH |
| 3359 | r | **M** | WC | *WC* | CS | | 3424 | | **M** | DB | *SR* | TO |
| 3360 | r | **M** | WC | *WC* | CS | | 3426 | r | **RV** | RV | *RV* | EH |
| 3362 | r | **M** | WC | *WC* | CS | | 3431 | r | **M** | WC | *WC* | CS |
| 3364 | r | **RV** | RV | *RV* | EH | | 3438 | r | **PC** | RA | *ST* | CS |
| 3366 | r | **BG** | DR | | BH | | | | | | | |

**Names:**

| | | | | |
|---|---|---|---|---|
| 3312 | HELVELLYN | | 3384 | DICKENS |
| 3330 | BRUNEL | | 3390 | CONSTABLE |
| 3348 | GAINSBOROUGH | | 3397 | WORDSWORTH |
| 3356 | TENNYSON | | 3426 | ELGAR |
| 3364 | SHAKESPEARE | | 3438 | BEN LOMOND |

# OPEN STANDARD

Mark 1. This coach has narrower seats than later vehicles. Built with BR Mark 1 bogies. –/64 2T. ETH 4.

Lot No. 30079 York 1953. Commonwealth bogies. 36 t.

3766   x   **M**   WC   *WC*   CS

# OPEN STANDARD

Mark 1. These vehicles are a development of the above with fluorescent lighting and modified design of seat headrest. Built with BR Mark 1 bogies. –/64 2T. ETH 4.

**4831–36.** Lot No. 30506 Wolverton 1959. Commonwealth bogies. 33 t.
**4856.** Lot No. 30525 Wolverton 1959–60. B4 bogies. 33 t.

| | | | | | | | | | | | |
|---|---|---|---|---|---|---|---|---|---|---|---|
| 4831 | x | **M** | BK | *BK* | BT | | 4836 | x | **M** | BK | *BK* | BT |
| 4832 | x | **CC** | BK | *BK* | BT | | 4856 | x | **M** | BK | *BK* | BT |

## OPEN STANDARD

Mark 1. Later vehicles built with Commonwealth bogies. –/64 2T. ETH 4.

**4905.** Lot No. 30646 Wolverton 1961. 36 t.
**4927–5044.** Lot No. 30690 Wolverton 1961–62. Aluminium window frames. 37 t.

| | | | | | | | | | | |
|---|---|---|---|---|---|---|---|---|---|---|
| 4905 | x | **M** | WC | *WC* | CS | 4994 | x | **M** | WC | *WC* | CS |
| 4927 | x | **CC** | RV | *RV* | EH | 4996 | x | **M** | RV | | CD |
| 4931 | v | **M** | WC | *WC* | CS | 4998 | | **CH** | RV | *RV* | EH |
| 4940 | x | **M** | WC | *WC* | CS | 5007 | | **G** | RV | | EH |
| 4946 | x | **M** | RV | *RV* | EH | 5008 | x | **M** | RV | *RV* | EH |
| 4949 | x | **CH** | RV | *RV* | EH | 5009 | x | **CH** | RV | *RV* | EH |
| 4951 | x | **M** | WC | *WC* | CS | 5027 | | **G** | RV | | EH |
| 4954 | v | **M** | WC | *WC* | CS | 5028 | x | **CC** | BK | *BK* | BT |
| 4959 | | **CH** | RV | *RV* | EH | 5032 | x | **M** | WC | *WC* | CS |
| 4960 | x | **M** | WC | *WC* | CS | 5033 | x | **M** | WC | *WC* | CS |
| 4973 | x | **M** | WC | *WC* | CS | 5035 | x | **M** | WC | *WC* | CS |
| 4984 | x | **M** | WC | *WC* | CS | 5040 | x | **CH** | RV | *RV* | EH |
| 4991 | | **CH** | RV | *RV* | EH | 5044 | x | **M** | WC | *WC* | CS |

## OPEN STANDARD

Mark 2. Pressure ventilated. –/64 2T. B4 bogies. ETH 4.

Lot No. 30751 Derby 1965–67. 32 t.

| | | | | | | | | | | |
|---|---|---|---|---|---|---|---|---|---|---|
| 5157 | v | **CH** | VT | *VT* | TM | 5200 | v | **M** | WC | *WC* | CS |
| 5171 | v | **M** | WC | *WC* | CS | 5212 | v | **CH** | VT | | TM |
| 5177 | v | **CH** | VT | *VT* | TM | 5216 | v | **M** | WC | *WC* | CS |
| 5191 | v | **CH** | VT | *VT* | TM | 5222 | v | **M** | WC | *WC* | CS |
| 5198 | v | **CH** | VT | *VT* | TM | | | | | | |

## OPEN STANDARD

Mark 2. Pressure ventilated. –/48 2T. B4 bogies. ETH 4.

Lot No. 30752 Derby 1966. 32 t.

| | | | | | | | | | | |
|---|---|---|---|---|---|---|---|---|---|---|
| 5229 | | **M** | WC | *WC* | CS | 5239 | | **M** | WC | *WC* | CS |
| 5236 | v | **M** | WC | *WC* | CS | 5249 | v | **G** | WC | *WC* | CS |
| 5237 | v | **M** | WC | *WC* | CS | | | | | | |

## OPEN STANDARD

Mark 2A. Pressure ventilated. –/64 2T (w –/62 2T). B4 bogies. ETH 4.

f  Facelifted vehicles.

**5276–5341.** Lot No. 30776 Derby 1967–68. 32 t.
**5350–5419.** Lot No. 30787 Derby 1968. 32 t.

| | | | | | | | | | | |
|---|---|---|---|---|---|---|---|---|---|---|
| 5276 | f | **RV** | RV | *RV* | EH | 5292 | f | **CC** | RV | *RV* | EH |
| 5278 | | **M** | WC | *WC* | CS | 5341 | f | **CC** | RV | *RV* | EH |

| 5350 | | **CH** | RV | | EH | | 5419 | w | **M** | WC | *WC* | CS |
| 5366 | f | **CH** | RV | *RV* | EH | | | | | | | |

## OPEN STANDARD

Mark 2D. Air conditioned. Stones equipment. Refurbished with new seats and end luggage stacks. –/58 2T. B4 bogies. d. ETH 5.

Lot No. 30822 Derby 1971. 33 t.

| 5631 | **M** | DB | *SR* | TO | | 5700 | **FP** | DR | | BH |
| 5632 | **M** | DB | *SR* | TO | | 5710 | **FP** | DR | | BH |
| 5657 | **M** | DB | *SR* | TO | | | | | | |

## OPEN STANDARD

Mark 2E. Air conditioned. Stones equipment. –/64 2T. B4 bogies. d. ETH 5.

r Refurbished with new interior panelling.
s Refurbished with new interior panelling, modified design of seat headrest and centre luggage stack. –/60 2T.

**5787–97**. Lot No. 30837 Derby 1972. 33.5 t.
**5810**. Lot No. 30844 Derby 1972–73. 33.5 t.

| 5787 | s | **V** | DR | | CR | | 5810 | s | **DS** | DR | | KM |
| 5797 | r★ | **IC** | RA | | BO | | | | | | | |

## OPEN STANDARD

Mark 2F. Air conditioned. Temperature Ltd equipment. InterCity 70 seats. All were refurbished in the 1980s with power-operated vestibule doors, new panels and seat trim. –/64 2T. B4 bogies. d. ETH 5X.

\* Early Mark 2 style seats. These vehicles have undergone a second refurbishment with carpets and new seat trim.
q Fitted with two wheelchair spaces. –/60 2T 2W.
s Fitted with centre luggage stack. –/60 2T.
t Fitted with centre luggage stack and wheelchair space. –/58 2T 1W.

**5910–55**. Lot No. 30846 Derby 1973. 33 t.
**5959–6158**. Lot No. 30860 Derby 1973–74. 33 t.
**6173–83**. Lot No. 30874 Derby 1974–75. 33 t.

| 5910 | q | **V** | RV | *RV* | EH | | 5945 | | **V** | RV | *RV* | EH |
| 5912 | | **PC** | RA | *ST* | CS | | 5950 | | **AR** | RV | *RV* | EH |
| 5919 | s pt | **BG** | DR | | ZK | | 5952 | | **V** | RV | *RV* | EH |
| 5921 | | **AR** | RV | *RV* | EH | | 5954 | | **M** | DB | *SR* | TO |
| 5922 | | **M** | DB | | BS | | 5955 | | **V** | RV | *RV* | EH |
| 5924 | | **M** | DB | | BS | | 5959 | n | **M** | DB | | BS |
| 5928 | | **CH** | VT | *WC* | CS | | 5961 | s pt | **V** | RV | *RV* | EH |
| 5929 | | **AR** | RV | *RV* | EH | | 5964 | | **AR** | RV | *RV* | EH |
| 5937 | | **V** | RV | *RV* | EH | | 5965 | t | **AW** | RV | | CD |

| | | | | | | | | | | |
|---|---|---|---|---|---|---|---|---|---|---|
| 5971 | | **DS** | DR | | KM | 6046 | | **DS** | DR | | KM |
| 5976 | t | **AW** | RV | | CD | 6051 | | **V** | RV | RV | EH |
| 5985 | | **AR** | RV | RV | EH | 6054 | | **V** | RV | RV | EH |
| 5987 | | **V** | RV | RV | EH | 6064 | s | **BG** | DR | | ZK |
| 5991 | | **PC** | RA | ST | CS | 6067 | s pt | **V** | RV | RV | EH |
| 5995 | | **DS** | DR | | KM | 6103 | | **M** | WC | WC | CS |
| 5997 | | **V** | RV | RV | EH | 6110 | | **M** | DB | SR | TO |
| 5998 | | **AR** | RV | RV | EH | 6115 | s | **M** | WC | WC | CS |
| 6000 | t | **M** | WC | WC | CS | 6117 | ★ | **DS** | DR | | KM |
| 6001 | | **DS** | DR | | KM | 6122 | ★ | **DS** | DR | | KM |
| 6006 | | **AR** | RV | RV | EH | 6137 | s pt | **AW** | RV | | CD |
| 6008 | | **DS** | DR | | KM | 6139 | n* | **M** | DB | SR | TO |
| 6012 | | **M** | WC | WC | CS | 6141 | q | **V** | RV | RV | EH |
| 6021 | | **M** | WC | WC | CS | 6152 | * | **V** | DB | | BS |
| 6022 | s | **M** | WC | WC | CS | 6158 | | **V** | RV | RV | EH |
| 6024 | s | **V** | RV | RV | EH | 6173 | ★ | **DS** | DR | | KM |
| 6027 | q | **V** | RV | RV | EH | 6176 | t | **V** | RV | RV | EH |
| 6036 | * | **M** | DB | | BS | 6177 | s | **V** | RV | RV | EH |
| 6042 | | **AR** | RV | RV | EH | 6183 | s | **AW** | RV | | CD |

# BRAKE GENERATOR VAN

Mark 1. Renumbered 1989 from BR departmental series. Converted from Gangwayed Brake Van in 1973 to three-phase supply brake generator van for use with HST trailers. Modified 1999 for use with loco-hauled stock. B5 bogies.

Lot No. 30400 Pressed Steel 1958.

| | | | | | |
|---|---|---|---|---|---|
| 6310 | (81448, 975325) | **CH** | RV | RV | EH |

# GENERATOR VAN

Mark 1. Converted from Gangwayed Brake Vans in 1992. B4 bogies. ETH 75.

**6311**. Lot No. 30162 Pressed Steel 1958. 37.25 t.
**6312**. Lot No. 30224 Cravens 1956. 37.25 t.
**6313**. Lot No. 30484 Pressed Steel 1958. 37.25 t.

| | | | | | |
|---|---|---|---|---|---|
| 6311 | (80903, 92911) | **B** | DB | | TO |
| 6312 | (81023, 92925) | **M** | WC | WC | CS |
| 6313 | (81553, 92167) | **PC** | OE | BP | SL |

# BUFFET STANDARD

Mark 2C. Converted from Open Standard by removal of one seating bay and replacing this by a counter with a space for a trolley, now replaced with a more substantial buffet. Adjacent toilet removed and converted to steward's washing area/store. Pressure ventilated. –/55 1T. B4 bogies. ETH 4.

Lot No. 30795 Derby 1969–70. 32.5 t.

| | | | | | |
|---|---|---|---|---|---|
| 6528 | (5592) | **M** | WC | WC | CS |

# SLEEPER RECEPTION CAR

Mark 2F. Converted from Open First. These vehicles consist of pantry, microwave cooking facilities, seating area for passengers (with loose chairs, staff toilet plus two bars). Now refurbished again with new "sofa" seating as well as the loose chairs. Converted at RTC, Derby (6700), Ilford (6701–05) and Derby (6706–08). Air conditioned. 6700/01/03/05–08 have Stones equipment and 6702/04 have Temperature Ltd equipment. The number of seats per coach can vary but typically is 25/– 1T (12 seats as "sofa" seating and 13 loose chairs). B4 bogies. d. ETH 5X.

**6700–02/04/08.** Lot No. 30859 Derby 1973–74. 33.5 t.
**6703/05–07.** Lot No. 30845 Derby 1973. 33.5 t.

| | | | | | |
|---|---|---|---|---|---|
| 6700 | (3347) | **FS** | E | *SR* | IS |
| 6701 | (3346) | **FS** | E | *SR* | IS |
| 6702 | (3421) | **FS** | E | *SR* | IS |
| 6703 | (3308) | **FS** | E | *SR* | IS |
| 6704 | (3341) | **FS** | E | *SR* | IS |
| 6705 | (3310, 6430) | **FS** | E | *SR* | IS |
| 6706 | (3283, 6421) | **FS** | E | *SR* | IS |
| 6707 | (3276, 6418) | **FS** | E | *SR* | IS |
| 6708 | (3370) | **FS** | E | *SR* | IS |

# BUFFET FIRST

Mark 2D. Converted from Buffet Standard by the removal of another seating bay and fitting a more substantial buffet counter with boiler and microwave oven. Now converted to First Class with new seating and end luggage stacks. Air conditioned. Stones equipment. 30/– 1T. B4 bogies. d. ETH 5.

Lot No. 30822 Derby 1971. 33 t.

| | | | | | |
|---|---|---|---|---|---|
| 6720 | (5622, 6652) | **M** | DB | | Eastleigh East Yard |
| 6722 | (5736, 6661) | **FP** | E | | LM |
| 6723 | (5641, 6662) | **M** | WC | | CS |
| 6724 | (5721, 6665) | **M** | WC | *WC* | CS |

# OPEN BRAKE STANDARD WITH TROLLEY SPACE

Mark 2. This vehicle uses the same body shell as the Mark 2 Corridor Brake First. Converted from Open Brake Standard by removal of one seating bay and replacing this with a counter with a space for a trolley. Adjacent toilet removed and converted to a steward's washing area/store. –/23. B4 bogies. ETH 4.

Lot No. 30757 Derby 1966. 31 t.

| | | | | | | |
|---|---|---|---|---|---|---|
| 9101 | (9398) | v | **CH** | VT | *VT* | TM |

## OPEN BRAKE STANDARD

Mark 2. These vehicles use the same body shell as the Mark 2 Corridor Brake First and have First Class seat spacing and wider tables. Pressure ventilated. –/31 1T. B4 bogies. ETH 4.

9104 was originally numbered 9401. It was renumbered when converted to Open Brake Standard with trolley space. Now returned to original layout.

Lot No. 30757 Derby 1966. 31.5 t.

| | | | | | | | | | |
|------|---|---|-----|-----|-----|------|---|-----|-----|-----|
| 9104 | v | **M** | WC | *WC* | CS | 9392 | v | **M** | WC | *WC* | CS |
| 9391 | | **M** | WC | *WC* | CS | | | | | |

## OPEN BRAKE STANDARD

Mark 2C. Pressure ventilated. –/31 1T. B4 bogies. d. ETH 4.

Lot No. 30798 Derby 1970. 32 t.

| | | | | |
|------|---|-----|-----|
| 9440 | **M** | WC | SH |

## OPEN BRAKE STANDARD

Mark 2D. Air conditioned. Stones Equipment. All now refurbished with new seating –/22 1TD. B4 bogies. d. pg. ETH 5.

Lot No. 30824 Derby 1971. 33 t.

| | | | | | | | | | | |
|------|----|-----|----|------|---|----|-----|-----|----|
| 9488 | **FP** | DR | | BH | 9494 | | **M** | DB | *SR* | TO |
| 9493 | **M** | WC | *WC* | CS | | | | | |

## OPEN BRAKE STANDARD

Mark 2E. Air conditioned. Stones Equipment. –/32 1T. B4 bogies. d. pg. ETH 5.

Lot No. 30838 Derby 1972. 33 t.

**Non-standard livery**: 9502 Pullman umber & cream.

r Refurbished with new interior panelling.
s Refurbished with modified design of seat headrest and new interior panelling.

| | | | | | | | | | | | |
|------|----|-----|-----|-----|----|------|----|-----|-----|-----|
| 9496 | r | **IC** | VT | *WC* | CS | 9507 | s | **V** | RV | *RV* | EH |
| 9502 | s | **O** | OE | *BP* | SL | 9508 | s | **BG** | DR | | BH |
| 9504 | s | **V** | RV | *RV* | EH | 9509 | s | **AV** | RV | | CD |
| 9506 | s★ | **BG** | DR | *SR* | TO | | | | | |

# OPEN BRAKE STANDARD

Mark 2F. Air conditioned. Temperature Ltd equipment. All were refurbished in the 1980s with power-operated vestibule doors, new panels and seat trim. All now further refurbished with carpets. –/32 1T. B4 bogies. d. pg. ETH 5X.

9537 has had all its seats removed and is used to carry luggage.

**Advertising livery:** 9537 CruiseSaver Express (dark blue).

Lot No. 30861 Derby 1974. 34 t.

| | | | | | | | | | | |
|---|---|---|---|---|---|---|---|---|---|---|
| 9520 | n | **AR** | RV | *RV* | EH | 9527 | n | **AR** | RV | *RV* | EH |
| 9521 | ★ | **AW** | RV | | CD | 9529 | n | **M** | DB | | BS |
| 9522 | | **M** | DB | *SR* | TO | 9531 | | **M** | DB | | BS |
| 9525 | | **DS** | DR | | KM | 9537 | n | **AL** | RV | *RV* | EH |
| 9526 | n★ | **IC** | RV | *RV* | EH | 9539 | | **AW** | RV | | CD |

# DRIVING OPEN BRAKE STANDARD

Mark 2F. Air conditioned. Temperature Ltd equipment. Push & pull (tdm system). Converted from Open Brake Standard, these vehicles originally had half cabs at the brake end. They have since been refurbished and have had their cabs widened and the cab-end gangways removed. Five vehicles (9701–03/08/14) have been converted for use in Network Rail test trains and can be found in the Service Stock section of this book. –/30 1W 1T. B4 bogies. d. pg. Cowcatchers. ETH 5X.

**9704–10.** Lot No. 30861 Derby 1974. Converted Glasgow 1979. Disc brakes. 34 t.
**9711/13.** Lot No. 30861 Derby 1974. Converted Glasgow 1985. 34 t.

| | | | | | | | | | |
|---|---|---|---|---|---|---|---|---|---|
| 9704 | (9512) | **AR** | BA | | ZG | 9710 | (9518) | **1** | BA | | ZG |
| 9705 | (9519) | **AR** | DR | | ZA | 9711 | (9532) | **AR** | VT | | TM |
| 9707 | (9511) | **AR** | DR | | ZA | 9713 | (9535) | **AR** | NR | | ZA |
| 9709 | (9515) | **AR** | BA | | ZG | | | | | | |

# OPEN BRAKE UNCLASSIFIED

Mark 2E. Converted from Open Standard with new seating for use on Anglo-Scottish overnight services by Railcare, Wolverton. Air conditioned. Stones equipment. –/31 2T. B4 bogies. d. ETH 4X.

**9801–03.** Lot No. 30837 Derby 1972. 33.5 t.
**9804–10.** Lot No. 30844 Derby 1972–73. 33.5 t.

| | | | | | | | | | | | |
|---|---|---|---|---|---|---|---|---|---|---|---|
| 9800 | (5751) | **FS** | E | *SR* | IS | 9806 | (5840) | **FS** | E | *SR* | IS |
| 9801 | (5760) | **FS** | E | *SR* | IS | 9807 | (5851) | **FS** | E | *SR* | IS |
| 9802 | (5772) | **FS** | E | *SR* | IS | 9808 | (5871) | **FS** | E | *SR* | IS |
| 9803 | (5799) | **FS** | E | *SR* | IS | 9809 | (5890) | **FS** | E | *SR* | IS |
| 9804 | (5826) | **FS** | E | *SR* | IS | 9810 | (5892) | **FS** | E | *SR* | IS |
| 9805 | (5833) | **FS** | E | *SR* | IS | | | | | | |

# KITCHEN BUFFET FIRST

Mark 3A. Air conditioned. Converted from HST catering vehicles and Mark 3 Open Firsts. Refurbished with table lamps and burgundy seat trim (except *). 18/– plus two seats for staff use (* 24/–, † 24/–, § 24/–, t 23/– 1W). BT10 bogies. d. ETH 14X.

§ First Great Western Sleeper "day coaches" that have been fitted with former HST First Class seats to a 2+1 layout.

**Non-standard livery:** 10211 EWS dark maroon.

**10200–211**. Lot No. 30884 Derby 1977. 39.8 t.
**10212–229**. Lot No. 30878 Derby 1975–76. 39.8 t.
**10232–259**. Lot No. 30890 Derby 1979. 39.8 t.

| | | | | | | |
|---|---|---|---|---|---|---|
| 10200 | (40519) | * | **1** | P | *GA* | NC |
| 10202 | (40504) | † | **BG** | AV | | LM |
| 10203 | (40506) | * | **1** | P | *GA* | NC |
| 10206 | (40507) | | **V** | P | | LM |
| 10211 | (40510) | | **0** | DB | *DB* | TO |
| 10212 | (11049) | | **VT** | P | *VW* | WB |
| 10214 | (11034) | * | **1** | P | *GA* | NC |
| 10215 | (11032) | | **BG** | AV | | LM |
| 10216 | (11041) | * | **1** | P | *GA* | NC |
| 10217 | (11051) | | **VT** | P | | LM |
| 10219 | (11047) | § | **FD** | P | *GW* | PZ |
| 10222 | (11063) | | **BG** | AV | | LM |
| 10223 | (11043) | * | **1** | P | *GA* | NC |
| 10225 | (11014) | § | **FD** | P | *GW* | PZ |
| 10226 | (11015) | | **V** | AV | | LM |
| 10228 | (11035) | * | **1** | P | *GA* | NC |
| 10229 | (11059) | * | **GA** | P | *GA* | NC |
| 10232 | (10027) | § | **FD** | P | *GW* | PZ |
| 10233 | (10013) | | **V** | AV | | LM |
| 10235 | (10015) | † | **BG** | AV | | LM |
| 10237 | (10022) | | **DR** | AV | | LM |
| 10241 | (10009) | * | **1** | P | | IL |
| 10242 | (10002) | | **BG** | AV | | LM |
| 10246 | (10014) | † | **BG** | AV | | CF |
| 10247 | (10011) | * | **NX** | P | *GA* | NC |
| 10249 | (10012) | | **AW** | AV | *AW* | CF |
| 10250 | (10020) | | **V** | AV | | LM |
| 10253 | (10026) | | **V** | P | | LM |
| 10257 | (10007) | † | **BG** | AV | | LM |
| 10259 | (10025) | t | **AW** | AV | *AW* | CF |

# KITCHEN BUFFET FIRST

Mark 3A. Air conditioned. Rebuilt for Chiltern Railways 2011–12 and fitted with sliding plug doors. Interiors originally refurbished for Wrexham & Shropshire with Primarius seating, a new kitchen area and universal-access toilet. 30/– 1TD 1W. BT10 bogies. ETH 14X.

**10271/273/274**. Lot No. 30890 Derby 1979. 41.3 t.
**10272**. Lot No. 30884 Derby 1977. 41.3 t.

| | | | | | |
|---|---|---|---|---|---|
| 10271 | (10018, 10236) | **CM** | AV | *CR* | AL |
| 10272 | (40517, 10208) | **CM** | AV | *CR* | AL |
| 10273 | (10021, 10230) | **CM** | AV | *CR* | AL |
| 10274 | (10010, 10255) | **CM** | AV | *CR* | AL |

# KITCHEN BUFFET STANDARD

Mark 4. Air conditioned. Rebuilt from First to Standard Class with bar adjacent to seating area instead of adjacent to end of coach. –/30 1T, BT41 bogies. ETH 6X.

**Advertising livery:** 10312 Sky 1 (blue).

Lot No. 31045 Metro-Cammell 1989–92. 43.2 t.

| | | | | | | | | |
|---|---|---|---|---|---|---|---|---|
| 10300 | **EC** | E | *EC* | BN | 10317 | **EC** | E | *EC* | BN |
| 10301 | **EC** | E | *EC* | BN | 10318 | **EC** | E | *EC* | BN |
| 10302 | **EC** | E | *EC* | BN | 10319 | **EC** | E | *EC* | BN |
| 10303 | **EC** | E | *EC* | BN | 10320 | **EC** | E | *EC* | BN |
| 10304 | **EC** | E | *EC* | BN | 10321 | **EC** | E | *EC* | BN |
| 10305 | **EC** | E | *EC* | BN | 10323 | **EC** | E | *EC* | BN |
| 10306 | **EC** | E | *EC* | BN | 10324 | **EC** | E | *EC* | BN |
| 10307 | **EC** | E | *EC* | BN | 10325 | **EC** | E | *EC* | BN |
| 10308 | **EC** | E | *EC* | BN | 10326 | **EC** | E | *EC* | BN |
| 10309 | **EC** | E | *EC* | BN | 10328 | **EC** | E | *EC* | BN |
| 10310 | **EC** | E | *EC* | BN | 10329 | **EC** | E | *EC* | BN |
| 10311 | **EC** | E | *EC* | BN | 10330 | **EC** | E | *EC* | BN |
| 10312 | **AL** | E | *EC* | BN | 10331 | **EC** | E | *EC* | BN |
| 10313 | **EC** | E | *EC* | BN | 10332 | **EC** | E | *EC* | BN |
| 10315 | **EC** | E | *EC* | BN | 10333 | **EC** | E | *EC* | BN |

# BUFFET STANDARD

Mark 3A. Air conditioned. Converted from Mark 3 Open Standards at Derby 2006. –/52 1T (including 6 Compin Pegasus seats for "priority" use). BT10 bogies. d. ETH 13X.

Lot No. 30877 Derby 1975–77. 37.8 t.

| | | | | | | | | | | |
|---|---|---|---|---|---|---|---|---|---|---|
| 10401 | (12168) | **NX** | P | *GA* | NC | 10404 | (12068) | **1** | P | *GA* | NC |
| 10402 | (12010) | **1** | P | *GA* | NC | 10405 | (12157) | **1** | P | *GA* | NC |
| 10403 | (12135) | **1** | P | *EA* | NC | 10406 | (12020) | **1** | P | *GA* | NC |

# SLEEPING CAR WITH PANTRY

Mark 3A. Air conditioned. Retention toilets. 12 compartments with a fixed lower berth and a hinged upper berth, plus an attendants compartment. 2T. BT10 bogies. d. ETH 7X.

**Non-standard livery:** 10546 EWS dark maroon.

Lot No. 30960 Derby 1981–83. 41 t.

| | | | | | | | | |
|---|---|---|---|---|---|---|---|---|
| 10501 | **FS** | P | *SR* | IS | 10507 | **FS** | P | *SR* | IS |
| 10502 | **FS** | P | *SR* | IS | 10508 | **FS** | P | *SR* | IS |
| 10504 | **FS** | P | *SR* | IS | 10513 | **FS** | P | *SR* | IS |
| 10506 | **FS** | P | *SR* | IS | 10516 | **FS** | P | *SR* | IS |

| 10519 | **FS** | P | *SR* | IS | | 10565 | **FS** | P | *SR* | IS |
|-------|--------|---|------|-----|--|-------|--------|---|------|-----|
| 10520 | **FS** | P | *SR* | IS | | 10580 | **FS** | P | *SR* | IS |
| 10522 | **FS** | P | *SR* | IS | | 10584 | **FD** | P | *GW* | PZ |
| 10523 | **FS** | P | *SR* | IS | | 10589 | **FD** | P | *GW* | PZ |
| 10526 | **FS** | P | *SR* | IS | | 10590 | **FD** | P | *GW* | PZ |
| 10527 | **FS** | P | *SR* | IS | | 10594 | **FD** | P | *GW* | PZ |
| 10529 | **FS** | P | *SR* | IS | | 10596 | **IC** | P | | ZN |
| 10531 | **FS** | P | *SR* | IS | | 10597 | **FS** | P | *SR* | IS |
| 10532 | **FD** | P | *GW* | PZ | | 10598 | **FS** | P | *SR* | IS |
| 10534 | **FD** | P | *GW* | PZ | | 10600 | **FS** | P | *SR* | IS |
| 10542 | **FS** | P | *SR* | IS | | 10601 | **FD** | P | *GW* | PZ |
| 10543 | **FS** | P | *SR* | IS | | 10605 | **FS** | P | *SR* | IS |
| 10544 | **FS** | P | *SR* | IS | | 10607 | **FS** | P | *SR* | IS |
| 10546 | **0** | DB | *DB* | TO | | 10610 | **FS** | P | *SR* | IS |
| 10548 | **FS** | P | *SR* | IS | | 10612 | **FD** | P | *GW* | PZ |
| 10551 | **FS** | P | *SR* | IS | | 10613 | **FS** | P | *SR* | IS |
| 10553 | **FS** | P | *SR* | IS | | 10614 | **FS** | P | *SR* | IS |
| 10561 | **FS** | P | *SR* | IS | | 10616 | **FD** | P | *GW* | PZ |
| 10562 | **FS** | P | *SR* | IS | | 10617 | **FS** | P | *SR* | IS |
| 10563 | **FD** | P | *GW* | PZ | | | | | | |

# SLEEPING CAR

Mark 3A. Air conditioned. Retention toilets. 13 compartments with a fixed lower berth and a hinged upper berth (* 11 compartments with a fixed lower berth and a hinged upper berth + one compartment for a disabled person. 1TD). 2T. BT10 bogies. ETH 6X.

10734 was originally 2914 and used as a Royal Train staff sleeping car. It has 12 berths and a shower room and is ETH 11X.

**10648–729**. Lot No. 30961 Derby 1980–84. 43.5 t.
**10734**. Lot No. 31002 Derby/Wolverton 1985. 42.5 t.

| 10648 | d* | **FS** | P | *SR* | IS | | 10699 | d* | **FS** | P | *SR* | IS |
|-------|-----|--------|---|------|-----|--|-------|-----|--------|----|------|-----|
| 10650 | d* | **FS** | P | *SR* | IS | | 10703 | d* | **FS** | P | *SR* | IS |
| 10666 | d* | **FS** | P | *SR* | IS | | 10706 | d* | **FS** | P | *SR* | IS |
| 10675 | d | **FS** | P | *SR* | IS | | 10714 | d* | **FS** | P | *SR* | IS |
| 10680 | d* | **FS** | P | *SR* | IS | | 10718 | d* | **FS** | P | *SR* | IS |
| 10683 | d | **FS** | P | *SR* | IS | | 10719 | d* | **FS** | P | *SR* | IS |
| 10688 | d | **FS** | P | *SR* | IS | | 10722 | d* | **FS** | P | *SR* | IS |
| 10689 | d* | **FS** | P | *SR* | IS | | 10723 | d* | **FS** | P | *SR* | IS |
| 10690 | | **FS** | P | *SR* | IS | | 10729 | | **VN** | OE | *NB* | CP |
| 10693 | d | **FS** | P | *SR* | IS | | 10734 | | **VN** | OE | *NB* | CP |

**Names:**

| 10729 | CREWE | | 10734 | BALMORAL |
|-------|-------|--|-------|----------|

# OPEN FIRST

Mark 3A. Air conditioned. All refurbished with table lamps and new seat cushions and trim. 48/– 2T (* 48/– 1T 1TD, † 47/– 2T 1W). BT10 bogies. d. ETH 6X.

§ 11029 has been reseated with Standard Class seats: –/68 2T 2W.

11006/007 were open composites 11906/907 for a time.

**Non-standard livery:** 11039 EWS dark maroon.

Lot No. 30878 Derby 1975–76. 34.3 t.

| | | | | | | | | | | |
|---|---|---|---|---|---|---|---|---|---|---|
| 11006 | | **V** | DR | | LM | 11028 | | **V** | AV | | ZB |
| 11007 | | **VT** | P | *VW* | WB | 11029 § | **BG** | AV | *CR* | AL |
| 11011 | * | **V** | DR | | LM | 11031 † | **BG** | AV | *CR* | AL |
| 11013 | | **DR** | AV | | LM | 11033 | | **DR** | AV | | LM |
| 11018 | | **VT** | P | *VW* | WB | 11039 | | **0** | DB | *DB* | TO |
| 11021 | | **V** | P | | LM | 11044 † | **DR** | AV | | LM |
| 11026 | | **V** | P | | LM | 11048 | | **VT** | P | *VW* | WB |
| 11027 † | **DR** | AV | | LM | | | | | | |

# OPEN FIRST

Mark 3B. Air conditioned. InterCity 80 seats. All refurbished with table lamps and new seat cushions and trim. 48/– 2T. BT10 bogies. d. ETH 6X.

† Greater Anglia vehicles fitted with disabled toilet and reduced seating including three Compin "Pegasus" seats of the same type as used in Standard Class (but regarded as First Class!). 34/3 1T 1TD 2W.

Lot No. 30982 Derby 1985. 36.5 t.

| | | | | | | | | | |
|---|---|---|---|---|---|---|---|---|---|
| 11066 | **1** | P | *GA* | NC | 11085 † | **1** | P | *GA* | NC |
| 11067 | **1** | P | *GA* | NC | 11087 † | **NX** | P | *GA* | NC |
| 11068 | **1** | P | *GA* | NC | 11088 † | **1** | P | *GA* | NC |
| 11069 | **1** | P | *GA* | NC | 11089 | **BG** | AV | | LM |
| 11070 | **1** | P | *GA* | NC | 11090 † | **1** | P | *GA* | NC |
| 11072 | **1** | P | *GA* | NC | 11091 | **NX** | P | *GA* | NC |
| 11073 | **1** | P | *GA* | NC | 11092 † | **1** | P | *GA* | NC |
| 11074 | **V** | P | | LM | 11093 † | **1** | P | *GA* | NC |
| 11075 | **1** | P | *GA* | NC | 11094 † | **1** | P | *GA* | NC |
| 11076 | **1** | P | *GA* | NC | 11095 † | **1** | P | *GA* | NC |
| 11077 | **1** | P | *GA* | NC | 11096 † | **1** | P | *GA* | NC |
| 11078 † | **1** | P | *GA* | NC | 11097 | **V** | AV | | LM |
| 11079 | **V** | AV | | LM | 11098 † | **1** | P | *GA* | NC |
| 11080 | **1** | P | *GA* | NC | 11099 † | **1** | P | *GA* | NC |
| 11081 | **1** | P | *GA* | NC | 11100 † | **1** | P | *GA* | NC |
| 11082 | **1** | P | *GA* | NC | 11101 † | **1** | P | *GA* | NC |

# OPEN FIRST

Mark 4. Air conditioned. Rebuilt with new interior by Bombardier Wakefield 2003–05 (some converted from Standard Class vehicles) 41/– 1T (plus 2 seats for staff use). BT41 bogies. ETH 6X.

**Advertising livery:** 11294 Sky 1 (blue).

**11201–11273.** Lot No. 31046 Metro-Cammell 1989–92. 41.3 t.
**11277–11299.** Lot No. 31049 Metro-Cammell 1989–92. 41.3 t.

| | | | | | | | | | | |
|---|---|---|---|---|---|---|---|---|---|---|
| 11201 | | **EC** | E | *EC* | BN | 11284 (12487) | **EC** | E | *EC* | BN |
| 11219 | | **EC** | E | *EC* | BN | 11285 (12537) | **EC** | E | *EC* | BN |
| 11229 | | **EC** | E | *EC* | BN | 11286 (12482) | **EC** | E | *EC* | BN |
| 11237 | | **EC** | E | *EC* | BN | 11287 (12527) | **EC** | E | *EC* | BN |
| 11241 | | **EC** | E | *EC* | BN | 11288 (12517) | **EC** | E | *EC* | BN |
| 11244 | | **EC** | E | *EC* | BN | 11289 (12528) | **EC** | E | *EC* | BN |
| 11273 | | **EC** | E | *EC* | BN | 11290 (12530) | **EC** | E | *EC* | BN |
| 11277 | (12408) | **EC** | E | *EC* | BN | 11291 (12535) | **EC** | E | *EC* | BN |
| 11278 | (12479) | **EC** | E | *EC* | BN | 11292 (12451) | **EC** | E | *EC* | BN |
| 11279 | (12521) | **EC** | E | *EC* | BN | 11293 (12536) | **EC** | E | *EC* | BN |
| 11280 | (12523) | **EC** | E | *EC* | BN | 11294 (12529) | **AL** | E | *EC* | BN |
| 11281 | (12418) | **EC** | E | *EC* | BN | 11295 (12475) | **EC** | E | *EC* | BN |
| 11282 | (12524) | **EC** | E | *EC* | BN | 11298 (12416) | **EC** | E | *EC* | BN |
| 11283 | (12435) | **EC** | E | *EC* | BN | 11299 (12532) | **EC** | E | *EC* | BN |

# OPEN FIRST (DISABLED)

Mark 4. Air conditioned. Rebuilt from Open First by Bombardier Wakefield 2003–05. 42/– 1W 1TD. BT41 bogies. ETH 6X.

**Advertising livery:** 11325 Sky 1 (blue).

Lot No. 31046 Metro-Cammell 1989–92. 40.7 t.

| | | | | | | | | | |
|---|---|---|---|---|---|---|---|---|---|
| 11301 (11215) | **EC** | E | *EC* | BN | 11316 (11227) | **EC** | E | *EC* | BN |
| 11302 (11203) | **EC** | E | *EC* | BN | 11317 (11223) | **EC** | E | *EC* | BN |
| 11303 (11211) | **EC** | E | *EC* | BN | 11318 (11251) | **EC** | E | *EC* | BN |
| 11304 (11257) | **EC** | E | *EC* | BN | 11319 (11247) | **EC** | E | *EC* | BN |
| 11305 (11261) | **EC** | E | *EC* | BN | 11320 (11255) | **EC** | E | *EC* | BN |
| 11306 (11276) | **EC** | E | *EC* | BN | 11321 (11245) | **EC** | E | *EC* | BN |
| 11307 (11217) | **EC** | E | *EC* | BN | 11322 (11228) | **EC** | E | *EC* | BN |
| 11308 (11263) | **EC** | E | *EC* | BN | 11323 (11235) | **EC** | E | *EC* | BN |
| 11309 (11259) | **EC** | E | *EC* | BN | 11324 (11253) | **EC** | E | *EC* | BN |
| 11310 (11272) | **EC** | E | *EC* | BN | 11325 (11231) | **AL** | E | *EC* | BN |
| 11311 (11221) | **EC** | E | *EC* | BN | 11326 (11206) | **EC** | E | *EC* | BN |
| 11312 (11225) | **EC** | E | *EC* | BN | 11327 (11236) | **EC** | E | *EC* | BN |
| 11313 (11210) | **EC** | E | *EC* | BN | 11328 (11274) | **EC** | E | *EC* | BN |
| 11314 (11207) | **EC** | E | *EC* | BN | 11329 (11243) | **EC** | E | *EC* | BN |
| 11315 (11238) | **EC** | E | *EC* | BN | 11330 (11249) | **EC** | E | *EC* | BN |

# OPEN FIRST

Mark 4. Air conditioned. Rebuilt from Open First by Bombardier Wakefield 2003–05. Separate area for 7 smokers, although smoking is no longer allowed. 46/– 1W 1TD. BT41 bogies. ETH 6X.

**Advertising livery:** 11425 Sky 1 (blue).

Lot No. 31046 Metro-Cammell 1989–92. 42.1 t.

| | | | | | | | | |
|---|---|---|---|---|---|---|---|---|
| 11401 (11214) | **EC** | E | *EC* | BN | 11416 (11254) | **EC** | E | *EC* | BN |
| 11402 (11216) | **EC** | E | *EC* | BN | 11417 (11226) | **EC** | E | *EC* | BN |
| 11403 (11258) | **EC** | E | *EC* | BN | 11418 (11222) | **EC** | E | *EC* | BN |
| 11404 (11202) | **EC** | E | *EC* | BN | 11419 (11250) | **EC** | E | *EC* | BN |
| 11405 (11204) | **EC** | E | *EC* | BN | 11420 (11242) | **EC** | E | *EC* | BN |
| 11406 (11205) | **EC** | E | *EC* | BN | 11421 (11220) | **EC** | E | *EC* | BN |
| 11407 (11256) | **EC** | E | *EC* | BN | 11422 (11232) | **EC** | E | *EC* | BN |
| 11408 (11218) | **EC** | E | *EC* | BN | 11423 (11230) | **EC** | E | *EC* | BN |
| 11409 (11262) | **EC** | E | *EC* | BN | 11424 (11239) | **EC** | E | *EC* | BN |
| 11410 (11260) | **EC** | E | *EC* | BN | 11425 (11234) | **AL** | E | *EC* | BN |
| 11411 (11240) | **EC** | E | *EC* | BN | 11426 (11252) | **EC** | E | *EC* | BN |
| 11412 (11209) | **EC** | E | *EC* | BN | 11427 (11200) | **EC** | E | *EC* | BN |
| 11413 (11212) | **EC** | E | *EC* | BN | 11428 (11233) | **EC** | E | *EC* | BN |
| 11414 (11246) | **EC** | E | *EC* | BN | 11429 (11275) | **EC** | E | *EC* | BN |
| 11415 (11208) | **EC** | E | *EC* | BN | 11430 (11248) | **EC** | E | *EC* | BN |

# OPEN FIRST

Mark 4. Air conditioned. Converted from Kitchen Buffet Standard with new interior by Bombardier Wakefield 2005. 46/– 1T. BT41 bogies. ETH 6X.

Lot No. 31046 Metro-Cammell 1989–92. 41.3 t.

| | | | | | | | | | |
|---|---|---|---|---|---|---|---|---|---|
| 11998 (10314) | **EC** | E | *EC* | BN | 11999 (10316) | **EC** | E | *EC* | BN |

# OPEN STANDARD

Mark 3A. Air conditioned. All refurbished with modified seat backs and new layout and further refurbished with new seat trim. –/76 2T (s –/70 2T 1W, t –/72 2T, z –/70 1TD 1T 2W. BT10 bogies. d. ETH 6X.

n   Greater Anglia modified coaches with eight Compin Pegasus seats at saloon ends for "priority" use and a high density layout with more unidirectional seating. –/80 2T.

§   First Great Western Sleeper "day coaches" that have been fitted with former HST First Class seats to a 2+1 layout and are effectively unclassified. –/45(2) 2T 1W.

12170/171 were converted from Open Composites 11909/910, formerly Open Firsts 11009/010.

**12005–167.** Lot No. 30877 Derby 1975–77. 34.3 t.
**12170/171.** Lot No. 30878 Derby 1975–76. 34.3 t.

| Nr. | | | | | Nr. | | | | |
|---|---|---|---|---|---|---|---|---|---|
| 12005 h | 1 | P | GA | NC | 12087 s | V | DR | | LM |
| 12008 | V | P | | LM | 12089 | 1 | P | GA | NC |
| 12009 h | 1 | P | GA | NC | 12090 h | 1 | P | GA | NC |
| 12011 | VT | P | VW | WB | 12091 h | 1 | P | GA | NC |
| 12012 h | 1 | P | GA | NC | 12092 | 1 | P | | LM |
| 12013 h | 1 | P | GA | NC | 12093 h | 1 | P | GA | NC |
| 12015 h | 1 | P | GA | NC | 12094 | V | AV | CR | AL |
| 12016 | 1 | P | GA | NC | 12095 | V | P | | LM |
| 12017 | BG | AV | CR | AL | 12097 h | 1 | P | GA | NC |
| 12019 h | 1 | P | GA | NC | 12098 | 1 | P | GA | NC |
| 12021 | NX | P | GA | NC | 12099 h | 1 | P | GA | NC |
| 12022 | V | P | | LM | 12100 § | FD | P | GW | PZ |
| 12024 h | 1 | P | GA | NC | 12101 s | V | P | | LM |
| 12026 h | 1 | P | GA | NC | 12103 | 1 | P | GA | NC |
| 12027 h | 1 | P | GA | NC | 12104 | V | AV | | LM |
| 12029 | V | P | | LM | 12105 h | 1 | P | GA | NC |
| 12030 h | 1 | P | GA | NC | 12107 h | 1 | P | GA | NC |
| 12031 | 1 | P | GA | NC | 12108 | 1 | P | GA | NC |
| 12032 h | 1 | P | GA | NC | 12109 h | 1 | P | GA | NC |
| 12034 | 1 | P | GA | NC | 12110 h | 1 | P | GA | NC |
| 12035 h | GA | P | GA | NC | 12111 | 1 | P | GA | NC |
| 12036 s | V | P | | LM | 12114 h | 1 | P | GA | NC |
| 12037 h | 1 | P | GA | NC | 12115 h | 1 | P | GA | NC |
| 12040 h | 1 | P | GA | NC | 12116 h | 1 | P | GA | NC |
| 12041 h | 1 | P | GA | NC | 12118 | 1 | P | GA | NC |
| 12042 h | 1 | P | GA | NC | 12119 t | BG | AV | CR | AL |
| 12043 s | BG | AV | CR | AL | 12120 h | 1 | P | GA | NC |
| 12045 | V | P | | LM | 12122 z | VT | P | VW | WB |
| 12046 h | 1 | P | GA | NC | 12125 h | 1 | P | GA | NC |
| 12047 z | V | DR | | LM | 12126 h | 1 | P | GA | NC |
| 12049 | 1 | P | GA | NC | 12129 h | NX | P | GA | NC |
| 12051 h | NX | P | GA | NC | 12130 h | 1 | P | GA | NC |
| 12054 s | BG | AV | CR | AL | 12132 | NX | P | GA | NC |
| 12056 h | 1 | P | GA | NC | 12133 | VT | P | VW | WB |
| 12057 h | 1 | P | GA | NC | 12134 | V | DR | | LM |
| 12058 | V | AV | | LM | 12137 h | 1 | P | GA | NC |
| 12060 h | 1 | P | GA | NC | 12138 | VT | P | VW | WB |
| 12061 h | 1 | P | GA | NC | 12139 | NC | P | GA | NC |
| 12062 h | 1 | P | GA | NC | 12141 | 1 | P | GA | NC |
| 12063 | 1 | DR | | LM | 12142 z | V | P | | ZN |
| 12064 | 1 | P | GA | NC | 12143 | 1 | P | GA | NC |
| 12065 | 1 | DR | | LM | 12144 s | V | P | | LM |
| 12066 h | 1 | P | GA | NC | 12146 | 1 | P | GA | NC |
| 12067 | 1 | P | GA | NC | 12147 | 1 | P | GA | NC |
| 12073 h | 1 | P | GA | NC | 12148 | GA | P | GA | NC |
| 12078 | VT | P | VW | WB | 12150 h | 1 | P | GA | NC |
| 12079 | 1 | P | GA | NC | 12151 | 1 | P | GA | NC |
| 12081 | 1 | P | GA | NC | 12153 | 1 | P | GA | NC |
| 12082 h | 1 | P | GA | NC | 12154 h | 1 | P | GA | NC |
| 12083 | V | P | | LM | 12156 | V | P | | LM |
| 12084 h | 1 | P | GA | NC | 12159 | 1 | P | GA | NC |

| | | | | | | | | | |
|---|---|---|---|---|---|---|---|---|---|
| 12160 | s | **V** | P | | LM | 12166 | **1** | P | *GA* | NC |
| 12161 | § | **FD** | P | *GW* | PZ | 12167 | h | **1** | P | *GA* | NC |
| 12163 | | **V** | P | | LM | 12170 | | **1** | P | *GA* | NC |
| 12164 | | **1** | P | *GA* | NC | 12171 | | **1** | P | *GA* | NC |
| 12165 | | **V** | AV | | LM | | | | | |

## OPEN STANDARD

Mark 3B. Air conditioned. BT10 bogies. d. ETH 6X. Converted from Mark 3B Open Firsts and fitted with new Grammer seating. –/70 2T 1W.

Lot No. 30982 Derby 1985. 38.5 t.

| | | | | | |
|---|---|---|---|---|---|
| 12176 | (11064) | **AW** | AV | *AW* | CF |
| 12177 | (11065) | **AW** | AV | *AW* | CF |
| 12178 | (11071) | **AW** | AV | *AW* | CF |
| 12179 | (11083) | **AW** | AV | *AW* | CF |
| 12180 | (11084) | **AW** | AV | *AW* | CF |
| 12181 | (11086) | **AW** | AV | *AW* | CF |

## OPEN STANDARD (END)

Mark 4. Air conditioned. Rebuilt with new interior by Bombardier Wakefield 2003–05. Separate area for 26 smokers, although smoking is no longer allowed. –/76 1T. BT41 bogies. ETH 6X.

12232 was converted from the original 12405.

**Advertising livery:** 11425 Sky 1 (blue).

**12200–231.** Lot No. 31047 Metro-Cammell 1989–91. 39.5 t.
**12232.** Lot No. 31049 Metro-Cammell 1989–92. 39.5 t.

| | | | | | | | | | |
|---|---|---|---|---|---|---|---|---|---|
| 12200 | **EC** | E | *EC* | BN | 12217 | **AL** | E | *EC* | BN |
| 12201 | **EC** | E | *EC* | BN | 12218 | **EC** | E | *EC* | BN |
| 12202 | **EC** | E | *EC* | BN | 12219 | **EC** | E | *EC* | BN |
| 12203 | **EC** | E | *EC* | BN | 12220 | **EC** | E | *EC* | BN |
| 12204 | **EC** | E | *EC* | BN | 12222 | **EC** | E | *EC* | BN |
| 12205 | **EC** | E | *EC* | BN | 12223 | **EC** | E | *EC* | BN |
| 12207 | **EC** | E | *EC* | BN | 12224 | **EC** | E | *EC* | BN |
| 12208 | **EC** | E | *EC* | BN | 12225 | **EC** | E | *EC* | BN |
| 12209 | **EC** | E | *EC* | BN | 12226 | **EC** | E | *EC* | BN |
| 12210 | **EC** | E | *EC* | BN | 12227 | **EC** | E | *EC* | BN |
| 12211 | **EC** | E | *EC* | BN | 12228 | **EC** | E | *EC* | BN |
| 12212 | **EC** | E | *EC* | BN | 12229 | **EC** | E | *EC* | BN |
| 12213 | **EC** | E | *EC* | BN | 12230 | **EC** | E | *EC* | BN |
| 12214 | **EC** | E | *EC* | BN | 12231 | **EC** | E | *EC* | BN |
| 12215 | **EC** | E | *EC* | BN | 12232 | **EC** | E | *EC* | BN |
| 12216 | **EC** | E | *EC* | BN | | | | | |

## OPEN STANDARD (DISABLED)

Mark 4. Air conditioned. Rebuilt with new interior by Bombardier Wakefield 2003–05. –/68 2W 1TD. BT41 bogies. ETH 6X.

12331 was converted from Open Standard 12531.

**Advertising livery:** 12322 Sky 1 (blue).

**12300–330.** Lot No. 31048 Metro-Cammell 1989–91. 39.4 t.
**12331.** Lot No. 31049 Metro-Cammell 1989–92. 39.4 t.

| | | | | | | | | | |
|---|---|---|---|---|---|---|---|---|---|
| 12300 | **EC** | E | *EC* | BN | 12317 | **EC** | E | *EC* | BN |
| 12301 | **EC** | E | *EC* | BN | 12318 | **EC** | E | *EC* | BN |
| 12302 | **EC** | E | *EC* | BN | 12319 | **EC** | E | *EC* | BN |
| 12303 | **EC** | E | *EC* | BN | 12320 | **EC** | E | *EC* | BN |
| 12304 | **EC** | E | *EC* | BN | 12321 | **EC** | E | *EC* | BN |
| 12305 | **EC** | E | *EC* | BN | 12322 | **AL** | E | *EC* | BN |
| 12307 | **EC** | E | *EC* | BN | 12323 | **EC** | E | *EC* | BN |
| 12308 | **EC** | E | *EC* | BN | 12324 | **EC** | E | *EC* | BN |
| 12309 | **EC** | E | *EC* | BN | 12325 | **EC** | E | *EC* | BN |
| 12310 | **EC** | E | *EC* | BN | 12326 | **EC** | E | *EC* | BN |
| 12311 | **EC** | E | *EC* | BN | 12327 | **EC** | E | *EC* | BN |
| 12312 | **EC** | E | *EC* | BN | 12328 | **EC** | E | *EC* | BN |
| 12313 | **EC** | E | *EC* | BN | 12329 | **EC** | E | *EC* | BN |
| 12315 | **EC** | E | *EC* | BN | 12330 | **EC** | E | *EC* | BN |
| 12316 | **EC** | E | *EC* | BN | 12331 | **EC** | E | *EC* | BN |

## OPEN STANDARD

Mark 4. Air conditioned. Rebuilt with new interior by Bombardier Wakefield 2003–05. –/76 1T. BT41 bogies. ETH 6X.

12405 is the second coach to carry that number. It was built from the bodyshell originally intended for 12221. The original 12405 is now 12232.

**Advertising livery:** 12446, 12464, 12519 Sky 1 (blue).

Lot No. 31049 Metro-Cammell 1989–92. 40.8 t.

| | | | | | | | | | |
|---|---|---|---|---|---|---|---|---|---|
| 12400 | **EC** | E | *EC* | BN | 12420 | **EC** | E | *EC* | BN |
| 12401 | **EC** | E | *EC* | BN | 12421 | **EC** | E | *EC* | BN |
| 12402 | **EC** | E | *EC* | BN | 12422 | **EC** | E | *EC* | BN |
| 12403 | **EC** | E | *EC* | BN | 12423 | **EC** | E | *EC* | BN |
| 12404 | **EC** | E | *EC* | BN | 12424 | **EC** | E | *EC* | BN |
| 12405 | **EC** | E | *EC* | BN | 12425 | **EC** | E | *EC* | BN |
| 12406 | **EC** | E | *EC* | BN | 12426 | **EC** | E | *EC* | BN |
| 12407 | **EC** | E | *EC* | BN | 12427 | **EC** | E | *EC* | BN |
| 12409 | **EC** | E | *EC* | BN | 12428 | **EC** | E | *EC* | BN |
| 12410 | **EC** | E | *EC* | BN | 12429 | **EC** | E | *EC* | BN |
| 12411 | **EC** | E | *EC* | BN | 12430 | **EC** | E | *EC* | BN |
| 12414 | **EC** | E | *EC* | BN | 12431 | **EC** | E | *EC* | BN |
| 12415 | **EC** | E | *EC* | BN | 12432 | **EC** | E | *EC* | BN |
| 12417 | **EC** | E | *EC* | BN | 12433 | **EC** | E | *EC* | BN |
| 12419 | **EC** | E | *EC* | BN | 12434 | **EC** | E | *EC* | BN |

| 12436 | **EC** | E | *EC* | BN | 12467 | **EC** | E | *EC* | BN |
|-------|--------|---|------|-----|-------|--------|---|------|-----|
| 12437 | **EC** | E | *EC* | BN | 12468 | **EC** | E | *EC* | BN |
| 12438 | **EC** | E | *EC* | BN | 12469 | **EC** | E | *EC* | BN |
| 12439 | **EC** | E | *EC* | BN | 12470 | **EC** | E | *EC* | BN |
| 12440 | **EC** | E | *EC* | BN | 12471 | **EC** | E | *EC* | BN |
| 12441 | **EC** | E | *EC* | BN | 12472 | **EC** | E | *EC* | BN |
| 12442 | **EC** | E | *EC* | BN | 12473 | **EC** | E | *EC* | BN |
| 12443 | **EC** | E | *EC* | BN | 12474 | **EC** | E | *EC* | BN |
| 12444 | **EC** | E | *EC* | BN | 12476 | **EC** | E | *EC* | BN |
| 12445 | **EC** | E | *EC* | BN | 12477 | **EC** | E | *EC* | BN |
| 12446 | **AL** | E | *EC* | BN | 12478 | **EC** | E | *EC* | BN |
| 12447 | **EC** | E | *EC* | BN | 12480 | **EC** | E | *EC* | BN |
| 12448 | **EC** | E | *EC* | BN | 12481 | **EC** | E | *EC* | BN |
| 12449 | **EC** | E | *EC* | BN | 12483 | **EC** | E | *EC* | BN |
| 12450 | **EC** | E | *EC* | BN | 12484 | **EC** | E | *EC* | BN |
| 12452 | **EC** | E | *EC* | BN | 12485 | **EC** | E | *EC* | BN |
| 12453 | **EC** | E | *EC* | BN | 12486 | **EC** | E | *EC* | BN |
| 12454 | **EC** | E | *EC* | BN | 12488 | **EC** | E | *EC* | BN |
| 12455 | **EC** | E | *EC* | BN | 12489 | **EC** | E | *EC* | BN |
| 12456 | **EC** | E | *EC* | BN | 12513 | **EC** | E | *EC* | BN |
| 12457 | **EC** | E | *EC* | BN | 12514 | **EC** | E | *EC* | BN |
| 12458 | **EC** | E | *EC* | BN | 12515 | **EC** | E | *EC* | BN |
| 12459 | **EC** | E | *EC* | BN | 12518 | **EC** | E | *EC* | BN |
| 12460 | **EC** | E | *EC* | BN | 12519 | **AL** | E | *EC* | BN |
| 12461 | **EC** | E | *EC* | BN | 12520 | **EC** | E | *EC* | BN |
| 12462 | **EC** | E | *EC* | BN | 12522 | **EC** | E | *EC* | BN |
| 12463 | **EC** | E | *EC* | BN | 12526 | **EC** | E | *EC* | BN |
| 12464 | **AL** | E | *EC* | BN | 12533 | **EC** | E | *EC* | BN |
| 12465 | **EC** | E | *EC* | BN | 12534 | **EC** | E | *EC* | BN |
| 12466 | **EC** | E | *EC* | BN | 12538 | **EC** | E | *EC* | BN |

# OPEN STANDARD

Mark 3A. Air conditioned. Rebuilt for Chiltern Railways 2011–13 and fitted with sliding plug doors and toilets with retention tanks. Original InterCity 70 seating retained but mainly arranged around tables. –/72(6) or * –/69(4) 1T. BT10 bogies. ETH 6X.

**12602–609/614–616/618/620.** Lot No. 30877 Derby 1975–77. 36.2 t (* 37.1 t).
**12601/613/617–619/621/623/625/627.** Lot No. 30878 Derby 1975–76. 36.2 t (* 37.1 t).

| 12602 | (12072) |   | **CM** | AV | *CR* | AL |
|-------|---------|---|--------|----|------|-----|
| 12603 | (12053) | * | **CM** | AV | *CR* | AL |
| 12604 | (12131) |   | **CM** | AV | *CR* | AL |
| 12605 | (11040) | * | **CM** | AV | *CR* | AL |
| 12606 | (12048) |   | **CM** | AV | *CR* | AL |
| 12607 | (12038) | * | **CM** | AV | *CR* | AL |
| 12608 | (12069) |   | **CM** | AV | *CR* | AL |
| 12609 | (12014) | * | **CM** | AV | *CR* | AL |
| 12610 | (12117) |   | **CM** | AV | *CR* | AL |
| 12613 | (11042, 12173) | * | **CM** | AV | *CR* | AL |

| | | | | | | |
|---|---|---|---|---|---|---|
| 12614 (12145) | | **CM** | AV | *CR* | AL | |
| 12615 (12059) | * | **CM** | AV | *CR* | AL | |
| 12616 (12127) | | **CM** | AV | *CR* | AL | |
| 12617 (11052, 12174) | * | **CM** | AV | *CR* | AL | |
| 12618 (11008, 12169) | | **CM** | AV | *CR* | AL | |
| 12619 (11058, 12175) | * | **CM** | AV | *CR* | AL | |
| 12620 (12124) | | **CM** | AV | *CR* | AL | |
| 12621 (11046) | * | **CM** | AV | *CR* | AL | |
| 12623 (11019) | * | **CM** | AV | *CR* | AL | |
| 12625 (11030) | * | **CM** | AV | *CR* | AL | |
| 12627 (11054) | * | **CM** | AV | *CR* | AL | |

# CORRIDOR FIRST

Mark 1. 42/– 2T. B4 bogies. ETH 3.

Lot No. 30381 Swindon 1959. 33 t.

| | | | | | | | | | | | |
|---|---|---|---|---|---|---|---|---|---|---|---|
| 13227 | x | **CH** | JH | *RV* | EH | | 13230 | xk | **M** | BK | *BK* | BT |
| 13229 | xk | **M** | BK | *BK* | BT | | | | | | |

# CORRIDOR FIRST

Mark 2A. Pressure ventilated. 42/– 2T. B4 bogies. ETH 4.

Lot No. 30774 Derby 1968. 33 t.

| | | | | | |
|---|---|---|---|---|---|
| 13440 | v | **M** | WC | *WC* | CS |

# CORRIDOR BRAKE FIRST

Mark 1. 24/– 1T. Commonwealth bogies. ETH 2.

Lot No. 30668 Swindon 1961. 36 t.

Originally numbered in 14xxx series and then renumbered in 17xxx series.

| | | | | | | | | | | | |
|---|---|---|---|---|---|---|---|---|---|---|---|
| 17015 | x | **CC** | RV | | TM | | 17018 | v | **CH** | VT | *VT* | TM |

# CORRIDOR BRAKE FIRST

Mark 2A. Pressure ventilated. 24/– 1T. B4 bogies. ETH 4.

Originally numbered 14056–102. 17080/090 were numbered 35516/503 for a time when declassified.

**17056/077**. Lot No. 30775 Derby 1967–8. 32 t.
**17080–102**. Lot No. 30786 Derby 1968. 32 t.

| | | | | | | | | | | |
|---|---|---|---|---|---|---|---|---|---|---|
| 17056 | **M** | RV | | EH | | 17090 | v | **CH** | VT | | TM |
| 17077 | **RV** | RV | | EH | | 17102 | | **M** | WC | *WC* | CS |
| 17080 | **PC** | RA | *ST* | CS | | | | | | |

# COUCHETTE/GENERATOR COACH

Mark 2B. Formerly part of Royal Train. Converted from Corridor Brake First built 1969. Consists of luggage accommodation, guard's compartment, 350 kW diesel generator and staff sleeping accommodation. Pressure ventilated. B5 bogies. ETH 5X.

**Non-standard livery:** 17105 Oxford blue.

Lot No. 30888 Wolverton 1977. 46 t.

17105  (14105, 2905)          **O**    RV    *RV*         EH

# CORRIDOR BRAKE FIRST

Mark 2D. Air conditioned. Stones equipment. 24/– 1T. B4 Bogies. ETH 5.

Lot No. 30823 Derby 1971–72. 33.5 t.

17159  (14159)      d      **DS**   DR                KM
17167  (14167)             **VN**   OE    *NB*         CP

# OPEN BRAKE UNCLASSIFIED

Mark 3B. Air conditioned. Fitted with hydraulic handbrake. Used by First Great Western as Sleeper "day coaches" that have been fitted with former HST First Class seats to a 2+1 layout and are effectively unclassified. 36/– 1T. BT10 bogies. pg. d. ETH 5X.

Lot No. 30990 Derby 1986. 35.81 t.

17173   **FD** P   *GW*   PZ   | 17175   **FD** P   *GW*   PZ
17174   **FD** P   *GW*   PZ   |

# CORRIDOR BRAKE COMPOSITE

Mark 1. There are two variants depending upon whether the Standard Class compartments have armrests. Each vehicle has two First Class and three Standard Class compartments. 12/18 2T (* 12/24 2T). Commonwealth bogies. ETH 2.

**21241–245.** Lot No. 30669 Swindon 1961–62. 36 t.
**21256.** Lot No. 30731 Derby 1963. 37 t.
**21266–272.** Lot No. 30732 Derby 1964. 37 t.

21241 x   **CC** BK  *BK*   BT   | 21266 x* **M**  WC  *WC*   CS
21245 x   **M**  RV  *RV*   EH   | 21269 *  **CC** RV  *RV*   EH
21256 x   **M**  WC  *WC*   CS   | 21272 x* **CH** RV  *RV*   EH

## CORRIDOR BRAKE STANDARD

Mark 1. Four compartments. Lot No. 30721 has metal window frames and melamine interior panelling. –/24 1T. ETH2.

**35185.** Lot No. 30427 Wolverton 1959. B4 bogies. 33 t.
**35459.** Lot No. 30721 Wolverton 1963. Commonwealth bogies. 37 t.

| | | | | | |
|---|---|---|---|---|---|
| 35185 | x | **M** | BK | *BK* | BT |
| 35459 | x | **M** | WC | *WC* | CS |

## CORRIDOR BRAKE GENERATOR STANDARD

Mark 1. Four compartments. Metal window frames and melamine interior panelling. Fitted with an ets generator in the former luggage compartment.

Lot No. 30721 Wolverton 1963. Commonwealth bogies. 37 t.

| | | | | | |
|---|---|---|---|---|---|
| 35469 | x | **CC** | RV | *RV* | EH |

## BRAKE/POWER KITCHEN

Mark 2C. Pressure ventilated. Converted from Corridor Brake First (declassified to Corridor Brake Standard) built 1970. Converted by West Coast Railway Company 2000–01. Consists of 60 kVA generator, guard's compartment and electric kitchen. B5 bogies. ETH 4.

**Non-standard livery:** British Racing Green with gold lining.

Lot No. 30796 Derby 1969–70. 32.5 t.

| | | | | |
|---|---|---|---|---|
| 35511 | (14130, 17130) | **O** | RA | BO |

## KITCHEN CAR

Mark 1. Converted 1989/2006 from Kitchen Buffet Unclassified. Buffet and seating area replaced with additional kitchen and food preparation area. Fluorescent lighting. Commonwealth bogies. ETH 2X.

Lot No. 30628 Pressed Steel 1960–61. 39 t.

| | | | | | | |
|---|---|---|---|---|---|---|
| 80041 | (1690) | x | **M** | RV | *RV* | EH |
| 80042 | (1646) | | **BG** | RV | *RV* | EH |

# DRIVING BRAKE VAN (110 mph)

Mark 3B. Air conditioned. T4 bogies. dg. ETH 5X. Driving Brake Vans converted for use by Network Rail can be found in the Service Stock section of this book.

**Non-standard livery:** 82146 All over silver with DB logos.

Lot No. 31042 Derby 1988. 45.18 t.

| | | | | | | | | | | |
|---|---|---|---|---|---|---|---|---|---|---|
| 82101 | **V** | DR | | CR | 82125 | **V** | P | | LM |
| 82102 | **1** | P | *GA* | NC | 82126 | **VT** | P | *VW* | WB |
| 82103 | **1** | P | *GA* | NC | 82127 | **1** | P | *GA* | NC |
| 82105 | **1** | P | *GA* | NC | 82132 | **1** | P | *GA* | NC |
| 82106 | **V** | AV | | LM | 82133 | **1** | P | *GA* | NC |
| 82107 | **NX** | P | *GA* | NC | 82136 | **1** | P | *GA* | NC |
| 82110 | **V** | AV | | LM | 82137 | **V** | AV | | LM |
| 82112 | **1** | P | *GA* | NC | 82138 | **V** | AV | | LM |
| 82113 | **V** | AV | | LM | 82139 | **1** | P | *GA* | NC |
| 82114 | **1** | P | *GA* | NC | 82140 | **V** | P | | LM |
| 82115 | **B** | NR | | ZN | 82141 | **V** | AV | | LM |
| 82116 | **V** | AV | | LM | 82143 | **1** | P | *GA* | NC |
| 82118 | **1** | P | *GA* | NC | 82146 | **0** | DB | *DB* | TO |
| 82120 | **V** | AV | | LM | 82148 | **V** | AV | | LM |
| 82121 | **1** | P | *GA* | NC | 82150 | **V** | AV | | LM |
| 82122 | **V** | AV | | LM | 82152 | **1** | P | *GA* | NC |
| 82123 | **V** | AV | | LM | | | | | |

# DRIVING BRAKE VAN (140 mph)

Mark 4. Air conditioned. Swiss-built (SIG) bogies. dg. ETH 6X.

**Non-standard livery:** 82205 Flying Scotsman (purple).

**Advertising livery:** 82216 Sky 1 (blue).

Lot No. 31043 Metro-Cammell 1988. 43.5 t.

| | | | | | | | | | |
|---|---|---|---|---|---|---|---|---|---|
| 82200 | **EC** | E | *EC* | BN | 82216 | **AL** | E | *EC* | BN |
| 82201 | **EC** | E | *EC* | BN | 82217 | **EC** | E | *EC* | BN |
| 82202 | **EC** | E | *EC* | BN | 82218 | **EC** | E | *EC* | BN |
| 82203 | **EC** | E | *EC* | BN | 82219 | **EC** | E | *EC* | BN |
| 82204 | **EC** | E | *EC* | BN | 82220 | **EC** | E | *EC* | BN |
| 82205 | **AL** | E | *EC* | BN | 82222 | **EC** | E | *EC* | BN |
| 82206 | **EC** | E | *EC* | BN | 82223 | **EC** | E | *EC* | BN |
| 82207 | **EC** | E | *EC* | BN | 82224 | **EC** | E | *EC* | BN |
| 82208 | **EC** | E | *EC* | BN | 82225 | **EC** | E | *EC* | BN |
| 82209 | **EC** | E | *EC* | BN | 82226 | **EC** | E | *EC* | BN |
| 82210 | **EC** | E | *EC* | BN | 82227 | **EC** | E | *EC* | BN |
| 82211 | **EC** | E | *EC* | BN | 82228 | **EC** | E | *EC* | BN |
| 82212 | **EC** | E | *EC* | BN | 82229 | **EC** | E | *EC* | BN |
| 82213 | **EC** | E | *EC* | BN | 82230 | **EC** | E | *EC* | BN |
| 82214 | **EC** | E | *EC* | BN | 82231 | **EC** | E | *EC* | BN |
| 82215 | **EC** | E | *EC* | BN | | | | | |

## DRIVING BRAKE VAN (110 mph)

Mark 3B. Air conditioned. T4 bogies. dg. ETH 6X.

82301–305 originally converted 2008 for use on Wrexham & Shropshire services. Now operated by Chiltern Railways in push-pull mode with Class 67s. 82309 was converted for Chiltern in 2013.

g  Fitted with a diesel generator.

Lot No. 31042 Derby 1988. 45.2 t.

| | | | | | |
|---|---|---|---|---|---|
| 82301 | (82117) | g | **CM** | AV | *CR* | AL |
| 82302 | (82151) | g | **CM** | AV | *CR* | AL |
| 82303 | (82135) | g | **CM** | AV | *CR* | AL |
| 82304 | (82130) | g | **CM** | AV | *CR* | AL |
| 82305 | (82134) | g | **CM** | AV | *CR* | AL |
| 82306 | (82144) | | **AW** | AV | *AW* | CF |
| 82307 | (82131) | | **AW** | AV | *AW* | CF |
| 82308 | (82108) | | **AW** | AV | *AW* | CF |
| 82309 | (82104) | g | **CM** | AV | *CR* | AL |

## GANGWAYED BRAKE VAN (100 mph)

Mark 1. Short frame (57 ft). Load 10 t. Adapted 199? for use as Brake Luggage Van. Guard's compartment retained and former baggage area adapted for secure stowage of passengers' luggage. B4 bogies. 100 mph. ETH 1X.

Lot No. 30162 Pressed Steel 1956–57. 30.5 t.

| | | | | |
|---|---|---|---|---|
| 92904 | (80867, 99554) | **VN** | OE | *NB* | CP |

## GENERAL UTILITY VAN (100 mph)

Mark 1. Short frame. Load 14 t. Screw couplers. Adapted 2013/2010 for use as a water carrier with 3000 gallon capacity.

**Non-standard livery:** 96100 GWR Brown.

**96100.** Lot No. 30565 Pressed Steel 1959. 30 t. B5 bogies.
**96175.** Lot No. 30403 York/Glasgow 1958–60. 30 t. Commonwealth bogies.

| | | | | | |
|---|---|---|---|---|---|
| 96100 | (86734, 93734) | x | **0** | VT | *VT* | TM |
| 96175 | (86628, 93628) | x | **M** | WC | *WC* | CS |

## KITCHEN CAR

Mark 1 converted from Corridor First in 2008 with staff accommodation. Commonwealth bogies. ETH 3.

Lot No. 30667 Swindon 1961. 35 t.

| | | | | | |
|---|---|---|---|---|---|
| 99316 | (13321) | x | **M** | WC | *WC* | CS |

## BUFFET STANDARD

Mark 1 converted from Open Standard in 2013 by the removal of two seating bays and fitting of a buffet. –/48 2T. Commonwealth bogies. ETH 4.

Lot No. 30646 Wolverton 1961. 36 t.

99318 (4912)          x          **M**    WC    *WC*              CS

## KITCHEN CAR

Mark 1 converted from Corridor Standard in 2011 with staff accommodation. Commonwealth bogies. ETH 3.

Lot No. 30685 Derby 1961–62. 34 t.

99712 (18893)        x          **M**    WC    *WC*              CS

## OPEN STANDARD

Mark 1 Corridor Standard rebuilt in 1997 as Open Standard using components from 4936. –/64 2T. Commonwealth bogies. ETH 4.

Lot No. 30685 Derby 1961–62. 36 t.

99722 (25806, 18806) x        **M**    WC    *WC*              CS

# NYMR REGISTERED COACHES

These coaches are permitted to operate on the national railway network but may only be used to convey fare-paying passengers between Middlesbrough and Whitby on the Esk Valley branch as an extension of North Yorkshire Moors Railway services between Pickering and Grosmont. Only NYMR coaches currently registered for use on the national network are listed.

## RESTAURANT FIRST

Mark 1. 24/–. Commonwealth bogies. ETH 2. Lot No. 30633 Swindon 1961. 42.5 t.

| 324 | x | **PC** | NY | *NY* | NY | JOS de CRAU |
|-----|---|--------|----|----|----|-------------|

## BUFFET STANDARD

Mark 1. –/44 2T. Commonwealth bogies. ETH 3.

Lot No. 30520 Wolverton 1960. 38 t.

| 1823 | v | **M** | NY | *NY* | NY |
|------|---|-------|----|----|----|

## OPEN STANDARD

Mark 1. –/64 2T (* –/60 2W 2T, † –/60 3W 1T). BR Mark 1 bogies. ETH 4.

**3798/3801.** Lot No. 30079 York 1953. 33 t.
**3860/72.** Lot No. 30080 York 1954. 33 t.
**3948.** Lot No. 30086 Eastleigh 1954–55. 33 t.
**4198/4252.** Lot No. 30172 York 1956. 33 t.
**4286/90.** Lot No. 30207 BRCW 1956. 33 t.
**4455.** Lot No. 30226 BRCW 1957. 33 t.

| 3798 | v | **M** | NY | *NY* | NY | | 4198 | v | **CC** | NY | *NY* | NY |
|------|----|-------|----|----|----|---|------|----|--------|----|----|----|
| 3801 | v | **CC** | NY | *NY* | NY | | 4252 | v* | **CC** | NY | *NY* | NY |
| 3860 | v* | **M** | NY | *NY* | NY | | 4286 | v | **CC** | NY | *NY* | NY |
| 3872 | v† | **BG** | NY | *NY* | NY | | 4290 | v | **M** | NY | *NY* | NY |
| 3948 | v | **CC** | NY | *NY* | NY | | 4455 | v | **CC** | NY | *NY* | NY |

## OPEN STANDARD

Mark 1. –/48 2T. BR Mark 1 bogies. ETH 4.

**4786.** Lot No. 30376 York 1957. 33 t.
**4817.** Lot No. 30473 BRCW 1959. 33 t.

| 4786 | v | **CH** | NY | *NY* | NY | | 4817 | v | **M** | NY | *NY* | NY |
|------|---|--------|----|----|----|---|------|---|-------|----|----|----|

## OPEN STANDARD

Mark 1. Later vehicles built with Commonwealth bogies. –/64 2T. ETH 4.

Lot No. 30690 Wolverton 1961–62. Aluminium window frames. 37 t.

| 4990 | v | **M** | NY | *NY* | NY | | 5000 | v | **M** | NY | *NY* | NY |
|------|---|-------|----|----|----|---|------|---|-------|----|----|----|
| 5029 | v | **CH** | NY | *NY* | NY | | | | | | | |

# OPEN BRAKE STANDARD

Mark 1. –/39 1T. BR Mark 1 bogies. ETH 4.

Lot No. 30170 Doncaster 1956. 34 t.

| | | | | | | | | | | |
|---|---|---|---|---|---|---|---|---|---|---|
| 9225 | v | **M** | NY | *NY* | NY | | 9267 | v | **BG** | NY | *NY* | NY |
| 9274 | v | **M** | NY | *NY* | NY | | | | | |

# CORRIDOR COMPOSITE

Mark 1. 24/18 1T. BR Mark 1 bogies. ETH 2.

**15745.** Lot No. 30179 Metro Cammell 1956. 36 t.
**16156.** Lot No. 30665 Derby 1961. 36 t.

| | | | | | | | | | | |
|---|---|---|---|---|---|---|---|---|---|---|
| 15745 | v | **M** | NY | *NY* | NY | | 16156 | v | **CC** | NY | *NY* | NY |

# CORRIDOR BRAKE COMPOSITE

Mark 1. Two First Class and three Standard Class compartments. 12/18 2T. BR Mark 1 bogies.

Lot No. 30185 Metro Cammell 1956. 36 t.

| | | | | | |
|---|---|---|---|---|---|
| 21100 | v | **CC** | NY | *NY* | NY |

# CORRIDOR BRAKE STANDARD

Mark 1. –/24 1T. BR Mark 1 bogies. ETH 2.

Lot No. 30233 Gloucester 1957. 35 t.

| | | | | | |
|---|---|---|---|---|---|
| 35089 | v | **CC** | NY | *NY* | NY |

# PULLMAN BRAKE THIRD

Built 1928 by Metropolitan Carriage & Wagon Company. –/30. Gresley bogies. 37.5 t.

| | | | | | | |
|---|---|---|---|---|---|---|
| 232 | v | **PC** | NY | *NY* | NY | CAR No. 79 |

# PULLMAN KITCHEN FIRST

Built by Metro-Cammell 1960–61 for ECML services. 20/– 2T. Commonwealth bogies. ETH 4. 41.2 t.

| | | | | | | |
|---|---|---|---|---|---|---|
| 318 | x | **PC** | NY | *NY* | NY | ROBIN |

# PULLMAN PARLOUR FIRST

Built by Metro-Cammell 1960–61 for ECML services. 29/– 2T. Commonwealth bogies. 38.5 t.

| | | | | | | |
|---|---|---|---|---|---|---|
| 328 | x | **PC** | NY | *NY* | NY | OPAL |

# 2.2. HIGH SPEED TRAIN TRAILER CARS

HSTs consist of a number of trailer cars (usually between six and nine) with a power car at each end. All trailers are classified Mark 3 and have BT10 bogies with disc brakes and central door locking. Heating is by a 415 V three-phase supply and vehicles have air conditioning. Maximum speed is 125 mph.

The trailer cars have one standard bodyshell for both First and Standard Class, thus facilitating easy conversion from one class to the other. As built all cars had facing seating around tables with Standard Class coaches having nine bays of seats per side which did not line up with the eight windows per side. This created a new unwelcome trend in British rolling stock of seats not lining up with windows.

All vehicles underwent a mid-life refurbishment in the 1980s with Standard Class seating layouts revised to incorporate unidirectional seating in addition to facing, in a somewhat higgledy-piggledy layout where seats did not line up either side of the aisle.

A further refurbishment programme was completed in November 2000, with each Train Operating Company having a different scheme as follows:

**Great Western Trains (later First Great Western).** Green seat covers and extra partitions between seat bays.

**Great North Eastern Railway.** New ceiling lighting panels and brown seat covers. First Class vehicles had table lamps and imitation walnut plastic end panels.

**Virgin CrossCountry.** Green seat covers. Standard Class vehicles had four seats in the centre of each carriage replaced with a luggage stack. All have now passed to other operators.

**Midland Mainline.** Grey seat covers, redesigned seat squabs, side carpeting and two seats in the centre of each Standard Class carriage and one in First Class carriages replaced with a luggage stack.

Since then the remaining three operators of HSTs have embarked on separate, and very different, refurbishment projects:

**Midland Mainline** was first to refurbish its vehicles a second time during 2003–04. This involved fitting new fluorescent and halogen ceiling lighting, although the original seats were retained in First and Standard Class, but with blue upholstery.

London St Pancras–Sheffield/Leeds and Nottingham services are now operated by **East Midlands Trains** and in late 2009 this operator embarked on another, less radical, refurbishment which included retention of the original seats but with red upholstery in Standard Class and blue in First Class. This programme was completed in 2010.

**First Great Western** started a major rebuild of its HST sets in late 2006, with the programme completed in 2008. With an increased fleet of 54 sets (since reduced to 53) the new interiors feature new lighting and seating throughout. First Class seats have leather upholstery, and are made by Primarius UK. Standard Class seats are of high-back design by Grammer. A number of sets operate without a full buffet or kitchen car, instead using one of 19 TS vehicles converted to include a "mini buffet" counter for use on shorter distance services. During 2012 15 402xx or 407xx buffet vehicles were converted to Trailer Standards to make the rakes formed as 7-cars up to 8-cars.

**GNER** modernised its buffet cars with new corner bars in 2004 and at the same time each HST set was made up to 9-cars with an extra Standard Class vehicle added with a disabled person's toilet.

At the end of 2006 **GNER** embarked on a major rebuild of its sets, with the work being carried out at Wabtec, Doncaster. All vehicles will have similar interiors to the Mark 4 "Mallard" fleet, with new Primarius seats throughout. The refurbishment of the 13 sets was completed by **National Express East Coast** in late 2009, these trains now operated by **East Coast**.

Ten sets ex-Virgin CrossCountry, and some spare vehicles, were temporarily allocated to Midland Mainline for the interim service to Manchester during 2003–04 and had a facelift. Buffet cars were converted from TSB to TFKB and renumbered in the 408xx series. These vehicles are now in use with First Great Western or East Coast.

Open access operator **Grand Central** started operation in December 2007 with a new service from Sunderland to London King's Cross. This operator has three sets mostly using stock converted from loco-hauled Mark 3s. The seats in Standard Class have First Class spacing and in most vehicles are all facing. Increases in the number of passengers on its services has seen rakes lengthened from 5-cars to 6-cars and they can also run as 7-cars at busy times.

**CrossCountry** reintroduced HSTs to the Cross-Country network from 2008. Five sets were refurbished at Wabtec, Doncaster principally for use on the Plymouth–Edinburgh route. Three of these sets use stock mostly converted from loco-hauled Mark 3s and two are sets ex-Midland Mainline. The interiors are similar to refurbished East Coast sets, although the seating layout is different and one toilet per coach has been removed in favour of a luggage stack.

### Operator Codes

Operator codes are shown in the heading before each set of vehicles. The first letter is always "T" for HST coaches, denoting a Trailer vehicle. The second letter denotes the passenger accommodation in that vehicle, for example "F" for First. "GS" denotes Guards accommodation and Standard Class seating. This is followed by catering provision, with "B" for buffet, and "K" for a kitchen and buffet:

| | | | | |
|---|---|---|---|---|
| TCK | Trailer Composite Kitchen | | TFKB | Trailer Kitchen Buffet First |
| TF | Trailer First | | TSB | Trailer Buffet Standard |
| TFB | Trailer Buffet First | | TS | Trailer Standard |
| TGS | Trailer Guard's Standard | | | |

## TRAILER STANDARD BUFFET                           TSB

19 vehicles converted at Laira 2009–10 from HST TSs for First Great Western. Refurbished with Grammer seating.

**40101–119.** For Lot No. details see TS. –/70 1T. 35.5 t.

| | | | | |
|---|---|---|---|---|
| 40101 | (42170) | **FD** | P | *GW* | LA |
| 40102 | (42223) | **FD** | P | *GW* | LA |
| 40103 | (42316) | **FD** | P | *GW* | LA |
| 40104 | (42254) | **FD** | P | *GW* | LA |
| 40105 | (42084) | **FD** | P | *GW* | LA |
| 40106 | (42162) | **FD** | P | *GW* | LA |
| 40107 | (42334) | **FD** | P | *GW* | LA |
| 40108 | (42314) | **FD** | P | *GW* | LA |
| 40109 | (42262) | **FD** | P | *GW* | LA |
| 40110 | (42187) | **FD** | P | *GW* | LA |
| 40111 | (42248) | **FD** | P | *GW* | LA |
| 40112 | (42336) | **FD** | P | *GW* | LA |
| 40113 | (42309) | **FD** | P | *GW* | LA |
| 40114 | (42086) | **FD** | P | *GW* | LA |
| 40115 | (42320) | **FD** | P | *GW* | LA |
| 40116 | (42147) | **FD** | P | *GW* | LA |
| 40117 | (42249) | **FD** | P | *GW* | LA |
| 40118 | (42338) | **FD** | P | *GW* | LA |
| 40119 | (42090) | **FD** | P | *GW* | LA |

## TRAILER BUFFET FIRST                              TFB

Converted from TSB by fitting First Class seats. Renumbered from 404xx series by subtracting 200. All refurbished by First Great Western and fitted with Primarius leather seating. 23/–.

**40204–221.** Lot No. 30883 Derby 1976–77. 36.12 t.
**40231.** Lot No. 30899 Derby 1978–79. 36.12 t.

| | | | | | | | | | |
|---|---|---|---|---|---|---|---|---|---|
| 40204 | **FD** | A | *GW* | LA | | 40210 | **FD** | A | *GW* | LA |
| 40205 | **FD** | A | *GW* | LA | | 40221 | **FD** | A | *GW* | LA |
| 40207 | **FD** | A | *GW* | LA | | 40231 | **FD** | A | *GW* | LA |

## TRAILER BUFFET STANDARD                           TSB

Renumbered from 400xx series by adding 400. –/33 1W.

40433 was numbered 40233 for a time when fitted with 23 First Class seats.

**40402–426.** Lot No. 30883 Derby 1976–77. 36.12 t.
**40433.** Lot No. 30899 Derby 1978–79. 36.12 t.

| | | | | | | | | | |
|---|---|---|---|---|---|---|---|---|---|
| 40402 | **V** | AV | | LM | | 40426 | **GC** | A | *GC* | HT |
| 40419 | **V** | AV | | LM | | 40433 | **GC** | A | *GC* | HT |
| 40424 | **GC** | A | *GC* | HT | | | | | | |

# TRAILER KITCHEN BUFFET FIRST TFKB

These vehicles have larger kitchens than the 402xx and 404xx series vehicles, and are used in trains where a full meal service is required. They were renumbered from the 403xx series (in which the seats were unclassified) by adding 400 to the previous number. 17/–.

\* Refurbished First Great Western vehicles. Primarius leather seating.
m Refurbished East Coast vehicles with Primarius seating.

**40700–721**. Lot No. 30921 Derby 1978–79. 38.16 t.
**40722–735**. Lot No. 30940 Derby 1979–80. 38.16 t.
**40737–753**. Lot No. 30948 Derby 1980–81. 38.16 t.
**40754–757**. Lot No. 30966 Derby 1982. 38.16 t.

| | | | | | | | | | | |
|---|---|---|---|---|---|---|---|---|---|---|
| 40700 | | **ST** | P | *EM* | NL | 40732 | | **ST** | P | *EC* | EC |
| 40701 | m | **NX** | P | *EC* | EC | 40733 | \* | **FD** | A | *GW* | LA |
| 40702 | | **NX** | P | *EC* | EC | 40734 | \* | **FD** | A | *GW* | LA |
| 40703 | \* | **FD** | A | *GW* | LA | 40735 | m | **NX** | A | *EC* | EC |
| 40704 | m | **NX** | A | *EC* | EC | 40737 | m | **NX** | A | *EC* | EC |
| 40705 | | **NX** | A | *EC* | EC | 40739 | \* | **FD** | A | *GW* | LA |
| 40706 | m | **NX** | A | *EC* | EC | 40740 | m | **NX** | A | *EC* | EC |
| 40707 | \* | **FD** | A | *GW* | LA | 40741 | | **ST** | P | *EM* | NL |
| 40708 | | **NX** | P | *EC* | EC | 40742 | m | **NX** | A | *EC* | EC |
| 40710 | \* | **FD** | A | *GW* | LA | 40743 | \* | **FD** | A | *GW* | LA |
| 40711 | m | **NX** | A | *EC* | EC | 40746 | | **ST** | P | *EM* | NL |
| 40713 | \* | **FD** | A | *GW* | LA | 40748 | m | **NX** | A | *EC* | EC |
| 40715 | \* | **FD** | A | *GW* | LA | 40749 | | **ST** | P | *EM* | NL |
| 40716 | \* | **FD** | A | *GW* | LA | 40750 | m | **NX** | A | *EC* | EC |
| 40718 | \* | **FD** | A | *GW* | LA | 40751 | | **ST** | P | *EM* | NL |
| 40720 | m | **NX** | A | *EC* | EC | 40752 | \* | **FD** | A | *GW* | LA |
| 40721 | \* | **FD** | A | *GW* | LA | 40753 | | **ST** | P | *EM* | NL |
| 40722 | \* | **FD** | A | *GW* | LA | 40754 | | **ST** | P | *EM* | NL |
| 40727 | \* | **FD** | A | *GW* | LA | 40755 | \* | **FD** | A | *GW* | LA |
| 40728 | | **ST** | P | *EM* | NL | 40756 | | **ST** | P | *EM* | NL |
| 40730 | | **ST** | P | *EM* | NL | 40757 | \* | **FD** | A | *GW* | LA |

# TRAILER KITCHEN BUFFET FIRST TFKB

These vehicles have been converted from TSBs in the 404xx series to be similar to the 407xx series vehicles. 17/–.

40802/804/811 were numbered 40212/232/211 for a time when fitted with 23 First Class seats.

\* Refurbished First Great Western vehicles. Primarius leather seating.
m Refurbished East Coast vehicle with Primarius seating.

**40801–803/805/808/809/811**. Lot No. 30883 Derby 1976–77. 38.16 t.
**40804/806/807/810**. Lot No. 30899 Derby 1978–79. 38.16 t.

| | | | | | | |
|---|---|---|---|---|---|---|
| 40801 | (40027, 40427) | \* | **FD** | P | *GW* | LA |
| 40802 | (40012, 40412) | \* | **FD** | P | *GW* | LA |

| | | | | | |
|---|---|---|---|---|---|
| 40803 | (40018, 40418) | * | **FD** | P | GW | LA |
| 40804 | (40032, 40432) | * | **FD** | P | GW | LA |
| 40805 | (40020, 40420) | m | **NX** | P | EC | EC |
| 40806 | (40029, 40429) | * | **FD** | P | GW | LA |
| 40807 | (40035, 40435) | * | **FD** | P | GW | LA |
| 40808 | (40015, 40415) | * | **FD** | P | GW | LA |
| 40809 | (40014, 40414) | * | **FD** | P | GW | LA |
| 40810 | (40030, 40430) | * | **FD** | P | GW | LA |
| 40811 | (40011, 40411) | * | **FD** | P | GW | LA |

## TRAILER BUFFET FIRST                                    TFB

Vehicles owned by First Group. Converted from TSB by First Great Western.
Refurbished with Primarius leather seating. 23/–.

**40900/902/904.** Lot No. 30883 Derby 1976–77. 36.12 t.
**40901/903.** Lot No. 30899 Derby 1978–79. 36.12 t.

| | | | | | |
|---|---|---|---|---|
| 40900 | (40022, 40422) | **FD** | FG | GW | LA |
| 40901 | (40036, 40436) | **FD** | FG | GW | LA |
| 40902 | (40023, 40423) | **FD** | FG | GW | LA |
| 40903 | (40037, 40437) | **FD** | FG | GW | LA |
| 40904 | (40001, 40401) | **FD** | FG | GW | LA |

## TRAILER FIRST                                    TF

As built and m 48/– 2T (m† 48/– 1T – one toilet removed for trolley space).
* Refurbished First Great Western vehicles. Primarius leather seating.
c Refurbished CrossCountry vehicles with Primarius seating and 2 tip-up seats. One toilet removed. 40/– 1TD 1W.
m Refurbished East Coast vehicles with Primarius seating.
s Fitted with centre luggage stack, disabled toilet and wheelchair space. 46/– 1T 1TD 1W.
w Wheelchair space. 47/– 2T 1W. (41154 47/– 1TD 1T 1W).
x Toilet removed for trolley space (FGW). 48/– 1T.

**41003–056.** Lot No. 30881 Derby 1976–77. 33.66 t.
**41057–120.** Lot No. 30896 Derby 1977–78. 33.66 t.
**41121–148.** Lot No. 30938 Derby 1979–80. 33.66 t.
**41149–166.** Lot No. 30947 Derby 1980. 33.66 t.
**41167–169.** Lot No. 30963 Derby 1982. 33.66 t.
**41170.** Lot No. 30967 Derby 1982. Former prototype vehicle. 33.66 t.
**41176.** Lot No. 30897 Derby 1977. 33.66 t.
**41179/180.** Lot No. 30884 Derby 1976–77. 33.66 t.
**41181–184/189.** Lot No. 30939 Derby 1979–80. 33.66 t.
**41185–187/191.** Lot No. 30969 Derby 1982. 33.66 t.
**41190.** Lot No. 30882 Derby 1976–77. 33.60 t.
**41192.** Lot No. 30897 Derby 1977–79. 33.60 t.
**41193–195/41201–206.** Lot No. 30878 Derby 1975–76. 34.3 t. Converted from Mark 3A Open First.

| | | | | | |
|---|---|---|---|---|---|
| 41003 | *x | **FD** | A | *GW* | LA |
| 41004 | *x | **FD** | A | *GW* | LA |
| 41005 | *x | **FD** | A | *GW* | LA |
| 41006 | *w | **FD** | A | *GW* | LA |
| 41007 | *x | **FD** | A | *GW* | LA |
| 41008 | *w | **FD** | A | *GW* | LA |
| 41009 | *x | **FD** | A | *GW* | LA |
| 41010 | *w | **FD** | A | *GW* | LA |
| 41011 | *x | **FD** | A | *GW* | LA |
| 41012 | *w | **FD** | A | *GW* | LA |
| 41015 | *x | **FD** | A | *GW* | LA |
| 41016 | *w | **FD** | A | *GW* | LA |
| 41017 | *x | **FD** | A | *GW* | LA |
| 41018 | *w | **FD** | A | *GW* | LA |
| 41019 | *x | **FD** | A | *GW* | LA |
| 41020 | *w | **FD** | A | *GW* | LA |
| 41021 | *x | **FD** | A | *GW* | LA |
| 41022 | *w | **FD** | A | *GW* | LA |
| 41023 | *x | **FD** | A | *GW* | LA |
| 41024 | *w | **FD** | A | *GW* | LA |
| 41026 | c | **XC** | A | *XC* | EC |
| 41027 | *x | **FD** | A | *GW* | LA |
| 41028 | *w | **FD** | A | *GW* | LA |
| 41029 | *x | **FD** | A | *GW* | LA |
| 41030 | *w | **FD** | A | *GW* | LA |
| 41031 | *x | **FD** | A | *GW* | LA |
| 41032 | *w | **FD** | A | *GW* | LA |
| 41033 | *x | **FD** | A | *GW* | LA |
| 41034 | *w | **FD** | A | *GW* | LA |
| 41035 | c | **XC** | A | *XC* | EC |
| 41037 | *x | **FD** | A | *GW* | LA |
| 41038 | *w | **FD** | A | *GW* | LA |
| 41039 | m† | **NX** | A | *EC* | EC |
| 41040 | mw | **NX** | A | *EC* | EC |
| 41041 | s | **ST** | P | *EM* | NL |
| 41044 | mw | **NX** | A | *EC* | EC |
| 41045 | *x | **FD** | FG | *GW* | LA |
| 41046 | s | **ST** | P | *EM* | NL |
| 41051 | *x | **FD** | A | *GW* | LA |
| 41052 | *w | **FD** | A | *GW* | LA |
| 41055 | *x | **FD** | A | *GW* | LA |
| 41056 | *w | **FD** | A | *GW* | LA |
| 41057 | | **ST** | P | *EM* | NL |
| 41059 | *w | **FD** | FG | *GW* | LA |
| 41061 | w | **ST** | P | *EM* | NL |
| 41062 | | **ST** | P | *EC* | EC |
| 41063 | | **ST** | P | *EM* | NL |
| 41064 | s | **ST** | P | *EM* | NL |
| 41065 | *x | **FD** | A | *GW* | LA |
| 41066 | m† | **NX** | A | *EC* | EC |
| 41067 | s | **ST** | P | *EM* | NL |
| 41068 | s | **ST** | P | *EM* | NL |
| 41069 | s | **ST** | P | *EM* | NL |
| 41070 | s | **ST** | P | *EM* | NL |
| 41071 | | **ST** | P | *EM* | NL |
| 41072 | s | **ST** | P | *EM* | NL |
| 41075 | | **ST** | P | *EM* | NL |
| 41076 | s | **ST** | P | *EM* | NL |
| 41077 | | **ST** | P | *EM* | NL |
| 41079 | | **ST** | P | *EM* | NL |
| 41081 | *x | **FD** | P | *GW* | LA |
| 41083 | mw | **NX** | P | *EC* | EC |
| 41084 | s | **ST** | P | *EM* | NL |
| 41085 | *x | **FD** | FG | *GW* | LA |
| 41086 | *x | **FD** | FG | *GW* | LA |
| 41087 | m† | **NX** | A | *EC* | EC |
| 41088 | mw | **NX** | A | *EC* | EC |
| 41089 | *w | **FD** | A | *GW* | LA |
| 41090 | m† | **NX** | A | *EC* | EC |
| 41091 | m† | **NX** | A | *EC* | EC |
| 41092 | mw | **NX** | A | *EC* | EC |
| 41093 | *x | **FD** | A | *GW* | LA |
| 41094 | *w | **FD** | A | *GW* | LA |
| 41095 | mw | **NX** | P | *EC* | EC |
| 41096 | *x | **FD** | P | *GW* | LA |
| 41097 | m† | **NX** | A | *EC* | EC |
| 41098 | mw | **NX** | A | *EC* | EC |
| 41099 | m† | **NX** | A | *EC* | EC |
| 41100 | mw | **NX** | A | *EC* | EC |
| 41101 | *x | **FD** | A | *GW* | LA |
| 41102 | *w | **FD** | A | *GW* | LA |
| 41103 | *x | **FD** | A | *GW* | LA |
| 41104 | *w | **FD** | A | *GW* | LA |
| 41105 | *x | **FD** | A | *GW* | LA |
| 41106 | *w | **FD** | A | *GW* | LA |
| 41108 | *w | **FD** | P | *GW* | LA |
| 41109 | *x | **FD** | P | *GW* | LA |
| 41110 | *w | **FD** | A | *GW* | LA |
| 41111 | | **ST** | P | *EM* | NL |
| 41112 | | **ST** | P | *EM* | NL |
| 41113 | s | **ST** | P | *EM* | NL |
| 41114 | *x | **FD** | FG | *GW* | LA |
| 41115 | m† | **NX** | P | *EC* | EC |
| 41116 | *x | **FD** | A | *GW* | LA |
| 41117 | | **ST** | P | *EM* | NL |
| 41118 | mw | **NX** | A | *EC* | EC |
| 41119 | *x | **FD** | P | *GW* | LA |
| 41120 | m† | **NX** | A | *EC* | EC |
| 41121 | *x | **FD** | A | *GW* | LA |
| 41122 | *w | **FD** | A | *GW* | LA |
| 41123 | *x | **FD** | A | *GW* | LA |
| 41124 | *w | **FD** | A | *GW* | LA |

| | | | | | | | | | | |
|---|---|---|---|---|---|---|---|---|---|---|
| 41125 | *x | **FD** | A | *GW* | LA | 41147 | *x | **FD** | P | *GW* | LA |
| 41126 | *w | **FD** | A | *GW* | LA | 41148 | *x | **FD** | P | *GW* | LA |
| 41127 | *x | **FD** | A | *GW* | LA | 41149 | *w | **FD** | P | *GW* | LA |
| 41128 | *w | **FD** | A | *GW* | LA | 41150 | mw | **NX** | A | *EC* | EC |
| 41129 | *x | **FD** | A | *GW* | LA | 41151 | mt | **NX** | A | *EC* | EC |
| 41130 | *w | **FD** | A | *GW* | LA | 41152 | mw | **NX** | A | *EC* | EC |
| 41131 | *x | **FD** | A | *GW* | LA | 41154 | w | **ST** | P | *EC* | EC |
| 41132 | *w | **FD** | A | *GW* | LA | 41155 | *x | **FD** | P | *GW* | LA |
| 41133 | *x | **FD** | A | *GW* | LA | 41156 | | **ST** | P | *EM* | NL |
| 41134 | *w | **FD** | A | *GW* | LA | 41157 | *x | **FD** | A | *GW* | LA |
| 41135 | *w | **FD** | A | *GW* | LA | 41158 | *w | **FD** | A | *GW* | LA |
| 41136 | *w | **FD** | A | *GW* | LA | 41159 | mt | **NX** | P | *EC* | EC |
| 41137 | *x | **FD** | A | *GW* | LA | 41160 | *w | **FD** | FG | *GW* | LA |
| 41138 | *w | **FD** | A | *GW* | LA | 41161 | *w | **FD** | P | *GW* | LA |
| 41139 | *x | **FD** | A | *GW* | LA | 41162 | *w | **FD** | FG | *GW* | LA |
| 41140 | *w | **FD** | A | *GW* | LA | 41163 | *x | **FD** | FG | *GW* | LA |
| 41141 | *x | **FD** | A | *GW* | LA | 41164 | mw | **NX** | A | *EC* | EC |
| 41142 | *w | **FD** | A | *GW* | LA | 41165 | mw | **NX** | P | *EC* | EC |
| 41143 | *x | **FD** | A | *GW* | LA | 41166 | *w | **FD** | FG | *GW* | LA |
| 41144 | *w | **FD** | A | *GW* | LA | 41167 | *w | **FD** | FG | *GW* | LA |
| 41145 | *x | **FD** | A | *GW* | LA | 41168 | *x | **FD** | P | *GW* | LA |
| 41146 | *w | **FD** | A | *GW* | LA | 41169 | *w | **FD** | P | *GW* | LA |

| | | | | | |
|---|---|---|---|---|---|
| 41170 (41001) | mt | **NX** | A | *EC* | EC |
| 41176 (42142, 42352) | *w | **FD** | P | *GW* | LA |
| 41179 (40505) | *x | **FD** | A | *GW* | LA |
| 41180 (40511) | *w | **FD** | A | *GW* | LA |
| 41181 (42282) | *x | **FD** | P | *GW* | LA |
| 41182 (42278) | *w | **FD** | P | *GW* | LA |
| 41183 (42274) | *w | **FD** | P | *GW* | LA |
| 41184 (42270) | *x | **FD** | P | *GW* | LA |
| 41185 (42313) | mt | **NX** | P | *EC* | EC |
| 41186 (42312) | *w | **FD** | P | *GW* | LA |
| 41187 (42311) | *w | **FD** | P | *GW* | LA |
| 41189 (42298) | *w | **FD** | P | *GW* | LA |
| 41190 (42088) | mt | **NX** | P | *EC* | EC |
| 41191 (42318) | *x | **FD** | P | *GW* | LA |
| 41192 (42246) | *w | **FD** | P | *GW* | LA |

The following coaches have been converted from loco-hauled Mark 3 vehicles for CrossCountry.

| | | | | | |
|---|---|---|---|---|---|
| 41193 (11060) | c | **XC** | P | *XC* | EC |
| 41194 (11016) | c | **XC** | P | *XC* | EC |
| 41195 (11020) | c | **XC** | P | *XC* | EC |

The following coaches have been converted from loco-hauled Mark 3 vehicles for Grand Central. 48/– 2T.

| | | | | |
|---|---|---|---|---|
| 41201 (11045) | **GC** | A | *GC* | HT |
| 41202 (11017) | **GC** | A | *GC* | HT |
| 41203 (11038) | **GC** | A | *GC* | HT |
| 41204 (11023) | **GC** | A | *GC* | HT |
| 41205 (11036) | **GC** | A | *GC* | HT |
| 41206 (11055) | **GC** | A | *GC* | HT |

# TRAILER STANDARD TS

42158 was numbered 41177 for a time when fitted with First Class seats.
42310 was numbered 41188 for a time when fitted with First Class seats.

Standard seating and m –/76 2T.
* Refurbished First Great Western vehicles. Grammer seating. –/80 2T (unless h – high density).
c Refurbished CrossCountry vehicles with Primarius seating. One toilet removed. –/82 1T.
§c Refurbished CrossCountry vehicles with Primarius seating and 2 tip-up seats. One toilet removed. –/66 1TD 2W. Note 42379/380 are –/71 1T 2W.
d FGW vehicles with disabled persons toilet and 5, 6 or 7 tip-up seats. –/68 1T 1TD 2W.
h "High density" FGW vehicles. –/84 2T.
k "High density" FGW refurbished vehicle with disabled persons toilet and 5, 6 or 7 tip-up seats. –/72 1T 1TD 2W.
m Refurbished East Coast vehicles with Primarius seating.
u Centre luggage stack (EMT) –/74 2T.
v First Great Western Volo entertainment coach. TV screens fitted to most seat backs.
w Centre luggage stack and wheelchair space (EMT) –72 2T 1W.
† Disabled persons toilet (East Coast) –/62 1T 1TD 1W.

**42003–089/362.** Lot No. 30882 Derby 1976–77. 33.6 t.
**42091–250.** Lot No. 30897 Derby 1977–79. 33.6 t.
**42251–305.** Lot No. 30939 Derby 1979–80. 33.6 t.
**42306–322.** Lot No. 30969 Derby 1982. 33.6 t.
**42323–341.** Lot No. 30983 Derby 1984–85. 33.6 t.
**42342/360.** Lot No. 30949 Derby 1982. 33.47 t. Converted from TGS.
**42343/345.** Lot No. 30970 Derby 1982. 33.47 t. Converted from TGS.
**42344/361.** Lot No. 30964 Derby 1982. 33.47 t. Converted from TGS.
**42346/347/350/351/379/380.** Lot No. 30881 Derby 1976–77. 33.66 t. Converted from TF.
**42348/349/363–365/381.** Lot No. 30896 Derby 1977–78. 33.66 t. Converted from TF.
**42354.** Lot No. 30897 Derby 1977. Was TF from 1983 to 1992. 33.66 t.
**42353/355–357.** Lot No. 30967 Derby 1982. Ex-prototype vehicles. 33.66 t.
**42366–378/382/383/401–409.** Lot No. 30877 Derby 1975–77. 34.3 t. Converted from Mark 3A Open Standard.
**42384.** Lot No. 30896 Derby 1977–78. 33.66 t. Converted from TF.
**42385.** Lot No. 30947 Derby 1980. 33.66 t. Converted from TF.
**42501/509/513/515/517.** Lot No. 30948 Derby 1980–81. 34.8 t. Converted from TFKB.
**42502/506/508/514/516.** Lot No. 30940 Derby 1979–80. 34.8 t. Converted from TFKB.
**42503/504/510/511.** Lot No. 30921 Derby 1978–79. 34.8 t. Converted from TFKB.
**42505/507/512/518/519.** Lot No. 30883 Derby 1976–77. 34.8 t. Converted from TSB.
**42520.** Lot No. 30899 Derby 1978–79. 34.8 t. Converted from TSB.

| | | | | | | | | | | |
|---|---|---|---|---|---|---|---|---|---|---|
| 42003 | *hv | **FD** | A | *GW* | LA | 42059 | m | **NX** | A | *EC* | EC |
| 42004 | *d | **FD** | A | *GW* | LA | 42060 | *h | **FD** | A | *GW* | LA |
| 42005 | *hv | **FD** | A | *GW* | LA | 42061 | *h | **FD** | A | *GW* | LA |
| 42006 | *h | **FD** | A | *GW* | LA | 42062 | *k | **FD** | A | *GW* | LA |
| 42007 | *d | **FD** | A | *GW* | LA | 42063 | m | **NX** | A | *EC* | EC |
| 42008 | *k | **FD** | A | *GW* | LA | 42064 | m | **NX** | A | *EC* | EC |
| 42009 | *hv | **FD** | A | *GW* | LA | 42065 | m | **NX** | A | *EC* | EC |
| 42010 | *hv | **FD** | A | *GW* | LA | 42066 | *k | **FD** | A | *GW* | LA |
| 42012 | *k | **FD** | A | *GW* | LA | 42067 | *h | **FD** | A | *GW* | LA |
| 42013 | *h | **FD** | A | *GW* | LA | 42068 | *h | **FD** | A | *GW* | LA |
| 42014 | *h | **FD** | A | *GW* | LA | 42069 | *k | **FD** | A | *GW* | LA |
| 42015 | *k | **FD** | A | *GW* | LA | 42070 | *hv | **FD** | A | *GW* | LA |
| 42016 | *h | **FD** | A | *GW* | LA | 42071 | *h | **FD** | A | *GW* | LA |
| 42019 | *v | **FD** | A | *GW* | LA | 42072 | * | **FD** | A | *GW* | LA |
| 42021 | *k | **FD** | A | *GW* | LA | 42073 | *hv | **FD** | A | *GW* | LA |
| 42023 | *h | **FD** | A | *GW* | LA | 42074 | *hv | **FD** | A | *GW* | LA |
| 42024 | *k | **FD** | A | *GW* | LA | 42075 | *v | **FD** | A | *GW* | LA |
| 42025 | *h | **FD** | A | *GW* | LA | 42076 | *v | **FD** | A | *GW* | LA |
| 42026 | *h | **FD** | A | *GW* | LA | 42077 | * | **FD** | A | *GW* | LA |
| 42027 | *hv | **FD** | A | *GW* | LA | 42078 | * | **FD** | A | *GW* | LA |
| 42028 | *h | **FD** | A | *GW* | LA | 42079 | *h | **FD** | A | *GW* | LA |
| 42029 | *h | **FD** | A | *GW* | LA | 42080 | *h | **FD** | A | *GW* | LA |
| 42030 | *k | **FD** | A | *GW* | LA | 42081 | *k | **FD** | A | *GW* | LA |
| 42031 | *h | **FD** | A | *GW* | LA | 42083 | *h | **FD** | A | *GW* | LA |
| 42032 | *h | **FD** | A | *GW* | LA | 42085 | *hv | **FD** | P | *GW* | LA |
| 42033 | *v | **FD** | A | *GW* | LA | 42087 | *h | **FD** | P | *GW* | LA |
| 42034 | * | **FD** | A | *GW* | LA | 42089 | *h | **FD** | A | *GW* | LA |
| 42035 | * | **FD** | A | *GW* | LA | 42091 | mt | **NX** | A | *EC* | EC |
| 42036 | c | **XC** | A | *XC* | EC | 42092 | *k | **FD** | FG | *GW* | LA |
| 42037 | c | **XC** | A | *XC* | EC | 42093 | *h | **FD** | FG | *GW* | LA |
| 42038 | c | **XC** | A | *XC* | EC | 42094 | *h | **FD** | FG | *GW* | LA |
| 42039 | *hv | **FD** | A | *GW* | LA | 42095 | * | **FD** | FG | *GW* | LA |
| 42040 | *h | **FD** | A | *GW* | LA | 42096 | *hv | **FD** | A | *GW* | LA |
| 42041 | *h | **FD** | A | *GW* | LA | 42097 | c | **XC** | A | *XC* | EC |
| 42042 | *hv | **FD** | A | *GW* | LA | 42098 | *hv | **FD** | A | *GW* | LA |
| 42043 | *h | **FD** | A | *GW* | LA | 42099 | *hv | **FD** | A | *GW* | LA |
| 42044 | *h | **FD** | A | *GW* | LA | 42100 | u | **ST** | P | *EM* | NL |
| 42045 | *v | **FD** | A | *GW* | LA | 42101 | *h | **FD** | P | *GW* | LA |
| 42046 | * | **FD** | A | *GW* | LA | 42102 | *hv | **FD** | P | *GW* | LA |
| 42047 | * | **FD** | A | *GW* | LA | 42103 | *k | **FD** | FG | *GW* | LA |
| 42048 | *hv | **FD** | A | *GW* | LA | 42104 | m | **NX** | A | *EC* | EC |
| 42049 | *h | **FD** | A | *GW* | LA | 42105 | *k | **FD** | FG | *GW* | LA |
| 42050 | *h | **FD** | A | *GW* | LA | 42106 | m | **NX** | A | *EC* | EC |
| 42051 | c | **XC** | A | *XC* | EC | 42107 | * | **FD** | A | *GW* | LA |
| 42052 | c | **XC** | A | *XC* | EC | 42108 | *h | **FD** | FG | *GW* | LA |
| 42053 | c | **XC** | A | *XC* | EC | 42109 | m | **NX** | P | *EC* | EC |
| 42054 | *v | **FD** | A | *GW* | LA | 42110 | m | **NX** | P | *EC* | EC |
| 42055 | * | **FD** | A | *GW* | LA | 42111 | u | **ST** | P | *EM* | NL |
| 42056 | * | **FD** | A | *GW* | LA | 42112 | u | **ST** | P | *EM* | NL |
| 42057 | m | **NX** | A | *EC* | EC | 42113 | u | **ST** | P | *EM* | NL |
| 42058 | m | **NX** | A | *EC* | EC | 42115 | *hv | **FD** | P | *GW* | LA |

| | | | | | | | | | | | |
|---|---|---|---|---|---|---|---|---|---|---|---|
| 42116 | mt | **NX** | A | *EC* | EC | | 42171 | m | **NX** | A | *EC* | EC |

| | | | | | |
|---|---|---|---|---|---|
| 42116 mt | **NX** | A | *EC* | EC |
| 42117 m | **NX** | P | *EC* | EC |
| 42118 *h | **FD** | A | *GW* | LA |
| 42119 u | **ST** | P | *EM* | NL |
| 42120 u | **ST** | P | *EM* | NL |
| 42121 u | **ST** | P | *EM* | NL |
| 42122 m | **NX** | A | *EC* | EC |
| 42123 | **ST** | P | *EC* | EC |
| 42124 u | **ST** | P | *EM* | NL |
| 42125 | **ST** | P | *EC* | EC |
| 42126 *h | **FD** | A | *GW* | LA |
| 42127 mt | **NX** | A | *EC* | EC |
| 42128 mt | **NX** | A | *EC* | EC |
| 42129 *v | **FD** | A | *GW* | LA |
| 42130 m | **NX** | P | *EC* | EC |
| 42131 u | **ST** | P | *EM* | NL |
| 42132 u | **ST** | P | *EM* | NL |
| 42133 u | **ST** | P | *EM* | NL |
| 42134 m | **NX** | A | *EC* | EC |
| 42135 u | **ST** | P | *EM* | NL |
| 42136 u | **ST** | P | *EM* | NL |
| 42137 u | **ST** | P | *EM* | NL |
| 42138 *k | **FD** | P | *GW* | LA |
| 42139 u | **ST** | P | *EM* | NL |
| 42140 u | **ST** | P | *EM* | NL |
| 42141 u | **ST** | P | *EM* | NL |
| 42143 *v | **FD** | A | *GW* | LA |
| 42144 * | **FD** | A | *GW* | LA |
| 42145 * | **FD** | A | *GW* | LA |
| 42146 m | **NX** | A | *EC* | EC |
| 42148 u | **ST** | P | *EM* | NL |
| 42149 u | **ST** | P | *EM* | NL |
| 42150 m | **NX** | A | *EC* | EC |
| 42151 w | **ST** | P | *EM* | NL |
| 42152 u | **ST** | P | *EM* | NL |
| 42153 u | **ST** | P | *EM* | NL |
| 42154 m | **NX** | A | *EC* | EC |
| 42155 w | **ST** | P | *EM* | NL |
| 42156 u | **ST** | P | *EM* | NL |
| 42157 u | **ST** | P | *EM* | NL |
| 42158 m | **NX** | A | *EC* | EC |
| 42159 mt | **NX** | P | *EC* | EC |
| 42160 m | **NX** | P | *EC* | EC |
| 42161 mt | **NX** | A | *EC* | EC |
| 42163 m | **NX** | P | *EC* | EC |
| 42164 | **ST** | P | *EM* | NL |
| 42165 | **ST** | P | *EM* | NL |
| 42166 *hv | **FD** | P | *GW* | LA |
| 42167 *h | **FD** | FG | *GW* | LA |
| 42168 *hv | **FD** | FG | *GW* | LA |
| 42169 *h | **FD** | FG | *GW* | LA |
| 42171 m | **NX** | A | *EC* | EC |
| 42172 m | **NX** | A | *EC* | EC |
| 42173 *k | **FD** | P | *GW* | LA |
| 42174 *k | **FD** | P | *GW* | LA |
| 42175 *h | **FD** | FG | *GW* | LA |
| 42176 *hv | **FD** | FG | *GW* | LA |
| 42177 *h | **FD** | FG | *GW* | LA |
| 42178 *hv | **FD** | P | *GW* | LA |
| 42179 m | **NX** | A | *EC* | EC |
| 42180 m | **NX** | A | *EC* | EC |
| 42181 m | **NX** | A | *EC* | EC |
| 42182 m | **NX** | A | *EC* | EC |
| 42183 *d | **FD** | A | *GW* | LA |
| 42184 *v | **FD** | A | *GW* | LA |
| 42185 * | **FD** | A | *GW* | LA |
| 42186 m | **NX** | A | *EC* | EC |
| 42188 mt | **NX** | A | *EC* | EC |
| 42189 mt | **NX** | A | *EC* | EC |
| 42190 m | **NX** | A | *EC* | EC |
| 42191 m | **NX** | A | *EC* | EC |
| 42192 m | **NX** | A | *EC* | EC |
| 42193 m | **NX** | A | *EC* | EC |
| 42194 w | **ST** | P | *EM* | NL |
| 42195 *k | **FD** | P | *GW* | LA |
| 42196 *h | **FD** | A | *GW* | LA |
| 42197 *hv | **FD** | A | *GW* | LA |
| 42198 m | **NX** | A | *EC* | EC |
| 42199 m | **NX** | A | *EC* | EC |
| 42200 *d | **FD** | A | *GW* | LA |
| 42201 *k | **FD** | A | *GW* | LA |
| 42202 *k | **FD** | A | *GW* | LA |
| 42203 *h | **FD** | A | *GW* | LA |
| 42204 *h | **FD** | A | *GW* | LA |
| 42205 | **ST** | P | *EC* | EC |
| 42206 *d | **FD** | A | *GW* | LA |
| 42207 *d | **FD** | A | *GW* | LA |
| 42208 * | **FD** | A | *GW* | LA |
| 42209 * | **FD** | A | *GW* | LA |
| 42210 | **ST** | P | *EC* | EC |
| 42211 *k | **FD** | A | *GW* | LA |
| 42212 *hv | **FD** | A | *GW* | LA |
| 42213 *h | **FD** | A | *GW* | LA |
| 42214 *h | **FD** | A | *GW* | LA |
| 42215 m | **NX** | A | *EC* | EC |
| 42216 *hv | **FD** | A | *GW* | LA |
| 42217 *k | **FD** | P | *GW* | LA |
| 42218 *k | **FD** | P | *GW* | LA |
| 42219 m | **NX** | A | *EC* | EC |
| 42220 w | **ST** | P | *EM* | NL |
| 42221 *hv | **FD** | A | *GW* | LA |
| 42222 *hv | **FD** | P | *GW* | LA |

| | | | | | | | | | |
|---|---|---|---|---|---|---|---|---|---|
| 42224 | *k | **FD** | P | *GW* | LA | 42280 | * | **FD** | A | *GW* | LA |

| | | | | | | | | | | | |
|---|---|---|---|---|---|---|---|---|---|---|---|
| 42224 | *k | **FD** | P | *GW* | LA | 42280 | * | **FD** | A | *GW* | LA |
| 42225 | u | **ST** | P | *EM* | NL | 42281 | * | **FD** | A | *GW* | LA |
| 42226 | m | **NX** | A | *EC* | EC | 42283 | *h | **FD** | A | *GW* | LA |
| 42227 | u | **ST** | P | *EM* | NL | 42284 | *h | **FD** | A | *GW* | LA |
| 42228 | m | **NX** | A | *EC* | EC | 42285 | *h | **FD** | A | *GW* | LA |
| 42229 | u | **ST** | P | *EM* | NL | 42286 | m† | **NX** | P | *EC* | EC |
| 42230 | u | **ST** | P | *EM* | NL | 42287 | *k | **FD** | A | *GW* | LA |
| 42231 | *h | **FD** | FG | *GW* | LA | 42288 | *h | **FD** | A | *GW* | LA |
| 42232 | *hv | **FD** | FG | *GW* | LA | 42289 | *h | **FD** | A | *GW* | LA |
| 42233 | *h | **FD** | FG | *GW* | LA | 42290 | c | **XC** | P | *XC* | EC |
| 42234 | c | **XC** | P | *XC* | EC | 42291 | *d | **FD** | A | *GW* | LA |
| 42235 | m | **NX** | A | *EC* | EC | 42292 | *d | **FD** | A | *GW* | LA |
| 42236 | *hv | **FD** | A | *GW* | LA | 42293 | * | **FD** | A | *GW* | LA |
| 42237 | m | **NX** | P | *EC* | EC | 42294 | * | **FD** | P | *GW* | LA |
| 42238 | m† | **NX** | A | *EC* | EC | 42295 | *d | **FD** | A | *GW* | LA |
| 42239 | m† | **NX** | A | *EC* | EC | 42296 | * | **FD** | A | *GW* | LA |
| 42240 | m | **NX** | A | *EC* | EC | 42297 | * | **FD** | A | *GW* | LA |
| 42241 | m | **NX** | A | *EC* | EC | 42299 | *d | **FD** | A | *GW* | LA |
| 42242 | m | **NX** | A | *EC* | EC | 42300 | * | **FD** | A | *GW* | LA |
| 42243 | m | **NX** | A | *EC* | EC | 42301 | * | **FD** | A | *GW* | LA |
| 42244 | m | **NX** | A | *EC* | EC | 42302 | *k | **FD** | FG | *GW* | LA |
| 42245 | * | **FD** | A | *GW* | LA | 42303 | *hv | **FD** | FG | *GW* | LA |
| 42247 | *hv | **FD** | P | *GW* | LA | 42304 | *h | **FD** | FG | *GW* | LA |
| 42250 | * | **FD** | A | *GW* | LA | 42305 | *h | **FD** | FG | *GW* | LA |
| 42251 | *k | **FD** | A | *GW* | LA | 42306 | m | **NX** | P | *EC* | EC |
| 42252 | * | **FD** | A | *GW* | LA | 42307 | m | **NX** | P | *EC* | EC |
| 42253 | * | **FD** | A | *GW* | LA | 42308 | *hv | **FD** | P | *GW* | LA |
| 42255 | *d | **FD** | A | *GW* | LA | 42310 | *k | **FD** | P | *GW* | LA |
| 42256 | * | **FD** | A | *GW* | LA | 42315 | *hv | **FD** | P | *GW* | LA |
| 42257 | * | **FD** | A | *GW* | LA | 42317 | *k | **FD** | P | *GW* | LA |
| 42258 | *hv | **FD** | P | *GW* | LA | 42319 | *hv | **FD** | P | *GW* | LA |
| 42259 | *k | **FD** | A | *GW* | LA | 42321 | *h | **FD** | P | *GW* | LA |
| 42260 | *h | **FD** | A | *GW* | LA | 42322 | m | **NX** | P | *EC* | EC |
| 42261 | *h | **FD** | A | *GW* | LA | 42323 | m | **NX** | A | *EC* | EC |
| 42263 | *v | **FD** | A | *GW* | LA | 42325 | *v | **FD** | A | *GW* | LA |
| 42264 | *k | **FD** | A | *GW* | LA | 42326 | m | **NX** | P | *EC* | EC |
| 42265 | *v | **FD** | A | *GW* | LA | 42327 | w | **ST** | P | *EM* | NL |
| 42266 | *k | **FD** | P | *GW* | LA | 42328 | w | **ST** | P | *EM* | NL |
| 42267 | *d | **FD** | A | *GW* | LA | 42329 | w | **ST** | P | *EM* | NL |
| 42268 | *d | **FD** | A | *GW* | LA | 42330 | m | **NX** | P | *EC* | EC |
| 42269 | * | **FD** | A | *GW* | LA | 42331 | w | **ST** | P | *EM* | NL |
| 42271 | *k | **FD** | A | *GW* | LA | 42332 | *v | **FD** | A | *GW* | LA |
| 42272 | *h | **FD** | A | *GW* | LA | 42333 | * | **FD** | A | *GW* | LA |
| 42273 | *h | **FD** | A | *GW* | LA | 42335 | w | **ST** | P | *EC* | EC |
| 42275 | *d | **FD** | A | *GW* | LA | 42337 | w | **ST** | P | *EM* | NL |
| 42276 | * | **FD** | A | *GW* | LA | 42339 | w | **ST** | P | *EM* | NL |
| 42277 | * | **FD** | A | *GW* | LA | 42340 | m | **NX** | A | *EC* | EC |
| 42279 | *d | **FD** | A | *GW* | LA | 42341 | u | **ST** | P | *EM* | NL |

| | | | | | | |
|---|---|---|---|---|---|---|
| 42342 | (44082) | | c | **XC** | A | *XC* | EC |
| 42343 | (44095) | | *v | **FD** | A | *GW* | LA |
| 42344 | (44092) | | *k | **FD** | A | *GW* | LA |

| 42345 | (44096) | *d | FD | A | GW | LA |
|---|---|---|---|---|---|---|
| 42346 | (41053) | *h | FD | A | GW | LA |
| 42347 | (41054) | *k | FD | A | GW | LA |
| 42348 | (41073) | *k | FD | A | GW | LA |
| 42349 | (41074) | *hv | FD | A | GW | LA |
| 42350 | (41047) | *v | FD | A | GW | LA |
| 42351 | (41048) | *v | FD | A | GW | LA |
| 42353 | (42001, 41171) | *k | FD | FG | GW | LA |
| 42354 | (42114, 41175) | m | NX | A | EC | EC |
| 42355 | (42000, 41172) | m | NX | A | EC | EC |
| 42356 | (42002, 41173) | *k | FD | A | GW | LA |
| 42357 | (41002, 41174) | m | NX | A | EC | EC |
| 42360 | (44084, 45084) | *hv | FD | A | GW | LA |
| 42361 | (44099, 42000) | *h | FD | A | GW | LA |
| 42362 | (42011, 41178) | *hv | FD | A | GW | LA |
| 42363 | (41082) | mt | NX | A | EC | EC |
| 42364 | (41080) | *k | FD | P | GW | LA |
| 42365 | (41107) | *h | FD | P | GW | LA |

42366–378 have been converted from loco-hauled Mark 3 vehicles for CrossCountry and 42382/383 for First Great Western.

| 42366 | (12007) | §c | XC | P | XC | EC |
|---|---|---|---|---|---|---|
| 42367 | (12025) | c | XC | P | XC | EC |
| 42368 | (12028) | c | XC | P | XC | EC |
| 42369 | (12050) | c | XC | P | XC | EC |
| 42370 | (12086) | c | XC | P | XC | EC |
| 42371 | (12052) | §c | XC | P | XC | EC |
| 42372 | (12055) | c | XC | P | XC | EC |
| 42373 | (12071) | c | XC | P | XC | EC |
| 42374 | (12075) | c | XC | P | XC | EC |
| 42375 | (12113) | c | XC | P | XC | EC |
| 42376 | (12085) | §c | XC | P | XC | EC |
| 42377 | (12102) | c | XC | P | XC | EC |
| 42378 | (12123) | c | XC | P | XC | EC |
| 42379 | (41036) | §c | XC | A | XC | EC |
| 42380 | (41025) | §c | XC | A | XC | EC |
| 42381 | (41058) | *k | FD | P | GW | LA |
| 42382 | (12128) | *h | FD | P | GW | LA |
| 42383 | (12172) | *h | FD | P | GW | LA |
| 42384 | (41078) | w | ST | P | EM | NL |
| 42385 | (41153) | *h | FD | P | GW | LA |

The following coaches have been converted from loco-hauled Mark 3 vehicles for Grand Central. They have a lower density seating layout (most seats arranged around tables). –/64 2T († –/60 1TD 1T 2W).

| 42401 | (12149) |   | GC | A | GC | HT |
|---|---|---|---|---|---|---|
| 42402 | (12155) |   | GC | A | GC | HT |
| 42403 | (12033) | † | GC | A | GC | HT |
| 42404 | (12152) |   | GC | A | GC | HT |
| 42405 | (12136) |   | GC | A | GC | HT |
| 42406 | (12112) | † | GC | A | GC | HT |

| | | | | | |
|---|---|---|---|---|---|
| 42407 | (12044) | **GC** | A | *GC* | HT |
| 42408 | (12121) | **GC** | A | *GC* | HT |
| 42409 | (12088) † | **GC** | A | *GC* | HT |

These coaches were converted or are being converted from TFKB or TSB buffet cars to TS vehicles in 2011–12 (42501–515) and 2013–14 (42516–520) at Wabtec Kilmarnock for First Great Western. –/84 1T. 34.8 t.

| | | | | | |
|---|---|---|---|---|---|
| 42501 | (40344, 40744) | * | **FD** | A | *GW* | LA |
| 42502 | (40331, 40731) | * | **FD** | A | *GW* | LA |
| 42503 | (40312, 40712) | * | **FD** | A | *GW* | LA |
| 42504 | (40314, 40714) | * | **FD** | A | *GW* | LA |
| 42505 | (40428, 40228) | * | **FD** | A | *GW* | LA |
| 42506 | (40324, 40724) | * | **FD** | A | *GW* | LA |
| 42507 | (40409, 40209) | * | **FD** | A | *GW* | LA |
| 42508 | (40325, 40725) | * | **FD** | A | *GW* | LA |
| 42509 | (40336, 40736) | * | **FD** | A | *GW* | LA |
| 42510 | (40317, 40717) | * | **FD** | A | *GW* | LA |
| 42511 | (40309, 40709) | * | **FD** | A | *GW* | LA |
| 42512 | (40408, 40208) | * | **FD** | A | *GW* | LA |
| 42513 | (40338, 40738) | * | **FD** | A | *GW* | LA |
| 42514 | (40326, 40726) | * | **FD** | A | *GW* | LA |
| 42515 | (40347, 40747) | * | **FD** | A | *GW* | LA |
| 42516 | (40323, 40723) | | | A | | ZK |
| 42517 | (40345, 40745) | | | A | | ZK |
| 42518 | (40003, 40403) | | | P | | ZK |
| 42519 | (40016, 40416) | | | P | | ZK |
| 42520 | (40234, 40434) | | | P | | ZK |

# TRAILER GUARD'S STANDARD                                    TGS

As built and m –/65 1T.
* Refurbished First Great Western vehicles. Grammer seating and toilet removed for trolley store. –/67 (unless h).
† Contains a mix of original seats and 20 new Grammer seats. –/65 1T.
c Refurbished CrossCountry vehicles with Primarius seating. –/67 1T.
h "High density" FGW vehicles. –/71.
m Refurbished East Coast vehicles with Primarius seating.
s Fitted with centre luggage stack (EMT) –/63 1T.
t Fitted with centre luggage stack –/61 1T.

**44000**. Lot No. 30953 Derby 1980. 33.47 t.
**44001–090**. Lot No. 30949 Derby 1980–82. 33.47 t.
**44091–094**. Lot No. 30964 Derby 1982. 33.47 t.
**44097–101**. Lot No. 30970 Derby 1982. 33.47 t.

| | | | | | | | | | | | |
|---|---|---|---|---|---|---|---|---|---|---|---|
| 44000 | *h | **FD** | P | *GW* | LA | | 44008 | *h | **FD** | A | *GW* | LA |
| 44001 | * | **FD** | A | *GW* | LA | | 44009 | *h | **FD** | A | *GW* | LA |
| 44002 | *h | **FD** | A | *GW* | LA | | 44010 | *h | **FD** | A | *GW* | LA |
| 44003 | *h | **FD** | A | *GW* | LA | | 44011 | * | **FD** | A | *GW* | LA |
| 44004 | *h | **FD** | A | *GW* | LA | | 44012 | c | **XC** | A | *XC* | EC |
| 44005 | *h | **FD** | A | *GW* | LA | | 44013 | *h | **FD** | A | *GW* | LA |
| 44006 | *h | **FD** | A | *GW* | LA | | 44014 | *h | **FD** | A | *GW* | LA |
| 44007 | *h | **FD** | A | *GW* | LA | | | | | | | |

| | | | | | | | | | | | |
|---|---|---|---|---|---|---|---|---|---|---|---|
| 44015 | * | **FD** | A | *GW* | LA | 44055 | *h | **FD** | FG | *GW* | LA |
| 44016 | *h | **FD** | A | *GW* | LA | 44056 | m | **NX** | A | *EC* | EC |
| 44017 | c | **XC** | A | *XC* | EC | 44057 | m | **NX** | P | *EC* | EC |
| 44018 | * | **FD** | A | *GW* | LA | 44058 | m | **NX** | A | *EC* | EC |
| 44019 | m | **NX** | A | *EC* | EC | 44059 | * | **FD** | A | *GW* | LA |
| 44020 | *h | **FD** | A | *GW* | LA | 44060 | *h | **FD** | P | *GW* | LA |
| 44021 | c | **XC** | P | *XC* | EC | 44061 | m | **NX** | A | *EC* | EC |
| 44022 | *h | **FD** | A | *GW* | LA | 44063 | m | **NX** | A | *EC* | EC |
| 44023 | *h | **FD** | A | *GW* | LA | 44064 | *h | **FD** | A | *GW* | LA |
| 44024 | *h | **FD** | A | *GW* | OO | 44065 | t | **V** | AV | | LM |
| 44025 | * | **FD** | A | *GW* | LA | 44066 | * | **FD** | A | *GW* | LA |
| 44026 | *h | **FD** | A | *GW* | LA | 44067 | | **FD** | A | *GW* | LA |
| 44027 | s | **ST** | P | *EM* | NL | 44068 | *h | **FD** | FG | *GW* | LA |
| 44028 | * | **FD** | A | *GW* | LA | 44069 | *h | **FD** | P | *GW* | LA |
| 44029 | * | **FD** | A | *GW* | LA | 44070 | s | **ST** | P | *EM* | NL |
| 44030 | *h | **FD** | A | *GW* | LA | 44071 | s | **ST** | P | *EM* | NL |
| 44031 | m | **NX** | A | *EC* | EC | 44072 | c | **XC** | P | *XC* | EC |
| 44032 | * | **FD** | A | *GW* | LA | 44073 | † | **ST** | P | *EC* | EC |
| 44033 | *h | **FD** | A | *GW* | LA | 44074 | *h | **FD** | FG | *GW* | LA |
| 44034 | * | **FD** | A | *GW* | LA | 44075 | m | **NX** | P | *EC* | EC |
| 44035 | * | **FD** | A | *GW* | LA | 44076 | *h | **FD** | FG | *GW* | LA |
| 44036 | *h | **FD** | A | *GW* | LA | 44077 | m | **NX** | A | *EC* | EC |
| 44037 | *h | **FD** | A | *GW* | LA | 44078 | *h | **FD** | P | *GW* | LA |
| 44038 | *h | **FD** | A | *GW* | LA | 44079 | *h | **FD** | P | *GW* | LA |
| 44039 | * | **FD** | A | *GW* | LA | 44080 | m | **NX** | A | *EC* | EC |
| 44040 | * | **FD** | A | *GW* | LA | 44081 | *h | **FD** | FG | *GW* | LA |
| 44041 | s | **ST** | P | *EM* | NL | 44083 | *h | **FD** | P | *GW* | LA |
| 44042 | *h | **FD** | P | *GW* | LA | 44085 | s | **ST** | P | *EM* | NL |
| 44043 | *h | **FD** | A | *GW* | LA | 44086 | * | **FD** | A | *GW* | LA |
| 44044 | s | **ST** | P | *EM* | NL | 44088 | t | **V** | AV | | LM |
| 44045 | m | **NX** | A | *EC* | EC | 44089 | t | **V** | AV | | LM |
| 44046 | s | **ST** | P | *EM* | NL | 44090 | *h | **FD** | P | *GW* | LA |
| 44047 | s | **ST** | P | *EM* | NL | 44091 | *h | **FD** | P | *GW* | LA |
| 44048 | s | **ST** | P | *EM* | NL | 44093 | *h | **FD** | A | *GW* | LA |
| 44049 | * | **FD** | A | *GW* | LA | 44094 | m | **NX** | A | *EC* | EC |
| 44050 | m | **NX** | P | *EC* | EC | 44097 | *h | **FD** | P | *GW* | LA |
| 44051 | s | **ST** | P | *EM* | NL | 44098 | m | **NX** | A | *EC* | EC |
| 44052 | c | **XC** | P | *XC* | EC | 44100 | *h | **FD** | FG | *GW* | PM |
| 44054 | s | **ST** | P | *EM* | NL | 44101 | *h | **FD** | P | *GW* | LA |

# TRAILER COMPOSITE KITCHEN TCK

**45001–005.** Lot No. 30877 Derby 1975–77. 34.3 t. Converted from Mark 3A Open Standard. Refurbished CrossCountry vehicles with Primarius seating. Small kitchen for the preparation of hot food and stowage space for two trolleys between First and Standard Class. One toilet removed. 30/10 1T.

| | | | | | |
|---|---|---|---|---|---|
| 45001 | (12004) | **XC** | P | *XC* | EC |
| 45002 | (12106) | **XC** | P | *XC* | EC |
| 45003 | (12076) | **XC** | P | *XC* | EC |
| 45004 | (12077) | **XC** | P | *XC* | EC |
| 45005 | (12080) | **XC** | P | *XC* | EC |

# 2.2. HST SET FORMATIONS

## FIRST GREAT WESTERN

The largest operator of HSTs is First Great Western with 53 sets to cover 49 diagrams (of these one is a "hot spare" at Old Oak Common and one a "hot spare" at Bristol St Philip's Marsh).

The sets are split into three types, as shown below. These are 16 "low density" sets mainly used on West Country services, 19 "high density" sets with a full kitchen or buffet vehicle and 18 "super high density" sets including a TSB vehicle (with just a small corner buffet counter).

Volo TV screens are fitted to Coach D TS vehicles.

Although some sets are prefixed "OC" for Old Oak Common, for maintenance purposes all trailers are now based at Laira apart from two spare vehicles.

**Number of sets:** 53.
**Maximum number of daily diagrams:** 49.
**Formations:** 8-cars.
**Allocation:** Laira (Plymouth) or Old Oak Common (London).
**Other maintenance and servicing depots:** Landore (Swansea), St Philip's Marsh (Bristol), Long Rock (Penzance).
**Operation:** London Paddington–Exeter/Paignton/Plymouth/(Newquay in the summer)/Penzance, Bristol, Cardiff/Swansea/West Wales, Oxford/Hereford/Great Malvern/Cheltenham Spa.

| Set | H | G | F | E | D | C | B | A | density |
|-----|-----|-----|-----|-----|-----|-----|-----|-----|---------|
| LA01 | 41023 | 41024 | 40755 | 42034 | 42033 | 42007 | 42035 | 44011 | L |
| LA02 | 41031 | 41032 | 40727 | 42046 | 42045 | 42047 | 42047 | 44015 | L |
| LA03 | 41037 | 41038 | 40757 | 42055 | 42343 | 42292 | 42056 | 44018 | L |
| LA04 | 41051 | 41052 | 40710 | 42077 | 42076 | 42004 | 42078 | 44025 | L |
| LA05 | 41093 | 41094 | 40707 | 42185 | 42184 | 42107 | 42107 | 44001 | L |
| LA06 | 41103 | 41104 | 40713 | 42208 | 42054 | 42206 | 42209 | 44066 | L |
| LA07 | 41121 | 41122 | 40722 | 42252 | 42019 | 42345 | 42253 | 44028 | L |
| LA08 | 41123 | 41124 | 40739 | 42256 | 42263 | 42255 | 42257 | 44029 | L |
| LA09 | 41129 | 41130 | 40716 | 42072 | 42325 | 42267 | 42269 | 44032 | L |
| LA10 | 41133 | 41134 | 40721 | 42276 | 42332 | 42275 | 42277 | 44034 | L |
| LA11 | 41116 | 41135 | 40703 | 42280 | 42265 | 42279 | 42281 | 44035 | L |
| LA12 | 41003 | 41136 | 40752 | 42144 | 42143 | 42268 | 42145 | 44049 | L |
| LA13 | 41141 | 41142 | 40734 | 42333 | 42075 | 42291 | 42293 | 44038 | L |
| LA14 | 41143 | 41144 | 40733 | 42296 | 42350 | 42295 | 42297 | 44039 | L |
| LA15 | 41145 | 41146 | 40715 | 42300 | 42351 | 42299 | 42301 | 44040 | L |
| LA16 | 41157 | 41158 | 40743 | 42245 | 42129 | 42200 | 42250 | 44086 | L |
| OC30 | 41007 | 41008 | 40807 | 42079 | 42236 | 42251 | 42080 | 44026 | H |
| OC31 | 41127 | 41128 | 40804 | 42060 | 42197 | 42347 | 42061 | 44020 | H |
| OC32 | 41017 | 41018 | 40801 | 42025 | 42362 | 42024 | 42026 | 44008 | H |
| OC33 | 41027 | 41028 | 40806 | 42040 | 42039 | 42348 | 42041 | 44013 | H |
| OC34 | 41101 | 41102 | 40803 | 42203 | 42027 | 42201 | 42204 | 44064 | H |
| OC35 | 41105 | 41106 | 40808 | 42213 | 42212 | 42211 | 42214 | 44067 | H |

▲ **Mark 1s:** Northern Belle-liveried Mark 1 Kitchen First 325 "DUART" is seen at Nappa, near Hellifield, on 25/05/13.  **Andrew Mason**

▼ BR Chocolate & Cream-liveried Mark 1 Open First 3100 at Bristol Temple Meads on 22/09/12.  **Steve Widdowson**

▲ BR Carmine & Cream-liveried Mark 1 Open First 3123 is seen at Kinloid in the West Highlands on 09/06/12.　**Andrew Mason**

▼ BR Maroon-liveried Mark 1 Open Standard 4960 is seen at Worcester Shrub Hill on 16/04/11.　**Dave Gommersall**

▲ BR Maroon-liveried Mark 1 Corridor First 13229 is seen near Mossend on 05/09/12.                                                         **Robin Ralston**

▼ **Mark 2s:** Pullman Car Company-liveried Mark 2E Open First 3231 "BEN CRUACHAN" is seen at Kirkby-in-Furness on 13/04/13.                **Andrew Mason**

▲ Riviera Trains-liveried Mark 2F Open First 3330 "BRUNEL" is seen at Cleghorn on 18/11/12.　　**Robin Ralston**

▼ Newly in traffic in DRS livery, Mark 2F Open Standard 6117 is seen near Derby on 26/08/13 in the formation of a Derby–Crewe service operated on behalf of East Midlands Trains.　　**Robert Pritchard**

▲ Pullman Car Company-liveried Mark 2A Corridor Brake First 17080 is seen near Carstairs on 02/03/13.                **Robin Ralston**

▼ First ScotRail-liveried Mark 2E Open Brake Unclassified 9807 is seen in the formation of the Euston–Glasgow Central Caledonian Sleeper service near Carstairs on 01/06/13.                **Robin Ralston**

▲ **Mark 3s:** Greater Anglia-liveried Mark 3A Kitchen Buffet First 10229 at Colchester on 25/04/13.                                                         **Antony Guppy**

▼ Still in "One" livery with a white (former National Express) stripe, Mark 3B Open First 11072 passes Pudding Mill Lane on 26/07/13.          **Robert Pritchard**

▲ Arriva Trains Wales dark blue-liveried Mark 3B Open Standard 12178 at Cardiff Central on 17/10/12. **Robert Pritchard**

▼ **Mark 3 Sleeping cars:** First ScotRail Mark 3A Sleeping Car With Pantry 10508 is seen near Carstairs on 01/06/13. **Robin Ralston**

▲ **Mark 3 HST vehicles:** In National Express livery with East Coast branding, Trailer Kitchen Buffet First 40701 is seen at Doncaster on 09/08/13. **Robert Pritchard**

▼ First Great Western-liveried Trailer First 41104 is seen at Plymouth on 05/04/13. **Robert Pritchard**

▲ Grand Central-liveried Trailer First 41206 at York on 06/08/12.
**Robert Pritchard**

▼ CrossCountry-liveried Trailer Standard 42374 is also seen at York, on 19/04/13.
**Robert Pritchard**

▲ East Midlands Trains Trailer Guard's Standard 44048 is seen at Dore & Totley on 14/10/12. **Robert Pritchard**

▼ **Mark 4s:** East Coast silver-liveried Mark 4 Kitchen Buffet Standard 10325 at York on 06/06/13. **Robert Pritchard**

▲ **DVTs:** National Express-liveried Mark 3B Driving Brake Van 82107 leads the 10.30 Liverpool Street–Norwich through Manor Park on 21/04/13. **Robert Pritchard**

▼ Arriva Trains Wales-liveried Mark 3B Driving Brake Van 82306 leads the 18.21 Cardiff–Holyhead near Leominster on 09/07/13.      **Dave Gommersall**

▲ **Pullman cars, saloons and other stock:** General Utility Van 96100 (converted for use as a water carrier with B5 bogies) is seen at Bishops Lydeard on 25/05/13.
**David Hunt**

▼ Royal Scotsman Saloon 99967 "Dining Car No. 1" is seen near Inverkeithing on 10/05/13.
**Ian Lothian**

▲ BR Maroon-liveried Pullman Parlour Second No. 347 is seen near Dawlish on 08/07/13.　　**Stewart Armstrong**

▼ BR Carmine & Cream-liveried Mark 1 Corridor Brake Composite 21249, converted to act as a Support Coach for New Build steam locomotive 60163 "Tornado", is seen at Worcester Shrub Hill on 14/09/13.　　**Steve Widdowson**

▲ **Service stock:** HSBC Rail-liveried EMU Translator Vehicle 975867 is seen at Greenhill Upper on 02/02/12.                                                    **Ian Lothian**

▼ Network Rail Driving Trailer Coach 9708 at Skegness after arrival on a test train (hauled by 31285) on 16/09/13.                                          **John Pink**

▲ Network Rail Track Recording Train Staff Coach 977969, converted from a Mark 2B Corridor Brake First, is seen at Carlisle on 17/08/13. **Robert Pritchard**

▼ Electrification Measurement Coach 977983, converted from Mark 2F 3407 (later Gatwick Express coach 72503) is seen at Eastleigh on 16/10/12.
**Tony Christie**

▲ New Measurement Train Track Recording Coach 977994 at York on 06/08/12.
**Robert Pritchard**

▼ Network Rail Ultrasonic Test Coach 999602 (converted from a Class 421 EMU motor coach) stands at Derby on 01/03/13.
**Mick Tindall**

| | | | | | | | | | |
|---|---|---|---|---|---|---|---|---|---|
| OC36 | 41004 | 41110 | 40809 | 42346 | 42349 | 42138 | 42089 | 44003 | H |
| OC37 | 41131 | 41132 | 40802 | 42272 | 42073 | 42271 | 42273 | 44033 | H |
| OC38 | 41137 | 41138 | 40810 | 42284 | 42003 | 42202 | 42285 | 44036 | H |
| OC40 | 41181 | 41149 | 40106 | 42502 | 42166 | 42218 | 42071 | 44079 | SH |
| OC41 | 41109 | 41182 | 40107 | 42505 | 42222 | 42224 | 42382 | 44101 | SH |
| OC42 | 41168 | 41183 | 40108 | 42511 | 42315 | 42317 | 42383 | 44090 | SH |
| OC43 | 41147 | 41186 | 40109 | 42515 | 42258 | 42266 | 42365 | 44000 | SH |
| OC44 | 41191 | 41192 | 40110 | 42514 | 42115 | 42174 | 42288 | 44097 | SH |
| OC45 | 41119 | 41187 | 40111 | 42501 | 42247 | 42173 | 42260 | 44078 | SH |
| OC46 | 41096 | 41161 | 40112 | 42512 | 42178 | 42195 | 42043 | 44042 | SH |
| OC47 | 41081 | 41108 | 40113 | 42509 | 42308 | 42217 | 42067 | 44060 | SH |
| OC48 | 41184 | 41189 | 40114 | 42101 | 42085 | 42310 | 42087 | 44069 | SH |
| OC49 | 41148 | 41169 | 40115 | 42385 | 42319 | 42364 | 42321 | 44091 | SH |
| OC50 | 41179 | 41180 | 40101 | 42196 | 42098 | 42264 | 42283 | 44093 | SH |
| OC51 | 41005 | 41006 | 40103 | 42513 | 42070 | 42069 | 42118 | 44023 | SH |
| OC52 | 41029 | 41030 | 40102 | 42510 | 42042 | 42008 | 42044 | 44014 | SH |
| OC53 | 41033 | 41034 | 40118 | 42506 | 42048 | 42066 | 42050 | 44016 | SH |
| OC54 | 41055 | 41056 | 40117 | 42503 | 42074 | 42081 | 42126 | 44043 | SH |
| OC55 | 41065 | 41089 | 40104 | 42504 | 42221 | 42062 | 42068 | 44022 | SH |
| OC56 | 41125 | 41126 | 40116 | 42508 | 42216 | 42344 | 42261 | 44030 | SH |
| OC57 | 41139 | 41140 | 40105 | 42507 | 42099 | 42287 | 42289 | 44037 | SH |
| LA60 | 41114 | 41162 | 40900 | 42231 | 42232 | 42353 | 42233 | 44074 | H |
| LA61 | 41086 | 41166 | 40901 | 42304 | 42303 | 42302 | 42305 | 44068 | H |
| LA62 | 41085 | 41167 | 40902 | 42167 | 42168 | 42103 | 42169 | 44055 | H |
| LA63 | 41045 | 41059 | 40903 | 42175 | 42176 | 42105 | 42177 | 44081 | H |
| LA64 | 41163 | 41166 | 40904 | 42094 | 42093 | 42092 | 42108 | 44076 | H |
| LA71 | 41009 | 41010 | 40204 | 42013 | 42360 | 42012 | 42014 | 44004 | H |
| LA72 | 41011 | 41012 | 40205 | 42016 | 42005 | 42015 | 42361 | 44005 | H |
| LA73 | 41015 | 41016 | 40207 | 42006 | 42096 | 42021 | 42023 | 44007 | H |
| LA74 | 41019 | 41020 | 40221 | 42028 | 42009 | 42259 | 42029 | 44009 | H |
| LA75 | 41021 | 41022 | 40210 | 42031 | 42010 | 42030 | 42032 | 44010 | H |

L = Low density; H = High density; SH = Super High density.

**Spares:**

| | | | | | | | | |
|---|---|---|---|---|---|---|---|---|
| LA: | 40119 | 40231 | 40718 | 40811 | 41155 | 41176 | 42049 | 42083 |
| | 42095 | 42102 | 42294 | 42356 | 42381 | 44002 | 44059 | 44083 |
| OO: | 44024 | | | | | | | |
| PM: | 44100 | | | | | | | |

# NETWORK RAIL: NEW MEASUREMENT TRAIN

The Network Rail "New Measurement Train" is used to test and evaluate Britain's main railway lines. Can run in 4-, 5- or 6-car formation depending on routes being taken (the 6-car formation is shown below).

977995     975984     977994     977993     975814     977984

# EAST COAST

East Coast operates 14 refurbished HST sets on the ECML. As well as serving non-electrified destinations such as Hull and Inverness the East Coast HSTs also work alongside Class 91s and Mark 4 sets on services to Leeds, Newcastle and Edinburgh. Set EC64 (ex-NL05) transferred from East Midlands Trains in 2011.

**Number of sets:** 14.
**Maximum number of daily diagrams:** 13.
**Formations:** 9-cars.
**Allocation:** Craigentinny (Edinburgh).
**Other maintenance depot:** Neville Hill (Leeds).
**Operation:** London King's Cross–Leeds/Harrogate/Skipton/Hull/Lincoln/Newcastle/Edinburgh/Aberdeen/Inverness.

| Set | M | L | J | G | F | E | D | C | B |
|-----|-----|-----|-----|-----|-----|-----|-----|-----|-----|
| EC51 | 41120 | 41150 | 40748 | 42215 | 42091 | 42146 | 42150 | 42154 | 44094 |
| EC52 | 41039 | 41040 | 40735 | 42323 | 42189 | 42057 | 42058 | 42059 | 44019 |
| EC53 | 41090 | 41044 | 40737 | 42340 | 42127 | 42063 | 42064 | 42065 | 44045 |
| EC54 | 41087 | 41088 | 40706 | 42104 | 42161 | 42171 | 42172 | 42219 | 44056 |
| EC55 | 41091 | 41092 | 40704 | 42179 | 42188 | 42180 | 42181 | 42106 | 44058 |
| EC56 | 41170 | 41118 | 40720 | 42241 | 42363 | 42242 | 42243 | 42244 | 44098 |
| EC57 | 41151 | 41152 | 40740 | 42226 | 42128 | 42182 | 42186 | 42190 | 44080 |
| EC58 | 41097 | 41098 | 40750 | 42158 | 42238 | 42191 | 42192 | 42193 | 44061 |
| EC59 | 41099 | 41100 | 40711 | 42235 | 42239 | 42240 | 42198 | 42199 | 44063 |
| EC60 | 41066 | 41164 | 40742 | 42122 | 42116 | 42357 | 42134 | 42355 | 44031 |
| EC61 | 41115 | 41165 | 40702 | 42117 | 42159 | 42160 | 42109 | 42110 | 44057 |
| EC62 | 41185 | 41095 | 40701 | 42306 | 42326 | 42330 | 42237 | 42307 | 44075 |
| EC63 | 41159 | 41083 | 40708 | 42163 | 42286 | 42228 | 42130 | 42322 | 44050 |
| EC64 | 41062 | 41154 | 40732 | 42125 | 42335 | 42123 | 42205 | 42210 | 44073 |

**Spares:**

EC:    40705    40805    41190    42354    44077

# GRAND CENTRAL

GC operates HSTs between Sunderland and King's Cross. Formations are flexible: there are enough vehicles to form three 6-car sets or one set can be disbanded to enable the sets to run as 7-cars at times of high demand.

**Number of sets:** 3.
**Maximum number of daily diagrams:** 2.
**Formations:** 6-cars or 7-cars.
**Allocation:** Heaton (Newcastle).
**Operation:** London King's Cross–Sunderland.

| Set | TF | TSB | TS | TS | TS | TF* |
|-----|-----|-----|-----|-----|-----|-----|
| GC01 | 41201 | 40424 | 42403 | 42402 | 42401 | 41204 |
| GC02 | 41202 | 40426 | 42406 | 42405 | 42404 | 41205 |
| GC03 | 41203 | 40433 | 42409 | 42408 | 42407 | 41206 |

* declassified.

# EAST MIDLANDS TRAINS

East Midlands Trains HSTs are concentrated on the Nottingham corridor during the day, with early morning and evening services to Leeds for servicing at Neville Hill.

**Number of sets:** 10.
**Maximum number of daily diagrams:** 9.
**Formations:** 8-cars.
**Allocation:** Neville Hill (Leeds).
**Other maintenance depot:** Derby Etches Park.
**Operation:** London St Pancras–Nottingham, Sheffield/Leeds.

| Set | J | G | F | E | D | C | B | A |
|-----|------|------|------|------|------|------|------|------|
| NL01 | 41057 | 41084 | 40730 | 42327 | 42111 | 42112 | 42113 | 44041 |
| NL02 | 41112 | 41067 | 40754 | 42194 | 42229 | 42227 | 42225 | 44027 |
| NL03 | 41061 | 41068 | 40741 | 42337 | 42119 | 42120 | 42121 | 44054 |
| NL04 | 41077 | 41064 | 40749 | 42151 | 42164 | 42165 | 42153 | 44047 |
| NL06 | 41156 | 41041 | 40746 | 42132 | 42131 | 42331 | 42133 | 44046 |
| NL07 | 41111 | 41070 | 40751 | 42339 | 42135 | 42136 | 42137 | 44044 |
| NL08 | 41071 | 41072 | 40753 | 42329 | 42139 | 42140 | 42141 | 44048 |
| NL10 | 41075 | 41076 | 40756 | 42328 | 42341 | 42148 | 42149 | 44051 |
| NL11 | 41117 | 41046 | 40728 | 42220 | 42100 | 42230 | 42124 | 44085 |
| NL12 | 41079 | 41069 | 40700 | 42155 | 42156 | 42157 | 42152 | 44070 |

**Spares:**

NL:    41063   41113   42384   44071

# CROSSCOUNTRY

CrossCountry reintroduced regular HST diagrams on its services from the December 2008 timetable. Trains run in 7-car formation with the spare TS coaches regularly used in traffic as coaches "C", "D" or "E".

**Number of sets:** 5.
**Maximum number of daily diagrams:** 4.
**Formations:** 7-cars.
**Allocation:** Craigentinny (Edinburgh).
**Other maintenance depots:** Laira (Plymouth) or Neville Hill (Leeds).
**Operation:** Edinburgh–Leeds–Plymouth is the core route with some services extending to Dundee or Penzance.

| Set | A | B | C | D | E | F | G |
|-----|------|------|------|------|------|------|------|
| XC01 | 41193 | 45001 | 42368 | 42369 | 42367 | 42366 | 44021 |
| XC02 | 41194 | 45002 | 42375 | 42373 | 42374 | 42371 | 44072 |
| XC03 | 41195 | 45003 | 42290 | 42378 | 42377 | 42376 | 44052 |
| XC04 | 41026 | 45004 | 42038 | 42037 | 42036 | 42380 | 44012 |
| XC05 | 41035 | 45005 | 42051 | 42053 | 42052 | 42379 | 44017 |

**Spares:**

EC:    42097   42234   42342   42370   42372

# 2.4. SALOONS

Several specialist passenger carrying vehicles, normally referred to as saloons are permitted to run on the National Rail system. Many of these are to pre-nationalisation designs.

## WCJS FIRST CLASS SALOON

Built 1892 by LNWR, Wolverton. Originally dining saloon mounted on six-wheel bogies. Rebuilt with new underframe with four-wheel bogies in 1927. Rebuilt 1960 as observation saloon with DMU end. Gangwayed at other end. The interior has a saloon, kitchen, guards vestibule and observation lounge. 19/– 1T. Gresley bogies. 28.5 t. 75 mph.

| 41 | (484, 45018) | x | **M** | WC | *WC* | CS |

## LNWR DINING SALOON

Built 1890 by LNWR, Wolverton. Mounted on the underframe of LMS General Utility Van 37908 in the 1980s. Contains kitchen and dining area seating 12 at tables for two. 10/–. Gresley bogies. 75 mph. 25.4 t.

| 159 | (5159) | x | **M** | WC | *WC* | CS |

## GNR FIRST CLASS SALOON

Built 1912 by GNR, Doncaster. Contains entrance vestibule, lavatory, two separate saloons, library and luggage space. 19/– 1T. Gresley bogies. 75 mph. 29.4 t.

**Non-standard livery:** Teak.

| 807 | (4807) | x | **0** | WC | *WC* | CS |

## LNER GENERAL MANAGERS SALOON

Built 1945 by LNER, York. Gangwayed at one end with a veranda at the other. The interior has a dining saloon seating 12, kitchen, toilet, office and nine seat lounge. 21/– 1T. B4 bogies. 75 mph. ETH 3. 35.7 t.

| 1999 | (902260) | | **M** | OE | | CS | DINING CAR No. 2 |

## GENERAL MANAGER'S SALOON

Renumbered 1989 from London Midland Region departmental series. Formerly the LMR General Manager's saloon. Rebuilt from LMS period 1 Corridor Brake First M5033M to dia 1654 and mounted on the underframe of BR suburban Brake Standard M43232. Screw couplings have been removed. B4 bogies. 100 mph. ETH 2X.

LMS Lot No. 326 Derby 1927. 27.5 t.

6320   (5033, DM 395707)   x   **M**   62   *62*       SK

## BRITISH PULLMAN SUPPORT CAR

Converted 199? from Courier vehicle converted from Mark 1 Corridor Brake Standard 1986–87. Toilet retained and former compartment area replaced with train manager's office, crew locker room, linen store and dry goods store. The former luggage area has been adapted for use as an engineers' compartment and workshop. Commonwealth bogies. 100 mph. ETH 2.

Lot No. 30721 Wolverton 1963. 37 t.

99545 (35466, 80207)      **PC**   OE   *BP*   SL   BAGGAGE CAR No. 11

## SERVICE CAR

Converted from BR Mark 1 Corridor Brake Standard. Commonwealth bogies. 100 mph. ETH 2.

Lot No. 30721 Wolverton 1963.

99886 (35407)      x   **M**   WC   *WC*   CS            SERVICE CAR No. 86

## ROYAL SCOTSMAN SALOONS

Built 1960 by Metro-Cammell as Pullman Kitchen First for East Coast Main Line services. Rebuilt 2013 as dining car. Commonwealth bogies. 38.5 t.

99960 (321 SWIFT)   **M**   OE   *RS*   CS            DINING CAR No. 2

Built 1960 by Metro-Cammell as Pullman Parlour First (§ Pullman Kitchen First) for East Coast Main Line services. Rebuilt 1990 as sleeping cars with four twin sleeping rooms (*§ three twin sleeping rooms and two single sleeping rooms at each end). Commonwealth bogies. 38.5 t.

99961 (324 AMBER) *   **M**   OE   *RS*   CS            STATE CAR 1
99962 (329 PEARL)    **M**   OE   *RS*   CS            STATE CAR 2
99963 (331 TOPAZ)    **M**   OE   *RS*   CS            STATE CAR 3
99964 (313 FINCH) §  **M**   OE   *RS*   CS            STATE CAR 4

Built 1960 by Metro-Cammell as Pullman Kitchen First for East Coast Main Line services. Rebuilt 1990 as observation car with open verandah seating 32. Commonwealth bogies. 38.5 t.

99965 (319 SNIPE)      **M**   OE   *RS*    CS         OBSERVATION CAR

Built 1960 by Metro-Cammell as Pullman Kitchen First for East Coast Main Line services. Rebuilt 1993 as dining car. Commonwealth bogies. 38.5 t.

99967 (317 RAVEN)      **M**   OE   *RS*    CS         DINING CAR No. 1

Mark 3A. Converted 1997 from a Sleeping Car at Carnforth Railway Restoration & Engineering Services. BT10 bogies. Attendant's and adjacent two sleeping compartments converted to generator room containing a 160 kW Volvo unit. In 99968 four sleeping compartments remain for staff use with another converted for use as a staff shower and toilet. The remaining five sleeping compartments have been replaced by two passenger cabins. In 99969 seven sleeping compartments remain for staff use. A further sleeping compartment, along with one toilet, have been converted to store rooms. The other two sleeping compartments have been combined to form a crew mess. ETH 7X. 41.5 t.

Lot No. 30960 Derby 1981–83.

99968 (10541)          **M**   OE   *RS*    CS         STATE CAR 5
99969 (10556)          **M**   OE   *RS*    CS         SERVICE CAR

# RAILFILMS "LMS CLUB CAR"

Converted from BR Mark 1 Open Standard at Carnforth Railway Restoration & Engineering Services in 1994. Contains kitchen, pantry and two dining saloons. 20/– 1T. Commonwealth bogies. 100 mph. ETH 4.

Lot No. 30724 York 1963. 37 t.

99993 (5067)        x  **M**   RA   *ST*    CS         LMS CLUB CAR

# BR INSPECTION SALOON

Mark 1. Short frames. Non-gangwayed. Observation windows at each end. The interior layout consists of two saloons interspersed by a central lavatory/kitchen/guards/luggage section. 90 mph.

BR Wagon Lot No. 3095 Swindon 1957. B4 bogies. 30.5 t.

999506                 **M**   WC   *WC*    CS

# 2.5. PULLMAN CAR COMPANY SERIES

Pullman cars have never generally been numbered as such, although many have carried numbers, instead they have carried titles. However, a scheme of schedule numbers exists which generally lists cars in chronological order. In this section those numbers are shown followed by the car's title. Cars described as "kitchen" contain a kitchen in addition to passenger accommodation and have gas cooking unless otherwise stated. Cars described as "parlour" consist entirely of passenger accommodation. Cars described as "brake" contain a compartment for the use of the guard and a luggage compartment in addition to passenger accommodation.

## PULLMAN PARLOUR FIRST

Built 1927 by Midland Carriage & Wagon Company. 26/– 2T. Gresley bogies. ETH 2. 41 t.

213     MINERVA      **PC**    OE    *BP*      SL

## PULLMAN PARLOUR FIRST

Built 1928 by Metropolitan Carriage & Wagon Company. 24/– 2T. Gresley bogies. ETH 4. 40 t.

239     AGATHA      **PC**    OE        SL
243     LUCILLE      **PC**    OE    *BP*      SL

## PULLMAN KITCHEN FIRST

Built 1925 by BRCW. Rebuilt by Midland Carriage & Wagon Company in 1928. 20/– 1T. Gresley bogies. ETH 4. 41 t.

245     IBIS      **PC**    OE    *BP*      SL

## PULLMAN PARLOUR FIRST

Built 1928 by Metropolitan Carriage & Wagon Company. 24/– 2T. Gresley bogies. ETH 4.

254     ZENA      **PC**    OE    *BP*      SL

## PULLMAN KITCHEN FIRST

Built 1928 by Metropolitan Carriage & Wagon Company. 20/– 1T. Gresley bogies. ETH 4. 42 t.

255     IONE      **PC**    OE    *BP*      SL

# PULLMAN KITCHEN COMPOSITE

Built 1932 by Metropolitan Carriage & Wagon Company. Originally included in 6-Pul EMU. Electric cooking. 12/16 1T. EMU bogies.

| 264 | RUTH | **PC** | OE | | SL |
|-----|------|--------|----|----|-----|

# PULLMAN KITCHEN FIRST

Built 1932 by Metropolitan Carriage & Wagon Company. Originally included in "Brighton Belle" EMUs but now used as hauled stock. Electric cooking. 20/– 1T. B5 (SR) bogies (§ EMU bogies). ETH 2. 44 t.

| 280 | AUDREY | | **PC** | OE | *BP* | SL |
|-----|--------|----|--------|----|------|-----|
| 281 | GWEN | | **PC** | OE | *BP* | SL |
| 283 | MONA | § | **PC** | OE | | SL |
| 284 | VERA | | **PC** | OE | *BP* | SL |

# PULLMAN PARLOUR THIRD

Built 1932 by Metropolitan Carriage & Wagon Company. Originally included in "Brighton Belle" EMUs. –/56 2T. EMU bogies.

| 286 | CAR No. 86 | **PC** | OE | | SL |
|-----|------------|--------|----|----|-----|

# PULLMAN BRAKE THIRD

Built 1932 by Metropolitan Carriage & Wagon Company. Originally driving motor cars in "Brighton Belle" EMUs. Traction and control equipment removed for use as hauled stock. –/48 1T. EMU bogies.

| 292 | CAR No. 92 | **PC** | OE | | SL |
|-----|------------|--------|----|----|-----|
| 293 | CAR No. 93 | **PC** | OE | | SL |

# PULLMAN PARLOUR FIRST

Built 1951 by Birmingham Railway Carriage & Wagon Company. 32/– 2T. Gresley bogies. ETH 3. 39 t.

| 301 | PERSEUS | **PC** | OE | *BP* | SL |
|-----|---------|--------|----|------|-----|

Built 1952 by Pullman Car Company, Preston Park using underframe and bogies from 176 RAINBOW, the body of which had been destroyed by fire. 26/– 2T. Gresley bogies. ETH 4. 38 t.

| 302 | PHOENIX | **PC** | OE | *BP* | SL |
|-----|---------|--------|----|------|-----|

# PULLMAN PARLOUR FIRST

Built 1951 by Birmingham Railway Carriage & Wagon Company. 32/– 2T. Gresley bogies. ETH 3. 39 t.

| 308 | CYGNUS | **PC** | OE | *BP* | SL |
|-----|--------|--------|----|------|-----|

## PULLMAN BAR FIRST

Built 1951 by Birmingham Railway Carriage & Wagon Company. Rebuilt 1999 by Blake Fabrications, Edinburgh with original timber-framed body replaced by a new fabricated steel body. Contains kitchen, bar, dining saloon and coupé. Electric cooking. 14/– 1T. Gresley bogies. ETH 3.

310     PEGASUS                    x   **PC**   RA    *ST*    CS

Also carries "THE TRIANON BAR" branding.

## PULLMAN PALOUR FIRST

Built 1960–61 by Metro-Cammell for East Coast Main Line services. –/36 2T. Commonwealth bogies. 38.5 t.

326     EMERALD                    x   **PC**   WC    *WC*    CS

## PULLMAN KITCHEN SECOND

Built 1960–61 by Metro-Cammell for East Coast Main Line services. Commonwealth bogies. –/30 1T. 40 t.

335     CAR No. 335                x   **PC**   VT    *VT*    TM

## PULLMAN PARLOUR SECOND

Built 1960–61 by Metro-Cammell for East Coast Main Line services. 347, 348 and 350 are used as Open Firsts. –/42 2T. Commonwealth bogies. 38.5 t.

| 347 | CAR No. 347 | x | **M**  | WC | *WC* | CS |          |
|-----|-------------|---|--------|----|------|----|----------|
| 348 | CAR No. 348 | x | **M**  | WC | *WC* | CS |          |
| 349 | CAR No. 349 | x | **PC** | VT | *VT* | TM |          |
| 350 | CAR No. 350 | x | **M**  | WC | *WC* | CS |          |
| 352 | CAR No. 352 | x | **PC** | WC | *WC* | CS | AMETHYST |
| 353 | CAR No. 353 | x | **PC** | VT | *VT* | TM |          |

## PULLMAN SECOND BAR

Built 1960–61 by Metro-Cammell for East Coast Main Line services. –/24+17 bar seats. Commonwealth bogies. 38.5 t.

354     THE HADRIAN BAR     x   **PC**   WC    *WC*    CS

# 2.6. LOCOMOTIVE SUPPORT COACHES

These carriages have been adapted from Mark 1s and Mark 2s for use as support coaches for heritage steam locomotives. Some seating is retained for the use of personnel supporting the locomotives operation with the remainder of the carriage adapted for storage, workshop, dormitory and catering purposes. These carriages can spend considerable periods of time off the national railway system when the locomotives they support are not being used on that system. No owner or operator details are included in this section. After the depot code, the locomotive(s) each carriage is usually used to support is given.

## CORRIDOR BRAKE FIRST

Mark 1. Commonwealth bogies. ETH 2.

**14007.** Lot No. 30382 Swindon 1959. 35 t.
**17013.** Lot No. 30668 Swindon 1961. 36 t.
**17025.** Lot No. 30718 Swindon 1963. Metal window frames. 36 t.

| | | | | | |
|---|---|---|---|---|---|
| 14007 | (14007, 17007) | x | **M** | NY | LNER 61264 |
| 17013 | (14013) | x | **PC** | SH | LNER 60019 | BOTAURUS |
| 17025 | (14025) | v | **M** | CS | LMS 45690 |

## CORRIDOR BRAKE FIRST

Mark 2A. Pressure ventilated. B4 bogies. ETH 4.

**14064.** Lot No. 30775 Derby 1967–68. 32 t.
**14099/17096.** Lot No. 30786 Derby 1968. 32 t.

| | | | | | |
|---|---|---|---|---|---|
| 14064 | (14064, 17064) | x | **M** | CS | LMS 45305/BR 70013 |
| 14099 | (14099, 17099) | v | **M** | CS | LMS 45305/BR 70013 |
| 17096 | (14096) | | **PC** | SL | SR 35028 | MERCATOR |

## CORRIDOR BRAKE COMPOSITE

Mark 1. ETH 2.

**21096.** Lot No. 30185 Metro-Cammell 1956. BR Mark 1 bogies. 32.5 t.
**21232.** Lot No. 30574 GRCW 1960. B4 bogies. 34 t.
**21249.** Lot No. 30669 Swindon 1961–62. Commonwealth bogies. 36 t.

| | | | | |
|---|---|---|---|---|
| 21096 | x | **M** | NY | LNER 60007 |
| 21232 | x | **M** | SK | LMS 46233 |
| 21249 | x | **CC** | BH | New Build 60163 |

## CORRIDOR BRAKE STANDARD

Mark 1. Metal window frames and melamine interior panelling. ETH 2.

**35317–333.** Lot No. 30699 Wolverton 1962–63. Commonwealth bogies. 37 t.
**35449.** Lot No. 30728 Wolverton 1963. Commonwealth bogies. 37 t.
**35451–486.** Lot No. 30721 Wolverton 1963. Commonwealth bogies. 37 t.

| | | | | |
|---|---|---|---|---|
| 35317 | x | **CC** | SH | LNER 60019 |
| 35322 | x | **M** | CS | WCRC Carnforth-based locomotives |
| 35333 | x | **CH** | MI | GWR 6024 |
| 35449 | x | **M** | BQ | LMS 45231 |
| 35451 | x | **G** | MI | SR 34046 |
| 35457 | v | **M** | WH | LNER 61306 |
| 35461 | x | **CH** | TM | GWR 5029 |
| 35463 | v | **M** | CS | WCRC Carnforth-based locomotives |
| 35465 | x | **CC** | SH | BR 70000 |
| 35468 | x | **M** | YK | National Railway Museum locomotives |
| 35470 | v | **CH** | TM | Tyseley Locomotive Works-based locos |
| 35476 | x | **M** | SK | LMS 46233 |
| 35486 | x | **M** | TN | LNER 60009/61994 |

## CORRIDOR BRAKE FIRST

Mark 2C. Pressure ventilated. Renumbered when declassified. B4 bogies. ETH 4.

Lot No. 30796 Derby 1969–70. 32.5 t.

| | | | |
|---|---|---|---|
| 35508 (14128, 17128) | **M** | BQ | LMS 44871/45407 |

## CORRIDOR BRAKE FIRST

Mark 2A. Pressure ventilated. Renumbered when declassified. B4 bogies. ETH 4.

Lot No. 30786 Derby 1968. 32 t.

| | | | | |
|---|---|---|---|---|
| 35517 (14088, 17088) | b | **M** | BQ | LMS 44871/45407 |
| 35518 (14097, 17097) | b | **G** | SH | SR 34067 |

## COURIER VEHICLE

Mark 1. Converted 1986–87 from Corridor Brake Standards. ETH 2.

**80204/217.** Lot No. 30699 Wolverton 1962. Commonwealth bogies. 37 t.
**80220.** Lot No. 30573 Gloucester 1960. B4 bogies. 33 t.

| | | | |
|---|---|---|---|
| 80204 (35297) | **M** | CS | WCRC Carnforth-based locomotives |
| 80217 (35299) | **M** | CS | WCRC Carnforth-based locomotives |
| 80220 (35276) | **M** | NY | LNER 62005 |

# 2.7. 95xxx & 99xxx RANGE NUMBER CONVERSION TABLE

The following table is presented to help readers identify vehicles which may still carry numbers in the 95xxx and 99xxx number ranges of the former private owner number series, which is no longer in general use.

| 9xxxx | BR No. | 9xxxx | BR No. | 9xxxx | BR No. |
|---|---|---|---|---|---|
| 95402 | Pullman 326 | 99349 | Pullman 349 | 99673 | 550 |
| 99035 | 35322 | 99350 | Pullman 350 | 99674 | 551 |
| 99040 | 21232 | 99352 | Pullman 352 | 99675 | 552 |
| 99041 | 35476 | 99353 | Pullman 353 | 99676 | 553 |
| 99052 | Saloon 41 | 99354 | Pullman 354 | 99677 | 586 |
| 99121 | 3105 | 99361 | Pullman 335 | 99678 | 504 |
| 99122 | 3106 | 99371 | 3128 | 99679 | 506 |
| 99125 | 3113 | 99405 | 35486 | 99680 | 17102 |
| 99127 | 3117 | 99530 | Pullman 301 | 99710 | 18767 |
| 99128 | 3130 | 99531 | Pullman 302 | 99716 * | 18808 |
| 99131 | Saloon 1999 | 99532 | Pullman 308 | 99718 | 18862 |
| 99241 | 35449 | 99534 | Pullman 245 | 99721 | 18756 |
| 99302 | 13323 | 99535 | Pullman 213 | 99723 | 35459 |
| 99304 | 21256 | 99536 | Pullman 254 | 99880 | Saloon 159 |
| 99311 | 1882 | 99537 | Pullman 280 | 99881 | Saloon 807 |
| 99312 | 35463 | 99539 | Pullman 255 | 99887 | 2127 |
| 99317 | 3766 | 99541 | Pullman 243 | 99953 | 35468 |
| 99319 | 17168 | 99543 | Pullman 284 | 99966 | 34525 |
| 99326 | 4954 | 99546 | Pullman 281 | 99970 | Pullman 232 |
| 99327 | 5044 | 99547 | Pullman 292 | 99972 | Pullman 318 |
| 99328 | 5033 | 99548 | Pullman 293 | 99973 | 324 |
| 99329 | 4931 | 99670 | 546 | 99974 | Pullman 328 |
| 99347 | Pullman 347 | 99671 | 548 | 99995 | 35457 |
| 99348 | Pullman 348 | 99672 | 549 | | |

* The number 99716 has also been applied to 3416 for filming purposes.

# 2.8. SET FORMATIONS

## CHILTERN MARK 3 SET FORMATIONS

Chiltern Railways uses a number of loco-hauled rakes on services principally between London Marylebone and Birmingham Moor Street. Rake AL04 is used on a commuter train between Marylebone and Banbury. All coaches apart from rake AL04 and 12094 have been rebuilt at Wabtec, Doncaster and fitted with sliding plug doors.

| Set | | | | | | DVT |
|---|---|---|---|---|---|---|
| AL01 | 12610 12613 12614 12615 12602 | | | | 10273 | 82301 |
| AL02 | 12603 12606 12607 12608 12609 | | | | 10272 | 82302 |
| AL03 | 12616 12617 12618 12619 12604 | | | | 10274 | 82303 |
| AL04 | 12119 12043 12017 11029 11031 | | | | 12054 | 82304 |
| AL05 | 12623 12605 12621 12627 12625 | | | | 10271 | 82305 |

Spare  12094 12620 82309

# EAST COAST MARK 4 SET FORMATIONS

The East Coast Mark 4 sets generally run in fixed formations since their refurbishment at Bombardier, Wakefield in 2003–05. These rakes are listed below. Class 91 locomotives are positioned next to Coach B.

| Set | B | C | D | E | F | H | K | L | M | DVT |
|---|---|---|---|---|---|---|---|---|---|---|
| BN01 | 12207 | 12417 | 12415 | 12414 | 12307 | 10307 | 11298 | 11301 | 11401 | 82207 |
| BN02 | 12232 | 12402 | 12450 | 12448 | 12302 | 10302 | 11299 | 11302 | 11402 | 82202 |
| BN03 | 12201 | 12401 | 12459 | 12478 | 12301 | 10320 | 11277 | 11303 | 11403 | 82219 |
| BN04 | 12202 | 12480 | 12421 | 12518 | 12327 | 10303 | 11278 | 11304 | 11404 | 82209 |
| BN05 | 12209 | 12486 | 12520 | 12522 | 12300 | 10326 | 11219 | 11305 | 11405 | 82210 |
| BN06 | 12208 | 12406 | 12420 | 12422 | 12313 | 10309 | 11279 | 11306 | 11406 | 82208 |
| BN07 | 12231 | 12411 | 12405 | 12489 | 12329 | 10323 | 11280 | 11307 | 11407 | 82204 |
| BN08 | 12205 | 12481 | 12485 | 12407 | 12328 | 10300 | 11229 | 11308 | 11408 | 82211 |
| BN09 | 12230 | 12513 | 12483 | 12514 | 12308 | 10304 | 11281 | 11309 | 11409 | 82215 |
| BN10 | 12214 | 12419 | 12488 | 12443 | 12305 | 10331 | 11282 | 11310 | 11410 | 82205 |
| BN11 | 12203 | 12437 | 12436 | 12484 | 12315 | 10308 | 11283 | 11311 | 11411 | 82218 |
| BN12 | 12212 | 12431 | 12404 | 12426 | 12330 | 10333 | 11284 | 11312 | 11412 | 82212 |
| BN13 | 12228 | 12469 | 12430 | 12424 | 12311 | 10313 | 11285 | 11313 | 11413 | 82213 |
| BN14 | 12229 | 12410 | 12526 | 12423 | 12312 | 10332 | 12201 | 11314 | 11414 | 82206 |
| BN15 | 12226 | 12442 | 12409 | 12515 | 12309 | 10306 | 11286 | 11315 | 11415 | 82214 |
| BN16 | 12213 | 12428 | 12445 | 12433 | 12304 | 10315 | 11287 | 11316 | 11416 | 82222 |
| BN17 | 12223 | 12444 | 12427 | 12432 | 12303 | 10324 | 11288 | 11317 | 11417 | 82225 |
| BN18 | 12215 | 12453 | 12468 | 12467 | 12324 | 10305 | 11289 | 11318 | 11418 | 82220 |
| BN19 | 12211 | 12434 | 12400 | 12470 | 12310 | 10318 | 11290 | 11319 | 11419 | 82201 |
| BN20 | 12224 | 12477 | 12439 | 12440 | 12326 | 10321 | 11241 | 11320 | 11420 | 82200 |
| BN21 | 12222 | 12461 | 12441 | 12476 | 12323 | 10330 | 11244 | 11321 | 11421 | 82227 |
| BN22 | 12210 | 12452 | 12460 | 12473 | 12316 | 10301 | 11291 | 11322 | 11422 | 82230 |
| BN23 | 12225 | 12454 | 12456 | 12455 | 12318 | 10325 | 11292 | 11323 | 11423 | 82226 |
| BN24 | 12219 | 12447 | 12425 | 12403 | 12319 | 10328 | 11293 | 11324 | 11424 | 82229 |
| BN25 | 12217 | 12446 | 12519 | 12464 | 12322 | 10312 | 11294 | 11325 | 11425 | 82216 |
| BN26 | 12220 | 12474 | 12465 | 12429 | 12325 | 10311 | 11295 | 11326 | 11426 | 82223 |
| BN27 | 12216 | 12449 | 12466 | 12538 | 12317 | 10319 | 11237 | 11327 | 11427 | 82228 |
| BN28 | 12218 | 12458 | 12463 | 12533 | 12320 | 10310 | 11273 | 11328 | 11428 | 82217 |
| BN29 | 12204 | 12462 | 12457 | 12438 | 12321 | 10317 | 11998 | 11329 | 11429 | 82231 |
| BN30 | 12227 | 12471 | 12534 | 12472 | 12331 | 10329 | 11999 | 11330 | 11430 | 82203 |
| Spare | 12200 | | | | | | | | | 82224 |

# 2.9. SERVICE STOCK

Most vehicles in this section are numbered in the former BR departmental number series. They are used for internal purposes within the railway industry, ie they do not generate revenue from outside the industry.

## BARRIER, ESCORT & TRANSLATOR VEHICLES

These vehicles are used to move multiple unit, HST and other vehicles around the national railway system.

**HST Barrier Vehicles.** Mark 1/2A. Renumbered from BR departmental series, or converted from various types. B4 bogies (* Commonwealth bogies).

**Non-standard livery:** 6340, 6344, 6346 All over dark blue.

**6330.** Mark 2A. Lot No. 30786 Derby 1968.
**6336/38/44.** Mark 1. Lot No. 30715 Gloucester 1962.
**6340.** Mark 1. Lot No. 30669 Swindon 1962.
**6346.** Mark 2A. Lot No. 30777 Derby 1967.
**6348.** Mark 1. Lot No. 30163 Pressed Steel 1957.

| | | | | | | |
|---|---|---|---|---|---|---|
| 6330 | (14084, 975629) | | **FB** | A | *GW* | LA |
| 6336 | (81591, 92185) | | **FB** | A | *GW* | LA |
| 6338 | (81581, 92180) | | **FB** | A | *GW* | LA |
| 6340 | (21251, 975678) | * | **0** | A | *EC* | EC |
| 6344 | (81263, 92080) | | **0** | A | *EC* | EC |
| 6346 | (9422) | | **0** | A | *EC* | EC |
| 6348 | (81233, 92963) | | **FB** | A | *GW* | LA |

**Mark 4 Barrier Vehicles.** Mark 2A/2C. Converted from Corridor First (*) or Open Brake Standard. B4 bogies.

**Non-standard livery:** 6358 All over dark blue.

**6352/53.** Mark 2A. Lot No. 30774 Derby 1968.
**6354/55.** Mark 2C. Lot No. 30820 Derby 1970.
**6358/59.** Mark 2A. Lot No. 30788 Derby 1968.

| | | | | | | |
|---|---|---|---|---|---|---|
| 6352 | (13465, 19465) | * | **GN** | E | *EC* | BN |
| 6353 | (13478, 19478) | * | **GN** | E | *EC* | BN |
| 6354 | (9459) | | **GN** | E | *EC* | BN |
| 6355 | (9477) | | **GN** | E | *EC* | BN |
| 6358 | (9432) | | **0** | E | *EC* | BN |
| 6359 | (9429) | | **GN** | E | *EC* | BN |

**EMU Translator Vehicles.** Mark 1. Converted 1980 from Restaurant Unclassified Opens. Commonwealth bogies.

Lot No. 30647 Wolverton 1959–61.

| | | | | | | |
|---|---|---|---|---|---|---|
| 6376 | (1021, 975973) | **PB** | P | *CS* | RU *(works with 6377)* |
| 6377 | (1042, 975975) | **PB** | P | *CS* | RU *(works with 6376)* |
| 6378 | (1054, 975971) | **PB** | P | *CS* | RU *(works with 6379)* |
| 6379 | (1059, 975972) | **PB** | P | *CS* | RU *(works with 6378)* |

**HST Barrier Vehicles**. Mark 1. Converted from Gangwayed Brake Vans in 1994–95. B4 bogies.

**6392**. Lot No. 30715 Gloucester 1962.
**6393/97**. Lot No. 30716 Gloucester 1962.
**6394**. Lot No. 30162 Pressed Steel 1956–57.
**6398/99**. Lot No. 30400 Pressed Steel 1957–58.

| | | | | |
|---|---|---|---|---|
| 6392 | (81588, 92183) | **PB** | P | *EM* | NL |
| 6393 | (81609, 92196) | **PB** | P | *EC* | EC |
| 6394 | (80878, 92906) | **P** | P | *EC* | EC |
| 6397 | (81600, 92190) | **PB** | P | *EM* | NL |
| 6398 | (81471, 92126) | **PB** | EM | *EM* | NL |
| 6399 | (81367, 92994) | **PB** | EM | *EM* | NL |

**Escort Coaches**. Converted from Mark 2A Open Brake Standards. These vehicles use the same bodyshell as the Mark 2A Corridor Brake First. B4 bogies.

**9419**. Lot No.30777 Derby 1970.
**9428**. Lot No.30820 Derby 1970.

| | | | | |
|---|---|---|---|---|
| 9419 | | **DS** | DR | *DR* | KM |
| 9428 | | **DS** | DR | *DR* | KM |

**Eurostar Barrier Vehicles**. Mark 1. Converted from General Utility Vans with bodies removed. Fitted with B4 bogies for use as Eurostar barrier vehicles.

**96380–381**. Lot No. 30417 Pressed Steel 1958–59.
**96383**. Lot No. 30565 Pressed Steel 1959.
**96384**. Lot No. 30616 Pressed Steel 1959–60.

| | | | | |
|---|---|---|---|---|
| 96380 | (86386, 6380) | **B** | EU | *EU* | TI |
| 96381 | (86187, 6381) | **B** | EU | *EU* | TI |
| 96383 | (86664, 6383) | **B** | EU | *EU* | TI |
| 96384 | (86955, 6384) | **B** | EU | *EU* | TI |

**EMU Translator Vehicles**. Converted from various Mark 1s.

**Non-standard livery**: All over blue.

**975864**. Lot No. 30054 Eastleigh 1951–54. Commonwealth bogies.
**975867**. Lot No. 30014 York 1950–51. Commonwealth bogies.
**975875**. Lot No. 30143 Charles Roberts 1954–55. Commonwealth bogies.
**975974/978**. Lot No. 30647 Wolverton 1959–61. B4 bogies.
**977087**. Lot No. 30229 Metro–Cammell 1955–57. Commonwealth bogies.

| | | | | | | | |
|---|---|---|---|---|---|---|---|
| 975864 | (3849) | **HB** | E | *GB* | PG | | *(works with 975867)* |
| 975867 | (1006) | **HB** | E | *GB* | PG | | *(works with 975864)* |
| 975875 | (34643) | **0** | E | *GB* | PG | | *(works with 977087)* |
| 975974 | (1030) | **AG** | A | *GB* | PG | Paschar | *(works with 975978)* |
| 975978 | (1025) | **AG** | A | *GB* | PG | Perpetiel | *(works with 975974)* |
| 977087 | (34971) | **0** | E | *GB* | PG | | *(works with 975875)* |

# LABORATORY, TESTING & INSPECTION COACHES

These coaches are used for research, development, testing and inspection on the national railway system. Many are fitted with sophisticated technical equipment.

**Plain Line Pattern Recognition Coaches.** Converted from BR Mark 2F Buffet First (*) or Open Standard. B4 bogies.

**1256.** Lot No. 30845 Derby 1973.
**5981.** Lot No. 30860 Derby 1973–74.

| | | | | | | |
|---|---|---|---|---|---|---|
| 1256 | (3296) | * | Y | NR | *DB* | ZA |
| 5981 | | | Y | NR | *DB* | ZA |

**Generator Vans.** Mark 1. Converted from BR Mark 1 Gangwayed Brake Vans. B5 bogies.

**6260.** Lot No. 30400 Pressed Steel 1957–58.
**6261.** Lot No. 30323 Pressed Steel 1957.
**6262.** Lot No. 30228 Metro-Cammell 1957–58.
**6263.** Lot No. 30163 Pressed Steel 1957.
**6264.** Lot No. 30173 York 1956.

| | | | | | |
|---|---|---|---|---|---|
| 6260 | (81450, 92116) | **NR** | NR | *DB* | ZA |
| 6261 | (81284, 92988) | Y | NR | *DB* | ZA |
| 6262 | (81064, 92928) | Y | NR | *DB* | ZA |
| 6263 | (81231, 92961) | Y | NR | *DB* | ZA |
| 6264 | (80971, 92923) | Y | NR | *DB* | ZA |

**Staff Coaches.** Mark 2D/2F. Converted from BR Mark 2D/2F Open Brake Standard. B4 bogies.

**9481.** Lot No. 30824 Derby 1971.
**9516/23.** Lot No. 30861 Derby 1974.

| | | | | |
|---|---|---|---|---|
| 9481 | Y | NR | *DB* | ZA |
| 9516 | Y | NR | *DB* | ZA |
| 9523 | Y | NR | *DB* | ZA |

**Driving Trailer Coaches.** Converted 2008 at Serco, Derby from Mark 2F Driving Open Brake Standards. Fitted with generator and modified to work in Blue Star push-pull mode. Disc brakes. B4 bogies.

**9701–08.** Lot No. 30861 Derby 1974. Converted to Driving Open Brake Standard Glasgow 1974.
**9714.** Lot No. 30861 Derby 1974. Converted to Driving Open Brake Standard Glasgow 1986.

| | | | | | |
|---|---|---|---|---|---|
| 9701 | (9528) | Y | NR | *DB* | ZA |
| 9702 | (9510) | Y | NR | *DB* | ZA |
| 9703 | (9517) | Y | NR | *DB* | ZA |
| 9708 | (9530) | Y | NR | *DB* | ZA |
| 9714 | (9536) | Y | NR | *DB* | ZA |

**Ultrasonic Test Coach**. Converted from Class 421 EMU MBSO.

**62287**. Lot No. 30808. York 1970. SR Mark 6 bogies.
**62384**. Lot No. 30816. York 1970. SR Mark 6 bogies.

| | | | | |
|---|---|---|---|---|
| 62287 | **Y** | NR | *DB* | ZA |
| 62384 | **Y** | NR | *DB* | ZA |

**Test Train Brake Force Runners**. Converted from Mark 2F Open Standard converted to Class 488/3 EMU TSOLH. These vehicles are included in test trains to provide brake force and are not used for any other purposes. Lot No. 30860 Derby 1973–74. B4 bogies.

| | | | | | |
|---|---|---|---|---|---|
| 72612 | (6156) | **Y** | NR | *DB* | ZA |
| 72616 | (6007) | **Y** | NR | *DB* | ZA |

**Structure Gauging Train Coach**. Converted from Mark 2F Open Standard converted to Class 488/3 EMU TSOLH. Lot No. 30860 Derby 1973–74. B4 bogies.

| | | | | | |
|---|---|---|---|---|---|
| 72630 | (6094) | **Y** | NR | *DB* | ZA *(works with 99666)* |

**Plain Line Pattern Recognition Coaches**. Converted from BR Mark 2F Open Standard converted to Class 488/3 EMU TSOLH. Lot No. 30860 Derby 1973–74. B4 bogies.

| | | | | | |
|---|---|---|---|---|---|
| 72631 | (6096) | **Y** | NR | *DB* | ZA |
| 72639 | (6070) | **Y** | NR | *DB* | ZA |

**Driving Trailer Coaches**. Converted from Mark 3B 110 mph Driving Brake Vans. Lot No. 31042 Derby 1988.

| | | | | |
|---|---|---|---|---|
| 82111 | **Y** | NR | | LB |
| 82124 | **Y** | NR | | ZA |
| 82129 | **Y** | NR | *DB* | ZA |
| 82145 | **Y** | NR | *DB* | ZA |

**Structure Gauging Train Coach**. Converted from BR Mark 2E Open First then converted to exhibition van. Lot No. 30843 Derby 1972–73. B4 bogies.

| | | | | | |
|---|---|---|---|---|---|
| 99666 | (3250) | **Y** | NR | *DB* | ZA *(works with 72630)* |

**Inspection Saloon**. Converted from Class 202 DEMU TRB at Stewarts Lane for use as a BR Southern Region General Manager's Saloon. Overhauled at FM Rail, Derby in 2004–05 for use as a New Trains Project Saloon. Can be used in push-pull mode with suitably equipped locomotives. Eastleigh 1958. SR Mark 4 bogies.

| | | | | | | |
|---|---|---|---|---|---|---|
| 975025 | (60755) | **G** | NR | *DB* | ZA | CAROLINE |

**Overhead Line Equipment Test Coach ("MENTOR")**. Converted from BR Mark 1 Corridor Brake Standard. Lot No. 30142 Gloucester 1954–55. Fitted with pantograph. B4 bogies.

| | | | | |
|---|---|---|---|---|
| 975091 | (34615) | **Y** | NR | *DB* | ZA |

**New Measurement Train Conference Coach**. Converted from prototype HST TF Lot No. 30848 Derby 1972. BT10 bogies.

| | | | | |
|---|---|---|---|---|
| 975814 | (11000, 41000) | **Y** | NR | *DB* | EC |

**New Measurement Train Lecture Coach**. Converted from prototype HST catering vehicle. Lot No. 30849 Derby 1972–73. BT10 bogies.

975984 (10000, 40000)          **Y**     NR     *DB*          EC

**Radio Survey Coach**. Converted from BR Mark 2E Open Standard. Lot No. 30844 Derby 1972–73. B4 bogies.

977868 (5846)          **Y**     NR     *DB*          ZA

**Winterisation Test Train Coach**. Converted from BR Mark 2E Open Standard. Lot No. 30844 Derby 1972–73. B4 bogies.

977869 (5858)          **Y**     NR     *DR*          ZA

**Track Recording Train Staff Coach**. Converted from Royal Household couchette Lot No. 30889, which in turn had been converted from BR Mark 2B Corridor Brake First. Lot No. 30790 Derby 1969. B5 bogies.

977969 (14112, 2906)          **Y**     NR     *DB*          ZA

**Track Inspection Train Coach**. Converted from BR Mark 2E Open Standard. Lot No. 30844 Derby 1972–73. B4 bogies.

977974  (5854)          **Y**     NR     *DB*          ZA

**Electrification Measurement Coach**. Converted from BR Mark 2F Open First converted to Class 488/2 EMU TFOH. Lot No. 30859 Derby 1973–74. B4 bogies.

977983  (3407, 72503)          **Y**     NR     *DB*          ZA

**New Measurement Train Staff Coach**. Converted from HST catering vehicle. Lot No. 30884 Derby 1976–77. BT10 bogies.

977984  (40501)          **Y**     P     *DB*          EC

**Structure Gauging Train Coaches**. Converted from Mark 2F Open Standard converted to Class 488/3 EMU TSOLH or from BR Mark 2D Open First subsequently declassified to Open Standard and then converted to exhibition van. B4 bogies.

**977985**. Lot No. 30860 Derby 1973–74.
**977986**. Lot No. 30821 Derby 1971.

977985  (6019, 72715)          **Y**     NR     *DB*          ZA *(works with 977986)*
977986  (3189, 99664)          **Y**     NR     *DB*          ZA *(works with 977985)*

**New Measurement Train Overhead Line Equipment Test Coach**. Converted from HST TGS. Lot No. 30949 Derby 1982. Fitted with pantograph. BT10 bogies.

977993  (44053)          **Y**     P     *DB*          EC

**New Measurement Train Track Recording Coach**. Converted from HST TGS. Lot No. 30949 Derby 1982. BT10 bogies.

977994  (44087)          **Y**     P     *DB*          EC

**New Measurement Train Coach.** Converted from HST catering vehicle. Lot No. 30921 Derby 1978–79. BT10 bogies. Fitted with generator.

| 977995 | (40719, 40619) | **Y** | P | *DB* | EC |
|--------|----------------|-------|---|------|-----|

**Radio Survey Coach.** Converted from Mark 2F Open Standard converted to Class 488/3 EMU TSOLH. Lot No. 30860 Derby 1973–74.

| 977997 | (72613, 6126) | **Y** | NR | *DB* | ZA |
|--------|---------------|-------|----|------|-----|

**Track Recording Coach.** Purpose built Mark 2. B4 bogies.

| 999550 | | **Y** | NR | *DB* | ZA |
|--------|--|-------|----|------|-----|

**Ultrasonic Test Coaches.** Converted from Class 421 EMU MBSO and Class 432 EMU MSO.

**999602/605.** Lot No. 30862 York 1974. SR Mk 6 bogies.
**999606.** Lot No. 30816. York 1970. SR Mk 6 bogies.

| 999602 | (62483) | **Y** | NR | *DB* | ZA |
|--------|---------|-------|----|------|-----|
| 999605 | (62482) | **Y** | NR | *DB* | ZA |
| 999606 | (62356) | **Y** | NR | *DB* | ZA |

# BREAKDOWN TRAIN COACHES

These coaches are formed in trains used for the recovery of derailed railway vehicles and were converted from BR Mark 1 Corridor Brake Standard and General Utility Van. The current use of each vehicle is given.

**971001/003/004.** Lot No. 30403 York/Glasgow 1958–60. Commonwealth bogies.
**971002.** Lot No. 30417 Pressed Steel 1958–59. Commonwealth bogies.
**975087.** Lot No. 30032 Wolverton 1951–52. BR Mark 1 bogies.
**975464.** Lot No. 30386 Charles Roberts 1956–58. Commonwealth bogies.
**975471.** Lot No. 30095 Wolverton 1953–55. Commonwealth bogies.
**975477.** Lot No. 30233 GRCW 1955–57. BR Mark 1 bogies.
**975486.** Lot No. 30025 Wolverton 1950–52. Commonwealth bogies.

| 971001 | (86560, 94150) | **Y** | NR | *DB* | BS | Tool & Generator Van |
|--------|----------------|-------|----|------|--------|----------------------|
| 971002 | (86624, 94190) | **Y** | NR | *DB* | SP | Tool Van |
| 971003 | (86596, 94191) | **Y** | NR | *DB* | BS | Tool Van |
| 971004 | (86194, 94168) | **Y** | NR | | Worksop | Tool Van |
| 975087 | (34289) | **Y** | NR | | Worksop | Tool & Generator Van |
| 975464 | (35171) | **Y** | NR | *DB* | SP | Staff Coach |
| 975471 | (34543) | **Y** | NR | *DB* | BS | Staff Coach |
| 975477 | (35108) | **Y** | NR | | Worksop | Staff Coach |
| 975486 | (34100) | **Y** | NR | *DB* | SP | Tool & Generator Van |

# INFRASTRUCTURE MAINTENANCE COACHES

### De-Icing Coaches

These coaches are used for removing ice from the conductor rail of DC lines. They were converted from Class 489 DMLVs that had originally been Class 414/3 DMBSOs.

Lot No. 30452 Ashford/Eastleigh 1959. Mk 4 bogies.

| | | | | | |
|---|---|---|---|---|---|
| 68501 | (61281) | **Y** | NR | *GB* | TW |
| 68504 | (61286) | **Y** | NR | *GB* | TW |
| 68505 | (61299) | **Y** | NR | *GB* | TW |

# INTERNAL USER VEHICLES

These vehicles are confined to yards and depots or do not normally move at all. Details are given of the internal user number (if allocated), type, former identity, current use and location. Many no longer see regular use.

975403 carries its original number 4598.

| | | | |
|---|---|---|---|
| 041379 | LMS CCT 35527 | Stores van | Leeman Road EY, York |
| 041947 | BR GUV 93425 | Stores van | IL |
| 042154 | BR GUV 93975 | Stores van | Ipswich Upper Yard |
| 061061 | BR CCT 94135 | Stores van | Oxford Station |
| 061223 | BR GUV 93714 | Stores van | Oxford Station |
| 083439 | BR CCT 94752 | Stores van | WD |
| 083602 | BR CCT 94494 | Stores van | Three Bridges Station |
| 083637 | BR NW 99203 | Stores van | SL |
| 083644 | BR Ferry Van 889201 | Stores van | EH |
| 083664 | BR Ferry Van 889203 | Stores van | EH |
| – | BR Open First 3186 | Instruction Coach | DY |
| – | BR Open First 3381 | Instruction Coach | HE |
| – | BR Open Standard 5636 | Instruction Coach | PM |
| – | BR BV 6360 | Barrier vehicle | NL |
| – | BR BV 6396 | Stores van | MA |
| – | BR RFKB 10256 | Instruction Coach | Yoker |
| – | BR RFKB 10260 | Instruction Coach | Yoker |
| – | BR BFK 17156 | Instruction Coach | DY |
| – | BR TSOLH 72614 | Instruction Coach | ZA |
| – | BR TSOLH 72615 | Instruction Coach | ZA |
| – | BR BG 92901 | Stores van | WB |
| – | BR NL 94003 | Stores van | OO |
| – | BR NL 94006 | Stores van | OO |
| – | BR NK 94121 | Stores van | TO |
| – | BR NB 94438 | Stores van | TO |
| – | BR GUV 96139 | Stores van | MA |
| – | BR Ferry Van 889200 | Stores van | SL |
| – | BR Ferry Van 889202 | Stores van | SL |
| – | BR Open Standard 975403 | Cinema Coach | PM |

**Abbreviations:**
BFK = Corridor Brake First                          BG = Gangwayed Brake Van
BV = Barrier Vehicle
CCT = Covered Carriage Truck (a 4-wheeled van similar to a GUV)
GUV = General Utility Van
NB = High Security Brake Van (converted from BG)
NK= High Security General Utility Van
NL = Newspaper Van (converted from a GUV)
NW = Bullion Van (converted from a Corridor Brake Standard)
RFKB = Kitchen Buffet First
TSOLH  = Trailer Standard Open with Lavatory and high density seating

# 9. COACHING STOCK AWAITING DISPOSAL

This list contains the last known locations of coaching stock awaiting disposal. The definition of which vehicles are "awaiting disposal" is somewhat vague, but generally speaking these are vehicles of types not now in normal service, those not expected to see further use or vehicles which have been damaged by fire, vandalism or collision.

| | | | | | | | |
|---|---|---|---|---|---|---|---|
| 1205 | ZA | 5463 | CS | 10554 | LM | 94106 | MH |
| 1252 | SH | 5478 | SH | 10588 | IS | 94116 | TY |
| 1253 | SH | 5487 | SH | 10647 | LM | 94137 | ME |
| 1258 | CS | 5491 | CS | 10681 | LM | 94147 | ME |
| 1644 | CS | 5569 | CS | 10682 | LM | 94153 | WE |
| 1650 | CS | 5737 | CS | 10701 | LM | 94160 | MH |
| 1652 | CS | 5740 | CS | 10709 | LM | 94166 | BS |
| 1655 | CS | 5756 | CS | 10710 | LM | 94170 | MH |
| 1658 | Totton | 5815 | SH | 10727 | LM | 94176 | BS |
| 1663 | CS | 5876 | SH | 10731 | LM | 94177 | TO |
| 1670 | CS | 5888 | SH | 11005 | LM | 94192 | ME |
| 1679 | EH | 5900 | CS | 12096 | ZN | 94195 | BS |
| 1680 | EH | 5903 | CS | 13306 | CS | 94196 | MH |
| 1696 | Totton | 5925 | SH | 13320 | CS | 94197 | BS |
| 2127 | CS | 5943 | SH | 13323 | CS | 94199 | MH |
| 3241 | CS | 5958 | SH | 13508 | BO | 94207 | TO |
| 3255 | Totton | 5978 | SH | 17168 | CS | 94208 | TO |
| 3269 | EH | 6009 | SH | 18756 | SH | 94213 | ME |
| 3303 | CE | 6029 | SH | 18767 | SH | 94214 | MH |
| 3309 | CS | 6041 | CS | 18808 | SH | 94217 | MH |
| 3338 | EH | 6045 | SH | 18862 | SH | 94221 | ME |
| 3368 | Totton | 6050 | CS | 34525 | CS | 94222 | MH |
| 3375 | EH | 6073 | SH | 40729 | NL | 94224 | CD |
| 3408 | CS | 6134 | SH | 41043 | ZB | 94225 | MH |
| 3414 | EH | 6151 | SH | 80211 | ZA | 94227 | Tees Yard |
| 3416 | CS | 6154 | SH | 80212 | CS | 94229 | MH |
| 4860 | CS | 6175 | SH | 80403 | CS | 94302 | TY |
| 4932 | CS | 6179 | CS | 80404 | CS | 94303 | TY |
| 4997 | CS | 6321 | NN | 84519 | CD | 94304 | MH |
| 5148 | TM | 6322 | NN | 92111 | CD | 94306 | TY |
| 5179 | TM | 6323 | NN | 92114 | ZA | 94308 | MH |
| 5183 | TM | 6324 | CP | 92159 | CS | 94310 | WE |
| 5186 | TM | 6325 | NN | 92303 | CD | 94311 | WE |
| 5193 | TM | 6361 | NL | 92400 | CD | 94313 | WE |
| 5194 | TM | 6364 | WH | 92908 | CS | 94316 | TO |
| 5221 | TM | 6365 | WH | 92929 | CD | 94317 | TO |
| 5331 | Totton | 9489 | CS | 92936 | CD | 94322 | MH |
| 5386 | Totton | 10201 | LM | 93723 | BY | 94323 | TY |
| 5420 | TM | 10245 | CS | 94101 | CS | 94326 | TY |
| 5453 | SH | 10540 | LM | 94104 | TO | 94332 | TY |

| | | | | | | | |
|---|---|---|---|---|---|---|---|
| 94333 | TY | 94476 | CD | 94541 | ME | 96604 | CF |
| 94334 | CD | 94479 | TO | 94542 | TY | 96605 | RU |
| 94335 | TY | 94482 | MH | 94543 | ME | 96606 | RU |
| 94336 | TY | 94488 | CD | 94544 | MH | 96607 | RU |
| 94337 | WE | 94490 | MH | 94545 | Tees Yard | 96608 | RU |
| 94338 | WE | 94492 | WE | 94546 | TY | 96609 | RU |
| 94340 | CD | 94495 | TY | 94547 | MH | 99019 | ZR |
| 94343 | MH | 94497 | ME | 94548 | TY | 889400 | ZA |
| 94344 | TO | 94498 | MH | 95300 | MH | 975081 | ZA |
| 94401 | MH | 94499 | CD | 95301 | MH | 975280 | ZA |
| 94406 | MH | 94501 | TO | 95400 | MH | 975454 | TO |
| 94408 | TY | 94504 | TY | 95410 | MH | 975484 | CS |
| 94410 | WE | 94512 | TY | 95727 | WE | 975639 | CS |
| 94412 | ME | 94514 | ME | 95754 | TY | 975681 | Portobello |
| 94413 | ME | 94515 | ** | 95761 | WE | 975682 | Portobello |
| 94416 | ME | 94517 | CD | 95763 | BS | 975685 | Portobello |
| 94420 | MH | 94518 | ME | 96110 | CS | 975686 | Portobello |
| 94422 | TO | 94519 | ME | 96132 | CS | 975687 | Portobello |
| 94423 | BS | 94520 | TY | 96135 | CS | 975688 | Portobello |
| 94427 | WE | 94521 | CD | 96164 | CS | 975918 | ME |
| 94428 | ME | 94522 | TY | 96165 | CS | 975920 | Portobello |
| 94429 | Tees Yard | 94525 | TY | 96170 | CS | 975991 | CD |
| 94431 | MH | 94526 | TY | 96178 | CS | 977077 | ** |
| 94432 | ME | 94527 | TY | 96182 | CS | 977085 | BO |
| 94433 | MH | 94528 | ME | 96191 | CS | 977095 | CS |
| 94434 | TY | 94529 | CD | 96192 | CS | 977111 | ** |
| 94435 | TO | 94530 | ME | 96371 | WB | 977112 | ** |
| 94440 | ME | 94531 | TY | 96372 | LM | 977618 | BY |
| 94445 | WE | 94534 | ME | 96373 | LM | 977989 | ZA |
| 94450 | WE | 94536 | ME | 96374 | ZB | 977990 | ZA |
| 94451 | WE | 94538 | CD | 96375 | LM | 999508 | ZA |
| 94462 | CD | 94539 | MH | 96602 | RU | | |
| 94463 | TY | 94540 | TJ | 96603 | CF | DS 70220 | ** |
| 94470 | TO | | | | | | |

** Other locations:

| | |
|---|---|
| 94515 | Eastleigh East Yard |
| 977077 | Ripple Lane Yard |
| 977111 | Ripple Lane Yard |
| 977112 | Ripple Lane Yard |
| DS 70220 | Western Trading Estate Siding, North Acton |

# 3. DIESEL MULTIPLE UNITS

# INTRODUCTION

## DMU CLASSES

DMU Classes are listed in class number order. Principal details and dimensions are quoted for each class in metric and/or imperial units as considered appropriate bearing in mind common usage in Great Britain.

All dimensions and weights are quoted for vehicles in an "as new" condition with all necessary supplies (eg oil, water, sand) on board. Dimensions are quoted in the order Length – Width. All lengths are quoted over buffers or couplers as appropriate. Where two lengths are quoted, the first refers to outer vehicles in a set and the second to inner vehicles. All width dimensions quoted are maxima. All weights are shown as metric tonnes (t = tonnes).

## NUMERICAL LISTINGS

DMUs are listed in numerical order of set – using current numbers as allocated by the RSL. Individual "loose" vehicles are listed in numerical order after vehicles formed into fixed formations. Where sets or vehicles have been renumbered in recent years, former numbering detail is shown in parentheses. Each entry is laid out as in the following example:

| RSL Set No. | Detail | Livery | Owner | Operator | Depot | Formation | Name |
|---|---|---|---|---|---|---|---|
| 153 309 | cr | **GA** | P | *EA* | NC | 52309 | GERALD FIENNES |

**Detail Differences**. Detail differences which currently affect the areas and types of train which vehicles may work are shown, plus differences in interior layout. Where such differences occur within a class, these are shown either in the heading information or alongside the individual set or vehicle number. The following standard abbreviations are used:

e European Railway Traffic Management System (ERTMS) signalling equipment fitted.

r Radio Electric Token Block signalling equipment fitted.

Use of the above abbreviations indicates the equipment fitted is normally operable. Meaning of non-standard abbreviations is detailed in individual class headings.

**Set Formations**. Regular set formations are shown where these are normally maintained. Readers should note set formations might be temporarily varied from time to time to suit maintenance and/or operational requirements. Vehicles shown as "Spare" are not formed in any regular set formation.

**Codes.** Codes are used to denote the livery, owner, operation and depot of each unit. Details of these will be found in section 6 of this book. Where a unit or spare car is off-lease, the operator column is left blank.

**Names.** Only names carried with official sanction are listed. Names are shown in UPPER/lower case characters as actually shown on the name carried on the vehicle(s). Unless otherwise shown, complete units are regarded as named rather than just the individual car(s) which carry the name.

# GENERAL INFORMATION

## CLASSIFICATION AND NUMBERING

First generation ("Heritage") DMUs were classified in the series 100–139.
Parry People Movers (not technically DMUs) are classified in the series 139.
Second generation DMUs are classified in the series 140–199.
Diesel-electric multiple units are classified in the series 200–249.
Service units are classified in the series 930–999.

First and second generation individual cars are numbered in the series 50000–59999 and 79000–79999.

Parry People Mover cars are numbered in the 39000 series.

DEMU individual cars are numbered in the series 60000–60999, except for a few former EMU vehicles which retain their EMU numbers.

Service stock individual cars are numbered in the series 975000–975999 and 977000–977999, although this series is not exclusively used for DMU vehicles.

## OPERATING CODES

These codes are used by train operating company staff to describe the various different types of vehicles and normally appear on data panels on the inner (ie non driving) ends of vehicles.

The first part of the code describes whether or not the car has a motor or a driving cab as follows:

DM  Driving motor.
M   Motor
DT  Driving trailer
T   Trailer

The next letter is a "B" for cars with a brake compartment.

This is followed by the saloon details:

F   First
S   Standard
C   Composite
so  denotes a semi-open vehicle (part compartments, part open). All other vehicles are assumed to consist solely of open saloons.

L denotes a vehicle with a toilet.
W denotes a wheelchair space.

Finally vehicles with a buffet or kitchen area are suffixed RB or RMB for a miniature buffet counter.

Where two vehicles of the same type are formed within the same unit, the above codes may be suffixed by (A) and (B) to differentiate between the vehicles.

A composite is a vehicle containing both First and Standard Class accommodation, whilst a brake vehicle is a vehicle containing separate specific accommodation for the conductor.

Where vehicles have been declassified, the correct operating code which describes the actual vehicle layout is quoted in this publication.

# BUILD DETAILS

**Lot Numbers**
Vehicles ordered under the auspices of BR were allocated a lot (batch) number when ordered and these are quoted in class headings and sub-headings.

**Builders**
These are shown in class headings. Abbreviations used are found in section 7.7.

Information on sub-contracting works which built parts of vehicles eg the underframes etc is not shown.

# ACCOMMODATION

The information given in class headings and sub-headings is in the form F/S nT (or TD) nW. For example 12/54 1T 1W denotes 12 First Class and 54 Standard Class seats, one toilet and one space for a wheelchair. A number in brackets (ie (2)) denotes tip-up seats (in addition to the fixed seats). Tip-up seats in vestibules do not count. The seating layout of open saloons is shown as 2+1, 2+2 or 3+2 as the case may be. Where units have First Class accommodation as well as Standard Class and the layout is different for each class then these are shown separately prefixed by "1:" and "2:". TD denotes a toilet suitable for use by a disabled person.

# 3.1. DIESEL MECHANICAL & DIESEL HYDRAULIC UNITS

## 3.1.1 FIRST GENERATION UNITS

## CLASS 121                  PRESSED STEEL SUBURBAN

First generation units. One set is used on weekdays by Chiltern Railways on peak-hour Aylesbury–Princes Risborough services.
**Construction:** Steel.
**Engines:** Two Leyland 1595 of 112 kW (150 hp) at 1800 rpm.
**Transmission:** Mechanical. Cardan shaft and freewheel to a four-speed epicyclic gearbox and final drive.
**Bogies:** DD10.
**Brakes:** Vacuum.
**Couplers:** Screw.
**Dimensions:** 20.45 x 2.82 m.
**Gangways:** Non gangwayed single cars with cabs at each end.
**Wheel arrangement:** 1-A + A-1.
**Doors:** Manually-operated slam.
**Maximum Speed:** 70 mph.
**Seating Layout:** 3+2 facing.
**Multiple Working:** "Blue Square" coupling code. First Generation vehicles cannot be coupled to Second Generation units.

Fitted with central door locking.

121 020 formerly in departmental use as unit 960 002 (977722).

121 034 returned to use with Chiltern Railways in 2011. Formerly in departmental use as 977828.

**Non-standard livery:** 121 020 All over Chiltern blue with a silver stripe.

**DMBS.** Lot No. 30518 1960–61. –/65. 38.0 t.

| | | | | | |
|---|---|---|---|---|---|
| 121 020 | **O** | CR | *CR* | AL | 55020 |
| 121 034 | **G** | CR | *CR* | AL | 55034 |

# 3.1.2 PARRY PEOPLE MOVERS

## CLASS 139                                                    PPM-60

Gas/flywheel hybrid drive Railcars used on the Stourbridge Junction–Stourbridge Town branch.

**Body construction:** Stainless steel framework.
**Chassis construction:** Welded mild steel box section.
**Primary Drive:** Ford MVH420 2.3 litre 64 kW (86 hp) LPG fuel engine driving through Newage marine gearbox, Tandler bevel box and 4 "V" belt driver to flywheel.
**Flywheel Energy Store:** 500 kg, 1 m diameter, normal operational speed range 1000–1500 rpm.
**Final transmission:** 4 "V" belt driver from flywheel to Tandler bevel box, Linde hydrostatic transmission and spiral bevel gearbox at No. 2 end axle.
**Braking:** Normal service braking by regeneration to flywheel (1 m/s/s); emergency/parking braking by sprung-on, air-off disc brakes (3 m/s/s).
**Maximum Speed:** 45 mph.
**Dimensions:** 8.7 x 2.4 m.
**Doors:** Deans powered doors, double-leaf folding (one per side).
**Seating Layout:** 1+1 unidirectional/facing.
**Multiple Working:** Not applicable.

**39001–002. DMS.** Main Road Sheet Metal, Leyland 2007–08. –/17(4) 1W. 12.5 t.

| | | | | | |
|---|---|---|---|---|---|
| 139 001 | **LM** | P | *LM* | SJ | 39001 |
| 139 002 | **LM** | P | *LM* | SJ | 39002 |

# 3.1.3 SECOND GENERATION UNITS

All units in this section have air brakes and are equipped with public address, with transmission equipment on driving vehicles and flexible diaphragm gangways. Except where otherwise stated, transmission is Voith 211r hydraulic with a cardan shaft to a Gmeinder GM190 final drive.

## CLASS 142          PACER          BREL DERBY/LEYLAND

DMS–DMSL.

**Construction:** Steel underframe, rivetted steel body and roof. Built from Leyland National bus parts on Leyland Bus four-wheeled underframes.
**Engines:** One Cummins LT10-R of 165 kW (225 hp) at 1950 rpm.
**Couplers:** BSI at outer ends, bar within unit.
**Dimensions:** 15.55 x 2.80 m.
**Gangways:** Within unit only.
**Doors:** Twin-leaf inward pivoting.
**Wheel Arrangement:** 1-A + A-1.
**Maximum Speed:** 75 mph.
**Seating Layout:** 3+2 mainly unidirectional bus/bench style unless stated.
**Multiple Working:** Within class and with Classes 143, 144, 150, 153, 155, 156, 158 and 159.

c Refurbished Arriva Trains Wales units. Fitted with 2+2 individual Chapman seating.
s Fitted with 2+2 individual high-back seating.
t Former First North Western facelifted units – DMS fitted with a luggage/bicycle rack and wheelchair space.
u Merseytravel units – Fitted with 3+2 individual low-back seating.

**55542–591. DMS.** Lot No. 31003 1985–86. –/62 (c –/46(6) 2W, s –/56, t –/53 or 55 1W, u –/52 or 54 1W). 24.5 t.
**55592–641. DMSL.** Lot No. 31004 1985–86. –/59 1T (c –/44(6) 1T 2W, s –/50 1T, u –/60 1T). 25.0 t.
**55701–746. DMS.** Lot No. 31013 1986–87. –/62 (c –/46(6) 2W, s –/56, t –/53 or 55 1W, u –/52 or 54 1W). 24.5 t.
**55747–792. DMSL.** Lot No. 31014 1986–87. –/59 1T (c –/44(6) 1T 2W, s –/50 1T, u –/60 1T). 25.0 t.

| | | | | | | |
|---|---|---|---|---|---|---|
| 142 001 | t | **NO** | A | *NO* | NH | 55542 | 55592 |
| 142 002 | c | **AV** | A | *AW* | CF | 55543 | 55593 |
| 142 003 |   | **NO** | A | *NO* | NH | 55544 | 55594 |
| 142 004 | t | **NO** | A | *NO* | NH | 55545 | 55595 |
| 142 005 | t | **NO** | A | *NO* | NH | 55546 | 55596 |
| 142 006 | c | **AV** | A | *AW* | CF | 55547 | 55597 |
| 142 007 | t | **NO** | A | *NO* | NH | 55548 | 55598 |
| 142 009 | t | **NO** | A | *NO* | HT | 55550 | 55600 |
| 142 010 | c | **AV** | A | *AW* | CF | 55551 | 55601 |
| 142 011 | t | **NO** | A | *NO* | NH | 55552 | 55602 |
| 142 012 | t | **NO** | A | *NO* | NH | 55553 | 55603 |
| 142 013 |   | **NO** | A | *NO* | NH | 55554 | 55604 |
| 142 014 | t | **NO** | A | *NO* | NH | 55555 | 55605 |
| 142 015 | s | **NO** | A | *NO* | HT | 55556 | 55606 |
| 142 016 | s | **NO** | A | *NO* | HT | 55557 | 55607 |
| 142 017 | s | **NO** | A | *NO* | HT | 55558 | 55608 |
| 142 018 | s | **NO** | A | *NO* | HT | 55559 | 55609 |
| 142 019 | s | **NO** | A | *NO* | HT | 55560 | 55610 |
| 142 020 | s | **NO** | A | *NO* | HT | 55561 | 55611 |
| 142 021 | s | **NO** | A | *NO* | HT | 55562 | 55612 |
| 142 022 | s | **NO** | A | *NO* | HT | 55563 | 55613 |
| 142 023 | t | **NO** | A | *NO* | HT | 55564 | 55614 |
| 142 024 | s | **NO** | A | *NO* | HT | 55565 | 55615 |
| 142 025 | s | **NO** | A | *NO* | HT | 55566 | 55616 |
| 142 026 | s | **NO** | A | *NO* | HT | 55567 | 55617 |
| 142 027 | t | **NO** | A | *NO* | HT | 55568 | 55618 |
| 142 028 | t | **NO** | A | *NO* | NH | 55569 | 55619 |
| 142 029 |   | **NO** | A | *NO* | HT | 55570 | 55620 |
| 142 030 |   | **NO** | A | *NO* | NH | 55571 | 55621 |
| 142 031 | t | **NO** | A | *NO* | NH | 55572 | 55622 |
| 142 032 | t | **NO** | A | *NO* | NH | 55573 | 55623 |
| 142 033 | t | **NO** | A | *NO* | NH | 55574 | 55624 |
| 142 034 | t | **NO** | A | *NO* | NH | 55575 | 55625 |
| 142 035 | t | **NO** | A | *NO* | NH | 55576 | 55626 |
| 142 036 | t | **NO** | A | *NO* | NH | 55577 | 55627 |
| 142 037 | t | **NO** | A | *NO* | NH | 55578 | 55628 |

| | | | | | | | |
|---|---|---|---|---|---|---|---|
| 142 038 | t | **NO** | A | *NO* | NH | 55579 | 55629 |
| 142 039 | t | **NO** | A | *NO* | NH | 55580 | 55630 |
| 142 040 | t | **NO** | A | *NO* | NH | 55581 | 55631 |
| 142 041 | u | **NO** | A | *NO* | NH | 55582 | 55632 |
| 142 042 | u | **NO** | A | *NO* | NH | 55583 | 55633 |
| 142 043 | u | **NO** | A | *NO* | NH | 55584 | 55634 |
| 142 044 | u | **NO** | A | *NO* | NH | 55585 | 55635 |
| 142 045 | u | **NO** | A | *NO* | NH | 55586 | 55636 |
| 142 046 | u | **NO** | A | *NO* | NH | 55587 | 55637 |
| 142 047 | u | **NO** | A | *NO* | NH | 55588 | 55638 |
| 142 048 | u | **NO** | A | *NO* | NH | 55589 | 55639 |
| 142 049 | u | **NO** | A | *NO* | NH | 55590 | 55640 |
| 142 050 | s | **NO** | A | *NO* | HT | 55591 | 55641 |
| 142 051 | u | **NO** | A | *NO* | NH | 55701 | 55747 |
| 142 052 | u | **NO** | A | *NO* | NH | 55702 | 55748 |
| 142 053 | u | **NO** | A | *NO* | NH | 55703 | 55749 |
| 142 054 | u | **NO** | A | *NO* | NH | 55704 | 55750 |
| 142 055 | u | **NO** | A | *NO* | NH | 55705 | 55751 |
| 142 056 | u | **NO** | A | *NO* | NH | 55706 | 55752 |
| 142 057 | u | **NO** | A | *NO* | NH | 55707 | 55753 |
| 142 058 | u | **NO** | A | *NO* | NH | 55708 | 55754 |
| 142 060 | t | **NO** | A | *NO* | NH | 55710 | 55756 |
| 142 061 | t | **NO** | A | *NO* | NH | 55711 | 55757 |
| 142 062 | t | **NO** | A | *NO* | NH | 55712 | 55758 |
| 142 063 | t | **NO** | A | *NO* | NH | 55713 | 55759 |
| 142 064 | t | **NO** | A | *NO* | HT | 55714 | 55760 |
| 142 065 | s | **NO** | A | *NO* | HT | 55715 | 55761 |
| 142 066 | s | **NO** | A | *NO* | HT | 55716 | 55762 |
| 142 067 | | **NO** | A | *NO* | HT | 55717 | 55763 |
| 142 068 | t | **NO** | A | *NO* | HT | 55718 | 55764 |
| 142 069 | c | **AV** | A | *AW* | CF | 55719 | 55765 |
| 142 070 | t | **NO** | A | *NO* | HT | 55720 | 55766 |
| 142 071 | s | **NO** | A | *NO* | HT | 55721 | 55767 |
| 142 072 | c | **AV** | A | *AW* | CF | 55722 | 55768 |
| 142 073 | c | **AV** | A | *AW* | CF | 55723 | 55769 |
| 142 074 | c | **AV** | A | *AW* | CF | 55724 | 55770 |
| 142 075 | c | **AV** | A | *AW* | CF | 55725 | 55771 |
| 142 076 | c | **AV** | A | *AW* | CF | 55726 | 55772 |
| 142 077 | c | **AV** | A | *AW* | CF | 55727 | 55773 |
| 142 078 | s | **NO** | A | *NO* | HT | 55728 | 55774 |
| 142 079 | s | **NO** | A | *NO* | HT | 55729 | 55775 |
| 142 080 | c | **AV** | A | *AW* | CF | 55730 | 55776 |
| 142 081 | c | **AV** | A | *AW* | CF | 55731 | 55777 |
| 142 082 | c | **AV** | A | *AW* | CF | 55732 | 55778 |
| 142 083 | c | **AV** | A | *AW* | CF | 55733 | 55779 |
| 142 084 | s | **NO** | A | *NO* | HT | 55734 | 55780 |
| 142 085 | c | **AV** | A | *AW* | CF | 55735 | 55781 |
| 142 086 | s | **NO** | A | *NO* | HT | 55736 | 55782 |
| 142 087 | s | **NO** | A | *NO* | HT | 55737 | 55783 |
| 142 088 | s | **NO** | A | *NO* | HT | 55738 | 55784 |
| 142 089 | s | **NO** | A | *NO* | HT | 55739 | 55785 |

| | | | | | | | | |
|---|---|---|---|---|---|---|---|---|
| 142 090 | s | **NO** | A | *NO* | HT | 55740 | 55786 | |
| 142 091 | s | **NO** | A | *NO* | HT | 55741 | 55787 | |
| 142 092 | s | **NO** | A | *NO* | HT | 55742 | 55788 | |
| 142 093 | s | **NO** | A | *NO* | HT | 55743 | 55789 | |
| 142 094 | s | **NO** | A | *NO* | HT | 55744 | 55790 | |
| 142 095 | s | **NO** | A | *NO* | HT | 55745 | 55791 | |
| 142 096 | s | **NO** | A | *NO* | HT | 55746 | 55792 | |

# CLASS 143    PACER    ALEXANDER/BARCLAY

DMS–DMSL. Similar design to Class 142, but bodies built by W Alexander with Barclay underframes.

**Construction:** Steel underframe, aluminium alloy body and roof. Alexander bus bodywork on four-wheeled underframes.
**Engines:** One Cummins LT10-R of 165 kW (225 hp) at 1950 rpm.
**Couplers:** BSI at outer ends, bar within unit.
**Dimensions:** 15.45 x 2.80 m.
**Gangways:** Within unit only.        **Wheel Arrangement:** 1-A + A-1.
**Doors:** Twin-leaf inward pivoting.    **Maximum Speed:** 75 mph.
**Seating Layout:** 2+2 high-back Chapman seating, mainly unidirectional.
**Multiple Working:** Within class and with Classes 142, 144, 150, 153, 155, 156, 158 and 159.

**DMS.** Lot No. 31005 Andrew Barclay 1985–86. –/48(6) 2W. 24.0 t.
**DMSL.** Lot No. 31006 Andrew Barclay 1985–86. –/44(6) 1T 2W. 24.5 t.

| | | | | | | | |
|---|---|---|---|---|---|---|---|
| 143 601 | **AV** | MG | *AW* | CF | 55642 | 55667 | |
| 143 602 | **AV** | P | *AW* | CF | 55651 | 55668 | |
| 143 603 | **FI** | P | *GW* | EX | 55658 | 55669 | |
| 143 604 | **AV** | P | *AW* | CF | 55645 | 55670 | |
| 143 605 | **AW** | P | *AW* | CF | 55646 | 55671 | |
| 143 606 | **AV** | P | *AW* | CF | 55647 | 55672 | |
| 143 607 | **AV** | P | *AW* | CF | 55648 | 55673 | |
| 143 608 | **AV** | P | *AW* | CF | 55649 | 55674 | |
| 143 609 | **AV** | SG | *AW* | CF | 55650 | 55675 | Sir Tom Jones |
| 143 610 | **AV** | MG | *AW* | CF | 55643 | 55676 | |
| 143 611 | **FI** | P | *GW* | EX | 55652 | 55677 | |
| 143 612 | **FI** | P | *GW* | EX | 55653 | 55678 | |
| 143 614 | **AV** | MG | *AW* | CF | 55655 | 55680 | |
| 143 616 | **AV** | P | *AW* | CF | 55657 | 55682 | |
| 143 617 | **FI** | FW | *GW* | EX | 55644 | 55683 | |
| 143 618 | **FI** | FW | *GW* | EX | 55659 | 55684 | |
| 143 619 | **FI** | FW | *GW* | EX | 55660 | 55685 | |
| 143 620 | **FI** | P | *GW* | EX | 55661 | 55686 | |
| 143 621 | **FI** | P | *GW* | EX | 55662 | 55687 | |
| 143 622 | **AV** | P | *AW* | CF | 55663 | 55688 | |
| 143 623 | **AV** | P | *AW* | CF | 55664 | 55689 | |
| 143 624 | **AW** | P | *AW* | CF | 55665 | 55690 | |
| 143 625 | **AV** | P | *AW* | CF | 55666 | 55691 | |

# CLASS 144    PACER    ALEXANDER/BREL DERBY

DMS–DMSL or DMS–MS–DMSL. As Class 143, but underframes built by BREL.

**Construction:** Steel underframe, aluminium alloy body and roof. Alexander bus bodywork on four-wheeled underframes.
**Engines:** One Cummins LT10-R of 165 kW (225 hp) at 1950 rpm.
**Couplers:** BSI at outer ends, bar within unit.
**Dimensions:** 15.45/15.43 x 2.80 m.
**Gangways:** Within unit only.      **Wheel Arrangement:** 1-A + A-1.
**Doors:** Twin-leaf inward pivoting.      **Maximum Speed:** 75 mph.
**Seating Layout:** 2+2 high-back Richmond seating, mainly unidirectional.
**Multiple Working:** Within class and with Classes 142, 143, 150, 153, 155, 156, 158 and 159.

**DMS.** Lot No. 31015 BREL Derby 1986–87. –/45(3) 1W 24.0 t.
**MS.** Lot No. BREL Derby 31037 1987. –/58. 23.5 t.
**DMSL.** Lot No. BREL Derby 31016 1986–87. –/41(3) 1T. 24.5 t.

| | | | | | | |
|---|---|---|---|---|---|---|
| 144 001 | **NO** | P | *NO* | NL | 55801 | | 55824 |
| 144 002 | **NO** | P | *NO* | NL | 55802 | | 55825 |
| 144 003 | **NO** | P | *NO* | NL | 55803 | | 55826 |
| 144 004 | **NO** | P | *NO* | NL | 55804 | | 55827 |
| 144 005 | **NO** | P | *NO* | NL | 55805 | | 55828 |
| 144 006 | **NO** | P | *NO* | NL | 55806 | | 55829 |
| 144 007 | **NO** | P | *NO* | NL | 55807 | | 55830 |
| 144 008 | **NO** | P | *NO* | NL | 55808 | | 55831 |
| 144 009 | **NO** | P | *NO* | NL | 55809 | | 55832 |
| 144 010 | **NO** | P | *NO* | NL | 55810 | | 55833 |
| 144 011 | **NO** | P | *NO* | NL | 55811 | | 55834 |
| 144 012 | **NO** | P | *NO* | NL | 55812 | | 55835 |
| 144 013 | **NO** | P | *NO* | NL | 55813 | | 55836 |
| 144 014 | **NO** | P | *NO* | NL | 55814 | 55850 | 55837 |
| 144 015 | **NO** | P | *NO* | NL | 55815 | 55851 | 55838 |
| 144 016 | **NO** | P | *NO* | NL | 55816 | 55852 | 55839 |
| 144 017 | **NO** | P | *NO* | NL | 55817 | 55853 | 55840 |
| 144 018 | **NO** | P | *NO* | NL | 55818 | 55854 | 55841 |
| 144 019 | **NO** | P | *NO* | NL | 55819 | 55855 | 55842 |
| 144 020 | **NO** | P | *NO* | NL | 55820 | 55856 | 55843 |
| 144 021 | **NO** | P | *NO* | NL | 55821 | 55857 | 55844 |
| 144 022 | **NO** | P | *NO* | NL | 55822 | 55858 | 55845 |
| 144 023 | **NO** | P | *NO* | NL | 55823 | 55859 | 55846 |

**Name:** 144 001 THE PENISTONE LINE PARTNERSHIP

# CLASS 150/0    SPRINTER    BREL YORK

DMSL–MS–DMS. Prototype Sprinter.

**Construction:** Steel.
**Engines:** One Cummins NT855R5 of 213 kW (285 hp) at 2100 rpm.
**Bogies:** BX8P (powered), BX8T (non-powered).
**Couplers:** BSI at outer end of driving vehicles, bar non-driving ends.

**Dimensions:** 19.93/19.92 x 2.73 m.
**Gangways:** Within unit only.
**Doors:** Twin-leaf sliding.
**Seating Layout:** 3+2 (mainly unidirectional).
**Wheel Arrangement:** 2-B + 2-B + B-2.
**Maximum Speed:** 75 mph.
**Multiple Working:** Within class and with Classes 142, 143, 144, 153, 155, 156, 158, 159, 170 and 172.

**DMSL.** Lot No. 30984 1984. –/72 1T. 35.4 t.
**MS.** Lot No. 30986 1984. –/92. 35.0 t.
**DMS.** Lot No. 30985 1984. –/69(6). 34.7 t.

| | | | | | | | |
|---|---|---|---|---|---|---|---|
| 150 001 | **FB** | A | *GW* | RG | 55200 | 55400 | 55300 |
| 150 002 | **FB** | A | *GW* | RG | 55201 | 55401 | 55301 |

# CLASS 150/1      SPRINTER      BREL YORK

DMSL–DMS.

**Construction:** Steel.
**Engines:** One Cummins NT855R5 of 213 kW (285 hp) at 2100 rpm.
**Bogies:** BP38 (powered), BT38 (non-powered).
**Couplers:** BSI.
**Dimensions:** 19.74 x 2.82 m.
**Gangways:** Within unit only.
**Doors:** Twin-leaf sliding.
**Seating Layout:** 3+2 facing as built but Centro units were reseated with mainly unidirectional seating.
**Wheel Arrangement:** 2-B (+ 2-B) + B-2.
**Maximum Speed:** 75 mph.
**Multiple Working:** Within class and with Classes 142, 143, 144, 153, 155, 156, 158, 159, 170 and 172.

c   3+2 Chapman seating.

**DMSL.** Lot No. 31011 1985–86. –/72 1T (c –/59 1TD (except 52144 which is –/62 1TD), t –/71 1T, u –/71 1T). 38.3 t.
**DMS.** Lot No. 31012 1985–86. –/76 (c –/65, t –/73, u –/70 (6)). 38.1 t.

| | | | | | | | |
|---|---|---|---|---|---|---|---|
| 150 101 | u | **FB** | A | *GW* | PM | 52101 | 57101 |
| 150 102 | u | **FB** | A | *GW* | PM | 52102 | 57102 |
| 150 103 | u | **NO** | A | *NO* | NH | 52103 | 57103 |
| 150 104 | u | **FB** | A | *GW* | PM | 52104 | 57104 |
| 150 105 | u | **LM** | A | *LM* | TS | 52105 | 57105 |
| 150 106 | u | **FB** | A | *GW* | PM | 52106 | 57106 |
| 150 107 | u | **LM** | A | *LM* | TS | 52107 | 57107 |
| 150 108 | u | **FB** | A | *GW* | PM | 52108 | 57108 |
| 150 109 | u | **LM** | A | *LM* | TS | 52109 | 57109 |
| 150 110 | u | **NO** | A | *NO* | NH | 52110 | 57110 |
| 150 111 | u | **NO** | A | *NO* | NH | 52111 | 57111 |
| 150 112 | u | **NO** | A | *NO* | NH | 52112 | 57112 |
| 150 113 | u | **NO** | A | *NO* | NH | 52113 | 57113 |
| 150 114 | u | **NO** | A | *NO* | NH | 52114 | 57114 |
| 150 115 | u | **NO** | A | *NO* | NH | 52115 | 57115 |
| 150 116 | u | **NO** | A | *NO* | NH | 52116 | 57116 |
| 150 117 | u | **NO** | A | *NO* | NH | 52117 | 57117 |
| 150 118 | u | **NO** | A | *NO* | NH | 52118 | 57118 |

▲ Northern-liveried 142 024 arrives at Doncaster with the 15.19 Scunthorpe–Lincoln (via Sheffield) on 09/08/13. **Robert Pritchard**

▼ Arriva Trains-liveried 143 610 leaves Cardiff Queen Street on 17/10/2012 with the 10.45 Coryton–Radyr City Line service. **Robert Pritchard**

▲ Northern-liveried 144 023 and 142 089 passes Rotherham Parkgate with the 17.48 Leeds–Sheffield on 01/08/13.  **Robert Pritchard**

▼ London Midland has kept three Class 150s, one of which is used on the Bedford–Bletchley line. On 06/06/13 150 105 arrives at Kempston Hardwicke with the 16.37 Bedford–Bletchley.  **Alisdair Anderson**

▲ In the new Arriva Trains Wales/Welsh Government livery 150 213 and 158 833 stand at Cardiff Central after arrival with the 13.29 from Fishguard Harbour on 05/04/13.
**Robert Pritchard**

▲ First Great Western plain blue-liveried 153 361 is coupled to "Local Lines"-liveried 153 370 as they pass Powderham Crossing with the 14.30 Exeter St Davids–Paignton on 27/04/13. **Tony Christie**

▼ Northern-liveried 155 341 and 153 358 pass Horbury with the 07.43 Selby–Wakefield Westgate on 19/03/10. **Andrew Wills**

▲ Greater Anglia-liveried 156 402 passes Haddiscoe Marina with the 15.50 Lowestoft–Norwich on 06/07/13. This unit was the first of Greater Anglia's nine 156s to have interior modifications to comply with the 2020 accessibility regulations, including fitting a new universal access toilet. **Peter Weber**

▲ ScotRail Saltire-liveried 158 786 pauses at Springburn with the 12.52 Glasgow Queen Street–Cumbernauld on 23/05/13. **Alexander Colley**

▼ First Great Western "Dynamic Lines"-liveried 165 112 leads a 5-car Turbo formation through Twyford cutting with the 08.11 Oxford–Paddington on 19/07/13. **Neil Gibson**

▲ CrossCountry-liveried 170 105 pauses at Melton Mowbray with the 10.22 Birmingham New Street–Stansted Airport on 26/06/13 as 170 522 leaves with the 09.21 Stansted–Birmingham. **Paul Biggs**

▼ Southern-liveried 171 728 pauses at Rye with the 11.32 Brighton–Ashford International on 15/08/13. **Nigel Gibbs**

▲ Chiltern Railways has a small fleet of four 172s. On 25/08/13 172 104 is paired with a Class 168 as it passes West Ruislip with the 10.40 Birmingham Snow Hill–London Marylebone. **Antony Guppy**

▼ London Midland's 172s have end gangway connections. 172 331 passes Bissell Wood, near Blakedown, with the 11.39 Whitlocks End–Kidderminster on 03/03/12. **Chris Wilson**

▲ Arriva Trains-liveried 175 007 leaves Llanelli with the 13.10 Milford Haven–Manchester Piccadilly on 04/04/13. **Robert Pritchard**

▼ Grand Central 180 105 arrives at Doncaster with the 15.37 Bradford Interchange–London King's Cross on 15/04/13. **Robert Pritchard**

▲ TransPennine Express 185 132 arrives at Sheffield with the 15.26 Cleethorpes–Manchester Airport on 01/08/13. **Robert Pritchard**

▼ CrossCountry-liveried 220 020 leaves Derby with the 14.36 Newcastle–Reading on 25/08/13. **Robert Pritchard**

▲ Virgin Trains Voyager 221 112 passes Greenfoot with a diverted 15.40 Edinburgh–
Birmingham New Street on 25/05/13.                                    **Robin Ralston**

▼ East Midlands Trains Meridian 222 020 passes Archer Road in Sheffield with
the 11.47 Sheffield–London St Pancras on 26/01/13.            **Robert Pritchard**

▲ Network Rail Track Assessment Unit 950 001 is seen at Cossington on the Midland Main Line with a trip from Derby to Bedford on 04/06/13. **Mick Tindall**

▼ Network Rail Plasser & Theurer 09-3X-Dynamic Tamper DR 73116 is seen near Alsager heading south on 19/07/13. **Cliff Beeton**

▲ Amey Infrastructure Services Plasser & Theurer 08-16/4x4C80-RT Tamper DR 73922 passes Chelmscote working from Warrington Bank Quay to Watford Junction on 04/07/13. **Mark Beal**

▼ Swietelsky Babcock Rail Plasser & Theurer 08-4x4/RS-RT Tamper DR 73940 passes Barrow-upon-Soar on 01/09/13 working from Burton-upon-Trent to Syston North Junction. **Paul Biggs**

▲ Volker Rail Matisa B 45 UE Tamper DR 75301 heads north from York on 18/01/12.                                                                    **Robert Pritchard**

▼ Volker Rail Matisa R 24 S Ballast Regulator DR 77801 passes Colton Junction on its way from York to Seamer via Hull on 05/04/12.          **Gavin Morrison**

▲ Cowans Sheldon Self-Propelled Heavy Duty Twin Jib Track Relayer DRC 78226 lowers a track panel at Ashchurch on 13/01/13 during a possession to relay S&C turnouts. **John Stretton**

▼ Harsco Track Technologies RGH20C Rail Grinding Train DR 79272+DR 79262 passes Wolverton heading north on 28/03/13. **Robert Pritchard**

▲ A Network Rail Overhead Line Equipment Renewal train, formed of Windhoff Multi Purpose Vehicle DR 98003 (on the rear) and DR 98010 leading is seen at Bradwell on its way from Ingatestone to Crewe on 29/04/13. **Mark Beal**

▼ Network Rail Cowans Sheldon 75-tonne Diesel Hydraulic (telescopic) Breakdown Crane ADRC 96713 is seen north of Barrow-upon-Soar engaged in recovering a derailed freight train on 05/01/13. **Robert Pritchard**

| | | | | | | | |
|---|---|---|---|---|---|---|---|
| 150 119 | u | **NO** | A | *NO* | NH | 52119 | 57119 |
| 150 120 | t | **FB** | A | *GW* | EX | 52120 | 57120 |
| 150 122 | u | **FB** | A | *GW* | EX | 52122 | 57122 |
| 150 123 | t | **FB** | A | *GW* | EX | 52123 | 57123 |
| 150 124 | u | **FB** | A | *GW* | EX | 52124 | 57124 |
| 150 125 | u | **FB** | A | *GW* | EX | 52125 | 57125 |
| 150 126 | u | **FB** | A | *GW* | EX | 52126 | 57126 |
| 150 128 | t | **FB** | A | *GW* | EX | 52128 | 57128 |
| 150 129 | t | **FB** | A | *GW* | EX | 52129 | 57129 |
| 150 130 | t | **FB** | A | *GW* | EX | 52130 | 57130 |
| 150 131 | t | **FB** | A | *GW* | EX | 52131 | 57131 |
| 150 132 | u | **NO** | A | *NO* | NH | 52132 | 57132 |
| 150 133 | c | **NO** | A | *NO* | NH | 52133 | 57133 |
| 150 134 | c | **NO** | A | *NO* | NH | 52134 | 57134 |
| 150 135 | c | **NO** | A | *NO* | NH | 52135 | 57135 |
| 150 136 | c | **NO** | A | *NO* | NH | 52136 | 57136 |
| 150 137 | c | **NO** | A | *NO* | NH | 52137 | 57137 |
| 150 138 | c | **NO** | A | *NO* | NH | 52138 | 57138 |
| 150 139 | c | **NO** | A | *NO* | NH | 52139 | 57139 |
| 150 140 | c | **NO** | A | *NO* | NH | 52140 | 57140 |
| 150 141 | c | **NO** | A | *NO* | NH | 52141 | 57141 |
| 150 142 | c | **NO** | A | *NO* | NH | 52142 | 57142 |
| 150 143 | c | **NO** | A | *NO* | NH | 52143 | 57143 |
| 150 144 | c | **NO** | A | *NO* | NH | 52144 | 57144 |
| 150 145 | c | **NO** | A | *NO* | NH | 52145 | 57145 |
| 150 146 | c | **NO** | A | *NO* | NH | 52146 | 57146 |
| 150 147 | c | **NO** | A | *NO* | NH | 52147 | 57147 |
| 150 148 | c | **NO** | A | *NO* | NH | 52148 | 57148 |
| 150 149 | c | **NO** | A | *NO* | NH | 52149 | 57149 |
| 150 150 | c | **NO** | A | *NO* | NH | 52150 | 57150 |

**Names:**

| | |
|---|---|
| 150 125 | THE HEART OF WESSEX LINE |
| 150 129 | Devon & Cornwall RAIL PARTNERSHIP |
| 150 130 | Severnside Community Rail Partnership |

## CLASS 150/2    SPRINTER    BREL YORK

DMSL–DMS.

**Construction:** Steel.
**Engines:** One Cummins NT855R5 of 213 kW (285 hp) at 2100 rpm.
**Bogies:** BP38 (powered), BT38 (non-powered).
**Couplers:** BSI.
**Dimensions:** 19.74 x 2.82 m.
**Gangways:** Throughout.
**Doors:** Twin-leaf sliding.
**Wheel Arrangement:** 2-B + B-2.
**Maximum Speed:** 75 mph.
**Seating Layout:** 3+2 mainly unidirectional seating as built, but most units have now been refurbished with new 2+2 seating.
**Multiple Working:** Within class and with Classes 142, 143, 144, 153, 155, 156, 158, 159, 170 and 172.

c  3+2 Chapman seating (former First North Western units).
p  Refurbished Arriva Trains Wales units with 2+2 Primarius seating.
v  Units refurbished for Valley Lines with 2+2 Chapman seating.
w  Units refurbished for First Great Western with 2+2 Chapman seating.

**Northern promotional vinyls:**

150 203/205/207/215/218/222/223/225/228/268–271/273–277 Welcome
to Yorkshire.
150 272 R&B Festival week, Colne.

**DMSL.** Lot No. 31017 1986–87. † –/68 1T 1W, c –/62 1TD, p –/60(4) 1T, u –/71
1T), v –/60(8) 1T, w –/60(8) 1T. 37.5 t.
**DMS.** Lot No. 31018 1986–87. † –/71(3), c –/70, p –/56(10) 1W, u –/70(6),
v –/56(15) 2W, w –/56(17) 2W, z –/68. 36.5 t.

| 150 201 | c | **N0** | A | *NO* | NH | 52201 | 57201 |
|---------|---|--------|---|------|----|-------|-------|
| 150 202 | u | **FB** | A | *GW* | PM | 52202 | 57202 |
| 150 203 | c | **N0** | A | *NO* | NH | 52203 | 57203 |
| 150 204 | u | **N0** | A | *NO* | NH | 52204 | 57204 |
| 150 205 | c | **N0** | A | *NO* | NH | 52205 | 57205 |
| 150 206 | u | **N0** | A | *NO* | NH | 52206 | 57206 |
| 150 207 | c | **N0** | A | *NO* | NH | 52207 | 57207 |
| 150 208 | p | **AV** | P | *AW* | CF | 52208 | 57208 |
| 150 210 | u | **N0** | A | *NO* | NH | 52210 | 57210 |
| 150 211 | c | **N0** | A | *NO* | NH | 52211 | 57211 |
| 150 213 | p | **AW** | P | *AW* | CF | 52213 | 57213 |
| 150 214 | u | **N0** | A | *NO* | NH | 52214 | 57214 |
| 150 215 | c | **N0** | A | *NO* | NH | 52215 | 57215 |
| 150 216 | u | **FB** | A | *GW* | PM | 52216 | 57216 |
| 150 217 | p | **AV** | P | *AW* | CF | 52217 | 57217 |
| 150 218 | c | **N0** | A | *NO* | NH | 52218 | 57218 |
| 150 219 | w | **FI** | P | *GW* | PM | 52219 | 57219 |
| 150 220 | u | **N0** | A | *NO* | NH | 52220 | 57220 |
| 150 221 | w | **FI** | P | *GW* | PM | 52221 | 57221 |
| 150 222 | c | **N0** | A | *NO* | NH | 52222 | 57222 |
| 150 223 | c | **N0** | A | *NO* | NH | 52223 | 57223 |
| 150 224 | c | **N0** | A | *NO* | NH | 52224 | 57224 |
| 150 225 | c | **N0** | A | *NO* | NH | 52225 | 57225 |
| 150 226 | u | **N0** | A | *NO* | NH | 52226 | 57226 |
| 150 227 | p | **AV** | P | *AW* | CF | 52227 | 57227 |
| 150 228 | † | **N0** | P | *NO* | NH | 52228 | 57228 |
| 150 229 | p | **AV** | P | *AW* | CF | 52229 | 57229 |
| 150 230 | w | **AV** | P | *AW* | CF | 52230 | 57230 |
| 150 231 | p | **AV** | P | *AW* | CF | 52231 | 57231 |
| 150 232 | w | **FI** | P | *GW* | PM | 52232 | 57232 |
| 150 233 | w | **FI** | P | *GW* | PM | 52233 | 57233 |
| 150 234 | w | **FI** | P | *GW* | PM | 52234 | 57234 |
| 150 235 | p | **AV** | P | *AW* | CF | 52235 | 57235 |
| 150 236 | w | **AW** | P | *AW* | CF | 52236 | 57236 |
| 150 237 | p | **AW** | P | *AW* | CF | 52237 | 57237 |
| 150 238 | w | **FI** | P | *GW* | PM | 52238 | 57238 |
| 150 239 | w | **FI** | P | *GW* | PM | 52239 | 57239 |

| | | | | | | | |
|---|---|---|---|---|---|---|---|
| 150 240 | w | **AV** | P | AW | CF | 52240 | 57240 |
| 150 241 | w | **AV** | P | AW | CF | 52241 | 57241 |
| 150 242 | w | **AV** | P | AW | CF | 52242 | 57242 |
| 150 243 | w | **FI** | P | GW | PM | 52243 | 57243 |
| 150 244 | w | **FI** | P | GW | PM | 52244 | 57244 |
| 150 245 | p | **AV** | P | AW | CF | 52245 | 57245 |
| 150 246 | w | **FI** | P | GW | PM | 52246 | 57246 |
| 150 247 | w | **FI** | P | GW | PM | 52247 | 57247 |
| 150 248 | w | **FI** | P | GW | PM | 52248 | 57248 |
| 150 249 | w | **FI** | P | GW | PM | 52249 | 57249 |
| 150 250 | p | **AW** | P | AW | CF | 52250 | 57250 |
| 150 251 | w | **AW** | P | AW | CF | 52251 | 57251 |
| 150 252 | p | **AV** | P | AW | CF | 52252 | 57252 |
| 150 253 | w | **AW** | P | AW | CF | 52253 | 57253 |
| 150 254 | w | **AV** | P | AW | CF | 52254 | 57254 |
| 150 255 | p | **AW** | P | AW | CF | 52255 | 57255 |
| 150 256 | p | **AV** | P | AW | CF | 52256 | 57256 |
| 150 257 | p | **AW** | P | AW | CF | 52257 | 57257 |
| 150 258 | p | **AV** | P | AW | CF | 52258 | 57258 |
| 150 259 | p | **AV** | P | AW | CF | 52259 | 57259 |
| 150 260 | p | **AV** | P | AW | CF | 52260 | 57260 |
| 150 261 | w | **FI** | P | GW | PM | 52261 | 57261 |
| 150 262 | p | **AV** | P | AW | CF | 52262 | 57262 |
| 150 263 | w | **FI** | P | GW | PM | 52263 | 57263 |
| 150 264 | p | **AV** | P | AW | CF | 52264 | 57264 |
| 150 265 | w | **FI** | P | GW | PM | 52265 | 57265 |
| 150 266 | w | **FI** | P | GW | PM | 52266 | 57266 |
| 150 267 | v | **AV** | P | AW | CF | 52267 | 57267 |
| 150 268 | † | **NO** | P | NO | NH | 52268 | 57268 |
| 150 269 | † | **NO** | P | NO | NH | 52269 | 57269 |
| 150 270 | † | **NO** | P | NO | NH | 52270 | 57270 |
| 150 271 | † | **NO** | P | NO | NH | 52271 | 57271 |
| 150 272 | † | **NO** | P | NO | NH | 52272 | 57272 |
| 150 273 | † | **NO** | P | NO | NH | 52273 | 57273 |
| 150 274 | † | **NO** | P | NO | NH | 52274 | 57274 |
| 150 275 | † | **NO** | P | NO | NH | 52275 | 57275 |
| 150 276 | † | **NO** | P | NO | NH | 52276 | 57276 |
| 150 277 | † | **NO** | P | NO | NH | 52277 | 57277 |
| 150 278 | v | **AW** | P | AW | CF | 52278 | 57278 |
| 150 279 | v | **AW** | P | AW | CF | 52279 | 57279 |
| 150 280 | v | **AV** | P | AW | CF | 52280 | 57280 |
| 150 281 | v | **AW** | P | AW | CF | 52281 | 57281 |
| 150 282 | v | **AV** | P | AW | CF | 52282 | 57282 |
| 150 283 | p | **AV** | P | AW | CF | 52283 | 57283 |
| 150 284 | p | **AW** | P | AW | CF | 52284 | 57284 |
| 150 285 | p | **AV** | P | AW | CF | 52285 | 57285 |

# CLASS 150/9      SPRINTER      BREL YORK

3-car First Great Western hybrids formed of a Class 150/1 with a 150/2 centre vehicle. DMSL–DMS–DMS. For details see Class 150/1 or Class 150/2.

| | | | | | | | |
|---|---|---|---|---|---|---|---|
| 150 921 | u | **FB** | A | *GW* | PM | 52121 57212 57121 |
| 150 927 | u | **FB** | A | *GW* | PM | 52127 57209 57127 |

# CLASS 153      SUPER SPRINTER      LEYLAND BUS

DMSL. Converted by Hunslet-Barclay, Kilmarnock from Class 155 2-car units.

**Construction:** Steel underframe, rivetted steel body and roof. Built from Leyland National bus parts on Leyland Bus bogied underframes.
**Engine:** One Cummins NT855R5 of 213 kW (285 hp) at 2100 rpm.
**Bogies:** One P3-10 (powered) and one BT38 (non-powered).
**Couplers:** BSI.
**Dimensions:** 23.21 x 2.70 m.
**Gangways:** Throughout.                    **Wheel Arrangement:** 2-B.
**Doors:** Single-leaf sliding plug.         **Maximum Speed:** 75 mph.
**Seating Layout:** 2+2 facing/unidirectional.
**Multiple Working:** Within class and with Classes 142, 143, 144, 150, 155, 156, 158, 159, 170 and 172.

Cars numbered in the 573xx series were renumbered by adding 50 to their original number so that the last two digits correspond with the set number.

† Uprated Cummins engine fitted (231 kW – 310 hp)
c Chapman seating.
d Richmond seating.

**52301–52335. DMSL.** Lot No. 31026 1987–88. Converted under Lot No. 31115 1991–92. –/72(3) 1T 1W. (s –/72 1T 1W, t –/72(2) 1T 1W). 41.2 t.
**57301–57335. DMSL.** Lot No. 31027 1987–88. Converted under Lot No. 31115 1991–92. –/72(3) 1T 1W (s –/72 1T 1W). 41.2 t.

| | | | | | | | |
|---|---|---|---|---|---|---|---|
| 153 301 | d | **NO** | A | *NO* | NL | 52301 | |
| 153 302 | c | **EM** | A | *EM* | NM | 52302 | |
| 153 303 | c | **AW** | A | *AW* | CF | 52303 | |
| 153 304 | ds | **NO** | A | *NO* | NL | 52304 | |
| 153 305 | d | **FI** | A | *GW* | EX | 52305 | |
| 153 306 | cr | **GA** | P | *GA* | NC | 52306 | |
| 153 307 | d | **NO** | A | *NO* | NL | 52307 | |
| 153 308 | c | **EM** | A | *EM* | NM | 52308 | |
| 153 309 | cr | **GA** | P | *GA* | NC | 52309 | GERARD FIENNES |
| 153 310 | c | **EM** | P | *EM* | NM | 52310 | |
| 153 311 | c | **EM** | P | *EM* | NM | 52311 | |
| 153 312 | s | **AV** | A | *AW* | CF | 52312 | |
| 153 313 | cs | **EM** | P | *EM* | NM | 52313 | |
| 153 314 | cr | **1** | P | *GA* | NC | 52314 | |
| 153 315 | ds | **NO** | A | *NO* | NL | 52315 | |
| 153 316 | c | **NO** | P | *NO* | NL | 52316 | |
| 153 317 | ds | **NO** | A | *NO* | NL | 52317 | |

| | | | | | | |
|---|---|---|---|---|---|---|
| 153 318 | d | **FI** | A | *GW* | EX | 52318 |
| 153 319 | c | **EM** | A | *EM* | NM | 52319 |
| 153 320 | †c | **AV** | P | *AW* | CF | 52320 |
| 153 321 | ct | **EM** | P | *EM* | NM | 52321 |
| 153 322 | cr | **GA** | P | *GA* | NC | 52322 | BENJAMIN BRITTEN |
| 153 323 | c | **AV** | P | *AW* | CF | 52323 |
| 153 324 | c | **NO** | P | *NO* | NL | 52324 |
| 153 325 | c | **LM** | P | *GW* | EX | 52325 |
| 153 326 | c | **EM** | P | *EM* | NM | 52326 |
| 153 327 | c | **AV** | A | *AW* | CF | 52327 |
| 153 328 | ds | **NO** | A | *NO* | NL | 52328 |
| 153 329 | c | **FB** | P | *GW* | EX | 52329 |
| 153 330 | cs | **NO** | P | *NO* | NL | 52330 |
| 153 331 | d | **NO** | A | *NO* | NL | 52331 |
| 153 332 | c | **NO** | P | *NO* | NL | 52332 |
| 153 333 | cs | **LM** | P | *GW* | EX | 52333 |
| 153 334 | ct | **LM** | P | *LM* | TS | 52334 |
| 153 335 | cr | **GA** | P | *GA* | NC | 52335 | MICHAEL PALIN |
| 153 351 | d | **NO** | A | *NO* | NL | 57351 |
| 153 352 | ds | **NO** | A | *NO* | NL | 57352 |
| 153 353 | c | **AW** | A | *AW* | CF | 57353 |
| 153 354 | c | **LM** | P | *LM* | TS | 57354 |
| 153 355 | c | **EM** | A | *EM* | NM | 57355 |
| 153 356 | c | **LM** | P | *LM* | TS | 57356 |
| 153 357 | c | **EM** | A | *EM* | NM | 57357 |
| 153 358 | c | **NO** | P | *NO* | NL | 57358 |
| 153 359 | c | **NO** | P | *NO* | NL | 57359 |
| 153 360 | c | **NO** | P | *NO* | NL | 57360 |
| 153 361 | cs | **FB** | P | *GW* | EX | 57361 |
| 153 362 | cs | **AV** | A | *AW* | CF | 57362 | Dylan Thomas 1914–1953 |
| 153 363 | cs | **NO** | P | *NO* | NL | 57363 |
| 153 364 | c | **LM** | P | *LM* | TS | 57364 |
| 153 365 | c | **LM** | P | *LM* | TS | 57365 |
| 153 366 | c | **LM** | P | *LM* | TS | 57366 |
| 153 367 | cs | **AV** | P | *AW* | CF | 57367 |
| 153 368 | d | **FI** | A | *GW* | EX | 57368 |
| 153 369 | c | **FB** | P | *GW* | EX | 57369 |
| 153 370 | d | **FI** | A | *GW* | EX | 57370 |
| 153 371 | c | **LM** | P | *LM* | TS | 57371 |
| 153 372 | d | **FI** | A | *GW* | EX | 57372 |
| 153 373 | d | **FI** | A | *GW* | EX | 57373 |
| 153 374 | c | **EM** | A | *EM* | NM | 57374 |
| 153 375 | c | **LM** | P | *LM* | TS | 57375 |
| 153 376 | c | **EM** | P | *EM* | NM | 57376 |
| 153 377 | d | **FI** | A | *GW* | EX | 57377 |
| 153 378 | d | **NO** | A | *NO* | NL | 57378 |
| 153 379 | c | **EM** | P | *EM* | NM | 57379 |
| 153 380 | d | **FI** | A | *GW* | EX | 57380 |
| 153 381 | c | **EM** | P | *EM* | NM | 57381 |
| 153 382 | d | **FI** | A | *GW* | EX | 57382 |
| 153 383 | c | **EM** | P | *EM* | NM | 57383 |

| 153 384 | c | **EM** | P | *EM* | NM | 57384 |
| 153 385 | c | **EM** | P | *EM* | NM | 57385 |

---

# CLASS 155   SUPER SPRINTER           LEYLAND BUS

DMSL–DMS.

**Construction:** Steel underframe, rivetted steel body and roof. Built from
Leyland National bus parts on Leyland Bus bogied underframes.
**Engines:** One Cummins NT855R5 of 213 kW (285 hp) at 2100 rpm.
**Bogies:** One P3-10 (powered) and one BT38 (non-powered).
**Couplers:** BSI.
**Dimensions:** 23.21 x 2.70 m.
**Gangways:** Throughout.          **Wheel Arrangement:** 2-B + B-2.
**Doors:** Single-leaf sliding plug.   **Maximum Speed:** 75 mph.
**Seating Layout:** 2+2 facing/unidirectional Chapman seating.
**Multiple Working:** Within class and with Classes 142, 143, 144, 150, 153,
156, 158, 159, 170 and 172.

**Northern promotional vinyls:**

155 341–347 Leeds–Bradford–Manchester route (the "Calder Valley").

**DMSL.** Lot No. 31057 1988. –/76 1TD 1W. 39.0 t.
**DMS.** Lot No. 31058 1988. –/80. 38.6 t.

| 155 341 | **NO** | P | *NO* | NL | 52341 | 57341 |
| 155 342 | **NO** | P | *NO* | NL | 52342 | 57342 |
| 155 343 | **NO** | P | *NO* | NL | 52343 | 57343 |
| 155 344 | **NO** | P | *NO* | NL | 52344 | 57344 |
| 155 345 | **NO** | P | *NO* | NL | 52345 | 57345 |
| 155 346 | **NO** | P | *NO* | NL | 52346 | 57346 |
| 155 347 | **NO** | P | *NO* | NL | 52347 | 57347 |

---

# CLASS 156   SUPER SPRINTER   METRO-CAMMELL

DMSL–DMS.

**Construction:** Steel.
**Engines:** One Cummins NT855R5 of 213 kW (285 hp) at 2100 rpm.
**Bogies:** One P3-10 (powered) and one BT38 (non-powered).
**Couplers:** BSI.
**Dimensions:** 23.03 x 2.73 m.
**Gangways:** Throughout.          **Wheel Arrangement:** 2-B + B-2.
**Doors:** Single-leaf sliding.     **Maximum Speed:** 75 mph.
**Seating Layout:** 2+2 facing/unidirectional.
**Multiple Working:** Within class and with Classes 142, 143, 144, 150, 153,
155, 158, 159, 170 and 172.

† Greater Anglia units fitted with new universal access toilet as part of the 2020 accessibility regulations.
c  Chapman seating.
d  Richmond seating.

**Northern promotional vinyls:**

| | |
|---|---|
| 156 441 | Manchester and Liverpool |
| 156 448 | Hadrians Wall Country (Newcastle–Carlisle line). |
| 156 461 | Ravenglass & Eskdale Railway. |
| 156 464 | Lancashire DalesRail |
| 156 484 | Settle & Carlisle line. |
| 156 490 | National Railway Museum. |

**DMSL.** Lot No. 31028 1988–89. –/74 1TD 1W (* –/72, c & t –/70, u –/68, † –/62 1TD 2W). 38.6 t.
**DMS.** Lot No. 31029 1987–89. –/76 (d –/78, † –/74, t & u –/72). 36.1 t.

| | | | | | | |
|---|---|---|---|---|---|---|
| 156 401 | c* | **EM** | P | *EM* | DY | 52401 | 57401 |
| 156 402 | †cr | **GA** | P | *GA* | NC | 52402 | 57402 |
| 156 403 | c* | **EM** | P | *EM* | DY | 52403 | 57403 |
| 156 404 | c* | **EM** | P | *EM* | DY | 52404 | 57404 |
| 156 405 | c* | **EM** | P | *EM* | DY | 52405 | 57405 |
| 156 406 | c* | **EM** | P | *EM* | DY | 52406 | 57406 |
| 156 407 | †cr | **GA** | P | *GA* | NC | 52407 | 57407 |
| 156 408 | c* | **EM** | P | *EM* | DY | 52408 | 57408 |
| 156 409 | †cr | **GA** | P | *GA* | NC | 52409 | 57409 |
| 156 410 | c* | **EM** | P | *EM* | DY | 52410 | 57410 |
| 156 411 | c* | **EM** | P | *EM* | DY | 52411 | 57411 |
| 156 412 | †cr | **GA** | P | *GA* | NC | 52412 | 57412 |
| 156 413 | c* | **EM** | P | *EM* | DY | 52413 | 57413 |
| 156 414 | c* | **EM** | P | *EM* | DY | 52414 | 57414 |
| 156 415 | c* | **EM** | P | *EM* | DY | 52415 | 57415 |
| 156 416 | cr | **1** | P | *GA* | NC | 52416 | 57416 |
| 156 417 | cr | **1** | P | *GA* | NC | 52417 | 57417 |
| 156 418 | †cr | **GA** | P | *GA* | NC | 52418 | 57418 |
| 156 419 | †cr | **GA** | P | *GA* | NC | 52419 | 57419 |
| 156 420 | c | **NO** | P | *NO* | AN | 52420 | 57420 |
| 156 421 | c | **NO** | P | *NO* | AN | 52421 | 57421 |
| 156 422 | †cr | **GA** | P | *GA* | NC | 52422 | 57422 |
| 156 423 | c | **NO** | P | *NO* | AN | 52423 | 57423 |
| 156 424 | c | **NO** | P | *NO* | AN | 52424 | 57424 |
| 156 425 | c | **NO** | P | *NO* | AN | 52425 | 57425 |
| 156 426 | c | **NO** | P | *NO* | AN | 52426 | 57426 |
| 156 427 | c | **NO** | P | *NO* | AN | 52427 | 57427 |
| 156 428 | c | **NO** | P | *NO* | AN | 52428 | 57428 |
| 156 429 | c | **NO** | P | *NO* | AN | 52429 | 57429 |
| 156 430 | t | **SR** | A | *SR* | CK | 52430 | 57430 |
| 156 431 | t | **SR** | A | *SR* | CK | 52431 | 57431 |
| 156 432 | t | **SR** | A | *SR* | CK | 52432 | 57432 |
| 156 433 | t | **SR** | A | *SR* | CK | 52433 | 57433 |
| 156 434 | t | **SR** | A | *SR* | CK | 52434 | 57434 |
| 156 435 | t | **SR** | A | *SR* | CK | 52435 | 57435 |

| 156 436 | †  | **SR** | A | *SR* | CK | 52436 | 57436 |
| 156 437 | t  | **SR** | A | *SR* | CK | 52437 | 57437 |
| 156 438 | d  | **NO** | A | *NO* | HT | 52438 | 57438 |
| 156 439 | t  | **SR** | A | *SR* | CK | 52439 | 57439 |
| 156 440 | c  | **NO** | P | *NO* | AN | 52440 | 57440 |
| 156 441 | c  | **NO** | P | *NO* | AN | 52441 | 57441 |
| 156 442 | t  | **SR** | A | *SR* | CK | 52442 | 57442 |
| 156 443 | d  | **NO** | A | *NO* | HT | 52443 | 57443 |
| 156 444 | d  | **NO** | A | *NO* | HT | 52444 | 57444 |
| 156 445 | u  | **SR** | A | *SR* | CK | 52445 | 57445 |
| 156 446 | t  | **FS** | A | *SR* | CK | 52446 | 57446 |
| 156 447 | ru | **FS** | A | *SR* | CK | 52447 | 57447 |
| 156 448 | d  | **NO** | A | *NO* | HT | 52448 | 57448 |
| 156 449 | u  | **FS** | A | *SR* | CK | 52449 | 57449 |
| 156 450 | ru | **FS** | A | *SR* | CK | 52450 | 57450 |
| 156 451 | d  | **NO** | A | *NO* | HT | 52451 | 57451 |
| 156 452 | c  | **NO** | P | *NO* | AN | 52452 | 57452 |
| 156 453 | ru | **FS** | A | *SR* | CK | 52453 | 57453 |
| 156 454 | d  | **NO** | A | *NO* | HT | 52454 | 57454 |
| 156 455 | c  | **NO** | P | *NO* | AN | 52455 | 57455 |
| 156 456 | rt | **FS** | A | *SR* | CK | 52456 | 57456 |
| 156 457 | rt | **FS** | A | *SR* | CK | 52457 | 57457 |
| 156 458 | rt | **FS** | A | *SR* | CK | 52458 | 57458 |
| 156 459 | c  | **NO** | P | *NO* | AN | 52459 | 57459 |
| 156 460 | c  | **NO** | P | *NO* | AN | 52460 | 57460 |
| 156 461 | c  | **NO** | P | *NO* | AN | 52461 | 57461 |
| 156 462 |    | **FS** | A | *SR* | CK | 52462 | 57462 |
| 156 463 | d  | **NO** | A | *NO* | HT | 52463 | 57463 |
| 156 464 | c  | **NO** | P | *NO* | AN | 52464 | 57464 |
| 156 465 | ru | **FS** | A | *SR* | CK | 52465 | 57465 |
| 156 466 | c  | **NO** | P | *NO* | AN | 52466 | 57466 |
| 156 467 | r  | **FS** | A | *SR* | CK | 52467 | 57467 |
| 156 468 | d  | **NO** | A | *NO* | AN | 52468 | 57468 |
| 156 469 | d  | **NO** | A | *NO* | HT | 52469 | 57469 |
| 156 470 | c  | **EM** | A | *EM* | DY | 52470 | 57470 |
| 156 471 | d  | **NO** | A | *NO* | AN | 52471 | 57471 |
| 156 472 | d  | **NO** | A | *NO* | AN | 52472 | 57472 |
| 156 473 | c  | **EM** | A | *EM* | DY | 52473 | 57473 |
| 156 474 | rt | **FS** | A | *SR* | CK | 52474 | 57474 |
| 156 475 | d  | **NO** | A | *NO* | HT | 52475 | 57475 |
| 156 476 | rt | **FS** | A | *SR* | CK | 52476 | 57476 |
| 156 477 | t  | **FS** | A | *SR* | CK | 52477 | 57477 |
| 156 478 | rt | **FS** | A | *SR* | CK | 52478 | 57478 |
| 156 479 | d  | **NO** | A | *NO* | HT | 52479 | 57479 |
| 156 480 | d  | **NO** | A | *NO* | HT | 52480 | 57480 |
| 156 481 | d  | **NO** | A | *NO* | HT | 52481 | 57481 |
| 156 482 | d  | **NO** | A | *NO* | AN | 52482 | 57482 |
| 156 483 | d  | **NO** | A | *NO* | AN | 52483 | 57483 |
| 156 484 | d  | **NO** | A | *NO* | HT | 52484 | 57484 |
| 156 485 | ru | **FS** | A | *SR* | CK | 52485 | 57485 |
| 156 486 | d  | **NO** | A | *NO* | AN | 52486 | 57486 |

| | | | | | | | |
|---|---|---|---|---|---|---|---|
| 156 487 | d | **NO** | A | *NO* | AN | 52487 | 57487 |
| 156 488 | d | **NO** | A | *NO* | AN | 52488 | 57488 |
| 156 489 | d | **NO** | A | *NO* | AN | 52489 | 57489 |
| 156 490 | d | **NO** | A | *NO* | HT | 52490 | 57490 |
| 156 491 | d | **NO** | A | *NO* | AN | 52491 | 57491 |
| 156 492 | r* | **SR** | A | *SR* | CK | 52492 | 57492 |
| 156 493 | rt | **FS** | A | *SR* | CK | 52493 | 57493 |
| 156 494 | u | **SR** | A | *SR* | CK | 52494 | 57494 |
| 156 495 | u | **SR** | A | *SR* | CK | 52495 | 57495 |
| 156 496 | u | **FS** | A | *SR* | CK | 52496 | 57496 |
| 156 497 | c | **EM** | A | *EM* | DY | 52497 | 57497 |
| 156 498 | c | **EM** | A | *EM* | DY | 52498 | 57498 |
| 156 499 | rt | **SR** | A | *SR* | CK | 52499 | 57499 |
| 156 500 | u | **SR** | A | *SR* | CK | 52500 | 57500 |
| 156 501 | | **SR** | A | *SR* | CK | 52501 | 57501 |
| 156 502 | | **SR** | A | *SR* | CK | 52502 | 57502 |
| 156 503 | | **SR** | A | *SR* | CK | 52503 | 57503 |
| 156 504 | | **SR** | A | *SR* | CK | 52504 | 57504 |
| 156 505 | | **SR** | A | *SR* | CK | 52505 | 57505 |
| 156 506 | | **SR** | A | *SR* | CK | 52506 | 57506 |
| 156 507 | | **SR** | A | *SR* | CK | 52507 | 57507 |
| 156 508 | | **SR** | A | *SR* | CK | 52508 | 57508 |
| 156 509 | | **SR** | A | *SR* | CK | 52509 | 57509 |
| 156 510 | | **SR** | A | *SR* | CK | 52510 | 57510 |
| 156 511 | | **SR** | A | *SR* | CK | 52511 | 57511 |
| 156 512 | | **SR** | A | *SR* | CK | 52512 | 57512 |
| 156 513 | | **SR** | A | *SR* | CK | 52513 | 57513 |
| 156 514 | | **SR** | A | *SR* | CK | 52514 | 57514 |

**Names:**

| | |
|---|---|
| 156 416 | Saint Edmund |
| 156 420 | LA' AL RATTY Ravenglass & Eskdale Railway |
| 156 438 | Timothy Hackworth |
| 156 440 | George Bradshaw |
| 156 441 | William Huskisson MP |
| 156 444 | Councillor Bill Cameron |
| 156 459 | Benny Rothman – The Manchester Rambler |
| 156 460 | Driver John Axon G.C. |
| 156 464 | Lancashire DalesRail |
| 156 466 | Gracie Fields |

# CLASS 158/0                                                         BREL

DMSL(B)–DMSL(A) or DMCL–DMSL or DMSL–MSL–DMSL.

**Construction:** Welded aluminium.
**Engines:** 158 701–813/158 880–890/158 950–961: One Cummins NTA855R1 of 260 kW (350 hp) at 2100 rpm.
158 815–862: One Perkins 2006-TWH of 260 kW (350 hp) at 2100 rpm.
158 863–872: One Cummins NTA855R3 of 300 kW (400 hp) at 1900 rpm.
**Bogies:** One BREL P4 (powered) and one BREL T4 (non-powered) per car.
**Couplers:** BSI.                                      **Dimensions:** 22.57 x 2.70 m.
**Gangways:** Throughout.                               **Wheel Arrangement:** 2-B + B-2.
**Doors:** Twin-leaf swing plug.                        **Maximum Speed:** 90 mph.
**Seating Layout:** 2+2 facing/unidirectional in all Standard and First Class except 2+1 in South West Trains First Class.
**Multiple Working:** Within class and with Classes 142, 143, 144, 150, 153, 155, 156, 159, 170 and 172.

ScotRail 158s 158 701–741 are "fitted" for RETB. When a unit arrives at Inverness the cab display unit is clipped on and plugged in.

Arriva Trains Wales units have ERTMS plugged in at Machynlleth for working the Cambrian Lines.

*    Refurbished ScotRail units fitted with Grammer seating, additional luggage racks and cycle stowage areas.
     ScotRail units 158 726–741 are fitted with Richmond seating.
†    Refurbished East Midlands Trains units with Grammer seating.
c    Chapman seating.
s    Refurbished Arriva Trains Wales units with Grammer seating.
u    Refurbished former South West Trains units with Class 159-style interiors, including First Class seating.
w    Refurbished First Great Western units. Units 158 745–749/751/762/767 (now formed into 3-car sets) have been fitted with Richmond seating.

**Northern promotional vinyls:**

158 784 PTEG: 40 years.
158 787, 158 792–796 Sheffield–Leeds fast service.
158 790 Rugby League (Northern Rail Cup).
158 860 Keighley & Brontë Country.
158 861 Yorkshire Wolds & Coast.
158 901–910 Leeds–Bradford–Manchester route (the "Calder Valley").

**DMSL(B).** Lot No. 31051 BREL Derby 1989–92. –/68 1TD 1W. († –/72 1TD 1W, c, w –/66 1TD 1W, s –/64(4) 1TD 2W, t –/64 1TD 1W). 38.5 t.
**MSL.** Lot No. 31050 BREL Derby 1991. –/66(3) 1T. 38.5 t.
**DMSL(A).** Lot No. 31052 BREL Derby 1989–92. –/70 1T († –/74, c, w –/68 1T, * –/64(2) 1T plus cycle stowage area, s –/70 1T, t –/66 1T). 38.5 t.

The above details refer to the "as built" condition. The following DMSL(B) have now been converted to DMCL as follows:

**52701–736/52738–741 (ScotRail).** 15/53 1TD 1W (* refurbished sets 14/46(6) 1TD 1W plus cycle stowage area).
**52786/789 (Former South West Trains units).** 13/44 1TD 1W.

| | | | | | | | | |
|---|---|---|---|---|---|---|---|---|
| 158 701 | * | **FS** | P | *SR* | IS | 52701 | 57701 | |
| 158 702 | * | **FS** | P | *SR* | IS | 52702 | 57702 | |
| 158 703 | * | **FS** | P | *SR* | IS | 52703 | 57703 | |
| 158 704 | * | **FS** | P | *SR* | IS | 52704 | 57704 | |
| 158 705 | * | **FS** | P | *SR* | IS | 52705 | 57705 | |
| 158 706 | * | **FS** | P | *SR* | IS | 52706 | 57706 | |
| 158 707 | * | **FS** | P | *SR* | IS | 52707 | 57707 | |
| 158 708 | * | **FS** | P | *SR* | IS | 52708 | 57708 | |
| 158 709 | * | **FS** | P | *SR* | IS | 52709 | 57709 | |
| 158 710 | * | **FS** | P | *SR* | IS | 52710 | 57710 | |
| 158 711 | * | **FS** | P | *SR* | IS | 52711 | 57711 | |
| 158 712 | * | **FS** | P | *SR* | IS | 52712 | 57712 | |
| 158 713 | * | **FS** | P | *SR* | IS | 52713 | 57713 | |
| 158 714 | * | **FS** | P | *SR* | IS | 52714 | 57714 | |
| 158 715 | * | **FS** | P | *SR* | IS | 52715 | 57715 | |
| 158 716 | * | **FS** | P | *SR* | IS | 52716 | 57716 | |
| 158 717 | * | **FS** | P | *SR* | IS | 52717 | 57717 | |
| 158 718 | * | **FS** | P | *SR* | IS | 52718 | 57718 | |
| 158 719 | * | **FS** | P | *SR* | IS | 52719 | 57719 | |
| 158 720 | * | **FS** | P | *SR* | IS | 52720 | 57720 | |
| 158 721 | * | **FS** | P | *SR* | IS | 52721 | 57721 | |
| 158 722 | * | **FS** | P | *SR* | IS | 52722 | 57722 | |
| 158 723 | * | **FS** | P | *SR* | IS | 52723 | 57723 | |
| 158 724 | * | **FS** | P | *SR* | IS | 52724 | 57724 | |
| 158 725 | * | **FS** | P | *SR* | IS | 52725 | 57725 | |
| 158 726 | | **FS** | P | *SR* | HA | 52726 | 57726 | |
| 158 727 | | **FS** | P | *SR* | HA | 52727 | 57727 | |
| 158 728 | | **FS** | P | *SR* | HA | 52728 | 57728 | |
| 158 729 | | **FS** | P | *SR* | HA | 52729 | 57729 | |
| 158 730 | | **FS** | P | *SR* | HA | 52730 | 57730 | |
| 158 731 | | **FS** | P | *SR* | HA | 52731 | 57731 | |
| 158 732 | | **FS** | P | *SR* | HA | 52732 | 57732 | |
| 158 733 | | **FS** | P | *SR* | HA | 52733 | 57733 | |
| 158 734 | | **FS** | P | *SR* | HA | 52734 | 57734 | |
| 158 735 | | **FS** | P | *SR* | HA | 52735 | 57735 | |
| 158 736 | | **FS** | P | *SR* | HA | 52736 | 57736 | |
| 158 738 | | **FS** | P | *SR* | HA | 52738 | 57738 | |
| 158 739 | | **FS** | P | *SR* | HA | 52739 | 57739 | |
| 158 740 | | **FS** | P | *SR* | HA | 52740 | 57740 | |
| 158 741 | | **FS** | P | *SR* | HA | 52741 | 57741 | |
| 158 752 | | **NO** | P | *NO* | NL | 52752 | 58716 | 57752 |
| 158 753 | | **NO** | P | *NO* | NL | 52753 | 58710 | 57753 |
| 158 754 | | **NO** | P | *NO* | NL | 52754 | 58708 | 57754 |
| 158 755 | | **NO** | P | *NO* | NL | 52755 | 58702 | 57755 |
| 158 756 | | **NO** | P | *NO* | NL | 52756 | 58712 | 57756 |
| 158 757 | | **NO** | P | *NO* | NL | 52757 | 58706 | 57757 |
| 158 758 | | **NO** | P | *NO* | NL | 52758 | 58714 | 57758 |
| 158 759 | | **NO** | P | *NO* | NL | 52759 | 58713 | 57759 |
| 158 763 | w | **FI** | P | *GW* | PM | 52763 | 57763 | |
| 158 766 | w | **FI** | P | *GW* | PM | 52766 | 57766 | |
| 158 770 | † | **ST** | P | *EM* | NM | 52770 | 57770 | |

| | | | | | | | |
|---|---|---|---|---|---|---|---|
| 158 773 | † | **ST** | P | *EM* | NM | 52773 | 57773 |
| 158 774 | † | **ST** | P | *EM* | NM | 52774 | 57774 |
| 158 777 | † | **ST** | P | *EM* | NM | 52777 | 57777 |
| 158 780 | † | **ST** | A | *EM* | NM | 52780 | 57780 |
| 158 782 | | **SR** | A | *SR* | HA | 52782 | 57782 |
| 158 783 | † | **ST** | A | *EM* | NM | 52783 | 57783 |
| 158 784 | | **NO** | A | *NO* | NL | 52784 | 57784 |
| 158 785 | † | **ST** | A | *EM* | NM | 52785 | 57785 |
| 158 786 | u | **SR** | A | *SR* | HA | 52786 | 57786 |
| 158 787 | | **NO** | A | *NO* | NL | 52787 | 57787 |
| 158 788 | † | **ST** | A | *EM* | NM | 52788 | 57788 |
| 158 789 | u | **SR** | A | *SR* | HA | 52789 | 57789 |
| 158 790 | | **NO** | A | *NO* | NL | 52790 | 57790 |
| 158 791 | | **NO** | A | *NO* | NL | 52791 | 57791 |
| 158 792 | | **NO** | A | *NO* | NL | 52792 | 57792 |
| 158 793 | | **NO** | A | *NO* | NL | 52793 | 57793 |
| 158 794 | | **NO** | A | *NO* | NL | 52794 | 57794 |
| 158 795 | | **NO** | A | *NO* | NL | 52795 | 57795 |
| 158 796 | | **NO** | A | *NO* | NL | 52796 | 57796 |
| 158 797 | | **NO** | A | *NO* | NL | 52797 | 57797 |
| 158 798 | w | **FI** | P | *GW* | PM | 52798 | 58715 | 57798 |
| 158 799 | † | **ST** | P | *EM* | NM | 52799 | 57799 |
| 158 806 | † | **ST** | P | *EM* | NM | 52806 | 57806 |
| 158 810 | † | **ST** | P | *EM* | NM | 52810 | 57810 |
| 158 812 | † | **ST** | P | *EM* | NM | 52812 | 57812 |
| 158 813 | † | **ST** | P | *EM* | NM | 52813 | 57813 |
| 158 815 | c | **NO** | A | *NO* | NL | 52815 | 57815 |
| 158 816 | c | **NO** | A | *NO* | NL | 52816 | 57816 |
| 158 817 | c | **NO** | A | *NO* | NL | 52817 | 57817 |
| 158 818 | es | **AW** | A | *AW* | MN | 52818 | 57818 |
| 158 819 | es | **AW** | A | *AW* | MN | 52819 | 57819 |
| 158 820 | es | **AW** | A | *AW* | MN | 52820 | 57820 |
| 158 821 | es | **AW** | A | *AW* | MN | 52821 | 57821 |
| 158 822 | es | **AW** | A | *AW* | MN | 52822 | 57822 |
| 158 823 | es | **AW** | A | *AW* | MN | 52823 | 57823 |
| 158 824 | es | **AW** | A | *AW* | MN | 52824 | 57824 |
| 158 825 | es | **AW** | A | *AW* | MN | 52825 | 57825 |
| 158 826 | es | **AW** | A | *AW* | MN | 52826 | 57826 |
| 158 827 | es | **AW** | A | *AW* | MN | 52827 | 57827 |
| 158 828 | es | **AW** | A | *AW* | MN | 52828 | 57828 |
| 158 829 | es | **AW** | A | *AW* | MN | 52829 | 57829 |
| 158 830 | es | **AW** | A | *AW* | MN | 52830 | 57830 |
| 158 831 | es | **AW** | A | *AW* | MN | 52831 | 57831 |
| 158 832 | es | **AW** | A | *AW* | MN | 52832 | 57832 |
| 158 833 | es | **AW** | A | *AW* | MN | 52833 | 57833 |
| 158 834 | es | **AW** | A | *AW* | MN | 52834 | 57834 |
| 158 835 | es | **AW** | A | *AW* | MN | 52835 | 57835 |
| 158 836 | es | **AW** | A | *AW* | MN | 52836 | 57836 |
| 158 837 | es | **AW** | A | *AW* | MN | 52837 | 57837 |
| 158 838 | es | **AW** | A | *AW* | MN | 52838 | 57838 |
| 158 839 | es | **AW** | A | *AW* | MN | 52839 | 57839 |

| 158 840 | es | **AW** | A | *AW* | MN | 52840 | 57840 |
| 158 841 | es | **AW** | A | *AW* | MN | 52841 | 57841 |
| 158 842 | c | **NO** | A | *NO* | NL | 52842 | 57842 |
| 158 843 | c | **NO** | A | *NO* | NL | 52843 | 57843 |
| 158 844 | | **NO** | A | *NO* | NL | 52844 | 57844 |
| 158 845 | | **NO** | A | *NO* | NL | 52845 | 57845 |
| 158 846 | † | **ST** | A | *EM* | NM | 52846 | 57846 |
| 158 847 | † | **ST** | A | *EM* | NM | 52847 | 57847 |
| 158 848 | | **NO** | A | *NO* | NL | 52848 | 57848 |
| 158 849 | | **NO** | A | *NO* | NL | 52849 | 57849 |
| 158 850 | | **NO** | A | *NO* | NL | 52850 | 57850 |
| 158 851 | | **NO** | A | *NO* | NL | 52851 | 57851 |
| 158 852 | † | **ST** | A | *EM* | NM | 52852 | 57852 |
| 158 853 | | **NO** | A | *NO* | NL | 52853 | 57853 |
| 158 854 | † | **ST** | A | *EM* | NM | 52854 | 57854 |
| 158 855 | | **NO** | A | *NO* | NL | 52855 | 57855 |
| 158 856 | † | **ST** | A | *EM* | NM | 52856 | 57856 |
| 158 857 | † | **ST** | A | *EM* | NM | 52857 | 57857 |
| 158 858 | † | **ST** | A | *EM* | NM | 52858 | 57858 |
| 158 859 | | **NO** | A | *NO* | NL | 52859 | 57859 |
| 158 860 | | **NO** | A | *NO* | NL | 52860 | 57860 |
| 158 861 | | **NO** | A | *NO* | NL | 52861 | 57861 |
| 158 862 | † | **ST** | A | *EM* | NM | 52862 | 57862 |
| 158 863 | † | **ST** | A | *EM* | NM | 52863 | 57863 |
| 158 864 | † | **ST** | A | *EM* | NM | 52864 | 57864 |
| 158 865 | † | **ST** | A | *EM* | NM | 52865 | 57865 |
| 158 866 | † | **ST** | A | *EM* | NM | 52866 | 57866 |
| 158 867 | c | **SR** | A | *SR* | HA | 52867 | 57867 |
| 158 868 | c | **SR** | A | *SR* | HA | 52868 | 57868 |
| 158 869 | c | **SR** | A | *SR* | HA | 52869 | 57869 |
| 158 870 | c | **SR** | A | *SR* | HA | 52870 | 57870 |
| 158 871 | c | **SR** | A | *SR* | HA | 52871 | 57871 |
| 158 872 | c | **NO** | A | *NO* | NL | 52872 | 57872 |

**Names (ScotRail units carry their names on the unit ends):**

| 158 702 | BBC Scotland 75 years |
| 158 707 | Far North Line 125th ANNIVERSARY |
| 158 715 | Haymarket |
| 158 720 | Inverness & Nairn Railway – 150 years |
| 158 784 | Barbara Castle |
| 158 791 | County of Nottinghamshire |
| 158 796 | Fred Trueman Cricketing Legend |
| 158 797 | Jane Tomlinson |
| 158 860 | Ian Dewhirst |

**Class 158/8. Refurbished South West Trains units.** Converted from former TransPennine Express units at Wabtec, Doncaster in 2007. 2+1 seating in First Class. Details as Class 158/0 except:

**DMCL.** Lot No. 31051 BREL Derby 1989–92. 13/44 1TD 1W. 38.5 t.
**DMSL.** Lot No. 31052 BREL Derby 1989–92. –/70 1T. 38.5 t.

| 158 880 | (158 737) | **ST** | P | *SW* | SA | 52737 | 57737 |
| 158 881 | (158 742) | **ST** | P | *SW* | SA | 52742 | 57742 |
| 158 882 | (158 743) | **ST** | P | *SW* | SA | 52743 | 57743 |
| 158 883 | (158 744) | **ST** | P | *SW* | SA | 52744 | 57744 |
| 158 884 | (158 772) | **ST** | P | *SW* | SA | 52772 | 57772 |
| 158 885 | (158 775) | **ST** | P | *SW* | SA | 52775 | 57775 |
| 158 886 | (158 779) | **ST** | P | *SW* | SA | 52779 | 57779 |
| 158 887 | (158 781) | **ST** | P | *SW* | SA | 52781 | 57781 |
| 158 888 | (158 802) | **ST** | P | *SW* | SA | 52802 | 57802 |
| 158 889 | (158 808) | **ST** | P | *SW* | SA | 52808 | 57808 |
| 158 890 | (158 814) | **ST** | P | *SW* | SA | 52814 | 57814 |

## CLASS 158/9                                                    BREL

DMSL–DMS. Units leased by West Yorkshire PTE but managed by Eversholt Rail. Details as Class 158/0 except for seating and toilets.

**DMSL**. Lot No. 31051 BREL Derby 1990–92. –/70 1TD 1W. 38.5 t.
**DMS**. Lot No. 31052 BREL Derby 1990–92. –/72 and parcels area. 38.5 t.

| 158 901 | **NO** | E | *NO* | NL | 52901 | 57901 |                     |
| 158 902 | **NO** | E | *NO* | NL | 52902 | 57902 |                     |
| 158 903 | **NO** | E | *NO* | NL | 52903 | 57903 |                     |
| 158 904 | **NO** | E | *NO* | NL | 52904 | 57904 |                     |
| 158 905 | **NO** | E | *NO* | NL | 52905 | 57905 |                     |
| 158 906 | **NO** | E | *NO* | NL | 52906 | 57906 |                     |
| 158 907 | **NO** | E | *NO* | NL | 52907 | 57907 |                     |
| 158 908 | **NO** | E | *NO* | NL | 52908 | 57908 |                     |
| 158 909 | **NO** | E | *NO* | NL | 52909 | 57909 |                     |
| 158 910 | **NO** | E | *NO* | NL | 52910 | 57910 | William Wilberforce |

## CLASS 158/0                                                    BREL

DMSL–DMSL–DMSL. Refurbished units reformed for First Great Western. For vehicle details see above. Formations can be flexible depending on when unit exams become due.

| 158 950 | w | **FI** | P | *GW* | PM | 57751 | 52761 | 57761 |
| 158 951 | w | **FI** | P | *GW* | PM | 52751 | 52764 | 57764 |
| 158 952 | w | **FI** | P | *GW* | PM | 57745 | 52762 | 57762 |
| 158 953 | w | **FI** | P | *GW* | PM | 52745 | 52750 | 57750 |
| 158 954 | w | **FI** | P | *GW* | PM | 57747 | 52760 | 57760 |
| 158 955 | w | **FI** | P | *GW* | PM | 52747 | 52765 | 57765 |
| 158 956 | w | **FI** | P | *GW* | PM | 52748 | 52768 | 57768 |
| 158 957 | w | **FI** | P | *GW* | PM | 57748 | 52771 | 57771 |
| 158 958 | w | **FI** | P | *GW* | PM | 57746 | 52776 | 57776 |
| 158 959 | w | **FI** | P | *GW* | PM | 52746 | 52778 | 57778 |
| 158 960 | w | **FI** | P | *GW* | PM | 57749 | 52769 | 57769 |
| 158 961 | w | **FI** | P | *GW* | PM | 52749 | 52767 | 57767 |

## CLASS 159/0                                 BREL

DMCL–MSL–DMSL. Built as Class 158. Converted before entering passenger service to Class 159 by Rosyth Dockyard.

**Construction:** Welded aluminium.
**Engines:** One Cummins NTA855R3 of 300 kW (400 hp) at 1900 rpm.
**Bogies:** One BREL P4 (powered) and one BREL T4 (non-powered) per car.
**Couplers:** BSI.               **Dimensions:** 22.16 x 2.70 m.
**Gangways:** Throughout.       **Wheel Arrangement:** 2-B + B-2 + B-2.
**Doors:** Twin-leaf swing plug.    **Maximum Speed:** 90 mph.
**Seating Layout:** 1: 2+1 facing, 2: 2+2 facing/unidirectional.
**Multiple Working:** Within class and with Classes 142, 143, 144, 150, 153, 155, 156, 158 and 170.

**DMCL.** Lot No. 31051 BREL Derby 1992–93. 23/28 1TD 1W. 38.5 t.
**MSL.** Lot No. 31050 BREL Derby 1992–93. –/70(6) 1T. 38.5 t.
**DMSL.** Lot No. 31052 BREL Derby 1992–93. –/72 1T. 38.5 t.

| | | | | | | | | |
|---|---|---|---|---|---|---|---|---|
| 159 001 | **ST** | P | *SW* | SA | 52873 | 58718 | 57873 | CITY OF EXETER |
| 159 002 | **ST** | P | *SW* | SA | 52874 | 58719 | 57874 | CITY OF SALISBURY |
| 159 003 | **ST** | P | *SW* | SA | 52875 | 58720 | 57875 | TEMPLECOMBE |
| 159 004 | **ST** | P | *SW* | SA | 52876 | 58721 | 57876 | BASINGSTOKE AND DEANE |
| 159 005 | **ST** | P | *SW* | SA | 52877 | 58722 | 57877 | WEST OF ENGLAND LINE |
| 159 006 | **ST** | P | *SW* | SA | 52878 | 58723 | 57878 | THE SEATON TRAMWAY Seaton–Colyford–Colyton |
| 159 007 | **ST** | P | *SW* | SA | 52879 | 58724 | 57879 | |
| 159 008 | **ST** | P | *SW* | SA | 52880 | 58725 | 57880 | |
| 159 009 | **ST** | P | *SW* | SA | 52881 | 58726 | 57881 | |
| 159 010 | **ST** | P | *SW* | SA | 52882 | 58727 | 57882 | |
| 159 011 | **ST** | P | *SW* | SA | 52883 | 58728 | 57883 | |
| 159 012 | **ST** | P | *SW* | SA | 52884 | 58729 | 57884 | |
| 159 013 | **ST** | P | *SW* | SA | 52885 | 58730 | 57885 | |
| 159 014 | **ST** | P | *SW* | SA | 52886 | 58731 | 57886 | |
| 159 015 | **ST** | P | *SW* | SA | 52887 | 58732 | 57887 | |
| 159 016 | **ST** | P | *SW* | SA | 52888 | 58733 | 57888 | |
| 159 017 | **ST** | P | *SW* | SA | 52889 | 58734 | 57889 | |
| 159 018 | **ST** | P | *SW* | SA | 52890 | 58735 | 57890 | |
| 159 019 | **ST** | P | *SW* | SA | 52891 | 58736 | 57891 | |
| 159 020 | **ST** | P | *SW* | SA | 52892 | 58737 | 57892 | |
| 159 021 | **ST** | P | *SW* | SA | 52893 | 58738 | 57893 | |
| 159 022 | **ST** | P | *SW* | SA | 52894 | 58739 | 57894 | |

## CLASS 159/1                                 BREL

DMCL–MSL–DMSL. Units converted from Class 158s at Wabtec, Doncaster in 2006–07 for South West Trains.

Details as Class 158/0 except:
**Seating Layout:** 1: 2+1 facing, 2: 2+2 facing/unidirectional.

**DMCL.** Lot No. 31051 BREL Derby 1989–92. 24/28 1TD 1W. 38.5 t.
**MSL.** Lot No. 31050 BREL Derby 1989–92. –/70 1T. 38.5 t.
**DMSL.** Lot No. 31052 BREL Derby 1989–92. –/72 1T. 38.5 t.

| | | | | | | | |
|---|---|---|---|---|---|---|---|
| 159 101 | (158 800) | **ST** | P | *SW* | SA | 52800 | 58717 | 57800 |
| 159 102 | (158 803) | **ST** | P | *SW* | SA | 52803 | 58703 | 57803 |
| 159 103 | (158 804) | **ST** | P | *SW* | SA | 52804 | 58704 | 57804 |
| 159 104 | (158 805) | **ST** | P | *SW* | SA | 52805 | 58705 | 57805 |
| 159 105 | (158 807) | **ST** | P | *SW* | SA | 52807 | 58707 | 57807 |
| 159 106 | (158 809) | **ST** | P | *SW* | SA | 52809 | 58709 | 57809 |
| 159 107 | (158 811) | **ST** | P | *SW* | SA | 52811 | 58711 | 57811 |
| 159 108 | (158 801) | **ST** | P | *SW* | SA | 52801 | 58701 | 57801 |

# CLASS 165/0     NETWORK TURBO     BREL

DMSL–DMS and DMSL–MS–DMS. Chiltern Railways units. Refurbished 2003–05 with First Class seats removed and air conditioning fitted.
**Construction:** Welded aluminium.
**Engines:** One Perkins 2006-TWH of 260 kW (350 hp) at 2100 rpm.
**Bogies:** BREL P3-17 (powered), BREL T3-17 (non-powered).
**Couplers:** BSI.
**Dimensions:** 23.50/23.25 x 2.81 m.

| | |
|---|---|
| **Gangways:** Within unit only. | **Wheel Arrangement:** 2-B (+ B-2) + B-2. |
| **Doors:** Twin-leaf swing plug. | **Maximum Speed:** 75 mph. |

**Seating Layout:** 2+2/3+2 facing/unidirectional.
**Multiple Working:** Within class and with Classes 166, 168, 170 and 172.

Fitted with tripcocks for working over London Underground tracks between Harrow-on-the-Hill and Amersham.

**58801–822/58873–878. DMSL.** Lot No. 31087 BREL York 1990. –/82(7) 1T 2W. 40.1 t.
**58823–833. DMSL.** Lot No. 31089 BREL York 1991–92. –/82(7) 1T 2W. 40.1 t.
**MS.** Lot No. 31090 BREL York 1991–92. –/106. 37.0 t.
**DMS.** Lot No. 31088 BREL York 1991–92. –/94. 39.4 t.

| | | | | | | |
|---|---|---|---|---|---|---|
| 165 001 | **CR** | A | *CR* | AL | 58801 | 58834 |
| 165 002 | **CR** | A | *CR* | AL | 58802 | 58835 |
| 165 003 | **CR** | A | *CR* | AL | 58803 | 58836 |
| 165 004 | **CR** | A | *CR* | AL | 58804 | 58837 |
| 165 005 | **CR** | A | *CR* | AL | 58805 | 58838 |
| 165 006 | **CR** | A | *CR* | AL | 58806 | 58839 |
| 165 007 | **CR** | A | *CR* | AL | 58807 | 58840 |
| 165 008 | **CR** | A | *CR* | AL | 58808 | 58841 |
| 165 009 | **CR** | A | *CR* | AL | 58809 | 58842 |
| 165 010 | **CR** | A | *CR* | AL | 58810 | 58843 |
| 165 011 | **CR** | A | *CR* | AL | 58811 | 58844 |
| 165 012 | **CR** | A | *CR* | AL | 58812 | 58845 |
| 165 013 | **CR** | A | *CR* | AL | 58813 | 58846 |
| 165 014 | **CR** | A | *CR* | AL | 58814 | 58847 |
| 165 015 | **CR** | A | *CR* | AL | 58815 | 58848 |
| 165 016 | **CR** | A | *CR* | AL | 58816 | 58849 |

| 165 017 | **CR** | A | *CR* | AL | 58817 |       | 58850 |
| 165 018 | **CR** | A | *CR* | AL | 58818 |       | 58851 |
| 165 019 | **CR** | A | *CR* | AL | 58819 |       | 58852 |
| 165 020 | **CR** | A | *CR* | AL | 58820 |       | 58853 |
| 165 021 | **CR** | A | *CR* | AL | 58821 |       | 58854 |
| 165 022 | **CR** | A | *CR* | AL | 58822 |       | 58855 |
| 165 023 | **CR** | A | *CR* | AL | 58873 |       | 58867 |
| 165 024 | **CR** | A | *CR* | AL | 58874 |       | 58868 |
| 165 025 | **CR** | A | *CR* | AL | 58875 |       | 58869 |
| 165 026 | **CR** | A | *CR* | AL | 58876 |       | 58870 |
| 165 027 | **CR** | A | *CR* | AL | 58877 |       | 58871 |
| 165 028 | **CR** | A | *CR* | AL | 58878 |       | 58872 |
| 165 029 | **CR** | A | *CR* | AL | 58823 | 55404 | 58856 |
| 165 030 | **CR** | A | *CR* | AL | 58824 | 55405 | 58857 |
| 165 031 | **CR** | A | *CR* | AL | 58825 | 55406 | 58858 |
| 165 032 | **CR** | A | *CR* | AL | 58826 | 55407 | 58859 |
| 165 033 | **CR** | A | *CR* | AL | 58827 | 55408 | 58860 |
| 165 034 | **CR** | A | *CR* | AL | 58828 | 55409 | 58861 |
| 165 035 | **CR** | A | *CR* | AL | 58829 | 55410 | 58862 |
| 165 036 | **CR** | A | *CR* | AL | 58830 | 55411 | 58863 |
| 165 037 | **CR** | A | *CR* | AL | 58831 | 55412 | 58864 |
| 165 038 | **CR** | A | *CR* | AL | 58832 | 55413 | 58865 |
| 165 039 | **CR** | A | *CR* | AL | 58833 | 55414 | 58866 |

## CLASS 165/1    NETWORK TURBO                                        BREL

First Great Western units. DMCL–MS–DMS or DMCL–DMS.

**Construction:** Welded aluminium.
**Engines:** One Perkins 2006-TWH of 260 kW (350 hp) at 2100 rpm.
**Bogies:** BREL P3-17 (powered), BREL T3-17 (non-powered).
**Couplers:** BSI.
**Dimensions:** 23.50/23.25 x 2.81 m.
**Gangways:** Within unit only.          **Wheel Arrangement:** 2-B (+ B-2) + B-2.
**Doors:** Twin-leaf swing plug.          **Maximum Speed:** 90 mph.
**Seating Layout:** 1: 2+2 facing, 2: 3+2 facing/unidirectional.
**Multiple Working:** Within class and with Classes 166, 168, 170 and 172.

**58953–969. DMCL.** Lot No. 31098 BREL York 1992. 16/66 1T. 38.0 t.
**58879–898. DMCL.** Lot No. 31096 BREL York 1992. 16/72 1T. 38.0 t.
**MS.** Lot No. 31099 BREL 1992. –/106. 37.0 t.
**DMS.** Lot No. 31097 BREL 1992. –/98. 37.0 t.

| 165 101 | **FD** | A | *GW* | RG | 58953 | 55415 | 58916 |
| 165 102 | **FD** | A | *GW* | RG | 58954 | 55416 | 58917 |
| 165 103 | **FD** | A | *GW* | RG | 58955 | 55417 | 58918 |
| 165 104 | **FD** | A | *GW* | RG | 58956 | 55418 | 58919 |
| 165 105 | **FD** | A | *GW* | RG | 58957 | 55419 | 58920 |
| 165 106 | **FD** | A | *GW* | RG | 58958 | 55420 | 58921 |
| 165 107 | **FD** | A | *GW* | RG | 58959 | 55421 | 58922 |
| 165 108 | **FD** | A | *GW* | RG | 58960 | 55422 | 58923 |
| 165 109 | **FD** | A | *GW* | RG | 58961 | 55423 | 58924 |

| | | | | | | | |
|---|---|---|---|---|---|---|---|
| 165 110 | FD | A | GW | RG | 58962 | 55424 | 58925 |
| 165 111 | FD | A | GW | RG | 58963 | 55425 | 58926 |
| 165 112 | FD | A | GW | RG | 58964 | 55426 | 58927 |
| 165 113 | FD | A | GW | RG | 58965 | 55427 | 58928 |
| 165 114 | FD | A | GW | RG | 58966 | 55428 | 58929 |
| 165 116 | FD | A | GW | RG | 58968 | 55430 | 58931 |
| 165 117 | FD | A | GW | RG | 58969 | 55431 | 58932 |
| 165 118 | FD | A | GW | RG | 58879 | | 58933 |
| 165 119 | FD | A | GW | RG | 58880 | | 58934 |
| 165 120 | FD | A | GW | RG | 58881 | | 58935 |
| 165 121 | FD | A | GW | RG | 58882 | | 58936 |
| 165 122 | FD | A | GW | RG | 58883 | | 58937 |
| 165 123 | FD | A | GW | RG | 58884 | | 58938 |
| 165 124 | FD | A | GW | RG | 58885 | | 58939 |
| 165 125 | FD | A | GW | RG | 58886 | | 58940 |
| 165 126 | FD | A | GW | RG | 58887 | | 58941 |
| 165 127 | FD | A | GW | RG | 58888 | | 58942 |
| 165 128 | FD | A | GW | RG | 58889 | | 58943 |
| 165 129 | FD | A | GW | RG | 58890 | | 58944 |
| 165 130 | FD | A | GW | RG | 58891 | | 58945 |
| 165 131 | FD | A | GW | RG | 58892 | | 58946 |
| 165 132 | FD | A | GW | RG | 58893 | | 58947 |
| 165 133 | FD | A | GW | RG | 58894 | | 58948 |
| 165 134 | FD | A | GW | RG | 58895 | | 58949 |
| 165 135 | FD | A | GW | RG | 58896 | | 58950 |
| 165 136 | FD | A | GW | RG | 58897 | | 58951 |
| 165 137 | FD | A | GW | RG | 58898 | | 58952 |

## CLASS 166      NETWORK EXPRESS TURBO      ABB

DMSL–MS–DMCL. First Great Western units, built for Paddington–Oxford/
Newbury services. Air conditioned and with additional luggage space
compared to the Class 165s. The DMSL vehicles have had their 16 First
Class seats declassified.

**Construction:** Welded aluminium.
**Engines:** One Perkins 2006-TWH of 260 kW (350 hp) at 2100 rpm.
**Bogies:** BREL P3-17 (powered), BREL T3-17 (non-powered).
**Couplers:** BSI.
**Dimensions:** 23.50 x 2.81 m.
**Gangways:** Within unit only.                **Wheel Arrangement:** 2-B + B-2 + B-2.
**Doors:** Twin-leaf swing plug.              **Maximum Speed:** 90 mph.
**Seating Layout:** 1: 2+2 facing, 2: 2+2/3+2 facing/unidirectional.
**Multiple Working:** Within class and with Classes 165, 168, 170 and 172.

**DMSL.** Lot No. 31116 ABB York 1992–93. –/84 1T. 39.6 t.
**MS.** Lot No. 31117 ABB York 1992–93. –/91. 38.0 t.
**DMCL.** Lot No. 31116 ABB York 1992–93. 16/68 1T. 39.6 t.

| | | | | | | | |
|---|---|---|---|---|---|---|---|
| 166 201 | FD | A | GW | RG | 58101 | 58601 | 58122 |
| 166 202 | FD | A | GW | RG | 58102 | 58602 | 58123 |
| 166 203 | FD | A | GW | RG | 58103 | 58603 | 58124 |

| 166 204 | **FD** | A | *GW* | RG | 58104 | 58604 | 58125 |
| 166 205 | **FD** | A | *GW* | RG | 58105 | 58605 | 58126 |
| 166 206 | **FD** | A | *GW* | RG | 58106 | 58606 | 58127 |
| 166 207 | **FD** | A | *GW* | RG | 58107 | 58607 | 58128 |
| 166 208 | **FD** | A | *GW* | RG | 58108 | 58608 | 58129 |
| 166 209 | **FD** | A | *GW* | RG | 58109 | 58609 | 58130 |
| 166 210 | **FD** | A | *GW* | RG | 58110 | 58610 | 58131 |
| 166 211 | **FD** | A | *GW* | RG | 58111 | 58611 | 58132 |
| 166 212 | **FD** | A | *GW* | RG | 58112 | 58612 | 58133 |
| 166 213 | **FD** | A | *GW* | RG | 58113 | 58613 | 58134 |
| 166 214 | **FD** | A | *GW* | RG | 58114 | 58614 | 58135 |
| 166 215 | **FD** | A | *GW* | RG | 58115 | 58615 | 58136 |
| 166 216 | **FD** | A | *GW* | RG | 58116 | 58616 | 58137 |
| 166 217 | **FD** | A | *GW* | RG | 58117 | 58617 | 58138 |
| 166 218 | **FD** | A | *GW* | RG | 58118 | 58618 | 58139 |
| 166 219 | **FD** | A | *GW* | RG | 58119 | 58619 | 58140 |
| 166 220 | **FD** | A | *GW* | RG | 58120 | 58620 | 58141 |
| 166 221 | **FD** | A | *GW* | RG | 58121 | 58621 | 58142 |

# CLASS 168   CLUBMAN   ADTRANZ/BOMBARDIER

Air conditioned.

**Construction:** Welded aluminium bodies with bolt-on steel ends.
**Engines:** One MTU 6R183TD13H of 315 kW (422 hp) at 1900 rpm.
**Transmission:** Hydraulic. Voith T211rzze to ZF final drive.
**Bogies:** One Adtranz P3–23 and one BREL T3–23 per car.
**Couplers:** BSI at outer ends, bar within unit.
**Dimensions:** Class 168/0: 24.10/23.61 x 2.69 m. Others: 23.62/23.61 x 2.69 m.
**Gangways:** Within unit only.   **Wheel Arrangement:** 2-B (+ B-2 + B-2) + B-2.
**Doors:** Twin-leaf swing plug.   **Maximum Speed:** 100 mph.
**Seating Layout:** 2+2 facing/unidirectional.
**Multiple Working:** Within class and with Classes 165 and 166.

Fitted with tripcocks for working over London Underground tracks between Harrow-on-the-Hill and Amersham.

**Class 168/0.** Original Design. DMSL(A)–MS–MSL–DMSL(B) or DMSL(A)–MSL–MS–DMSL(B).

58451–455 were numbered 58656–660 for a time when used in 168 106–110.

**58151–155. DMSL(A).** Adtranz Derby 1997–98. –/57 1TD 1W. 44.0 t.
**58651–655. MSL.** Adtranz Derby 1998. –/73 1T. 41.0 t.
**58451–455. MS.** Adtranz Derby 1998. –/77. 41.0 t.
**58251–255. DMSL(B).** Adtranz Derby 1998. –/68 1T. 43.6 t.

| 168 001 | **CR** | P | *CR* | AL | 58151 | 58451 | 58651 | 58251 |
| 168 002 | **CL** | P | *CR* | AL | 58152 | 58652 | 58452 | 58252 |
| 168 003 | **CL** | P | *CR* | AL | 58153 | 58453 | 58653 | 58253 |
| 168 004 | **CL** | P | *CR* | AL | 58154 | 58654 | 58454 | 58254 |
| 168 005 | **CR** | P | *CR* | AL | 58155 | 58655 | 58455 | 58255 |

**Class 168/1.** These units are effectively Class 170s. DMSL(A)–MSL–MS–DMSL(B) or DMSL(A)–MS–DMSL(B).

58461–463 have been renumbered from 58661–663.

**58156–163. DMSL(A).** Adtranz Derby 2000. –/57 1TD 2W. 45.2 t.
**58456–460. MS.** Bombardier Derby 2002. –/76. 41.8 t.
**58756–757. MSL.** Bombardier Derby 2002. –/73 1T. 42.9 t.
**58461–463. MS.** Adtranz Derby 2000. –/76. 42.4 t.
**58256–263. DMSL(B).** Adtranz Derby 2000. –/69 1T. 45.2 t.

| 168 106 | **CR** | P | *CR* | AL | 58156 | 58456 | 58756 | 58256 |
|---------|--------|---|------|----|-------|-------|-------|-------|
| 168 107 | **CR** | P | *CR* | AL | 58157 | 58757 | 58457 | 58257 |
| 168 108 | **CR** | P | *CR* | AL | 58158 |       | 58458 | 58258 |
| 168 109 | **CR** | P | *CR* | AL | 58159 |       | 58459 | 58259 |
| 168 110 | **CR** | P | *CR* | AL | 58160 |       | 58460 | 58260 |
| 168 111 | **CR** | E | *CR* | AL | 58161 |       | 58461 | 58261 |
| 168 112 | **CR** | E | *CR* | AL | 58162 |       | 58462 | 58262 |
| 168 113 | **CR** | E | *CR* | AL | 58163 |       | 58463 | 58263 |

**Class 168/2.** These units are effectively Class 170s. DMSL(A)–(MS)–MS–DMSL(B).

**58164–169. DMSL(A).** Bombardier Derby 2003–04. –/57 1TD 2W. 45.4 t.
**58365–367. MS.** Bombardier Derby 2006. –/76. 43.3 t.
**58464/468/469. MS.** Bombardier Derby 2003–04. –/76. 44.0 t.
**58465–467. MS.** Bombardier Derby 2006. –/76. 43.3 t.
**58264–269. DMSL(B).** Bombardier Derby 2003–04. –/69 1T. 45.5 t.

| 168 214 | **CR** | P | *CR* | AL | 58164 |       | 58464 | 58264 |
|---------|--------|---|------|----|-------|-------|-------|-------|
| 168 215 | **CR** | P | *CR* | AL | 58165 | 58365 | 58465 | 58265 |
| 168 216 | **CL** | P | *CR* | AL | 58166 | 58366 | 58466 | 58266 |
| 168 217 | **CL** | P | *CR* | AL | 58167 | 58367 | 58467 | 58267 |
| 168 218 | **CR** | P | *CR* | AL | 58168 |       | 58468 | 58268 |
| 168 219 | **CL** | P | *CR* | AL | 58169 |       | 58469 | 58269 |

# CLASS 170   TURBOSTAR ADTRANZ/BOMBARDIER

Various formations. Air conditioned.

**Construction:** Welded aluminium bodies with bolt-on steel ends.
**Engines:** One MTU 6R183TD13H of 315 kW (422 hp) at 1900 rpm.
**Transmission:** Hydraulic. Voith T211rzze to ZF final drive.
**Bogies:** One Adtranz P3–23 and one BREL T3–23 per car.
**Couplers:** BSI at outer ends, bar within later build units.
**Dimensions:** 23.62/23.61 x 2.69 m.
**Gangways:** Within unit only.          **Wheel Arrangement:** 2-B (+ B-2) + B-2.
**Doors:** Twin-leaf sliding plug.        **Maximum Speed:** 100 mph.
**Seating Layout:** 1: 2+1 facing/unidirectional. 2: 2+2 unidirectional/facing.
**Multiple Working:** Within class and with Classes 150, 153, 155, 156, 158, 159 and 172.

**Class 170/1. CrossCountry (former Midland Mainline) units.** Lazareni seating. DMSL–MS–DMCL/DMSL–DMCL.

**DMSL.** Adtranz Derby 1998–99. –/59 1TD 2W. 45.0 t.
**MS.** Adtranz Derby 2001. –/80. 43.0 t.
**DMCL.** Adtranz Derby 1998–99. 9/52 1T. 44.8 t

| | | | | | | | |
|---|---|---|---|---|---|---|---|
| 170 101 | **XC** | P | *XC* | TS | 50101 | 55101 | 79101 |
| 170 102 | **XC** | P | *XC* | TS | 50102 | 55102 | 79102 |
| 170 103 | **XC** | P | *XC* | TS | 50103 | 55103 | 79103 |
| 170 104 | **XC** | P | *XC* | TS | 50104 | 55104 | 79104 |
| 170 105 | **XC** | P | *XC* | TS | 50105 | 55105 | 79105 |
| 170 106 | **XC** | P | *XC* | TS | 50106 | 55106 | 79106 |
| 170 107 | **XC** | P | *XC* | TS | 50107 | 55107 | 79107 |
| 170 108 | **XC** | P | *XC* | TS | 50108 | 55108 | 79108 |
| 170 109 | **XC** | P | *XC* | TS | 50109 | 55109 | 79109 |
| 170 110 | **XC** | P | *XC* | TS | 50110 | 55110 | 79110 |
| 170 111 | **XC** | P | *XC* | TS | 50111 | | 79111 |
| 170 112 | **XC** | P | *XC* | TS | 50112 | | 79112 |
| 170 113 | **XC** | P | *XC* | TS | 50113 | | 79113 |
| 170 114 | **XC** | P | *XC* | TS | 50114 | | 79114 |
| 170 115 | **XC** | P | *XC* | TS | 50115 | | 79115 |
| 170 116 | **XC** | P | *XC* | TS | 50116 | | 79116 |
| 170 117 | **XC** | P | *XC* | TS | 50117 | | 79117 |

**Class 170/2. Greater Anglia 3-car units.** Chapman seating. DMCL–MSL–DMSL.

**Advertising livery:** 170 208 Breckland Line (Norwich–Cambridge).

**DMCL.** Adtranz Derby 1999. 7/39 1TD 2W. 45.0 t.
**MSL.** Adtranz Derby 1999. –/68 1T. Guard's office. 45.3 t.
**DMSL.** Adtranz Derby 1999. –/66 1T. 43.4 t.

| | | | | | | | |
|---|---|---|---|---|---|---|---|
| 170 201 | r | **1** | P | *GA* | NC | 50201 | 56201 | 79201 |
| 170 202 | r | **1** | P | *GA* | NC | 50202 | 56202 | 79202 |
| 170 203 | r | **1** | P | *GA* | NC | 50203 | 56203 | 79203 |
| 170 204 | r | **1** | P | *GA* | NC | 50204 | 56204 | 79204 |
| 170 205 | r | **1** | P | *GA* | NC | 50205 | 56205 | 79205 |
| 170 206 | r | **1** | P | *GA* | NC | 50206 | 56206 | 79206 |
| 170 207 | r | **1** | P | *GA* | NC | 50207 | 56207 | 79207 |
| 170 208 | r | **AL** | P | *GA* | NC | 50208 | 56208 | 79208 |

**Class 170/2. Greater Anglia 2-car units.** Chapman seating. DMSL–DMCL.

**DMSL.** Bombardier Derby 2002. –/57 1TD 2W. 45.7 t.
**DMCL.** Bombardier Derby 2002. 9/53 1T. 45.7 t.

| | | | | | | | |
|---|---|---|---|---|---|---|---|
| 170 270 | r | **1** | P | *GA* | NC | 50270 | 79270 |
| 170 271 | r | **AN** | P | *GA* | NC | 50271 | 79271 |
| 170 272 | r | **AN** | P | *GA* | NC | 50272 | 79272 |
| 170 273 | r | **AN** | P | *GA* | NC | 50273 | 79273 |

**Class 170/3. TransPennine Express units.** Chapman seating. DMCL–DMSL.
170 309 renumbered from 170 399.

**50301–308/399. DMCL.** Adtranz Derby 2000–01. 8/43 1TD 2W. 45.8 t.
**79301–308/399. DMSL.** Adtranz Derby 2000–01. –/65 1T. 45.8 t.

| 170 301 | **FT** | P | *TP* | XW | 50301 | 79301 |
| 170 302 | **FT** | P | *TP* | XW | 50302 | 79302 |
| 170 303 | **FT** | P | *TP* | XW | 50303 | 79303 |
| 170 304 | **FT** | P | *TP* | XW | 50304 | 79304 |
| 170 305 | **FT** | P | *TP* | XW | 50305 | 79305 |
| 170 306 | **FT** | P | *TP* | XW | 50306 | 79306 |
| 170 307 | **FT** | P | *TP* | XW | 50307 | 79307 |
| 170 308 | **FT** | P | *TP* | XW | 50308 | 79308 |
| 170 309 | **FT** | P | *TP* | XW | 50399 | 79399 |

**Class 170/3. Units built for Hull Trains, now in use with ScotRail.** Chapman seating. DMSL–MSLRB–DMSL.

**DMSL(A)**. Bombardier Derby 2004. –/55 1TD 2W. 46.5 t.
**MSLRB**. Bombardier Derby 2004. –/57 1T. Buffet and guard's office 44.7 t.
**DMSL(B)**. Bombardier Derby 2004. –/67 1T. 47.0 t.

| 170 393 | **SR** | P | *SR* | HA | 50393 | 56393 | 79393 |
| 170 394 | **SR** | P | *SR* | HA | 50394 | 56394 | 79394 |
| 170 395 | **SR** | P | *SR* | HA | 50395 | 56395 | 79395 |
| 170 396 | **SR** | P | *SR* | HA | 50396 | 56396 | 79396 |

**Class 170/3. CrossCountry units.** Lazareni seating. DMSL–MS–DMCL.

**DMSL**. Bombardier Derby 2002. –/59 1TD 2W. 45.4 t.
**MS**. Bombardier Derby 2002. –/80. 43.0 t.
**DMCL**. Bombardier Derby 2002. 9/52 1T. 45.8 t.

| 170 397 | **XC** | P | *XC* | TS | 50397 | 56397 | 79397 |
| 170 398 | **XC** | P | *XC* | TS | 50398 | 56398 | 79398 |

**Class 170/4. ScotRail "express" units.** Chapman seating. DMCL–MS–DMCL.

**DMCL(A)**. Adtranz Derby 1999–2001. 9/43 1TD 2W. 45.2 t.
**MS**. Adtranz Derby 1999–2001. –/76. 42.5 t.
**DMCL(B)**. Adtranz Derby 1999–2001. 9/49 1T. 45.2 t.

| 170 401 | **FS** | P | *SR* | HA | 50401 | 56401 | 79401 |
| 170 402 | **SR** | P | *SR* | HA | 50402 | 56402 | 79402 |
| 170 403 | **FS** | P | *SR* | HA | 50403 | 56403 | 79403 |
| 170 404 | **FS** | P | *SR* | HA | 50404 | 56404 | 79404 |
| 170 405 | **FS** | P | *SR* | HA | 50405 | 56405 | 79405 |
| 170 406 | **FS** | P | *SR* | HA | 50406 | 56406 | 79406 |
| 170 407 | **FS** | P | *SR* | HA | 50407 | 56407 | 79407 |
| 170 408 | **FS** | P | *SR* | HA | 50408 | 56408 | 79408 |
| 170 409 | **FS** | P | *SR* | HA | 50409 | 56409 | 79409 |
| 170 410 | **FS** | P | *SR* | HA | 50410 | 56410 | 79410 |
| 170 411 | **FS** | P | *SR* | HA | 50411 | 56411 | 79411 |
| 170 412 | **SR** | P | *SR* | HA | 50412 | 56412 | 79412 |
| 170 413 | **FS** | P | *SR* | HA | 50413 | 56413 | 79413 |
| 170 414 | **FS** | P | *SR* | HA | 50414 | 56414 | 79414 |
| 170 415 | **SR** | P | *SR* | HA | 50415 | 56415 | 79415 |
| 170 416 | **FS** | E | *SR* | HA | 50416 | 56416 | 79416 |
| 170 417 | **FS** | E | *SR* | HA | 50417 | 56417 | 79417 |
| 170 418 | **SR** | E | *SR* | HA | 50418 | 56418 | 79418 |

| 170 419 | **FS** | E | *SR* | HA | 50419 | 56419 | 79419 |
| 170 420 | **FS** | E | *SR* | HA | 50420 | 56420 | 79420 |
| 170 421 | **FS** | E | *SR* | HA | 50421 | 56421 | 79421 |
| 170 422 | **FS** | E | *SR* | HA | 50422 | 56422 | 79422 |
| 170 423 | **FS** | E | *SR* | HA | 50423 | 56423 | 79423 |
| 170 424 | **FS** | E | *SR* | HA | 50424 | 56424 | 79424 |

**Names (carried on end cars):**

| 170 401 | Sir Moir Lockhead OBE |
| 170 405 | Riverside Museum |
| 170 407 | UNIVERSITY OF ABERDEEN |

**Class 170/4. ScotRail "express" units.** Chapman seating. DMCL–MS–DMCL.

**DMCL.** Bombardier Derby 2003–05. 9/43 1TD 2W. 46.8 t.
**MS.** Bombardier Derby 2003–05. –/76. 43.7 t.
**DMCL.** Bombardier Derby 2003–05. 9/49 1T. 46.5 t.

| 170 425 | **SR** | P | *SR* | HA | 50425 | 56425 | 79425 | |
| 170 426 | **SR** | P | *SR* | HA | 50426 | 56426 | 79426 | |
| 170 427 | **SR** | P | *SR* | HA | 50427 | 56427 | 79427 | |
| 170 428 | **SR** | P | *SR* | HA | 50428 | 56428 | 79428 | |
| 170 429 | **SR** | P | *SR* | HA | 50429 | 56429 | 79429 | |
| 170 430 | **SR** | P | *SR* | HA | 50430 | 56430 | 79430 | |
| 170 431 | **SR** | P | *SR* | HA | 50431 | 56431 | 79431 | |
| 170 432 | **SR** | P | *SR* | HA | 50432 | 56432 | 79432 | |
| 170 433 | **FS** | P | *SR* | HA | 50433 | 56433 | 79433 | Investor in People |
| 170 434 | **SR** | P | *SR* | HA | 50434 | 56434 | 79434 | |

**Class 170/4. ScotRail units.** Originally built as Standard Class only units.
170 450–457 have been retro-fitted with First Class. Chapman seating.
DMSL–MS–DMSL or † DMCL–MS–DMCL.

**DMSL.** Bombardier Derby 2004–05. –/55 1TD 2W († 9/47 1TD 2W). 46.3 t.
**MS.** Bombardier Derby 2004–05. –/76. 43.4 t.
**DMSL.** Bombardier Derby 2004–05. –/67 1T († 9/49 1T 1W). 46.4 t.

| 170 450 | † | **SR** | P | *SR* | HA | 50450 | 56450 | 79450 |
| 170 451 | † | **SR** | P | *SR* | HA | 50451 | 56451 | 79451 |
| 170 452 | † | **SR** | P | *SR* | HA | 50452 | 56452 | 79452 |
| 170 453 | † | **SR** | P | *SR* | HA | 50453 | 56453 | 79453 |
| 170 454 | † | **SR** | P | *SR* | HA | 50454 | 56454 | 79454 |
| 170 455 | † | **SR** | P | *SR* | HA | 50455 | 56455 | 79455 |
| 170 456 | † | **SR** | P | *SR* | HA | 50456 | 56456 | 79456 |
| 170 457 | † | **SR** | P | *SR* | HA | 50457 | 56457 | 79457 |
| 170 458 | | **SR** | P | *SR* | HA | 50458 | 56458 | 79458 |
| 170 459 | | **SR** | P | *SR* | HA | 50459 | 56459 | 79459 |
| 170 460 | | **SR** | P | *SR* | HA | 50460 | 56460 | 79460 |
| 170 461 | | **FS** | P | *SR* | HA | 50461 | 56461 | 79461 |

**Class 170/4. ScotRail units.** Standard Class only units. Chapman seating.
DMSL–MS–DMSL.

**50470–471. DMSL(A).** Adtranz Derby 2001. –/55 1TD 2W. 45.1 t.
**50472–478. DMSL(A).** Bombardier Derby 2004–05. –/57 1TD 2W. 46.3 t.

**56470–471. MS**. Adtranz Derby 2001. –/76. 42.4 t.
**56472–478. MS**. Bombardier Derby 2004–05. –/76. 43.4 t.
**79470–471. DMSL(B)**. Adtranz Derby 2001. –/67 1T. 45.1 t.
**79472–478. DMSL(B)**. Bombardier Derby 2004–05. –/67 1T. 46.4 t.

| | | | | | | | |
|---|---|---|---|---|---|---|---|
| 170 470 | **SR** | P | *SR* | HA | 50470 | 56470 | 79470 |
| 170 471 | **SR** | P | *SR* | HA | 50471 | 56471 | 79471 |
| 170 472 | **SR** | P | *SR* | HA | 50472 | 56472 | 79472 |
| 170 473 | **SR** | P | *SR* | HA | 50473 | 56473 | 79473 |
| 170 474 | **SR** | P | *SR* | HA | 50474 | 56474 | 79474 |
| 170 475 | **SR** | P | *SR* | HA | 50475 | 56475 | 79475 |
| 170 476 | **SR** | P | *SR* | HA | 50476 | 56476 | 79476 |
| 170 477 | **SR** | P | *SR* | HA | 50477 | 56477 | 79477 |
| 170 478 | **SP** | P | *SR* | HA | 50478 | 56478 | 79478 |

**Class 170/5. London Midland and CrossCountry 2-car units.** Lazareni seating. DMSL–DMSL or * DMSL–DMCL (CrossCountry).

**DMSL(A)**. Adtranz Derby 1999–2000. –/55 1TD 2W (* –/59 1TD 2W). 45.8 t.
**DMSL(B)**. Adtranz Derby 1999–2000. –/67 1T (* DMCL 9/52 1T). 45.9 t.

| | | | | | | |
|---|---|---|---|---|---|---|
| 170 501 | | **LM** | P | *LM* | TS | 50501 | 79501 |
| 170 502 | | **LM** | P | *LM* | TS | 50502 | 79502 |
| 170 503 | | **LM** | P | *LM* | TS | 50503 | 79503 |
| 170 504 | | **LM** | P | *LM* | TS | 50504 | 79504 |
| 170 505 | | **LM** | P | *LM* | TS | 50505 | 79505 |
| 170 506 | | **LM** | P | *LM* | TS | 50506 | 79506 |
| 170 507 | | **LM** | P | *LM* | TS | 50507 | 79507 |
| 170 508 | | **LM** | P | *LM* | TS | 50508 | 79508 |
| 170 509 | | **LM** | P | *LM* | TS | 50509 | 79509 |
| 170 510 | | **LM** | P | *LM* | TS | 50510 | 79510 |
| 170 511 | | **LM** | P | *LM* | TS | 50511 | 79511 |
| 170 512 | | **LM** | P | *LM* | TS | 50512 | 79512 |
| 170 513 | | **LM** | P | *LM* | TS | 50513 | 79513 |
| 170 514 | | **LM** | P | *LM* | TS | 50514 | 79514 |
| 170 515 | | **LM** | P | *LM* | TS | 50515 | 79515 |
| 170 516 | | **LM** | P | *LM* | TS | 50516 | 79516 |
| 170 517 | | **LM** | P | *LM* | TS | 50517 | 79517 |
| 170 518 | * | **XC** | P | *XC* | TS | 50518 | 79518 |
| 170 519 | * | **XC** | P | *XC* | TS | 50519 | 79519 |
| 170 520 | * | **XC** | P | *XC* | TS | 50520 | 79520 |
| 170 521 | * | **XC** | P | *XC* | TS | 50521 | 79521 |
| 170 522 | * | **XC** | P | *XC* | TS | 50522 | 79522 |
| 170 523 | * | **XC** | P | *XC* | TS | 50523 | 79523 |

**Class 170/6. London Midland and CrossCountry 3-car units.** Lazareni seating. DMSL–MS–DMSL or * DMSL–MS–DMCL (CrossCountry).

**DMSL(A)**. Adtranz Derby 2000. –/55 1TD 2W (* –/59 1TD 2W). 45.8 t.
**MS**. Adtranz Derby 2000. –/74 (* –/80). 42.4 t.
**DMSL(B)**. Adtranz Derby 2000. –/67 1T (* DMCL 9/52 1T). 45.9 t.

| | | | | | | | |
|---|---|---|---|---|---|---|---|
| 170 630 | **LM** | P | *LM* | TS | 50630 | 56630 | 79630 |
| 170 631 | **LM** | P | *LM* | TS | 50631 | 56631 | 79631 |

| 170 632 | **LM** | P | *LM* | TS | 50632 | 56632 | 79632 |
| 170 633 | **LM** | P | *LM* | TS | 50633 | 56633 | 79633 |
| 170 634 | **LM** | P | *LM* | TS | 50634 | 56634 | 79634 |
| 170 635 | **LM** | P | *LM* | TS | 50635 | 56635 | 79635 |
| 170 636 | * **XC** | P | *XC* | TS | 50636 | 56636 | 79636 |
| 170 637 | * **XC** | P | *XC* | TS | 50637 | 56637 | 79637 |
| 170 638 | * **XC** | P | *XC* | TS | 50638 | 56638 | 79638 |
| 170 639 | * **XC** | P | *XC* | TS | 50639 | 56639 | 79639 |

# CLASS 171            TURBOSTAR            BOMBARDIER

DMCL–DMSL or DMCL–MS–MS–DMCL. Southern units. Air conditioned. Chapman seating.

**Construction:** Welded aluminium bodies with bolt-on steel ends.
**Engines:** One MTU 6R183TD13H of 315 hp (422 hp) at 1900 rpm.
**Transmission:** Hydraulic. Voith T211rzze to ZF final drive.
**Bogies:** One Adtranz P3–23 and one BREL T3–23 per car.
**Couplers:** Dellner 12 at outer ends, bar within unit (Class 171/8s).
**Dimensions:** 23.62/23.61 x 2.69 m.
**Gangways:** Within unit only.    **Wheel Arrangement:** 2-B (+ B-2 + B-2) + B-2.
**Doors:** Twin-leaf swing plug.    **Maximum Speed:** 100 mph.
**Seating Layout:** 1: 2+1 facing/unidirectional. 2: 2+2 facing/unidirectional.
**Multiple Working:** Within class and with EMU Classes 375 and 377 in an emergency.

**Class 171/7. 2-car units.** DMCL–DMSL.

171 721–726 were built as Class 170s (170 721–726), but renumbered as Class 171s on fitting with Dellner couplers.

171 730 was formerly South West Trains unit 170 392, before transferring to Southern in 2007.

**50721–726. DMCL.** Bombardier Derby 2003. 9/43 1TD 2W. 47.6 t.
**50727–729. DMCL.** Bombardier Derby 2005. 9/43 1TD 2W. 46.3 t.
**50392. DMCL.** Bombardier Derby 2003. 9/43 1TD 2W. 46.6 t.
**79721–726. DMSL.** Bombardier Derby 2003. –/64 1T. 47.8 t.
**79727–729. DMSL.** Bombardier Derby 2005. –/64 1T. 46.2 t.
**79392. DMSL.** Bombardier Derby 2003. –/64 1T. 46.5 t.

| 171 721 | **SN** | P | *SN* | SU | 50721 | 79721 |
| 171 722 | **SN** | P | *SN* | SU | 50722 | 79722 |
| 171 723 | **SN** | P | *SN* | SU | 50723 | 79723 |
| 171 724 | **SN** | P | *SN* | SU | 50724 | 79724 |
| 171 725 | **SN** | P | *SN* | SU | 50725 | 79725 |
| 171 726 | **SN** | P | *SN* | SU | 50726 | 79726 |
| 171 727 | **SN** | P | *SN* | SU | 50727 | 79727 |
| 171 728 | **SN** | P | *SN* | SU | 50728 | 79728 |
| 171 729 | **SN** | P | *SN* | SU | 50729 | 79729 |
| 171 730 | **SN** | P | *SN* | SU | 50392 | 79392 |

**Class 171/8. 4-car units.** DMCL(A)–MS–MS–DMCL(B).

**DMCL(A).** Bombardier Derby 2004. 9/43 1TD 2W. 46.5 t.
**MS.** Bombardier Derby 2004. –/74. 43.7 t.
**DMCL(B).** Bombardier Derby 2004. 9/50 1T. 46.5 t.

| 171 801 | **SN** | P | *SN* | SU | 50801 | 54801 | 56801 | 79801 |
|---------|--------|---|------|----|-------|-------|-------|-------|
| 171 802 | **SN** | P | *SN* | SU | 50802 | 54802 | 56802 | 79802 |
| 171 803 | **SN** | P | *SN* | SU | 50803 | 54803 | 56803 | 79803 |
| 171 804 | **SN** | P | *SN* | SU | 50804 | 54804 | 56804 | 79804 |
| 171 805 | **SN** | P | *SN* | SU | 50805 | 54805 | 56805 | 79805 |
| 171 806 | **SN** | P | *SN* | SU | 50806 | 54806 | 56806 | 79806 |

# CLASS 172          TURBOSTAR          BOMBARDIER

New generation London Overground, Chiltern Railways and London Midland Turbostars. Air conditioned.

**Construction:** Welded aluminium bodies with bolt-on steel ends.
**Engines:** One MTU 6H1800R83 of 360 kW (483 hp) at 1800 rpm.
**Transmission:** Mechanical. Supplied by ZF, Germany.
**Bogies:** B5006 type "lightweight" bogies.
**Couplers:** BSI at outer ends, bar within unit.
**Dimensions:** 23.62/23.0 × 2.69 m.
**Gangways:** London Overground & Chiltern units: Within unit only. London Midland units: Throughout.
**Wheel Arrangement:** 2-B (+ B-2) + B-2.
**Doors:** Twin-leaf sliding plug.
**Maximum Speed:** 100 mph (London Overground units 75 mph).
**Seating Layout:** 2+2 facing/unidirectional.
**Multiple Working:** Within class and with Classes 150, 153, 155, 156, 158, 159, 165, 166 and 170.

**Class 172/0. London Overground units.** Used on the Gospel Oak–Barking line. DMS–DMS.

**59311–318. DMS(W).** Bombardier Derby 2009–10. –/60 2W. 41.6 t.
**59411–418. DMS.** Bombardier Derby 2009–10. –/64. 41.5 t.

| 172 001 | **LO** | A | *LO* | WN | 59311 | 59411 |
|---------|--------|---|------|----|-------|-------|
| 172 002 | **LO** | A | *LO* | WN | 59312 | 59412 |
| 172 003 | **LO** | A | *LO* | WN | 59313 | 59413 |
| 172 004 | **LO** | A | *LO* | WN | 59314 | 59414 |
| 172 005 | **LO** | A | *LO* | WN | 59315 | 59415 |
| 172 006 | **LO** | A | *LO* | WN | 59316 | 59416 |
| 172 007 | **LO** | A | *LO* | WN | 59317 | 59417 |
| 172 008 | **LO** | A | *LO* | WN | 59318 | 59418 |

**Class 172/1. Chiltern Railways units.** DMSL–DMS.

**59111–114. DMSL.** Bombardier Derby 2009–10. –/60(5) 1TD 2W. 42.4 t.
**59211–214. DMS.** Bombardier Derby 2009–10. –/80. 41.8 t.

| 172 101 | **CR** | A | *CR* | AL | 59111 | 59211 |
|---------|--------|---|------|----|-------|-------|
| 172 102 | **CR** | A | *CR* | AL | 59112 | 59212 |

| 172 103 | **CR** | A | *CR* | AL | 59113 | 59213 |
| 172 104 | **CR** | A | *CR* | AL | 59114 | 59214 |

**Class 172/2. London Midland 2-car units.** DMSL–DMS. Used on local services via Birmingham Snow Hill.

**50211–222. DMSL.** Bombardier Derby 2010–11. –/52(11) 1TD 2W. 42.5 t.
**79211–222. DMS.** Bombardier Derby 2010–11. –/68(8). 41.9 t.

| 172 211 | **LM** | P | *LM* | TS | 50211 | 79211 |
| 172 212 | **LM** | P | *LM* | TS | 50212 | 79212 |
| 172 213 | **LM** | P | *LM* | TS | 50213 | 79213 |
| 172 214 | **LM** | P | *LM* | TS | 50214 | 79214 |
| 172 215 | **LM** | P | *LM* | TS | 50215 | 79215 |
| 172 216 | **LM** | P | *LM* | TS | 50216 | 79216 |
| 172 217 | **LM** | P | *LM* | TS | 50217 | 79217 |
| 172 218 | **LM** | P | *LM* | TS | 50218 | 79218 |
| 172 219 | **LM** | P | *LM* | TS | 50219 | 79219 |
| 172 220 | **LM** | P | *LM* | TS | 50220 | 79220 |
| 172 221 | **LM** | P | *LM* | TS | 50221 | 79221 |
| 172 222 | **LM** | P | *LM* | TS | 50222 | 79222 |

**Class 172/3. London Midland 3-car units.** DMSL–MS–DMS. Used on local services via Birmingham Snow Hill.

**50331–345. DMSL.** Bombardier Derby 2010–11. –/52(11) 1TD 2W. 42.5 t.
**56331–345. MS.** Bombardier Derby 2010–11. –/72(8). 38.8 t.
**79331–345. DMS.** Bombardier Derby 2010–11. –/68(8). 41.9 t.

| 172 331 | **LM** | P | *LM* | TS | 50331 | 56331 | 79331 |
| 172 332 | **LM** | P | *LM* | TS | 50332 | 56332 | 79332 |
| 172 333 | **LM** | P | *LM* | TS | 50333 | 56333 | 79333 |
| 172 334 | **LM** | P | *LM* | TS | 50334 | 56334 | 79334 |
| 172 335 | **LM** | P | *LM* | TS | 50335 | 56335 | 79335 |
| 172 336 | **LM** | P | *LM* | TS | 50336 | 56336 | 79336 |
| 172 337 | **LM** | P | *LM* | TS | 50337 | 56337 | 79337 |
| 172 338 | **LM** | P | *LM* | TS | 50338 | 56338 | 79338 |
| 172 339 | **LM** | P | *LM* | TS | 50339 | 56339 | 79339 |
| 172 340 | **LM** | P | *LM* | TS | 50340 | 56340 | 79340 |
| 172 341 | **LM** | P | *LM* | TS | 50341 | 56341 | 79341 |
| 172 342 | **LM** | P | *LM* | TS | 50342 | 56342 | 79342 |
| 172 343 | **LM** | P | *LM* | TS | 50343 | 56343 | 79343 |
| 172 344 | **LM** | P | *LM* | TS | 50344 | 56344 | 79344 |
| 172 345 | **LM** | P | *LM* | TS | 50345 | 56345 | 79345 |

# CLASS 175          CORADIA 1000          ALSTOM

Air conditioned.

**Construction:** Steel.
**Engines:** One Cummins N14 of 335 kW (450 hp).
**Transmission:** Hydraulic. Voith T211rzze to ZF Voith final drive.
**Bogies:** ACR (Alstom FBO) – LTB-MBS1, TB-MB1, MBS1-LTB.
**Couplers:** Scharfenberg outer ends and bar within unit (Class 175/1).

**Dimensions:** 23.7 x 2.73 m.
**Gangways:** Within unit only.    **Wheel Arrangement:** 2-B (+ B-2) + B-2.
**Doors:** Single-leaf swing plug.    **Maximum Speed:** 100 mph.
**Seating Layout:** 2+2 facing/unidirectional.
**Multiple Working:** Within class and with Class 180.

**Class 175/0.** DMSL–DMSL. 2-car units.

**DMSL(A).** Alstom Birmingham 1999–2000. –/54 1TD 2W. 48.8 t.
**DMSL(B).** Alstom Birmingham 1999–2000. –/64 1T. 50.7 t.

| | | | | | | |
|---|---|---|---|---|---|---|
| 175 001 | **AV** | A | *AW* | CH | 50701 | 79701 |
| 175 002 | **AV** | A | *AW* | CH | 50702 | 79702 |
| 175 003 | **AV** | A | *AW* | CH | 50703 | 79703 |
| 175 004 | **AV** | A | *AW* | CH | 50704 | 79704 |
| 175 005 | **AV** | A | *AW* | CH | 50705 | 79705 |
| 175 006 | **AV** | A | *AW* | CH | 50706 | 79706 |
| 175 007 | **AV** | A | *AW* | CH | 50707 | 79707 |
| 175 008 | **AV** | A | *AW* | CH | 50708 | 79708 |
| 175 009 | **AV** | A | *AW* | CH | 50709 | 79709 |
| 175 010 | **AV** | A | *AW* | CH | 50710 | 79710 |
| 175 011 | **AV** | A | *AW* | CH | 50711 | 79711 |

**Class 175/1.** DMSL–MSL–DMSL. 3-car units.

**DMSL(A).** Alstom Birmingham 1999–2001. –/54 1TD 2W. 50.7 t.
**MSL.** Alstom Birmingham 1999–2001. –/68 1T. 47.5 t.
**DMSL(B).** Alstom Birmingham 1999–2001. –/64 1T. 49.5 t.

| | | | | | | | |
|---|---|---|---|---|---|---|---|
| 175 101 | **AV** | A | *AW* | CH | 50751 | 56751 | 79751 |
| 175 102 | **AV** | A | *AW* | CH | 50752 | 56752 | 79752 |
| 175 103 | **AV** | A | *AW* | CH | 50753 | 56753 | 79753 |
| 175 104 | **AV** | A | *AW* | CH | 50754 | 56754 | 79754 |
| 175 105 | **AV** | A | *AW* | CH | 50755 | 56755 | 79755 |
| 175 106 | **AV** | A | *AW* | CH | 50756 | 56756 | 79756 |
| 175 107 | **AV** | A | *AW* | CH | 50757 | 56757 | 79757 |
| 175 108 | **AV** | A | *AW* | CH | 50758 | 56758 | 79758 |
| 175 109 | **AV** | A | *AW* | CH | 50759 | 56759 | 79759 |
| 175 110 | **AV** | A | *AW* | CH | 50760 | 56760 | 79760 |
| 175 111 | **AV** | A | *AW* | CH | 50761 | 56761 | 79761 |
| 175 112 | **AV** | A | *AW* | CH | 50762 | 56762 | 79762 |
| 175 113 | **AV** | A | *AW* | CH | 50763 | 56763 | 79763 |
| 175 114 | **AV** | A | *AW* | CH | 50764 | 56764 | 79764 |
| 175 115 | **AV** | A | *AW* | CH | 50765 | 56765 | 79765 |
| 175 116 | **AV** | A | *AW* | CH | 50766 | 56766 | 79766 |

# CLASS 180          ADELANTE                    ALSTOM

Air conditioned.

**Construction:** Steel.
**Engines:** One Cummins QSK19 of 560 kW (750 hp) at 2100 rpm.
**Transmission:** Hydraulic. Voith T312br to Voith final drive.
**Bogies:** ACR (Alstom FBO): LTB1-MBS2, TB1-MB2, TB1-MB2, TB2-MB2, MBS2-LTB1.

**Couplers:** Scharfenberg outer ends, bar within unit.
**Dimensions:** 23.71/23.03 x 2.73 m.
**Gangways:** Within unit only.
**Wheel Arrangement:** 2-B + B-2 + B-2 + B-2 + B-2.
**Doors:** Single-leaf swing plug.          **Maximum Speed:** 125 mph.
**Seating Layout:** 1: 2+1 facing/unidirectional, 2: 2+2 facing/unidirectional.
**Multiple Working:** Within class and with Class 175.

**DMSL(A).** Alstom Birmingham 2000–01. –/46 2W 1TD. 51.7 t.
**MFL.** Alstom Birmingham 2000–01. 42/– 1T 1W + catering point. 49.6 t.
**MSL.** Alstom Birmingham 2000–01. –/68 1T. 49.5 t.
**MSLRB.** Alstom Birmingham 2000–01. –/56 1T. 50.3 t.
**DMSL(B).** Alstom Birmingham 2000–01. –/56 1T. 51.4 t.

| | | | | | | | | | |
|---|---|---|---|---|---|---|---|---|---|
| 180 101 | **GC** | A | *GC* | HT | 50901 | 54901 | 55901 | 56901 | 59901 |
| 180 102 | **FD** | A | *GW* | OO | 50902 | 54902 | 55902 | 56902 | 59902 |
| 180 103 | **FD** | A | *GW* | OO | 50903 | 54903 | 55903 | 56903 | 59903 |
| 180 104 | **FD** | A | *GW* | OO | 50904 | 54904 | 55904 | 56904 | 59904 |
| 180 105 | **GC** | A | *GC* | HT | 50905 | 54905 | 55905 | 56905 | 59905 |
| 180 106 | **FD** | A | *GW* | OO | 50906 | 54906 | 55906 | 56906 | 59906 |
| 180 107 | **GC** | A | *GC* | HT | 50907 | 54907 | 55907 | 56907 | 59907 |
| 180 108 | **FD** | A | *GW* | OO | 50908 | 54908 | 55908 | 56908 | 59908 |
| 180 109 | **FD** | A | *HT* | OO | 50909 | 54909 | 55909 | 56909 | 59909 |
| 180 110 | **FD** | A | *HT* | OO | 50910 | 54910 | 55910 | 56910 | 59910 |
| 180 111 | **FD** | A | *HT* | OO | 50911 | 54911 | 55911 | 56911 | 59911 |
| 180 112 | **GC** | A | *GC* | HT | 50912 | 54912 | 55912 | 56912 | 59912 |
| 180 113 | **FD** | A | *HT* | OO | 50913 | 54913 | 55913 | 56913 | 59913 |
| 180 114 | **GC** | A | *GC* | HT | 50914 | 54914 | 55914 | 56914 | 59914 |

**Names (carried on DMSL(A):**

| | |
|---|---|
| 180 105 | THE YORKSHIRE ARTIST ASHLEY JACKSON |
| 180 107 | HART OF THE NORTH |
| 180 112 | JAMES HERRIOT |

## CLASS 185          DESIRO UK          SIEMENS

Air conditioned. Grammer seating.

**Construction:** Aluminium.
**Engines:** One Cummins QSK19 of 560 kW (750 hp) at 2100 rpm.
**Transmission:** Voith.
**Bogies:** Siemens.
**Couplers:** Dellner 12.               **Dimensions:** 23.76/23.75 x 2.66 m.
**Gangways:** Within unit only.         **Wheel Arrangement:** 2-B + 2-B + B-2.
**Doors:** Double-leaf sliding plug.    **Maximum Speed:** 100 mph.
**Seating Layout:** 1: 2+1 facing/unidirectional, 2: 2+2 facing/unidirectional.
**Multiple Working:** Within class only.

**DMCL.** Siemens Krefeld 2005–06. 15/18(8) 2W 1TD + catering point. 55.4 t.
**MSL.** Siemens Krefeld 2005–06. –/72 1T. 52.7 t.
**DMS.** Siemens Krefeld 2005–06. –/64(4). 54.9 t.

| 185 101 | **FT** | E | *TP* | AK | 51101 | 53101 | 54101 |
| 185 102 | **FT** | E | *TP* | AK | 51102 | 53102 | 54102 |
| 185 103 | **FT** | E | *TP* | AK | 51103 | 53103 | 54103 |
| 185 104 | **FT** | E | *TP* | AK | 51104 | 53104 | 54104 |
| 185 105 | **FT** | E | *TP* | AK | 51105 | 53105 | 54105 |
| 185 106 | **FT** | E | *TP* | AK | 51106 | 53106 | 54106 |
| 185 107 | **FT** | E | *TP* | AK | 51107 | 53107 | 54107 |
| 185 108 | **FT** | E | *TP* | AK | 51108 | 53108 | 54108 |
| 185 109 | **FT** | E | *TP* | AK | 51109 | 53109 | 54109 |
| 185 110 | **FT** | E | *TP* | AK | 51110 | 53110 | 54110 |
| 185 111 | **FT** | E | *TP* | AK | 51111 | 53111 | 54111 |
| 185 112 | **FT** | E | *TP* | AK | 51112 | 53112 | 54112 |
| 185 113 | **FT** | E | *TP* | AK | 51113 | 53113 | 54113 |
| 185 114 | **FT** | E | *TP* | AK | 51114 | 53114 | 54114 |
| 185 115 | **FT** | E | *TP* | AK | 51115 | 53115 | 54115 |
| 185 116 | **FT** | E | *TP* | AK | 51116 | 53116 | 54116 |
| 185 117 | **FT** | E | *TP* | AK | 51117 | 53117 | 54117 |
| 185 118 | **FT** | E | *TP* | AK | 51118 | 53118 | 54118 |
| 185 119 | **FT** | E | *TP* | AK | 51119 | 53119 | 54119 |
| 185 120 | **FT** | E | *TP* | AK | 51120 | 53120 | 54120 |
| 185 121 | **FT** | E | *TP* | AK | 51121 | 53121 | 54121 |
| 185 122 | **FT** | E | *TP* | AK | 51122 | 53122 | 54122 |
| 185 123 | **FT** | E | *TP* | AK | 51123 | 53123 | 54123 |
| 185 124 | **FT** | E | *TP* | AK | 51124 | 53124 | 54124 |
| 185 125 | **FT** | E | *TP* | AK | 51125 | 53125 | 54125 |
| 185 126 | **FT** | E | *TP* | AK | 51126 | 53126 | 54126 |
| 185 127 | **FT** | E | *TP* | AK | 51127 | 53127 | 54127 |
| 185 128 | **FT** | E | *TP* | AK | 51128 | 53128 | 54128 |
| 185 129 | **FT** | E | *TP* | AK | 51129 | 53129 | 54129 |
| 185 130 | **FT** | E | *TP* | AK | 51130 | 53130 | 54130 |
| 185 131 | **FT** | E | *TP* | AK | 51131 | 53131 | 54131 |
| 185 132 | **FT** | E | *TP* | AK | 51132 | 53132 | 54132 |
| 185 133 | **FT** | E | *TP* | AK | 51133 | 53133 | 54133 |
| 185 134 | **FT** | E | *TP* | AK | 51134 | 53134 | 54134 |
| 185 135 | **FT** | E | *TP* | AK | 51135 | 53135 | 54135 |
| 185 136 | **FT** | E | *TP* | AK | 51136 | 53136 | 54136 |
| 185 137 | **FT** | E | *TP* | AK | 51137 | 53137 | 54137 |
| 185 138 | **FT** | E | *TP* | AK | 51138 | 53138 | 54138 |
| 185 139 | **FT** | E | *TP* | AK | 51139 | 53139 | 54139 |
| 185 140 | **FT** | E | *TP* | AK | 51140 | 53140 | 54140 |
| 185 141 | **FT** | E | *TP* | AK | 51141 | 53141 | 54141 |
| 185 142 | **FT** | E | *TP* | AK | 51142 | 53142 | 54142 |
| 185 143 | **FT** | E | *TP* | AK | 51143 | 53143 | 54143 |
| 185 144 | **FT** | E | *TP* | AK | 51144 | 53144 | 54144 |
| 185 145 | **FT** | E | *TP* | AK | 51145 | 53145 | 54145 |
| 185 146 | **FT** | E | *TP* | AK | 51146 | 53146 | 54146 |
| 185 147 | **FT** | E | *TP* | AK | 51147 | 53147 | 54147 |
| 185 148 | **FT** | E | *TP* | AK | 51148 | 53148 | 54148 |
| 185 149 | **FT** | E | *TP* | AK | 51149 | 53149 | 54149 |
| 185 150 | **FT** | E | *TP* | AK | 51150 | 53150 | 54150 |
| 185 151 | **FT** | E | *TP* | AK | 51151 | 53151 | 54151 |

# 3.2. DIESEL ELECTRIC UNITS

## CLASS 201/202    PRESERVED "HASTINGS" UNIT    BR

DMBS–TSL–TSL–TSRB–TSL–DMBS.

Preserved unit made up from two Class 201 short-frame cars and three Class 202 long-frame cars. The "Hastings" units were made with narrow body-profiles for use on the section between Tonbridge and Battle which had tunnels of restricted loading gauge. These tunnels were converted to single track operation in the 1980s thus allowing standard loading gauge stock to be used. The set also contains a Class 411 EMU trailer (not Hastings line gauge) and a Class 422 EMU buffet car.

**Construction:** Steel.
**Engine:** One English Electric 4SRKT Mk. 2 of 450 kW (600 hp) at 850 rpm.
**Main Generator:** English Electric EE824.
**Traction Motors:** Two English Electric EE507 mounted on the inner bogie.
**Bogies:** SR Mk 4. (Former EMU TSL vehicles have Commonwealth bogies).
**Couplers:** Drophead buckeye.
**Dimensions:** 18.40 x 2.50 m (60000), 20.35 x 2.50 m (60116/118/529), 18.36 x 2.50 m (60501), 20.35 x 2.82 (69337), 20.30 x 2.82 (70262).
**Gangways:** Within unit only.          **Doors:** Manually operated slam.
**Brakes:** Electro-pneumatic and automatic air.
**Maximum Speed:** 75 mph.          **Seating Layout:** 2+2 facing.
**Multiple Working:** Other ex-BR Southern Region DEMU vehicles.

**60000. DMBS.** Lot No. 30329 Eastleigh 1957. –/22. 55.0 t.
**60116. DMBS.** Lot No. 30395 Eastleigh 1957. –/31. 56.0 t.
**60118. DMBS.** Lot No. 30395 Eastleigh 1957. –/30. 56.0 t.
**60501. TSL.** Lot No. 30331 Eastleigh 1957. –/52 2T. 29.5 t.
**60529. TSL.** Lot No. 30397 Eastleigh 1957. –/60 2T. 30.5 t.
**69337. TSRB (ex-Class 422 EMU).** Lot No. 30805 York 1970. –/40. 35.0 t.
**70262. TSL (ex-Class 411/5 EMU).** Lot No. 30455 Eastleigh 1958. –/64 2T. 31.5 t.

| | | | | | | | | | | |
|---|---|---|---|---|---|---|---|---|---|---|
| 201 001 | G | HD | *HD* | SE | 60116 | 60529 | 70262 | 69337 | 60501 | 60118 |
| Spare | G | HD | *HD* | SE | 60000 | | | | | |

**Names:**

| | |
|---|---|
| 60000 | Hastings |
| 60116 | Mountfield |
| 60118 | Tunbridge Wells |

## CLASS 220          VOYAGER          BOMBARDIER

DMS–MS–MS–DMF. All engines have been derated from 750 hp to 700 hp.

**Construction:** Steel.
**Engine:** Cummins QSK19 of 520 kW (700 hp) at 1800 rpm.
**Transmission:** Two Alstom Onix 800 three-phase traction motors of 275 kW.
**Braking:** Rheostatic and electro-pneumatic.

**Bogies:** Bombardier B5005.
**Couplers:** Dellner 12 at outer ends, bar within unit.
**Dimensions:** 23.85/23.00 (602xx) x 2.73 m.
**Gangways:** Within unit only.
**Wheel Arrangement:** 1A-A1 + 1A-A1 + 1A-A1 + 1A-A1.
**Doors:** Single-leaf swing plug.
**Maximum Speed:** 125 m.p.h.
**Seating Layout:** 1: 2+1 facing/unidirectional, 2: 2+2 mainly unidirectional.
**Multiple Working:** Within class and with Classes 221 and 222 (in an emergency). Also can be controlled from Class 57/3 locomotives.

**DMS**. Bombardier Bruges/Wakefield 2000–01. –/42 1TD 1W. 51.1 t.
**MS(A)**. Bombardier Bruges/Wakefield 2000–01. –/66. 45.9 t.
**MS(B)**. Bombardier Bruges/Wakefield 2000–01. –/66 1TD. 46.7 t.
**DMF**. Bombardier Bruges/Wakefield 2000–01. 26/– 1TD 1W. 50.9 t.

| 220 001 | **XC** | VL | *XC* | CZ | 60301 | 60701 | 60201 | 60401 |
|---------|--------|----|------|----|-------|-------|-------|-------|
| 220 002 | **XC** | VL | *XC* | CZ | 60302 | 60702 | 60202 | 60402 |
| 220 003 | **XC** | VL | *XC* | CZ | 60303 | 60703 | 60203 | 60403 |
| 220 004 | **XC** | VL | *XC* | CZ | 60304 | 60704 | 60204 | 60404 |
| 220 005 | **XC** | VL | *XC* | CZ | 60305 | 60705 | 60205 | 60405 |
| 220 006 | **XC** | VL | *XC* | CZ | 60306 | 60706 | 60206 | 60406 |
| 220 007 | **XC** | VL | *XC* | CZ | 60307 | 60707 | 60207 | 60407 |
| 220 008 | **XC** | VL | *XC* | CZ | 60308 | 60708 | 60208 | 60408 |
| 220 009 | **XC** | VL | *XC* | CZ | 60309 | 60709 | 60209 | 60409 |
| 220 010 | **XC** | VL | *XC* | CZ | 60310 | 60710 | 60210 | 60410 |
| 220 011 | **XC** | VL | *XC* | CZ | 60311 | 60711 | 60211 | 60411 |
| 220 012 | **XC** | VL | *XC* | CZ | 60312 | 60712 | 60212 | 60412 |
| 220 013 | **XC** | VL | *XC* | CZ | 60313 | 60713 | 60213 | 60413 |
| 220 014 | **XC** | VL | *XC* | CZ | 60314 | 60714 | 60214 | 60414 |
| 220 015 | **XC** | VL | *XC* | CZ | 60315 | 60715 | 60215 | 60415 |
| 220 016 | **XC** | VL | *XC* | CZ | 60316 | 60716 | 60216 | 60416 |
| 220 017 | **XC** | VL | *XC* | CZ | 60317 | 60717 | 60217 | 60417 |
| 220 018 | **XC** | VL | *XC* | CZ | 60318 | 60718 | 60218 | 60418 |
| 220 019 | **XC** | VL | *XC* | CZ | 60319 | 60719 | 60219 | 60419 |
| 220 020 | **XC** | VL | *XC* | CZ | 60320 | 60720 | 60220 | 60420 |
| 220 021 | **XC** | VL | *XC* | CZ | 60321 | 60721 | 60221 | 60421 |
| 220 022 | **XC** | VL | *XC* | CZ | 60322 | 60722 | 60222 | 60422 |
| 220 023 | **XC** | VL | *XC* | CZ | 60323 | 60723 | 60223 | 60423 |
| 220 024 | **XC** | VL | *XC* | CZ | 60324 | 60724 | 60224 | 60424 |
| 220 025 | **XC** | VL | *XC* | CZ | 60325 | 60725 | 60225 | 60425 |
| 220 026 | **XC** | VL | *XC* | CZ | 60326 | 60726 | 60226 | 60426 |
| 220 027 | **XC** | VL | *XC* | CZ | 60327 | 60727 | 60227 | 60427 |
| 220 028 | **XC** | VL | *XC* | CZ | 60328 | 60728 | 60228 | 60428 |
| 220 029 | **XC** | VL | *XC* | CZ | 60329 | 60729 | 60229 | 60429 |
| 220 030 | **XC** | VL | *XC* | CZ | 60330 | 60730 | 60230 | 60430 |
| 220 031 | **XC** | VL | *XC* | CZ | 60331 | 60731 | 60231 | 60431 |
| 220 032 | **XC** | VL | *XC* | CZ | 60332 | 60732 | 60232 | 60432 |
| 220 033 | **XC** | VL | *XC* | CZ | 60333 | 60733 | 60233 | 60433 |
| 220 034 | **XC** | VL | *XC* | CZ | 60334 | 60734 | 60234 | 60434 |

# CLASS 221       SUPER VOYAGER       BOMBARDIER

\* DMS–MS–MS–MSRMB–DMF (Virgin Trains units) or DMS–MS–MS–MS–DMF (CrossCountry units). Built as tilting units but tilt now isolated on CrossCountry sets. All engines have been derated from 750 hp to 700 hp.

**Construction:** Steel.
**Engine:** Cummins QSK19 of 520 kW (700 hp) at 1800 rpm.
**Transmission:** Two Alstom Onix 800 three-phase traction motors of 275 kW.
**Braking:** Rheostatic and electro-pneumatic.
**Bogies:** Bombardier HVP.
**Couplers:** Dellner 12 at outer ends, bar within unit.
**Dimensions:** 23.67 x 2.73 m.
**Gangways:** Within unit only.
**Wheel Arrangement:** 1A-A1 + 1A-A1 + 1A-A1 (+ 1A-A1) + 1A-A1.
**Doors:** Single-leaf swing plug.
**Maximum Speed:** 125 mph.
**Seating Layout:** 1: 2+1 facing/unidirectional, 2: 2+2 mainly unidirectional.
**Multiple Working:** Within class and with Classes 220 and 222 (in an emergency). Also can be controlled from Class 57/3 locomotives.

\* Virgin Trains units. MSRMB moved adjacent to the DMF. The seating in this vehicle (2+2 facing) can be used by First or Standard Class passengers depending on demand.

**Advertising livery:** 221 115 Dark grey Bombardier branding on end vehicles.

**DMS.** Bombardier Bruges/Wakefield 2001–02. –/42 1TD 1W. 58.5 t (\* 58.9 t.)
**60751–794 MS (\* MSRMB).** Bombardier Bruges/Wakefield 2001–02. –/66 (\* –/52). 54.1 t (\* 55.9 t.)
**60951–994. MS.** Bombardier Bruges/Wakefield 2001–02. –/66 1TD (\* –/68 1TD). 54.8 t (\* 54.3 t.)
**60851–890. MS.** Bombardier Bruges/Wakefield 2001–02. –/62 1TD (\* –/68 1TD). 54.4 t (\* 55.0 t.)
**DMF.** Bombardier Bruges/Wakefield 2001–02. 26/– 1TD 1W. 58.9 t (\* 59.1 t.)

| | | | | | | | | | |
|---|---|---|---|---|---|---|---|---|---|
| 221 101 | \* | **VT** | VL | *VW* | CZ | 60351 | 60951 | 60851 | 60751 | 60451 |
| 221 102 | \* | **VT** | VL | *VW* | CZ | 60352 | 60952 | 60852 | 60752 | 60452 |
| 221 103 | \* | **VT** | VL | *VW* | CZ | 60353 | 60953 | 60853 | 60753 | 60453 |
| 221 104 | \* | **VT** | VL | *VW* | CZ | 60354 | 60954 | 60854 | 60754 | 60454 |
| 221 105 | \* | **VT** | VL | *VW* | CZ | 60355 | 60955 | 60855 | 60755 | 60455 |
| 221 106 | \* | **VT** | VL | *VW* | CZ | 60356 | 60956 | 60856 | 60756 | 60456 |
| 221 107 | \* | **VT** | VL | *VW* | CZ | 60357 | 60957 | 60857 | 60757 | 60457 |
| 221 108 | \* | **VT** | VL | *VW* | CZ | 60358 | 60958 | 60858 | 60758 | 60458 |
| 221 109 | \* | **VT** | VL | *VW* | CZ | 60359 | 60959 | 60859 | 60759 | 60459 |
| 221 110 | \* | **VT** | VL | *VW* | CZ | 60360 | 60960 | 60860 | 60760 | 60460 |
| 221 111 | \* | **VT** | VL | *VW* | CZ | 60361 | 60961 | 60861 | 60761 | 60461 |
| 221 112 | \* | **VT** | VL | *VW* | CZ | 60362 | 60962 | 60862 | 60762 | 60462 |
| 221 113 | \* | **VT** | VL | *VW* | CZ | 60363 | 60963 | 60863 | 60763 | 60463 |
| 221 114 | \* | **VT** | VL | *VW* | CZ | 60364 | 60764 | 60964 | 60864 | 60464 |
| 221 115 | \* | **AL** | VL | *VW* | CZ | 60365 | 60765 | 60965 | 60865 | 60465 |
| 221 116 | \* | **VT** | VL | *VW* | CZ | 60366 | 60766 | 60966 | 60866 | 60466 |
| 221 117 | \* | **VT** | VL | *VW* | CZ | 60367 | 60767 | 60967 | 60867 | 60467 |

| | | | | | | | | | | |
|---|---|---|---|---|---|---|---|---|---|---|
| 221 118 | * | **VT** | VL | *VW* | CZ | 60368 | 60768 | 60968 | 60868 | 60468 |
| 221 119 | | **XC** | VL | *XC* | CZ | 60369 | 60769 | 60969 | 60869 | 60469 |
| 221 120 | | **XC** | VL | *XC* | CZ | 60370 | 60770 | 60970 | 60870 | 60470 |
| 221 121 | | **XC** | VL | *XC* | CZ | 60371 | 60771 | 60971 | 60871 | 60471 |
| 221 122 | | **XC** | VL | *XC* | CZ | 60372 | 60772 | 60972 | 60872 | 60472 |
| 221 123 | | **XC** | VL | *XC* | CZ | 60373 | 60773 | 60973 | 60873 | 60473 |
| 221 124 | | **XC** | VL | *XC* | CZ | 60374 | 60774 | 60974 | 60874 | 60474 |
| 221 125 | | **XC** | VL | *XC* | CZ | 60375 | 60775 | 60975 | 60875 | 60475 |
| 221 126 | | **XC** | VL | *XC* | CZ | 60376 | 60776 | 60976 | 60876 | 60476 |
| 221 127 | | **XC** | VL | *XC* | CZ | 60377 | 60777 | 60977 | 60877 | 60477 |
| 221 128 | | **XC** | VL | *XC* | CZ | 60378 | 60778 | 60978 | 60878 | 60478 |
| 221 129 | | **XC** | VL | *XC* | CZ | 60379 | 60779 | 60979 | 60879 | 60479 |
| 221 130 | | **XC** | VL | *XC* | CZ | 60380 | 60780 | 60980 | 60880 | 60480 |
| 221 131 | | **XC** | VL | *XC* | CZ | 60381 | 60781 | 60981 | 60881 | 60481 |
| 221 132 | | **XC** | VL | *XC* | CZ | 60382 | 60782 | 60982 | 60882 | 60482 |
| 221 133 | | **XC** | VL | *XC* | CZ | 60383 | 60783 | 60983 | 60883 | 60483 |
| 221 134 | | **XC** | VL | *XC* | CZ | 60384 | 60784 | 60984 | 60884 | 60484 |
| 221 135 | | **XC** | VL | *XC* | CZ | 60385 | 60785 | 60985 | 60885 | 60485 |
| 221 136 | | **XC** | VL | *XC* | CZ | 60386 | 60786 | 60986 | 60886 | 60486 |
| 221 137 | | **XC** | VL | *XC* | CZ | 60387 | 60787 | 60987 | 60887 | 60487 |
| 221 138 | | **XC** | VL | *XC* | CZ | 60388 | 60788 | 60988 | 60888 | 60488 |
| 221 139 | | **XC** | VL | *XC* | CZ | 60389 | 60789 | 60989 | 60889 | 60489 |
| 221 140 | | **XC** | VL | *XC* | CZ | 60390 | 60790 | 60990 | 60890 | 60490 |
| 221 141 | | **XC** | VL | *XC* | CZ | 60391 | 60791 | 60991 | | 60491 |
| 221 142 | * | **VT** | VL | *VW* | CZ | 60392 | 60992 | 60994 | 60792 | 60492 |
| 221 143 | * | **VT** | VL | *VW* | CZ | 60393 | 60993 | 60794 | 60793 | 60493 |
| Spare | * | **VT** | VL | | CZ | 60394 | | | | 60494 |

**Names (carried on MS No. 609xx):**

| | | | |
|---|---|---|---|
| 221 101 | Louis Bleriot | 221 109 | Marco Polo |
| 221 102 | John Cabot | 221 110 | James Cook |
| 221 103 | Christopher Columbus | 221 111 | Roald Amundsen |
| 221 104 | Sir John Franklin | 221 112 | Ferdinand Magellan |
| 221 105 | William Baffin | 221 113 | Sir Walter Raleigh |
| 221 106 | Willem Barents | 221 115 | Polmadie Depot |
| 221 107 | Sir Martin Frobisher | 221 142 | BOMBARDIER Voyager |
| 221 108 | Sir Ernest Shackleton | 221 143 | Auguste Picard |

# CLASS 222        MERIDIAN        BOMBARDIER

**Construction:** Steel.
**Engine:** Cummins QSK19 of 560 kW (750 hp) at 1800 rpm.
**Transmission:** Two Alstom Onix 800 three-phase traction motors of 275 kW.
**Braking:** Rheostatic and electro-pneumatic.
**Bogies:** Bombardier B5005.          **Dimensions:** 23.85/23.00 x 2.73 m.
**Couplers:** Dellner at outer ends, bar within unit.
**Gangways:** Within unit only.          **Wheel Arrangement:** All cars 1A-A1.
**Doors:** Single-leaf swing plug.        **Maximum Speed:** 125 mph.
**Seating Layout:** 1: 2+1, 2: 2+2 facing/unidirectional.
**Multiple Working:** Within class and with Classes 220 and 221 (in an emergency).

**222 001–006.** 7-car units. DMF–MF–MF–MSRMB–MS–MS–DMS.

The 7-car units were built as 9-car units, before being reduced to 8-car sets and then later to 7-car sets to strengthen all 4-car units to 5-cars. 222 007 was built as a 9-car unit but later reduced to a 5-car unit.

**DMRF.** Bombardier Bruges 2004–05. 22/– 1TD 1W. 52.8 t.
**MF.** Bombardier Bruges 2004–05. 42/– 1T. 46.8 t.
**MSRMB.** Bombardier Bruges 2004–05. –/62. 48.0 t.
**MS.** Bombardier Bruges 2004–05. –/68 1T. 47.0 t.
**DMS.** Bombardier Bruges 2004–05. –/38 1TD 1W. 49.4 t.

| 222 001 | **ST** | E | *EM* | DY | 60241 | 60445 | 60341 | 60621 |
|---|---|---|---|---|---|---|---|---|
|  |  |  |  |  | 60561 | 60551 | 60161 |  |
| 222 002 | **ST** | E | *EM* | DY | 60242 | 60346 | 60342 | 60622 |
|  |  |  |  |  | 60562 | 60544 | 60162 |  |
| 222 003 | **ST** | E | *EM* | DY | 60243 | 60446 | 60343 | 60623 |
|  |  |  |  |  | 60563 | 60553 | 60163 |  |
| 222 004 | **ST** | E | *EM* | DY | 60244 | 60345 | 60342 | 60624 |
|  |  |  |  |  | 60564 | 60554 | 60164 |  |
| 222 005 | **ST** | E | *EM* | DY | 60245 | 60347 | 60443 | 60625 |
|  |  |  |  |  | 60565 | 60555 | 60165 |  |
| 222 006 | **ST** | E | *EM* | DY | 60246 | 60447 | 60441 | 60626 |
|  |  |  |  |  | 60566 | 60556 | 60166 |  |

**Names (carried on MSRMB or DMS (222 003)):**

222 001   THE ENTREPRENEUR EXPRESS
222 002   THE CUTLERS' COMPANY
222 003   TORNADO
222 004   CHILDREN'S HOSPITAL SHEFFIELD
222 006   THE CARBON CUTTER

**222 007–023.** 5-car units. DMF–MC–MSRMB–MS–DMS.

**DMRF.** Bombardier Bruges 2003–04. 22/– 1TD 1W. 52.8 t.
**MC.** Bombardier Bruges 2003–04. 28/22 1T. 48.6 t.
**MSRMB.** Bombardier Bruges 2003–04. –/62. 49.6 t.
**MS.** Bombardier Bruges 2004–05. –/68 1T. 47.0 t.
**DMS.** Bombardier Bruges 2003–04. –/40 1TD 1W. 51.0 t.

| 222 007 | **ST** | E | *EM* | DY | 60247 | 60442 | 60627 | 60567 | 60167 |
|---|---|---|---|---|---|---|---|---|---|

| 222 008 | **ST** | E | *EM* | DY | 60248 60918 60628 60545 60168 |
| 222 009 | **ST** | E | *EM* | DY | 60249 60919 60629 60557 60169 |
| 222 011 | **ST** | E | *EM* | DY | 60250 60920 60630 60546 60170 |
| 222 012 | **ST** | E | *EM* | DY | 60251 60921 60631 60531 60171 |
| 222 013 | **ST** | E | *EM* | DY | 60252 60922 60632 60532 60172 |
| 222 014 | **ST** | E | *EM* | DY | 60253 60923 60633 60533 60173 |
| 222 015 | **ST** | E | *EM* | DY | 60254 60924 60634 60534 60174 |
| 222 016 | **ST** | E | *EM* | DY | 60255 60925 60635 60535 60175 |
| 222 017 | **ST** | E | *EM* | DY | 60256 60926 60636 60536 60176 |
| 222 018 | **ST** | E | *EM* | DY | 60257 60927 60637 60537 60177 |
| 222 019 | **ST** | E | *EM* | DY | 60258 60928 60638 60444 60178 |
| 222 020 | **ST** | E | *EM* | DY | 60259 60929 60639 60547 60179 |
| 222 021 | **ST** | E | *EM* | DY | 60260 60930 60640 60543 60180 |
| 222 022 | **ST** | E | *EM* | DY | 60261 60931 60641 60552 60181 |
| 222 023 | **ST** | E | *EM* | DY | 60262 60932 60642 60542 60182 |
| | | | | | 60263 60933 60643 60541 60183 |

**Name (carried on MSRMB):** 222 022  INVEST IN NOTTINGHAM

**222 101–104. 4-car former Hull Trains units.** DMF–MC–MSRMB–DMS.

**DMRF.** Bombardier Bruges 2005. 22/– 1TD 1W. 52.8 t.
**MC.** Bombardier Bruges 2005. 11/46 1T. 47.1 t.
**MSRMB.** Bombardier Bruges 2005. –/62. 48.0 t.
**DMS.** Bombardier Bruges 2005.  –/40 1TD 1W. 49.4 t.

| 222 101 | **ST** | E | *EM* | DY | 60271 60571 60681 60191 |
| 222 102 | **ST** | E | *EM* | DY | 60272 60572 60682 60192 |
| 222 103 | **ST** | E | *EM* | DY | 60273 60573 60683 60193 |
| 222 104 | **ST** | E | *EM* | DY | 60274 60574 60684 60194 |

# 3.3. SERVICE DMUS

This section lists vehicles not used for passenger-carrying purposes. Vehicles are numbered in the special service stock number series.

## CLASS 950                          TRACK ASSESSMENT UNIT

DM–DM. Purpose built service unit based on the Class 150/1 design. Gangwayed within unit.

**Construction:** Steel.
**Engine:** One Cummins NT-855-RT5 of 213 kW (285 hp) at 2100 rpm per power car.
**Transmission:** Hydraulic. Voith T211r with cardan shafts to Gmeinder GM190 final drive.
**Maximum Speed:** 75 mph.          **Couplers:** BSI automatic.
**Bogies:** BP38 (powered), BT38 (non-powered).
**Brakes:** Electro-pneumatic.          **Dimensions:** 20.06 x 2.82 m.
**Doors:** Manually operated slam & power operated sliding.
**Multiple Working:** Classes 142, 143, 144, 150, 153, 155, 156, 158, 159 and 170.

**999600. DM.** Lot No. 4060 BREL York 1987. 35.0 t.
**999601. DM.** Lot No. 4061 BREL York 1987. 35.0 t.

| 950 001 | **Y** | NR | *DB* | ZA | 999600 999601 |

## CLASS 960                    ROUTE LEARNING UNIT

DMB. Converted from Class 121. Non-gangwayed.

**For details see Page 191.**

This unit is available for hire to other operators for route learning if required.

Lot No. 30518 Pressed Steel 1960. 38.0 t.

| 960 014 | **BG** | CR | *CR* | AL | 977873 (55022) |

## CLASS 960                    WATER-JETTING UNIT

DMB–MS–DMB. Converted 2003–04 from Class 117. Non-gangwayed.

**Construction:** Steel.
**Engines:** Two Leyland 1595 of 112 kW (150 hp) at 1800 rpm.
**Transmission:** Mechanical. Cardan shaft and freewheel to a four-speed epicyclic gearbox with a further cardan shaft to the final drive, each engine driving the inner axle of one bogie.
**Maximum Speed:** 70 mph.
**Bogies:** DD10.
**Brakes:** Twin pipe vacuum.
**Doors:** Manually operated slam.
**Couplings:** Screw.
**Multiple Working:** Blue Square.
**Dimensions:** 20.45 x 2.84 m.

**977987/988. DMB.** Lot No. 30546/30548 Pressed Steel 1959–60. 36.5 t.
**977992. MS.** Lot No. 30548 Pressed Steel 1959–60. 36.5 t.

| 960 301 | **G** | CR | *CR* | AL | 977987 (51371) 977992 (51375) |
|         |       |    |      |    | 977988 (51413)                |

# 3.4. DMUS AWAITING DISPOSAL

The list below comprises vehicles which are stored awaiting disposal.

**Class 121**

| 121 032 | **AV** | CR | TM | 55032 |

**Class 960**

Converted from Class 121 or 122. 960 302/303 converted for use as Severn Tunnel Emergency Train units, but never actually used as such.

| 960 011 | **RK** | CR | TM | 977859 | (55025) |
| 960 302 | **Y**  | AV | CF | 977975 | (55027) |
| 960 303 | **Y**  | AV | CF | 977976 | (55031) |

# 4. ELECTRIC MULTIPLE UNITS

# INTRODUCTION

## EMU CLASSES

Principal details and dimensions are quoted for each class in metric and/or imperial units as considered appropriate bearing in mind common UK usage.

All dimensions and weights are quoted for vehicles in an "as new" condition with all necessary supplies on board. Dimensions are quoted in the order length x overall width. All lengths quoted are over buffers or couplers as appropriate. Where two lengths are quoted, the first refers to outer vehicles in a set and the second to inner vehicles. All weights are shown as metric tonnes (t = tonnes).

Bogie Types are quoted in the format motored/non-motored (eg BP20/BT13 denotes BP20 motored bogies and BT non-motored bogies).

Unless noted to the contrary, all vehicles listed have bar couplers at non-driving ends.

Vehicles ordered under the auspices of BR were allocated a Lot (batch) number when ordered and these are quoted in class headings and sub-headings. Vehicles ordered since 1995 have no Lot Numbers, but the manufacturer and location that they were built is given.

## NUMERICAL LISTINGS

25 kV AC 50 Hz overhead Electric Multiple Units (EMUs) and dual voltage EMUs are listed in numerical order of set numbers. Individual "loose" vehicles are listed in numerical order after vehicles formed into fixed formations.

750 V DC third rail EMUs are listed in numerical order of class number, then in numerical order of set number. Some of these use the former Southern Region four-digit set numbers. These are derived from theoretical six digit set numbers which are the four-digit set number prefixed by the first two numbers of the class.

Where sets or vehicles have been renumbered in recent years, former numbering detail is shown alongside current detail. Each entry is laid out as in the following example:

| Set No. | Detail | Livery | Owner | Operator | Allocation | Formation |
|---------|--------|--------|-------|----------|------------|-----------|
| 315803  | †      | **GA** | E     | *GA*     | IL         | 64465 71283 71391 64466 |

**Detail Differences**. Only detail differences which currently affect the areas and types of train which vehicles may work are shown. All other detail differences are specifically excluded. Where such differences occur within a class or part class, these are shown alongside the individual set or vehicle number. Meaning of abbreviations are detailed in individual class headings.

**Set Formations.** Set formations shown are those normally maintained. Readers should note some set formations might be temporarily varied from time to time to suit maintenance and/or operational requirements. Vehicles shown as "Spare" are not formed in any regular set formation.

**Codes.** Codes are used to denote the livery, owner, operator and depot of each unit. Details of these will be found in section 7 of this book. Where a unit or spare car is off-lease, the operator column will be left blank.

**Names.** Only names carried with official sanction are listed. As far as possible names are shown in UPPER/lower case characters as actually shown on the name carried on the vehicle(s). Unless otherwise shown, complete units are regarded as named rather than just the individual car(s) which carry the name.

# GENERAL INFORMATION

## CLASSIFICATION AND NUMBERING

25 kV AC 50 Hz overhead and "Versatile" EMUs are classified in the series 300–399.

750 V DC third rail EMUs are classified in the series 400–599.

Service units are classified in the series 900–949.

EMU individual cars are numbered in the series 61000–78999, except for vehicles used on the Isle of Wight – which are numbered in a separate series, and the Class 378s, 380s and 395s, which take up 38xxx and 39xxx series'.

Any vehicle constructed or converted to replace another vehicle following accident damage and carrying the same number as the original vehicle is denoted by the suffix[II] in this publication.

## OPERATING CODES

These codes are used by train operating company staff to describe the various different types of vehicles and normally appear on data panels on the inner (ie non driving) ends of vehicles.

A "B" prefix indicates a battery vehicle.
A "P" prefix indicates a trailer vehicle on which is mounted the pantograph, instead of the default case where the pantograph is mounted on a motor vehicle.

The first part of the code describes whether or not the car has a motor or a driving cab as follows:

DM Driving motor.
M Motor
DT Driving trailer
T Trailer
The next letter is a "B" for cars with a brake compartment.

This is followed by the saloon details:

F    First
S    Standard
C    Composite

The next letter denotes the style of accommodation as follows:

O    Open
K    Side compartment with lavatory
so   Semi-open (part compartments, part open). All other vehicles are
     assumed to consist solely of open saloons.

Finally vehicles with a buffet or kitchen area are suffixed RB or RMB for a
miniature buffet counter.

Where two vehicles of the same type are formed within the same unit,
the above codes may be suffixed by (A) and (B) to differentiate between the
vehicles.

A composite is a vehicle containing both First and Standard Class
accommodation, whilst a brake vehicle is a vehicle containing separate
specific accommodation for the conductor.

# BUILD DETAILS

### Lot Numbers

Vehicles ordered under the auspices of BR were allocated a Lot (batch)
number when ordered and these are quoted in class headings and sub-
headings.

### Builders

These are shown in class headings. Abbreviations used are found in section
7.6.

Information on sub-contracting works which built parts of vehicles eg the
underframes etc is not shown.

# ACCOMMODATION

The information given in class headings and sub-headings is in the form
F/S nT (or TD) nW. For example 12/54 1T 1W denotes 12 First Class and 54
Standard Class seats, one toilet and one space for a wheelchair. A number
in brackets (ie (2)) denotes tip-up seats (in addition to the fixed seats). Tip-
up seats in vestibules do not count. The seating layout of open saloons is
shown as 2+1, 2+2 or 3+2 as the case may be. Where units have first class
accommodation as well as standard and the layout is different for each class
then these are shown separately prefixed by "1:" and "2:". Compartments
are three seats a side in First Class and mostly four a side in Standard Class in
EMUs. TD denotes a toilet suitable for use by a disabled person.

# 4.1. 25 kV AC 50 Hz OVERHEAD & DUAL VOLTAGE UNITS

Except where otherwise stated, all units in this section operate on 25 kV AC 50 Hz overhead only.

## CLASS 313 BREL YORK

Inner suburban units.

**Formation:** DMSO–PTSO–BDMSO or DMSO–TSO–BDMSO.
**Systems:** 25 kV AC overhead/750 V DC third rail.
**Construction:** Steel underframe, aluminium alloy body and roof.
**Traction Motors:** Four GEC G310AZ of 82.125 kW.
**Wheel Arrangement:** Bo-Bo + 2-2 + Bo-Bo.
**Braking:** Disc & rheostatic. **Dimensions:** 20.33/20.18 x 2.82 m.
**Bogies:** BX1. **Couplers:** Tightlock.
**Gangways:** Within unit + end doors. **Control System:** Camshaft.
**Doors:** Sliding. **Maximum Speed:** 75 mph.
**Seating Layout:** Various, see sub-class headings.
**Multiple Working:** Within class.

**DMSO.** Lot No. 30879 1976–77. –/74. 36.0 t.
**PTSO.** Lot No. 30880 1976–77. –/83. 31.0 t.
**BDMSO.** Lot No. 30885 1976–77. –/74. 37.5 t.

**Class 313/0. Standard Design.** Refurbished with high back seats (3+2 facing).

| | | | | | | | |
|---|---|---|---|---|---|---|---|
| 313018 | **FU** | E | *FC* | HE | 62546 | 71230 | 62610 |
| 313024 | **FU** | E | *FC* | HE | 62552 | 71236 | 62616 |
| 313025 | **FU** | E | *FC* | HE | 62553 | 71237 | 62617 |
| 313026 | **FU** | E | *FC* | HE | 62554 | 71238 | 62618 |
| 313027 | **FU** | E | *FC* | HE | 62555 | 71239 | 62619 |
| 313028 | **FU** | E | *FC* | HE | 62556 | 71240 | 62620 |
| 313029 | **FU** | E | *FC* | HE | 62557 | 71241 | 62621 |
| 313030 | **FU** | E | *FC* | HE | 62558 | 71242 | 62622 |
| 313031 | **FU** | E | *FC* | HE | 62559 | 71243 | 62623 |
| 313032 | **FU** | E | *FC* | HE | 62560 | 71244 | 62643 |
| 313033 | **FU** | E | *FC* | HE | 62561 | 71245 | 62625 |
| 313035 | **FU** | E | *FC* | HE | 62563 | 71247 | 62627 |
| 313036 | **FU** | E | *FC* | HE | 62564 | 71248 | 62628 |
| 313037 | **FU** | E | *FC* | HE | 62565 | 71249 | 62629 |
| 313038 | **FU** | E | *FC* | HE | 62566 | 71250 | 62630 |
| 313039 | **FU** | E | *FC* | HE | 62567 | 71251 | 62631 |
| 313040 | **FU** | E | *FC* | HE | 62568 | 71252 | 62632 |
| 313041 | **FU** | E | *FC* | HE | 62569 | 71253 | 62633 |
| 313042 | **FU** | E | *FC* | HE | 62570 | 71254 | 62634 |
| 313043 | **FU** | E | *FC* | HE | 62571 | 71255 | 62635 |
| 313044 | **FU** | E | *FC* | HE | 62572 | 71256 | 62636 |
| 313045 | **FU** | E | *FC* | HE | 62573 | 71257 | 62637 |
| 313046 | **FU** | E | *FC* | HE | 62574 | 71258 | 62638 |

| 313047 | **FU** | E | *FC* | HE | 62575 | 71259 | 62639 |
| 313048 | **FU** | E | *FC* | HE | 62576 | 71260 | 62640 |
| 313049 | **FU** | E | *FC* | HE | 62577 | 71261 | 62641 |
| 313050 | **FU** | E | *FC* | HE | 62578 | 71262 | 62649 |
| 313051 | **FU** | E | *FC* | HE | 62579 | 71263 | 62624 |
| 313052 | **FU** | E | *FC* | HE | 62580 | 71264 | 62644 |
| 313053 | **FU** | E | *FC* | HE | 62581 | 71265 | 62645 |
| 313054 | **FU** | E | *FC* | HE | 62582 | 71266 | 62646 |
| 313055 | **FU** | E | *FC* | HE | 62583 | 71267 | 62647 |
| 313056 | **FU** | E | *FC* | HE | 62584 | 71268 | 62648 |
| 313057 | **FU** | E | *FC* | HE | 62585 | 71269 | 62642 |
| 313058 | **FU** | E | *FC* | HE | 62586 | 71270 | 62650 |
| 313059 | **FU** | E | *FC* | HE | 62587 | 71271 | 62651 |
| 313060 | **FU** | E | *FC* | HE | 62588 | 71272 | 62652 |
| 313061 | **FU** | E | *FC* | HE | 62589 | 71273 | 62653 |
| 313062 | **FU** | E | *FC* | HE | 62590 | 71274 | 62654 |
| 313063 | **FU** | E | *FC* | HE | 62591 | 71275 | 62655 |
| 313064 | **FU** | E | *FC* | HE | 62592 | 71276 | 62656 |

**Name (carried on PTSO):** 313054    Captain William Leefe Robinson V.C.

**Class 313/1. Former London Overground units.** Original low back seats (3+2 facing). Details as Class 313/0.

| 313122 | **FU** | E | *FC* | HE | 62550 | 71234 | 62614 |
| 313123 | **FU** | E | *FC* | HE | 62551 | 71235 | 62615 |
| 313134 | **FU** | E | *FC* | HE | 62562 | 71246 | 62626 |

**Names (carried on PTSO):**

313122    Eric Roberts 1946–2012 "The Flying Nottsman"
313134    City of London

**Class 313/2. Southern units.** Units refurbished for Southern for Brighton Coastway services. Fitted with 2+2 mainly facing high-back seating. 750 V DC only (pantographs removed).

**DMSO.** Lot No. 30879 1976–77. –/64. 36.0 t.
**TSO.** Lot No. 30880 1976–77. –/68.    . t.
**BDMSO.** Lot No. 30885 1976–77. –/64. 37.5 t.

| 313201 | (313101) | **SN** | BN | *SN* | BI | 62529 | 71213 | 62593 |
| 313202 | (313102) | **SN** | BN | *SN* | BI | 62530 | 71214 | 62594 |
| 313203 | (313103) | **SN** | BN | *SN* | BI | 62531 | 71215 | 62595 |
| 313204 | (313104) | **SN** | BN | *SN* | BI | 62532 | 71216 | 62596 |
| 313205 | (313105) | **SN** | BN | *SN* | BI | 62533 | 71217 | 62597 |
| 313206 | (313106) | **SN** | BN | *SN* | BI | 62534 | 71218 | 62598 |
| 313207 | (313107) | **SN** | BN | *SN* | BI | 62535 | 71219 | 62599 |
| 313208 | (313108) | **SN** | BN | *SN* | BI | 62536 | 71220 | 62600 |
| 313209 | (313109) | **SN** | BN | *SN* | BI | 62537 | 71221 | 62601 |
| 313210 | (313110) | **SN** | BN | *SN* | BI | 62538 | 71222 | 62602 |
| 313211 | (313111) | **SN** | BN | *SN* | BI | 62539 | 71223 | 62603 |
| 313212 | (313112) | **SN** | BN | *SN* | BI | 62540 | 71224 | 62604 |
| 313213 | (313113) | **SN** | BN | *SN* | BI | 62541 | 71225 | 62605 |
| 313214 | (313114) | **SN** | BN | *SN* | BI | 62542 | 71226 | 62606 |

| 313215 | (313115) | **SN** | BN | *SN* | BI | 62543 | 71227 | 62607 |
| 313216 | (313116) | **SN** | BN | *SN* | BI | 62544 | 71228 | 62608 |
| 313217 | (313117) | **SN** | BN | *SN* | BI | 62545 | 71229 | 62609 |
| 313219 | (313119) | **SN** | BN | *SN* | BI | 62547 | 71231 | 62611 |
| 313220 | (313120) | **SN** | BN | *SN* | BI | 62548 | 71232 | 62612 |

## CLASS 314                                                    BREL YORK

Inner suburban units.

**Formation:** DMSO–PTSO–DMSO.
**Construction:** Steel underframe, aluminium alloy body and roof.
**Traction Motors:** Four GEC G310AZ (* Brush TM61-53) of 82.125 kW.
**Wheel Arrangement:** Bo-Bo + 2-2 + Bo-Bo.
**Braking:** Disc & rheostatic.          **Dimensions:** 20.33/20.18 x 2.82 m.
**Bogies:** BX1.                          **Couplers:** Tightlock.
**Gangways:** Within unit + end doors.   **Control System:** Thyristor.
**Doors:** Sliding.                       **Maximum Speed:** 70 mph.
**Seating Layout:** 3+2 low-back facing.
**Multiple Working:** Within class and with Class 315.

**DMSO.** Lot No. 30912 1979. –/68. 34.5 t.
**64588[II]. DMSO.** Lot No. 30908 1978–80. Rebuilt Railcare Glasgow 1996 from Class 507 No. 64426. The original 64588 was scrapped. –/74. 34.5 t.
**PTSO.** Lot No. 30913 1979. –/76. 33.0 t.

| 314201 | * | **SC** | A | *SR* | GW | 64583 | 71450 | 64584 |
| 314202 | * | **SC** | A | *SR* | GW | 64585 | 71451 | 64586 |
| 314203 | * | **SR** | A | *SR* | GW | 64587 | 71452 | 64588[II] |
| 314204 | * | **SR** | A | *SR* | GW | 64589 | 71453 | 64590 |
| 314205 | * | **SC** | A | *SR* | GW | 64591 | 71454 | 64592 |
| 314206 | * | **SC** | A | *SR* | GW | 64593 | 71455 | 64594 |
| 314207 |   | **SC** | A | *SR* | GW | 64595 | 71456 | 64596 |
| 314208 |   | **SR** | A | *SR* | GW | 64597 | 71457 | 64598 |
| 314209 |   | **SC** | A | *SR* | GW | 64599 | 71458 | 64600 |
| 314210 |   | **SC** | A | *SR* | GW | 64601 | 71459 | 64602 |
| 314211 |   | **SR** | A | *SR* | GW | 64603 | 71460 | 64604 |
| 314212 |   | **SR** | A | *SR* | GW | 64605 | 71461 | 64606 |
| 314213 |   | **SC** | A | *SR* | GW | 64607 | 71462 | 64608 |
| 314214 |   | **SC** | A | *SR* | GW | 64609 | 71463 | 64610 |
| 314215 |   | **SC** | A | *SR* | GW | 64611 | 71464 | 64612 |
| 314216 |   | **SC** | A | *SR* | GW | 64613 | 71465 | 64614 |

## CLASS 315                                                    BREL YORK

Inner suburban units.

**Formation:** DMSO–TSO–PTSO–DMSO.
**Construction:** Steel underframe, aluminium alloy body and roof.
**Traction Motors:** Four Brush TM61-53 (* GEC G310AZ) of 82.125 kW.
**Wheel Arrangement:** Bo-Bo + 2-2 + 2-2 + Bo-Bo.
**Braking:** Disc & rheostatic.          **Dimensions:** 20.18 x 2.82 m.
**Bogies:** BX1.                          **Couplers:** Tightlock.

**Gangways:** Within unit + end doors. **Control System:** Thyristor.
**Doors:** Sliding.                    **Maximum Speed:** 75 mph.
**Seating Layout:** 3+2 low-back facing.
**Multiple Working:** Within class and with Class 314.

**DMSO.** Lot No. 30902 1980–81. –/74. 35.0 t († 38.2 t).
**TSO.** Lot No. 30904 1980–81. –/86. 25.5 t († 27.4 t).
**PTSO.** Lot No. 30903 1980–81. –/84 († –/75(7) 2W). 32.0 t († 33.8 t).

| | | | | | | | | |
|---|---|---|---|---|---|---|---|---|
| 315801 | † | **GA** | E | *GA* | IL | 64461 | 71281 | 71389 | 64462 |
| 315802 | † | **GA** | E | *GA* | IL | 64463 | 71282 | 71390 | 64464 |
| 315803 | † | **GA** | E | *GA* | IL | 64465 | 71283 | 71391 | 64466 |
| 315804 | † | **GA** | E | *GA* | IL | 64467 | 71284 | 71392 | 64468 |
| 315805 | † | **GA** | E | *GA* | IL | 64469 | 71285 | 71393 | 64470 |
| 315806 | † | **GA** | E | *GA* | IL | 64471 | 71286 | 71394 | 64472 |
| 315807 | | **1** | E | *GA* | IL | 64473 | 71287 | 71395 | 64474 |
| 315808 | † | **GA** | E | *GA* | IL | 64475 | 71288 | 71396 | 64476 |
| 315809 | | **GA** | E | *GA* | IL | 64477 | 71289 | 71397 | 64478 |
| 315810 | † | **GA** | E | *GA* | IL | 64479 | 71290 | 71398 | 64480 |
| 315811 | | **1** | E | *GA* | IL | 64481 | 71291 | 71399 | 64482 |
| 315812 | † | **GA** | E | *GA* | IL | 64483 | 71292 | 71400 | 64484 |
| 315813 | † | **GA** | E | *GA* | IL | 64485 | 71293 | 71401 | 64486 |
| 315814 | † | **GA** | E | *GA* | IL | 64487 | 71294 | 71402 | 64488 |
| 315815 | † | **GA** | E | *GA* | IL | 64489 | 71295 | 71403 | 64490 |
| 315816 | † | **GA** | E | *GA* | IL | 64491 | 71296 | 71404 | 64492 |
| 315817 | † | **GA** | E | *GA* | IL | 64493 | 71297 | 71405 | 64494 |
| 315818 | | **1** | E | *GA* | IL | 64495 | 71298 | 71406 | 64496 |
| 315819 | | **1** | E | *GA* | IL | 64497 | 71299 | 71407 | 64498 |
| 315820 | | **1** | E | *GA* | IL | 64499 | 71300 | 71408 | 64500 |
| 315821 | | **1** | E | *GA* | IL | 64501 | 71301 | 71409 | 64502 |
| 315822 | † | **GA** | E | *GA* | IL | 64503 | 71302 | 71410 | 64504 |
| 315823 | † | **GA** | E | *GA* | IL | 64505 | 71303 | 71411 | 64506 |
| 315824 | | **1** | E | *GA* | IL | 64507 | 71304 | 71412 | 64508 |
| 315825 | | **1** | E | *GA* | IL | 64509 | 71305 | 71413 | 64510 |
| 315826 | | **1** | E | *GA* | IL | 64511 | 71306 | 71414 | 64512 |
| 315827 | † | **GA** | E | *GA* | IL | 64513 | 71307 | 71415 | 64514 |
| 315828 | † | **GA** | E | *GA* | IL | 64515 | 71308 | 71416 | 64516 |
| 315829 | † | **GA** | E | *GA* | IL | 64517 | 71309 | 71417 | 64518 |
| 315830 | | **GA** | E | *GA* | IL | 64519 | 71310 | 71418 | 64520 |
| 315831 | † | **GA** | E | *GA* | IL | 64521 | 71311 | 71419 | 64522 |
| 315832 | † | **GA** | E | *GA* | IL | 64523 | 71312 | 71420 | 64524 |
| 315833 | | **1** | E | *GA* | IL | 64525 | 71313 | 71421 | 64526 |
| 315834 | | **1** | E | *GA* | IL | 64527 | 71314 | 71422 | 64528 |
| 315835 | | **1** | E | *GA* | IL | 64529 | 71315 | 71423 | 64530 |
| 315836 | | **1** | E | *GA* | IL | 64531 | 71316 | 71424 | 64532 |
| 315837 | | **1** | E | *GA* | IL | 64533 | 71317 | 71425 | 64534 |
| 315838 | | **1** | E | *GA* | IL | 64535 | 71318 | 71426 | 64536 |
| 315839 | | **1** | E | *GA* | IL | 64537 | 71319 | 71427 | 64538 |
| 315840 | | **1** | E | *GA* | IL | 64539 | 71320 | 71428 | 64540 |
| 315841 | | **1** | E | *GA* | IL | 64541 | 71321 | 71429 | 64542 |
| 315842 | * | **1** | E | *GA* | IL | 64543 | 71322 | 71430 | 64544 |
| 315843 | * | **1** | E | *GA* | IL | 64545 | 71323 | 71431 | 64546 |

| | | | | | | | | |
|---|---|---|---|---|---|---|---|---|
| 315844 | * | **1** | E | *GA* | IL | 64547 | 71324 | 71432 | 64548 |
| 315845 | *† | **GA** | E | *GA* | IL | 64549 | 71325 | 71433 | 64550 |
| 315846 | * | **1** | E | *GA* | IL | 64551 | 71326 | 71434 | 64552 |
| 315847 | * | **1** | E | *GA* | IL | 64553 | 71327 | 71435 | 64554 |
| 315848 | * | **1** | E | *GA* | IL | 64555 | 71328 | 71436 | 64556 |
| 315849 | * | **1** | E | *GA* | IL | 64557 | 71329 | 71437 | 64558 |
| 315850 | * | **1** | E | *GA* | IL | 64559 | 71330 | 71438 | 64560 |
| 315851 | * | **1** | E | *GA* | IL | 64561 | 71331 | 71439 | 64562 |
| 315852 | * | **1** | E | *GA* | IL | 64563 | 71332 | 71440 | 64564 |
| 315853 | * | **1** | E | *GA* | IL | 64565 | 71333 | 71441 | 64566 |
| 315854 | * | **1** | E | *GA* | IL | 64567 | 71334 | 71442 | 64568 |
| 315855 | *† | **GA** | E | *GA* | IL | 64569 | 71335 | 71443 | 64570 |
| 315856 | * | **1** | E | *GA* | IL | 64571 | 71336 | 71444 | 64572 |
| 315857 | * | **1** | E | *GA* | IL | 64573 | 71337 | 71445 | 64574 |
| 315858 | *† | **GA** | E | *GA* | IL | 64575 | 71338 | 71446 | 64576 |
| 315859 | * | **1** | E | *GA* | IL | 64577 | 71339 | 71447 | 64578 |
| 315860 | * | **1** | E | *GA* | IL | 64579 | 71340 | 71448 | 64580 |
| 315861 | * | **1** | E | *GA* | IL | 64581 | 71341 | 71449 | 64582 |

**Names (carried on DMSO):**

| | |
|---|---|
| 315817 | Transport for London |
| 315829 | London Borough of Havering Celebrating 40 years |
| 315845 | Herbie Woodward |
| 315857 | Stratford Connections |

# CLASS 317                                      BREL YORK/DERBY

Outer suburban units.

**Formation:** Various, see sub-class headings.
**Construction:** Steel.
**Traction Motors:** Four GEC G315BZ of 247.5 kW (except 317 722, see below).
**Wheel Arrangement:** 2-2 + Bo-Bo + 2-2 + 2-2.
**Braking:** Disc.                          **Dimensions:** 19.83/20.18 x 2.82 m.
**Bogies:** BP20 (MSO), BT13 (others).     **Couplers:** Tightlock.
**Gangways:** Throughout                    **Control System:** Thyristor.
**Doors:** Sliding.                         **Maximum Speed:** 100 mph.
**Seating Layout:** Various, see sub-class headings.
**Multiple Working:** Within class & with Classes 318, 319, 320, 321, 322 and 323.

**Class 317/1.** Pressure ventilated.

**Formation:** DTSO–MSO–TCO–DTSO.
**Seating Layout:** 1: 2+2 facing, 2: 3+2 facing.

**DTSO(A)** Lot No. 30955 York 1981–82. –/74. 29.5 t.
**MSO.** Lot No. 30958 York 1981–82. –/79. 49.0 t.
**TCO.** Lot No. 30957 Derby 1981–82. 22/46 2T. 29.0 t.
**DTSO(B)** Lot No. 30956 York 1981–82. –/71. 29.5 t.

| | | | | | | | | |
|---|---|---|---|---|---|---|---|---|
| 317337 | **FU** | A | *FC* | HE | 77036 | 62671 | 71613 | 77084 |
| 317338 | **FU** | A | *FC* | HE | 77037 | 62698 | 71614 | 77085 |
| 317339 | **FU** | A | *FC* | HE | 77038 | 62699 | 71615 | 77086 |

| 317340 | **FU** | A | *FC* | HE | 77039 | 62700 | 71616 | 77087 |
| 317341 | **FU** | A | *FC* | HE | 77040 | 62701 | 71617 | 77088 |
| 317342 | **FU** | A | *FC* | HE | 77041 | 62702 | 71618 | 77089 |
| 317343 | **FU** | A | *FC* | HE | 77042 | 62703 | 71619 | 77090 |
| 317344 | **FU** | A | *FC* | HE | 77029 | 62690 | 71620 | 77091 |
| 317345 | **FU** | A | *FC* | HE | 77044 | 62705 | 71621 | 77092 |
| 317346 | **FU** | A | *FC* | HE | 77045 | 62706 | 71622 | 77093 |
| 317347 | **FU** | A | *FC* | HE | 77046 | 62707 | 71623 | 77094 |
| 317348 | **FU** | A | *FC* | HE | 77047 | 62708 | 71624 | 77095 |

**Names (carried on TCO):**

317345 Driver John Webb | 317348 Richard A Jenner

**Class 317/5**. Pressure ventilated. Units renumbered from Class 317/1 in 2005 for West Anglia Metro services. Refurbished with new upholstery and Passenger Information Systems. Details as Class 317/1.

The original DTSO 77048 was written off after the Cricklewood accident of 1983. A replacement vehicle was built (at Wolverton) in 1987 and given the same number.

| 317501 | **NX** | A | *GA* | IL | 77024 | 62661 | 71577 | 77048 |
| 317502 | **NX** | A | *GA* | IL | 77001 | 62662 | 71578 | 77049 |
| 317503 | **NX** | A | *GA* | IL | 77002 | 62663 | 71579 | 77050 |
| 317504 | **NX** | A | *GA* | IL | 77003 | 62664 | 71580 | 77051 |
| 317505 | **NX** | A | *GA* | IL | 77004 | 62665 | 71581 | 77052 |
| 317506 | **NX** | A | *GA* | IL | 77005 | 62666 | 71582 | 77053 |
| 317507 | **NX** | A | *GA* | IL | 77006 | 62667 | 71583 | 77054 |
| 317508 | **NX** | A | *GA* | IL | 77010 | 62697 | 71587 | 77058 |
| 317509 | **NX** | A | *GA* | IL | 77011 | 62672 | 71588 | 77059 |
| 317510 | **NX** | A | *GA* | IL | 77012 | 62673 | 71589 | 77060 |
| 317511 | **NC** | A | *GA* | IL | 77014 | 62675 | 71591 | 77062 |
| 317512 | **NC** | A | *GA* | IL | 77015 | 62676 | 71592 | 77063 |
| 317513 | **NX** | A | *GA* | IL | 77016 | 62677 | 71593 | 77064 |
| 317514 | **NX** | A | *GA* | IL | 77017 | 62678 | 71594 | 77065 |
| 317515 | **NX** | A | *GA* | IL | 77019 | 62680 | 71596 | 77067 |

**Name (carried on TCO):**

317507 University of Cambridge 800 Years 1209–2009

**Class 317/6**. Convection heating. Units converted from Class 317/2 by Railcare, Wolverton 1998–99 with new Chapman seating.

**Formation:** DTSO–MSO–TSO–DTCO.
**Seating Layout:** 2+2 facing.

**77200–219. DTSO**. Lot No. 30994 York 1985–86. –/64. 29.5 t.
**77280–283. DTSO**. Lot No. 31007 York 1987. –/64. 29.5 t.
**62846–865. MSO**. Lot No. 30996 York 1985–86. –/70. 49.0 t.
**62886–889. MSO**. Lot No. 31009 York 1987. –/70. 49.0 t.
**71734–753. TSO**. Lot No. 30997 York 1985–86. –/62 2T. 29.0 t.
**71762–765. TSO**. Lot No. 31010 York 1987. –/62 2T. 29.0 t.
**77220–239. DTCO**. Lot No. 30995 York 1985–86. 24/48. 29.5 t.
**77284–287. DTCO**. Lot No. 31008 York 1987. 24/48. 29.5 t.

| | | | | | | | |
|---|---|---|---|---|---|---|---|
| 317649 | **NC** | A | *GA* | IL | 77200 | 62846 | 71734 | 77220 |
| 317650 | **NC** | A | *GA* | IL | 77201 | 62847 | 71735 | 77221 |
| 317651 | **NC** | A | *GA* | IL | 77202 | 62848 | 71736 | 77222 |
| 317652 | **NC** | A | *GA* | IL | 77203 | 62849 | 71739 | 77223 |
| 317653 | **NC** | A | *GA* | IL | 77204 | 62850 | 71738 | 77224 |
| 317654 | **NC** | A | *GA* | IL | 77205 | 62851 | 71737 | 77225 |
| 317655 | **NC** | A | *GA* | IL | 77206 | 62852 | 71740 | 77226 |
| 317656 | **NC** | A | *GA* | IL | 77207 | 62853 | 71742 | 77227 |
| 317657 | **NC** | A | *GA* | IL | 77208 | 62854 | 71741 | 77228 |
| 317658 | **NC** | A | *GA* | IL | 77209 | 62855 | 71743 | 77229 |
| 317659 | **GA** | A | *GA* | IL | 77210 | 62856 | 71744 | 77230 |
| 317660 | **GA** | A | *GA* | IL | 77211 | 62857 | 71745 | 77231 |
| 317661 | **GA** | A | *GA* | IL | 77212 | 62858 | 71746 | 77232 |
| 317662 | **GA** | A | *GA* | IL | 77213 | 62859 | 71747 | 77233 |
| 317663 | **GA** | A | *GA* | IL | 77214 | 62860 | 71748 | 77234 |
| 317664 | **GA** | A | *GA* | IL | 77215 | 62861 | 71749 | 77235 |
| 317665 | **GA** | A | *GA* | IL | 77216 | 62862 | 71750 | 77236 |
| 317666 | **NC** | A | *GA* | IL | 77217 | 62863 | 71752 | 77237 |
| 317667 | **GA** | A | *GA* | IL | 77218 | 62864 | 71751 | 77238 |
| 317668 | **GA** | A | *GA* | IL | 77219 | 62865 | 71753 | 77239 |
| 317669 | **NC** | A | *GA* | IL | 77280 | 62886 | 71762 | 77284 |
| 317670 | **GA** | A | *GA* | IL | 77281 | 62887 | 71763 | 77285 |
| 317671 | **NC** | A | *GA* | IL | 77282 | 62888 | 71764 | 77286 |
| 317672 | **GA** | A | *GA* | IL | 77283 | 62889 | 71765 | 77287 |

**Name (carried on DTCO):** 317654   Richard Wells

**Class 317/7.** Units converted from Class 317/1 by Railcare, Wolverton 2000 for Stansted Express services between London Liverpool Street and Stansted. Air conditioning. Fitted with luggage stacks. Displaced from Stansted services in 2011 by Class 379s.

* 317722 has received new Bombardier MJA 280-8 AC traction motors as part of an Angel trial. Two vehicles (77021 and 62682, now in **GA** livery) have also received an interior refurbishment with new Fainsa seating whilst the other two vehicles have been left in their former Stansted Express condition (and are still in **NX** livery). The unit will return to use with Greater Anglia as a demonstrator during 2014.

**Formation:** DTSO–MSO–TSO–DTCO.
**Seating Layout:** 1: 2+1 facing, 2: 2+2 facing.

**DTSO** Lot No. 30955 York 1981–82. –/52 + catering point. 31.4 t.
**MSO.** Lot No. 30958 York 1981–82. –/62 (* –/64). 51.3 t.
**TSO.** Lot No. 30957 Derby 1981–82. –/42(5) 1W 1T 1TD. 30.2 t.
**DTCO** Lot No. 30956 York 1981–82. 22/16 + catering point. 31.6 t.

| | | | | | | | |
|---|---|---|---|---|---|---|---|
| 317708 | **NX** | | A | ZG | 77007 | 62668 | 71584 | 77055 |
| 317709 | **NX** | | A | ZI | 77008 | 62669 | 71585 | 77056 |
| 317710 | **NX** | | A | ZG | 77009 | 62670 | 71586 | 77057 |
| 317714 | **NX** | | A | ZG | 77013 | 62674 | 71590 | 77061 |
| 317719 | **NX** | | A | ZI | 77018 | 62679 | 71595 | 77066 |
| 317722 | * | **GA/NX** | A | ZI | 77021 | 62682 | 71598 | 77069 |
| 317723 | **NX** | | A | ZG | 77022 | 62683 | 71599 | 77070 |

| | | | | | | | | |
|---|---|---|---|---|---|---|---|---|
| 317729 | **NX** | A | | ZG | 77028 | 62689 | 71605 | 77076 |
| 317732 | **NX** | A | | ZI | 77031 | 62692 | 71608 | 77079 |

**Names (carried on DTCO):**

| | | |
|---|---|---|
| 317709 Len Camp | | 317723 The Tottenham Flyer |

**Class 317/8**. Pressure Ventilated. Units refurbished and renumbered from Class 317/1 in 2005–06 at Wabtec, Doncaster for use on Stansted Express services. Displaced from Stansted services in 2011.

**Formation:** DTSO–MSO–TCO–DTSO.
**Seating Layout:** 1: 2+2 facing, 2: 3+2 facing.

**DTSO(A)** Lot No. 30955 York 1981–82. –/66. 29.5 t.
**MSO.** Lot No. 30958 York 1981–82. –/71. 49.0 t.
**TCO.** Lot No. 30957 Derby 1981–82. 20/42 2T. 29.0 t.
**DTSO(B)** Lot No. 30956 York 1981–82. –/66. 29.5 t.

| | | | | | | | | | |
|---|---|---|---|---|---|---|---|---|---|
| 317881 | **NX** | A | *GA* | IL | 77020 | 62681 | 71597 | 77068 | |
| 317882 | **NC** | A | *GA* | IL | 77023 | 62684 | 71600 | 77071 | |
| 317883 | **NC** | A | *GA* | IL | 77000 | 62685 | 71601 | 77072 | |
| 317884 | **NC** | A | *GA* | IL | 77025 | 62686 | 71602 | 77073 | |
| 317885 | **NC** | A | *GA* | IL | 77026 | 62687 | 71603 | 77074 | |
| 317886 | **NC** | A | *GA* | IL | 77027 | 62688 | 71604 | 77075 | |
| 317887 | **NX** | A | *GA* | IL | 77043 | 62704 | 71606 | 77077 | |
| 317888 | **NX** | A | *GA* | IL | 77030 | 62691 | 71607 | 77078 | |
| 317889 | **NX** | A | *GA* | IL | 77032 | 62693 | 71609 | 77080 | |
| 317890 | **NX** | A | *GA* | IL | 77033 | 62694 | 71610 | 77081 | |
| 317891 | **NX** | A | *GA* | IL | 77034 | 62695 | 71611 | 77082 | |
| 317892 | **NX** | A | *GA* | IL | 77035 | 62696 | 71612 | 77083 | Ilford Depot |

# CLASS 318                                           BREL YORK

Outer suburban units. An overhaul programme started in October 2013 with 318 251 and this will see a new large toilet fitted. Revised seating details awaited.

**Formation:** DTSO–MSO–DTSO.
**Construction:** Steel.
**Traction Motors:** Four Brush TM 2141 of 268 kW.
**Wheel Arrangement:** 2-2 + Bo-Bo + 2-2.
**Braking:** Disc.
**Dimensions:** 19.83/19.92 x 2.82 m.
**Bogies:** BP20 (MSO), BT13 (others).
**Couplers:** Tightlock.
**Gangways:** Within unit.
**Control System:** Thyristor.
**Doors:** Sliding.
**Maximum Speed:** 90 mph.
**Seating Layout:** 3+2 facing.
**Multiple Working:** Within class & with Classes 317, 319, 320, 321, 322 and 323.

**77240–259. DTSO.** Lot No. 30999 1985–86. –/64 1T. 30.0 t.
**77288. DTSO.** Lot No. 31020 1987. –/64 1T. 30.0 t.
**62866–885. MSO.** Lot No. 30998 1985–86. –/77. 50.9 t.
**62890. MSO.** Lot No. 31019 1987. –/77. 50.9 t.
**77260–279. DTSO.** Lot No. 31000 1985–86. –/72. 29.6 t.
**77289. DTSO.** Lot No. 31021 1987. –/72. 29.6 t.

| | | | | | | | | |
|---|---|---|---|---|---|---|---|---|
| 318250 | **SC** | E | *SR* | GW | 77240 | 62866 | 77260 | |
| 318251 | **SR** | E | *SR* | GW | 77241 | 62867 | 77261 | |
| 318252 | **SC** | E | *SR* | GW | 77242 | 62868 | 77262 | |
| 318253 | **SC** | E | *SR* | GW | 77243 | 62869 | 77263 | |
| 318254 | **SC** | E | *SR* | GW | 77244 | 62870 | 77264 | |
| 318255 | **SC** | E | *SR* | GW | 77245 | 62871 | 77265 | |
| 318256 | **SC** | E | *SR* | GW | 77246 | 62872 | 77266 | |
| 318257 | **SC** | E | *SR* | GW | 77247 | 62873 | 77267 | |
| 318258 | **SC** | E | *SR* | GW | 77248 | 62874 | 77268 | |
| 318259 | **SC** | E | *SR* | GW | 77249 | 62875 | 77269 | Citizens' Network |
| 318260 | **SC** | E | *SR* | GW | 77250 | 62876 | 77270 | |
| 318261 | **SC** | E | *SR* | GW | 77251 | 62877 | 77271 | |
| 318262 | **SC** | E | *SR* | GW | 77252 | 62878 | 77272 | |
| 318263 | **SC** | E | *SR* | GW | 77253 | 62879 | 77273 | |
| 318264 | **SC** | E | *SR* | GW | 77254 | 62880 | 77274 | |
| 318265 | **SC** | E | *SR* | GW | 77255 | 62881 | 77275 | |
| 318266 | **SC** | E | *SR* | GW | 77256 | 62882 | 77276 | STRATHCLYDER |
| 318267 | **SC** | E | *SR* | GW | 77257 | 62883 | 77277 | |
| 318268 | **SC** | E | *SR* | GW | 77258 | 62884 | 77278 | |
| 318269 | **SC** | E | *SR* | GW | 77259 | 62885 | 77279 | |
| 318270 | **SC** | E | *SR* | GW | 77288 | 62890 | 77289 | |

## CLASS 319      BREL YORK

Express and outer suburban units.

**Formation:** Various, see sub-class headings.
**Systems:** 25 kV AC overhead/750 V DC third rail.
**Construction:** Steel.
**Traction Motors:** Four GEC G315BZ of 268 kW.
**Wheel Arrangement:** 2-2 + Bo-Bo + 2-2 + 2-2.
**Braking:** Disc.      **Dimensions:** 20.17/20.16 x 2.82 m.
**Bogies:** P7-4 (MSO), T3-7 (others).      **Couplers:** Tightlock.
**Gangways:** Within unit + end doors. **Control System:** GTO chopper.
**Doors:** Sliding.      **Maximum Speed:** 100 mph.
**Seating Layout:** Various, see sub-class headings.
**Multiple Working:** Within class & with Classes 317, 318, 320, 321, 322 and 323.

**Class 319/0.** DTSO–MSO–TSO–DTSO.

**Seating Layout:** 3+2 facing.

**DTSO(A).** Lot No. 31022 (odd nos.) 1987–88. –/82. 28.2 t.
**MSO.** Lot No. 31023 1987–88. –/82. 49.2 t.
**TSO.** Lot No. 31024 1987–88. –/77 2T. 31.0 t.
**DTSO(B).** Lot No. 31025 (even nos.) 1987–88. –/78. 28.1 t.

| | | | | | | | | |
|---|---|---|---|---|---|---|---|---|
| 319001 | **FU** | P | *FC* | BF | 77291 | 62891 | 71772 | 77290 |
| 319002 | **FU** | P | *FC* | BF | 77293 | 62892 | 71773 | 77292 |
| 319003 | **FU** | P | *FC* | BF | 77295 | 62893 | 71774 | 77294 |
| 319004 | **FU** | P | *FC* | BF | 77297 | 62894 | 71775 | 77296 |
| 319005 | **FU** | P | *FC* | BF | 77299 | 62895 | 71776 | 77298 |
| 319006 | **FU** | P | *FC* | BF | 77301 | 62896 | 71777 | 77300 |
| 319007 | **FU** | P | *FC* | BF | 77303 | 62897 | 71778 | 77302 |

| | | | | | | | | |
|---|---|---|---|---|---|---|---|---|
| 319008 | **SN** | P | *FC* | BF | 77305 | 62898 | 71779 | 77304 |
| 319009 | **SN** | P | *FC* | BF | 77307 | 62899 | 71780 | 77306 |
| 319010 | **FU** | P | *FC* | BF | 77309 | 62900 | 71781 | 77308 |
| 319011 | **SN** | P | *FC* | BF | 77311 | 62901 | 71782 | 77310 |
| 319012 | **SN** | P | *FC* | BF | 77313 | 62902 | 71783 | 77312 |
| 319013 | **SN** | P | *FC* | BF | 77315 | 62903 | 71784 | 77314 |

**Names (carried on TSO):**

| | |
|---|---|
| 319001 Driver Mick Winnett | 319011 John Ruskin College |
| 319008 Cheriton | 319013 The Surrey Hills |
| 319009 Coquelles | |

**Class 319/2.** DTSO–MSO–TSO–DTCO. Units converted from Class 319/0.

**Seating Layout:** 1: 2+1 facing, 2: 2+2 facing.

**Advertising liveries:** 319215 Visit Switzerland (red).
319 218 Lycamobile (white).

**DTSO.** Lot No. 31022 (odd nos.) 1987–88. –/64. 28.2 t.
**MSO.** Lot No. 31023 1987–88. –/73 2T. 49.2 t.
**TSO.** Lot No. 31024 1987–88. –/52 1T 1TD. 31.0 t.
**DTCO.** Lot No. 31025 (even nos.) 1987–88. 18/36. 28.1 t.

| | | | | | | | | |
|---|---|---|---|---|---|---|---|---|
| 319214 | **SN** | P | *FC* | BF | 77317 | 62904 | 71785 | 77316 |
| 319215 | **AL** | P | *FC* | BF | 77319 | 62905 | 71786 | 77318 |
| 319216 | **SN** | P | *FC* | BF | 77321 | 62906 | 71787 | 77320 |
| 319217 | **SN** | P | *FC* | BF | 77323 | 62907 | 71788 | 77322 Brighton |
| 319218 | **AL** | P | *FC* | BF | 77325 | 62908 | 71789 | 77324 Croydon |
| 319219 | **SN** | P | *FC* | BF | 77327 | 62909 | 71790 | 77326 |
| 319220 | **SN** | P | *FC* | BF | 77329 | 62910 | 71791 | 77328 |

**Class 319/3.** DTSO–MSO–TSO–DTSO. Converted from Class 319/1 by replacing First Class seats with Standard Class seats. Used mainly on the Luton–Sutton/Wimbledon routes.

**Seating Layout:** 3+2 facing.
**Dimensions:** 19.33 x 2.82 m.

**DTSO(A).** Lot No. 31063 1990. –/70. 29.0 t.
**MSO.** Lot No. 31064 1990. –/78. 50.6 t.
**TSO.** Lot No. 31065 1990. –/74 2T. 31.0 t.
**DTSO(B).** Lot No. 31066 1990. –/75. 29.7 t.

| | | | | | | | | |
|---|---|---|---|---|---|---|---|---|
| 319361 | **FU** | P | *FC* | BF | 77459 | 63043 | 71929 | 77458 |
| 319362 | **FU** | P | *FC* | BF | 77461 | 63044 | 71930 | 77460 |
| 319363 | **FU** | P | *FC* | BF | 77463 | 63045 | 71931 | 77462 |
| 319364 | **FU** | P | *FC* | BF | 77465 | 63046 | 71932 | 77464 |
| 319365 | **FU** | P | *FC* | BF | 77467 | 63047 | 71933 | 77466 |
| 319366 | **FU** | P | *FC* | BF | 77469 | 63048 | 71934 | 77468 |
| 319367 | **FU** | P | *FC* | BF | 77471 | 63049 | 71935 | 77470 |
| 319368 | **FU** | P | *FC* | BF | 77473 | 63050 | 71936 | 77472 |
| 319369 | **FU** | P | *FC* | BF | 77475 | 63051 | 71937 | 77474 |
| 319370 | **FU** | P | *FC* | BF | 77477 | 63052 | 71938 | 77476 |
| 319371 | **FU** | P | *FC* | BF | 77479 | 63053 | 71939 | 77478 |

| | | | | | | | |
|---|---|---|---|---|---|---|---|
| 319372 | **FU** | P | *FC* | BF | 77481 | 63054 | 71940 | 77480 |
| 319373 | **FU** | P | *FC* | BF | 77483 | 63055 | 71941 | 77482 |
| 319374 | **FU** | P | *FC* | BF | 77485 | 63056 | 71942 | 77484 |
| 319375 | **FU** | P | *FC* | BF | 77487 | 63057 | 71943 | 77486 |
| 319376 | **FU** | P | *FC* | BF | 77489 | 63058 | 71944 | 77488 |
| 319377 | **FU** | P | *FC* | BF | 77491 | 63059 | 71945 | 77490 |
| 319378 | **FU** | P | *FC* | BF | 77493 | 63060 | 71946 | 77492 |
| 319379 | **FU** | P | *FC* | BF | 77495 | 63061 | 71947 | 77494 |
| 319380 | **FU** | P | *FC* | BF | 77497 | 63062 | 71948 | 77496 |
| 319381 | **FU** | P | *FC* | BF | 77973 | 63093 | 71979 | 77974 |
| 319382 | **FU** | P | *FC* | BF | 77975 | 63094 | 71980 | 77976 |
| 319383 | **FU** | P | *FC* | BF | 77977 | 63095 | 71981 | 77978 |
| 319384 | **FU** | P | *FC* | BF | 77979 | 63096 | 71982 | 77980 |
| 319385 | **FU** | P | *FC* | BF | 77981 | 63097 | 71983 | 77982 |
| 319386 | **FU** | P | *FC* | BF | 77983 | 63098 | 71984 | 77984 |

**Names (carried on TSO):**

319364 Transforming Blackfriars
319365 Transforming Farringdon
319374 Bedford Cauldwell TMD

**Class 319/4.** DTCO–MSO–TSO–DTSO. Converted from Class 319/0. Refurbished with carpets. DTSO(A) converted to composite. Used mainly on the Bedford–Gatwick–Brighton route.

**Seating Layout:** 1: 2+1 facing 2: 2+2/3+2 facing.

**77331–381. DTCO.** Lot No. 31022 (odd nos.) 1987–88. 12/51. 28.2t.
**77431–457. DTCO.** Lot No. 31038 (odd nos.) 1988. 12/51. 28.2t.
**62911–936. MSO.** Lot No. 31023 1987–88. –/74. 49.2t.
**62961–974. MSO.** Lot No. 31039 1988. –/74. 49.2t.
**71792–817. TSO.** Lot No. 31024 1987–88. –/67 2T. 31.0t.
**71866–879. TSO.** Lot No. 31040 1988. –67 2T. 31.0t.
**77330–380. DTSO.** Lot No. 31025 (even nos.) 1987–88. –/71 1W. 28.1t.
**77430–456. DTSO.** Lot No. 31041 (even nos.) 1988. –/71 1W. 28.1t.

| | | | | | | | |
|---|---|---|---|---|---|---|---|
| 319421 | **FU** | P | *FC* | BF | 77331 | 62912 | 71792 | 77330 |
| 319422 | **FU** | P | *FC* | BF | 77333 | 62912 | 71793 | 77332 |
| 319423 | **FU** | P | *FC* | BF | 77335 | 62913 | 71794 | 77334 |
| 319424 | **FU** | P | *FC* | BF | 77337 | 62914 | 71795 | 77336 |
| 319425 | **FU** | P | *FC* | BF | 77339 | 62915 | 71796 | 77338 |
| 319426 | **FU** | P | *FC* | BF | 77341 | 62916 | 71797 | 77340 |
| 319427 | **FU** | P | *FC* | BF | 77343 | 62917 | 71798 | 77342 |
| 319428 | **FU** | P | *FC* | BF | 77345 | 62918 | 71799 | 77344 |
| 319429 | **FU** | P | *FC* | BF | 77347 | 62919 | 71800 | 77346 |
| 319430 | **FU** | P | *FC* | BF | 77349 | 62920 | 71801 | 77348 |
| 319431 | **FU** | P | *FC* | BF | 77351 | 62921 | 71802 | 77350 |
| 319432 | **FU** | P | *FC* | BF | 77353 | 62922 | 71803 | 77352 |
| 319433 | **FU** | P | *FC* | BF | 77355 | 62923 | 71804 | 77354 |
| 319434 | **FU** | P | *FC* | BF | 77357 | 62924 | 71805 | 77356 |
| 319435 | **FU** | P | *FC* | BF | 77359 | 62925 | 71806 | 77358 |
| 319436 | **FU** | P | *FC* | BF | 77361 | 62926 | 71807 | 77360 |
| 319437 | **FU** | P | *FC* | BF | 77363 | 62927 | 71808 | 77362 |

| | | | | | | | | |
|---|---|---|---|---|---|---|---|---|
| 319438 | **FU** | P | *FC* | BF | 77365 | 62928 | 71809 | 77364 |
| 319439 | **FU** | P | *FC* | BF | 77367 | 62929 | 71810 | 77366 |
| 319440 | **FU** | P | *FC* | BF | 77369 | 62930 | 71811 | 77368 |
| 319441 | **FU** | P | *FC* | BF | 77371 | 62931 | 71812 | 77370 |
| 319442 | **FU** | P | *FC* | BF | 77373 | 62932 | 71813 | 77372 |
| 319443 | **FU** | P | *FC* | BF | 77375 | 62933 | 71814 | 77374 |
| 319444 | **FU** | P | *FC* | BF | 77377 | 62934 | 71815 | 77376 |
| 319445 | **FU** | P | *FC* | BF | 77379 | 62935 | 71816 | 77378 |
| 319446 | **FU** | P | *FC* | BF | 77381 | 62936 | 71817 | 77380 |
| 319447 | **FU** | P | *FC* | BF | 77431 | 62961 | 71866 | 77430 |
| 319448 | **FU** | P | *FC* | BF | 77433 | 62962 | 71867 | 77432 |
| 319449 | **FU** | P | *FC* | BF | 77435 | 62963 | 71868 | 77434 |
| 319450 | **FU** | P | *FC* | BF | 77437 | 62964 | 71869 | 77436 |
| 319451 | **FU** | P | *FC* | BF | 77439 | 62965 | 71870 | 77438 |
| 319452 | **FU** | P | *FC* | BF | 77441 | 62966 | 71871 | 77440 |
| 319453 | **FU** | P | *FC* | BF | 77443 | 62967 | 71872 | 77442 |
| 319454 | **FU** | P | *FC* | BF | 77445 | 62968 | 71873 | 77444 |
| 319455 | **FU** | P | *FC* | BF | 77447 | 62969 | 71874 | 77446 |
| 319456 | **FU** | P | *FC* | BF | 77449 | 62970 | 71875 | 77448 |
| 319457 | **FU** | P | *FC* | BF | 77451 | 62971 | 71876 | 77450 |
| 319458 | **FU** | P | *FC* | BF | 77453 | 62972 | 71877 | 77452 |
| 319459 | **FU** | P | *FC* | BF | 77455 | 62973 | 71878 | 77454 |
| 319460 | **FU** | P | *FC* | BF | 77457 | 62974 | 71879 | 77456 |

**Names (carried on TSO):**

319425  Transforming Travel
319435  Adrian Jackson-Robbins Chairman 1987–2007 Association of Public
            Transport Users
319446  St Pancras International
319448  Elstree Studios The Home of British Film and Television production
319449  King's Cross Thameslink

# CLASS 320                                     BREL YORK

Suburban units. All refurbished 2011–13 and fitted with a new universal access toilet to comply with the 2020 accessibility regulations.

**Formation:** DTSO–MSO–DTSO.
**Construction:** Steel
**Traction Motors:** Four Brush TM2141B of 268 kW.
**Wheel Arrangement:** 2-2 + Bo-Bo + 2-2.

| | |
|---|---|
| **Braking:** Disc. | **Dimensions:** 19.95 x 2.82 m. |
| **Bogies:** P7-4 (MSO), T3-7 (others). | **Couplers:** Tightlock. |
| **Gangways:** Within unit. | **Control System:** Thyristor. |
| **Doors:** Sliding. | **Maximum Speed:** 90 mph. |

**Seating Layout:** 3+2 facing.
**Multiple Working:** Within class & with Classes 317, 318, 319, 321, 322 and 323.

DTSO (A). Lot No. 31060 1990. –/51(4) 1TD 2W. 31.7 t.
MSO. Lot No. 31062 1990. –/78. 52.6 t.
DTSO (B). Lot No. 31061 1990. –/77. 31.6 t.

| 320301 | **SR** | E | *SR* | GW | 77899 | 63021 | 77921 |
| 320302 | **SR** | E | *SR* | GW | 77900 | 63022 | 77922 |
| 320303 | **SR** | E | *SR* | GW | 77901 | 63023 | 77923 |
| 320304 | **SR** | E | *SR* | GW | 77902 | 63024 | 77924 |
| 320305 | **SR** | E | *SR* | GW | 77903 | 63025 | 77925 |
| 320306 | **SR** | E | *SR* | GW | 77904 | 63026 | 77926 |
| 320307 | **SR** | E | *SR* | GW | 77905 | 63027 | 77927 |
| 320308 | **SR** | E | *SR* | GW | 77906 | 63028 | 77928 |
| 320309 | **SR** | E | *SR* | GW | 77907 | 63029 | 77929 |
| 320310 | **SR** | E | *SR* | GW | 77908 | 63030 | 77930 |
| 320311 | **SR** | E | *SR* | GW | 77909 | 63031 | 77931 |
| 320312 | **SR** | E | *SR* | GW | 77910 | 63032 | 77932 |
| 320313 | **SR** | E | *SR* | GW | 77911 | 63033 | 77933 |
| 320314 | **SR** | E | *SR* | GW | 77912 | 63034 | 77934 |
| 320315 | **SR** | E | *SR* | GW | 77913 | 63035 | 77935 |
| 320316 | **SR** | E | *SR* | GW | 77914 | 63036 | 77936 |
| 320317 | **SR** | E | *SR* | GW | 77915 | 63037 | 77937 |
| 320318 | **SR** | E | *SR* | GW | 77916 | 63038 | 77938 |
| 320319 | **SR** | E | *SR* | GW | 77917 | 63039 | 77939 |
| 320320 | **SR** | E | *SR* | GW | 77918 | 63040 | 77940 |
| 320321 | **SR** | E | *SR* | GW | 77919 | 63041 | 77941 |
| 320322 | **SR** | E | *SR* | GW | 77920 | 63042 | 77942 |

# CLASS 321                                              BREL YORK

Outer suburban units.

**Formation:** DTCO (DTSO on Class 321/9)–MSO–TSO–DTSO.
**Construction:** Steel.
**Traction Motors:** Four Brush TM2141C of 268 kW.
**Wheel Arrangement:** 2-2 + Bo-Bo + 2-2 + 2-2.
**Braking:** Disc.                          **Dimensions:** 19.95 x 2.82 m.
**Bogies:** P7-4 (MSO), T3-7 (others).      **Couplers:** Tightlock.
**Gangways:** Within unit.                  **Control System:** Thyristor.
**Doors:** Sliding.                         **Maximum Speed:** 100 mph.
**Seating Layout:** 1: 2+2 facing, 2: 3+2 facing.
**Multiple Working:** Within class & with Classes 317, 318, 319, 320, 322 and 323.

**Class 321/3.**

**DTCO.** Lot No. 31053 1988–90. 16/57. 29.7 t.
**MSO.** Lot No. 31054 1988–90. –/82. 51.5 t.
**TSO.** Lot No. 31055 1988–90. –/75 2T. 29.1 t.
**DTSO.** Lot No. 31056 1988–90. –/78. 29.7 t.

| 321301 | **NX** | E | *GA* | IL | 78049 | 62975 | 71880 | 77853 |
| 321302 | **NX** | E | *GA* | IL | 78050 | 62976 | 71881 | 77854 |
| 321303 | **NX** | E | *GA* | IL | 78051 | 62977 | 71882 | 77855 |
| 321304 | **NX** | E | *GA* | IL | 78052 | 62978 | 71883 | 77856 |
| 321305 | **NX** | E | *GA* | IL | 78053 | 62979 | 71884 | 77857 |
| 321306 | **NX** | E | *GA* | IL | 78054 | 62980 | 71885 | 77858 |
| 321307 | **NX** | E | *GA* | IL | 78055 | 62981 | 71886 | 77859 |
| 321308 | **NX** | E | *GA* | IL | 78056 | 62982 | 71887 | 77860 |

| | | | | | | | | |
|---|---|---|---|---|---|---|---|---|
| 321 309 | NX | E | GA | IL | 78057 | 62983 | 71888 | 77861 |
| 321 310 | NX | E | GA | IL | 78058 | 62984 | 71889 | 77862 |
| 321 311 | NX | E | GA | IL | 78059 | 62985 | 71890 | 77863 |
| 321 312 | NX | E | GA | IL | 78060 | 62986 | 71891 | 77864 |
| 321 313 | NX | E | GA | IL | 78061 | 62987 | 71892 | 77865 |
| 321 314 | NX | E | GA | IL | 78062 | 62988 | 71893 | 77866 |
| 321 315 | NX | E | GA | IL | 78063 | 62989 | 71894 | 77867 |
| 321 316 | NX | E | GA | IL | 78064 | 62990 | 71895 | 77868 |
| 321 317 | NX | E | GA | IL | 78065 | 62991 | 71896 | 77869 |
| 321 318 | NX | E | GA | IL | 78066 | 62992 | 71897 | 77870 |
| 321 319 | NX | E | GA | IL | 78067 | 62993 | 71898 | 77871 |
| 321 320 | NX | E | GA | IL | 78068 | 62994 | 71899 | 77872 |
| 321 321 | NX | E | GA | IL | 78069 | 62995 | 71900 | 77873 |
| 321 322 | NX | E | GA | IL | 78070 | 62996 | 71901 | 77874 |
| 321 323 | NX | E | GA | IL | 78071 | 62997 | 71902 | 77875 |
| 321 324 | NX | E | GA | IL | 78072 | 62998 | 71903 | 77876 |
| 321 325 | NX | E | GA | IL | 78073 | 62999 | 71904 | 77877 |
| 321 326 | NX | E | GA | IL | 78074 | 63000 | 71905 | 77878 |
| 321 327 | NC | E | GA | IL | 78075 | 63001 | 71906 | 77879 |
| 321 328 | NX | E | GA | IL | 78076 | 63002 | 71907 | 77880 |
| 321 329 | NX | E | GA | IL | 78077 | 63003 | 71908 | 77881 |
| 321 330 | NC | E | GA | IL | 78078 | 63004 | 71909 | 77882 |
| 321 331 | NC | E | GA | IL | 78079 | 63005 | 71910 | 77883 |
| 321 332 | NC | E | GA | IL | 78080 | 63006 | 71911 | 77884 |
| 321 333 | NC | E | GA | IL | 78081 | 63007 | 71912 | 77885 |
| 321 334 | NC | E | GA | IL | 78082 | 63008 | 71913 | 77886 |
| 321 335 | NC | E | GA | IL | 78083 | 63009 | 71914 | 77887 |
| 321 336 | NC | E | GA | IL | 78084 | 63010 | 71915 | 77888 |
| 321 337 | NC | E | GA | IL | 78085 | 63011 | 71916 | 77889 |
| 321 338 | NC | E | GA | IL | 78086 | 63012 | 71917 | 77890 |
| 321 339 | NC | E | GA | IL | 78087 | 63013 | 71918 | 77891 |
| 321 340 | NC | E | GA | IL | 78088 | 63014 | 71919 | 77892 |
| 321 341 | NC | E | GA | IL | 78089 | 63015 | 71920 | 77893 |
| 321 342 | NC | E | GA | IL | 78090 | 63016 | 71921 | 77894 |
| 321 343 | NC | E | GA | IL | 78091 | 63017 | 71922 | 77895 |
| 321 344 | NC | E | GA | IL | 78092 | 63018 | 71923 | 77896 |
| 321 345 | NC | E | GA | IL | 78093 | 63019 | 71924 | 77897 |
| 321 346 | NC | E | GA | IL | 78094 | 63020 | 71925 | 77898 |
| 321 347 | NC | E | GA | IL | 78131 | 63105 | 71991 | 78280 |
| 321 348 | NC | E | GA | IL | 78132 | 63106 | 71992 | 78281 |
| 321 349 | NC | E | GA | IL | 78133 | 63107 | 71993 | 78282 |
| 321 350 | NC | E | GA | IL | 78134 | 63108 | 71994 | 78283 |
| 321 351 | NC | E | GA | IL | 78135 | 63109 | 71995 | 78284 |
| 321 352 | NC | E | GA | IL | 78136 | 63110 | 71996 | 78285 |
| 321 353 | NC | E | GA | IL | 78137 | 63111 | 71997 | 78286 |
| 321 354 | NC | E | GA | IL | 78138 | 63112 | 71998 | 78287 |
| 321 355 | NC | E | GA | IL | 78139 | 63113 | 71999 | 78288 |
| 321 356 | NC | E | GA | IL | 78140 | 63114 | 72000 | 78289 |
| 321 357 | NC | E | GA | IL | 78141 | 63115 | 72001 | 78290 |
| 321 358 | NC | E | GA | IL | 78142 | 63116 | 72002 | 78291 |
| 321 359 | GA | E | GA | IL | 78143 | 63117 | 72003 | 78292 |

| | | | | | | | |
|---|---|---|---|---|---|---|---|
| 321360 | **NC** | E | *GA* | IL | 78144 | 63118 | 72004 | 78293 |
| 321361 | **GA** | E | *GA* | IL | 78145 | 63119 | 72005 | 78294 |
| 321362 | **GA** | E | *GA* | IL | 78146 | 63120 | 72006 | 78295 |
| 321363 | **GA** | E | *GA* | IL | 78147 | 63121 | 72007 | 78296 |
| 321364 | **GA** | E | *GA* | IL | 78148 | 63122 | 72008 | 78297 |
| 321365 | **GA** | E | *GA* | IL | 78149 | 63123 | 72009 | 78298 |
| 321366 | **GA** | E | *GA* | IL | 78150 | 63124 | 72010 | 78299 |

**Names (carried on TSO):**

| | |
|---|---|
| 321312 | Southend-on-Sea |
| 321313 | University of Essex |
| 321321 | NSPCC ESSEX FULL STOP |
| 321334 | Amsterdam |
| 321336 | GEOFFREY FREEMAN ALLEN |
| 321342 | R. Barnes |
| 321343 | RSA RAILWAY STUDY ASSOCIATION |
| 321351 | London Southend Airport |
| 321361 | Phoenix |

**Class 321/4.**

The original vehicles 71966 and 77960 from 321418 and 78114 and 63082 from 321420 were written off after the Watford Junction accident in 1996. The undamaged vehicles were formed together as 321418 whilst four new vehicles were built in 1997, taking the same numbers as the scrapped vehicles, and these became the second 321420.

The DTCOs of 321438–447 have had 12 First Class seats declassified.

\* 321448 has received an interior refurbishment as an Eversholt demonstrator unit. It has been fitted with two different types of interior using seats supplied by ATD. 78130 and 63104 have a "suburban" interior with a 3+2 seating layout and 78279 and 71990 have a "metro" interior with 2+2 seating. The unit is in normal service with Greater Anglia.

**Non-standard livery:** 321448 Eversholt demonstrator (silver with blue doors and multi-coloured stripes).

**DTCO.** Lot No. 31067 1989–90. 28/40. 29.8 t (\* 16/30(4) 1TD 2W. 33.9 t).
**MSO.** Lot No. 31068 1989–90. –/79. 51.6 t (\* –/82. 54.0 t).
**TSO.** Lot No. 31069 1989–90. –/74 2T. 29.2 t (\* –/62 1T. 31.7 t).
**DTSO.** Lot No. 31070 1989–90. –/78. 29.8 t. (\* –/58. 33.2 t).

| | | | | | | | |
|---|---|---|---|---|---|---|---|
| 321401 | **FU** | E | *FC* | HE | 78095 | 63063 | 71949 | 77943 |
| 321402 | **FU** | E | *FC* | HE | 78096 | 63064 | 71950 | 77944 |
| 321403 | **FU** | E | *FC* | HE | 78097 | 63065 | 71951 | 77945 |
| 321404 | **FU** | E | *FC* | HE | 78098 | 63066 | 71952 | 77946 |
| 321405 | **FU** | E | *FC* | HE | 78099 | 63067 | 71953 | 77947 |
| 321406 | **FU** | E | *FC* | HE | 78100 | 63068 | 71954 | 77948 |
| 321407 | **FU** | E | *FC* | HE | 78101 | 63069 | 71955 | 77949 |
| 321408 | **FU** | E | *FC* | HE | 78102 | 63070 | 71956 | 77950 |
| 321409 | **FU** | E | *FC* | HE | 78103 | 63071 | 71957 | 77951 |
| 321410 | **FU** | E | *FC* | HE | 78104 | 63072 | 71958 | 77952 |
| 321411 | **LM** | E | *LM* | NN | 78105 | 63073 | 71959 | 77953 |

| | | | | | | | | |
|---|---|---|---|---|---|---|---|---|
| 321412 | **LM** | E | *LM* | NN | 78106 | 63074 | 71960 | 77954 |
| 321413 | **LM** | E | *LM* | NN | 78107 | 63075 | 71961 | 77955 |
| 321414 | **LM** | E | *LM* | NN | 78108 | 63076 | 71962 | 77956 |
| 321415 | **LM** | E | *LM* | NN | 78109 | 63077 | 71963 | 77957 |
| 321416 | **LM** | E | *LM* | NN | 78110 | 63078 | 71964 | 77958 |
| 321417 | **LM** | E | *LM* | NN | 78111 | 63079 | 71965 | 77959 |
| 321418 | **FU** | E | *FC* | HE | 78112 | 63080 | 71968 | 77962 |
| 321419 | **FU** | E | *FC* | HE | 78113 | 63081 | 71967 | 77961 |
| 321420 | **FU** | E | *FC* | HE | 78114 | 63082 | 71966 | 77960 |
| 321421 | **NC** | E | *GA* | IL | 78115 | 63083 | 71969 | 77963 |
| 321422 | **NC** | E | *GA* | IL | 78116 | 63084 | 71970 | 77964 |
| 321423 | **NC** | E | *GA* | IL | 78117 | 63085 | 71971 | 77965 |
| 321424 | **NX** | E | *GA* | IL | 78118 | 63086 | 71972 | 77966 |
| 321425 | **NC** | E | *GA* | IL | 78119 | 63087 | 71973 | 77967 |
| 321426 | **NX** | E | *GA* | IL | 78120 | 63088 | 71974 | 77968 |
| 321427 | **NX** | E | *GA* | IL | 78121 | 63089 | 71975 | 77969 |
| 321428 | **NX** | E | *GA* | IL | 78122 | 63090 | 71976 | 77970 |
| 321429 | **NX** | E | *GA* | IL | 78123 | 63091 | 71977 | 77971 |
| 321430 | **NX** | E | *GA* | IL | 78124 | 63092 | 71978 | 77972 |
| 321431 | **NX** | E | *GA* | IL | 78151 | 63125 | 72011 | 78300 |
| 321432 | **NC** | E | *GA* | IL | 78152 | 63126 | 72012 | 78301 |
| 321433 | **NC** | E | *GA* | IL | 78153 | 63127 | 72013 | 78302 |
| 321434 | **NC** | E | *GA* | IL | 78154 | 63128 | 72014 | 78303 |
| 321435 | **NC** | E | *GA* | IL | 78155 | 63129 | 72015 | 78304 |
| 321436 | **NC** | E | *GA* | IL | 78156 | 63130 | 72016 | 78305 |
| 321437 | **NC** | E | *GA* | IL | 78157 | 63131 | 72017 | 78306 |
| 321438 | **GA** | E | *GA* | IL | 78158 | 63132 | 72018 | 78307 |
| 321439 | **GA** | E | *GA* | IL | 78159 | 63133 | 72019 | 78308 |
| 321440 | **GA** | E | *GA* | IL | 78160 | 63134 | 72020 | 78309 |
| 321441 | **GA** | E | *GA* | IL | 78161 | 63135 | 72021 | 78310 |
| 321442 | **GA** | E | *GA* | IL | 78162 | 63136 | 72022 | 78311 |
| 321443 | **GA** | E | *GA* | IL | 78125 | 63099 | 71985 | 78274 |
| 321444 | **NC** | E | *GA* | IL | 78126 | 63100 | 71986 | 78275 |
| 321445 | **NC** | E | *GA* | IL | 78127 | 63101 | 71987 | 78276 |
| 321446 | **NC** | E | *GA* | IL | 78128 | 63102 | 71988 | 78277 |
| 321447 | **GA** | E | *GA* | IL | 78129 | 63103 | 71989 | 78278 |
| 321448 | * **O** | E | *GA* | IL | 78130 | 63104 | 71990 | 78279 |

**Names (carried on TSO):**

321403 Stewart Fleming Signalman King's Cross
321409 Dame Alice Owen's School 400 Years of Learning
321418 The Poppy Express Supporting The Royal British Legion
321428 The Essex Commuter
321444 Essex Lifeboats
321446 George Mullings

**Class 321/9**. DTSO(A)–MSO–TSO–DTSO(B).

**DTSO(A)**. Lot No. 31108 1991. –/70(8). 29.2 t.
**MSO**. Lot No. 31109 1991. –/79. 51.1 t.
**TSO**. Lot No. 31110 1991. –/74 2T. 29.0 t.
**DTSO(B)**. Lot No. 31111 1991. –/70(7) 1W. 29.2 t.

| 321901 | **YR** | E | *NO* | NL | 77990 | 63153 | 72128 | 77993 |
| 321902 | **YR** | E | *NO* | NL | 77991 | 63154 | 72129 | 77994 |
| 321903 | **YR** | E | *NO* | NL | 77992 | 63155 | 72130 | 77995 |

# CLASS 322                        BREL YORK

Units built for use on Stansted Airport services, used for a number of years with ScotRail before transfer to Northern.

**Formation:** DTSO–MSO–TSO–DTSO.
**Construction:** Steel.
**Traction Motors:** Four Brush TM2141C of 268 kW.
**Wheel Arrangement:** 2-2 + Bo-Bo + 2-2 + 2-2.
**Braking:** Disc.                     **Dimensions:** 19.95/19.92 x 2.82 m.
**Bogies:** P7-4 (MSO), T3-7 (others).    **Couplers:** Tightlock.
**Gangways:** Within unit.               **Control System:** Thyristor.
**Doors:** Sliding.                   **Maximum Speed:** 100 mph.
**Seating Layout:** 3+2 facing.
**Multiple Working:** Within class & with Classes 317, 318, 319, 320, 321 and 323.

**DTSO(A).** Lot No. 31094 1990. –/58. 29.3 t.
**MSO.** Lot No. 31092 1990. –/83. 51.5 t.
**TSO.** Lot No. 31093 1990. –/76 2T. 28.8 t.
**DTSO(B).** Lot No. 31091 1990. –/89(3) 1W. 29.1 t.

| 322481 | **FB** | E | *NO* | NL | 78163 | 63137 | 72023 | 77985 |
| 322482 | **FB** | E | *NO* | NL | 78164 | 63138 | 72024 | 77986 |
| 322483 | **FB** | E | *NO* | NL | 78165 | 63139 | 72025 | 77987 |
| 322484 | **FB** | E | *NO* | NL | 78166 | 63140 | 72026 | 77988 |
| 322485 | **FB** | E | *NO* | NL | 78167 | 63141 | 72027 | 77989 |

# CLASS 323   HUNSLET TRANSPORTATION PROJECTS

Suburban units.

**Formation:** DMSO–PTSO–DMSO.
**Construction:** Welded aluminium alloy.
**Traction Motors:** Four Holec DMKT 52/24 asynchronous of 146 kW.
**Wheel Arrangement:** Bo-Bo + 2-2 + Bo-Bo.
**Braking:** Disc.                     **Dimensions:** 23.37/23.44 x 2.80 m.
**Bogies:** SRP BP62 (DMSO), BT52 (PTSO). **Couplers:** Tightlock.
**Gangways:** Within unit.               **Control System:** GTO Inverter.
**Doors:** Sliding plug.             **Maximum Speed:** 90 mph.
**Seating Layout:** 3+2 facing/unidirectional.
**Multiple Working:** Within class & with Classes 317, 318, 319, 320, 321 and 322.

**DMSO(A).** Lot No. 31112 Hunslet 1992–93. –/98 (* –/82). 41.0 t.
**TSO.** Lot No. 31113 Hunslet 1992–93. –/88(5) 1T 2W. (* –/80 1T 2W). 39.4t.
**DMSO(B).** Lot No. 31114 Hunslet 1992–93. –/98 (* –/82). 41.0 t.

| 323201 | **LM** | P | *LM* | SO | 64001 | 72201 | 65001 |
| 323202 | **LM** | P | *LM* | SO | 64002 | 72202 | 65002 |
| 323203 | **LM** | P | *LM* | SO | 64003 | 72203 | 65003 |
| 323204 | **LM** | P | *LM* | SO | 64004 | 72204 | 65004 |

| | | | | | | | |
|---|---|---|---|---|---|---|---|
| 323 205 | | LM | P | LM | SO | 64005 | 72205 | 65005 |
| 323 206 | | LM | P | LM | SO | 64006 | 72206 | 65006 |
| 323 207 | | LM | P | LM | SO | 64007 | 72207 | 65007 |
| 323 208 | | LM | P | LM | SO | 64008 | 72208 | 65008 |
| 323 209 | | LM | P | LM | SO | 64009 | 72209 | 65009 |
| 323 210 | | LM | P | LM | SO | 64010 | 72210 | 65010 |
| 323 211 | | LM | P | LM | SO | 64011 | 72211 | 65011 |
| 323 212 | | LM | P | LM | SO | 64012 | 72212 | 65012 |
| 323 213 | | LM | P | LM | SO | 64013 | 72213 | 65013 |
| 323 214 | | LM | P | LM | SO | 64014 | 72214 | 65014 |
| 323 215 | | LM | P | LM | SO | 64015 | 72215 | 65015 |
| 323 216 | | LM | P | LM | SO | 64016 | 72216 | 65016 |
| 323 217 | | LM | P | LM | SO | 64017 | 72217 | 65017 |
| 323 218 | | LM | P | LM | SO | 64018 | 72218 | 65018 |
| 323 219 | | LM | P | LM | SO | 64019 | 72219 | 65019 |
| 323 220 | | LM | P | LM | SO | 64020 | 72220 | 65020 |
| 323 221 | | LM | P | LM | SO | 64021 | 72221 | 65021 |
| 323 222 | | LM | P | LM | SO | 64022 | 72222 | 65022 |
| 323 223 | * | NO | P | NO | LG | 64023 | 72223 | 65023 |
| 323 224 | * | NO | P | NO | LG | 64024 | 72224 | 65024 |
| 323 225 | * | NO | P | NO | LG | 64025 | 72225 | 65025 |
| 323 226 | | NO | P | NO | LG | 64026 | 72226 | 65026 |
| 323 227 | | NO | P | NO | LG | 64027 | 72227 | 65027 |
| 323 228 | | NO | P | NO | LG | 64028 | 72228 | 65028 |
| 323 229 | | NO | P | NO | LG | 64029 | 72229 | 65029 |
| 323 230 | | NO | P | NO | LG | 64030 | 72230 | 65030 |
| 323 231 | | NO | P | NO | LG | 64031 | 72231 | 65031 |
| 323 232 | | NO | P | NO | LG | 64032 | 72232 | 65032 |
| 323 233 | | NO | P | NO | LG | 64033 | 72233 | 65033 |
| 323 234 | | NO | P | NO | LG | 64034 | 72234 | 65034 |
| 323 235 | | NO | P | NO | LG | 64035 | 72235 | 65035 |
| 323 236 | | NO | P | NO | LG | 64036 | 72236 | 65036 |
| 323 237 | | NO | P | NO | LG | 64037 | 72237 | 65037 |
| 323 238 | | NO | P | NO | LG | 64038 | 72238 | 65038 |
| 323 239 | | NO | P | NO | LG | 64039 | 72239 | 65039 |
| 323 240 | | LM | P | LM | SO | 64040 | 72340 | 65040 |
| 323 241 | | LM | P | LM | SO | 64041 | 72341 | 65041 |
| 323 242 | | LM | P | LM | SO | 64042 | 72342 | 65042 |
| 323 243 | | LM | P | LM | SO | 64043 | 72343 | 65043 |

# CLASS 325                                    ABB DERBY

Postal units based on Class 319s. Compatible with diesel or electric locomotive haulage.

**Formation:** DTPMV–MPMV–TPMV–DTPMV.
**System:** 25 kV AC overhead/750 V DC third rail.
**Construction:** Steel.
**Traction Motors:** Four GEC G315BZ of 268 kW.
**Wheel Arrangement:** 2-2 + Bo-Bo + 2-2 + 2-2.
**Braking:** Disc.                    **Dimensions:** 19.33 x 2.82 m.

**Bogies:** P7-4 (MSO), T3-7 (others).
**Gangways:** None.
**Doors:** Roller shutter.
**Multiple Working:** Within class.

**Couplers:** Drop-head buckeye.
**Control System:** GTO Chopper.
**Maximum Speed:** 100 mph.

**DTPMV.** Lot No. 31144 1995. 29.1 t.
**MPMV.** Lot No. 31145 1995. 49.5 t.
**TPMV.** Lot No. 31146 1995. 30.7 t.

| | | | | | | | | |
|---|---|---|---|---|---|---|---|---|
| 325001 | **RM** | RM | *DB* | CE | 68300 | 68340 | 68360 | 68301 |
| 325002 | **RM** | RM | *DB* | CE | 68302 | 68341 | 68361 | 68303 |
| 325003 | **RM** | RM | *DB* | CE | 68304 | 68342 | 68362 | 68305 |
| 325004 | **RM** | RM | *DB* | CE | 68306 | 68343 | 68363 | 68307 |
| 325005 | **RM** | RM | *DB* | CE | 68308 | 68344 | 68364 | 68309 |
| 325006 | **RM** | RM | *DB* | CE | 68310 | 68345 | 68365 | 68311 |
| 325007 | **RM** | RM | *DB* | CE | 68312 | 68346 | 68366 | 68313 |
| 325008 | **RM** | RM | *DB* | CE | 68314 | 68347 | 68367 | 68315 |
| 325009 | **RM** | RM | *DB* | CE | 68316 | 68349 | 68369 | 68317 |
| 325011 | **RM** | RM | *DB* | CE | 68320 | 68350 | 68370 | 68321 |
| 325012 | **RM** | RM | *DB* | CE | 68322 | 68351 | 68371 | 68323 |
| 325013 | **RM** | RM | *DB* | CE | 68324 | 68352 | 68372 | 68325 |
| 325014 | **RM** | RM | *DB* | CE | 68326 | 68353 | 68373 | 68327 |
| 325015 | **RM** | RM | *DB* | CE | 68328 | 68354 | 68374 | 68329 |
| 325016 | **RM** | RM | *DB* | CE | 68330 | 68355 | 68375 | 68331 |

**Names (carried on one side of each DTPMV):**

325002 Royal Mail North Wales & North West
325006 John Grierson
325008 Peter Howarth CBE

# CLASS 332    HEATHROW EXPRESS CAF/SIEMENS

Dedicated Heathrow Express units. Five units were increased from 4-car to 5-car in 2002. Usually operate in coupled pairs.

**Formations:** DMSO–TSO–PTSO–(TSO)–DMFO.
**Construction:** Steel.
**Traction Motors:** Two Siemens monomotors asynchronous of 350 kW.
**Wheel Arrangement:** B-B + 2-2 + 2-2 (+ 2-2) + B-B.
**Braking:** Disc.
**Bogies:** CAF.
**Gangways:** Within unit.
**Doors:** Sliding plug.

**Dimensions:** 23.74/23.35/23.14 x 2.75 m.
**Couplers:** Scharfenberg 10L.
**Control System:** IGBT Inverter.
**Maximum Speed:** 100 mph.

**Heating & ventilation:** Air conditioning.
**Seating:** 1: 1+1 facing/unidirectional, 2: 2+2 mainly unidirectional.
**Multiple Working:** Within class.

**Advertising livery:** Vehicles 78401, 78403, 78405, 78407, 78409, 78411, 78413, 78415, 78417, 78419, 78421, 78423, 78425, 78427 Vodafone (red).

**DMSO.** CAF 1997–98. –/43 (8). 49.9 t.
**72400–413. TSO.** CAF 1997–98. –/64 (11). 38.4 t.
**72414–418. TSO.** CAF 2002. –/56 35.8 t.

**PTSO**. CAF 1997–98. –/39 (11) 1TD 2W. 47.6 t.
**DMFO**. CAF 1997–98. 20/–. 49.5 t.

| | | | | | | | | |
|---|---|---|---|---|---|---|---|---|
| 332001 | **HE** | HE | _HE_ | OH | 78400 | 72412 | 63400 | | 78401 |
| 332002 | **HE** | HE | _HE_ | OH | 78402 | 72409 | 63406 | | 78403 |
| 332003 | **HE** | HE | _HE_ | OH | 78404 | 72407 | 63402 | | 78405 |
| 332004 | **HE** | HE | _HE_ | OH | 78406 | 72405 | 63403 | | 78407 |
| 332005 | **HE** | HE | _HE_ | OH | 78408 | 72411 | 63404 | 72417 | 78409 |
| 332006 | **HE** | HE | _HE_ | OH | 78410 | 72410 | 63405 | 72415 | 78411 |
| 332007 | **HE** | HE | _HE_ | OH | 78412 | 72401 | 63401 | 72414 | 78413 |
| 332008 | **HE** | HE | _HE_ | OH | 78414 | 72413 | 63407 | 72418 | 78415 |
| 332009 | **HE** | HE | _HE_ | OH | 78416 | 72400 | 63408 | 72416 | 78417 |
| 332010 | **HE** | HE | _HE_ | OH | 78418 | 72402 | 63409 | | 78419 |
| 332011 | **HE** | HE | _HE_ | OH | 78420 | 72403 | 63410 | | 78421 |
| 332012 | **HE** | HE | _HE_ | OH | 78422 | 72404 | 63411 | | 78423 |
| 332013 | **HE** | HE | _HE_ | OH | 78424 | 72408 | 63412 | | 78425 |
| 332014 | **HE** | HE | _HE_ | OH | 78426 | 72406 | 63413 | | 78427 |

# CLASS 333                                          CAF/SIEMENS

West Yorkshire area suburban units.

**Formation:** DMSO–PTSO–TSO–DMSO.
**Construction:** Steel.
**Traction Motors:** Two Siemens monomotors asynchronous of 350 kW.
**Wheel Arrangement:** B-B + 2-2 + 2-2 + B-B.
**Braking:** Disc.
**Dimensions:** 23.74 (outer ends)/23.35 (TSO) x 2.75 m.
**Bogies:** CAF.                          **Couplers:** Dellner 10L.
**Gangways:** Within unit.               **Control System:** IGBT Inverter.
**Doors:** Sliding plug.                  **Maximum Speed:** 100 mph.
**Heating & ventilation:** Air conditioning.
**Seating Layout:** 3+2 facing/unidirectional.
**Multiple Working:** Within class.

333001–008 were made up to 4-car units from 3-car units in 2002.

333009–016 were made up to 4-car units from 3-car units in 2003.

**DMSO(A)**. (Odd Nos.) CAF 2001. –/90. 50.6 t.
**PTSO**. CAF 2001. –/73(6) 1TD 2W. 46.0 t.
**TSO**. CAF 2002–03. –/100. 38.5 t.
**DMSO(B)**. (Even Nos.) CAF 2001. –/90. 50.0 t.

| | | | | | | | | |
|---|---|---|---|---|---|---|---|---|
| 333001 | **YR** | A | _NO_ | NL | 78451 | 74461 | 74477 | 78452 |
| 333002 | **YR** | A | _NO_ | NL | 78453 | 74462 | 74478 | 78454 |
| 333003 | **YR** | A | _NO_ | NL | 78455 | 74463 | 74479 | 78456 |
| 333004 | **YR** | A | _NO_ | NL | 78457 | 74464 | 74480 | 78458 |
| 333005 | **YR** | A | _NO_ | NL | 78459 | 74465 | 74481 | 78460 |
| 333006 | **YR** | A | _NO_ | NL | 78461 | 74466 | 74482 | 78462 |
| 333007 | **YR** | A | _NO_ | NL | 78463 | 74467 | 74483 | 78464 |
| 333008 | **YR** | A | _NO_ | NL | 78465 | 74468 | 74484 | 78466 |
| 333009 | **YR** | A | _NO_ | NL | 78467 | 74469 | 74485 | 78468 |
| 333010 | **YR** | A | _NO_ | NL | 78469 | 74470 | 74486 | 78470 |

| 333011 | **YR** | A | *NO* | NL | 78471 | 74471 | 74487 | 78472 |
| 333012 | **YR** | A | *NO* | NL | 78473 | 74472 | 74488 | 78474 |
| 333013 | **YR** | A | *NO* | NL | 78475 | 74473 | 74489 | 78476 |
| 333014 | **YR** | A | *NO* | NL | 78477 | 74474 | 74490 | 78478 |
| 333015 | **YR** | A | *NO* | NL | 78479 | 74475 | 74491 | 78480 |
| 333016 | **YR** | A | *NO* | NL | 78481 | 74476 | 74492 | 78482 |

**Name (carried on end cars):**

333007 Alderman J Arthur Godwin First Lord Mayor of Bradford 1907

# CLASS 334    JUNIPER    ALSTOM BIRMINGHAM

Outer suburban units.

**Formation:** DMSO–PTSO–DMSO.
**Construction:** Steel.
**Traction Motors:** Two Alstom ONIX 800 asynchronous of 270 kW.
**Wheel Arrangement:** 2-Bo + 2-2 + Bo-2.
**Braking:** Disc.                                    **Dimensions:** 21.01/19.94 x 2.80 m.
**Bogies:** Alstom LTB3/TBP3.           **Couplers:** Tightlock.
**Gangways:** Within unit.                    **Control System:** IGBT Inverter.
**Doors:** Sliding plug.                          **Maximum Speed:** 90 mph.
**Heating & ventilation:** Pressure heating and ventilation.
**Seating Layout:** 2+2 facing/unidirectional (3+2 in PTSO).
**Multiple Working:** Within class.

**DMSO(A).** Alstom Birmingham 1999–2001. –/64. 42.6 t.
**PTSO.** Alstom Birmingham 1999–2001. –/55 1TD 1W. 39.4 t.
**DMSO(B).** Alstom Birmingham 1999–2001. –/64. 42.6 t.

| 334001 | **SP** | E | *SR* | GW | 64101 | 74301 | 65101 | Donald Dewar |
| 334002 | **SR** | E | *SR* | GW | 64102 | 74302 | 65102 | |
| 334003 | **SR** | E | *SR* | GW | 64103 | 74303 | 65103 | |
| 334004 | **SP** | E | *SR* | GW | 64104 | 74304 | 65104 | |
| 334005 | **SR** | E | *SR* | GW | 64105 | 74305 | 65105 | |
| 334006 | **SR** | E | *SR* | GW | 64106 | 74306 | 65106 | |
| 334007 | **SP** | E | *SR* | GW | 64107 | 74307 | 65107 | |
| 334008 | **SR** | E | *SR* | GW | 64108 | 74308 | 65108 | |
| 334009 | **SR** | E | *SR* | GW | 64109 | 74309 | 65109 | |
| 334010 | **SP** | E | *SR* | GW | 64110 | 74310 | 65110 | |
| 334011 | **SP** | E | *SR* | GW | 64111 | 74311 | 65111 | |
| 334012 | **SR** | E | *SR* | GW | 64112 | 74312 | 65112 | |
| 334013 | **SR** | E | *SR* | GW | 64113 | 74313 | 65113 | |
| 334014 | **SR** | E | *SR* | GW | 64114 | 74314 | 65114 | |
| 334015 | **SR** | E | *SR* | GW | 64115 | 74315 | 65115 | |
| 334016 | **SP** | E | *SR* | GW | 64116 | 74316 | 65116 | |
| 334017 | **SR** | E | *SR* | GW | 64117 | 74317 | 65117 | |
| 334018 | **SR** | E | *SR* | GW | 64118 | 74318 | 65118 | |
| 334019 | **SP** | E | *SR* | GW | 64119 | 74319 | 65119 | |
| 334020 | **SR** | E | *SR* | GW | 64120 | 74320 | 65120 | |
| 334021 | **SR** | E | *SR* | GW | 64121 | 74321 | 65121 | |
| 334022 | **SR** | E | *SR* | GW | 64122 | 74322 | 65122 | |

| | | | | | | | |
|---|---|---|---|---|---|---|---|
| 334023 | **SR** | E | *SR* | GW | 64123 | 74323 | 65123 |
| 334024 | **SR** | E | *SR* | GW | 64124 | 74324 | 65124 |
| 334025 | **SR** | E | *SR* | GW | 64125 | 74325 | 65125 |
| 334026 | **SP** | E | *SR* | GW | 64126 | 74326 | 65126 |
| 334027 | **SR** | E | *SR* | GW | 64127 | 74327 | 65127 |
| 334028 | **SR** | E | *SR* | GW | 64128 | 74328 | 65128 |
| 334029 | **SR** | E | *SR* | GW | 64129 | 74329 | 65129 |
| 334030 | **SR** | E | *SR* | GW | 64130 | 74330 | 65130 |
| 334031 | **SR** | E | *SR* | GW | 64131 | 74331 | 65131 |
| 334032 | **SP** | E | *SR* | GW | 64132 | 74332 | 65132 |
| 334033 | **SR** | E | *SR* | GW | 64133 | 74333 | 65133 |
| 334034 | **SP** | E | *SR* | GW | 64134 | 74334 | 65134 |
| 334035 | **SR** | E | *SR* | GW | 64135 | 74335 | 65135 |
| 334036 | **SR** | E | *SR* | GW | 64136 | 74336 | 65136 |
| 334037 | **SR** | E | *SR* | GW | 64137 | 74337 | 65137 |
| 334038 | **SR** | E | *SR* | GW | 64138 | 74338 | 65138 |
| 334039 | **SR** | E | *SR* | GW | 64139 | 74339 | 65139 |
| 334040 | **SR** | E | *SR* | GW | 64140 | 74340 | 65140 |

# CLASS 350      DESIRO UK      SIEMENS

Outer suburban and long distance units.

**Formation:** DMCO–TCO–PTSO–DMCO.
**Systems:** 25 kV AC overhead (350/1s built with 750 V DC).
**Construction:** Welded aluminium.
**Traction Motors:** 4 Siemens 1TB2016-0GB02 asynchronous of 250 kW.
**Wheel Arrangement:** Bo-Bo + 2-2 + 2-2 + Bo-Bo.
**Braking:** Disc & regenerative.    **Dimensions:** 20.34 x 2.79 m.
**Bogies:** SGP SF5000.    **Couplers:** Dellner 12.
**Gangways:** Throughout.    **Control System:** IGBT Inverter.
**Doors:** Sliding plug.
**Maximum Speed:** 110 mph (350/1, 350/3 and 350/4) and 100 mph (350/2).
**Heating & ventilation:** Air conditioning.
**Seating Layout:** Various, see sub-class headings.
**Multiple Working:** Within class.

**Class 350/1.** Original build units owned by Angel Trains. Formerly part of an aborted South West Trains 5-car Class 450/2 order. 2+2 seating.

**Seating Layout:** 1: 2+2 facing, 2: 2+2 facing/unidirectional.

**Advertising livery:** 350 110 Project 110 (centre cars are silver).

**DMSO(A).** Siemens Krefeld 2004–05. –/60. 48.7 t.
**TCO.** Siemens Krefeld/Prague 2004–05. 24/32 1T. 36.2 t.
**PTSO.** Siemens Krefeld/Prague 2004–05. –/50(9) 1TD 2W. 45.2 t.
**DMSO(B).** Siemens Krefeld/Prague 2004–05. –/60. 49.2 t.

| | | | | | | | | |
|---|---|---|---|---|---|---|---|---|
| 350101 | **LM** | A | *LM* | NN | 63761 | 66811 | 66861 | 63711 |
| 350102 | **LM** | A | *LM* | NN | 63762 | 66812 | 66862 | 63712 |
| 350103 | **LM** | A | *LM* | NN | 63765 | 66813 | 66863 | 63713 |
| 350104 | **LM** | A | *LM* | NN | 63764 | 66814 | 66864 | 63714 |
| 350105 | **LM** | A | *LM* | NN | 63763 | 66815 | 66868 | 63715 |

| 350 106 | **LM** | A | *LM* | NN | 63766 | 66816 | 66866 | 63716 |
| 350 107 | **LM** | A | *LM* | NN | 63767 | 66817 | 66867 | 63717 |
| 350 108 | **LM** | A | *LM* | NN | 63768 | 66818 | 66865 | 63718 |
| 350 109 | **LM** | A | *LM* | NN | 63769 | 66819 | 66869 | 63719 |
| 350 110 | **AL** | A | *LM* | NN | 63770 | 66820 | 66870 | 63720 |
| 350 111 | **LM** | A | *LM* | NN | 63771 | 66821 | 66871 | 63721 |
| 350 112 | **LM** | A | *LM* | NN | 63772 | 66822 | 66872 | 63722 |
| 350 113 | **LM** | A | *LM* | NN | 63773 | 66823 | 66873 | 63723 |
| 350 114 | **LM** | A | *LM* | NN | 63774 | 66824 | 66874 | 63724 |
| 350 115 | **LM** | A | *LM* | NN | 63775 | 66825 | 66875 | 63725 |
| 350 116 | **LM** | A | *LM* | NN | 63776 | 66826 | 66876 | 63726 |
| 350 117 | **LM** | A | *LM* | NN | 63777 | 66827 | 66877 | 63727 |
| 350 118 | **LM** | A | *LM* | NN | 63778 | 66828 | 66878 | 63728 |
| 350 119 | **LM** | A | *LM* | NN | 63779 | 66829 | 66879 | 63729 |
| 350 120 | **LM** | A | *LM* | NN | 63780 | 66830 | 66880 | 63730 |
| 350 121 | **LM** | A | *LM* | NN | 63781 | 66831 | 66881 | 63731 |
| 350 122 | **LM** | A | *LM* | NN | 63782 | 66832 | 66882 | 63732 |
| 350 123 | **LM** | A | *LM* | NN | 63783 | 66833 | 66883 | 63733 |
| 350 124 | **LM** | A | *LM* | NN | 63784 | 66834 | 66884 | 63734 |
| 350 125 | **LM** | A | *LM* | NN | 63785 | 66835 | 66885 | 63735 |
| 350 126 | **LM** | A | *LM* | NN | 63786 | 66836 | 66886 | 63736 |
| 350 127 | **LM** | A | *LM* | NN | 63787 | 66837 | 66887 | 63737 |
| 350 128 | **LM** | A | *LM* | NN | 63788 | 66838 | 66888 | 63738 |
| 350 129 | **LM** | A | *LM* | NN | 63789 | 66839 | 66889 | 63739 |
| 350 130 | **LM** | A | *LM* | NN | 63790 | 66840 | 66890 | 63740 |

**Class 350/2.** Owned by Porterbrook Leasing.

**Seating Layout:** 1: 2+2 facing, 2: 3+2 facing/unidirectional.

**DMSO(A).** Siemens Krefeld 2008–09. –/70. 43.7 t.
**TCO.** Siemens Prague 2008–09. 24/42 1T. 35.3 t.
**PTSO.** Siemens Prague 2008–09. –/61(9) 1TD 2W. 42.9 t.
**DMSO(B).** Siemens Krefeld 2008–09. –/70. 44.2 t.

| 350 231 | **LM** | P | *LM* | NN | 61431 | 65231 | 67531 | 61531 |
| 350 232 | **LM** | P | *LM* | NN | 61432 | 65232 | 67532 | 61532 |
| 350 233 | **LM** | P | *LM* | NN | 61433 | 65233 | 67533 | 61533 |
| 350 234 | **LM** | P | *LM* | NN | 61434 | 65234 | 67534 | 61534 |
| 350 235 | **LM** | P | *LM* | NN | 61435 | 65235 | 67535 | 61535 |
| 350 236 | **LM** | P | *LM* | NN | 61436 | 65236 | 67536 | 61536 |
| 350 237 | **LM** | P | *LM* | NN | 61437 | 65237 | 67537 | 61537 |
| 350 238 | **LM** | P | *LM* | NN | 61438 | 65238 | 67538 | 61538 |
| 350 239 | **LM** | P | *LM* | NN | 61439 | 65239 | 67539 | 61539 |
| 350 240 | **LM** | P | *LM* | NN | 61440 | 65240 | 67540 | 61540 |
| 350 241 | **LM** | P | *LM* | NN | 61441 | 65241 | 67541 | 61541 |
| 350 242 | **LM** | P | *LM* | NN | 61442 | 65242 | 67542 | 61542 |
| 350 243 | **LM** | P | *LM* | NN | 61443 | 65243 | 67543 | 61543 |
| 350 244 | **LM** | P | *LM* | NN | 61444 | 65244 | 67544 | 61544 |
| 350 245 | **LM** | P | *LM* | NN | 61445 | 65245 | 67545 | 61545 |
| 350 246 | **LM** | P | *LM* | NN | 61446 | 65246 | 67546 | 61546 |
| 350 247 | **LM** | P | *LM* | NN | 61447 | 65247 | 67547 | 61547 |
| 350 248 | **LM** | P | *LM* | NN | 61448 | 65248 | 67548 | 61548 |

| | | | | | | | | |
|---|---|---|---|---|---|---|---|---|
| 350 249 | **LM** | P | *LM* | NN | 61449 | 65249 | 67549 | 61549 |
| 350 250 | **LM** | P | *LM* | NN | 61450 | 65250 | 67550 | 61550 |
| 350 251 | **LM** | P | *LM* | NN | 61451 | 65251 | 67551 | 61551 |
| 350 252 | **LM** | P | *LM* | NN | 61452 | 65252 | 67552 | 61552 |
| 350 253 | **LM** | P | *LM* | NN | 61453 | 65253 | 67553 | 61553 |
| 350 254 | **LM** | P | *LM* | NN | 61454 | 65254 | 67554 | 61554 |
| 350 255 | **LM** | P | *LM* | NN | 61455 | 65255 | 67555 | 61555 |
| 350 256 | **LM** | P | *LM* | NN | 61456 | 65256 | 67556 | 61556 |
| 350 257 | **LM** | P | *LM* | NN | 61457 | 65257 | 67557 | 61557 |
| 350 258 | **LM** | P | *LM* | NN | 61458 | 65258 | 67558 | 61558 |
| 350 259 | **LM** | P | *LM* | NN | 61459 | 65259 | 67559 | 61559 |
| 350 260 | **LM** | P | *LM* | NN | 61460 | 65260 | 67560 | 61560 |
| 350 261 | **LM** | P | *LM* | NN | 61461 | 65261 | 67561 | 61561 |
| 350 262 | **LM** | P | *LM* | NN | 61462 | 65262 | 67562 | 61562 |
| 350 263 | **LM** | P | *LM* | NN | 61463 | 65263 | 67563 | 61563 |
| 350 264 | **LM** | P | *LM* | NN | 61464 | 65264 | 67564 | 61564 |
| 350 265 | **LM** | P | *LM* | NN | 61465 | 65265 | 67565 | 61565 |
| 350 266 | **LM** | P | *LM* | NN | 61466 | 65266 | 67566 | 61566 |
| 350 267 | **LM** | P | *LM* | NN | 61467 | 65267 | 67567 | 61567 |

**Name (carried on one side of PTSO):** 350 232   Chad Varah

**Class 350/3.** Owned by Angel Trains. On order for London Midland and due for delivery summer 2014. Full details awaited.

**DMSO(A).** Siemens Krefeld 2014.             .       t.
**TCO.** Siemens Krefeld 2014.             .       t.
**PTSO.** Siemens Krefeld 2014.             .       t.
**DMSO(B).** Siemens Krefeld 2014.             .       t.

| | | | | | |
|---|---|---|---|---|---|
| 350 301 | A | 60141 | 60511 | 60651 | 60151 |
| 350 302 | A | 60142 | 60512 | 60652 | 60152 |
| 350 303 | A | 60143 | 60513 | 60653 | 60153 |
| 350 304 | A | 60144 | 60514 | 60654 | 60154 |
| 350 305 | A | 60145 | 60515 | 60655 | 60155 |
| 350 306 | A | 60146 | 60516 | 60656 | 60156 |
| 350 307 | A | 60147 | 60517 | 60657 | 60157 |
| 350 308 | A | 60148 | 60518 | 60658 | 60158 |
| 350 309 | A | 60149 | 60519 | 60659 | 60159 |
| 350 310 | A | 60150 | 60520 | 60660 | 60160 |

**Class 350/4.** Owned by Angel Trains. Currently being delivered for use on TransPennine Express Manchester Airport–Edinburgh/Glasgow services.

**Seating Layout:** 1: 2+1 facing, 2: 2+2 facing/unidirectional.

**Non-standard livery:** Light grey with dark grey doors.

**DMSO(A).** Siemens Krefeld 2013–14. –/56. 44.2 t.
**TCO.** Siemens Krefeld 2013–14. 19/24 1T. 36.2 t.
**PTSO.** Siemens Krefeld 2013–14. –/42 1TD 1T. 44.6 t.
**DMSO(B).** Siemens Krefeld 2013–14. –/56. 45.0 t.

| | | | | | | | | |
|---|---|---|---|---|---|---|---|---|
| 350 401 | **0** | A | *TP* | AK | 60691 | 60901 | 60941 | 60671 |
| 350 402 | **0** | A | *TP* | AK | 60692 | 60902 | 60942 | 60672 |

| | | | | | | | | |
|---|---|---|---|---|---|---|---|---|
| 350 403 | **0** | A | *TP* | AK | 60693 | 60903 | 60943 | 60673 |
| 350 404 | **0** | A | | | 60694 | 60904 | 60944 | 60674 |
| 350 405 | **0** | A | | | 60695 | 60905 | 60945 | 60675 |
| 350 406 | | A | | | 60696 | 60906 | 60946 | 60676 |
| 350 407 | | A | | | 60697 | 60907 | 60947 | 60677 |
| 350 408 | | A | | | 60698 | 60908 | 60948 | 60678 |
| 350 409 | | A | | | 60699 | 60909 | 60949 | 60679 |
| 350 410 | | A | | | 60700 | 60910 | 60950 | 60680 |

# CLASS 357 ELECTROSTAR
## ADTRANZ/BOMBARDIER DERBY

Provision for 750 V DC supply if required.

**Formation:** DMSO–MSO–PTSO–DMSO.
**Construction:** Welded aluminium alloy underframe, sides and roof with steel ends. All sections bolted together.
**Traction Motors:** Two Adtranz asynchronous of 250 kW.
**Wheel Arrangement:** 2-Bo + 2-Bo + 2-2 + Bo-2.
**Braking:** Disc & regenerative.    **Dimensions:** 20.40/19.99 x 2.80 m.
**Bogies:** Adtranz P3-25/T3-25.    **Couplers:** Tightlock.
**Gangways:** Within unit.    **Control System:** IGBT Inverter.
**Doors:** Sliding plug.    **Maximum Speed:** 100 mph.
**Heating & ventilation:** Air conditioning.
**Seating Layout:** 3+2 facing/unidirectional.
**Multiple Working:** Within class.

Class 357/0. Owned by Porterbrook Leasing.

**DMSO(A).** Adtranz Derby 1999–2001. –/71. 40.7 t.
**MSO.** Adtranz Derby 1999–2001. –/78. 36.7 t.
**PTSO.** Adtranz Derby 1999–2001. –/58(4) 1TD 2W. 39.5 t.
**DMSO(B).** Adtranz Derby 1999–2001. –/71. 40.7 t.

| | | | | | | | | |
|---|---|---|---|---|---|---|---|---|
| 357 001 | **NC** | P | *C2* | EM | 67651 | 74151 | 74051 | 67751 |
| 357 002 | **NC** | P | *C2* | EM | 67652 | 74152 | 74052 | 67752 |
| 357 003 | **NC** | P | *C2* | EM | 67653 | 74153 | 74053 | 67753 |
| 357 004 | **NC** | P | *C2* | EM | 67654 | 74154 | 74054 | 67754 |
| 357 005 | **NC** | P | *C2* | EM | 67655 | 74155 | 74055 | 67755 |
| 357 006 | **NC** | P | *C2* | EM | 67656 | 74156 | 74056 | 67756 |
| 357 007 | **NC** | P | *C2* | EM | 67657 | 74157 | 74057 | 67757 |
| 357 008 | **NC** | P | *C2* | EM | 67658 | 74158 | 74058 | 67758 |
| 357 009 | **NC** | P | *C2* | EM | 67659 | 74159 | 74059 | 67759 |
| 357 010 | **NC** | P | *C2* | EM | 67660 | 74160 | 74060 | 67760 |
| 357 011 | **NC** | P | *C2* | EM | 67661 | 74161 | 74061 | 67761 |
| 357 012 | **NC** | P | *C2* | EM | 67662 | 74162 | 74062 | 67762 |
| 357 013 | **NC** | P | *C2* | EM | 67663 | 74163 | 74063 | 67763 |
| 357 014 | **NC** | P | *C2* | EM | 67664 | 74164 | 74064 | 67764 |
| 357 015 | **NC** | P | *C2* | EM | 67665 | 74165 | 74065 | 67765 |
| 357 016 | **NC** | P | *C2* | EM | 67666 | 74166 | 74066 | 67766 |
| 357 017 | **NC** | P | *C2* | EM | 67667 | 74167 | 74067 | 67767 |
| 357 018 | **NC** | P | *C2* | EM | 67668 | 74168 | 74068 | 67768 |

| | | | | | | | | |
|---|---|---|---|---|---|---|---|---|
| 357019 | **NC** | P | *C2* | EM | 67669 | 74169 | 74069 | 67769 |
| 357020 | **NC** | P | *C2* | EM | 67670 | 74170 | 74070 | 67770 |
| 357021 | **NC** | P | *C2* | EM | 67671 | 74171 | 74071 | 67771 |
| 357022 | **NC** | P | *C2* | EM | 67672 | 74172 | 74072 | 67772 |
| 357023 | **NC** | P | *C2* | EM | 67673 | 74173 | 74073 | 67773 |
| 357024 | **NC** | P | *C2* | EM | 67674 | 74174 | 74074 | 67774 |
| 357025 | **NC** | P | *C2* | EM | 67675 | 74175 | 74075 | 67775 |
| 357026 | **NC** | P | *C2* | EM | 67676 | 74176 | 74076 | 67776 |
| 357027 | **NC** | P | *C2* | EM | 67677 | 74177 | 74077 | 67777 |
| 357028 | **NC** | P | *C2* | EM | 67678 | 74178 | 74078 | 67778 |
| 357029 | **NC** | P | *C2* | EM | 67679 | 74179 | 74079 | 67779 |
| 357030 | **NC** | P | *C2* | EM | 67680 | 74180 | 74080 | 67780 |
| 357031 | **NC** | P | *C2* | EM | 67681 | 74181 | 74081 | 67781 |
| 357032 | **NC** | P | *C2* | EM | 67682 | 74182 | 74082 | 67782 |
| 357033 | **NC** | P | *C2* | EM | 67683 | 74183 | 74083 | 67783 |
| 357034 | **NC** | P | *C2* | EM | 67684 | 74184 | 74084 | 67784 |
| 357035 | **NC** | P | *C2* | EM | 67685 | 74185 | 74085 | 67785 |
| 357036 | **NC** | P | *C2* | EM | 67686 | 74186 | 74086 | 67786 |
| 357037 | **NC** | P | *C2* | EM | 67687 | 74187 | 74087 | 67787 |
| 357038 | **NC** | P | *C2* | EM | 67688 | 74188 | 74088 | 67788 |
| 357039 | **NC** | P | *C2* | EM | 67689 | 74189 | 74089 | 67789 |
| 357040 | **NC** | P | *C2* | EM | 67690 | 74190 | 74090 | 67790 |
| 357041 | **NC** | P | *C2* | EM | 67691 | 74191 | 74091 | 67791 |
| 357042 | **NC** | P | *C2* | EM | 67692 | 74192 | 74092 | 67792 |
| 357043 | **NC** | P | *C2* | EM | 67693 | 74193 | 74093 | 67793 |
| 357044 | **NC** | P | *C2* | EM | 67694 | 74194 | 74094 | 67794 |
| 357045 | **NC** | P | *C2* | EM | 67695 | 74195 | 74095 | 67795 |
| 357046 | **NC** | P | *C2* | EM | 67696 | 74196 | 74096 | 67796 |

**Names (carried on DMSO(A) and DMSO(B) (one plate on each)):**

357001 BARRY FLAXMAN
357002 ARTHUR LEWIS STRIDE 1841–1922
357003 SOUTHEND city.on.sea
357004 TONY AMOS
357006 DIAMOND JUBILEE 1952–2012
357011 JOHN LOWING
357028 London, Tilbury & Southend Railway 1854–2004
357029 THOMAS WHITELEGG 1840–1922
357030 ROBERT HARBEN WHITELEGG 1871–1957

**Class 357/2.** Owned by Angel Trains.

**DMSO(A).** Bombardier Derby 2001–02. –/71. 40.7 t.
**MSO.** Bombardier Derby 2001–02. –/78. 36.7 t.
**PTSO.** Bombardier Derby 2001–02. –/58(4) 1TD 2W. 39.5 t.
**DMSO(B).** Bombardier Derby 2001–02. –/71. 40.7 t.

| | | | | | | | | |
|---|---|---|---|---|---|---|---|---|
| 357201 | **NC** | A | *C2* | EM | 68601 | 74701 | 74601 | 68701 |
| 357202 | **NC** | A | *C2* | EM | 68602 | 74702 | 74602 | 68702 |
| 357203 | **NC** | A | *C2* | EM | 68603 | 74703 | 74603 | 68703 |
| 357204 | **NC** | A | *C2* | EM | 68604 | 74704 | 74604 | 68704 |
| 357205 | **NC** | A | *C2* | EM | 68605 | 74705 | 74605 | 68705 |

| 357 206 | **NC** | A | *C2* | EM | 68606 | 74706 | 74606 | 68706 |
| 357 207 | **NC** | A | *C2* | EM | 68607 | 74707 | 74607 | 68707 |
| 357 208 | **NC** | A | *C2* | EM | 68608 | 74708 | 74608 | 68708 |
| 357 209 | **NC** | A | *C2* | EM | 68609 | 74709 | 74609 | 68709 |
| 357 210 | **NC** | A | *C2* | EM | 68610 | 74710 | 74610 | 68710 |
| 357 211 | **NC** | A | *C2* | EM | 68611 | 74711 | 74611 | 68711 |
| 357 212 | **NC** | A | *C2* | EM | 68612 | 74712 | 74612 | 68712 |
| 357 213 | **NC** | A | *C2* | EM | 68613 | 74713 | 74613 | 68713 |
| 357 214 | **NC** | A | *C2* | EM | 68614 | 74714 | 74614 | 68714 |
| 357 215 | **NC** | A | *C2* | EM | 68615 | 74715 | 74615 | 68715 |
| 357 216 | **NC** | A | *C2* | EM | 68616 | 74716 | 74616 | 68716 |
| 357 217 | **NC** | A | *C2* | EM | 68617 | 74717 | 74617 | 68717 |
| 357 218 | **NC** | A | *C2* | EM | 68618 | 74718 | 74618 | 68718 |
| 357 219 | **NC** | A | *C2* | EM | 68619 | 74719 | 74619 | 68719 |
| 357 220 | **NC** | A | *C2* | EM | 68620 | 74720 | 74620 | 68720 |
| 357 221 | **NC** | A | *C2* | EM | 68621 | 74721 | 74621 | 68721 |
| 357 222 | **NC** | A | *C2* | EM | 68622 | 74722 | 74622 | 68722 |
| 357 223 | **NC** | A | *C2* | EM | 68623 | 74723 | 74623 | 68723 |
| 357 224 | **NC** | A | *C2* | EM | 68624 | 74724 | 74624 | 68724 |
| 357 225 | **NC** | A | *C2* | EM | 68625 | 74725 | 74625 | 68725 |
| 357 226 | **NC** | A | *C2* | EM | 68626 | 74726 | 74626 | 68726 |
| 357 227 | **NC** | A | *C2* | EM | 68627 | 74727 | 74627 | 68727 |
| 357 228 | **NC** | A | *C2* | EM | 68628 | 74728 | 74628 | 68728 |

**Names (carried on DMSO(A) and DMSO(B) (one plate on each)):**

| | | | | |
|---|---|---|---|---|
| 357 201 | KEN BIRD | | 357 207 | JOHN PAGE |
| 357 202 | KENNY MITCHELL | | 357 208 | DAVE DAVIS |
| 357 203 | HENRY PUMFRETT | | 357 209 | JAMES SNELLING |
| 357 204 | DEREK FOWERS | | 357 213 | UPMINSTER I.E.C.C. |
| 357 205 | JOHN D'SILVA | | 357 217 | ALLAN BURNELL |
| 357 206 | MARTIN AUNGIER | | 357 227 | SOUTHEND UNITED |

## CLASS 360/0          DESIRO UK          SIEMENS

Outer suburban/express units.

**Formation:** DMCO–PTSO–TSO–DMCO.
**Construction:** Welded aluminium.
**Traction Motors:** Four Siemens 1TB2016-0GB02 asynchronous of 250 kW.
**Wheel Arrangement:** Bo-Bo + 2-2 + 2-2 + Bo-Bo.
**Braking:** Disc & regenerative.          **Dimensions:** 20.34 x 2.80 m.
**Bogies:** SGP SF5000.                    **Couplers:** Dellner 12.
**Gangways:** Within unit.                 **Control System:** IGBT Inverter.
**Doors:** Sliding plug.                   **Maximum Speed:** 100 mph.
**Heating & ventilation:** Air conditioning.
**Seating Layout:** 1: 2+2 facing, 2: 3+2 facing/unidirectional.
**Multiple Working:** Within class.

**DMCO(A).** Siemens Krefeld 2002–03. 8/59. 45.0 t.
**PTSO.** Siemens Vienna 2002–03. –/60(9) 1TD 2W. 43.0 t.
**TSO.** Siemens Vienna 2002–03. –/78. 35.0 t.
**DMCO(B).** Siemens Krefeld 2002–03. 8/59. 45.0 t.

| 360 101 | **FB** | A | *GA* | IL | 65551 | 72551 | 74551 | 68551 |
| 360 102 | **FB** | A | *GA* | IL | 65552 | 72552 | 74552 | 68552 |
| 360 103 | **FB** | A | *GA* | IL | 65553 | 72553 | 74553 | 68553 |
| 360 104 | **FB** | A | *GA* | IL | 65554 | 72554 | 74554 | 68554 |
| 360 105 | **FB** | A | *GA* | IL | 65555 | 72555 | 74555 | 68555 |
| 360 106 | **FB** | A | *GA* | IL | 65556 | 72556 | 74556 | 68556 |
| 360 107 | **FB** | A | *GA* | IL | 65557 | 72557 | 74557 | 68557 |
| 360 108 | **FB** | A | *GA* | IL | 65558 | 72558 | 74558 | 68558 |
| 360 109 | **FB** | A | *GA* | IL | 65559 | 72559 | 74559 | 68559 |
| 360 110 | **FB** | A | *GA* | IL | 65560 | 72560 | 74560 | 68560 |
| 360 111 | **FB** | A | *GA* | IL | 65561 | 72561 | 74561 | 68561 |
| 360 112 | **FB** | A | *GA* | IL | 65562 | 72562 | 74562 | 68562 |
| 360 113 | **FB** | A | *GA* | IL | 65563 | 72563 | 74563 | 68563 |
| 360 114 | **FB** | A | *GA* | IL | 65564 | 72564 | 74564 | 68564 |
| 360 115 | **FB** | A | *GA* | IL | 65565 | 72565 | 74565 | 68565 |
| 360 116 | **FB** | A | *GA* | IL | 65566 | 72566 | 74566 | 68566 |
| 360 117 | **FB** | A | *GA* | IL | 65567 | 72567 | 74567 | 68567 |
| 360 118 | **FB** | A | *GA* | IL | 65568 | 72568 | 74568 | 68568 |
| 360 119 | **FB** | A | *GA* | IL | 65569 | 72569 | 74569 | 68569 |
| 360 120 | **FB** | A | *GA* | IL | 65570 | 72570 | 74570 | 68570 |
| 360 121 | **FB** | A | *GA* | IL | 65571 | 72571 | 74571 | 68571 |

## CLASS 360/2     DESIRO UK                                    SIEMENS

4-car Class 350 testbed units rebuilt for use by Heathrow Express on Paddington–Heathrow Airport stopping services ("Heathrow Connect").

Original 4-car sets 360 201–204 were made up to 5-cars during 2007 using additional TSOs. A fifth unit (360 205) was delivered in late 2005 as a 5-car set. This set is normally used on Terminals 1&3–Terminal 4 shuttle services.

**Formation:** DMSO–PTSO–TSO–TSO–DMSO.
**Construction:** Welded aluminium.
**Traction Motors:** Four Siemens 1TB2016-0GB02 asynchronous of 250 kW.
**Wheel Arrangement:** Bo-Bo + 2-2 + 2-2 + 2-2 + Bo-Bo.

| | |
|---|---|
| **Braking:** Disc & regenerative. | **Dimensions:** 20.34 x 2.80 m. |
| **Bogies:** SGP SF5000. | **Couplers:** Dellner 12. |
| **Gangways:** Within unit. | **Control System:** IGBT Inverter. |
| **Doors:** Sliding plug. | **Maximum Speed:** 100 mph. |

**Heating & ventilation:** Air conditioning.
**Seating Layout:** 3+2 (* 2+2) facing/unidirectional.
**Multiple Working:** Within class.

**DMSO(A).** Siemens Krefeld 2002–06. –/63 (* –/54). 44.8 t.
**PTSO.** Siemens Krefeld 2002–06. –/57(9) 1TD 2W (* –/48(9) 2W). 44.2 t.
**TSO.** Siemens Krefeld 2005–06. –/74 (* –/62). 35.3 t.
**TSO.** Siemens Krefeld 2002–06. –/74 (* –/62). 34.1 t.
**DMSO(B).** Siemens Krefeld 2002–06. –/63 (* –/54). 44.4 t.

| 360 201 | | **HC** | HE | *HC* | OH | 78431 | 63421 | 72431 | 72421 | 78441 |
| 360 202 | | **HC** | HE | *HC* | OH | 78432 | 63422 | 72432 | 72422 | 78442 |
| 360 203 | | **HC** | HE | *HC* | OH | 78433 | 63423 | 72433 | 72423 | 78443 |
| 360 204 | | **HC** | HE | *HC* | OH | 78434 | 63424 | 72434 | 72424 | 78444 |
| 360 205 | * | **HE** | HE | *HE* | OH | 78435 | 63425 | 72435 | 72425 | 78445 |

# CLASS 365     NETWORKER EXPRESS     ABB YORK

Outer suburban units.

**Formations:** DMCO–TSO–PTSO–DMCO.
**Systems:** 25 kV AC overhead but with 750 V DC third rail capability (units marked * were formerly used on DC lines in the South-East).
**Construction:** Welded aluminium alloy.
**Traction Motors:** Four GEC-Alsthom G354CX asynchronous of 157 kW.
**Wheel Arrangement:** Bo-Bo + 2-2 + 2-2 + Bo-Bo.
**Braking:** Disc & rheostatic.
**Dimensions:** 20.89/20.06 x 2.81 m.
**Bogies:** ABB P3-16/T3-16.     **Couplers:** Tightlock.
**Gangways:** Within unit.     **Control System:** GTO Inverter.
**Doors:** Sliding plug.     **Maximum Speed:** 100 mph.
**Seating Layout:** 1: 2+2 facing, 2: 2+2 facing.
**Multiple Working:** Within class only.

**Advertising liveries:**

365510 Cambridge & Ely; Cathedral cities (blue & white with various images).
365519 Peterborough; environment capital (blue & white with various images).
365531 Nelson's County; Norfolk (blue & white with various images).
365540 Garden cities of Hertfordshire (blue & white with various images).

**DMCO(A).** Lot No. 31133 1994–95. 12/56. 41.7 t.
**TSO.** Lot No. 31134 1994–95. –/65 1TD (* –/64 1TD) 32.9 t.
**PTSO.** Lot No. 31135 1994–95. –/68 1T. 34.6 t.
**DMCO(B).** Lot No. 31136 1994–95. 12/56. 41.7 t.

| | | | | | | | | |
|---|---|---|---|---|---|---|---|---|
| 365501 | * | FU | E | FC | HE | 65894 | 72241 | 72240 | 65935 |
| 365502 | * | FU | E | FC | HE | 65895 | 72243 | 72242 | 65936 |
| 365503 | * | FU | E | FC | HE | 65896 | 72245 | 72244 | 65937 |
| 365504 | * | FU | E | FC | HE | 65897 | 72247 | 72246 | 65938 |
| 365505 | * | FU | E | FC | HE | 65898 | 72249 | 72248 | 65939 |
| 365506 | * | FU | E | FC | HE | 65899 | 72251 | 72250 | 65940 |
| 365507 | * | FU | E | FC | HE | 65900 | 72253 | 72252 | 65941 |
| 365508 | * | FU | E | FC | HE | 65901 | 72255 | 72254 | 65942 |
| 365509 | * | FU | E | FC | HE | 65902 | 72257 | 72256 | 65943 |
| 365510 | * | AL | E | FC | HE | 65903 | 72259 | 72258 | 65944 |
| 365511 | * | FU | E | FC | HE | 65904 | 72261 | 72260 | 65945 |
| 365512 | * | FU | E | FC | HE | 65905 | 72263 | 72262 | 65946 |
| 365513 | * | FU | E | FC | HE | 65906 | 72265 | 72264 | 65947 |
| 365514 | * | FU | E | FC | HE | 65907 | 72267 | 72266 | 65948 |
| 365515 | * | FU | E | FC | HE | 65908 | 72269 | 72268 | 65949 |
| 365516 | * | FU | E | FC | HE | 65909 | 72271 | 72270 | 65950 |
| 365517 | | TL | E | FC | HE | 65910 | 72273 | 72272 | 65951 |
| 365518 | | FU | E | FC | HE | 65911 | 72275 | 72274 | 65952 |
| 365519 | | AL | E | FC | HE | 65912 | 72277 | 72276 | 65953 |
| 365520 | | FU | E | FC | HE | 65913 | 72279 | 72278 | 65954 |
| 365521 | | FU | E | FC | HE | 65914 | 72281 | 72280 | 65955 |
| 365522 | | FU | E | FC | HE | 65915 | 72283 | 72282 | 65956 |
| 365523 | | FU | E | FC | HE | 65916 | 72285 | 72284 | 65957 |

| | | | | | | | | |
|---|---|---|---|---|---|---|---|---|
| 365 524 | **FU** | E | *FC* | HE | 65917 | 72287 | 72286 | 65958 |
| 365 525 | **FU** | E | *FC* | HE | 65918 | 72289 | 72288 | 65959 |
| 365 527 | **FU** | E | *FC* | HE | 65920 | 72293 | 72292 | 65961 |
| 365 528 | **FU** | E | *FC* | HE | 65921 | 72295 | 72294 | 65962 |
| 365 529 | **FU** | E | *FC* | HE | 65922 | 72297 | 72296 | 65963 |
| 365 530 | **FU** | E | *FC* | HE | 65923 | 72299 | 72298 | 65964 |
| 365 531 | **AL** | E | *FC* | HE | 65924 | 72301 | 72300 | 65965 |
| 365 532 | **FU** | E | *FC* | HE | 65925 | 72303 | 72302 | 65966 |
| 365 533 | **FU** | E | *FC* | HE | 65926 | 72305 | 72304 | 65967 |
| 365 534 | **FU** | E | *FC* | HE | 65927 | 72307 | 72306 | 65968 |
| 365 535 | **FU** | E | *FC* | HE | 65928 | 72309 | 72308 | 65969 |
| 365 536 | **FU** | E | *FC* | HE | 65929 | 72311 | 72310 | 65970 |
| 365 537 | **FU** | E | *FC* | HE | 65930 | 72313 | 72312 | 65971 |
| 365 538 | **FU** | E | *FC* | HE | 65931 | 72315 | 72314 | 65972 |
| 365 539 | **FU** | E | *FC* | HE | 65932 | 72317 | 72316 | 65973 |
| 365 540 | **AL** | E | *FC* | HE | 65933 | 72319 | 72318 | 65974 |
| 365 541 | **FU** | E | *FC* | HE | 65934 | 72321 | 72320 | 65975 |

**Names (carried on each DMCO):**

| | |
|---|---|
| 365 506 | The Royston Express |
| 365 513 | Hornsey Depot |
| 365 514 | Captain George Vancouver |
| 365 518 | The Fenman |
| 365 527 | Robert Stripe Passengers' Champion |
| 365 530 | The Intalink Partnership promoting integrated transport in Hertfordshire since 1999 |
| 365 536 | Rufus Barnes Chief Executive of London TravelWatch for 25 years |
| 365 537 | Daniel Edwards (1974–2010) Cambridge Driver |

# CLASS 375 ELECTROSTAR
## ADTRANZ/BOMBARDIER DERBY

Express and outer suburban units.

**Formations:** Various.
**Systems:** 25 kV AC overhead/750 V DC third rail (some third rail only with provision for retro-fitting of AC equipment).
**Construction:** Welded aluminium alloy underframe, sides and roof with steel ends. All sections bolted together.
**Traction Motors:** Two Adtranz asynchronous of 250 kW.
**Wheel Arrangement:** 2-Bo (+ 2-Bo) + 2-2 + Bo-2.
**Braking:** Disc & regenerative.    **Dimensions:** 20.40/19.99 x 2.80 m.
**Bogies:** Adtranz P3-25/T3-25.    **Couplers:** Dellner 12.
**Gangways:** Throughout.    **Control System:** IGBT Inverter.
**Doors:** Sliding plug.    **Maximum Speed:** 100 mph.
**Heating & ventilation:** Air conditioning.
**Seating Layout:** 1: 2+2 facing/unidirectional (seats behind drivers cab in each DMCO). 2: 2+2 facing/unidirectional (except 375/9 – 3+2 facing/unidirectional).
**Multiple Working:** Within class and with Classes 376, 377, 378 and 379.

**Class 375/3.** Express units. 750 V DC only. DMCO–TSO–DMCO.

**DMCO(A).** Bombardier Derby 2001–02. 12/48. 43.8 t.
**TSO.** Bombardier Derby 2001–02. –/56 1TD 2W. 35.5 t.
**DMCO(B).** Bombardier Derby 2001–02. 12/48. 43.8 t.

| | | | | | | | |
|---|---|---|---|---|---|---|---|
| 375301 | **CN** | E | *SE* | RM | 67921 | 74351 | 67931 |
| 375302 | **CN** | E | *SE* | RM | 67922 | 74352 | 67932 |
| 375303 | **CN** | E | *SE* | RM | 67923 | 74353 | 67933 |
| 375304 | **CN** | E | *SE* | RM | 67924 | 74354 | 67934 |
| 375305 | **CN** | E | *SE* | RM | 67925 | 74355 | 67935 |
| 375306 | **CN** | E | *SE* | RM | 67926 | 74356 | 67936 |
| 375307 | **CN** | E | *SE* | RM | 67927 | 74357 | 67937 |
| 375308 | **SE** | E | *SE* | RM | 67928 | 74358 | 67938 |
| 375309 | **CN** | E | *SE* | RM | 67929 | 74359 | 67939 |
| 375310 | **CN** | E | *SE* | RM | 67930 | 74360 | 67940 |

**Name (carried on TSO):** 375304 Medway Valley Line 1856–2006

**Class 375/6.** Express units. 25 kV AC/750 V DC. DMCO–MSO–PTSO–DMCO.

**DMCO(A).** Adtranz Derby 1999–2001. 12/48. 46.2 t.
**MSO.** Adtranz Derby 1999–2001. –/66 1T. 40.5 t.
**PTSO.** Adtranz Derby 1999–2001. –/56 1TD 2W. 40.7 t.
**DMCO(B).** Adtranz Derby 1999–2001. 12/48. 46.2 t.

| | | | | | | | | |
|---|---|---|---|---|---|---|---|---|
| 375601 | **CN** | E | *SE* | RM | 67801 | 74251 | 74201 | 67851 |
| 375602 | **CN** | E | *SE* | RM | 67802 | 74252 | 74202 | 67852 |
| 375603 | **CN** | E | *SE* | RM | 67803 | 74253 | 74203 | 67853 |
| 375604 | **CN** | E | *SE* | RM | 67804 | 74254 | 74204 | 67854 |
| 375605 | **CN** | E | *SE* | RM | 67805 | 74255 | 74205 | 67855 |
| 375606 | **CN** | E | *SE* | RM | 67806 | 74256 | 74206 | 67856 |
| 375607 | **CN** | E | *SE* | RM | 67807 | 74257 | 74207 | 67857 |
| 375608 | **CN** | E | *SE* | RM | 67808 | 74258 | 74208 | 67858 |
| 375609 | **SE** | E | *SE* | RM | 67809 | 74259 | 74209 | 67859 |
| 375610 | **CN** | E | *SE* | RM | 67810 | 74260 | 74210 | 67860 |
| 375611 | **CN** | E | *SE* | RM | 67811 | 74261 | 74211 | 67861 |
| 375612 | **CN** | E | *SE* | RM | 67812 | 74262 | 74212 | 67862 |
| 375613 | **CN** | E | *SE* | RM | 67813 | 74263 | 74213 | 67863 |
| 375614 | **CN** | E | *SE* | RM | 67814 | 74264 | 74214 | 67864 |
| 375615 | **CN** | E | *SE* | RM | 67815 | 74265 | 74215 | 67865 |
| 375616 | **CN** | E | *SE* | RM | 67816 | 74266 | 74216 | 67866 |
| 375617 | **CN** | E | *SE* | RM | 67817 | 74267 | 74217 | 67867 |
| 375618 | **CN** | E | *SE* | RM | 67818 | 74268 | 74218 | 67868 |
| 375619 | **CN** | E | *SE* | RM | 67819 | 74269 | 74219 | 67869 |
| 375620 | **CN** | E | *SE* | RM | 67820 | 74270 | 74220 | 67870 |
| 375621 | **CN** | E | *SE* | RM | 67821 | 74271 | 74221 | 67871 |
| 375622 | **CN** | E | *SE* | RM | 67822 | 74272 | 74222 | 67872 |
| 375623 | **CN** | E | *SE* | RM | 67823 | 74273 | 74223 | 67873 |
| 375624 | **SE** | E | *SE* | RM | 67824 | 74274 | 74224 | 67874 |
| 375625 | **CN** | E | *SE* | RM | 67825 | 74275 | 74225 | 67875 |
| 375626 | **CN** | E | *SE* | RM | 67826 | 74276 | 74226 | 67876 |
| 375627 | **CN** | E | *SE* | RM | 67827 | 74277 | 74227 | 67877 |
| 375628 | **CN** | E | *SE* | RM | 67828 | 74278 | 74228 | 67878 |

| | | | | | | | | |
|---|---|---|---|---|---|---|---|---|
| 375 629 | **CN** | E | *SE* | RM | 67829 | 74279 | 74229 | 67879 |
| 375 630 | **CN** | E | *SE* | RM | 67830 | 74280 | 74230 | 67880 |

**Names (carried on one side of each MSO or PTSO):**

| | | | |
|---|---|---|---|
| 375 608 | Bromley Travelwise | 375 619 | Driver John Neve |
| 375 610 | Royal Tunbridge Wells | 375 623 | Hospice in the Weald |
| 375 611 | Dr. William Harvey | | |

**Class 375/7.** Express units. 750 V DC only. DMCO–MSO–TSO–DMCO.

**DMCO(A).** Bombardier Derby 2001–02. 12/48. 43.8 t.
**MSO.** Bombardier Derby 2001–02. –/66 1T. 36.4 t.
**TSO.** Bombardier Derby 2001–02. –/56 1TD 2W. 34.1 t.
**DMCO(B).** Bombardier Derby 2001–02. 12/48. 43.8 t.

| | | | | | | | | |
|---|---|---|---|---|---|---|---|---|
| 375 701 | **CN** | E | *SE* | RM | 67831 | 74281 | 74231 | 67881 |
| 375 702 | **CN** | E | *SE* | RM | 67832 | 74282 | 74232 | 67882 |
| 375 703 | **CN** | E | *SE* | RM | 67833 | 74283 | 74233 | 67883 |
| 375 704 | **CN** | E | *SE* | RM | 67834 | 74284 | 74234 | 67884 |
| 375 705 | **SE** | E | *SE* | RM | 67835 | 74285 | 74235 | 67885 |
| 375 706 | **CN** | E | *SE* | RM | 67836 | 74286 | 74236 | 67886 |
| 375 707 | **CN** | E | *SE* | RM | 67837 | 74287 | 74237 | 67887 |
| 375 708 | **CN** | E | *SE* | RM | 67838 | 74288 | 74238 | 67888 |
| 375 709 | **CN** | E | *SE* | RM | 67839 | 74289 | 74239 | 67889 |
| 375 710 | **CN** | E | *SE* | RM | 67840 | 74290 | 74240 | 67890 |
| 375 711 | **CN** | E | *SE* | RM | 67841 | 74291 | 74241 | 67891 |
| 375 712 | **CN** | E | *SE* | RM | 67842 | 74292 | 74242 | 67892 |
| 375 713 | **CN** | E | *SE* | RM | 67843 | 74293 | 74243 | 67893 |
| 375 714 | **CN** | E | *SE* | RM | 67844 | 74294 | 74244 | 67894 |
| 375 715 | **CN** | E | *SE* | RM | 67845 | 74295 | 74245 | 67895 |

**Name (carried on one side of each MSO or TSO):**

375 701   Kent Air Ambulance Explorer

**Class 375/8.** Express units. 750 V DC only. DMCO–MSO–TSO–DMCO.

375 801–820 are fitted with de-icing equipment. TSO weighs 36.5 t.

**DMCO(A).** Bombardier Derby 2004. 12/48. 43.3 t.
**MSO.** Bombardier Derby 2004. –/66 1T. 39.8 t.
**TSO.** Bombardier Derby 2004. –/52 1TD 2W. 35.9 t.
**DMCO(B).** Bombardier Derby 2004. 12/52. 43.3 t.

| | | | | | | | | |
|---|---|---|---|---|---|---|---|---|
| 375 801 | **CN** | E | *SE* | RM | 73301 | 79001 | 78201 | 73701 |
| 375 802 | **CN** | E | *SE* | RM | 73302 | 79002 | 78202 | 73702 |
| 375 803 | **CN** | E | *SE* | RM | 73303 | 79003 | 78203 | 73703 |
| 375 804 | **CN** | E | *SE* | RM | 73304 | 79004 | 78204 | 73704 |
| 375 805 | **CN** | E | *SE* | RM | 73305 | 79005 | 78205 | 73705 |
| 375 806 | **CN** | E | *SE* | RM | 73306 | 79006 | 78206 | 73706 |
| 375 807 | **CN** | E | *SE* | RM | 73307 | 79007 | 78207 | 73707 |
| 375 808 | **CN** | E | *SE* | RM | 73308 | 79008 | 78208 | 73708 |
| 375 809 | **CN** | E | *SE* | RM | 73309 | 79009 | 78209 | 73709 |
| 375 810 | **CN** | E | *SE* | RM | 73310 | 79010 | 78210 | 73710 |
| 375 811 | **CN** | E | *SE* | RM | 73311 | 79011 | 78211 | 73711 |

| 375812 | **CN** | E | *SE* | RM | 73312 | 79012 | 78212 | 73712 |
| 375813 | **CN** | E | *SE* | RM | 73313 | 79013 | 78213 | 73713 |
| 375814 | **CN** | E | *SE* | RM | 73314 | 79014 | 78214 | 73714 |
| 375815 | **CN** | E | *SE* | RM | 73315 | 79015 | 78215 | 73715 |
| 375816 | **CN** | E | *SE* | RM | 73316 | 79016 | 78216 | 73716 |
| 375817 | **CN** | E | *SE* | RM | 73317 | 79017 | 78217 | 73717 |
| 375818 | **CN** | E | *SE* | RM | 73318 | 79018 | 78218 | 73718 |
| 375819 | **CN** | E | *SE* | RM | 73319 | 79019 | 78219 | 73719 |
| 375820 | **CN** | E | *SE* | RM | 73320 | 79020 | 78220 | 73720 |
| 375821 | **CN** | E | *SE* | RM | 73321 | 79021 | 78221 | 73721 |
| 375822 | **CN** | E | *SE* | RM | 73322 | 79022 | 78222 | 73722 |
| 375823 | **CN** | E | *SE* | RM | 73323 | 79023 | 78223 | 73723 |
| 375824 | **CN** | E | *SE* | RM | 73324 | 79024 | 78224 | 73724 |
| 375825 | **CN** | E | *SE* | RM | 73325 | 79025 | 78225 | 73725 |
| 375826 | **CN** | E | *SE* | RM | 73326 | 79026 | 78226 | 73726 |
| 375827 | **CN** | E | *SE* | RM | 73327 | 79027 | 78227 | 73727 |
| 375828 | **CN** | E | *SE* | RM | 73328 | 79028 | 78228 | 73728 |
| 375829 | **CN** | E | *SE* | RM | 73329 | 79029 | 78229 | 73729 |
| 375830 | **CN** | E | *SE* | RM | 73330 | 79030 | 78230 | 73730 |

**Name (carried on one side of each MSO or TSO):**

375830  City of London

**Class 375/9.** Outer suburban units. 750 V DC only. DMCO–MSO–TSO–DMCO.

**DMCO(A).** Bombardier Derby 2003–04. 12/59. 43.4 t.
**MSO.** Bombardier Derby 2003–04. –/73 1T. 39.3 t.
**TSO.** Bombardier Derby 2003–04. –/59 1TD 2W. 35.6 t.
**DMCO(B).** Bombardier Derby 2003–04. 12/59. 43.4 t.

| 375901 | **CN** | E | *SE* | RM | 73331 | 79031 | 79061 | 73731 |
| 375902 | **CN** | E | *SE* | RM | 73332 | 79032 | 79062 | 73732 |
| 375903 | **CN** | E | *SE* | RM | 73333 | 79033 | 79063 | 73733 |
| 375904 | **CN** | E | *SE* | RM | 73334 | 79034 | 79064 | 73734 |
| 375905 | **CN** | E | *SE* | RM | 73335 | 79035 | 79065 | 73735 |
| 375906 | **CN** | E | *SE* | RM | 73336 | 79036 | 79066 | 73736 |
| 375907 | **CN** | E | *SE* | RM | 73337 | 79037 | 79067 | 73737 |
| 375908 | **CN** | E | *SE* | RM | 73338 | 79038 | 79068 | 73738 |
| 375909 | **CN** | E | *SE* | RM | 73339 | 79039 | 79069 | 73739 |
| 375910 | **CN** | E | *SE* | RM | 73340 | 79040 | 79070 | 73740 |
| 375911 | **CN** | E | *SE* | RM | 73341 | 79041 | 79071 | 73741 |
| 375912 | **CN** | E | *SE* | RM | 73342 | 79042 | 79072 | 73742 |
| 375913 | **CN** | E | *SE* | RM | 73343 | 79043 | 79073 | 73743 |
| 375914 | **CN** | E | *SE* | RM | 73344 | 79044 | 79074 | 73744 |
| 375915 | **CN** | E | *SE* | RM | 73345 | 79045 | 79075 | 73745 |
| 375916 | **CN** | E | *SE* | RM | 73346 | 79046 | 79076 | 73746 |
| 375917 | **CN** | E | *SE* | RM | 73347 | 79047 | 79077 | 73747 |
| 375918 | **CN** | E | *SE* | RM | 73348 | 79048 | 79078 | 73748 |
| 375919 | **CN** | E | *SE* | RM | 73349 | 79049 | 79079 | 73749 |
| 375920 | **CN** | E | *SE* | RM | 73350 | 79050 | 79080 | 73750 |
| 375921 | **CN** | E | *SE* | RM | 73351 | 79051 | 79081 | 73751 |
| 375922 | **CN** | E | *SE* | RM | 73352 | 79052 | 79082 | 73752 |

| | | | | | | | | |
|---|---|---|---|---|---|---|---|---|
| 375923 | **CN** | E | *SE* | RM | 73353 | 79053 | 79083 | 73753 |
| 375924 | **CN** | E | *SE* | RM | 73354 | 79054 | 79084 | 73754 |
| 375925 | **CN** | E | *SE* | RM | 73355 | 79055 | 79085 | 73755 |
| 375926 | **CN** | E | *SE* | RM | 73356 | 79056 | 79086 | 73756 |
| 375927 | **CN** | E | *SE* | RM | 73357 | 79057 | 79087 | 73757 |

# CLASS 376   ELECTROSTAR   BOMBARDIER DERBY

Inner suburban units.

**Formation:** DMSO–MSO–TSO–MSO–DMSO.
**System:** 750 V DC third rail.
**Construction:** Welded aluminium alloy underframe, sides and roof with steel ends. All sections bolted together.
**Traction Motors:** Two Bombardier asynchronous of 200 kW.
**Wheel Arrangement:** 2-Bo + 2-Bo + 2-2 + Bo-2 + Bo-2.
**Braking:** Disc & regenerative.            **Dimensions:** 20.40/19.99 x 2.80 m.
**Bogies:** Bombardier P3-25/T3-25.        **Couplers:** Dellner 12.
**Gangways:** Within unit.                         **Control System:** IGBT Inverter.
**Doors:** Sliding.                                      **Maximum Speed:** 75 mph.
**Heating & ventilation:** Pressure heating and ventilation.
**Seating Layout:** 2+2 low density facing.
**Multiple Working:** Within class and with Classes 375, 377, 378 and 379.

**DMSO(A).** Bombardier Derby 2004–05. –/36(6) 1W. 42.1 t.
**MSO.** Bombardier Derby 2004–05. –/48. 36.2 t.
**TSO.** Bombardier Derby 2004–05. –/48. 36.3 t.
**DMSO(B).** Bombardier Derby 2004–05. –/36(6) 1W. 42.1 t.

| | | | | | | | | | |
|---|---|---|---|---|---|---|---|---|---|
| 376001 | **CN** | E | *SE* | SG | 61101 | 63301 | 64301 | 63501 | 61601 |
| 376002 | **CN** | E | *SE* | SG | 61102 | 63302 | 64302 | 63502 | 61602 |
| 376003 | **CN** | E | *SE* | SG | 61103 | 63303 | 64303 | 63503 | 61603 |
| 376004 | **CN** | E | *SE* | SG | 61104 | 63304 | 64304 | 63504 | 61604 |
| 376005 | **CN** | E | *SE* | SG | 61105 | 63305 | 64305 | 63505 | 61605 |
| 376006 | **CN** | E | *SE* | SG | 61106 | 63306 | 64306 | 63506 | 61606 |
| 376007 | **CN** | E | *SE* | SG | 61107 | 63307 | 64307 | 63507 | 61607 |
| 376008 | **CN** | E | *SE* | SG | 61108 | 63308 | 64308 | 63508 | 61608 |
| 376009 | **CN** | E | *SE* | SG | 61109 | 63309 | 64309 | 63509 | 61609 |
| 376010 | **CN** | E | *SE* | SG | 61110 | 63310 | 64310 | 63510 | 61610 |
| 376011 | **CN** | E | *SE* | SG | 61111 | 63311 | 64311 | 63511 | 61611 |
| 376012 | **CN** | E | *SE* | SG | 61112 | 63312 | 64312 | 63512 | 61612 |
| 376013 | **CN** | E | *SE* | SG | 61113 | 63313 | 64313 | 63513 | 61613 |
| 376014 | **CN** | E | *SE* | SG | 61114 | 63314 | 64314 | 63514 | 61614 |
| 376015 | **CN** | E | *SE* | SG | 61115 | 63315 | 64315 | 63515 | 61615 |
| 376016 | **CN** | E | *SE* | SG | 61116 | 63316 | 64316 | 63516 | 61616 |
| 376017 | **CN** | E | *SE* | SG | 61117 | 63317 | 64317 | 63517 | 61617 |
| 376018 | **CN** | E | *SE* | SG | 61118 | 63318 | 64318 | 63518 | 61618 |
| 376019 | **CN** | E | *SE* | SG | 61119 | 63319 | 64319 | 63519 | 61619 |
| 376020 | **CN** | E | *SE* | SG | 61120 | 63320 | 64320 | 63520 | 61620 |
| 376021 | **CN** | E | *SE* | SG | 61121 | 63321 | 64321 | 63521 | 61621 |
| 376022 | **CN** | E | *SE* | SG | 61122 | 63322 | 64322 | 63522 | 61622 |
| 376023 | **CN** | E | *SE* | SG | 61123 | 63323 | 64323 | 63523 | 61623 |

| 376024 | **CN** | E | *SE* | SG | 61124 | 63324 | 64324 | 63524 | 61624 |
| 376025 | **CN** | E | *SE* | SG | 61125 | 63325 | 64325 | 63525 | 61625 |
| 376026 | **CN** | E | *SE* | SG | 61126 | 63326 | 64326 | 63526 | 61626 |
| 376027 | **CN** | E | *SE* | SG | 61127 | 63327 | 64327 | 63527 | 61627 |
| 376028 | **CN** | E | *SE* | SG | 61128 | 63328 | 64328 | 63528 | 61628 |
| 376029 | **CN** | E | *SE* | SG | 61129 | 63329 | 64329 | 63529 | 61629 |
| 376030 | **CN** | E | *SE* | SG | 61130 | 63330 | 64330 | 63530 | 61630 |
| 376031 | **CN** | E | *SE* | SG | 61131 | 63331 | 64331 | 63531 | 61631 |
| 376032 | **CN** | E | *SE* | SG | 61132 | 63332 | 64332 | 63532 | 61632 |
| 376033 | **CN** | E | *SE* | SG | 61133 | 63333 | 64333 | 63533 | 61633 |
| 376034 | **CN** | E | *SE* | SG | 61134 | 63334 | 64334 | 63534 | 61634 |
| 376035 | **CN** | E | *SE* | SG | 61135 | 63335 | 64335 | 63535 | 61635 |
| 376036 | **CN** | E | *SE* | SG | 61136 | 63336 | 64336 | 63536 | 61636 |

# CLASS 377   ELECTROSTAR   BOMBARDIER DERBY

Express and outer suburban units.

**Formations:** Various.
**Systems:** 25 kV AC overhead/750 V DC third rail or third rail only with provision for retro-fitting of AC equipment.
**Construction:** Welded aluminium alloy underframe, sides and roof with steel ends. All sections bolted together.
**Traction Motors:** Two Bombardier asynchronous of 250 kW.
**Wheel Arrangement:** 2-Bo(+ 2-Bo) + 2-2 + Bo-2.
**Braking:** Disc & regenerative.       **Dimensions:** 20.39/20.00 x 2.80 m.
**Bogies:** Bombardier P3-25/T3-25.     **Couplers:** Dellner 12.
**Gangways:** Throughout.               **Control System:** IGBT Inverter.
**Doors:** Sliding plug.                **Maximum Speed:** 100 mph.
**Heating & ventilation:** Air conditioning.
**Seating Layout:** Various, see sub-class headings.
**Multiple Working:** Within class and with Classes 375, 376, 378 and 379.

**Class 377/1.** 750 V DC only. DMCO–MSO–TSO–DMCO.
**Seating layout:** 1: 2+2 facing/unidirectional, 2: 2+2 facing/unidirectional (377 101–119), 3+2 and 2+2 facing/unidirectional (377 120–164) (3+2 seating in middle cars only 377 140–164).

**DMCO(A).** Bombardier Derby 2002–03. 12/48 (s 12/56). 44.8 t.
**MSO.** Bombardier Derby 2002–03. –/62 (s –/70, t –/69). 1T. 39.0 t.
**TSO.** Bombardier Derby 2002–03. –/52 (s –/60, t –/57). 1TD 2W. 35.4 t.
**DMCO(B).** Bombardier Derby 2002–03. 12/48 (s 12/56). 43.4 t.

| 377 101 | **SN** | P | *SN* | BI | 78501 | 77101 | 78901 | 78701 |
| 377 102 | **SN** | P | *SN* | BI | 78502 | 77102 | 78902 | 78702 |
| 377 103 | **SN** | P | *SN* | BI | 78503 | 77103 | 78903 | 78703 |
| 377 104 | **SN** | P | *SN* | BI | 78504 | 77104 | 78904 | 78704 |
| 377 105 | **SN** | P | *SN* | BI | 78505 | 77105 | 78905 | 78705 |
| 377 106 | **SN** | P | *SN* | BI | 78506 | 77106 | 78906 | 78706 |
| 377 107 | **SN** | P | *SN* | BI | 78507 | 77107 | 78907 | 78707 |
| 377 108 | **SN** | P | *SN* | BI | 78508 | 77108 | 78908 | 78708 |
| 377 109 | **SN** | P | *SN* | BI | 78509 | 77109 | 78909 | 78709 |
| 377 110 | **SN** | P | *SN* | BI | 78510 | 77110 | 78910 | 78710 |

| | | | | | | | | |
|---|---|---|---|---|---|---|---|---|
| 377 111 | | **SN** | P | *SN* | BI | 78511 | 77111 | 78911 | 78711 |
| 377 112 | | **SN** | P | *SN* | BI | 78512 | 77112 | 78912 | 78712 |
| 377 113 | | **SN** | P | *SN* | BI | 78513 | 77113 | 78913 | 78713 |
| 377 114 | | **SN** | P | *SN* | BI | 78514 | 77114 | 78914 | 78714 |
| 377 115 | | **SN** | P | *SN* | BI | 78515 | 77115 | 78915 | 78715 |
| 377 116 | | **SN** | P | *SN* | BI | 78516 | 77116 | 78916 | 78716 |
| 377 117 | | **SN** | P | *SN* | BI | 78517 | 77117 | 78917 | 78717 |
| 377 118 | | **SN** | P | *SN* | BI | 78518 | 77118 | 78918 | 78718 |
| 377 119 | | **SN** | P | *SN* | BI | 78519 | 77119 | 78919 | 78719 |
| 377 120 | s | **SN** | P | *SN* | BI | 78520 | 77120 | 78920 | 78720 |
| 377 121 | s | **SN** | P | *SN* | BI | 78521 | 77121 | 78921 | 78721 |
| 377 122 | s | **SN** | P | *SN* | BI | 78522 | 77122 | 78922 | 78722 |
| 377 123 | s | **SN** | P | *SN* | BI | 78523 | 77123 | 78923 | 78723 |
| 377 124 | s | **SN** | P | *SN* | BI | 78524 | 77124 | 78924 | 78724 |
| 377 125 | s | **SN** | P | *SN* | BI | 78525 | 77125 | 78925 | 78725 |
| 377 126 | s | **SN** | P | *SN* | BI | 78526 | 77126 | 78926 | 78726 |
| 377 127 | s | **SN** | P | *SN* | BI | 78527 | 77127 | 78927 | 78727 |
| 377 128 | s | **SN** | P | *SN* | BI | 78528 | 77128 | 78928 | 78728 |
| 377 129 | s | **SN** | P | *SN* | BI | 78529 | 77129 | 78929 | 78729 |
| 377 130 | s | **SN** | P | *SN* | BI | 78530 | 77130 | 78930 | 78730 |
| 377 131 | s | **SN** | P | *SN* | BI | 78531 | 77131 | 78931 | 78731 |
| 377 132 | s | **SN** | P | *SN* | BI | 78532 | 77132 | 78932 | 78732 |
| 377 133 | s | **SN** | P | *SN* | BI | 78533 | 77133 | 78933 | 78733 |
| 377 134 | s | **SN** | P | *SN* | BI | 78534 | 77134 | 78934 | 78734 |
| 377 135 | s | **SN** | P | *SN* | BI | 78535 | 77135 | 78935 | 78735 |
| 377 136 | s | **SN** | P | *SN* | BI | 78536 | 77136 | 78936 | 78736 |
| 377 137 | s | **SN** | P | *SN* | BI | 78537 | 77137 | 78937 | 78737 |
| 377 138 | s | **SN** | P | *SN* | BI | 78538 | 77138 | 78938 | 78738 |
| 377 139 | s | **SN** | P | *SN* | BI | 78539 | 77139 | 78939 | 78739 |
| 377 140 | t | **SN** | P | *SN* | BI | 78540 | 77140 | 78940 | 78740 |
| 377 141 | t | **SN** | P | *SN* | BI | 78541 | 77141 | 78941 | 78741 |
| 377 142 | t | **SN** | P | *SN* | BI | 78542 | 77142 | 78942 | 78742 |
| 377 143 | t | **SN** | P | *SN* | BI | 78543 | 77143 | 78943 | 78743 |
| 377 144 | t | **SN** | P | *SN* | BI | 78544 | 77144 | 78944 | 78744 |
| 377 145 | t | **SN** | P | *SN* | BI | 78545 | 77145 | 78945 | 78745 |
| 377 146 | t | **SN** | P | *SN* | BI | 78546 | 77146 | 78946 | 78746 |
| 377 147 | t | **SN** | P | *SN* | BI | 78547 | 77147 | 78947 | 78747 |
| 377 148 | t | **SN** | P | *SN* | BI | 78548 | 77148 | 78948 | 78748 |
| 377 149 | t | **SN** | P | *SN* | BI | 78549 | 77149 | 78949 | 78749 |
| 377 150 | t | **SN** | P | *SN* | BI | 78550 | 77150 | 78950 | 78750 |
| 377 151 | t | **SN** | P | *SN* | BI | 78551 | 77151 | 78951 | 78751 |
| 377 152 | t | **SN** | P | *SN* | BI | 78552 | 77152 | 78952 | 78752 |
| 377 153 | t | **SN** | P | *SN* | BI | 78553 | 77153 | 78953 | 78753 |
| 377 154 | t | **SN** | P | *SN* | BI | 78554 | 77154 | 78954 | 78754 |
| 377 155 | t | **SN** | P | *SN* | BI | 78555 | 77155 | 78955 | 78755 |
| 377 156 | t | **SN** | P | *SN* | BI | 78556 | 77156 | 78956 | 78756 |
| 377 157 | t | **SN** | P | *SN* | BI | 78557 | 77157 | 78957 | 78757 |
| 377 158 | t | **SN** | P | *SN* | BI | 78558 | 77158 | 78958 | 78758 |
| 377 159 | t | **SN** | P | *SN* | BI | 78559 | 77159 | 78959 | 78759 |
| 377 160 | t | **SN** | P | *SN* | BI | 78560 | 77160 | 78960 | 78760 |
| 377 161 | t | **SN** | P | *SN* | BI | 78561 | 77161 | 78961 | 78761 |

| | | | | | | | | |
|---|---|---|---|---|---|---|---|---|
| 377 162 | t | **SN** | P | *SN* | Bl | 78562 | 77162 | 78962 | 78762 |
| 377 163 | t | **SN** | P | *SN* | Bl | 78563 | 77163 | 78963 | 78763 |
| 377 164 | t | **SN** | P | *SN* | Bl | 78564 | 77164 | 78964 | 78764 |

**Class 377/2.** 25 kV AC/750 V DC. DMCO–MSO–PTSO–DMCO. These dual-voltage units are used on the South Croydon–Milton Keynes cross-London service. Three units were sub-leased to First Capital Connect in 2011.
**Seating layout:** 1: 2+2 facing/unidirectional, 2: 2+2 and 3+2 facing/unidirectional (3+2 seating in middle cars only).

**DMCO(A).** Bombardier Derby 2003–04. 12/48. 44.2 t.
**MSO.** Bombardier Derby 2003–04. –/69 1T. 39.8 t.
**PTSO.** Bombardier Derby 2003–04. –/57 1TD 2W. 40.1 t.
**DMCO(B).** Bombardier Derby 2003–04. 12/48. 44.2 t.

| | | | | | | | | |
|---|---|---|---|---|---|---|---|---|
| 377 201 | **SN** | P | *SN* | SU | 78571 | 77171 | 78971 | 78771 |
| 377 202 | **SN** | P | *SN* | SU | 78572 | 77172 | 78972 | 78772 |
| 377 203 | **SN** | P | *SN* | SU | 78573 | 77173 | 78973 | 78773 |
| 377 204 | **SN** | P | *SN* | SU | 78574 | 77174 | 78974 | 78774 |
| 377 205 | **SN** | P | *SN* | SU | 78575 | 77175 | 78975 | 78775 |
| 377 206 | **SN** | P | *SN* | SU | 78576 | 77176 | 78976 | 78776 |
| 377 207 | **FU** | P | *FC* | BF | 78577 | 77177 | 78977 | 78777 |
| 377 208 | **SN** | P | *SN* | SU | 78578 | 77178 | 78978 | 78778 |
| 377 209 | **SN** | P | *SN* | SU | 78579 | 77179 | 78979 | 78779 |
| 377 210 | **SN** | P | *SN* | SU | 78580 | 77180 | 78980 | 78780 |
| 377 211 | **FU** | P | *FC* | BF | 78581 | 77181 | 78981 | 78781 |
| 377 212 | **FU** | P | *FC* | BF | 78582 | 77182 | 78982 | 78782 |
| 377 213 | **SN** | P | *SN* | SU | 78583 | 77183 | 78983 | 78783 |
| 377 214 | **SN** | P | *SN* | SU | 78584 | 77184 | 78984 | 78784 |
| 377 215 | **SN** | P | *SN* | SU | 78585 | 77185 | 78985 | 78785 |

**Class 377/3.** 750 V DC only. DMCO–TSO–DMCO.
**Seating Layout:** 1: 2+2 facing/unidirectional, 2: 2+2 facing/unidirectional.

Units built as Class 375, but renumbered in the Class 377/3 range when fitted with Dellner couplers.

**DMCO(A).** Bombardier Derby 2001–02. 12/48. 43.5 t.
**TSO.** Bombardier Derby 2001–02. –/56 1TD 2W. 35.4 t.
**DMCO(B).** Bombardier Derby 2001–02. 12/48. 43.5 t.

| | | | | | | | | |
|---|---|---|---|---|---|---|---|---|
| 377 301 | (375 311) | **SN** | P | *SN* | SU | 68201 | 74801 | 68401 |
| 377 302 | (375 312) | **SN** | P | *SN* | SU | 68202 | 74802 | 68402 |
| 377 303 | (375 313) | **SN** | P | *SN* | SU | 68203 | 74803 | 68403 |
| 377 304 | (375 314) | **SN** | P | *SN* | SU | 68204 | 74804 | 68404 |
| 377 305 | (375 315) | **SN** | P | *SN* | SU | 68205 | 74805 | 68405 |
| 377 306 | (375 316) | **SN** | P | *SN* | SU | 68206 | 74806 | 68406 |
| 377 307 | (375 317) | **SN** | P | *SN* | SU | 68207 | 74807 | 68407 |
| 377 308 | (375 318) | **SN** | P | *SN* | SU | 68208 | 74808 | 68408 |
| 377 309 | (375 319) | **SN** | P | *SN* | SU | 68209 | 74809 | 68409 |
| 377 310 | (375 320) | **SN** | P | *SN* | SU | 68210 | 74810 | 68410 |
| 377 311 | (375 321) | **SN** | P | *SN* | SU | 68211 | 74811 | 68411 |
| 377 312 | (375 322) | **SN** | P | *SN* | SU | 68212 | 74812 | 68412 |
| 377 313 | (375 323) | **SN** | P | *SN* | SU | 68213 | 74813 | 68413 |

| | | | | | | | |
|---|---|---|---|---|---|---|---|
| 377 314 | (375 324) | **SN** | P | *SN* | SU | 68214 74814 68414 |
| 377 315 | (375 325) | **SN** | P | *SN* | SU | 68215 74815 68415 |
| 377 316 | (375 326) | **SN** | P | *SN* | SU | 68216 74816 68416 |
| 377 317 | (375 327) | **SN** | P | *SN* | SU | 68217 74817 68417 |
| 377 318 | (375 328) | **SN** | P | *SN* | SU | 68218 74818 68418 |
| 377 319 | (375 329) | **SN** | P | *SN* | SU | 68219 74819 68419 |
| 377 320 | (375 330) | **SN** | P | *SN* | SU | 68220 74820 68420 |
| 377 321 | (375 331) | **SN** | P | *SN* | SU | 68221 74821 68421 |
| 377 322 | (375 332) | **SN** | P | *SN* | SU | 68222 74822 68422 |
| 377 323 | (375 333) | **SN** | P | *SN* | SU | 68223 74823 68423 |
| 377 324 | (375 334) | **SN** | P | *SN* | SU | 68224 74824 68424 |
| 377 325 | (375 335) | **SN** | P | *SN* | SU | 68225 74825 68425 |
| 377 326 | (375 336) | **SN** | P | *SN* | SU | 68226 74826 68426 |
| 377 327 | (375 337) | **SN** | P | *SN* | SU | 68227 74827 68427 |
| 377 328 | (375 338) | **SN** | P | *SN* | SU | 68228 74828 68428 |

**Class 377/4**. 750 V DC only. DMCO–MSO–TSO–DMCO.
**Seating Layout:** 1: 2+2 facing/two seats longitudinal, 2: 2+2 and 3+2 facing/unidirectional (3+2 seating in middle cars only).

**DMCO(A)**. Bombardier Derby 2004–05. 10/48. 43.1 t.
**MSO**. Bombardier Derby 2004–05. –/69 1T. 39.3 t.
**TSO**. Bombardier Derby 2004–05. –/56 1TD 2W. 35.3 t.
**DMCO(B)**. Bombardier Derby 2004–05. 10/48. 43.2 t.

| | | | | | | | | |
|---|---|---|---|---|---|---|---|---|
| 377 401 | **SN** | P | *SN* | BI | 73401 | 78801 | 78601 | 73801 |
| 377 402 | **SN** | P | *SN* | BI | 73402 | 78802 | 78602 | 73802 |
| 377 403 | **SN** | P | *SN* | BI | 73403 | 78803 | 78603 | 73803 |
| 377 404 | **SN** | P | *SN* | BI | 73404 | 78804 | 78604 | 73804 |
| 377 405 | **SN** | P | *SN* | BI | 73405 | 78805 | 78605 | 73805 |
| 377 406 | **SN** | P | *SN* | BI | 73406 | 78806 | 78606 | 73806 |
| 377 407 | **SN** | P | *SN* | BI | 73407 | 78807 | 78607 | 73807 |
| 377 408 | **SN** | P | *SN* | BI | 73408 | 78808 | 78608 | 73808 |
| 377 409 | **SN** | P | *SN* | BI | 73409 | 78809 | 78609 | 73809 |
| 377 410 | **SN** | P | *SN* | BI | 73410 | 78810 | 78610 | 73810 |
| 377 411 | **SN** | P | *SN* | BI | 73411 | 78811 | 78611 | 73811 |
| 377 412 | **SN** | P | *SN* | BI | 73412 | 78812 | 78612 | 73812 |
| 377 413 | **SN** | P | *SN* | BI | 73413 | 78813 | 78613 | 73813 |
| 377 414 | **SN** | P | *SN* | BI | 73414 | 78814 | 78614 | 73814 |
| 377 415 | **SN** | P | *SN* | BI | 73415 | 78815 | 78615 | 73815 |
| 377 416 | **SN** | P | *SN* | BI | 73416 | 78816 | 78616 | 73816 |
| 377 417 | **SN** | P | *SN* | BI | 73417 | 78817 | 78617 | 73817 |
| 377 418 | **SN** | P | *SN* | BI | 73418 | 78818 | 78618 | 73818 |
| 377 419 | **SN** | P | *SN* | BI | 73419 | 78819 | 78619 | 73819 |
| 377 420 | **SN** | P | *SN* | BI | 73420 | 78820 | 78620 | 73820 |
| 377 421 | **SN** | P | *SN* | BI | 73421 | 78821 | 78621 | 73821 |
| 377 422 | **SN** | P | *SN* | BI | 73422 | 78822 | 78622 | 73822 |
| 377 423 | **SN** | P | *SN* | BI | 73423 | 78823 | 78623 | 73823 |
| 377 424 | **SN** | P | *SN* | BI | 73424 | 78824 | 78624 | 73824 |
| 377 425 | **SN** | P | *SN* | BI | 73425 | 78825 | 78625 | 73825 |
| 377 426 | **SN** | P | *SN* | BI | 73426 | 78826 | 78626 | 73826 |
| 377 427 | **SN** | P | *SN* | BI | 73427 | 78827 | 78627 | 73827 |

| | | | | | | | | |
|---|---|---|---|---|---|---|---|---|
| 377 428 | **SN** | P | *SN* | Bl | 73428 | 78828 | 78628 | 73828 |
| 377 429 | **SN** | P | *SN* | Bl | 73429 | 78829 | 78629 | 73829 |
| 377 430 | **SN** | P | *SN* | Bl | 73430 | 78830 | 78630 | 73830 |
| 377 431 | **SN** | P | *SN* | Bl | 73431 | 78831 | 78631 | 73831 |
| 377 432 | **SN** | P | *SN* | Bl | 73432 | 78832 | 78632 | 73832 |
| 377 433 | **SN** | P | *SN* | Bl | 73433 | 78833 | 78633 | 73833 |
| 377 434 | **SN** | P | *SN* | Bl | 73434 | 78834 | 78634 | 73834 |
| 377 435 | **SN** | P | *SN* | Bl | 73435 | 78835 | 78635 | 73835 |
| 377 436 | **SN** | P | *SN* | Bl | 73436 | 78836 | 78636 | 73836 |
| 377 437 | **SN** | P | *SN* | Bl | 73437 | 78837 | 78637 | 73837 |
| 377 438 | **SN** | P | *SN* | Bl | 73438 | 78838 | 78638 | 73838 |
| 377 439 | **SN** | P | *SN* | Bl | 73439 | 78839 | 78639 | 73839 |
| 377 440 | **SN** | P | *SN* | Bl | 73440 | 78840 | 78640 | 73840 |
| 377 441 | **SN** | P | *SN* | Bl | 73441 | 78841 | 78641 | 73841 |
| 377 442 | **SN** | P | *SN* | Bl | 73442 | 78842 | 78642 | 73842 |
| 377 443 | **SN** | P | *SN* | Bl | 73443 | 78843 | 78643 | 73843 |
| 377 444 | **SN** | P | *SN* | Bl | 73444 | 78844 | 78644 | 73844 |
| 377 445 | **SN** | P | *SN* | Bl | 73445 | 78845 | 78645 | 73845 |
| 377 446 | **SN** | P | *SN* | Bl | 73446 | 78846 | 78646 | 73846 |
| 377 447 | **SN** | P | *SN* | Bl | 73447 | 78847 | 78647 | 73847 |
| 377 448 | **SN** | P | *SN* | Bl | 73448 | 78848 | 78648 | 73848 |
| 377 449 | **SN** | P | *SN* | Bl | 73449 | 78849 | 78649 | 73849 |
| 377 450 | **SN** | P | *SN* | Bl | 73450 | 78850 | 78650 | 73850 |
| 377 451 | **SN** | P | *SN* | Bl | 73451 | 78851 | 78651 | 73851 |
| 377 452 | **SN** | P | *SN* | Bl | 73452 | 78852 | 78652 | 73852 |
| 377 453 | **SN** | P | *SN* | Bl | 73453 | 78853 | 78653 | 73853 |
| 377 454 | **SN** | P | *SN* | Bl | 73454 | 78854 | 78654 | 73854 |
| 377 455 | **SN** | P | *SN* | Bl | 73455 | 78855 | 78655 | 73855 |
| 377 456 | **SN** | P | *SN* | Bl | 73456 | 78856 | 78656 | 73856 |
| 377 457 | **SN** | P | *SN* | Bl | 73457 | 78857 | 78657 | 73857 |
| 377 458 | **SN** | P | *SN* | Bl | 73458 | 78858 | 78658 | 73858 |
| 377 459 | **SN** | P | *SN* | Bl | 73459 | 78859 | 78659 | 73859 |
| 377 460 | **SN** | P | *SN* | Bl | 73460 | 78860 | 78660 | 73860 |
| 377 461 | **SN** | P | *SN* | Bl | 73461 | 78861 | 78661 | 73861 |
| 377 462 | **SN** | P | *SN* | Bl | 73462 | 78862 | 78662 | 73862 |
| 377 463 | **SN** | P | *SN* | Bl | 73463 | 78863 | 78663 | 73863 |
| 377 464 | **SN** | P | *SN* | Bl | 73464 | 78864 | 78664 | 73864 |
| 377 465 | **SN** | P | *SN* | Bl | 73465 | 78865 | 78665 | 73865 |
| 377 466 | **SN** | P | *SN* | Bl | 73466 | 78866 | 78666 | 73866 |
| 377 467 | **SN** | P | *SN* | Bl | 73467 | 78867 | 78667 | 73867 |
| 377 468 | **SN** | P | *SN* | Bl | 73468 | 78868 | 78668 | 73868 |
| 377 469 | **SN** | P | *SN* | Bl | 73469 | 78869 | 78669 | 73869 |
| 377 470 | **SN** | P | *SN* | Bl | 73470 | 78870 | 78670 | 73870 |
| 377 471 | **SN** | P | *SN* | Bl | 73471 | 78871 | 78671 | 73871 |
| 377 472 | **SN** | P | *SN* | Bl | 73472 | 78872 | 78672 | 73872 |
| 377 473 | **SN** | P | *SN* | Bl | 73473 | 78873 | 78673 | 73873 |
| 377 474 | **SN** | P | *SN* | Bl | 73474 | 78874 | 78674 | 73874 |
| 377 475 | **SN** | P | *SN* | Bl | 73475 | 78875 | 78675 | 73875 |

**Class 377/5**. 25 kV AC/750 V DC. DMCO–MSO–PTSO–DMCO. Dual voltage FCC units (sub-leased from Southern). Details as Class 377/2 unless stated.

**DMCO(A)**. Bombardier Derby 2008–09. 10/48. 43.1t.
**MSO**. Bombardier Derby 2008–09. –/69 1T. 40.3t.
**PTSO**. Bombardier Derby 2008–09. –/56 1TD 2W. 40.6 t.
**DMCO(B)**. Bombardier Derby 2008–09. 10/48. 43.1t.

| | | | | | | | | |
|---|---|---|---|---|---|---|---|---|
| 377501 | **FU** | P | *FC* | BF | 73501 | 75901 | 74901 | 73601 |
| 377502 | **FU** | P | *FC* | BF | 73502 | 75902 | 74902 | 73602 |
| 377503 | **FU** | P | *FC* | BF | 73503 | 75903 | 74903 | 73603 |
| 377504 | **FU** | P | *FC* | BF | 73504 | 75904 | 74904 | 73604 |
| 377505 | **FU** | P | *FC* | BF | 73505 | 75905 | 74905 | 73605 |
| 377506 | **FU** | P | *FC* | BF | 73506 | 75906 | 74906 | 73606 |
| 377507 | **FU** | P | *FC* | BF | 73507 | 75907 | 74907 | 73607 |
| 377508 | **FU** | P | *FC* | BF | 73508 | 75908 | 74908 | 73608 |
| 377509 | **FU** | P | *FC* | BF | 73509 | 75909 | 74909 | 73609 |
| 377510 | **FU** | P | *FC* | BF | 73510 | 75910 | 74910 | 73610 |
| 377511 | **FU** | P | *FC* | BF | 73511 | 75911 | 74911 | 73611 |
| 377512 | **FU** | P | *FC* | BF | 73512 | 75912 | 74912 | 73612 |
| 377513 | **FU** | P | *FC* | BF | 73513 | 75913 | 74913 | 73613 |
| 377514 | **FU** | P | *FC* | BF | 73514 | 75914 | 74914 | 73614 |
| 377515 | **FU** | P | *FC* | BF | 73515 | 75915 | 74915 | 73615 |
| 377516 | **FU** | P | *FC* | BF | 73516 | 75916 | 74916 | 73616 |
| 377517 | **FU** | P | *FC* | BF | 73517 | 75917 | 74917 | 73617 |
| 377518 | **FU** | P | *FC* | BF | 73518 | 75918 | 74918 | 73618 |
| 377519 | **FU** | P | *FC* | BF | 73519 | 75919 | 74919 | 73619 |
| 377520 | **FU** | P | *FC* | BF | 73520 | 75920 | 74920 | 73620 |
| 377521 | **FU** | P | *FC* | BF | 73521 | 75921 | 74921 | 73621 |
| 377522 | **FU** | P | *FC* | BF | 73522 | 75922 | 74922 | 73622 |
| 377523 | **FU** | P | *FC* | BF | 73523 | 75923 | 74923 | 73623 |

**Class 377/6**. 750 V DC. DMSO–MSO–TSO–MSO–DMSO. Southern 5-car suburban units fitted with Fainsa seating. Technically the same as the 377/5s but using the slightly modified Class 379-style bodyshell.
**Seating Layout:** 2+2 facing/unidirectional.

**DMSO**. Bombardier Derby 2012–13. –/60. 44.7 t.
**MSO**. Bombardier Derby 2012–13. –/64 1T. 38.8 t.
**TSO**. Bombardier Derby 2012–13. –/46(2) 1TD 2W. 37.8 t.
**MSO**. Bombardier Derby 2012–13. –/66. 38.3 t.
**DMSO**. Bombardier Derby 2012–13. –/62. 44.7 t.

| | | | | | | | | | |
|---|---|---|---|---|---|---|---|---|---|
| 377601 | **SN** | P | *SN* | SU | 70101 | 70201 | 70301 | 70401 | 70501 |
| 377602 | **SN** | P | *SN* | SU | 70102 | 70202 | 70302 | 70402 | 70502 |
| 377603 | **SN** | P | *SN* | SU | 70103 | 70203 | 70303 | 70403 | 70503 |
| 377604 | **SN** | P | *SN* | SU | 70104 | 70204 | 70304 | 70404 | 70504 |
| 377605 | **SN** | P | *SN* | SU | 70105 | 70205 | 70305 | 70405 | 70505 |
| 377606 | **SN** | P | *SN* | SU | 70106 | 70206 | 70306 | 70406 | 70506 |
| 377607 | **SN** | P | *SN* | SU | 70107 | 70207 | 70307 | 70407 | 70507 |
| 377608 | **SN** | P | *SN* | SU | 70108 | 70208 | 70308 | 70408 | 70508 |
| 377609 | **SN** | P | *SN* | SU | 70109 | 70209 | 70309 | 70409 | 70509 |
| 377610 | **SN** | P | *SN* | SU | 70110 | 70210 | 70310 | 70410 | 70510 |
| 377611 | **SN** | P | *SN* | SU | 70111 | 70211 | 70311 | 70411 | 70511 |

| | | | | | | | | | |
|---|---|---|---|---|---|---|---|---|---|
| 377612 | **SN** | P | *SN* | SU | 70112 | 70212 | 70312 | 70412 | 70512 |
| 377613 | **SN** | P | *SN* | SU | 70113 | 70213 | 70313 | 70413 | 70513 |
| 377614 | **SN** | P | *SN* | SU | 70114 | 70214 | 70314 | 70414 | 70514 |
| 377615 | **SN** | P | *SN* | SU | 70115 | 70215 | 70315 | 70415 | 70515 |
| 377616 | **SN** | P | *SN* | SU | 70116 | 70216 | 70316 | 70416 | 70516 |
| 377617 | **SN** | P | *SN* | SU | 70117 | 70217 | 70317 | 70417 | 70517 |
| 377618 | **SN** | P | *SN* | SU | 70118 | 70218 | 70318 | 70418 | 70518 |
| 377619 | **SN** | P | *SN* | SU | 70119 | 70219 | 70319 | 70419 | 70519 |
| 377620 | **SN** | P | *SN* | SU | 70120 | 70220 | 70320 | 70420 | 70520 |
| 377621 | **SN** | P | *SN* | SU | 70121 | 70221 | 70321 | 70421 | 70521 |
| 377622 | **SN** | P | *SN* | SU | 70122 | 70222 | 70322 | 70422 | 70522 |
| 377623 | **SN** | P | *SN* | SU | 70123 | 70223 | 70323 | 70423 | 70523 |
| 377624 | **SN** | P | *SN* | SU | 70124 | 70224 | 70324 | 70424 | 70524 |
| 377625 | **SN** | P | *SN* | SU | 70125 | 70225 | 70325 | 70425 | 70525 |
| 377626 | **SN** | P | *SN* | SU | 70126 | 70226 | 70326 | 70426 | 70526 |

**Class 377/7.** 25kV AC/750V DC. DMSO–MSO–TSO–MSO–DMSO. Eight new dual-voltage units under construction for Southern. Due for delivery 2014. Full details awaited.

**DMSO.** Bombardier Derby 2013–14.      .    t.
**MSO.** Bombardier Derby 2013–14.      .    t.
**TSO.** Bombardier Derby 2013–14.      .    t.
**MSO.** Bombardier Derby 2013–14.      .    t.
**DMSO.** Bombardier Derby 2013–14.      .    t.

| | | | | | | | |
|---|---|---|---|---|---|---|---|
| 377701 | **SN** | P | | 65201 | 70601 | 65601 | 70701 | 65401 |
| 377702 | **SN** | P | | 65202 | 70602 | 65602 | 70702 | 65402 |
| 377703 | **SN** | P | | 65203 | 70603 | 65603 | 70703 | 65403 |
| 377704 | **SN** | P | | 65204 | 70604 | 65604 | 70704 | 65404 |
| 377705 | **SN** | P | | 65205 | 70605 | 65605 | 70705 | 65405 |
| 377706 | **SN** | P | | 65206 | 70606 | 65606 | 70706 | 65406 |
| 377707 | **SN** | P | | 65207 | 70607 | 65607 | 70707 | 65407 |
| 377708 | **SN** | P | | 65208 | 70608 | 65608 | 70708 | 65408 |

# CLASS 378    CAPITALSTAR    BOMBARDIER DERBY

57 Class 378 suburban Electrostars (designated Capitalstars by TfL).

**Formation:** DMSO–MSO–TSO–DMSO or DMSO–MSO–PTSO–DMSO.
**System:** Class 378/1 750 V DC third rail only. Class 378/2 25 kV AC overhead and 750 V DC third rail.
**Construction:** Welded aluminium alloy underframe, sides and roof with steel ends. All sections bolted together.
**Traction Motors:** Two Bombardier asynchronous of 200 kW.
**Wheel Arrangement:** 1A-Bo + 1A-Bo + 2-2 + Bo-1A.
**Braking:** Disc & regenerative.       **Dimensions:** 20.46/20.14 x 2.80 m.
**Bogies:** Bombardier P3-25/T3-25.    **Couplers:** Dellner 12.
**Gangways:** Within unit + end doors.    **Control System:** IGBT Inverter.
**Doors:** Sliding.       **Maximum Speed:** 75 mph.
**Heating & ventilation:** Air conditioning.
**Seating Layout:** Longitudinal ("tube style") low density.
**Multiple Working:** Within class and with Classes 375, 376, 377 and 379.

57 extra vehicles are on order to make all units up to 5-cars. This will take place in 2014–15, starting with units 378 135–154. The extra vehicles will be numbered in the 38401–457 series and should be inserted between the TSO and DMSO(B).

**Class 378/1.** 750 V DC. DMSO–MSO–TSO–DMSO. Third rail only units used on East London Line services. Provision for retro-fitting as dual voltage.

378 150–154 are fitted with de-icing equipment.

**DMSO(A).** Bombardier Derby 2009–10. –/36. 43.1 t.
**MSO.** Bombardier Derby 2009–10. –/40. 39.3 t.
**TSO.** Bombardier Derby 2009–10. –/34(6) 2W. 34.3 t.
**DMSO(B).** Bombardier Derby 2009–10. –/36. 42.7 t.

| | | | | | | | | |
|---|---|---|---|---|---|---|---|---|
| 378 135 | **LO** | QW | *LO* | NG | 38035 | 38235 | 38335 | 38135 |
| 378 136 | **LO** | QW | *LO* | NG | 38036 | 38236 | 38336 | 38136 |
| 378 137 | **LO** | QW | *LO* | NG | 38037 | 38237 | 38337 | 38137 |
| 378 138 | **LO** | QW | *LO* | NG | 38038 | 38238 | 38338 | 38138 |
| 378 139 | **LO** | QW | *LO* | NG | 38039 | 38239 | 38339 | 38139 |
| 378 140 | **LO** | QW | *LO* | NG | 38040 | 38240 | 38340 | 38140 |
| 378 141 | **LO** | QW | *LO* | NG | 38041 | 38241 | 38341 | 38141 |
| 378 142 | **LO** | QW | *LO* | NG | 38042 | 38242 | 38342 | 38142 |
| 378 143 | **LO** | QW | *LO* | NG | 38043 | 38243 | 38343 | 38143 |
| 378 144 | **LO** | QW | *LO* | NG | 38044 | 38244 | 38344 | 38144 |
| 378 145 | **LO** | QW | *LO* | NG | 38045 | 38245 | 38345 | 38145 |
| 378 146 | **LO** | QW | *LO* | NG | 38046 | 38246 | 38346 | 38146 |
| 378 147 | **LO** | QW | *LO* | NG | 38047 | 38247 | 38347 | 38147 |
| 378 148 | **LO** | QW | *LO* | NG | 38048 | 38248 | 38348 | 38148 |
| 378 149 | **LO** | QW | *LO* | NG | 38049 | 38249 | 38349 | 38149 |
| 378 150 | **LO** | QW | *LO* | NG | 38050 | 38250 | 38350 | 38150 |
| 378 151 | **LO** | QW | *LO* | NG | 38051 | 38251 | 38351 | 38151 |
| 378 152 | **LO** | QW | *LO* | NG | 38052 | 38252 | 38352 | 38152 |
| 378 153 | **LO** | QW | *LO* | NG | 38053 | 38253 | 38353 | 38153 |
| 378 154 | **LO** | QW | *LO* | NG | 38054 | 38254 | 38354 | 38154 |

**Class 378/2.** 25 kV AC/750 V DC. DMSO–MSO–PTSO–DMSO. Dual voltage units mainly used on North London Railway services. 378 201–224 built as 378 001–024 (3-car units) and extended to 4-car units in 2010.

378 216–220 are fitted with de-icing equipment.

**Advertising livery:** 378 211 and 378 221 Lycamobile (white).

**DMSO(A).** Bombardier Derby 2008–11. –/36. 43.4 t.
**MSO.** Bombardier Derby 2008–11. –/40. 39.6 t.
**PTSO.** Bombardier Derby 2008–11. –/34(6) 2W. 39.2 t.
**DMSO(B).** Bombardier Derby 2008–11. –/36. 43.1 t.

| | | | | | | | | |
|---|---|---|---|---|---|---|---|---|
| 378 201 | **LO** | QW | *LO* | NG | 38001 | 38201 | 38301 | 38101 |
| 378 202 | **LO** | QW | *LO* | NG | 38002 | 38202 | 38302 | 38102 |
| 378 203 | **LO** | QW | *LO* | NG | 38003 | 38203 | 38303 | 38103 |
| 378 204 | **LO** | QW | *LO* | NG | 38004 | 38204 | 38304 | 38104 |
| 378 205 | **LO** | QW | *LO* | NG | 38005 | 38205 | 38305 | 38105 |
| 378 206 | **LO** | QW | *LO* | NG | 38006 | 38206 | 38306 | 38106 |
| 378 207 | **LO** | QW | *LO* | NG | 38007 | 38207 | 38307 | 38107 |

| 378208 | LO | QW | LO | NG | 38008 38208 38308 | 38108 |
|--------|----|----|----|----|-------------------|-------|
| 378209 | LO | QW | LO | NG | 38009 38209 38309 | 38109 |
| 378210 | LO | QW | LO | NG | 38010 38210 38310 | 38110 |
| 378211 | AL | QW | LO | NG | 38011 38211 38311 | 38111 |
| 378212 | LO | QW | LO | NG | 38012 38212 38312 | 38112 |
| 378213 | LO | QW | LO | NG | 38013 38213 38313 | 38113 |
| 378214 | LO | QW | LO | NG | 38014 38214 38314 | 38114 |
| 378215 | LO | QW | LO | NG | 38015 38215 38315 | 38115 |
| 378216 | LO | QW | LO | NG | 38016 38216 38316 | 38116 |
| 378217 | LO | QW | LO | NG | 38017 38217 38317 | 38117 |
| 378218 | LO | QW | LO | NG | 38018 38218 38318 | 38118 |
| 378219 | LO | QW | LO | NG | 38019 38219 38319 | 38119 |
| 378220 | LO | QW | LO | NG | 38020 38220 38320 | 38120 |
| 378221 | AL | QW | LO | NG | 38021 38221 38321 | 38121 |
| 378222 | LO | QW | LO | NG | 38022 38222 38322 | 38122 |
| 378223 | LO | QW | LO | NG | 38023 38223 38323 | 38123 |
| 378224 | LO | QW | LO | NG | 38024 38224 38324 | 38124 |
| 378225 | LO | QW | LO | NG | 38025 38225 38325 | 38125 |
| 378226 | LO | QW | LO | NG | 38026 38226 38326 | 38126 |
| 378227 | LO | QW | LO | NG | 38027 38227 38327 | 38127 |
| 378228 | LO | QW | LO | NG | 38028 38228 38328 | 38128 |
| 378229 | LO | QW | LO | NG | 38029 38229 38329 | 38129 |
| 378230 | LO | QW | LO | NG | 38030 38230 38330 | 38130 |
| 378231 | LO | QW | LO | NG | 38031 38231 38331 | 38131 |
| 378232 | LO | QW | LO | NG | 38032 38232 38332 | 38132 |
| 378233 | LO | QW | LO | NG | 38033 38233 38333 | 38133 |
| 378234 | LO | QW | LO | NG | 38034 38234 38334 | 38134 |
| 378255 | LO | QW | LO | NG | 38055 38255 38355 | 38155 |
| 378256 | LO | QW | LO | NG | 38056 38256 38356 | 38156 |
| 378257 | LO | QW | LO | NG | 38057 38257 38357 | 38157 |

**Name (carried on 38033):** 378233   Ian Brown CBE

## CLASS 379   ELECTROSTAR   BOMBARDIER DERBY

New EMUs used on Liverpool Street–Stansted Airport and Liverpool Street–Cambridge services.

**Formation:** DMSO–MSO–PTSO–DMCO.
**System:** 25 kV AC overhead.
**Construction:** Welded aluminium alloy underframe, sides and roof with steel ends. All sections bolted together.
**Traction Motors:** Two Bombardier asynchronous of 200 kW.
**Wheel Arrangement:** 2-Bo + 2-Bo + 2-2 + Bo-2.

| | |
|---|---|
| **Braking:** Disc & regenerative. | **Dimensions:** 20.00 x 2.80 m. |
| **Bogies:** Bombardier P3-25/T3-25. | **Couplers:** Dellner 12. |
| **Gangways:** Throughout. | **Control System:** IGBT Inverter. |
| **Doors:** Sliding plug. | **Maximum Speed:** 100 mph. |

**Heating & ventilation:** Air conditioning.
**Seating Layout:** 1: 2+1 facing. 2: 2+2 facing/unidirectional.
**Multiple Working:** Within class and with Classes 375, 376, 377 and 378.

**DMSO**. Bombardier Derby 2010–11. –/60. 42.1 t.
**MSO**. Bombardier Derby 2010–11. –/62 1T. 38.6 t.
**PTSO**. Bombardier Derby 2010–11. –/43(2) 1TD 2W. 40.9 t.
**DMCO**. Bombardier Derby 2010–11. 20/24. 42.3 t.

| | | | | | | | | |
|---|---|---|---|---|---|---|---|---|
| 379001 | **NC** | MQ | *GA* | IL | 61201 | 61701 | 61901 | 62101 |
| 379002 | **NC** | MQ | *GA* | IL | 61202 | 61702 | 61902 | 62102 |
| 379003 | **NC** | MQ | *GA* | IL | 61203 | 61703 | 61903 | 62103 |
| 379004 | **NC** | MQ | *GA* | IL | 61204 | 61704 | 61904 | 62104 |
| 379005 | **NC** | MQ | *GA* | IL | 61205 | 61705 | 61905 | 62105 |
| 379006 | **NC** | MQ | *GA* | IL | 61206 | 61706 | 61906 | 62106 |
| 379007 | **NC** | MQ | *GA* | IL | 61207 | 61707 | 61907 | 62107 |
| 379008 | **NC** | MQ | *GA* | IL | 61208 | 61708 | 61908 | 62108 |
| 379009 | **NC** | MQ | *GA* | IL | 61209 | 61709 | 61909 | 62109 |
| 379010 | **NC** | MQ | *GA* | IL | 61210 | 61710 | 61910 | 62110 |
| 379011 | **NC** | MQ | *GA* | IL | 61211 | 61711 | 61911 | 62111 |
| 379012 | **NC** | MQ | *GA* | IL | 61212 | 61712 | 61912 | 62112 |
| 379013 | **NC** | MQ | *GA* | IL | 61213 | 61713 | 61913 | 62113 |
| 379014 | **NC** | MQ | *GA* | IL | 61214 | 61714 | 61914 | 62114 |
| 379015 | **NC** | MQ | *GA* | IL | 61215 | 61715 | 61915 | 62115 |
| 379016 | **NC** | MQ | *GA* | IL | 61216 | 61716 | 61916 | 62116 |
| 379017 | **NC** | MQ | *GA* | IL | 61217 | 61717 | 61917 | 62117 |
| 379018 | **NC** | MQ | *GA* | IL | 61218 | 61718 | 61918 | 62118 |
| 379019 | **NC** | MQ | *GA* | IL | 61219 | 61719 | 61919 | 62119 |
| 379020 | **NC** | MQ | *GA* | IL | 61220 | 61720 | 61920 | 62120 |
| 379021 | **NC** | MQ | *GA* | IL | 61221 | 61721 | 61921 | 62121 |
| 379022 | **NC** | MQ | *GA* | IL | 61222 | 61722 | 61922 | 62122 |
| 379023 | **NC** | MQ | *GA* | IL | 61223 | 61723 | 61923 | 62123 |
| 379024 | **NC** | MQ | *GA* | IL | 61224 | 61724 | 61924 | 62124 |
| 379025 | **NC** | MQ | *GA* | IL | 61225 | 61725 | 61925 | 62125 |
| 379026 | **NC** | MQ | *GA* | IL | 61226 | 61726 | 61926 | 62126 |
| 379027 | **NC** | MQ | *GA* | IL | 61227 | 61727 | 61927 | 62127 |
| 379028 | **NC** | MQ | *GA* | IL | 61228 | 61728 | 61928 | 62128 |
| 379029 | **NC** | MQ | *GA* | IL | 61229 | 61729 | 61929 | 62129 |
| 379030 | **NC** | MQ | *GA* | IL | 61230 | 61730 | 61930 | 62130 |

**Names (carried on end cars):**

| | | |
|---|---|---|
| 379005 | Stansted Express | 379015 City of Cambridge |
| 379011 | Ely Cathedral | 379025 Go Discover |
| 379012 | The West Anglian | |

---

## CLASS 380          DESIRO UK          SIEMENS

Used on Strathclyde area services and the Edinburgh–North Berwick route.

**Formation**: DMSO–PTSO–DMSO or DMSO–PTSO–TSO–DMSO.
**System**: 25 kV AC overhead.
**Construction**: Welded aluminium with steel ends.
**Traction Motors**: Four Siemens 1TB2016-0GB02 asynchronous of 250 kW.
**Wheel Arrangement**: Bo-Bo + 2-2 (+2-2) + Bo-Bo
**Braking**: Disc & regenerative.          **Dimensions**: 23.78/23.57 x 2.80 m.
**Bogies**: SGP SF5000.          **Couplers**: Voith.

**Gangways:** Throughout.
**Doors:** Sliding plug.
**Heating & ventilation:** Air conditioning.
**Multiple Working:** Within class.

**Control System:** IGBT Inverter.
**Maximum Speed:** 100 mph.
**Seating Layout:** 2+2 facing/unidirectional.

**DMSO(A).** Siemens Krefeld 2009–10. –/70. 45.0t.
**PTSO.** Siemens Krefeld 2009–10. –/57(12) 1TD 2W. 42.7t.
**TSO.** Siemens Krefeld 2009–10. –/74 1T. 34.8t.
**DMSO(B).** Siemens Krefeld 2009–10. –/64(5). 44.9t.

**Class 380/0.** 3-car units.

| | | | | | | | |
|---|---|---|---|---|---|---|---|
| 380001 | **SR** | E | *SR* | GW | 38501 | 38601 | 38701 |
| 380002 | **SR** | E | *SR* | GW | 38502 | 38602 | 38702 |
| 380003 | **SR** | E | *SR* | GW | 38503 | 38603 | 38703 |
| 380004 | **SR** | E | *SR* | GW | 38504 | 38604 | 38704 |
| 380005 | **SR** | E | *SR* | GW | 38505 | 38605 | 38705 |
| 380006 | **SR** | E | *SR* | GW | 38506 | 38606 | 38706 |
| 380007 | **SR** | E | *SR* | GW | 38507 | 38607 | 38707 |
| 380008 | **SR** | E | *SR* | GW | 38508 | 38608 | 38708 |
| 380009 | **SR** | E | *SR* | GW | 38509 | 38609 | 38709 |
| 380010 | **SR** | E | *SR* | GW | 38510 | 38610 | 38710 |
| 380011 | **SR** | E | *SR* | GW | 38511 | 38611 | 38711 |
| 380012 | **SR** | E | *SR* | GW | 38512 | 38612 | 38712 |
| 380013 | **SR** | E | *SR* | GW | 38513 | 38613 | 38713 |
| 380014 | **SR** | E | *SR* | GW | 38514 | 38614 | 38714 |
| 380015 | **SR** | E | *SR* | GW | 38515 | 38615 | 38715 |
| 380016 | **SR** | E | *SR* | GW | 38516 | 38616 | 38716 |
| 380017 | **SR** | E | *SR* | GW | 38517 | 38617 | 38717 |
| 380018 | **SR** | E | *SR* | GW | 38518 | 38618 | 38718 |
| 380019 | **SR** | E | *SR* | GW | 38519 | 38619 | 38719 |
| 380020 | **SR** | E | *SR* | GW | 38520 | 38620 | 38720 |
| 380021 | **SR** | E | *SR* | GW | 38521 | 38621 | 38721 |
| 380022 | **SR** | E | *SR* | GW | 38522 | 38622 | 38722 |

**Class 380/1.** 4-car units. 380 101–108 are fitted with NRN radios for working to North Berwick.

| | | | | | | | | |
|---|---|---|---|---|---|---|---|---|
| 380101 | **SR** | E | *SR* | GW | 38551 | 38651 | 38851 | 38751 |
| 380102 | **SR** | E | *SR* | GW | 38552 | 38652 | 38852 | 38752 |
| 380103 | **SR** | E | *SR* | GW | 38553 | 38653 | 38853 | 38753 |
| 380104 | **SR** | E | *SR* | GW | 38554 | 38654 | 38854 | 38754 |
| 380105 | **SR** | E | *SR* | GW | 38555 | 38655 | 38855 | 38755 |
| 380106 | **SR** | E | *SR* | GW | 38556 | 38656 | 38856 | 38756 |
| 380107 | **SR** | E | *SR* | GW | 38557 | 38657 | 38857 | 38757 |
| 380108 | **SR** | E | *SR* | GW | 38558 | 38658 | 38858 | 38758 |
| 380109 | **SR** | E | *SR* | GW | 38559 | 38659 | 38859 | 38759 |
| 380110 | **SR** | E | *SR* | GW | 38560 | 38660 | 38860 | 38760 |
| 380111 | **SR** | E | *SR* | GW | 38561 | 38661 | 38861 | 38761 |
| 380112 | **SR** | E | *SR* | GW | 38562 | 38662 | 38862 | 38762 |
| 380113 | **SR** | E | *SR* | GW | 38563 | 38663 | 38863 | 38763 |
| 380114 | **SR** | E | *SR* | GW | 38564 | 38664 | 38864 | 38764 |
| 380115 | **SR** | E | *SR* | GW | 38565 | 38665 | 38865 | 38765 |
| 380116 | **SR** | E | *SR* | GW | 38566 | 38666 | 38866 | 38766 |

# CLASS 387   ELECTROSTAR   BOMBARDIER DERBY

These 110 mph Electrostar units are on order to act as stop-gap rolling stock on the main Thameslink route until the new Class 700s are available. The Class 387s will be the first units to feature 6-digit vehicle numbers. Under construction and due for delivery 2014–15. Full details awaited.

**Formation:** DMSO–MSO–PTSO–DMSO.
**System:** 25 kV AC overhead and 750 V DC third rail.
**Construction:** Welded aluminium alloy underframe, sides and roof with steel ends. All sections bolted together.
**Traction Motors:**
**Wheel Arrangement:**
**Braking:** Disc & regenerative.          **Dimensions:**
**Bogies:**                                **Couplers:**
**Gangways:** Throughout.                  **Control System:** IGBT Inverter.
**Doors:** Sliding plug.                   **Maximum Speed:** 110 mph.
**Heating & ventilation:** Air conditioning.
**Seating Layout:**                        **Multiple Working:**

**DMSO.** Bombardier Derby 2014–15.     .     t.
**MSO.** Bombardier Derby 2014–15.      .     t.
**PTSO.** Bombardier Derby 2014–15.     .     t.
**DMSO.** Bombardier Derby 2014–15.     .     t.

| | | | |
|---|---|---|---|
| 387 101 | 421101 | 422101 | 423101 | 424101 |
| 387 102 | 421102 | 422102 | 423102 | 424102 |
| 387 103 | 421103 | 422103 | 423103 | 424103 |
| 387 104 | 421104 | 422104 | 423104 | 424104 |
| 387 105 | 421105 | 422105 | 423105 | 424105 |
| 387 106 | 421106 | 422106 | 423106 | 424106 |
| 387 107 | 421107 | 422107 | 423107 | 424107 |
| 387 108 | 421108 | 422108 | 423108 | 424108 |
| 387 109 | 421109 | 422109 | 423109 | 424109 |
| 387 110 | 421110 | 422110 | 423110 | 424110 |
| 387 111 | 421111 | 422111 | 423111 | 424111 |
| 387 112 | 421112 | 422112 | 423112 | 424112 |
| 387 113 | 421113 | 422113 | 423113 | 424113 |
| 387 114 | 421114 | 422114 | 423114 | 424114 |
| 387 115 | 421115 | 422115 | 423115 | 424115 |
| 387 116 | 421116 | 422116 | 423116 | 424116 |
| 387 117 | 421117 | 422117 | 423117 | 424117 |
| 387 118 | 421118 | 422118 | 423118 | 424118 |
| 387 119 | 421119 | 422119 | 423119 | 424119 |
| 387 120 | 421120 | 422120 | 423120 | 424120 |
| 387 121 | 421121 | 422121 | 423121 | 424121 |
| 387 122 | 421122 | 422122 | 423122 | 424122 |
| 387 123 | 421123 | 422123 | 423123 | 424123 |
| 387 124 | 421124 | 422124 | 423124 | 424124 |
| 387 125 | 421125 | 422125 | 423125 | 424125 |
| 387 126 | 421126 | 422126 | 423126 | 424126 |
| 387 127 | 421127 | 422127 | 423127 | 424127 |

| 387 128 | | | | 421128 | 422128 | 423128 | 424128 |
| 387 129 | | | | 421129 | 422129 | 423129 | 424129 |

## CLASS 390      PENDOLINO      ALSTOM

Tilting West Coast Main Line units.

**Formations:** As listed below.
**Construction:** Welded aluminium alloy.
**Traction Motors:** Two Alstom ONIX 800 of 425 kW.
**Wheel Arrangement:** 1A-A1 + 1A-A1 + 2-2 + 1A-A1 (+ 2-2 + 1A-A1) + 2-2 + 1A-A1 + 2-2 + 1A-A1 + 1A-A1.
**Braking:** Disc, rheostatic & regenerative.
**Dimensions:** 24.80/23.90 x 2.73 m.
**Couplers:** Dellner 12.
**Bogies:** Fiat-SIG.
**Control System:** IGBT Inverter.
**Gangways:** Within unit.
**Maximum Speed:** 125 mph.
**Doors:** Sliding plug.
**Heating & ventilation:** Air conditioning.
**Seating Layout:** 1: 2+1 facing/unidirectional, 2: 2+2 facing/unidirectional.
**Multiple Working:** Within class. Can also be controlled from Class 57/3 locos.

Units up to 390034 were delivered as 8-car sets, without the TSO (688xx). During 2004–05 these units were increased to 9-cars.

62 extra vehicles were built 2010–12 to lengthen 31 sets to 11-cars. On renumbering units were renumbered by adding 100 to the set number. Four new complete 11-car units were also delivered. All these extra vehicles were built at Savigliano in Italy (all original Pendolino vehicles were built at Birmingham).

390033 was written off in the Lambrigg accident of February 2007.

**Advertising livery:** 390 104 – Black Alstom vinyls on Virgin silver livery.

**DMRFO:** Alstom Birmingham/Savigliano 2001–05/2010–12. 18/–. 56.3 t.
**MFO(A):** Alstom Birmingham/Savigliano 2001–05/2010–12. 37/–(2) 1TD 1W. 52.3 t.
**PTFO:** Alstom Birmingham/Savigliano 2001–05/2010–12. 44/– 1T. 51.2 t.
**MFO(B):** Alstom Birmingham/Savigliano 2001–05/2010–12. 46/– 1T. 52.3 t.
**(TSO:** Alstom Savigliano 2010–12. –/74 1T. 49.2 t.)
**(MSO:** Alstom Savigliano 2010–12. –/76 1T. 52.2 t.)
**TSO:** Alstom Birmingham/Savigliano 2001–05/2010–12. –/76 1T. 45.5 t.
**MSO(A):** Alstom Birmingham/Savigliano 2001–05/2010–12. –/62(4) 1TD 1W. 52.0 t.
**PTSRMB:** Alstom Birmingham/Savigliano 2001–05/2010–12. –/48. 53.2 t.
**MSO(B):** Alstom Birmingham/Savigliano 2001–05/2010–12. –/62(2) 1TD 1W. 52.5 t.
**DMSO:** Alstom Birmingham/Savigliano 2001–05/2010–12. –/46 1T. 54.5 t.

**Class 390/0.** Original build 9-car units.
**Formation:** DMRFO–MFO–PTFO–MFO–TSO–MSO–PTSRMB–MSO–DMSO.

| 390 001 | **VT** | A | *VW* | MA | 69101 | 69401 | 69501 | 69601 | 68801 |
| | | | | | 69701 | 69801 | 69901 | 69201 | |
| 390 002 | **VT** | A | *VW* | MA | 69102 | 69402 | 69502 | 69602 | 68802 |
| | | | | | 69702 | 69802 | 69902 | 69202 | |
| 390 005 | **VT** | A | *VW* | MA | 69105 | 69405 | 69505 | 69605 | 68805 |
| | | | | | 69705 | 69805 | 69905 | 69205 | |
| 390 006 | **VT** | A | *VW* | MA | 69106 | 69406 | 69506 | 69606 | 68806 |
| | | | | | 69706 | 69806 | 69906 | 69206 | |
| 390 008 | **VT** | A | *VW* | MA | 69108 | 69408 | 69508 | 69608 | 68808 |
| | | | | | 69708 | 69808 | 69908 | 69208 | |

| 390 009 | **VT** | A | *VW* MA | 69109 | 69409 | 69509 | 69609 | 68809 |
| | | | | 69709 | 69809 | 69909 | 69209 | |
| 390 010 | **VT** | A | *VW* MA | 69110 | 69410 | 69510 | 69610 | 68810 |
| | | | | 69710 | 69810 | 69910 | 69210 | |
| 390 011 | **VT** | A | *VW* MA | 69111 | 69411 | 69511 | 69611 | 68811 |
| | | | | 69711 | 69811 | 69911 | 69211 | |
| 390 013 | **VT** | A | *VW* MA | 69113 | 69413 | 69513 | 69613 | 68813 |
| | | | | 69713 | 69813 | 69913 | 69213 | |
| 390 016 | **VT** | A | *VW* MA | 69116 | 69416 | 69516 | 69616 | 68816 |
| | | | | 69716 | 69816 | 69916 | 69216 | |
| 390 020 | **VT** | A | *VW* MA | 69120 | 69420 | 69520 | 69620 | 68820 |
| | | | | 69720 | 69820 | 69920 | 69220 | |
| 390 039 | **VT** | A | *VW* MA | 69139 | 69439 | 69539 | 69639 | 68839 |
| | | | | 69739 | 69839 | 69939 | 69239 | |
| 390 040 | **VT** | A | *VW* MA | 69140 | 69440 | 69540 | 69640 | 68840 |
| | | | | 69740 | 69840 | 69940 | 69240 | |
| 390 042 | **VT** | A | *VW* MA | 69142 | 69442 | 69542 | 69642 | 68842 |
| | | | | 69742 | 69842 | 69942 | 69242 | |
| 390 043 | **VT** | A | *VW* MA | 69143 | 69443 | 69543 | 69643 | 68843 |
| | | | | 69743 | 69843 | 69943 | 69243 | |
| 390 044 | **VT** | A | *VW* MA | 69144 | 69444 | 69544 | 69644 | 68844 |
| | | | | 69744 | 69844 | 69944 | 69244 | |
| 390 045 | **VT** | A | *VW* MA | 69145 | 69445 | 69545 | 69645 | 68845 |
| | | | | 69745 | 69845 | 69945 | 69245 | |
| 390 046 | **VT** | A | *VW* MA | 69146 | 69446 | 69546 | 69646 | 68846 |
| | | | | 69746 | 69846 | 69946 | 69246 | |
| 390 047 | **VT** | A | *VW* MA | 69147 | 69447 | 69547 | 69647 | 68847 |
| | | | | 69747 | 69847 | 69947 | 69247 | |
| 390 049 | **VT** | A | *VW* MA | 69149 | 69449 | 69549 | 69649 | 68849 |
| | | | | 69749 | 69849 | 69949 | 69249 | |
| 390 050 | **VT** | A | *VW* MA | 69150 | 69450 | 69550 | 69650 | 68850 |
| | | | | 69750 | 69850 | 69950 | 69250 | |

**Class 390/1**. Original build 9-car units now extended to 11-cars, except 390 154–157 which were built new as 11-cars.
**Formation**: DMRFO–MFO–PTFO–MFO–TSO–MSO–TSO–MSO–PTSRMB–MSO–DMSO.

| 390 103 | **VT** | A | *VW* MA | 69103 | 69403 | 69503 | 69603 | 65303 | 68903 |
| | | | | 68803 | 69703 | 69803 | 69903 | 69203 | |
| 390 104 | **AL** | A | *VW* MA | 69104 | 69404 | 69504 | 69604 | 65304 | 68904 |
| | | | | 68804 | 69704 | 69804 | 69904 | 69204 | |
| 390 107 | **VT** | A | *VW* MA | 69107 | 69407 | 69507 | 69607 | 65307 | 68907 |
| | | | | 68807 | 69707 | 69807 | 69907 | 69207 | |
| 390 112 | **VT** | A | *VW* MA | 69112 | 69412 | 69512 | 69612 | 65312 | 68912 |
| | | | | 68812 | 69712 | 69812 | 69912 | 69212 | |
| 390 114 | **VT** | A | *VW* MA | 69114 | 69414 | 69514 | 69614 | 65314 | 68914 |
| | | | | 68814 | 69714 | 69814 | 69914 | 69214 | |
| 390 115 | **VT** | A | *VW* MA | 69115 | 69415 | 69515 | 69615 | 65315 | 68915 |
| | | | | 68815 | 69715 | 69815 | 69915 | 69215 | |
| 390 117 | **VT** | A | *VW* MA | 69117 | 69417 | 69517 | 69617 | 65317 | 68917 |
| | | | | 68817 | 69717 | 69817 | 69917 | 69217 | |

| | | | | | | | | | | |
|---|---|---|---|---|---|---|---|---|---|---|
| 390 118 | **VT** | A | *VW* MA | 69118 | 69418 | 69518 | 69618 | 65318 | 68918 | |
| | | | | 68818 | 69718 | 69818 | 69918 | 69218 | | |
| 390 119 | **VT** | A | *VW* MA | 69119 | 69419 | 69519 | 69619 | 65319 | 68919 | |
| | | | | 68819 | 69719 | 69819 | 69919 | 69219 | | |
| 390 121 | **VT** | A | *VW* MA | 69121 | 69421 | 69521 | 69621 | 65321 | 68921 | |
| | | | | 68821 | 69721 | 69821 | 69921 | 69221 | | |
| 390 122 | **VT** | A | *VW* MA | 69122 | 69422 | 69522 | 69622 | 65322 | 68922 | |
| | | | | 68822 | 69722 | 69822 | 69922 | 69222 | | |
| 390 123 | **VT** | A | *VW* MA | 69123 | 69423 | 69523 | 69623 | 65323 | 68923 | |
| | | | | 68823 | 69723 | 69823 | 69923 | 69223 | | |
| 390 124 | **VT** | A | *VW* MA | 69124 | 69424 | 69524 | 69624 | 65324 | 68924 | |
| | | | | 68824 | 69724 | 69824 | 69924 | 69224 | | |
| 390 125 | **VT** | A | *VW* MA | 69125 | 69425 | 69525 | 69625 | 65325 | 68925 | |
| | | | | 68825 | 69725 | 69825 | 69925 | 69225 | | |
| 390 126 | **VT** | A | *VW* MA | 69126 | 69426 | 69526 | 69626 | 65326 | 68926 | |
| | | | | 68826 | 69726 | 69826 | 69926 | 69226 | | |
| 390 127 | **VT** | A | *VW* MA | 69127 | 69427 | 69527 | 69627 | 65327 | 68927 | |
| | | | | 68827 | 69727 | 69827 | 69927 | 69227 | | |
| 390 128 | **VT** | A | *VW* MA | 69128 | 69428 | 69528 | 69628 | 65328 | 68928 | |
| | | | | 68828 | 69728 | 69828 | 69928 | 69228 | | |
| 390 129 | **VT** | A | *VW* MA | 69129 | 69429 | 69529 | 69629 | 65329 | 68929 | |
| | | | | 68829 | 69729 | 69829 | 69929 | 69229 | | |
| 390 130 | **VT** | A | *VW* MA | 69130 | 69430 | 69530 | 69630 | 65330 | 68930 | |
| | | | | 68830 | 69730 | 69830 | 69930 | 69230 | | |
| 390 131 | **VT** | A | *VW* MA | 69131 | 69431 | 69531 | 69631 | 65331 | 68931 | |
| | | | | 68831 | 69731 | 69831 | 69931 | 69231 | | |
| 390 132 | **VT** | A | *VW* MA | 69132 | 69432 | 69532 | 69632 | 65332 | 68932 | |
| | | | | 68832 | 69732 | 69832 | 69932 | 69232 | | |
| 390 134 | **VT** | A | *VW* MA | 69134 | 69434 | 69534 | 69634 | 65334 | 68934 | |
| | | | | 68834 | 69734 | 69834 | 69934 | 69234 | | |
| 390 135 | **VT** | A | *VW* MA | 69135 | 69435 | 69535 | 69635 | 65335 | 68935 | |
| | | | | 68835 | 69735 | 69835 | 69935 | 69235 | | |
| 390 136 | **VT** | A | *VW* MA | 69136 | 69436 | 69536 | 69636 | 65336 | 68936 | |
| | | | | 68836 | 69736 | 69836 | 69936 | 69236 | | |
| 390 137 | **VT** | A | *VW* MA | 69137 | 69437 | 69537 | 69637 | 65337 | 68937 | |
| | | | | 68837 | 69737 | 69837 | 69937 | 69237 | | |
| 390 138 | **VT** | A | *VW* MA | 69138 | 69438 | 69538 | 69638 | 65338 | 68938 | |
| | | | | 68838 | 69738 | 69838 | 69938 | 69238 | | |
| 390 141 | **VT** | A | *VW* MA | 69141 | 69441 | 69541 | 69641 | 65341 | 68941 | |
| | | | | 68841 | 69741 | 69841 | 69941 | 69241 | | |
| 390 148 | **VT** | A | *VW* MA | 69148 | 69448 | 69548 | 69648 | 65348 | 68948 | |
| | | | | 68848 | 69748 | 69848 | 69948 | 69248 | | |
| 390 151 | **VT** | A | *VW* MA | 69151 | 69451 | 69551 | 69651 | 65351 | 68951 | |
| | | | | 68851 | 69751 | 69851 | 69951 | 69251 | | |
| 390 152 | **VT** | A | *VW* MA | 69152 | 69452 | 69552 | 69652 | 65352 | 68952 | |
| | | | | 68852 | 69752 | 69852 | 69952 | 69252 | | |
| 390 153 | **VT** | A | *VW* MA | 69153 | 69453 | 69553 | 69653 | 65353 | 68953 | |
| | | | | 68853 | 69753 | 69853 | 69953 | 69253 | | |
| 390 154 | **VT** | A | *VW* MA | 69154 | 69454 | 69554 | 69654 | 65354 | 68954 | |
| | | | | 68854 | 69754 | 69854 | 69954 | 69254 | | |

| 390 155 | **VT** | A | *VW* MA | 69155 69455 69555 69655 65355 68955 |
| | | | | 68855 69755 69855 69955 69255 |
| 390 156 | **VT** | A | *VW* MA | 69156 69456 69556 69656 65356 68956 |
| | | | | 68856 69756 69856 69956 69256 |
| 390 157 | **VT** | A | *VW* MA | 69157 69457 69557 69657 65357 68957 |
| | | | | 68857 69757 69857 69957 69257 |

## Names (carried on MFO No. 696xx):

| | | | |
|---|---|---|---|
| 390 001 | Virgin Pioneer | 390 117 | Virgin Prince |
| 390 002 | Virgin Angel | 390 118 | Virgin Princess |
| 390 005 | City of Wolverhampton | 390 119 | Virgin Warrior |
| 390 006 | Tate Liverpool | 390 121 | Virgin Dream |
| 390 008 | Virgin King | 390 122 | Penny the Pendolino |
| 390 009 | Treaty of Union | 390 123 | Virgin Glory |
| 390 010 | A Decade of Progress | 390 124 | Virgin Venturer |
| 390 011 | City of Lichfield | 390 125 | Virgin Stagecoach |
| 390 013 | Virgin Spirit | 390 126 | Virgin Enterprise |
| 390 016 | Virgin Champion | 390 127 | Virgin Buccaneer |
| 390 020 | Virgin Cavalier | 390 128 | City of Preston |
| 390 039 | Virgin Quest | 390 129 | City of Stoke-on-Trent |
| 390 040 | Virgin Pathfinder | 390 130 | City of Edinburgh |
| 390 042 | City of Bangor/Dinas Bangor | 390 131 | City of Liverpool |
| 390 043 | Virgin Explorer | 390 132 | City of Birmingham |
| 390 044 | Virgin Lionheart | 390 134 | City of Carlisle |
| 390 045 | 101 Squadron | 390 135 | City of Lancaster |
| 390 046 | Virgin Soldiers | 390 136 | City of Coventry |
| 390 047 | CLIC Sargent | 390 137 | Virgin Difference |
| 390 049 | Virgin Express | 390 138 | City of London |
| 390 050 | Virgin Invader | 390 141 | City of Chester |
| 390 103 | Virgin Hero | 390 148 | Virgin Harrier |
| 390 104 | Alstom Pendolino | 390 151 | Virgin Ambassador |
| 390 107 | Virgin Lady | 390 152 | Virgin Knight |
| 390 112 | Virgin Star | 390 153 | Mission Accomplished |
| 390 114 | City of Manchester | 390 156 | Stockport 170 |
| 390 115 | Virgin Crusader | 390 157 | Chad Varah |

## Additional names (carried on the front ends):

| | | | |
|---|---|---|---|
| 390 107 | Abigail Irozuru | 390 127 | Jessica Varnish |
| 390 122 | Beth Tweddle MBE | 390 152 | Alison Waters |

# CLASS 395   HS1 DOMESTIC SETS   HITACHI JAPAN

6-car dual-voltage units used on Southeastern High Speed services from St Pancras to Ashford/Dover/Margate via Ramsgate and Faversham.

**Formation:** PDTSO–MSO–MSO–MSO–MSO–PDTSO.
**Systems:** 25 kV AC overhead/750 V DC third rail.
**Construction:** Aluminium.
**Traction Motors:** Hitachi asynchronous of 210 kW.
**Wheel Arrangement:** 2-2 + Bo-Bo + Bo-Bo + Bo-Bo + Bo-Bo + 2-2.
**Braking:** Disc, rheostatic & regenerative braking.
**Dimensions:** 20.88/20.0 x 2.81 m.    **Couplers:** Scharfenberg.
**Bogies:** Hitachi.                     **Control System:** IGBT Inverter.

**Gangways:** Within unit.
**Doors:** Single-leaf sliding.
**Maximum Speed:** 140 mph.
**Multiple Working:** Within class only.
**Heating & ventilation:** Air conditioning.
**Seating Layout:** 2+2 facing/unidirectional (mainly unidirectional).

**PDTSO(A):** Hitachi Kasado, Japan 2006–09. –/28(12) 1TD 2W. 46.7 t.
**MSO:** Hitachi Kasado, Japan 2006–09. –/66. 45.0t–45.7 t.
**PDTSO(B):** Hitachi Kasado, Japan 2006–09. –/48 1T. 46.7 t.

| | | | | | | | | | | |
|---|---|---|---|---|---|---|---|---|---|---|
| 395001 | **SB** | E | *SE* | AD | 39011 | 39012 | 39013 | 39014 | 39015 | 39016 |
| 395002 | **SB** | E | *SE* | AD | 39021 | 39022 | 39023 | 39024 | 39025 | 39026 |
| 395003 | **SB** | E | *SE* | AD | 39031 | 39032 | 39033 | 39034 | 39035 | 39036 |
| 395004 | **SB** | E | *SE* | AD | 39041 | 39042 | 39043 | 39044 | 39045 | 39046 |
| 395005 | **SB** | E | *SE* | AD | 39051 | 39052 | 39053 | 39054 | 39055 | 39056 |
| 395006 | **SB** | E | *SE* | AD | 39061 | 39062 | 39063 | 39064 | 39065 | 39066 |
| 395007 | **SB** | E | *SE* | AD | 39071 | 39072 | 39073 | 39074 | 39075 | 39076 |
| 395008 | **SB** | E | *SE* | AD | 39081 | 39082 | 39083 | 39084 | 39085 | 39086 |
| 395009 | **SB** | E | *SE* | AD | 39091 | 39092 | 39093 | 39094 | 39095 | 39096 |
| 395010 | **SB** | E | *SE* | AD | 39101 | 39102 | 39103 | 39104 | 39105 | 39106 |
| 395011 | **SB** | E | *SE* | AD | 39111 | 39112 | 39113 | 39114 | 39115 | 39116 |
| 395012 | **SB** | E | *SE* | AD | 39121 | 39122 | 39123 | 39124 | 39125 | 39126 |
| 395013 | **SB** | E | *SE* | AD | 39131 | 39132 | 39133 | 39134 | 39135 | 39136 |
| 395014 | **SB** | E | *SE* | AD | 39141 | 39142 | 39143 | 39144 | 39145 | 39146 |
| 395015 | **SB** | E | *SE* | AD | 39151 | 39152 | 39153 | 39154 | 39155 | 39156 |
| 395016 | **SB** | E | *SE* | AD | 39161 | 39162 | 39163 | 39164 | 39165 | 39166 |
| 395017 | **SB** | E | *SE* | AD | 39171 | 39172 | 39173 | 39174 | 39175 | 39176 |
| 395018 | **SB** | E | *SE* | AD | 39181 | 39182 | 39183 | 39184 | 39185 | 39186 |
| 395019 | **SB** | E | *SE* | AD | 39191 | 39192 | 39193 | 39194 | 39195 | 39196 |
| 395020 | **SB** | E | *SE* | AD | 39201 | 39202 | 39203 | 39204 | 39205 | 39206 |
| 395021 | **SB** | E | *SE* | AD | 39211 | 39212 | 39213 | 39214 | 39215 | 39216 |
| 395022 | **SB** | E | *SE* | AD | 39221 | 39222 | 39223 | 39224 | 39225 | 39226 |
| 395023 | **SB** | E | *SE* | AD | 39231 | 39232 | 39233 | 39234 | 39235 | 39236 |
| 395024 | **SB** | E | *SE* | AD | 39241 | 39242 | 39243 | 39244 | 39245 | 39246 |
| 395025 | **SB** | E | *SE* | AD | 39251 | 39252 | 39253 | 39254 | 39255 | 39256 |
| 395026 | **SB** | E | *SE* | AD | 39261 | 39262 | 39263 | 39264 | 39265 | 39266 |
| 395027 | **SB** | E | *SE* | AD | 39271 | 39272 | 39273 | 39274 | 39275 | 39276 |
| 395028 | **SB** | E | *SE* | AD | 39281 | 39282 | 39283 | 39284 | 39285 | 39286 |
| 395029 | **SB** | E | *SE* | AD | 39291 | 39292 | 39293 | 39294 | 39295 | 39296 |

**Names (carried on end cars):**

| | | | |
|---|---|---|---|
| 395001 | Dame Kelly Holmes | 395018 | Mo Farah |
| 395002 | Sebastian Coe | 395019 | Jessica Ennis |
| 395003 | Sir Steve Redgrave | 395020 | Jason Kenny |
| 395004 | Sir Chris Hoy | 395021 | Ed Clancy MBE |
| 395005 | Dame Tanni Grey-Thompson | 395022 | Alistair Brownlee |
| 395006 | Daley Thompson | 395023 | Ellie Simmonds |
| 395007 | Steve Backley | 395024 | Jonnie Peacock |
| 395008 | Ben Ainslie | 395025 | Victoria Pendleton |
| 395009 | Rebecca Adlington | 395026 | Marc Woods |
| 395010 | Duncan Goodhew | 395027 | Hannah Cockcroft |
| 395011 | Katherine Grainger | 395028 | Laura Trott |
| 395016 | Jamie Staff | 395029 | David Weir |
| 395017 | Dame Sarah Storey | | |

# 4.2. 750 V DC THIRD RAIL EMUs

These classes use the third rail system at 750 V DC (unless stated). Outer couplers are buckeyes on units built before 1982 with bar couplers within the units. Newer units generally have Dellner outer couplers.

## CLASS 442        WESSEX EXPRESS        BREL DERBY

Stock built for Waterloo–Bournemouth–Weymouth services. Previously used by South West Trains, all units now used by Southern, principally on Victoria–Gatwick Airport–Brighton services.

**Formation:** DTSO(A)–TSO–MBC–TSO(W)–DTSO(B).
**Construction:** Steel.
**Traction Motors:** Four EE546 of 300 kW recovered from Class 432s.
**Wheel Arrangement:** 2-2 + 2-2 + Bo-Bo + 2-2 + 2-2.
**Braking:** Disc.                          **Dimensions:** 23.15/23.00 x 2.74 m.
**Bogies:** Two BREL P7 motor bogies (MBSO). T4 bogies (trailer cars).
**Couplers:** Buckeye.                      **Control System:** 1986-type.
**Gangways:** Throughout.                   **Maximum Speed:** 100 mph.
**Doors:** Sliding plug.                    **Heating & Ventilation:** Air conditioning.
**Seating Layout:** 1: 2+1 facing, 2: 2+2 mainly unidirectional.
**Multiple Working:** Within class and Class 33/1 & 73 locos in an emergency.

DTSO(A). Lot No. 31030 Derby 1988–89. –/74. 38.5 t.
TSO. Lot No. 31032 Derby 1988–89. –/76 2T. 34.5 t.
MBC. Lot No. 31034 Derby 1988–89. 24/28. 55.0 t.
TSO(W). Lot No. 31033 Derby 1988–89. –/66(4) 1TD 1T 2W. 37.8 t.
DTSO(B). Lot No. 31031 Derby 1988–89. –/74. 37.3 t.

| | | | | | | | | |
|---|---|---|---|---|---|---|---|---|
| 442 401 | GV | A | SN | SL | 77382 | 71818 | 62937 | 71842 77414 |
| 442 402 | GV | A | SN | SL | 77383 | 71819 | 62938 | 71843 77407 |
| 442 403 | GV | A | SN | SL | 77384 | 71820 | 62941 | 71844 77408 |
| 442 404 | GV | A | SN | SL | 77385 | 71821 | 62939 | 71845 77409 |
| 442 405 | GV | A | SN | SL | 77386 | 71822 | 62944 | 71846 77410 |
| 442 406 | GV | A | SN | SL | 77389 | 71823 | 62942 | 71847 77411 |
| 442 407 | GV | A | SN | SL | 77388 | 71824 | 62943 | 71848 77412 |
| 442 408 | GV | A | SN | SL | 77387 | 71825 | 62945 | 71849 77413 |
| 442 409 | GV | A | SN | SL | 77390 | 71826 | 62946 | 71850 77406 |
| 442 410 | GV | A | SN | SL | 77391 | 71827 | 62948 | 71851 77415 |
| 442 411 | GV | A | SN | SL | 77392 | 71828 | 62940 | 71858 77422 |
| 442 412 | GV | A | SN | SL | 77393 | 71829 | 62947 | 71853 77417 |
| 442 413 | GV | A | SN | SL | 77394 | 71830 | 62949 | 71854 77418 |
| 442 414 | GV | A | SN | SL | 77395 | 71831 | 62950 | 71855 77419 |
| 442 415 | GV | A | SN | SL | 77396 | 71832 | 62951 | 71856 77420 |
| 442 416 | GV | A | SN | SL | 77397 | 71833 | 62952 | 71857 77421 |
| 442 417 | GV | A | SN | SL | 77398 | 71834 | 62953 | 71852 77416 |
| 442 418 | GV | A | SN | SL | 77399 | 71835 | 62954 | 71859 77423 |
| 442 419 | GV | A | SN | SL | 77400 | 71836 | 62955 | 71860 77424 |
| 442 420 | GV | A | SN | SL | 77401 | 71837 | 62956 | 71861 77425 |
| 442 421 | GV | A | SN | SL | 77402 | 71838 | 62957 | 71862 77426 |

| 442422 | **GV** | A | *SN* | SL | 77403 71839 62958 71863 77427 |
| 442423 | **GV** | A | *SN* | SL | 77404 71840 62959 71864 77428 |
| 442424 | **GV** | A | *SN* | SL | 77405 71841 62960 71865 77429 |

## CLASS 444          DESIRO UK          SIEMENS

Express units.

**Formation:** DMCO–TSO–TSO–TSORMB–DMSO.
**Construction:** Aluminium.
**Traction Motors:** 4 Siemens 1TB2016-0GB02 asynchronous of 250 kW.
**Wheel Arrangement:** Bo-Bo + 2-2 + 2-2 + 2-2 + Bo-Bo.
**Braking:** Disc, rheostatic & regenerative. **Dimensions:** 23.57 x 2.80 m.
**Bogies:** SGP SF5000.                    **Couplers:** Dellner 12.
**Gangways:** Throughout.                 **Control System:** IGBT Inverter.
**Doors:** Single-leaf sliding plug.       **Maximum Speed:** 100 mph.
**Heating & Ventilation:** Air conditioning.
**Seating Layout:** 1: 2+1 facing/unidirectional, 2: 2+2 facing/unidirectional.
**Multiple Working:** Within class and with Class 450.

**DMSO.** Siemens Vienna/Krefeld 2003–04. –/76. 51.3t.
**TSO 67101–145.** Siemens Vienna/Krefeld 2003–04. –/76 1T. 40.3t.
**TSO 67151–195.** Siemens Vienna/Krefeld 2003–04. –/76 1T. 36.8t.
**TSORMB.** Siemens Vienna/Krefeld 2003–04. –/47 1T 1TD 2W. 42.1t.
**DMCO.** Siemens Vienna/Krefeld 2003–04. 35/24. 51.3t.

| 444001 | **ST** | A | *SW* | NT | 63801 67101 67151 67201 63851 |
| 444002 | **ST** | A | *SW* | NT | 63802 67102 67152 67202 63852 |
| 444003 | **ST** | A | *SW* | NT | 63803 67103 67153 67203 63853 |
| 444004 | **ST** | A | *SW* | NT | 63804 67104 67154 67204 63854 |
| 444005 | **ST** | A | *SW* | NT | 63805 67105 67155 67205 63855 |
| 444006 | **ST** | A | *SW* | NT | 63806 67106 67156 67206 63856 |
| 444007 | **ST** | A | *SW* | NT | 63807 67107 67157 67207 63857 |
| 444008 | **ST** | A | *SW* | NT | 63808 67108 67158 67208 63858 |
| 444009 | **ST** | A | *SW* | NT | 63809 67109 67159 67209 63859 |
| 444010 | **ST** | A | *SW* | NT | 63810 67110 67160 67210 63860 |
| 444011 | **ST** | A | *SW* | NT | 63811 67111 67161 67211 63861 |
| 444012 | **ST** | A | *SW* | NT | 63812 67112 67162 67212 63862 |
| 444013 | **ST** | A | *SW* | NT | 63813 67113 67163 67213 63863 |
| 444014 | **ST** | A | *SW* | NT | 63814 67114 67164 67214 63864 |
| 444015 | **ST** | A | *SW* | NT | 63815 67115 67165 67215 63865 |
| 444016 | **ST** | A | *SW* | NT | 63816 67116 67166 67216 63866 |
| 444017 | **ST** | A | *SW* | NT | 63817 67117 67167 67217 63867 |
| 444018 | **ST** | A | *SW* | NT | 63818 67118 67168 67218 63868 |
| 444019 | **ST** | A | *SW* | NT | 63819 67119 67169 67219 63869 |
| 444020 | **ST** | A | *SW* | NT | 63820 67120 67170 67220 63870 |
| 444021 | **ST** | A | *SW* | NT | 63821 67121 67171 67221 63871 |
| 444022 | **ST** | A | *SW* | NT | 63822 67122 67172 67222 63872 |
| 444023 | **ST** | A | *SW* | NT | 63823 67123 67173 67223 63873 |
| 444024 | **ST** | A | *SW* | NT | 63824 67124 67174 67224 63874 |
| 444025 | **ST** | A | *SW* | NT | 63825 67125 67175 67225 63875 |
| 444026 | **ST** | A | *SW* | NT | 63826 67126 67176 67226 63876 |

| 444027 | **ST** | A | *SW* | NT | 63827 67127 67177 67227 63877 |
| 444028 | **ST** | A | *SW* | NT | 63828 67128 67178 67228 63878 |
| 444029 | **ST** | A | *SW* | NT | 63829 67129 67179 67229 63879 |
| 444030 | **ST** | A | *SW* | NT | 63830 67130 67180 67230 63880 |
| 444031 | **ST** | A | *SW* | NT | 63831 67131 67181 67231 63881 |
| 444032 | **ST** | A | *SW* | NT | 63832 67132 67182 67232 63882 |
| 444033 | **ST** | A | *SW* | NT | 63833 67133 67183 67233 63883 |
| 444034 | **ST** | A | *SW* | NT | 63834 67134 67184 67234 63884 |
| 444035 | **ST** | A | *SW* | NT | 63835 67135 67185 67235 63885 |
| 444036 | **ST** | A | *SW* | NT | 63836 67136 67186 67236 63886 |
| 444037 | **ST** | A | *SW* | NT | 63837 67137 67187 67237 63887 |
| 444038 | **ST** | A | *SW* | NT | 63838 67138 67188 67238 63888 |
| 444039 | **ST** | A | *SW* | NT | 63839 67139 67189 67239 63889 |
| 444040 | **ST** | A | *SW* | NT | 63840 67140 67190 67240 63890 |
| 444041 | **ST** | A | *SW* | NT | 63841 67141 67191 67241 63891 |
| 444042 | **ST** | A | *SW* | NT | 63842 67142 67192 67242 63892 |
| 444043 | **ST** | A | *SW* | NT | 63843 67143 67193 67243 63893 |
| 444044 | **ST** | A | *SW* | NT | 63844 67144 67194 67244 63894 |
| 444045 | **ST** | A | *SW* | NT | 63845 67145 67195 67245 63895 |

**Names (carried on TSORMB):**

| | | | |
|---|---|---|---|
| 444001 | NAOMI HOUSE | 444018 | THE FAB 444 |
| 444012 | DESTINATION WEYMOUTH | 444038 | SOUTH WESTERN RAILWAY |

## CLASS 450      DESIRO UK      SIEMENS

Outer suburban units.

**Formation:** DMSO–TCO–TSO–DMSO (DMSO–TSO–TCO–DMSO 450 111–127).
**Construction:** Aluminium.
**Traction Motors:** 4 Siemens 1TB2016-0GB02 asynchronous of 250 kW.
**Wheel Arrangement:** Bo-Bo + 2-2 + 2-2 + Bo-Bo.
**Braking:** Disc, rheostatic & regenerative. **Dimensions:** 20.34 x 2.79 m.
**Bogies:** SGP SF5000. **Couplers:** Dellner 12.
**Gangways:** Throughout. **Control System:** IGBT Inverter.
**Doors:** Sliding plug. **Maximum Speed:** 100 mph.
**Heating & Ventilation:** Air conditioning.
**Seating Layout:** 1: 2+2 facing/unidirectional, 2: 3+2 facing/unidirectional.
**Multiple Working:** Within class and with Class 444.

**Class 450/0. Standard units.**

**DMSO(A).** Siemens Krefeld/Vienna 2002–06. –/70. 48.0 t.
**TCO.** Siemens Krefeld/Vienna 2002–06. 24/32(4) 1T. 35.8 t.
**TSO.** Siemens Krefeld/Vienna 2002–06. –/61(9) 1TD 2W. 39.8 t.
**DMSO(B).** Siemens Krefeld/Vienna 2002–06. –/70. 48.6 t.

| 450001 | **SD** | A | *SW* | NT | 63201 64201 68101 63601 |
| 450002 | **SD** | A | *SW* | NT | 63202 64202 68102 63602 |
| 450003 | **SD** | A | *SW* | NT | 63203 64203 68103 63603 |
| 450004 | **SD** | A | *SW* | NT | 63204 64204 68104 63604 |
| 450005 | **SD** | A | *SW* | NT | 63205 64205 68105 63605 |
| 450006 | **SD** | A | *SW* | NT | 63206 64206 68106 63606 |

| | | | | | | | | |
|---|---|---|---|---|---|---|---|---|
| 450 007 | **SD** | A | *SW* | NT | 63207 | 64207 | 68107 | 63607 |
| 450 008 | **SD** | A | *SW* | NT | 63208 | 64208 | 68108 | 63608 |
| 450 009 | **SD** | A | *SW* | NT | 63209 | 64209 | 68109 | 63609 |
| 450 010 | **SD** | A | *SW* | NT | 63210 | 64210 | 68110 | 63610 |
| 450 011 | **SD** | A | *SW* | NT | 63211 | 64211 | 68111 | 63611 |
| 450 012 | **SD** | A | *SW* | NT | 63212 | 64212 | 68112 | 63612 |
| 450 013 | **SD** | A | *SW* | NT | 63213 | 64213 | 68113 | 63613 |
| 450 014 | **SD** | A | *SW* | NT | 63214 | 64214 | 68114 | 63614 |
| 450 015 | **SD** | A | *SW* | NT | 63215 | 64215 | 68115 | 63615 |
| 450 016 | **SD** | A | *SW* | NT | 63216 | 64216 | 68116 | 63616 |
| 450 017 | **SD** | A | *SW* | NT | 63217 | 64217 | 68117 | 63617 |
| 450 018 | **SD** | A | *SW* | NT | 63218 | 64218 | 68118 | 63618 |
| 450 019 | **SD** | A | *SW* | NT | 63219 | 64219 | 68119 | 63619 |
| 450 020 | **SD** | A | *SW* | NT | 63220 | 64220 | 68120 | 63620 |
| 450 021 | **SD** | A | *SW* | NT | 63221 | 64221 | 68121 | 63621 |
| 450 022 | **SD** | A | *SW* | NT | 63222 | 64222 | 68122 | 63622 |
| 450 023 | **SD** | A | *SW* | NT | 63223 | 64223 | 68123 | 63623 |
| 450 024 | **SD** | A | *SW* | NT | 63224 | 64224 | 68124 | 63624 |
| 450 025 | **SD** | A | *SW* | NT | 63225 | 64225 | 68125 | 63625 |
| 450 026 | **SD** | A | *SW* | NT | 63226 | 64226 | 68126 | 63626 |
| 450 027 | **SD** | A | *SW* | NT | 63227 | 64227 | 68127 | 63627 |
| 450 028 | **SD** | A | *SW* | NT | 63228 | 64228 | 68128 | 63628 |
| 450 029 | **SD** | A | *SW* | NT | 63229 | 64229 | 68129 | 63629 |
| 450 030 | **SD** | A | *SW* | NT | 63230 | 64230 | 68130 | 63630 |
| 450 031 | **SD** | A | *SW* | NT | 63231 | 64231 | 68131 | 63631 |
| 450 032 | **SD** | A | *SW* | NT | 63232 | 64232 | 68132 | 63632 |
| 450 033 | **SD** | A | *SW* | NT | 63233 | 64233 | 68133 | 63633 |
| 450 034 | **SD** | A | *SW* | NT | 63234 | 64234 | 68134 | 63634 |
| 450 035 | **SD** | A | *SW* | NT | 63235 | 64235 | 68135 | 63635 |
| 450 036 | **SD** | A | *SW* | NT | 63236 | 64236 | 68136 | 63636 |
| 450 037 | **SD** | A | *SW* | NT | 63237 | 64237 | 68137 | 63637 |
| 450 038 | **SD** | A | *SW* | NT | 63238 | 64238 | 68138 | 63638 |
| 450 039 | **SD** | A | *SW* | NT | 63239 | 64239 | 68139 | 63639 |
| 450 040 | **SD** | A | *SW* | NT | 63240 | 64240 | 68140 | 63640 |
| 450 041 | **SD** | A | *SW* | NT | 63241 | 64241 | 68141 | 63641 |
| 450 042 | **SD** | A | *SW* | NT | 63242 | 64242 | 68142 | 63642 |
| 450 071 | **SD** | A | *SW* | NT | 63271 | 64271 | 68171 | 63671 |
| 450 072 | **SD** | A | *SW* | NT | 63272 | 64272 | 68172 | 63672 |
| 450 073 | **SD** | A | *SW* | NT | 63273 | 64273 | 68173 | 63673 |
| 450 074 | **SD** | A | *SW* | NT | 63274 | 64274 | 68174 | 63674 |
| 450 075 | **SD** | A | *SW* | NT | 63275 | 64275 | 68175 | 63675 |
| 450 076 | **SD** | A | *SW* | NT | 63276 | 64276 | 68176 | 63676 |
| 450 077 | **SD** | A | *SW* | NT | 63277 | 64277 | 68177 | 63677 |
| 450 078 | **SD** | A | *SW* | NT | 63278 | 64278 | 68178 | 63678 |
| 450 079 | **SD** | A | *SW* | NT | 63279 | 64279 | 68179 | 63679 |
| 450 080 | **SD** | A | *SW* | NT | 63280 | 64280 | 68180 | 63680 |
| 450 081 | **SD** | A | *SW* | NT | 63281 | 64281 | 68181 | 63681 |
| 450 082 | **SD** | A | *SW* | NT | 63282 | 64282 | 68182 | 63682 |
| 450 083 | **SD** | A | *SW* | NT | 63283 | 64283 | 68183 | 63683 |
| 450 084 | **SD** | A | *SW* | NT | 63284 | 64284 | 68184 | 63684 |
| 450 085 | **SD** | A | *SW* | NT | 63285 | 64285 | 68185 | 63685 |

| | | | | | | | | |
|---|---|---|---|---|---|---|---|---|
| 450086 | **SD** | A | *SW* | NT | 63286 | 64286 | 68186 | 63686 |
| 450087 | **SD** | A | *SW* | NT | 63287 | 64287 | 68187 | 63687 |
| 450088 | **SD** | A | *SW* | NT | 63288 | 64288 | 68188 | 63688 |
| 450089 | **SD** | A | *SW* | NT | 63289 | 64289 | 68189 | 63689 |
| 450090 | **SD** | A | *SW* | NT | 63290 | 64290 | 68190 | 63690 |
| 450091 | **SD** | A | *SW* | NT | 63291 | 64291 | 68191 | 63691 |
| 450092 | **SD** | A | *SW* | NT | 63292 | 64292 | 68192 | 63692 |
| 450093 | **SD** | A | *SW* | NT | 63293 | 64293 | 68193 | 63693 |
| 450094 | **SD** | A | *SW* | NT | 63294 | 64294 | 68194 | 63694 |
| 450095 | **SD** | A | *SW* | NT | 63295 | 64295 | 68195 | 63695 |
| 450096 | **SD** | A | *SW* | NT | 63296 | 64296 | 68196 | 63696 |
| 450097 | **SD** | A | *SW* | NT | 63297 | 64297 | 68197 | 63697 |
| 450098 | **SD** | A | *SW* | NT | 63298 | 64298 | 68198 | 63698 |
| 450099 | **SD** | A | *SW* | NT | 63299 | 64299 | 68199 | 63699 |
| 450100 | **SD** | A | *SW* | NT | 63300 | 64300 | 68200 | 63700 |
| 450101 | **SD** | A | *SW* | NT | 63701 | 66851 | 66801 | 63751 |
| 450102 | **SD** | A | *SW* | NT | 63702 | 66852 | 66802 | 63752 |
| 450103 | **SD** | A | *SW* | NT | 63703 | 66853 | 66803 | 63753 |
| 450104 | **SD** | A | *SW* | NT | 63704 | 66854 | 66804 | 63754 |
| 450105 | **SD** | A | *SW* | NT | 63705 | 66855 | 66805 | 63755 |
| 450106 | **SD** | A | *SW* | NT | 63706 | 66856 | 66806 | 63756 |
| 450107 | **SD** | A | *SW* | NT | 63707 | 66857 | 66807 | 63757 |
| 450108 | **SD** | A | *SW* | NT | 63708 | 66858 | 66808 | 63758 |
| 450109 | **SD** | A | *SW* | NT | 63709 | 66859 | 66809 | 63759 |
| 450110 | **SD** | A | *SW* | NT | 63710 | 66860 | 66810 | 63760 |
| 450111 | **SD** | A | *SW* | NT | 63901 | 66921 | 66901 | 63921 |
| 450112 | **SD** | A | *SW* | NT | 63902 | 66922 | 66902 | 63922 |
| 450113 | **SD** | A | *SW* | NT | 63903 | 66923 | 66903 | 63923 |
| 450114 | **SD** | A | *SW* | NT | 63904 | 66924 | 66904 | 63924 |
| 450115 | **SD** | A | *SW* | NT | 63905 | 66925 | 66905 | 63925 |
| 450116 | **SD** | A | *SW* | NT | 63906 | 66926 | 66906 | 63926 |
| 450117 | **SD** | A | *SW* | NT | 63907 | 66927 | 66907 | 63927 |
| 450118 | **SD** | A | *SW* | NT | 63908 | 66928 | 66908 | 63928 |
| 450119 | **SD** | A | *SW* | NT | 63909 | 66929 | 66909 | 63929 |
| 450120 | **SD** | A | *SW* | NT | 63910 | 66930 | 66910 | 63930 |
| 450121 | **SD** | A | *SW* | NT | 63911 | 66931 | 66911 | 63931 |
| 450122 | **SD** | A | *SW* | NT | 63912 | 66932 | 66912 | 63932 |
| 450123 | **SD** | A | *SW* | NT | 63913 | 66933 | 66913 | 63933 |
| 450124 | **SD** | A | *SW* | NT | 63914 | 66934 | 66914 | 63934 |
| 450125 | **SD** | A | *SW* | NT | 63915 | 66935 | 66915 | 63935 |
| 450126 | **SD** | A | *SW* | NT | 63916 | 66936 | 66916 | 63936 |
| 450127 | **SD** | A | *SW* | NT | 63917 | 66937 | 66917 | 63937 |

**Names (carried on DMSO(B)):**

450015  DESIRO
450042  TRELOAR COLLEGE

450114  FAIRBRIDGE investing in the future

**Class 450/5.** 28 units converted 2007–08 with First Class removed and a modified seating layout with more standing room (some Standard Class seats were taken out). First Class was refitted in 2013 but the removed Standard Class seats were not refitted so the units have kept their 450 5xx numbers.

▲ Converted for use as an ERTMS test unit, Network Rail 313 121 is seen on the ERTMS National Integration Facility (the Hertford Loop) at Watton-at-Stone on 14/08/13. **John Pink**

▼ ScotRail Saltire liveried-314 208 leaves Glasgow Central with the 16.34 to Newton on 02/06/13. **Robert Pritchard**

▲ The Greater Anglia Class 315s are currently being refurbished and repainted into the white & red livery. On 26/07/13 315 812 leads old "One"-liveried 315 839 past Pudding Mill Lane with the 09.50 Liverpool Street–Shenfield. **Robert Pritchard**

▼ First Capital Connect-liveried 319 443 is on the rear of the 15.26 Kentish Town–Sevenoaks (led by 319 424) at Crofton Road Jn on 02/04/13. **Antony Guppy**

▲ London Midland has a small fleet of seven Class 321s. On 30/06/13 321 415 passes Wolverton with an empty stock from Northampton depot to Watford Junction (for use on the St Albans Abbey branch the next day). **Mark Beal**

▼ The well-travelled 322s are now operated by Northern, working services in West Yorkshire and Leeds–Doncaster alongside the 321/9s. On 09/08/13 322 484 arrives at Doncaster with the 15.20 ex-Leeds. **Robert Pritchard**

▲ Northern-liveried 323 237 is seen near Longport with the 18.57 Stoke-on-Trent–Manchester Piccadilly stopping service on 19/06/13. **Cliff Beeton**

▼ Royal Mail EMUs 325 004 and 325 003 are seen near Claypole, between Grantham and Newark, with the diverted 1S96 16.20 Willesden–Shieldmuir mail train on 18/07/13. **Lindsay Atkinson**

▲ In the West Yorkshire PTE/Northern livery, 333 015 arrives at Menston with the 11.51 Ilkley–Bradford Forster Square on 27/10/12. **Tony Christie**

▼ ScotRail Saltire-liveried 334 025 arrives at Hyndland with the 13.55 Helensburgh Central–Edinburgh Waverley on 02/06/13. **Robert Pritchard**

▲ c2c-liveried 357 205 and 357 225 pass Pudding Mill Lane DLR stop with an empty stock working from Fenchurch Street to Shoeburyness via Stratford on 26/07/13. **Robert Pritchard**

▼ In plain First blue livery, although operated by Greater Anglia, 360 118 and 360 111 pass Manor Park with the 10.18 London Liverpool Street–Clacton on 26/07/13. **Robert Pritchard**

▲ First Capital Connect-liveried 365 508 passes Hadley Wood on 13/05/12 with the 16.32 London King's Cross–Peterborough. **Robert Pritchard**

▼ In Connex livery with Southeastern brandings, 375 827 passes Clapham High Street with the 10.07 London Victoria–Ashford on 07/12/11. **Robert Pritchard**

▲ First Capital Connect "Urban Lights"-liveried 377 503 and 377 508 pass Stoats Nest Junction, on the Brighton main line, with the 14.40 Bedford–Brighton on 15/03/12.                                                                    **Robert Pritchard**

▼ London Overground 378 151 arrives at Honor Oak Park with the 18.10 Dalston Junction–West Croydon on 26/07/13.                                          **Robert Pritchard**

▲ In National Express white livery with Greater Anglia branding, 379 025 and 379 009 pass Lea Bridge with the diverted 15.30 Stansted Airport–London Liverpool Street on 12/05/12. **Antony Guppy**

▼ ScotRail Saltire-liveried 380 018 passes Hillington West with the 13.48 Glasgow Central–Largs on 05/11/12. **Robert Pritchard**

▲ 11-car Virgin Trains Pendolino 390 153 passes Lamington with the 16.40 Glasgow Central–London Euston on 19/04/13. **Robin Ralston**

▼ Southeastern 395 029 passes Singlewell loops with the 15.44 Dover Priory–London St Pancras on 29/03/12. **William Turvill**

▲ Southern-operated and Gatwick Express-liveried 442 410 approaches Clapham Junction with the 11.15 London Victoria–Gatwick Airport on 04/03/13.
**Brian Denton**

▼ South West Trains white-liveried 444 044 passes Eastleigh with the 14.35 London Waterloo–Weymouth on 22/07/13. **Stewart Armstrong**

▲ Converted back from a High Capacity 450/5 to a standard 450 (but still numbered in the 450/5 series), 450 566 leaves Basingstoke with the 13.39 London Waterloo–Poole on 24/09/13. **Chris Wilson**

▼ SWT red-liveried Class 455s 5863 and 5738 leave Wimbledon with a London Waterloo–Hampton Court service on 27/07/11. **Brian Denton**

▲ SWT white-liveried Class 458 8027 approaches Wimbledon for London Waterloo on 27/07/11.　**Brian Denton**

▼ Southeastern-liveried 466 020+465 921+465 934 pass St Johns with an empty stock working from Orpington to London Charing Cross on 26/07/13.　**Robert Pritchard**

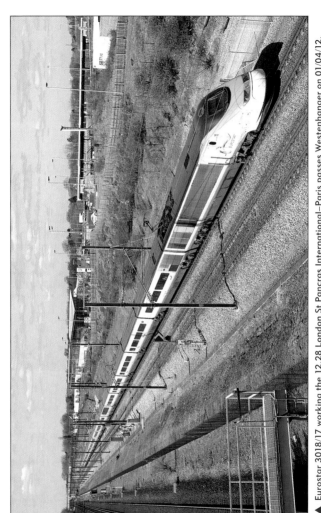

▲ Eurostar 3018/17 working the 12.28 London St Pancras International–Paris passes Westenhanger on 01/04/12.
**Antony Guppy**

▲ Merseyrail operates a fleet of 59 Class 507s and 508s. On 06/11/11 508 120 stands at Bootle Oriel Road with the 13.28 Southport–Hunts Cross.
**Robert Pritchard**

▼ Bombardier Flexity 2 014, one of 16 such trams operated by Blackpool Transport, arrives at Bispham working from Fleetwood to Starr Gate on 27/10/12.
**Robert Pritchard**

▲ Docklands Light Railway B07 cars 155 and 101 arrive at Bow Church working from Stratford to Canary Wharf on 16/09/10.          **Robert Pritchard**

▼ Nottingham Express Transit 213, in the new livery, stands at the Forest headed for Station Street on 26/08/13. Nottingham now has 22 new Alstom Citadis trams being delivered to supplement the fleet of 15 Incentro cars.          **Robert Pritchard**

**DMSO(A).** Siemens Krefeld/Vienna 2002–04. –/64. 48.0 t.
**TCO.** Siemens Krefeld/Vienna 2002–04. 24/30(4) 1T. 35.5 t.
**TSO.** Siemens Krefeld/Vienna 2002–04. –/56(9) 1TD 2W. 39.8 t.
**DMSO(B).** Siemens Krefeld/Vienna 2002–04. –/64. 48.6 t.

| | | | | | | | | |
|---|---|---|---|---|---|---|---|---|
| 450543 | (450043) | **SD** | A | *SW* | NT | 63243 | 64243 | 68143 | 63643 |
| 450544 | (450044) | **SD** | A | *SW* | NT | 63244 | 64244 | 68144 | 63644 |
| 450545 | (450045) | **SD** | A | *SW* | NT | 63245 | 64245 | 68145 | 63645 |
| 450546 | (450046) | **SD** | A | *SW* | NT | 63246 | 64246 | 68146 | 63646 |
| 450547 | (450047) | **SD** | A | *SW* | NT | 63247 | 64247 | 68147 | 63647 |
| 450548 | (450048) | **SD** | A | *SW* | NT | 63248 | 64248 | 68148 | 63648 |
| 450549 | (450049) | **SD** | A | *SW* | NT | 63249 | 64249 | 68149 | 63649 |
| 450550 | (450050) | **SD** | A | *SW* | NT | 63250 | 64250 | 68150 | 63650 |
| 450551 | (450051) | **SD** | A | *SW* | NT | 63251 | 64251 | 68151 | 63651 |
| 450552 | (450052) | **SD** | A | *SW* | NT | 63252 | 64252 | 68152 | 63652 |
| 450553 | (450053) | **SD** | A | *SW* | NT | 63253 | 64253 | 68153 | 63653 |
| 450554 | (450054) | **SD** | A | *SW* | NT | 63254 | 64254 | 68154 | 63654 |
| 450555 | (450055) | **SD** | A | *SW* | NT | 63255 | 64255 | 68155 | 63655 |
| 450556 | (450056) | **SD** | A | *SW* | NT | 63256 | 64256 | 68156 | 63656 |
| 450557 | (450057) | **SD** | A | *SW* | NT | 63257 | 64257 | 68157 | 63657 |
| 450558 | (450058) | **SD** | A | *SW* | NT | 63258 | 64258 | 68158 | 63658 |
| 450559 | (450059) | **SD** | A | *SW* | NT | 63259 | 64259 | 68159 | 63659 |
| 450560 | (450060) | **SD** | A | *SW* | NT | 63260 | 64260 | 68160 | 63660 |
| 450561 | (450061) | **SD** | A | *SW* | NT | 63261 | 64261 | 68161 | 63661 |
| 450562 | (450062) | **SD** | A | *SW* | NT | 63262 | 64262 | 68162 | 63662 |
| 450563 | (450063) | **SD** | A | *SW* | NT | 63263 | 64263 | 68163 | 63663 |
| 450564 | (450064) | **SD** | A | *SW* | NT | 63264 | 64264 | 68164 | 63664 |
| 450565 | (450065) | **SD** | A | *SW* | NT | 63265 | 64265 | 68165 | 63665 |
| 450566 | (450066) | **SD** | A | *SW* | NT | 63266 | 64266 | 68166 | 63666 |
| 450567 | (450067) | **SD** | A | *SW* | NT | 63267 | 64267 | 68167 | 63667 |
| 450568 | (450068) | **SD** | A | *SW* | NT | 63268 | 64268 | 68168 | 63668 |
| 450569 | (450069) | **SD** | A | *SW* | NT | 63269 | 64269 | 68169 | 63669 |
| 450570 | (450070) | **SD** | A | *SW* | NT | 63270 | 64270 | 68170 | 63670 |

# CLASS 455                                             BREL YORK

Inner suburban units.

**Formation:** DTSO–MSO–TSO–DTSO.
**Construction:** Steel. Class 455/7 TSO have a steel underframe and an aluminium alloy body & roof.
**Traction Motors:** Four GEC507-20J of 185 kW, some recovered from Class 405s.
**Wheel Arrangement:** 2-2 + Bo-Bo + 2-2 + 2-2.
**Braking:** Disc.                              **Dimensions:** 19.92/19.83 x 2.82 m.
**Bogies:** P7 (motor) and T3 (455/8 & 455/9) BX1 (455/7) trailer.
**Gangways:** Within unit + end doors (sealed on Southern units).
**Couplers:** Tightlock.                        **Control System:** 1982-type, camshaft.
**Doors:** Sliding.                             **Maximum Speed:** 75 mph.
**Heating & Ventilation:** Various.
**Seating Layout:** All units refurbished. SWT units: 2+2 high-back unidirectional/facing seating. Southern units: 3+2 high back mainly facing seating.
**Multiple Working:** Within class and with Class 456.

**Class 455/7. South West Trains units.** Second series with TSOs originally in Class 508s. Pressure heating & ventilation.

**DTSO**. Lot No. 30976 1984–85. –/50(4) 1W. 30.8t.
**MSO**. Lot No. 30975 1984–85. –/68. 45.7t.
**TSO**. Lot No. 30944 1979–80. –/68. 26.1t.

| | | | | | | | | |
|---|---|---|---|---|---|---|---|---|
| 5701 | **SS** | P | *SW* | WD | 77727 | 62783 | 71545 | 77728 |
| 5702 | **SS** | P | *SW* | WD | 77729 | 62784 | 71547 | 77730 |
| 5703 | **SS** | P | *SW* | WD | 77731 | 62785 | 71540 | 77732 |
| 5704 | **SS** | P | *SW* | WD | 77733 | 62786 | 71548 | 77734 |
| 5705 | **SS** | P | *SW* | WD | 77735 | 62787 | 71565 | 77736 |
| 5706 | **SS** | P | *SW* | WD | 77737 | 62788 | 71534 | 77738 |
| 5707 | **SS** | P | *SW* | WD | 77739 | 62789 | 71536 | 77740 |
| 5708 | **SS** | P | *SW* | WD | 77741 | 62790 | 71560 | 77742 |
| 5709 | **SS** | P | *SW* | WD | 77743 | 62791 | 71532 | 77744 |
| 5710 | **SS** | P | *SW* | WD | 77745 | 62792 | 71566 | 77746 |
| 5711 | **SS** | P | *SW* | WD | 77747 | 62793 | 71542 | 77748 |
| 5712 | **SS** | P | *SW* | WD | 77749 | 62794 | 71546 | 77750 |
| 5713 | **SS** | P | *SW* | WD | 77751 | 62795 | 71567 | 77752 |
| 5714 | **SS** | P | *SW* | WD | 77753 | 62796 | 71539 | 77754 |
| 5715 | **SS** | P | *SW* | WD | 77755 | 62797 | 71535 | 77756 |
| 5716 | **SS** | P | *SW* | WD | 77757 | 62798 | 71564 | 77758 |
| 5717 | **SS** | P | *SW* | WD | 77759 | 62799 | 71528 | 77760 |
| 5718 | **SS** | P | *SW* | WD | 77761 | 62800 | 71557 | 77762 |
| 5719 | **SS** | P | *SW* | WD | 77763 | 62801 | 71558 | 77764 |
| 5720 | **SS** | P | *SW* | WD | 77765 | 62802 | 71568 | 77766 |
| 5721 | **SS** | P | *SW* | WD | 77767 | 62803 | 71553 | 77768 |
| 5722 | **SS** | P | *SW* | WD | 77769 | 62804 | 71533 | 77770 |
| 5723 | **SS** | P | *SW* | WD | 77771 | 62805 | 71526 | 77772 |
| 5724 | **SS** | P | *SW* | WD | 77773 | 62806 | 71561 | 77774 |
| 5725 | **SS** | P | *SW* | WD | 77775 | 62807 | 71541 | 77776 |
| 5726 | **SS** | P | *SW* | WD | 77777 | 62808 | 71556 | 77778 |
| 5727 | **SS** | P | *SW* | WD | 77779 | 62809 | 71562 | 77780 |
| 5728 | **SS** | P | *SW* | WD | 77781 | 62810 | 71527 | 77782 |
| 5729 | **SS** | P | *SW* | WD | 77783 | 62811 | 71550 | 77784 |
| 5730 | **SS** | P | *SW* | WD | 77785 | 62812 | 71551 | 77786 |
| 5731 | **SS** | P | *SW* | WD | 77787 | 62813 | 71555 | 77788 |
| 5732 | **SS** | P | *SW* | WD | 77789 | 62814 | 71552 | 77790 |
| 5733 | **SS** | P | *SW* | WD | 77791 | 62815 | 71549 | 77792 |
| 5734 | **SS** | P | *SW* | WD | 77793 | 62816 | 71531 | 77794 |
| 5735 | **SS** | P | *SW* | WD | 77795 | 62817 | 71563 | 77796 |
| 5736 | **SS** | P | *SW* | WD | 77797 | 62818 | 71554 | 77798 |
| 5737 | **SS** | P | *SW* | WD | 77799 | 62819 | 71544 | 77800 |
| 5738 | **SS** | P | *SW* | WD | 77801 | 62820 | 71529 | 77802 |
| 5739 | **SS** | P | *SW* | WD | 77803 | 62821 | 71537 | 77804 |
| 5740 | **SS** | P | *SW* | WD | 77805 | 62822 | 71530 | 77806 |
| 5741 | **SS** | P | *SW* | WD | 77807 | 62823 | 71559 | 77808 |
| 5742 | **SS** | P | *SW* | WD | 77809 | 62824 | 71543 | 77810 |
| 5750 | **SS** | P | *SW* | WD | 77811 | 62825 | 71538 | 77812 |

**Class 455/8. Southern units**. First series. Pressure heating & ventilation. Fitted with in-cab air conditioning systems meaning that the end door has been sealed.

**DTSO.** Lot No. 30972 York 1982–84. –/74. 33.6 t.
**MSO.** Lot No. 30973 York 1982–84. –/84. 45.6 t.
**TSO.** Lot No. 30974 York 1982–84. –/75(3) 2W. 34.0 t.

| | | | | | | | | |
|---|---|---|---|---|---|---|---|---|
| 455801 | **SN** | E | *SN* | SU | 77627 | 62709 | 71657 | 77580 |
| 455802 | **SN** | E | *SN* | SU | 77581 | 62710 | 71664 | 77582 |
| 455803 | **SN** | E | *SN* | SU | 77583 | 62711 | 71639 | 77584 |
| 455804 | **SN** | E | *SN* | SU | 77585 | 62712 | 71640 | 77586 |
| 455805 | **SN** | E | *SN* | SU | 77587 | 62713 | 71641 | 77588 |
| 455806 | **SN** | E | *SN* | SU | 77589 | 62714 | 71642 | 77590 |
| 455807 | **SN** | E | *SN* | SU | 77591 | 62715 | 71643 | 77592 |
| 455808 | **SN** | E | *SN* | SU | 77637 | 62716 | 71644 | 77594 |
| 455809 | **SN** | E | *SN* | SU | 77623 | 62717 | 71648 | 77602 |
| 455810 | **SN** | E | *SN* | SU | 77597 | 62718 | 71646 | 77598 |
| 455811 | **SN** | E | *SN* | SU | 77599 | 62719 | 71647 | 77600 |
| 455812 | **SN** | E | *SN* | SU | 77595 | 62720 | 71645 | 77626 |
| 455813 | **SN** | E | *SN* | SU | 77603 | 62721 | 71649 | 77604 |
| 455814 | **SN** | E | *SN* | SU | 77605 | 62722 | 71650 | 77606 |
| 455815 | **SN** | E | *SN* | SU | 77607 | 62723 | 71651 | 77608 |
| 455816 | **SN** | E | *SN* | SU | 77609 | 62724 | 71652 | 77633 |
| 455817 | **SN** | E | *SN* | SU | 77611 | 62725 | 71653 | 77612 |
| 455818 | **SN** | E | *SN* | SU | 77613 | 62726 | 71654 | 77632 |
| 455819 | **SN** | E | *SN* | SU | 77615 | 62727 | 71637 | 77616 |
| 455820 | **SN** | E | *SN* | SU | 77617 | 62728 | 71656 | 77618 |
| 455821 | **SN** | E | *SN* | SU | 77619 | 62729 | 71655 | 77620 |
| 455822 | **SN** | E | *SN* | SU | 77621 | 62730 | 71658 | 77622 |
| 455823 | **SN** | E | *SN* | SU | 77601 | 62731 | 71659 | 77596 |
| 455824 | **SN** | E | *SN* | SU | 77593 | 62732 | 71660 | 77624 |
| 455825 | **SN** | E | *SN* | SU | 77579 | 62733 | 71661 | 77628 |
| 455826 | **SN** | E | *SN* | SU | 77630 | 62734 | 71662 | 77629 |
| 455827 | **SN** | E | *SN* | SU | 77610 | 62735 | 71663 | 77614 |
| 455828 | **SN** | E | *SN* | SU | 77631 | 62736 | 71638 | 77634 |
| 455829 | **SN** | E | *SN* | SU | 77635 | 62737 | 71665 | 77636 |
| 455830 | **SN** | E | *SN* | SU | 77625 | 62743 | 71666 | 77638 |
| 455831 | **SN** | E | *SN* | SU | 77639 | 62739 | 71667 | 77640 |
| 455832 | **SN** | E | *SN* | SU | 77641 | 62740 | 71668 | 77642 |
| 455833 | **SN** | E | *SN* | SU | 77643 | 62741 | 71669 | 77644 |
| 455834 | **SN** | E | *SN* | SU | 77645 | 62742 | 71670 | 77646 |
| 455835 | **SN** | E | *SN* | SU | 77647 | 62738 | 71671 | 77648 |
| 455836 | **SN** | E | *SN* | SU | 77649 | 62744 | 71672 | 77650 |
| 455837 | **SN** | E | *SN* | SU | 77651 | 62745 | 71673 | 77652 |
| 455838 | **SN** | E | *SN* | SU | 77653 | 62746 | 71674 | 77654 |
| 455839 | **SN** | E | *SN* | SU | 77655 | 62747 | 71675 | 77656 |
| 455840 | **SN** | E | *SN* | SU | 77657 | 62748 | 71676 | 77658 |
| 455841 | **SN** | E | *SN* | SU | 77659 | 62749 | 71677 | 77660 |
| 455842 | **SN** | E | *SN* | SU | 77661 | 62750 | 71678 | 77662 |
| 455843 | **SN** | E | *SN* | SU | 77663 | 62751 | 71679 | 77664 |
| 455844 | **SN** | E | *SN* | SU | 77665 | 62752 | 71680 | 77666 |

| 455845 | **SN** | E | *SN* | SU | 77667 | 62753 | 71681 | 77668 |
| 455846 | **SN** | E | *SN* | SU | 77669 | 62754 | 71682 | 77670 |

**Class 455/8. South West Trains units.** First series. Pressure heating & ventilation.

**DTSO.** Lot No. 30972 York 1982–84. −50(4) 1W. 29.5 t.
**MSO.** Lot No. 30973 York 1982–84. –/84 –/68. 45.6 t.
**TSO.** Lot No. 30974 York 1982–84. –/84 –/68. 27.1 t.

| 5847 | **SS** | P | *SW* | WD | 77671 | 62755 | 71683 | 77672 |
| 5848 | **SS** | P | *SW* | WD | 77673 | 62756 | 71684 | 77674 |
| 5849 | **SS** | P | *SW* | WD | 77675 | 62757 | 71685 | 77676 |
| 5850 | **SS** | P | *SW* | WD | 77677 | 62758 | 71686 | 77678 |
| 5851 | **SS** | P | *SW* | WD | 77679 | 62759 | 71687 | 77680 |
| 5852 | **SS** | P | *SW* | WD | 77681 | 62760 | 71688 | 77682 |
| 5853 | **SS** | P | *SW* | WD | 77683 | 62761 | 71689 | 77684 |
| 5854 | **SS** | P | *SW* | WD | 77685 | 62762 | 71690 | 77686 |
| 5855 | **SS** | P | *SW* | WD | 77687 | 62763 | 71691 | 77688 |
| 5856 | **SS** | P | *SW* | WD | 77689 | 62764 | 71692 | 77690 |
| 5857 | **SS** | P | *SW* | WD | 77691 | 62765 | 71693 | 77692 |
| 5858 | **SS** | P | *SW* | WD | 77693 | 62766 | 71694 | 77694 |
| 5859 | **SS** | P | *SW* | WD | 77695 | 62767 | 71695 | 77696 |
| 5860 | **SS** | P | *SW* | WD | 77697 | 62768 | 71696 | 77698 |
| 5861 | **SS** | P | *SW* | WD | 77699 | 62769 | 71697 | 77700 |
| 5862 | **SS** | P | *SW* | WD | 77701 | 62770 | 71698 | 77702 |
| 5863 | **SS** | P | *SW* | WD | 77703 | 62771 | 71699 | 77704 |
| 5864 | **SS** | P | *SW* | WD | 77705 | 62772 | 71700 | 77706 |
| 5865 | **SS** | P | *SW* | WD | 77707 | 62773 | 71701 | 77708 |
| 5866 | **SS** | P | *SW* | WD | 77709 | 62774 | 71702 | 77710 |
| 5867 | **SS** | P | *SW* | WD | 77711 | 62775 | 71703 | 77712 |
| 5868 | **SS** | P | *SW* | WD | 77713 | 62776 | 71704 | 77714 |
| 5869 | **SS** | P | *SW* | WD | 77715 | 62777 | 71705 | 77716 |
| 5870 | **SS** | P | *SW* | WD | 77717 | 62778 | 71706 | 77718 |
| 5871 | **SS** | P | *SW* | WD | 77719 | 62779 | 71707 | 77720 |
| 5872 | **SS** | P | *SW* | WD | 77721 | 62780 | 71708 | 77722 |
| 5873 | **SS** | P | *SW* | WD | 77723 | 62781 | 71709 | 77724 |
| 5874 | **SS** | P | *SW* | WD | 77725 | 62782 | 71710 | 77726 |

**Class 455/9. South West Trains units.** Third series. Convection heating.
**Dimensions:** 19.96/20.18 x 2.82 m.

Vehicles 67301 and 67400 were converted from Class 210 DEMU vehicles to replace accident damaged cars.

**DTSO.** Lot No. 30991 York 1985. –/50(4) 1W. 30.7 t.
**MSO.** Lot No. 30992 York 1985. –/68. 46.3 t.
**TSO.** Lot No. 30993 York 1985. –/68. 28.3 t.
**TSO†.** Lot No. 30932 Derby 1981. –/68. 26.5 t.

| 5901 | **SS** | P | *SW* | WD | 77813 | 62826 | 71714 | 77814 |
| 5902 | **SS** | P | *SW* | WD | 77815 | 62827 | 71715 | 77816 |
| 5903 | **SS** | P | *SW* | WD | 77817 | 62828 | 71716 | 77818 |
| 5904 | **SS** | P | *SW* | WD | 77819 | 62829 | 71717 | 77820 |
| 5905 | **SS** | P | *SW* | WD | 77821 | 62830 | 71725 | 77822 |

| 5906 |   | **SS** | P | *SW* | WD | 77823 | 62831 | 71719 | 77824 |
| 5907 |   | **SS** | P | *SW* | WD | 77825 | 62832 | 71720 | 77826 |
| 5908 |   | **SS** | P | *SW* | WD | 77827 | 62833 | 71721 | 77828 |
| 5909 |   | **SS** | P | *SW* | WD | 77829 | 62834 | 71722 | 77830 |
| 5910 |   | **SS** | P | *SW* | WD | 77831 | 62835 | 71723 | 77832 |
| 5911 |   | **SS** | P | *SW* | WD | 77833 | 62836 | 71724 | 77834 |
| 5912 | † | **SS** | P | *SW* | WD | 77835 | 62837 | 67400 | 77836 |
| 5913 | † | **SS** | P | *SW* | WD | 77837 | 67301 | 71726 | 77838 |
| 5914 |   | **SS** | P | *SW* | WD | 77839 | 62839 | 71727 | 77840 |
| 5915 |   | **SS** | P | *SW* | WD | 77841 | 62840 | 71728 | 77842 |
| 5916 |   | **SS** | P | *SW* | WD | 77843 | 62841 | 71729 | 77844 |
| 5917 |   | **SS** | P | *SW* | WD | 77845 | 62842 | 71730 | 77846 |
| 5918 |   | **SS** | P | *SW* | WD | 77847 | 62843 | 71732 | 77848 |
| 5919 |   | **SS** | P | *SW* | WD | 77849 | 62844 | 71718 | 77850 |
| 5920 |   | **SS** | P | *SW* | WD | 77851 | 62845 | 71733 | 77852 |

# CLASS 456                                                       BREL YORK

Inner suburban units. These units were withdrawn from traffic with
Southern in late 2013. Following overhaul and refurbishment at Wolverton
they will re-enter traffic with South West Trains during 2014.

**Formation:** DMSO–DTSO.
**Construction:** Steel underframe, aluminium alloy body & roof.
**Traction Motors:** Two GEC507-20J of 185 kW, some recovered from Class 405s.
**Wheel Arrangement:** 2-Bo + 2-2.   **Dimensions:** 20.61 x 2.82 m.
**Braking:** Disc.   **Couplers:** Tightlock.
**Bogies:** P7 (motor) and T3 (trailer).   **Control System:** GTO Chopper.
**Gangways:** Within unit.   **Maximum Speed:** 75 mph.
**Doors:** Sliding.   **Seating Layout:** 3+2 facing.
**Heating & Ventilation:** Convection heating.
**Multiple Working:** Within class and with Class 455.

**Advertising livery:** 456 006 TfL/City of London (blue & green with various
images).

**DMSO.** Lot No. 31073 1990–91. –/79. 41.1 t.
**DTSO.** Lot No. 31074 1990–91. –/73. 31.4 t.

| 456 001 | **SN** | P |   | WD | 64735 | 78250 |
| 456 002 | **SN** | P |   | ZN | 64736 | 78251 |
| 456 003 | **SN** | P |   | ZN | 64737 | 78252 |
| 456 004 | **SN** | P |   | ZN | 64738 | 78253 |
| 456 005 | **SN** | P |   | SL | 64739 | 78254 |
| 456 006 | **AL** | P |   | ZN | 64740 | 78255 |
| 456 007 | **SN** | P |   | WD | 64741 | 78256 |
| 456 008 | **SN** | P |   | SL | 64742 | 78257 |
| 456 009 | **SN** | P |   | WD | 64743 | 78258 |
| 456 010 | **SN** | P |   | ZN | 64744 | 78259 |
| 456 011 | **SN** | P |   | SL | 64745 | 78260 |
| 456 012 | **SN** | P |   | ZN | 64746 | 78261 |
| 456 013 | **SN** | P |   | WD | 64747 | 78262 |
| 456 014 | **SN** | P |   | ZN | 64748 | 78263 |

| 456015 | **SN** | P | | ZN | 64749 | 78264 |
|--------|--------|---|---|----|-------|-------|
| 456016 | **SN** | P | | WD | 64750 | 78265 |
| 456017 | **SN** | P | | ZN | 64751 | 78266 |
| 456018 | **SN** | P | | ZN | 64752 | 78267 |
| 456019 | **SN** | P | | ZN | 64753 | 78268 |
| 456020 | **SN** | P | | WD | 64754 | 78269 |
| 456021 | **SN** | P | | WD | 64755 | 78270 |
| 456022 | **SN** | P | | WD | 64756 | 78271 |
| 456023 | **SN** | P | | WD | 64757 | 78272 |
| 456024 | **SN** | P | | ZN | 64758 | 78273 |

# CLASS 458     JUNIPER     ALSTOM BIRMINGHAM

Outer suburban units. Between 2013 and 2015 the fleet of 30 4-car Class 458 units and the former Gatwick Express fleet of eight 8-car Class 460 units is to be combined to form a fleet of 36 5-car Standard Class only Class 458/5s. The work is being carried out at Wabtec Doncaster and Brush Loughborough. Former Class 460 driving cars 67901/903/907/908 are not included in this programme and are shown in the EMUs Awaiting Disposal section of this book.

The first six units to be completed will be 458 531–536, which use former Class 460 vehicles. Once these are in traffic (by spring 2014) 8001–30 will then be augmented to 5-cars. Former Class 460 vehicles to be added to the 4-car 458s have been allocated but are subject to change. For this reason all of the extra 460 vehicles are listed at the end of this section, with a space left in the formations of 8001–30 for them to be inserted.

After lengthening each unit will be renumbered into the 458 5xx series (eg 8001 will become 458 501). All individual vehicles will retain their original numbers.

**Formation:** DMCO–TSO–MSO–DMCO (as built) or 5-cars DMSO–TSO–TSO–MSO–DMSO.
**Construction:** Steel.                    **Dimensions:** 21.16 or 21.06 x 2.80 m.
**Traction Motors:** Two Alstom ONIX 800 asynchronous of 270 kW.
**Wheel Arrangement:** 2-Bo + 2-2 (+ 2-2) + Bo-2 + Bo-2.
**Braking:** Disc & regenerative.          **Control System:** IGBT Inverter.
**Bogies:** ACR.                            **Doors:** Sliding plug.
**Gangways:** Throughout.
**Couplers:** Scharfenberg AAR (458/5 Voith 136).
**Maximum Speed:** 100 mph (458/5 units being regeared to 75 mph).
**Heating & Ventilation:** Air conditioning. **Multiple Working:** Within class.
**Seating Layout:** 1: 2+2 facing, 2: 3+2 facing/unidirectional (458/5 units Standard Class only, 2+2 facing/unidirectional).

**DMCO(A).** Alstom 1998–2000. 12/63 (458/5 –/60). 46.4 t/45.7 t.
**TSO** (ex-460): Alstom 1998–99. 458 531–536 –/52 1T (for 8001–30 –/56). 34.4 t.
**TSO.** Alstom 1998–2000. –/54(6) 1TD 2W (458/5 –/42 1TD 2W). 34.6 t/34.1 t.
**MSO.** Alstom 1998–2000. –/75 1T (458 531–536 –/56, 8001–30 to be –56 1T). 42.1 t/39.3 t.
**DMCO(B).** Alstom 1998–2000. 12/63 (458/5 –/60). 46.4 t/45.7 t.

| 8001 | **ST** | P | *SW* | WD | 67601 | 74001 | 74101 | 67701 |
|------|--------|---|------|----|-------|-------|-------|-------|
| 8002 | **ST** | P | *SW* | WD | 67602 | 74002 | 74102 | 67702 |
| 8003 | **ST** | P | *SW* | WD | 67603 | 74003 | 74103 | 67703 |
| 8004 | **ST** | P | *SW* | WD | 67604 | 74004 | 74104 | 67704 |
| 8005 | **ST** | P | *SW* | WD | 67605 | 74005 | 74105 | 67705 |
| 8006 | **ST** | P | *SW* | WD | 67606 | 74006 | 74106 | 67706 |
| 8007 | **ST** | P | *SW* | WD | 67607 | 74007 | 74107 | 67707 |
| 8008 | **ST** | P | *SW* | WD | 67608 | 74008 | 74108 | 67708 |
| 8009 | **ST** | P | *SW* | WD | 67609 | 74009 | 74109 | 67709 |
| 8010 | **ST** | P | *SW* | WD | 67610 | 74010 | 74110 | 67710 |
| 8011 | **ST** | P | *SW* | WD | 67611 | 74011 | 74111 | 67711 |
| 8012 | **ST** | P | *SW* | WD | 67612 | 74012 | 74112 | 67712 |
| 8013 | **ST** | P | *SW* | WD | 67613 | 74013 | 74113 | 67713 |
| 8014 | **ST** | P | *SW* | WD | 67614 | 74014 | 74114 | 67714 |
| 8015 | **ST** | P | *SW* | WD | 67615 | 74015 | 74115 | 67715 |
| 8016 | **ST** | P | *SW* | WD | 67616 | 74016 | 74116 | 67716 |
| 8017 | **ST** | P | *SW* | WD | 67617 | 74017 | 74117 | 67717 |
| 8018 | **ST** | P | *SW* | WD | 67618 | 74018 | 74118 | 67718 |
| 8019 | **ST** | P | *SW* | WD | 67619 | 74019 | 74119 | 67719 |
| 8020 | **ST** | P | *SW* | WD | 67620 | 74020 | 74120 | 67720 |
| 8021 | **ST** | P | *SW* | WD | 67621 | 74021 | 74121 | 67721 |
| 8022 | **ST** | P | *SW* | WD | 67622 | 74022 | 74122 | 67722 |
| 8023 | **ST** | P | *SW* | WD | 67623 | 74023 | 74123 | 67723 |
| 8024 | **ST** | P | *SW* | WD | 67624 | 74024 | 74124 | 67724 |
| 8025 | **ST** | P | *SW* | WD | 67625 | 74025 | 74125 | 67725 |
| 8026 | **ST** | P | *SW* | WD | 67626 | 74026 | 74126 | 67726 |
| 8027 | **ST** | P | *SW* | WD | 67627 | 74027 | 74127 | 67727 |
| 8028 | **ST** | P | *SW* | WD | 67628 | 74028 | 74128 | 67728 |
| 8029 | **ST** | P | *SW* | WD | 67629 | 74029 | 74129 | 67729 |
| 8030 | **ST** | P | *SW* | WD | 67630 | 74030 | 74130 | 67730 |

The following Class 460 vehicles will be added to sets 8001–30 during 2014 and early 2015:

| 74401 | 74402 | 74403 | 74404 | 74405 | 74406 | 74407 | 74408 | 74411 |
|-------|-------|-------|-------|-------|-------|-------|-------|-------|
| 74412 | 74421 | 74422 | 74423 | 74424 | 74425 | 74426 | 74427 | 74428 |
| 74431 | 74432 | 74433 | 74434 | 74435 | 74436 | 74437 | 74438 | 74441 |
| 74442 | 74451 | 74452 | | | | | | |

The following units have been converted or are undergoing conversion from Class 460s.

| 458 531 | **SD** | P | *SW* | WD | 67913 | 74418 | 74446 | 74458 | 67912 |
|---------|--------|---|------|-------|-------|-------|-------|-------|-------|
| 458 532 | **SD** | P | | ZB/LB | 67904 | 74417 | 74447 | 74457 | 67905 |
| 458 533 | **SD** | P | | ZB | 67917 | 74413 | 74443 | 74453 | 67916 |
| 458 534 | **SD** | P | *SW* | WD | 67914 | 74414 | 74444 | 74454 | 67914 |
| 458 535 | **SD** | P | | ZB | 67915 | 74415 | 74445 | 74455 | 67911 |
| 458 536 | **SD** | P | | ZB/LB | 67906 | 74416 | 74448 | 74456 | 67902 |

# CLASS 465                                    NETWORKER

Inner/outer suburban units.

**Formation:** DMSO–TSO–TSO–DMSO.
**Construction:** Welded aluminium alloy.
**Traction Motors:** Hitachi asynchronous of 280 kW (Classes 465/0 and 465/1) or GEC-Alsthom G352BY (Classes 465/2 and 465/9).
**Wheel Arrangement:** Bo-Bo + 2-2 + 2-2 + Bo-Bo.
**Braking:** Disc & rheostatic and regenerative (Classes 465/0 and 465/1 only).
**Bogies:** BREL P3/T3 (465/0 and 465/1), SRP BP62/BT52 (465/2 and 465/9).
**Dimensions:** 20.89/20.06 x 2.81 m.
**Control System:** IGBT Inverter (465/0 and 465/1) or 1992-type GTO Inverter.
**Gangways:** Within unit.                **Couplers:** Tightlock.
**Doors:** Sliding plug.                   **Maximum Speed:** 75 mph.
**Seating Layout:** 3+2 facing/unidirectional.
**Multiple Working:** Within class and with Class 466.

**64759–808. DMSO(A).** Lot No. 31100 BREL York 1991–93. –/86. 39.2t.
**64809–858. DMSO(B).** Lot No. 31100 BREL York 1991–93. –/86. 39.2t.
**65734–749. DMSO(A).** Lot No. 31103 Metro-Cammell 1991–93. –/86. 39.2t.
**65784–799. DMSO(B).** Lot No. 31103 Metro-Cammell 1991–93. –/86. 39.2t.
**65800–846. DMSO(A).** Lot No. 31130 ABB York 1993–94. –/86. 39.2t.
**65847–893. DMSO(B).** Lot No. 31130 ABB York 1993–94. –/86. 39.2t.
**72028–126 (even nos.) TSO.** Lot No. 31102 BREL York 1991–93. –/90. 27.2t.
**72029–127 (odd nos.) TSO.** Lot No. 31101 BREL York 1991–93. –/86 1T. 28.0t.
**72787–817 (odd nos.) TSO.** Lot No. 31104 Metro-Cammell 1991–92. –/86 1T. 28.0t.
**72788–818 (even nos.) TSO.** Lot No. 31105 Metro-Cammell 1991–92. –/90. 27.2t.
**72900–992 (even nos.) TSO.** Lot No. 31102 ABB York 1993–94. –/90. 27.2t.
**72901–993 (odd nos.) TSO.** Lot No. 31101 ABB York 1993–94. –/86 1T. 28.0t.

**Class 465/0.** Built by BREL/ABB.

| | | | | | | | |
|---|---|---|---|---|---|---|---|
| 465001 | **SE** | E | *SE* | SG | 64759 | 72028 | 72029 | 64809 |
| 465002 | **SE** | E | *SE* | SG | 64760 | 72030 | 72031 | 64810 |
| 465003 | **SE** | E | *SE* | SG | 64761 | 72032 | 72033 | 64811 |
| 465004 | **SE** | E | *SE* | SG | 64762 | 72034 | 72035 | 64812 |
| 465005 | **SE** | E | *SE* | SG | 64763 | 72036 | 72037 | 64813 |
| 465006 | **SE** | E | *SE* | SG | 64764 | 72038 | 72039 | 64814 |
| 465007 | **SE** | E | *SE* | SG | 64765 | 72040 | 72041 | 64815 |
| 465008 | **SE** | E | *SE* | SG | 64766 | 72042 | 72043 | 64816 |
| 465009 | **SE** | E | *SE* | SG | 64767 | 72044 | 72045 | 64817 |
| 465010 | **SE** | E | *SE* | SG | 64768 | 72046 | 72047 | 64818 |
| 465011 | **SE** | E | *SE* | SG | 64769 | 72048 | 72049 | 64819 |
| 465012 | **SE** | E | *SE* | SG | 64770 | 72050 | 72051 | 64820 |
| 465013 | **SE** | E | *SE* | SG | 64771 | 72052 | 72053 | 64821 |
| 465014 | **SE** | E | *SE* | SG | 64772 | 72054 | 72055 | 64822 |
| 465015 | **SE** | E | *SE* | SG | 64773 | 72056 | 72057 | 64823 |
| 465016 | **SE** | E | *SE* | SG | 64774 | 72058 | 72059 | 64824 |
| 465017 | **SE** | E | *SE* | SG | 64775 | 72060 | 72061 | 64825 |
| 465018 | **SE** | E | *SE* | SG | 64776 | 72062 | 72063 | 64826 |
| 465019 | **SE** | E | *SE* | SG | 64777 | 72064 | 72065 | 64827 |

| 465 020 | **SE** | E | *SE* | SG | 64778 | 72066 | 72067 | 64828 |
|---------|--------|---|------|----|-------|-------|-------|-------|
| 465 021 | **SE** | E | *SE* | SG | 64779 | 72068 | 72069 | 64829 |
| 465 022 | **SE** | E | *SE* | SG | 64780 | 72070 | 72071 | 64830 |
| 465 023 | **SE** | E | *SE* | SG | 64781 | 72072 | 72073 | 64831 |
| 465 024 | **SE** | E | *SE* | SG | 64782 | 72074 | 72075 | 64832 |
| 465 025 | **SE** | E | *SE* | SG | 64783 | 72076 | 72077 | 64833 |
| 465 026 | **SE** | E | *SE* | SG | 64784 | 72078 | 72079 | 64834 |
| 465 027 | **SE** | E | *SE* | SG | 64785 | 72080 | 72081 | 64835 |
| 465 028 | **SE** | E | *SE* | SG | 64786 | 72082 | 72083 | 64836 |
| 465 029 | **SE** | E | *SE* | SG | 64787 | 72084 | 72085 | 64837 |
| 465 030 | **SE** | E | *SE* | SG | 64788 | 72086 | 72087 | 64838 |
| 465 031 | **SE** | E | *SE* | SG | 64789 | 72088 | 72089 | 64839 |
| 465 032 | **SE** | E | *SE* | SG | 64790 | 72090 | 72091 | 64840 |
| 465 033 | **SE** | E | *SE* | SG | 64791 | 72092 | 72093 | 64841 |
| 465 034 | **SE** | E | *SE* | SG | 64792 | 72094 | 72095 | 64842 |
| 465 035 | **SE** | E | *SE* | SG | 64793 | 72096 | 72097 | 64843 |
| 465 036 | **SE** | E | *SE* | SG | 64794 | 72098 | 72099 | 64844 |
| 465 037 | **SE** | E | *SE* | SG | 64795 | 72100 | 72101 | 64845 |
| 465 038 | **SE** | E | *SE* | SG | 64796 | 72102 | 72103 | 64846 |
| 465 039 | **SE** | E | *SE* | SG | 64797 | 72104 | 72105 | 64847 |
| 465 040 | **SE** | E | *SE* | SG | 64798 | 72106 | 72107 | 64848 |
| 465 041 | **SE** | E | *SE* | SG | 64799 | 72108 | 72109 | 64849 |
| 465 042 | **SE** | E | *SE* | SG | 64800 | 72110 | 72111 | 64850 |
| 465 043 | **SE** | E | *SE* | SG | 64801 | 72112 | 72113 | 64851 |
| 465 044 | **SE** | E | *SE* | SG | 64802 | 72114 | 72115 | 64852 |
| 465 045 | **SE** | E | *SE* | SG | 64803 | 72116 | 72117 | 64853 |
| 465 046 | **SE** | E | *SE* | SG | 64804 | 72118 | 72119 | 64854 |
| 465 047 | **SE** | E | *SE* | SG | 64805 | 72120 | 72121 | 64855 |
| 465 048 | **SE** | E | *SE* | SG | 64806 | 72122 | 72123 | 64856 |
| 465 049 | **SE** | E | *SE* | SG | 64807 | 72124 | 72125 | 64857 |
| 465 050 | **SE** | E | *SE* | SG | 64808 | 72126 | 72127 | 64858 |

**Class 465**/1. Built by BREL/ABB. Similar to Class 465/0 but with detail differences.

| 465 151 | **SE** | E | *SE* | SG | 65800 | 72900 | 72901 | 65847 |
|---------|--------|---|------|----|-------|-------|-------|-------|
| 465 152 | **SE** | E | *SE* | SG | 65801 | 72902 | 72903 | 65848 |
| 465 153 | **SE** | E | *SE* | SG | 65802 | 72904 | 72905 | 65849 |
| 465 154 | **SE** | E | *SE* | SG | 65803 | 72906 | 72907 | 65850 |
| 465 155 | **SE** | E | *SE* | SG | 65804 | 72908 | 72909 | 65851 |
| 465 156 | **SE** | E | *SE* | SG | 65805 | 72910 | 72911 | 65852 |
| 465 157 | **SE** | E | *SE* | SG | 65806 | 72912 | 72913 | 65853 |
| 465 158 | **SE** | E | *SE* | SG | 65807 | 72914 | 72915 | 65854 |
| 465 159 | **SE** | E | *SE* | SG | 65808 | 72916 | 72917 | 65855 |
| 465 160 | **SE** | E | *SE* | SG | 65809 | 72918 | 72919 | 65856 |
| 465 161 | **SE** | E | *SE* | SG | 65810 | 72920 | 72921 | 65857 |
| 465 162 | **SE** | E | *SE* | SG | 65811 | 72922 | 72923 | 65858 |
| 465 163 | **SE** | E | *SE* | SG | 65812 | 72924 | 72925 | 65859 |
| 465 164 | **SE** | E | *SE* | SG | 65813 | 72926 | 72927 | 65860 |
| 465 165 | **SE** | E | *SE* | SG | 65814 | 72928 | 72929 | 65861 |
| 465 166 | **SE** | E | *SE* | SG | 65815 | 72930 | 72931 | 65862 |
| 465 167 | **SE** | E | *SE* | SG | 65816 | 72932 | 72933 | 65863 |
| 465 168 | **SE** | E | *SE* | SG | 65817 | 72934 | 72935 | 65864 |

| 465 169 | **SE** | E | *SE* | SG | 65818 | 72936 | 72937 | 65865 |
| 465 170 | **SE** | E | *SE* | SG | 65819 | 72938 | 72939 | 65866 |
| 465 171 | **SE** | E | *SE* | SG | 65820 | 72940 | 72941 | 65867 |
| 465 172 | **SE** | E | *SE* | SG | 65821 | 72942 | 72943 | 65868 |
| 465 173 | **SE** | E | *SE* | SG | 65822 | 72944 | 72945 | 65869 |
| 465 174 | **SE** | E | *SE* | SG | 65823 | 72946 | 72947 | 65870 |
| 465 175 | **SE** | E | *SE* | SG | 65824 | 72948 | 72949 | 65871 |
| 465 176 | **SE** | E | *SE* | SG | 65825 | 72950 | 72951 | 65872 |
| 465 177 | **SE** | E | *SE* | SG | 65826 | 72952 | 72953 | 65873 |
| 465 178 | **SE** | E | *SE* | SG | 65827 | 72954 | 72955 | 65874 |
| 465 179 | **SE** | E | *SE* | SG | 65828 | 72956 | 72957 | 65875 |
| 465 180 | **SE** | E | *SE* | SG | 65829 | 72958 | 72959 | 65876 |
| 465 181 | **SE** | E | *SE* | SG | 65830 | 72960 | 72961 | 65877 |
| 465 182 | **SE** | E | *SE* | SG | 65831 | 72962 | 72963 | 65878 |
| 465 183 | **SE** | E | *SE* | SG | 65832 | 72964 | 72965 | 65879 |
| 465 184 | **SE** | E | *SE* | SG | 65833 | 72966 | 72967 | 65880 |
| 465 185 | **SE** | E | *SE* | SG | 65834 | 72968 | 72969 | 65881 |
| 465 186 | **SE** | E | *SE* | SG | 65835 | 72970 | 72971 | 65882 |
| 465 187 | **SE** | E | *SE* | SG | 65836 | 72972 | 72973 | 65883 |
| 465 188 | **SE** | E | *SE* | SG | 65837 | 72974 | 72975 | 65884 |
| 465 189 | **SE** | E | *SE* | SG | 65838 | 72976 | 72977 | 65885 |
| 465 190 | **SE** | E | *SE* | SG | 65839 | 72978 | 72979 | 65886 |
| 465 191 | **SE** | E | *SE* | SG | 65840 | 72980 | 72981 | 65887 |
| 465 192 | **SE** | E | *SE* | SG | 65841 | 72982 | 72983 | 65888 |
| 465 193 | **SE** | E | *SE* | SG | 65842 | 72984 | 72985 | 65889 |
| 465 194 | **SE** | E | *SE* | SG | 65843 | 72986 | 72987 | 65890 |
| 465 195 | **SE** | E | *SE* | SG | 65844 | 72988 | 72989 | 65891 |
| 465 196 | **SE** | E | *SE* | SG | 65845 | 72990 | 72991 | 65892 |
| 465 197 | **SE** | E | *SE* | SG | 65846 | 72992 | 72993 | 65893 |

**Class 465/2**. Built by Metro-Cammell. **Dimensions**: 20.80/20.15 x 2.81 m.

| 465 235 | **SE** | A | *SE* | SG | 65734 | 72787 | 72788 | 65784 |
| 465 236 | **CN** | A | *SE* | SG | 65735 | 72789 | 72790 | 65785 |
| 465 237 | **SE** | A | *SE* | SG | 65736 | 72791 | 72792 | 65786 |
| 465 238 | **SE** | A | *SE* | SG | 65737 | 72793 | 72794 | 65787 |
| 465 239 | **CN** | A | *SE* | SG | 65738 | 72795 | 72796 | 65788 |
| 465 240 | **SE** | A | *SE* | SG | 65739 | 72797 | 72798 | 65789 |
| 465 241 | **SE** | A | *SE* | SG | 65740 | 72799 | 72800 | 65790 |
| 465 242 | **CN** | A | *SE* | SG | 65741 | 72801 | 72802 | 65791 |
| 465 243 | **SE** | A | *SE* | SG | 65742 | 72803 | 72804 | 65792 |
| 465 244 | **CN** | A | *SE* | SG | 65743 | 72805 | 72806 | 65793 |
| 465 245 | **CN** | A | *SE* | SG | 65744 | 72807 | 72808 | 65794 |
| 465 246 | **CN** | A | *SE* | SG | 65745 | 72809 | 72810 | 65795 |
| 465 247 | **CN** | A | *SE* | SG | 65746 | 72811 | 72812 | 65796 |
| 465 248 | **CN** | A | *SE* | SG | 65747 | 72813 | 72814 | 65797 |
| 465 249 | **CN** | A | *SE* | SG | 65748 | 72815 | 72816 | 65798 |
| 465 250 | **CN** | A | *SE* | SG | 65749 | 72817 | 72818 | 65799 |

**Class 465/9.** Built by Metro-Cammell. Refurbished 2005 for longer distance services, with the addition of First Class. Details as Class 465/0 unless stated.
**Formation:** DMCO–TSO(A)–TSO(B)–DMCO.
**Seating Layout:** 1: 2+2 facing/unidirectional, 2: 3+2 facing/unidirectional.

**65700–733. DMCO(A).** Lot No. 31103 Metro-Cammell 1991–93. 12/68. 39.2t.
**72719–785 (odd nos.) TSO(A).** Lot No. 31104 Metro-Cammell 1991–92. –/76 1T 2W. 30.3t.
**72720–786 (even nos.) TSO(B).** Lot No. 31105 Metro-Cammell 1991–92. –/90. 29.5t.
**65750–783. DMCO(B).** Lot No. 31103 Metro-Cammell 1991–93. 12/68. 39.2t.

| | | | | | | | | |
|---|---|---|---|---|---|---|---|---|
| 465 901 | (465 201) | **CN** | A | *SE* | SG | 65700 | 72719 72720 | 65750 |
| 465 902 | (465 202) | **CN** | A | *SE* | SG | 65701 | 72721 72722 | 65751 |
| 465 903 | (465 203) | **CN** | A | *SE* | SG | 65702 | 72723 72724 | 65752 |
| 465 904 | (465 204) | **SE** | A | *SE* | SG | 65703 | 72725 72726 | 65753 |
| 465 905 | (465 205) | **SE** | A | *SE* | SG | 65704 | 72727 72728 | 65754 |
| 465 906 | (465 206) | **CN** | A | *SE* | SG | 65705 | 72729 72730 | 65755 |
| 465 907 | (465 207) | **SE** | A | *SE* | SG | 65706 | 72731 72732 | 65756 |
| 465 908 | (465 208) | **CN** | A | *SE* | SG | 65707 | 72733 72734 | 65757 |
| 465 909 | (465 209) | **CN** | A | *SE* | SG | 65708 | 72735 72736 | 65758 |
| 465 910 | (465 210) | **SE** | A | *SE* | SG | 65709 | 72737 72738 | 65759 |
| 465 911 | (465 211) | **CN** | A | *SE* | SG | 65710 | 72739 72740 | 65760 |
| 465 912 | (465 212) | **SE** | A | *SE* | SG | 65711 | 72741 72742 | 65761 |
| 465 913 | (465 213) | **SE** | A | *SE* | SG | 65712 | 72743 72744 | 65762 |
| 465 914 | (465 214) | **CN** | A | *SE* | SG | 65713 | 72745 72746 | 65763 |
| 465 915 | (465 215) | **SE** | A | *SE* | SG | 65714 | 72747 72748 | 65764 |
| 465 916 | (465 216) | **SE** | A | *SE* | SG | 65715 | 72749 72750 | 65765 |
| 465 917 | (465 217) | **SE** | A | *SE* | SG | 65716 | 72751 72752 | 65766 |
| 465 918 | (465 218) | **SE** | A | *SE* | SG | 65717 | 72753 72754 | 65767 |
| 465 919 | (465 219) | **CN** | A | *SE* | SG | 65718 | 72755 72756 | 65768 |
| 465 920 | (465 220) | **SE** | A | *SE* | SG | 65719 | 72757 72758 | 65769 |
| 465 921 | (465 221) | **SE** | A | *SE* | SG | 65720 | 72759 72760 | 65770 |
| 465 922 | (465 222) | **SE** | A | *SE* | SG | 65721 | 72761 72762 | 65771 |
| 465 923 | (465 223) | **SE** | A | *SE* | SG | 65722 | 72763 72764 | 65772 |
| 465 924 | (465 224) | **SE** | A | *SE* | SG | 65723 | 72765 72766 | 65773 |
| 465 925 | (465 225) | **CN** | A | *SE* | SG | 65724 | 72767 72768 | 65774 |
| 465 926 | (465 226) | **CN** | A | *SE* | SG | 65725 | 72769 72770 | 65775 |
| 465 927 | (465 227) | **CN** | A | *SF* | SG | 65726 | 72771 72772 | 65776 |
| 465 928 | (465 228) | **SE** | A | *SE* | SG | 65727 | 72773 72774 | 65777 |
| 465 929 | (465 229) | **CN** | A | *SE* | SG | 65728 | 72775 72776 | 65778 |
| 465 930 | (465 230) | **CN** | A | *SE* | SG | 65729 | 72777 72778 | 65779 |
| 465 931 | (465 231) | **SE** | A | *SE* | SG | 65730 | 72779 72780 | 65780 |
| 465 932 | (465 232) | **SE** | A | *SE* | SG | 65731 | 72781 72782 | 65781 |
| 465 933 | (465 233) | **SE** | A | *SE* | SG | 65732 | 72783 72784 | 65782 |
| 465 934 | (465 234) | **CN** | A | *SE* | SG | 65733 | 72785 72786 | 65783 |

**Name:** 465 903 Remembrance

# CLASS 466          NETWORKER          GEC-ALSTHOM

Inner/outer suburban units.

**Formation:** DMSO–DTSO.
**Construction:** Welded aluminium alloy.
**Traction Motors:** Two GEC-Alsthom G352AY asynchronous of 280kW.
**Wheel Arrangement:** Bo-Bo + 2-2.    **Couplers:** Tightlock.
**Braking:** Disc, rheostatic & regen.    **Control System:** 1992-type GTO Inverter.
**Dimensions:** 20.80 x 2.80 m.    **Maximum Speed:** 75 mph.
**Bogies:** BREL P3/T3.    **Doors:** Sliding plug.
**Gangways:** Within unit.    **Seating Layout:** 3+2 facing/unidirectional.
**Multiple Working:** Within class and with Class 465.

**DMSO.** Lot No. 31128 Birmingham 1993–94. –/86. 40.6t.
**DTSO.** Lot No. 31129 Birmingham 1993–94. –/82 1T. 31.4t.

| | | | | | | |
|---|---|---|---|---|---|---|
| 466001 | **SE** | A | *SE* | SG | 64860 | 78312 |
| 466002 | **SE** | A | *SE* | SG | 64861 | 78313 |
| 466003 | **SE** | A | *SE* | SG | 64862 | 78314 |
| 466004 | **SE** | A | *SE* | SG | 64863 | 78315 |
| 466005 | **SE** | A | *SE* | SG | 64864 | 78316 |
| 466006 | **SE** | A | *SE* | SG | 64865 | 78317 |
| 466007 | **SE** | A | *SE* | SG | 64866 | 78318 |
| 466008 | **SE** | A | *SE* | SG | 64867 | 78319 |
| 466009 | **SE** | A | *SE* | SG | 64868 | 78320 |
| 466010 | **SE** | A | *SE* | SG | 64869 | 78321 |
| 466011 | **SE** | A | *SE* | SG | 64870 | 78322 |
| 466012 | **SE** | A | *SE* | SG | 64871 | 78323 |
| 466013 | **SE** | A | *SE* | SG | 64872 | 78324 |
| 466014 | **SE** | A | *SE* | SG | 64873 | 78325 |
| 466015 | **SE** | A | *SE* | SG | 64874 | 78326 |
| 466016 | **SE** | A | *SE* | SG | 64875 | 78327 |
| 466017 | **SE** | A | *SE* | SG | 64876 | 78328 |
| 466018 | **SE** | A | *SE* | SG | 64877 | 78329 |
| 466019 | **SE** | A | *SE* | SG | 64878 | 78330 |
| 466020 | **SE** | A | *SE* | SG | 64879 | 78331 |
| 466021 | **SE** | A | *SE* | SG | 64880 | 78332 |
| 466022 | **SE** | A | *SE* | SG | 64881 | 78333 |
| 466023 | **SE** | A | *SE* | SG | 64882 | 78334 |
| 466024 | **SE** | A | *SE* | SG | 64883 | 78335 |
| 466025 | **SE** | A | *SE* | SG | 64884 | 78336 |
| 466026 | **SE** | A | *SE* | SG | 64885 | 78337 |
| 466027 | **SE** | A | *SE* | SG | 64886 | 78338 |
| 466028 | **SE** | A | *SE* | SG | 64887 | 78339 |
| 466029 | **SE** | A | *SE* | SG | 64888 | 78340 |
| 466030 | **SE** | A | *SE* | SG | 64889 | 78341 |
| 466031 | **SE** | A | *SE* | SG | 64890 | 78342 |
| 466032 | **SE** | A | *SE* | SG | 64891 | 78343 |
| 466033 | **SE** | A | *SE* | SG | 64892 | 78344 |
| 466034 | **SE** | A | *SE* | SG | 64893 | 78345 |
| 466035 | **SE** | A | *SE* | SG | 64894 | 78346 |

| 466036 | **SE** | A | *SE* | SG | 64895 | 78347 |
| 466037 | **SE** | A | *SE* | SG | 64896 | 78348 |
| 466038 | **SE** | A | *SE* | SG | 64897 | 78349 |
| 466039 | **SE** | A | *SE* | SG | 64898 | 78350 |
| 466040 | **SE** | A | *SE* | SG | 64899 | 78351 |
| 466041 | **SE** | A | *SE* | SG | 64900 | 78352 |
| 466042 | **SE** | A | *SE* | SG | 64901 | 78353 |
| 466043 | **SE** | A | *SE* | SG | 64902 | 78354 |

## CLASS 483 METRO-CAMMELL

Built 1938 onwards for LTE. Converted 1989–90 for the Isle of Wight Line.

**Formation:** DMSO–DMSO.
**System:** 660 V DC third rail.
**Construction:** Steel.
**Traction Motors:** Two Crompton Parkinson/GEC/BTH LT100 of 125 kW.
**Braking:** Tread. **Dimensions:** 16.15 x 2.69 m.
**Bogies:** LT design. **Couplers:** Wedglock.
**Gangways:** None. End doors.
**Control System:** Pneumatic Camshaft Motor (PCM).
**Doors:** Sliding. **Maximum Speed:** 45 mph.
**Seating Layout:** Longitudinal or 2+2 facing/unidirectional.
**Multiple Working:** Within class.
**Notes:** The last three numbers of the unit number only are carried.

Former London Underground numbers are shown in parentheses.

**DMSO (A).** Lot No. 31071. –/40. 27.4 t.
**DMSO (B).** Lot No. 31072. –/42. 27.4 t.

| 483002 | **LT** | SW | | RY | 122 | (10221) | 225 | (11142) | RAPTOR |
| 483004 | **LT** | SW | *SW* | RY | 124 | (10205) | 224 | (11205) | |
| 483006 | **LT** | SW | *SW* | RY | 126 | (10297) | 226 | (11297) | |
| 483007 | **LT** | SW | *SW* | RY | 127 | (10291) | 227 | (11291) | |
| 483008 | **LT** | SW | *SW* | RY | 128 | (10255) | 228 | (11255) | |
| 483009 | **LT** | SW | *SW* | RY | 129 | (10229) | 229 | (11229) | |

## CLASS 507 BREL YORK

**Formation:** BDMSO–TSO–DMSO.
**Construction:** Steel underframe, aluminium alloy body and roof.
**Traction Motors:** Four GEC G310AZ of 82.125 kW.
**Wheel Arrangement:** Bo-Bo + 2-2 + Bo-Bo.
**Braking:** Disc & rheostatic. **Dimensions:** 20.18 x 2.82 m.
**Bogies:** BX1. **Couplers:** Tightlock.
**Gangways:** Within unit + end doors. **Control System:** Camshaft.
**Doors:** Sliding. **Maximum Speed:** 75 mph.
**Seating Layout:** All refurbished with 2+2 high-back facing seating.
**Multiple Working:** Within class and with Class 508.

**Advertising livery:** 507 002 Liverpool Hope University (white).

**BDMSO.** Lot No. 30906 1978–80. –/56(3) 1W. 37.0 t.
**TSO.** Lot No. 30907 1978–80. –/74. 25.5 t.
**DMSO.** Lot No. 30908 1978–80. –/56(3) 1W. 35.5 t.

| | | | | | | | |
|---|---|---|---|---|---|---|---|
| 507 001 | **ME** | A | *ME* | BD | 64367 | 71342 | 64405 |
| 507 002 | **AL** | A | *ME* | BD | 64368 | 71343 | 64406 |
| 507 003 | **ME** | A | *ME* | BD | 64369 | 71344 | 64407 |
| 507 004 | **ME** | A | *ME* | BD | 64388 | 71345 | 64408 |
| 507 005 | **ME** | A | *ME* | BD | 64371 | 71346 | 64409 |
| 507 006 | **ME** | A | *ME* | BD | 64372 | 71347 | 64410 |
| 507 007 | **ME** | A | *ME* | BD | 64373 | 71348 | 64411 |
| 507 008 | **ME** | A | *ME* | BD | 64374 | 71349 | 64412 |
| 507 009 | **ME** | A | *ME* | BD | 64375 | 71350 | 64413 |
| 507 010 | **ME** | A | *ME* | BD | 64376 | 71351 | 64414 |
| 507 011 | **ME** | A | *ME* | BD | 64377 | 71352 | 64415 |
| 507 012 | **ME** | A | *ME* | BD | 64378 | 71353 | 64416 |
| 507 013 | **ME** | A | *ME* | BD | 64379 | 71354 | 64417 |
| 507 014 | **ME** | A | *ME* | BD | 64380 | 71355 | 64418 |
| 507 015 | **ME** | A | *ME* | BD | 64381 | 71356 | 64419 |
| 507 016 | **ME** | A | *ME* | BD | 64382 | 71357 | 64420 |
| 507 017 | **ME** | A | *ME* | BD | 64383 | 71358 | 64421 |
| 507 018 | **ME** | A | *ME* | BD | 64384 | 71359 | 64422 |
| 507 019 | **ME** | A | *ME* | BD | 64385 | 71360 | 64423 |
| 507 020 | **ME** | A | *ME* | BD | 64386 | 71361 | 64424 |
| 507 021 | **ME** | A | *ME* | BD | 64387 | 71362 | 64425 |
| 507 023 | **ME** | A | *ME* | BD | 64389 | 71364 | 64427 |
| 507 024 | **ME** | A | *ME* | BD | 64390 | 71365 | 64428 |
| 507 025 | **ME** | A | *ME* | BD | 64391 | 71366 | 64429 |
| 507 026 | **ME** | A | *ME* | BD | 64392 | 71367 | 64430 |
| 507 027 | **ME** | A | *ME* | BD | 64393 | 71368 | 64431 |
| 507 028 | **ME** | A | *ME* | BD | 64394 | 71369 | 64432 |
| 507 029 | **ME** | A | *ME* | BD | 64395 | 71370 | 64433 |
| 507 030 | **ME** | A | *ME* | BD | 64396 | 71371 | 64434 |
| 507 031 | **ME** | A | *ME* | BD | 64397 | 71372 | 64435 |
| 507 032 | **ME** | A | *ME* | BD | 64398 | 71373 | 64436 |
| 507 033 | **ME** | A | *ME* | BD | 64399 | 71374 | 64437 |

**Names:**

| | |
|---|---|
| 507 004 | Bob Paisley |
| 507 008 | Harold Wilson |
| 507 009 | Dixie Dean |
| 507 020 | John Peel |
| 507 021 | Red Rum |
| 507 023 | Operations Inspector Stuart Mason |
| 507 016 | Merseyrail – celebrating the first ten years 2003–2013 |
| 507 033 | Councillor Jack Spriggs |

# CLASS 508                                                    BREL YORK

**Formation:** DMSO–TSO–BDMSO.
**Construction:** Steel underframe, aluminium alloy body and roof.
**Traction Motors:** Four GEC G310AZ of 82.125 kW.
**Wheel Arrangement:** Bo-Bo + 2-2 + Bo-Bo.
**Braking:** Disc & rheostatic.          **Dimensions:** 20.18 x 2.82 m.
**Bogies:** BX1.                          **Couplers:** Tightlock.
**Gangways:** Within unit + end doors.   **Control System:** Camshaft.
**Doors:** Sliding.                       **Maximum Speed:** 75 mph.
**Seating Layout:** All refurbished with 2+2 high-back facing seating.
**Multiple Working:** Within class and with Class 507.

**Advertising livery:** 508 111 Beatles Story (blue).

**DMSO.** Lot No. 30979 1979–80. –/56(3) 1W. 36.0 t.
**TSO.** Lot No. 30980 1979–80. –/74. 26.5 t.
**BDMSO.** Lot No. 30981 1979–80. –/56(3) 1W. 36.5 t.

| | | | | | | | |
|---|---|---|---|---|---|---|---|
| 508 103 | **ME** | A | *ME* | BD | 64651 | 71485 | 64694 |
| 508 104 | **ME** | A | *ME* | BD | 64652 | 71486 | 64695 |
| 508 108 | **ME** | A | *ME* | BD | 64656 | 71490 | 64699 |
| 508 110 | **ME** | A | *ME* | BD | 64658 | 71492 | 64701 |
| 508 111 | **AL** | A | *ME* | BD | 64659 | 71493 | 64702 |
| 508 112 | **ME** | A | *ME* | BD | 64660 | 71494 | 64703 |
| 508 114 | **ME** | A | *ME* | BD | 64662 | 71496 | 64705 |
| 508 115 | **ME** | A | *ME* | BD | 64663 | 71497 | 64706 |
| 508 117 | **ME** | A | *ME* | BD | 64665 | 71499 | 64708 |
| 508 120 | **ME** | A | *ME* | BD | 64668 | 71502 | 64711 |
| 508 122 | **ME** | A | *ME* | BD | 64670 | 71504 | 64713 |
| 508 123 | **ME** | A | *ME* | BD | 64671 | 71505 | 64714 |
| 508 124 | **ME** | A | *ME* | BD | 64672 | 71506 | 64715 |
| 508 125 | **ME** | A | *ME* | BD | 64673 | 71507 | 64716 |
| 508 126 | **ME** | A | *ME* | BD | 64674 | 71508 | 64717 |
| 508 127 | **ME** | A | *ME* | BD | 64675 | 71509 | 64718 |
| 508 128 | **ME** | A | *ME* | BD | 64676 | 71510 | 64719 |
| 508 130 | **ME** | A | *ME* | BD | 64678 | 71512 | 64721 |
| 508 131 | **ME** | A | *ME* | BD | 64679 | 71513 | 64722 |
| 508 134 | **ME** | A | *ME* | BD | 64682 | 71516 | 64725 |
| 508 136 | **ME** | A | *ME* | BD | 64684 | 71518 | 64727 |
| 508 137 | **ME** | A | *ME* | BD | 64685 | 71519 | 64728 |
| 508 138 | **ME** | A | *ME* | BD | 64686 | 71520 | 64729 |
| 508 139 | **ME** | A | *ME* | BD | 64687 | 71521 | 64730 |
| 508 140 | **ME** | A | *ME* | BD | 64688 | 71522 | 64731 |
| 508 141 | **ME** | A | *ME* | BD | 64689 | 71523 | 64732 |
| 508 143 | **ME** | A | *ME* | BD | 64691 | 71525 | 64734 |

# 4.3. DUAL VOLTAGE THAMESLINK UNITS

The large fleet of EMUs currently under construction for the Thameslink routes have been designated Class 700. The first of these units should be delivered for testing in mid 2014 and the fleet will enter traffic between early 2016 and late 2018. They are being financed by Cross London Trains (a consortium of Siemens Project Ventures, Innisfree Ltd and 3i Infrastructure Ltd) and will be based at new depots being built at Three Bridges and Hornsey. The units will have 6-digit vehicle numbers.

## CLASS 700      DESIRO CITY      SIEMENS

**Formations (8-car):** DMCO–PTSO–MSO–TSO–TSO–MSO–PTSO–DMCO or **(12-car):** DMCO–PTSO–MSO–MSO–TSO–TSO–TSO–TSO–MSO–MSO–PTSO–DMCO.
**Systems:** 25 kV AC overhead/750 V DC third rail.
**Construction:** Aluminium.
**Traction Motors:**
**Wheel Arrangement (8-car):** Bo-Bo + 2-2 + Bo-Bo + 2-2 + 2-2 + Bo-Bo + 2-2 + Bo-Bo. **(12-car):** Bo-Bo + 2-2 + Bo-Bo + Bo-Bo + 2-2 + 2-2 + 2-2 + 2-2 + Bo-Bo + Bo-Bo + 2-2 + Bo-Bo.
**Braking:**                **Dimensions:** 20.0 m x 2.80 m.
**Bogies:** Siemens SF7000 inside-frame. **Couplers:**
**Gangways:** Within unit.        **Control System:** IGBT Inverter.
**Doors:**                  **Maximum Speed:** 100 mph.
**Heating & ventilation:** Air conditioning.
**Seating Layout:**
**Multiple Working:** Within class.

**Class 700/0.** 8-car units. Full details awaited.

**DMCO(A).** Siemens Krefeld 2014–18.     .    t.
**PTSO.** Siemens Krefeld 2014–18.      .    t.
**MSO.** Siemens Krefeld 2014–18.      .    t.
**TSO.** Siemens Krefeld 2014–18.      .    t.
**TSO.** Siemens Krefeld 2014–18.      .    t.
**MSO.** Siemens Krefeld 2014–18.      .    t.
**PTSO.** Siemens Krefeld 2014–18.      .    t.
**DMCO(B).** Siemens Krefeld 2014–18.     .    t.

| | | | | |
|---|---|---|---|---|
| 700 001 | 401001 | 402001 | 403001 | 406001 |
| | 407001 | 410001 | 411001 | 412001 |
| 700 002 | 401002 | 402002 | 403002 | 406002 |
| | 407002 | 410002 | 411002 | 412002 |
| 700 003 | 401003 | 402003 | 403003 | 406003 |
| | 407003 | 410003 | 411003 | 412003 |
| 700 004 | 401004 | 402004 | 403004 | 406004 |
| | 407004 | 410004 | 411004 | 412004 |

| 700005 | 401005 | 402005 | 403005 | 406005 |
|        | 407005 | 410005 | 411005 | 412005 |
| 700006 | 401006 | 402006 | 403006 | 406006 |
|        | 407006 | 410006 | 411006 | 412006 |
| 700007 | 401007 | 402007 | 403007 | 406007 |
|        | 407007 | 410007 | 411007 | 412007 |
| 700008 | 401008 | 402008 | 403008 | 406008 |
|        | 407008 | 410008 | 411008 | 412008 |
| 700009 | 401009 | 402009 | 403009 | 406009 |
|        | 407009 | 410009 | 411009 | 412009 |
| 700010 | 401010 | 402010 | 403010 | 406010 |
|        | 407010 | 410010 | 411010 | 412010 |
| 700011 | 401011 | 402011 | 403011 | 406011 |
|        | 407011 | 410011 | 411011 | 412011 |
| 700012 | 401012 | 402012 | 403012 | 406012 |
|        | 407012 | 410012 | 411012 | 412012 |
| 700013 | 401013 | 402013 | 403013 | 406013 |
|        | 407013 | 410013 | 411013 | 412013 |
| 700014 | 401014 | 402014 | 403014 | 406014 |
|        | 407014 | 410014 | 411014 | 412014 |
| 700015 | 401015 | 402015 | 403015 | 406015 |
|        | 407015 | 410015 | 411015 | 412015 |
| 700016 | 401016 | 402016 | 403016 | 406016 |
|        | 407016 | 410016 | 411016 | 412016 |
| 700017 | 401017 | 402017 | 403017 | 406017 |
|        | 407017 | 410017 | 411017 | 412017 |
| 700018 | 401018 | 402018 | 403018 | 406018 |
|        | 407018 | 410018 | 411018 | 412018 |
| 700019 | 401019 | 402019 | 403019 | 406019 |
|        | 407019 | 410019 | 411019 | 412019 |
| 700020 | 401020 | 402020 | 403020 | 406020 |
|        | 407020 | 410020 | 411020 | 412020 |
| 700021 | 401021 | 402021 | 403021 | 406021 |
|        | 407021 | 410021 | 411021 | 412021 |
| 700022 | 401022 | 402022 | 403022 | 406022 |
|        | 407022 | 410022 | 411022 | 412022 |
| 700023 | 401023 | 402023 | 403023 | 406023 |
|        | 407023 | 410023 | 411023 | 412023 |
| 700024 | 401024 | 402024 | 403024 | 406024 |
|        | 407024 | 410024 | 411024 | 412024 |
| 700025 | 401025 | 402025 | 403025 | 406025 |
|        | 407025 | 410025 | 411025 | 412025 |
| 700026 | 401026 | 402026 | 403026 | 406026 |
|        | 407026 | 410026 | 411026 | 412026 |
| 700027 | 401027 | 402027 | 403027 | 406027 |
|        | 407027 | 410027 | 411027 | 412027 |
| 700028 | 401028 | 402028 | 403028 | 406028 |
|        | 407028 | 410028 | 411028 | 412028 |
| 700029 | 401029 | 402029 | 403029 | 406029 |
|        | 407029 | 410029 | 411029 | 412029 |

| 700 030 | 401030 | 402030 | 403030 | 406030 |
|         | 407030 | 410030 | 411030 | 412030 |
| 700 031 | 401031 | 402031 | 403031 | 406031 |
|         | 407031 | 410031 | 411031 | 412031 |
| 700 032 | 401032 | 402032 | 403032 | 406032 |
|         | 407032 | 410032 | 411032 | 412032 |
| 700 033 | 401033 | 402033 | 403033 | 406033 |
|         | 407033 | 410033 | 411033 | 412033 |
| 700 034 | 401034 | 402034 | 403034 | 406034 |
|         | 407034 | 410034 | 411034 | 412034 |
| 700 035 | 401035 | 402035 | 403035 | 406035 |
|         | 407035 | 410035 | 411035 | 412035 |
| 700 036 | 401036 | 402036 | 403036 | 406036 |
|         | 407036 | 410036 | 411036 | 412036 |
| 700 037 | 401037 | 402037 | 403037 | 406037 |
|         | 407037 | 410037 | 411037 | 412037 |
| 700 038 | 401038 | 402038 | 403038 | 406038 |
|         | 407038 | 410038 | 411038 | 412038 |
| 700 039 | 401039 | 402039 | 403039 | 406039 |
|         | 407039 | 410039 | 411039 | 412039 |
| 700 040 | 401040 | 402040 | 403040 | 406040 |
|         | 407040 | 410040 | 411040 | 412040 |
| 700 041 | 401041 | 402041 | 403041 | 406041 |
|         | 407041 | 410041 | 411041 | 412041 |
| 700 042 | 401042 | 402042 | 403042 | 406042 |
|         | 407042 | 410042 | 411042 | 412042 |
| 700 043 | 401043 | 402043 | 403043 | 406043 |
|         | 407043 | 410043 | 411043 | 412043 |
| 700 044 | 401044 | 402044 | 403044 | 406044 |
|         | 407044 | 410044 | 411044 | 412044 |
| 700 045 | 401045 | 402045 | 403045 | 406045 |
|         | 407045 | 410045 | 411045 | 412045 |
| 700 046 | 401046 | 402046 | 403046 | 406046 |
|         | 407046 | 410046 | 411046 | 412046 |
| 700 047 | 401047 | 402047 | 403047 | 406047 |
|         | 407047 | 410047 | 411047 | 412047 |
| 700 048 | 401048 | 402048 | 403048 | 406048 |
|         | 407048 | 410048 | 411048 | 412048 |
| 700 049 | 401049 | 402049 | 403049 | 406049 |
|         | 407049 | 410049 | 411049 | 412049 |
| 700 050 | 401050 | 402050 | 403050 | 406050 |
|         | 407050 | 410050 | 411050 | 412050 |
| 700 051 | 401051 | 402051 | 403051 | 406051 |
|         | 407051 | 410051 | 411051 | 412051 |
| 700 052 | 401052 | 402052 | 403052 | 406052 |
|         | 407052 | 410052 | 411052 | 412052 |
| 700 053 | 401053 | 402053 | 403053 | 406053 |
|         | 407053 | 410053 | 411053 | 412053 |
| 700 054 | 401054 | 402054 | 403054 | 406054 |
|         | 407054 | 410054 | 411054 | 412054 |

| 700055 | 401055 402055 403055 406055 |
|--------|------------------------------|
|        | 407055 410055 411055 412055 |
| 700056 | 401056 402056 403056 406056 |
|        | 407056 410056 411056 412056 |
| 700057 | 401057 402057 403057 406057 |
|        | 407057 410057 411057 412057 |
| 700058 | 401058 402058 403058 406058 |
|        | 407058 410058 411058 412058 |
| 700059 | 401059 402059 403059 406059 |
|        | 407059 410059 411059 412059 |
| 700060 | 401060 402060 403060 406060 |
|        | 407060 410060 411060 412060 |

**Class 700/1**. 12-car units. Full details awaited.

**DMCO(A).** Siemens Krefeld 2013–18.      .     t.
**PTSO.** Siemens Krefeld 2013–18.      .     t.
**MSO.** Siemens Krefeld 2013–18.      .     t.
**MSO.** Siemens Krefeld 2013–18.      .     t.
**TSO.** Siemens Krefeld 2013–18.      .     t.
**TSO.** Siemens Krefeld 2013–18.      .     t.
**TSO.** Siemens Krefeld 2013–18.      .     t.
**TSO.** Siemens Krefeld 2013–18.      .     t.
**MSO.** Siemens Krefeld 2013–18.      .     t.
**MSO.** Siemens Krefeld 2013–18.      .     t.
**PTSO.** Siemens Krefeld 2013–18.      .     t.
**DMCO(B).** Siemens Krefeld 2013–18.      .     t.

| 700101 | 401101 402101 403101 404101 405101 406101 |
|--------|---------------------------------------------|
|        | 407101 408101 409101 410101 411101 412101 |
| 700102 | 401102 402102 403102 404102 405102 406102 |
|        | 407102 408102 409102 410102 411102 412102 |
| 700103 | 401103 402103 403103 404103 405103 406103 |
|        | 407103 408103 409103 410103 411103 412103 |
| 700104 | 401104 402104 403104 404104 405104 406104 |
|        | 407104 408104 409104 410104 411104 412104 |
| 700105 | 401105 402105 403105 404105 405105 406105 |
|        | 407105 408105 409105 410105 411105 412105 |
| 700106 | 401106 402106 403106 404106 405106 406106 |
|        | 407106 408106 409106 410106 411106 412106 |
| 700107 | 401107 402107 403107 404107 405107 406107 |
|        | 407107 408107 409107 410107 411107 412107 |
| 700108 | 401108 402108 403108 404108 405108 406108 |
|        | 407108 408108 409108 410108 411108 412108 |
| 700109 | 401109 402109 403109 404109 405109 406109 |
|        | 407109 408109 409109 410109 411109 412109 |
| 700110 | 401110 402110 403110 404110 405110 406110 |
|        | 407110 408110 409110 410110 411110 412110 |
| 700111 | 401111 402111 403111 404111 405111 406111 |
|        | 407111 408111 409111 410111 411111 412111 |
| 700112 | 401112 402112 403112 404112 405112 406112 |
|        | 407112 408112 409112 410112 411112 412112 |

| | |
|---|---|
| 700 113 | 401113 402113 403113 404113 405113 406113 |
| | 407113 408113 409113 410113 411113 412113 |
| 700 114 | 401114 402114 403114 404114 405114 406114 |
| | 407114 408114 409114 410114 411114 412114 |
| 700 115 | 401115 402115 403115 404115 405115 406115 |
| | 407115 408115 409115 410115 411115 412115 |
| 700 116 | 401116 402116 403116 404116 405116 406116 |
| | 407116 408116 409116 410116 411116 412116 |
| 700 117 | 401117 402117 403117 404117 405117 406117 |
| | 407117 408117 409117 410117 411117 412117 |
| 700 118 | 401118 402118 403118 404118 405118 406118 |
| | 407118 408118 409118 410118 411118 412118 |
| 700 119 | 401119 402119 403119 404119 405119 406119 |
| | 407119 408119 409119 410119 411119 412119 |
| 700 120 | 401120 402120 403120 404120 405120 406120 |
| | 407120 408120 409120 410120 411120 412120 |
| 700 121 | 401121 402121 403121 404121 405121 406121 |
| | 407121 408121 409121 410121 411121 412121 |
| 700 122 | 401122 402122 403122 404122 405122 406122 |
| | 407122 408122 409122 410122 411122 412122 |
| 700 123 | 401123 402123 403123 404123 405123 406123 |
| | 407123 408123 409123 410123 411123 412123 |
| 700 124 | 401124 402124 403124 404124 405124 406124 |
| | 407124 408124 409124 410124 411124 412124 |
| 700 125 | 401125 402125 403125 404125 405125 406125 |
| | 407125 408125 409125 410125 411125 412125 |
| 700 126 | 401126 402126 403126 404126 405126 406126 |
| | 407126 408126 409126 410126 411126 412126 |
| 700 127 | 401127 402127 403127 404127 405127 406127 |
| | 407127 408127 409127 410127 411127 412127 |
| 700 128 | 401128 402128 403128 404128 405128 406128 |
| | 407128 408128 409128 410128 411128 412128 |
| 700 129 | 401129 402129 403129 404129 405129 406129 |
| | 407129 408129 409129 410129 411129 412129 |
| 700 130 | 401130 402130 403130 404130 405130 406130 |
| | 407130 408130 409130 410130 411130 412130 |
| 700 131 | 401131 402131 403131 404131 405131 406131 |
| | 407131 408131 409131 410131 411131 412131 |
| 700 132 | 401132 402132 403132 404132 405132 406132 |
| | 407132 408132 409132 410132 411132 412132 |
| 700 133 | 401133 402133 403133 404133 405133 406133 |
| | 407133 408133 409133 410133 411133 412133 |
| 700 134 | 401134 402134 403134 404134 405134 406134 |
| | 407134 408134 409134 410134 411134 412134 |
| 700 135 | 401135 402135 403135 404135 405135 406135 |
| | 407135 408135 409135 410135 411135 412135 |
| 700 136 | 401136 402136 403136 404136 405136 406136 |
| | 407136 408136 409136 410136 411136 412136 |
| 700 137 | 401137 402137 403137 404137 405137 406137 |
| | 407137 408137 409137 410137 411137 412137 |

| 700 138 | 401138 402138 403138 404138 405138 406138 |
|---------|-------------------------------------------|
|         | 407138 408138 409138 410138 411138 412138 |
| 700 139 | 401139 402139 403139 404139 405139 406139 |
|         | 407139 408139 409139 410139 411139 412139 |
| 700 140 | 401140 402140 403140 404140 405140 406140 |
|         | 407140 408140 409140 410140 411140 412140 |
| 700 141 | 401141 402141 403141 404141 405141 406141 |
|         | 407141 408141 409141 410141 411141 412141 |
| 700 142 | 401142 402142 403142 404142 405142 406142 |
|         | 407142 408142 409142 410142 411142 412142 |
| 700 143 | 401143 402143 403143 404143 405143 406143 |
|         | 407143 408143 409143 410143 411143 412143 |
| 700 144 | 401144 402144 403144 404144 405144 406144 |
|         | 407144 408144 409144 410144 411144 412144 |
| 700 145 | 401145 402145 403145 404145 405145 406145 |
|         | 407145 408145 409145 410145 411145 412145 |
| 700 146 | 401146 402146 403146 404146 405146 406146 |
|         | 407146 408146 409146 410146 411146 412146 |
| 700 147 | 401147 402147 403147 404147 405147 406147 |
|         | 407147 408147 409147 410147 411147 412147 |
| 700 148 | 401148 402148 403148 404148 405148 406148 |
|         | 407148 408148 409148 410148 411148 412148 |
| 700 149 | 401149 402149 403149 404149 405149 406149 |
|         | 407149 408149 409149 410149 411149 412149 |
| 700 150 | 401150 402150 403150 404150 405150 406150 |
|         | 407150 408150 409150 410150 411150 412150 |
| 700 151 | 401151 402151 403151 404151 405151 406151 |
|         | 407151 408151 409151 410151 411151 412151 |
| 700 152 | 401152 402152 403152 404152 405152 406152 |
|         | 407152 408152 409152 410152 411152 412152 |
| 700 153 | 401153 402153 403153 404153 405153 406153 |
|         | 407153 408153 409153 410153 411153 412153 |
| 700 154 | 401154 402154 403154 404154 405154 406154 |
|         | 407154 408154 409154 410154 411154 412154 |
| 700 155 | 401155 402155 403155 404155 405155 406155 |
|         | 407155 408155 409155 410155 411155 412155 |

# 4.4. EUROSTAR UNITS

The original Eurostar Class 373 units were built for and are normally used on services between Britain and continental Europe via the Channel Tunnel. SNCF-owned units 3203/04, 3225/26 and 3227/28 have been removed from the Eurostar pool and only operate SNCF internal services between Paris and Lille. As they are not now permitted through the Channel Tunnel they are not listed here.

Each Class 373 train consists of two 10-car units coupled, with a motor car at each driving end. All units are articulated with an extra motor bogie on the coach adjacent to the motor car.

All Class 373 sets can be used between London St Pancras and Paris, Brussels and Disneyland Paris. Certain sets (shown *) are equipped for 1500 V DC operation and are used for the winter service to Bourg Saint Maurice and the summer service to Avignon.

Seven 8-car Class 373 sets were built for Regional Eurostar services, but all except one power car (3308) and one half set are on long-term hire to SNCF for use on French internal services so are not listed here. The spare half set (from 3308/07) is stored at Temple Mills depot.

The second generation Eurostar trains, Class 374s, are currently under construction, although these will supplement rather than replace the 373s.

**Formation:** DM–MSO–4TSO–RB–2TFO–TBFO. Gangwayed within pair of units. Air conditioned.
**Construction:** Steel.
**Supply Systems:** 25 kV AC 50 Hz overhead or 3000 V DC overhead (* also equipped for 1500 V DC overhead operation).
**Control System:** GTO–GTO Inverter on UK 750 V DC and 25 kV AC, GTO Chopper on SNCB 3000 V DC.
**Wheel Arrangement:** Bo-Bo + Bo–2–2–2–2–2–2–2–2.
**Length:** 22.15 m (DM), 21.85 m (MS & TBF), 18.70 m (other cars).
**Couplers:** Schaku 10S at outer ends, Schaku 10L at inner end of each DM and outer ends of each sub set.
**Maximum Speed:** 186 mph (300 km/h)
**Built:** 1992–93 by GEC-Alsthom/Brush/ANF/De Dietrich/BN Construction/ACEC.
DM vehicles carry the set numbers indicated below.

## CLASS 373                    ORIGINAL-BUILD UNITS

**10-car sets.** Built for services starting from or terminating in London Waterloo (now St Pancras). Individual vehicles in each set are allocated numbers 373xxx0 + 373xxx1 + 373xxx2 + 373xxx3 + 373xxx4 + 373xxx5 + 373xxx6 + 373xxx7 + 373xxx8 + 373xxx9, where 3xxx denotes the set number.

**373xxx0 series. DM.** Lot No. 31118 1992–95. 68.5 t.
**373xxx1 series. MSO.** Lot No. 31119 1992–95. –/48 2T. 44.6 t.
**373xxx2 series. TSO.** Lot No. 31120 1992–95. –/56 1T. 28.1 t.

**373xxx3 series. TSO.** Lot No. 31121 1992–95. –/56 2T. 29.7 t.
**373xxx4 series. TSO.** Lot No. 31122 1992–95. –/56 1T. 28.3 t.
**373xxx5 series. TSO.** Lot No. 31123 1992–95. –/56 2T. 29.2 t.
**373xxx6 series. RB.** Lot No.31124 1992–95. 31.1 t.
**373xxx7 series. TFO.** Lot No. 31125 1992–95. 39/– 1T. 29.6 t.
**373xxx8 series. TFO.** Lot No. 31126 1992–95. 39/– 1T. 32.2 t.
**373xxx9 series. TBFO.** Lot No. 31127 1992–95. 25/– 1TD. 39.4 t.

| | | | | | | | | | | |
|---|---|---|---|---|---|---|---|---|---|---|
| 3001 | **EU** | EU | *EU* | TI | | 3107 | | **EU** | SB | *EU* | FF |
| 3002 | **EU** | EU | *EU* | TI | | 3108 | | **EU** | SB | *EU* | FF |
| 3003 | **EU** | EU | *EU* | TI | | 3201 | * | **EU** | SF | *EU* | LY |
| 3004 | **EU** | EU | *EU* | TI | | 3202 | * | **EU** | SF | *EU* | LY |
| 3005 | **EU** | EU | *EU* | TI | | 3205 | | **EU** | SF | *EU* | LY |
| 3006 | **EU** | EU | *EU* | TI | | 3206 | | **EU** | SF | *EU* | LY |
| 3007 | **EU** | EU | *EU* | TI | | 3207 | * | **EU** | SF | *EU* | LY |
| 3008 | **EU** | EU | *EU* | TI | | 3208 | * | **EU** | SF | *EU* | LY |
| 3009 | **EU** | EU | *EU* | TI | | 3209 | * | **EU** | SF | *EU* | LY |
| 3010 | **EU** | EU | *EU* | TI | | 3210 | * | **EU** | SF | *EU* | LY |
| 3011 | **EU** | EU | *EU* | TI | | 3211 | | **EU** | SF | *EU* | LY |
| 3012 | **EU** | EU | *EU* | TI | | 3212 | | **EU** | SF | *EU* | LY |
| 3013 | **EU** | EU | *EU* | TI | | 3213 | * | **EU** | SF | *EU* | LY |
| 3014 | **EU** | EU | *EU* | TI | | 3214 | * | **EU** | SF | *EU* | LY |
| 3015 | **EU** | EU | *EU* | TI | | 3215 | * | **EU** | SF | *EU* | LY |
| 3016 | **EU** | EU | *EU* | TI | | 3216 | * | **EU** | SF | *EU* | LY |
| 3017 | **EU** | EU | *EU* | TI | | 3217 | | **EU** | SF | *EU* | LY |
| 3018 | **EU** | EU | *EU* | TI | | 3218 | | **EU** | SF | *EU* | LY |
| 3019 | **EU** | EU | *EU* | TI | | 3219 | | **EU** | SF | *EU* | LY |
| 3020 | **EU** | EU | *EU* | TI | | 3220 | | **EU** | SF | *EU* | LY |
| 3021 | **EU** | EU | *EU* | TI | | 3221 | | **EU** | SF | *EU* | LY |
| 3022 | **EU** | EU | *EU* | TI | | 3222 | | **EU** | SF | *EU* | LY |
| 3101 | **EU** | SB | | TI | | 3223 | * | **EU** | SF | *EU* | LY |
| 3102 | **EU** | SB | | TI | | 3224 | * | **EU** | SF | *EU* | LY |
| 3103 | **EU** | SB | *EU* | FF | | 3229 | * | **EU** | SF | *EU* | LY |
| 3104 | **EU** | SB | *EU* | FF | | 3230 | * | **EU** | SF | *EU* | LY |
| 3105 | **EU** | SB | *EU* | FF | | 3231 | | **EU** | SF | *EU* | LY |
| 3106 | **EU** | SB | *EU* | FF | | 3232 | | **EU** | SF | *EU* | LY |

**Spare Regional Eurostar DM:**

| | | | | |
|---|---|---|---|---|
| 3308 | **EU** | EU | | LB |

**Spare DM:**

| | | | | |
|---|---|---|---|---|
| 3999 | **EU** | EU | *EU* | TI |

**Names:**

| | | | |
|---|---|---|---|
| 3001/02 | Tread Lightly/Voyage Vert | 3013/14 | LONDON 2012 |
| 3003/04 | Tri-City-Athlon 2010 | 3207/08 | MICHEL HOLLARD |
| 3007/08 | Waterloo Sunset | 3209/10 | THE DA VINCI CODE |
| 3009/10 | REMEMBERING FROMELLES | | |

# CLASS 374                                SIEMENS VELARO e320

**8-car sets.** Under construction for Eurostar. These units are similar to the DB Class 407 ICE sets. Due to enter service in 2015 ahead of a proposed St Pancras–Amsterdam service starting in 2016. Full details awaited.

**Formation (provisional):** DMFO–TBFO–MFO–TSO–TSO–MSO–TSO–MSORB. Gangwayed within pair of units. Air conditioned.
**Construction:** Aluminium.
**Supply Systems:** 25 kV AC 50 Hz overhead, 15 kV AC 16.7 Hz overhead, 1500 V DC overhead and 3000 V DC overhead.
**Control System:**
**Wheel Arrangement:** Bo-Bo + 2-2 + Bo-Bo + 2-2 + 2-2 + Bo-Bo + 2-2 + Bo-Bo.
**Length:**
**Couplers:**
**Maximum Speed:** 200 mph (320 km/h).
**Built:** 2012–14 by Siemens, Krefeld, Germany.

DM vehicles carry the full 12-digit European Vehicle Numbers as indicated below. For example set 4001/02 carries the numbers 93 70 3740 011-9 + 93 70 3740 012-7 + 93 70 3740 013-5 + 93 70 3740 014-3 + 93 70 3740 015-0 + 93 70 3740 016-8 + 93 70 3740 017-6 + 93 70 3740 018-4 + 93 70 3740 028-3 + 93 70 3740 027-5 + 93 70 3740 026-7 + 93 70 3740 025-9 + 93 70 3740 024-2 + 93 70 3740 023-4 + 93 70 3740 022-6 + 93 70 3740 021-8.

**93 70 3740 xx1-c series. DMFO.** Siemens Krefeld 2012–14.         t.
**93 70 3740 xx2-c series. TBFO.** Siemens Krefeld 2012–14.       t.
**93 70 3740 xx3-c series. MFO.** Siemens Krefeld 2012–14.       t.
**93 70 3740 xx4-c series. TSO.** Siemens Krefeld 2012–14.       t.
**93 70 3740 xx5-c series. TSO.** Siemens Krefeld 2012–14.       t.
**93 70 3740 xx6-c series. MSO.** Siemens Krefeld 2012–14.       t.
**93 70 3740 xx7-c series. TSO.** Siemens Krefeld 2012–14.       t.
**93 70 3740 xx8-c series. MSORB.** Siemens Krefeld 2012–14.         t.

| | | | |
|---|---|---|---|
| 4001 | **ER** | 4011 | |
| 4002 | **ER** | 4012 | |
| 4003 | **ER** | 4013 | |
| 4004 | **ER** | 4014 | |
| 4005 | | 4015 | |
| 4006 | | 4016 | |
| 4007 | | 4017 | |
| 4008 | | 4018 | |
| 4009 | | 4019 | |
| 4010 | | 4020 | |

# 4.5. SERVICE EMUS

The following unit is used by Network Rail for ERTMS testing on the Hertford Loop. The unit has been heavily modified from its original condition, and now includes a toilet.

313121 **Y** BN *GB* WB 62549 71233 62613

# 4.6. EMU VEHICLES IN INDUSTRIAL SERVICE

This list comprises EMU vehicles that have been withdrawn from active service but continue to be used in industrial service.

| | | | | |
|---|---|---|---|---|
| Cl. 390 | 69133 | 69833 | | Virgin Trains Training Centre, Westmere Drive, Crewe, Cheshire |
| Cl. 390 | 69633 | 69733 | | The Fire Service College, Moreton-in-Marsh, Gloucestershire |
| Cl. 390 | 69933 | | | Safety & Accident Investigation Centre, Cranfield University, Cranfield, Bedfordshire |
| Cl. 508 | 64649 | 64712 | | Emergency Services Training Centre, Seacombe, Merseyside |
| Cl. 508 | 64681 | 71511 | 64724 | The Fire Service College, Moreton-in-Marsh, Gloucestershire |

# 4.7. EMUS AWAITING DISPOSAL

This list comprises vehicles awaiting disposal which are stored on the national railway network.

## 25 kV AC 50 Hz OVERHEAD UNITS:

| | | | | |
|---|---|---|---|---|
| Cl. 309 | **RR** | WC | CS | 71758 |
| Cl. 365 | **N** | FC | ZN | 65919 |

## 750 V DC THIRD RAIL UNITS:

| | | | | | | | |
|---|---|---|---|---|---|---|---|
| Cl. 460 | **GV** | P | LB | 67901 | 67903 | 67907 | 67908 |
| Cl. 508 | **CN** | A | ZG | 64664 | 64667 | 64680 | 64707 |
| | | | | 64723 | | | |
| Cl. 508 | **CN** | A | ZI | 64710 | 64720 | | |

64664 and 64707 are undergoing conversion to barrier vehicles.

# 5. ON-TRACK MACHINES

These machines are used for maintaining, renewing and enhancing the infrastructure of the national railway network. With the exception of snowploughs all can be self-propelled. They are permitted to operate either under their own power or in train formations throughout the network both within and outside engineering possessions. Machines only permitted to be used within engineering possessions, referred to as On-Track Plant, are not included. For each machine its Network Rail registered number, owner/ responsible custodian and type is given, plus its name if carried. In addition, for snow clearance equipment, the berthing location is also given. Actual operation of each machine is undertaken by either the owner/responsible custodian or a contracted responsible custodian.

(S) after the registered number designates a machine that is currently stored (the storage location of each is given at the end of this section).

## DYNAMIC TRACK STABILISERS

| | | |
|---|---|---|
| DR 72211 | BB | Plasser & Theurer DGS 62-N |
| DR 72213 | BB | Plasser & Theurer DGS 62-N |

## TAMPERS

| | | | |
|---|---|---|---|
| DR 73108 | CS | Plasser & Theurer 09-32-RT | Tiger |
| DR 73109 | SK | Plasser & Theurer 09-3X-RT | |
| DR 73110 | SK | Plasser & Theurer 09-3X-RT | Peter White |
| DR 73111 | NR | Plasser & Theurer 09-3X-Dynamic | Reading Panel 1965–2005 |
| DR 73113 | NR | Plasser & Theurer 09-3X-Dynamic | |
| DR 73114 | NR | Plasser & Theurer 09-3X-Dynamic | Ron Henderson |
| DR 73115 | NR | Plasser & Theurer 09-3X-Dynamic | |
| DR 73116 | NR | Plasser & Theurer 09-3X Dynamic | |
| DR 73117 | NR | Plasser & Theurer 09-3X Dynamic | |
| DR 73118 | NR | Plasser & Theurer 09-3X Dynamic | |
| DR 73803 | SK | Plasser & Theurer 08-32U-RT | Alexander Graham Bell |
| DR 73804 | SK | Plasser & Theurer 08-32U-RT | James Watt |
| DR 73805 | CS | Plasser & Theurer 08-16/32U-RT | |
| DR 73806 | CS | Plasser & Theurer 08-16/32U-RT | Karine |
| DR 73904 | SK | Plasser & Theurer 08-4x4/4S-RT | Thomas Telford |
| DR 73905 | CS | Plasser & Theurer 08-4x4/4S-RT | Eddie King |
| DR 73906 | CS | Plasser & Theurer 08-4x4/4S-RT | Panther |
| DR 73907 | CS | Plasser & Theurer 08-4x4/4S-RT | |
| DR 73908 | CS | Plasser & Theurer 08-4x4/4S-RT | |
| DR 73909 | CS | Plasser & Theurer 08-4x4/4S-RT | Saturn |
| DR 73910 | CS | Plasser & Theurer 08-4x4/4S-RT | Jupiter |
| DR 73911 (S) | CS | Plasser & Theurer 08-16/4x4C-RT | Puma |
| DR 73912 | CS | Plasser & Theurer 08-16/4x4C-RT | Lynx |
| DR 73913 | CS | Plasser & Theurer 08-12/4x4C-RT | |
| DR 73914 | SK | Plasser & Theurer 08-4x4/4S-RT | Robert McAlpine |
| DR 73915 | SK | Plasser & Theurer 08-16/4x4C-RT | William Arrol |

| DR 73916 | SK | Plasser & Theurer 08-16/4x4C-RT | First Engineering |
| DR 73917 | BB | Plasser & Theurer 08-4x4/4S-RT | |
| DR 73918 | BB | Plasser & Theurer 08-4x4/4S-RT | |
| DR 73919 | CS | Plasser & Theurer 08-16/4x4C100-RT | |
| DR 73920 | CS | Plasser & Theurer 08-16/4x4C80-RT | |
| DR 73921 | CS | Plasser & Theurer 08-16/4x4C80-RT | |
| DR 73922 | CS | Plasser & Theurer 08-16/4x4C80-RT | John Snowdon |
| DR 73923 | CS | Plasser & Theurer 08-4x4/4S-RT | Mercury |
| DR 73924 | CS | Plasser & Theurer 08-16/4x4C100-RT | Atlas |
| DR 73925 | CS | Plasser & Theurer 08-16/4x4C100-RT | Europa |
| DR 73926 | BB | Plasser & Theurer 08-16/4x4C100-RT | Stephen Keith Blanchard |
| DR 73927 | BB | Plasser & Theurer 08-16/4x4C100-RT | |
| DR 73928 | BB | Plasser & Theurer 08-16/4x4C100-RT | |
| DR 73929 | CS | Plasser & Theurer 08-4x4/4S-RT | |
| DR 73930 | CS | Plasser & Theurer 08-4x4/4S-RT | |
| DR 73931 | CS | Plasser & Theurer 08-16/4x4C100-RT | |
| DR 73932 | SK | Plasser & Theurer 08-4x4/4S-RT | |
| DR 73933 | SK | Plasser & Theurer 08-16/4x4/C100-RT | |
| DR 73934 | SK | Plasser & Theurer 08-16/4x4/C100-RT | |
| DR 73935 | CS | Plasser & Theurer 08-4x4/4S-RT | |
| DR 73936 | CS | Plasser & Theurer 08-4x4/4S-RT | |
| DR 73937 | BB | Plasser & Theurer 08-16/4x4C100-RT | |
| DR 73938 | BB | Plasser & Theurer 08-16/4x4C100-RT | |
| DR 73939 | BB | Plasser & Theurer 08-16/4x4C100-RT | Pat Best |
| DR 73940 | SK | Plasser & Theurer 08-4x4/4S-RT | |
| DR 73941 | SK | Plasser & Theurer 08-4x4/4S-RT | |
| DR 73942 | CS | Plasser & Theurer 08-4x4/4S-RT | |
| DR 73943 | BB | Plasser & Theurer 08-16/4x4C100-RT | |
| DR 73944 | BB | Plasser & Theurer 08-16/4x4C100-RT | |
| DR 73945 | BB | Plasser & Theurer 08-16/4x4C100-RT | |
| DR 73946 | VO | Plasser & Theurer Euromat 08-4x4/4S | |
| DR 73947 | CS | Plasser & Theurer 08-4x4/4S-RT | |
| DR 73948 | CS | Plasser & Theurer 08-4x4/4S-RT | |
| DR 75301 | VO | Matisa B 45 UE | |
| DR 75302 | VO | Matisa B 45 UE | |
| DR 75303 | VO | Matisa B 45 UE | |
| DR 75401 | VO | Matisa B 41 UE | |
| DR 75402 | VO | Matisa B 41 UE | |
| DR 75403 | VO | Matisa B 41 UE | |
| DR 75404 | VO | Matisa B 41 UE | |
| DR 75405 | VO | Matisa B 41 UE | |
| DR 75406 | CS | Matisa B 41 UE | Eric Machell |
| DR 75407 | CS | Matisa B 41 UE | |
| DR 75408 | BB | Matisa B 41 UE | |
| DR 75409 | BB | Matisa B 41 UE | |
| DR 75410 | BB | Matisa B 41 UE | |
| DR 75411 | BB | Matisa B 41 UE | |
| DR 75501 | BB | Matisa B 66 UC | |
| DR 75502 | BB | Matisa B 66 UC | |
| 99 70 9128 001-3 | SK | Plasser & Theurer Unimat 09-4x4/4S Dynamic | |

# BALLAST CLEANERS

| | | |
|---|---|---|
| DR 76323 | NR | Plasser & Theurer RM95-RT *(works with DR 92263/DR 92264)* |
| DR 76324 (S) | NR | Plasser & Theurer RM95-RT |
| DR 76501 | NR | Plasser & Theurer RM-900-RT *(works with DR 92285/DR 92286)* |
| DR 76502 | NR | Plasser & Theurer RM-900-RT *(works with DR 92331/DR 92332)* |
| DR 76503 | NR | Plasser & Theurer RM-900-RT *(works with DR 76701/DR 76801/ DR 92431/DR 92432)* |

# VACUUM PREPARATION MACHINES

| | | |
|---|---|---|
| DR 76701 | NR | Plasser & Theurer VM80-NR *(works with DR 76503/DR 76801/ DR 92431/DR 92432)* |
| DR 76702 (S) | NR | Plasser & Theurer VM80-NR |
| DR 76703 (S) | NR | Plasser & Theurer VM80-NR |
| DR 76710 (S) | NR | Plasser & Theurer VM80-TRS |
| DR 76711 (S) | NR | Plasser & Theurer VM80-TRS |

# RAIL VACUUM MACHINE

| | | |
|---|---|---|
| 99 70 9515 001-4 | BY | Railcare RA7-UK RailVac |

# BALLAST TRANSFER MACHINES

| | | |
|---|---|---|
| DR 76750 | NR | Matisa D75 *(works with DR 78802/DR 78812/ DR 78822/DR 78832)* |
| DR 76751 | NR | Matisa D75 *(works with DR 78801/DR 78811/ DR 78821/DR 78831)* |

# CONSOLIDATION MACHINE

| | | |
|---|---|---|
| DR 76801 | NR | Plasser & Theurer 09-CM-NR *(works with DR 76503/DR 76701/ DR 92431/DR 92432)* |

# FINISHING MACHINES & BALLAST REGULATORS

| | | |
|---|---|---|
| DR 77001 | SK | Plasser & Theurer AFM 2000-RT Finishing Machine |
| DR 77002 | SK | Plasser & Theurer AFM 2000-RT Finishing Machine |
| DR 77315 (S) | BB | Plasser & Theurer USP 5000C Regulator |
| DR 77316 (S) | BB | Plasser & Theurer USP 5000C Regulator |
| DR 77322 | BB | Plasser & Theurer USP 5000C Regulator |
| DR 77327 | CS | Plasser & Theurer USP 5000C Regulator |
| DR 77336 (S) | BB | Plasser & Theurer USP 5000C Regulator |
| DR 77801 | VO | Matisa R 24 S Regulator |
| DR 77802 | VO | Matisa R 24 S Regulator |
| DR 77901 | CS | Plasser & Theurer USP 5000-RT Regulator |
| DR 77903 | NR | Plasser & Theurer USP 5000-RT Regulator  Frank Jones |
| DR 77904 | NR | Plasser & Theurer USP 5000-RT Regulator |

| DR 77905 | NR | Plasser & Theurer USP 5000-RT Regulator |
| DR 77906 | NR | Plasser & Theurer USP 5000-RT Regulator |
| DR 77907 | NR | Plasser & Theurer USP 5000-RT Regulator |
| DR 77908 | SK | Plasser & Theurer USP 5000-RT Regulator |

# TWIN JIB TRACK RELAYERS

| DRP 78211 (S) | NR | Plasser & Theurer Self-Propelled Heavy Duty |
| DRP 78212 (S) | NR | Plasser & Theurer Self-Propelled Heavy Duty |
| DRP 78213 | VO | Plasser & Theurer Self-Propelled Heavy Duty |
| DRP 78215 | SK | Plasser & Theurer Self-Propelled Heavy Duty |
| DRP 78216 | BB | Plasser & Theurer Self-Propelled Heavy Duty |
| DRP 78217 (S) | SK | Plasser & Theurer Self-Propelled Heavy Duty |
| DRP 78218 (S) | BB | Plasser & Theurer Self-Propelled Heavy Duty |
| DRP 78219 | SK | Plasser & Theurer Self-Propelled Heavy Duty |
| DRP 78221 | BB | Plasser & Theurer Self-Propelled Heavy Duty |
| DRP 78222 | BB | Plasser & Theurer Self-Propelled Heavy Duty |
| DRP 78223 (S) | BB | Plasser & Theurer Self-Propelled Heavy Duty |
| DRP 78224 (S) | BB | Plasser & Theurer Self-Propelled Heavy Duty |
| DRC 78226 | CS | Cowans Sheldon Self-Propelled Heavy Duty |
| DRC 78229 (S) | NR | Cowans Sheldon Self-Propelled Heavy Duty |
| DRC 78231 (S) | NR | Cowans Sheldon Self-Propelled Heavy Duty |
| DRC 78234 (S) | NR | Cowans Sheldon Self-Propelled Heavy Duty |
| DRC 78235 | CS | Cowans Sheldon Self-Propelled Heavy Duty |
| DRC 78237 (S) | NR | Cowans Sheldon Self-Propelled Heavy Duty |

# TRACK RENEWAL MACHINES

**Matisa P95 Track Renewals Trains**
DR 78801+DR 78811+DR 78821+DR 78831 NR *(works with DR 76751)*
DR 78802+DR 78812+DR 78822+DR 78832 NR *(works with DR 76750)*

# RAIL GRINDING TRAINS

**Loram SPML 15**
DR 79200A + DR 79200B + DR 79200C   NR

**Loram SPML 17**
DR 79201A + DR 79201B                NR

**Speno RPS-32**
DR 79221 + DR 79222 + DR 79223 + DR 79224 + DR 79225 + DR 79226   SI

**Loram C21**
DR 79231 + DR 79232 + DR 79233 + DR 79234 + DR 79235 + DR 79236 + DR 79237   NR
DR 79241 + DR 79242 + DR 79243 + DR 79244 + DR 79245 + DR 79246 + DR 79247   NR
DR 79251 + DR 79252 + DR 79253 + DR 79254 + DR 79255 + DR 79256 + DR 79257   NR

**Name:** DR 79241/247   Roger South *(one plate on opposite sides of each)*

**Harsco Track Technologies RGH20C**

| | |
|---|---|
| DR 79261 + DR 79271 | NR |
| DR 79262 + DR 79272 | NR |
| DR 79263 + DR 79273 | NR |
| DR 79264 + DR 79274 | NR |
| DR 79265 (S) | NR spare vehicle |
| DR 79267 + DR 79277 | NR |

# STONEBLOWERS

| | | |
|---|---|---|
| DR 80200 (S) | NR | Pandrol Jackson Plain Line |
| DR 80201 | NR | Pandrol Jackson Plain Line |
| DR 80202 (S) | NR | Pandrol Jackson Plain Line |
| DR 80203 (S) | NR | Pandrol Jackson Plain Line |
| DR 80204 (S) | NR | Pandrol Jackson Plain Line |
| DR 80205 | NR | Pandrol Jackson Plain Line |
| DR 80206 | NR | Pandrol Jackson Plain Line |
| DR 80207 (S) | NR | Pandrol Jackson Plain Line |
| DR 80208 | NR | Pandrol Jackson Plain Line |
| DR 80209 | NR | Pandrol Jackson Plain Line |
| DR 80210 | NR | Pandrol Jackson Plain Line |
| DR 80211 | NR | Pandrol Jackson Plain Line |
| DR 80212 (S) | NR | Pandrol Jackson Plain Line |
| DR 80213 | NR | Harsco Track Technologies Plain Line |
| DR 80214 | NR | Harsco Track Technologies Plain Line |
| DR 80215 | NR | Harsco Track Technologies Plain Line |
| DR 80216 | NR | Harsco Track Technologies Plain Line |
| DR 80217 | NR | Harsco Track Technologies Plain Line |
| DR 80301 | NR | Harsco Track Technologies Multi-purpose Stephen Cornish |
| DR 80302 | NR | Harsco Track Technologies Multi-purpose |
| DR 80303 | NR | Harsco Track Technologies Multi-purpose |

# CRANES

| | | |
|---|---|---|
| DRP 81505 | BB | Plasser & Theurer 12 tonne Heavy Duty Diesel Hydraulic |
| DRP 81507 (S) | BB | Plasser & Theurer 12 tonne Heavy Duty Diesel Hydraulic |
| DRP 81508 (S) | BB | Plasser & Theurer 12 tonne Heavy Duty Diesel Hydraulic |
| DRP 81511 (S) | BB | Plasser & Theurer 12 tonne Heavy Duty Diesel Hydraulic |
| DRP 81513 | BB | Plasser & Theurer 12 tonne Heavy Duty Diesel Hydraulic |
| DRP 81517 | BB | Plasser & Theurer 12 tonne Heavy Duty Diesel Hydraulic |
| DRP 81519 (S) | BB | Plasser & Theurer 12 tonne Heavy Duty Diesel Hydraulic |
| DRP 81522 | BB | Plasser & Theurer 12 tonne Heavy Duty Diesel Hydraulic |
| DRP 81525 | BB | Plasser & Theurer 12 tonne Heavy Duty Diesel Hydraulic |
| DRP 81532 | BB | Plasser & Theurer 12 tonne Heavy Duty Diesel Hydraulic |
| DRK 81601 | VO | Kirow KRC810UK 100 tonne Heavy Duty Diesel Hydraulic |
| DRK 81602 | BB | Kirow KRC810UK 100 tonne Heavy Duty Diesel Hydraulic |
| DRK 81611 | BB | Kirow KRC1200UK 125 tonne Heavy Duty Diesel Hydraulic |
| DRK 81612 | CS | Kirow KRC1200UK 125 tonne Heavy Duty Diesel Hydraulic |
| DRK 81613 | VO | Kirow KRC1200UK 125 tonne Heavy Duty Diesel Hydraulic |

| DRK 81621 | VO | Kirow KRC250UK 25 tonne Diesel Hydraulic |
| DRK 81622 | VO | Kirow KRC250UK 25 tonne Diesel Hydraulic |
| DRK 81623 | SK | Kirow KRC250UK 25 tonne Diesel Hydraulic |
| DRK 81624 | SK | Kirow KRC250UK 25 tonne Diesel Hydraulic |
| DRK 81625 | SK | Kirow KRC250UK 25 tonne Diesel Hydraulic |
| ADRC 96710 | NR | Cowans Sheldon 75 tonne Diesel Hydraulic (telescopic) Breakdown |
| ADRC 96713 | NR | Cowans Sheldon 75 tonne Diesel Hydraulic (telescopic) Breakdown |
| ADRC 96714 | NR | Cowans Sheldon 75 tonne Diesel Hydraulic (telescopic) Breakdown |
| ADRC 96715 | NR | Cowans Sheldon 75 tonne Diesel Hydraulic (telescopic) Breakdown |

**Names:**

DRK 81601 Nigel Chester | DRK 81611 Malcolm L. Pearce

# BALLAST SYSTEM PROPULSION MACHINES

| DR 92263 | NR | Plasser & Theurer MFS-PW *(works with DR 76323/DR 92264)* |
| DR 92264 | NR | Plasser & Theurer NB-PW *(works with DR 76323/DR 92263)* |
| DR 92285 | NR | Plasser & Theurer PW-RT *(works with DR 76501/DR 92286)* |
| DR 92286 | NR | Plasser & Theurer NPW-RT *(works with DR 76501/DR 92285)* |
| DR 92331 | NR | Plasser & Theurer PW-RT *(works with DR 76502/DR 92332)* |
| DR 92332 | NR | Plasser & Theurer NPW-RT *(works with DR 76502/DR 92331)* |
| DR 92431 | NR | Plasser & Theurer PW-RT *(works with DR 76503/DR 76701/ DR 76801/DR 92432)* |
| DR 92432 | NR | Plasser & Theurer NPW-RT *(works with DR 76503/DR 76701/ DR 76801/DR 92431)* |

# GENERAL PURPOSE VEHICLES

| DR 97001 | HI | Eiv de Brieve DU94BA TRAMM with Crane  DU 94 B 001 URS |
| DR 97011 | HI | Windhoff MPV Master |
| DR 97012 | HI | Windhoff MPV Master |
| DR 97013 | HI | Windhoff MPV Master |
| DR 97014 | HI | Windhoff MPV Master |
| DR 98001 | NR | Windhoff Electrification MPV Master with Piling Equipment |
| DR 98002 (S) | NR | Windhoff MPV Master with Piling Equipment |
| DR 98003 | NR | Windhoff MPV Master with Overhead Line Renewal Equipment |
| DR 98004 | NR | Windhoff MPV Master with Overhead Line Renewal Equipment |
| DR 98005 (S) | NR | Windhoff MPV Master with Piling Equipment |
| DR 98006 | NR | Windhoff Electrification MPV Master with Piling Equipment |
| DR 98007 | NR | Windhoff Electrification MPV Master with Piling Equipment |
| DR 98008 | NR | Windhoff MPV Twin-cab Master with test equipment |
| DR 98009 | NR | Windhoff MPV Master with Overhead Line Renewal Equipment |
| DR 98010 | NR | Windhoff MPV Master with Overhead Line Renewal Equipment |
| DR 98011 | NR | Windhoff MPV Master with Overhead Line Renewal Equipment |
| DR 98012 | NR | Windhoff MPV Master with Overhead Line Renewal Equipment |
| DR 98013 | NR | Windhoff MPV Master with Overhead Line Renewal Equipment |
| DR 98014 | NR | Windhoff MPV Master with Overhead Line Renewal Equipment |

| | | |
|---|---|---|
| DR 98215A + DR 98215B | BB | Plasser & Theurer GP-TRAMM with Trailer |
| DR 98216A + DR 98216B | BB | Plasser & Theurer GP-TRAMM with Trailer |
| DR 98217A + DR 98217B | BB | Plasser & Theurer GP-TRAMM with Trailer |
| DR 98218A + DR 98218B | BB | Plasser & Theurer GP-TRAMM with Trailer |
| DR 98219A + DR 98219B | BB | Plasser & Theurer GP-TRAMM with Trailer |
| DR 98220A + DR 98220B | BB | Plasser & Theurer GP-TRAMM with Trailer |

| | | |
|---|---|---|
| DR 98305 (S) NR | | Geismar GP-TRAMM VMT 860 PL/UM |
| DR 98306 (S) NR | | Geismar GP-TRAMM VMT 860 PL/UM |

| | | |
|---|---|---|
| DR 98307A + DR 98307B (S) CS | | Geismar GP-TRAMM VMT 860 PL/UM with Trailer |
| DR 98308A + DR 98308B (S) CS | | Geismar GP-TRAMM VMT 860 PL/UM with Trailer |

| | | |
|---|---|---|
| DR 98901 + DR 98951 | NR | Windhoff MPV Master & Slave |
| DR 98902 + DR 98952 | NR | Windhoff MPV Master & Slave |
| DR 98903 + DR 98953 | NR | Windhoff MPV Master & Slave |
| DR 98904 + DR 98954 | NR | Windhoff MPV Master & Slave |
| DR 98905 + DR 98955 | NR | Windhoff MPV Master & Slave |
| DR 98906 + DR 98956 | NR | Windhoff MPV Master & Slave |
| DR 98907 + DR 98957 | NR | Windhoff MPV Master & Slave |
| DR 98908 + DR 98958 | NR | Windhoff MPV Master & Slave |
| DR 98909 + DR 98959 | NR | Windhoff MPV Master & Slave |
| DR 98910 + DR 98960 | NR | Windhoff MPV Master & Slave |
| DR 98911 + DR 98961 | NR | Windhoff MPV Master & Slave |
| DR 98912 + DR 98962 | NR | Windhoff MPV Master & Slave |
| DR 98913 + DR 98963 | NR | Windhoff MPV Master & Slave |
| DR 98914 + DR 98964 | NR | Windhoff MPV Master & Slave |
| DR 98915 + DR 98965 | NR | Windhoff MPV Master & Slave |
| DR 98916 + DR 98966 | NR | Windhoff MPV Master & Slave |
| DR 98917 + DR 98967 | NR | Windhoff MPV Master & Slave |
| DR 98918 + DR 98968 | NR | Windhoff MPV Master & Slave |
| DR 98919 + DR 98969 | NR | Windhoff MPV Master & Slave |
| DR 98920 + DR 98970 | NR | Windhoff MPV Master & Slave |
| DR 98921 + DR 98971 | NR | Windhoff MPV Master & Slave |
| DR 98922 + DR 98972 | NR | Windhoff MPV Master & Slave |
| DR 98923 + DR 98973 | NR | Windhoff MPV Master & Slave |
| DR 98924 + DR 98974 | NR | Windhoff MPV Master & Slave |
| DR 98925 + DR 98975 | NR | Windhoff MPV Master & Slave |
| DR 98926 + DR 98976 | NR | Windhoff MPV Master & Powered Slave |
| DR 98927 + DR 98977 | NR | Windhoff MPV Master & Powered Slave |
| DR 98928 + DR 98978 | NR | Windhoff MPV Master & Powered Slave |
| DR 98929 + DR 98979 | NR | Windhoff MPV Master & Powered Slave |
| DR 98930 + DR 98980 | NR | Windhoff MPV Master & Powered Slave |
| DR 98931 + DR 98981 | NR | Windhoff MPV Master & Powered Slave |
| DR 98932 + DR 98982 | NR | Windhoff MPV Master & Powered Slave |

**Names:**

| | |
|---|---|
| DR 97012 | Geoff Bell |
| DR 98003 | ANTHONY WRIGHTON 1944–2011 |
| DR 98004 | PHILIP CATTRELL 1961–2011 |
| DR 98009 | MELVYN SMITH 1953–2011 |
| DR 98010 | BENJAMIN GAUTREY 1992–2011 |

| 99 70 9131 001-8 | NR | Windhoff Electrification MPV Master |
| 99 70 9131 003-4 | NR | Windhoff Electrification MPV Master |
| 99 70 9131 005-9 | NR | Windhoff Electrification MPV Master |
| 99 70 9131 006-7 | NR | Windhoff Electrification MPV Master |
| 99 70 9131 010-9 | NR | Windhoff Electrification MPV Master |
| 99 70 9131 011-7 | NR | Windhoff Electrification MPV Master |
| 99 70 9131 013-3 | NR | Windhoff Electrification MPV Master |
| 99 70 9131 014-1 | NR | Windhoff Electrification MPV Master |
| 99 70 9131 015-8 | NR | Windhoff Electrification MPV Master |
| 99 70 9131 018-2 | NR | Windhoff Electrification MPV Master |
| 99 70 9131 020-8 | NR | Windhoff Electrification MPV Master |
| 99 70 9131 021-6 | NR | Windhoff Electrification MPV Master |
| 99 70 9131 022-4 | NR | Windhoff Electrification MPV Master |
| 99 70 9131 023-2 | NR | Windhoff Electrification MPV Master |

## SNOWPLOUGHS

| ADB 965203 | NR | Independent Drift Plough | Tees Yard |
| ADB 965206 | NR | Independent Drift Plough | Doncaster Carr Depot |
| ADB 965208 | NR | Independent Drift Plough | Inverness Millburn Yard |
| ADB 965209 | NR | Independent Drift Plough | Bristol Barton Hill Depot |
| ADB 965210 | NR | Independent Drift Plough | Tonbridge West Yard |
| ADB 965211 | NR | Independent Drift Plough | March Depot |
| ADB 965217 | NR | Independent Drift Plough | Edinburgh Slateford Depot |
| ADB 965219 | NR | Independent Drift Plough | Edinburgh Slateford Depot |
| ADB 965223 | NR | Independent Drift Plough | Margam Wagon Works |
| ADB 965224 | NR | Independent Drift Plough | Carlisle Kingmoor Yard |
| ADB 965230 | NR | Independent Drift Plough | Carlisle Kingmoor Yard |
| ADB 965231 | NR | Independent Drift Plough | Bristol Barton Hill Depot |
| ADB 965234 | NR | Independent Drift Plough | Inverness Millburn Yard |
| ADB 965235 | NR | Independent Drift Plough | Margam Wagon Works |
| ADB 965236 | NR | Independent Drift Plough | Tonbridge West Yard |
| ADB 965237 | NR | Independent Drift Plough | March Depot |
| ADB 965240 | NR | Independent Drift Plough | Inverness Millburn Yard |
| ADB 965241 | NR | Independent Drift Plough | Doncaster Carr Depot |
| ADB 965242 | NR | Independent Drift Plough | Tees Yard |
| ADB 965243 | NR | Independent Drift Plough | Inverness Millburn Yard |
| ADB 965576 | NR | Beilhack Type PB600 Plough | Doncaster Carr Depot |
| ADB 965577 | NR | Beilhack Type PB600 Plough | Doncaster Carr Depot |
| ADB 965578 | NR | Beilhack Type PB600 Plough | Carlisle Kingmoor Yard |
| ADB 965579 | NR | Beilhack Type PB600 Plough | Carlisle Kingmoor Yard |
| ADB 965580 | NR | Beilhack Type PB600 Plough | Wigan Springs Branch |
| ADB 965581 | NR | Beilhack Type PB600 Plough | Wigan Springs Branch |
| ADB 966098 | NR | Beilhack Type PB600 Plough | Doncaster Carr Depot |
| ADB 966099 | NR | Beilhack Type PB600 Plough | Doncaster Carr Depot |

## SNOWBLOWERS

| ADB 968500 | NR | Beilhack Self-Propelled Rotary | Edinburgh Slateford Depot |
| ADB 968501 | NR | Beilhack Self-Propelled Rotary | Edinburgh Slateford Depot |

# INFRASTRUCTURE MONITORING VEHICLES

| 999800 | NR | Plasser & Theurer EM-SAT 100/RT Track Survey Car |
| 999801 | NR | Plasser & Theurer EM-SAT 100/RT Track Survey Car |

**Name:** 999800 Richard Spoors

# ON-TRACK MACHINES AWAITING DISPOSAL

**Tampers**

| DR 73105 | Plasser & Theurer 09-32 CSM | Rugby Depot |
| DR 73428 | Plasser & Theurer 07-32 Duomatic | Russell Storage, Hillington |
| DR 73503 | Plasser & Theurer 08-16/90 ZW | Ashford OTM Depot |
| DR 75201 | Plasser & Theurer 08-275 S&C | Hither Green Depot |
| DR 75202 | Plasser & Theurer 08-275 S&C | Hither Green Depot |

**Ballast Cleaners**

| DR 76304 | Plasser & Theurer RM74 | Plasser UK, West Ealing |
| DR 76318 | Plasser & Theurer RM74 | Plasser UK, West Ealing |

**Twin Jib track relayer**

| DRB 78123 | British Hoist & Crane Non-Self-Propelled | Polmadie DHS |

# LOCATIONS OF STORED ON-TRACK MACHINES

The locations of machines shown above as stored (S) are shown here.

| DR 73911 | Leeds Holbeck Depot | DR 79265 | Eastleigh Works |
| DR 76324 | Plasser UK, West Ealing | DR 80200 | East Dereham |
| DR 76702 | Toton Yard | DR 80202 | Eastleigh Works |
| DR 76703 | Taunton Fairwater Yard | DR 80203 | Eastleigh Works |
| DR 76710 | Willesden Euroterminal | DR 80204 | East Dereham |
| DR 76711 | Taunton Fairwater Yard | DR 80207 | Eastleigh Works |
| DR 77315 | Ashford OTM Depot | DR 80212 | Eastleigh Works |
| DR 77316 | Ashford OTM Depot | DRP 81507 | Ashford OTM Depot |
| DR 77336 | Hither Green Depot | DRP 81508 | Ashford OTM Depot |
| DRP 78211 | Doncaster Marshgate Depot | DRP 81511 | Ashford OTM Depot |
| DRP 78212 | Doncaster Marshgate Depot | DRP 81519 | Woking OTM Depot |
| DRP 78217 | Glasgow Rutherglen Depot | DR 98002 | York Holgate Works |
| DRP 78218 | Ashford OTM Depot | DR 98005 | York Holgate Works |
| DRP 78223 | Ashford OTM Depot | DR 98305 | Eastleigh Works |
| DRP 78224 | Hither Green Depot | DR 98306 | Eastleigh Works |
| DRC 78229 | Cardiff Canton Depot | DR 98307A+ | |
| DRC 78231 | Cardiff Canton Depot | DR 98307B | Rugby Depot |
| DRC 78234 | Cardiff Canton Depot | DR 98308A+ | |
| DRC 78237 | York Holgate Works | DR 98308B | Rugby Depot |

# 6. UK LIGHT RAIL & METRO SYSTEMS

This section lists the rolling stock of the various light rail and metro systems in Great Britain. Passenger carrying vehicles only are covered (not works vehicles). This listing does not cover the London Underground network.

## 6.1. BLACKPOOL & FLEETWOOD TRAMWAY

Until the opening of Manchester Metrolink, the Blackpool tramway was the only urban/inter-urban tramway system left in Britain. The infrastructure is owned by Blackpool Corporation, and the tramway is operated by Blackpool Transport Services Ltd. The 11 miles from Fleetwood to Starr Gate reopened in spring 2012 following rebuilding as a modern light rail system with a new fleet of 16 Bombardier Flexity 2 trams.

**System:** 600 V DC overhead.
**Depot & Workshops:** Starr Gate and Rigby Road (heritage fleet).
**Standard livery:** Flexity 2s and **F**: White, black & purple.

## FLEXITY 2                                    5-SECTION TRAMS

16 new articulated Supertrams. These form the "A" fleet of trams used in normal daily service.

**Built:** 2011–12 by Bombardier Transportation, Bautzen, Germany.
**Wheel arrangement:** Bo-2-Bo.
**Traction Motors:** 4 x Bombardier 3-phase asynchronous of 120 kW.
**Dimensions:** 32.2 x 2.65 m.          **Seats:** 70 (4).
**Doors:** Sliding plug.                     **Couplers:**
**Weight:** 40.9 t.                          **Maximum Speed:** 43 mph.
**Braking:** Regenerative, disc and magnetic track.

| | | | |
|---|---|---|---|
| 001 | 005 | 009 | 013 |
| 002 | 006 | 010 | 014 |
| 003 | 007 | 011 | 015 |
| 004 | 008 | 012 | 016 |

**Name:** 002  "Alderman E.E. Wynne"

## "BALLOON" DOUBLE DECKERS                           A1-1A

The nine cars listed have partial exemption from the Rail Vehicle Accessibility Regulations and form the "B" fleet to supplement the Flexity 2 trams. All have been fitted with wider doors.

**Built:** 1934–35 by English Electric.
**Traction Motors:** 2 x EE305 of 40 kW. **Seats:** 94 (*† 92).

* Rebuilt with a flat front end design and air-conditioned cabs. Known as "Millennium Class".

**Advertising liveries:**

707: Coral Island: The Jewel on the Mile (black)    718: Madame Tussaud's (purple & red)
709: Blackpool Sealife Centre (blue)                720: Walls ice cream (red)
713: Houndshill Shopping Centre (purple & white)    724: Lyndene Hotel (blue)

| | | | | | |
|---|---|---|---|---|---|
| 700 | **F** | 711 † | **F** | 719 | **F** |
| 707 * | **AL** | 713 | **AL** | 720 | **AL** |
| 709 * | **AL** | 718 * | **AL** | 724 * | **AL** |

**Names:** 711 Ray Roberts    | 719 Donna's Dream House

# HERITAGE FLEET of VINTAGE CARS

The following trams have exemption from the RVAR for Heritage use.

| | | |
|---|---|---|
| Blackpool & Fleetwood 40 | Single-deck Fleetwood Box car | Built: 1914 |
| Bolton 66 | Bogie double-decker | Built: 1901 |
| Blackpool 147 MICHAEL AIREY | Standard double-decker | Built: 1924 |
| Blackpool 227 (602) | Open boat car | Built: 1934 |
| Blackpool 230 (604) GEORGE FORMBY OBE | Open boat car | Built: 1934 |
| Blackpool 272+T2 (672+682) | Progress Twin Car | Rebuilt: 1960 |
| Blackpool 600 THE DUCHESS OF CORNWALL | Open boat car | Built: 1934 |
| Blackpool 631 | Brush car | Built: 1937 |
| Blackpool 642 | Centenary car | Built: 1986 |
| Blackpool 648 | Centenary car | Built: 1987 |
| Blackpool 701 | Balloon double-decker | Built: 1934 |
| Blackpool 706 PRINCESS ALICE | Balloon open-top double-decker | Built: 1934 |
| Blackpool 717 PHILLIP R THORPE | Balloon double-decker | Built: 1935 |
| Blackpool 723 | Balloon double-decker | Built: 1935 |

**Illuminated cars**

| | | | |
|---|---|---|---|
| Blackpool 733 | Western Train loco & tender | | Rebuilt: 1962 |
| Blackpool 734 | Western Train coach | | Rebuilt: 1962 |
| Blackpool 736 | "Warship" HMS Blackpool | | Rebuilt: 1965 |
| Blackpool 737 | Illuminated Trawler – "Fisherman's Friend" | | Rebuilt: 2001 |

# STORED VEHICLES

The following vehicles are stored at Rigby Road depot.

| | | |
|---|---|---|
| Blackpool 8 (S) | BCT One Man Car | Rebuilt: 1974 |
| Blackpool 143 (S) | Standard double-decker | Built: 1924 |
| Blackpool 259 (S) | Brush car | Built: 1937 |
| Blackpool 279 (S) | English Electric Railcoach | Rebuilt: 1960 |
| Blackpool 304 (S) | Coronation Class single-decker | Built: 1952 |
| Blackpool 622 (S) | Brush car | Built: 1937 |
| Blackpool 632 (S) | Brush car | Built: 1937 |
| Blackpool 660 (S) | Coronation Class single-decker | Built: 1953 |
| Blackpool 663 (S) | Coronation Class single-decker | Built: 1953 |
| Blackpool 675+685 (S) | Progress Twin Car | Rebuilt: 1958/60 |
| Blackpool 676+686 (S) | Progress Twin Car | Rebuilt: 1958/60 |
| Blackpool 715 (S) | Balloon double-decker | Built: 1935 |
| Blackpool 761 (S) | Jubilee Class double-decker | Rebuilt: 1979 |

# 6.2. DOCKLANDS LIGHT RAILWAY

This system runs for a total of approximately 23 route miles from termini at Bank and Tower Gateway in central London to Lewisham, Stratford, Beckton and Woolwich Arsenal. A new line from Canning Town to Stratford International also opened in 2011. The first part of the network opened in 1987 from Tower Gateway to Island Gardens. Originally owned by London Transport, it is now part of the London Rail division of Transport for London and operated by Serco Docklands. Cars are normally driven automatically using the Alcatel Seltrack moving block signalling system.

Original P86 and P89 Class vehicles 01–21 were withdrawn from service in 1991 (01–11) and 1995 (12–21) and sold for use in Essen, Germany.

55 new cars from Bombardier in Germany entered traffic between 2008 and 2010. Along with platform extensions, these new vehicles have enabled 3-unit trains to operate on all routes.

**System:** 750 V DC third rail (bottom contact). High-floor.
**Depots:** Beckton (main depot) and Poplar.
**Livery:** Red with a curving blue stripe to represent the River Thames.

## CLASS B90                                    2-SECTION UNITS

**Built:** 1991–92 by BN Construction, Bruges, Belgium. Chopper control.
**Wheel Arrangement:** B-2-B.              **Traction Motors:** 2 x Brush 140 kW.
**Seats:** 52 (4).                          **Weight:** 37 t.
**Dimensions:** 28.80 x 2.65 m.            **Braking:** Rheostatic.
**Couplers:** Scharfenberg.                 **Maximum Speed:** 50 mph.
**Doors:** Sliding. End doors for staff use.

| | | | | | |
|---|---|---|---|---|---|
| 22 | 26 | 30 | 34 | 38 | 42 |
| 23 | 27 | 31 | 35 | 39 | 43 |
| 24 | 28 | 32 | 36 | 40 | 44 |
| 25 | 29 | 33 | 37 | 41 | |

## CLASS B92                                    2-SECTION UNITS

**Built:** 1992–95 by BN Construction, Bruges, Belgium. Chopper control.
**Wheel Arrangement:** B-2-B.              **Traction Motors:** 2 x Brush 140 kW.
**Seats:** 52 (4).                          **Weight:** 37 t.
**Dimensions:** 28.80 x 2.65 m.            **Braking:** Rheostatic.
**Couplers:** Scharfenberg.                 **Maximum Speed:** 50 mph.
**Doors:** Sliding. End doors for staff use.

| | | | | | |
|---|---|---|---|---|---|
| 45 | 53 | 61 | 69 | 77 | 85 |
| 46 | 54 | 62 | 70 | 78 | 86 |
| 47 | 55 | 63 | 71 | 79 | 87 |
| 48 | 56 | 64 | 72 | 80 | 88 |
| 49 | 57 | 65 | 73 | 81 | 89 |
| 50 | 58 | 66 | 74 | 82 | 90 |
| 51 | 59 | 67 | 75 | 83 | 91 |
| 52 | 60 | 68 | 76 | 84 | |

## CLASS B2K                                     2-SECTION UNITS

**Built:** 2002–03 by Bombardier Transportation, Bruges, Belgium.
**Wheel Arrangement:** B-2-B.        **Traction Motors:** 2 x Brush 140 kW.
**Seats:** 52 (4).                   **Weight:** 37 t.
**Dimensions:** 28.80 x 2.65 m.      **Braking:** Rheostatic.
**Couplers:** Scharfenberg.          **Maximum Speed:** 50 mph.
**Doors:** Sliding. End doors for staff use.

| | | | | | |
|---|---|---|---|---|---|
| 92 | 96 | 01 | 05 | 09 | 13 |
| 93 | 97 | 02 | 06 | 10 | 14 |
| 94 | 98 | 03 | 07 | 11 | 15 |
| 95 | 99 | 04 | 08 | 12 | 16 |

## CLASS B07                                     2-SECTION UNITS

**Built:** 2007–10 by Bombardier Transportation, Bautzen, Germany.
**Wheel Arrangement:** B-2-B.        **Traction Motors:** 2 x Brush 140 kW.
**Seats:** 52 (4).                   **Weight:** 37 t.
**Dimensions:**                      **Braking:** Rheostatic.
**Couplers:** Scharfenberg.          **Maximum Speed:** 50 mph.
**Doors:** Sliding. End doors for staff use.

| | | | | | |
|---|---|---|---|---|---|
| 101 | 111 | 120 | 129 | 138 | 147 |
| 102 | 112 | 121 | 130 | 139 | 148 |
| 103 | 113 | 122 | 131 | 140 | 149 |
| 104 | 114 | 123 | 132 | 141 | 150 |
| 105 | 115 | 124 | 133 | 142 | 151 |
| 106 | 116 | 125 | 134 | 143 | 152 |
| 107 | 117 | 126 | 135 | 144 | 153 |
| 108 | 118 | 127 | 136 | 145 | 154 |
| 109 | 119 | 128 | 137 | 146 | 155 |
| 110 | | | | | |

# 6.3. EDINBURGH TRAMWAY

A new tramway is under construction in Edinburgh, however the scheme has been dogged by construction problems, with the originally planned terminus of Newhaven in the north of the city cut back to York Place in the city centre. In the west side of the city trams will run to Edinburgh Airport. At the time of writing the tramway is due to open by May 2014, although not all of the 27 trams (all now delivered) will be required for the reduced system. The trams will be the longest to operate in the UK.

**System:** 750 V DC overhead.
**Platform Height:** 350 mm.
**Depot & Workshops:** Gogar.
**Livery:** White, red & black.

## CAF                              7-SECTION TRAMS

**Built:** 2009–11 by CAF, Irun, Spain.
**Wheel Arrangement:** Bo-Bo-2-Bo.    **Traction Motors:** 12 x CAF 80 kW.
**Seats:** 78.                                    **Weight:** 56.25 t.
**Dimensions:** 42.8 x 2.65 m.         **Braking:** Regenerative & electro hydraulic.
**Couplers:** Albert.                      **Maximum Speed:** 50 mph.
**Doors:** Sliding plug.

| | | | | |
|---|---|---|---|---|
| 251 | 257 | 263 | 268 | 273 |
| 252 | 258 | 264 | 269 | 274 |
| 253 | 259 | 265 | 270 | 275 |
| 254 | 260 | 266 | 271 | 276 |
| 255 | 261 | 267 | 272 | 277 |
| 256 | 262 | | | |

# 6.4. GLASGOW SUBWAY

This circular 4 ft gauge underground line is the smallest metro system in the UK, running for just over six miles. Operated by Strathclyde PTE the system has 15 stations. The entire passenger railway is underground, contained in twin tunnels, allowing for clockwise operation on the "outer" circle and anti-clockwise operation on the "inner" circle.

Trains are formed of 3-cars – either three power cars or two power cars sandwiching one of the newer trailer cars.

**System:** 600 V DC third rail.
**Depot & Workshops:** Broomloan.
**Livery:** All cars now carry the new orange & grey Subway livery.

## SINGLE POWER CARS

**Built:** 1977–79 by Metro-Cammell, Birmingham. Refurbished 1993–95 by ABB Derby.
**Wheel Arrangement:** Bo-Bo.
**Traction Motors:** 4 x GEC G312AZ of 35.6 kW.
**Seats:** 36.
**Couplers:** Wedglock.
**Weight:** 19.6 t.
**Dimensions:** 12.81 m x 2.34 m.
**Doors:** Sliding.
**Maximum Speed:** 33.5 mph.

| | | | | |
|---|---|---|---|---|
| 101 | 108 | 115 | 122 | 128 |
| 102 | 109 | 116 | 123 | 129 |
| 103 | 110 | 117 | 124 | 130 |
| 104 | 111 | 118 | 125 | 131 |
| 105 | 112 | 119 | 126 | 132 |
| 106 | 113 | 120 | 127 | 133 |
| 107 | 114 | 121 | | |

## INTERMEDIATE BOGIE TRAILERS

**Built:** 1992 by Hunslet Barclay, Kilmarnock.
**Seats:** 40.
**Couplers:** Wedglock.
**Weight:** 17.2 t.
**Dimensions:** 12.70 m x 2.34 m.
**Doors:** Sliding.
**Maximum Speed:** 33.5 mph.

| | | | | |
|---|---|---|---|---|
| 201 | 203 | 205 | 207 | 208 |
| 202 | 204 | 206 | | |

# 6.5. GREATER MANCHESTER METROLINK

Metrolink was the first modern tramway system in the UK, combining street running with longer distance running over former BR lines. The system opened in 1992 from Bury to Altrincham with a street section through the centre of Manchester and a spur to Piccadilly station. A second line opened in 2000 from Cornbrook to Eccles.

A short spur off the Eccles line to MediaCityUK opened in September 2010 whilst the first part of the South Manchester Line to Chorlton and St Werburgh's Road opened in July 2011. This was followed by a further extension to East Didsbury in May 2013. In June 2012 the former National Rail line from Manchester to Oldham Mumps opened as a Metrolink line and this was extended to Shaw & Crompton in December 2012 and to Rochdale station in February 2013. The East Manchester Line reached Droylsden in February 2013 and this was followed by Droylsden–Ashton-under-Lyne in October 2013, extending the total route mileage to approximately 48 miles.

Further extensions will see Metrolink reach Oldham town centres in early 2014 and this will be followed by the Rochdale town centre link, whilst the St Werburgh's Road–Manchester Airport extension is planned to open in 2016. Work has also now started on a second city crossing in Manchester.

**Operator:** RATP Dev.
**System:** 750 V DC overhead. High floor.
**Depot & Workshops:** Queens Road and Trafford.

# T68 1000 SERIES                    2-SECTION TRAMS

The remaining T68 trams were all due to be withdrawn from traffic during early 2014.
**Built:** 1991–92 by Firema, Italy. Chopper control.
**Wheel Arrangement:** Bo-2-Bo.          **Traction Motors:** 4 x GEC 130 kW.
**Dimensions:** 29.0 x 2.65 m.            **Seats:** 82 (4).
**Doors:** Sliding.                       **Couplers:** Scharfenberg.
**Weight:** 45 t.                         **Maximum Speed:** 50 mph.
**Braking:** Regenerative, disc and emergency track.

**Liveries:** White, dark grey & blue with light blue doors.
**M:** New Manchester Metrolink silver & yellow.

* Fitted with front-end valances, retractable couplers and controllable magnetic track brakes for on-street running mixed with private vehicles.

† Fitted with a special "ice-breaking" pantograph for use in the winter months.

(S) Stored at Trafford depot (except 1012 at Queens Road).

| | | | | | | |
|---|---|---|---|---|---|---|
| 1001 | * | (S) | | 1015 | * | (S) |
| 1002 | * | (S) | | 1016 | * | |
| 1003 | **M**\* | (S) | | 1017 | * | |
| 1004 | * | (S) | | 1018 | | (S) |
| 1005 | * | (S) | | 1019 | | (S) |
| 1006 | * | (S) | | 1020 | | (S) |
| 1007 | * | EAST LANCASHIRE RAILWAY | | 1021 | *† | |
| 1008 | * | (S) | | 1022 | * | POPPY APPEAL |
| 1009 | * | (S) | | 1023 | * | |
| 1010 | * | (S) | | 1024 | * | (S) |
| 1012 | * | (S) | | 1025 | * | (S) |
| 1013 | * | (S) | | 1026 | * | (S) |
| 1014 | * | (S) | | | | |

# T68 2000 SERIES                    2-SECTION TRAMS

**Built:** 1999 by Ansaldo, Italy. Chopper control. Fitted with front-end valances, retractable couplers and controllable magnetic track brakes for on-street running mixed with private vehicles.
**Wheel Arrangement:** Bo-2-Bo.          **Traction Motors:** 4 x GEC 130 kW.
**Dimensions:** 29.0 x 2.65 m.            **Seats:** 82 (4).
**Doors:** Sliding.                       **Couplers:** Scharfenberg.
**Weight:** 45 t.                         **Maximum Speed:** 50 mph.
**Braking:** Regenerative, disc and magnetic track.

**Livery:** White, dark grey & blue with light blue doors.

| | | | | |
|---|---|---|---|---|
| 2001 | | | 2004 | (S) |
| 2002 | (S) | | 2005 | (S) |
| 2003 | DAVE HANSFORD | | 2006 | (S) |

## 3000 SERIES   FLEXITY SWIFT   2-SECTION TRAMS

A total of 104 Bombardier M5000 "Flexity Swift" trams are currently being delivered to strengthen services on existing routes, for the new extensions and to replace the T68 series trams. Deliveries had reached 3077 by the end of 2013. Trams from 3075 upwards feature 8 more seats.

**Built:** 2009–14 by Bombardier, Vienna, Austria.
**Wheel Arrangement:** Bo-2-Bo.
**Traction Motors:** 4 x Bombardier 3-phase asynchronous of 120 kW.
**Dimensions:** 28.4 x 2.65 m.          **Seats:** 52.
**Doors:** Sliding.                      **Couplers:** Scharfenberg.
**Weight:** 39.7 t.                      **Maximum Speed:** 50 mph.
**Braking:** Regenerative, disc and magnetic track.

**Livery:** New Manchester Metrolink silver & yellow.

| | | | | |
|---|---|---|---|---|
| 3001 | 3022 | 3043 | 3064 | 3085 |
| 3002 | 3023 | 3044 | 3065 | 3086 |
| 3003 | 3024 | 3045 | 3066 | 3087 |
| 3004 | 3025 | 3046 | 3067 | 3088 |
| 3005 | 3026 | 3047 | 3068 | 3089 |
| 3006 | 3027 | 3048 | 3069 | 3090 |
| 3007 | 3028 | 3049 | 3070 | 3091 |
| 3008 | 3029 | 3050 | 3071 | 3092 |
| 3009 | 3030 | 3051 | 3072 | 3093 |
| 3010 | 3031 | 3052 | 3073 | 3094 |
| 3011 | 3032 | 3053 | 3074 | 3095 |
| 3012 | 3033 | 3054 | 3075 | 3096 |
| 3013 | 3034 | 3055 | 3076 | 3097 |
| 3014 | 3035 | 3056 | 3077 | 3098 |
| 3015 | 3036 | 3057 | 3078 | 3099 |
| 3016 | 3037 | 3058 | 3079 | 3100 |
| 3017 | 3038 | 3059 | 3080 | 3101 |
| 3018 | 3039 | 3060 | 3081 | 3102 |
| 3019 | 3040 | 3061 | 3082 | 3103 |
| 3020 | 3041 | 3062 | 3083 | 3104 |
| 3021 | 3042 | 3063 | 3084 | |

**Name:** 3020   LANCASHIRE FUSILIER

## 6.6. LONDON TRAMLINK

This system runs through central Croydon via a one-way loop, with lines radiating out to Wimbledon, New Addington and Beckenham Junction/ Elmers End, the total route mileage being 18½ miles. It opened in 2000 and is now operated by Transport for London. Six new Stadler trams entered traffic in spring 2012 and four more are on order.

**System:** 750 V DC overhead.          **Platform Height:** 350 mm.
**Depot & Workshops:** Therapia Lane, Croydon.

**Livery:** Light grey & lime green with a blue solebar.
**Advertising liveries:** 2534 – McMillan Williams Solicitors (white & red).
2554 – Love Croydon (purple & blue)

## BOMBARDIER                          3-SECTION TRAMS

**Built:** 1998–99 by Bombardier, Vienna, Austria.
**Wheel Arrangement:** Bo-2-Bo.          **Traction Motors:** 4 x 120 kW.
**Dimensions:** 30.1 x 2.65 m.           **Seats:** 70.
**Doors:** Sliding plug.                 **Couplers:** Scharfenberg.
**Weight:** 36.3 t.                      **Maximum Speed:** 50 mph.
**Braking:** Disc, regenerative and magnetic track.

| | | | | | |
|---|---|---|---|---|---|
| 2530 | 2534 **AL** | 2538 | 2542 | 2546 | 2550 |
| 2531 | 2535 | 2539 | 2543 | 2547 | 2551 |
| 2532 | 2536 | 2540 | 2544 | 2548 | 2552 |
| 2533 | 2537 | 2541 | 2545 | 2549 | 2553 |

**Name:** 2535 STEPHEN PARASCANDOLO 1980–2007

## STADLER                             5-SECTION TRAMS

Six new Variobahn trams entered traffic in 2012.
**Built:** 2011–12 by Stadler, Berlin, Germany.
**Wheel Arrangement:**                   **Traction Motors:** 8 x 45 kW.
**Dimensions:** 32.4 x 2.65 m.           **Seats:** 74.
**Doors:** Sliding plug.                 **Couplers:** Albert.
**Weight:** 41.5 t.                      **Maximum Speed:** 50 mph.
**Braking:** Disc, regenerative and magnetic track.

| | | | | | |
|---|---|---|---|---|---|
| 2554 **AL** | 2555 | 2556 | 2557 | 2558 | 2559 |

On order and due for delivery 2015–16:

| | | | |
|---|---|---|---|
| 2560 | 2561 | 2562 | 2563 |

# 6.7. NOTTINGHAM EXPRESS TRANSIT

This light rail system opened in 2004. Line 1 runs for 8¾ miles from Station Street, Nottingham (alongside Nottingham station) to Hucknall, including a short spur to Phoenix Park. There is around three miles of street running through Nottingham. Extensions are under construction to Clifton Lane (Line 2) to the south of Nottingham, and Toton Lane (Chilwell) via Beeston to the west (Line 3). These are due to open in December 2014. 22 new Alstom Citadis trams are now being delivered for these extensions.

The system is operated by the Tramlink Nottingham consortium (formed of Alstom Transport, Keolis, Wellglade, Meridiam Infrastructure, InfraVia and VINCI Construction).

**System:** 750 V DC overhead.        **Platform Height:** 350 mm.
**Depot & Workshops:** Wilkinson Street.

## BOMBARDIER INCENTRO 5-SECTION TRAMS

**Built:** 2002–03 by Bombardier, Derby Litchurch Lane Works.

| | |
|---|---|
| **Wheel Arrangement:** Bo-2-Bo. | **Traction Motors:** 8 x 45 kW wheelmotors. |
| **Dimensions:** 33.0 x 2.4 m | **Seats:** 54 (4). |
| **Doors:** Sliding plug. | **Couplers:** Not equipped. |
| **Weight:** 36.7 t. | **Maximum Speed:** 50 mph. |

**Braking:** Disc, regenerative and magnetic track for emergency use.

**Standard livery:** Revised NET livery (silver & green with black window surrounds).

**Advertising liveries:**

201 – Nottinghamcontemporary.org (yellow/light blue & white).
206 – e.on (red).
209 – Interski (white & blue).
211 – Alstom (pale blue).

| | | | | | |
|---|---|---|---|---|---|
| 201 | **AL** | Torvill and Dean | 209 | **AL** | Sid Standard |
| 202 | | DH Lawrence | 210 | | Sir Jesse Boot |
| 203 | | Bendigo Thompson | 211 | **AL** | Robin Hood |
| 204 | | Erica Beardsmore | 212 | | William Booth |
| 205 | | Lord Byron | 213 | | Mary Potter |
| 206 | **AL** | Angela Alcock | 214 | | Dennis McCarthy |
| 207 | **Blue** | Mavis Worthington | 215 | | Brian Clough |
| 208 | **Red** | Dinah Minton | | | |

## ALSTOM CITADIS 402 5-SECTION TRAMS

These cars are being delivered 2013–14 and are principally for the new extensions, although the first should be in traffic on Line 1 from spring 2014.

**Built:** 2013–14 by Alstom, Barcelona, Spain.

| | |
|---|---|
| **Wheel Arrangement:** Bo-2-Bo. | **Traction Motors:** 4 x 120 kW. |
| **Dimensions:** 32.0 x 2.4 m | **Seats:** 58 (6). |
| **Doors:** Sliding plug. | **Couplers:** Not equipped. |
| **Weight:** 40.8 t. | **Maximum Speed:** 43 mph. |

**Braking:** Disc, regenerative and magnetic track for emergency use.

| | | | | |
|---|---|---|---|---|
| 216 | 221 | 226 | 230 | 234 |
| 217 | 222 | 227 | 231 | 235 |
| 218 | 223 | 228 | 232 | 236 |
| 219 | 224 | 229 | 233 | 237 |
| 220 | 225 | | | |

## 6.8. MIDLAND METRO

Opened in 1999 and operated by Travel West Midlands, this consists of a 12½ mile line from Birmingham Snow Hill to Wolverhampton along the old GWR route to Wolverhampton Low Level. Approaching Wolverhampton it leaves the old railway for street-running to the St George's terminus. 20 CAF trams are now being delivered to replace the Ansaldo trams and to serve an extension being built from Snow Hill to New Street station.

**System:** 750 V DC overhead.  **Platform Height:** 350 mm.
**Depot & Workshops:** Wednesbury.

## ANSALDO                    2-SECTION TRAMS

**Built:** 1998–99 by Ansaldo Transporti, Italy.
**Wheel Arrangement:** Bo-2-Bo.  **Traction Motors:** 4 x 105 kW.
**Dimensions:** 24.00 x 2.65 m.  **Seats:** 52.
**Doors:** Sliding plug.  **Couplers:** Not equipped.
**Weight:** 35.6 t.  **Maximum Speed:** 43 mph.
**Braking:** Regenerative, disc and magnetic track.

**Standard livery:** Dark blue & light grey with a green stripe & red front end.

**MW:** New Network West Midlands tram livery (silver & pink).
**0:** Original Birmingham Corporation tram livery (cream & blue).

01 and 02 have been withdrawn and are stored at Wednesbury depot.

| 01 | (S) | | 09 | MW | JEFF ASTLE |
|----|-----|--|----|----|-----------|
| 02 | (S) | | 10 | MW | JOHN STANLEY WEBB |
| 03 | | RAY LEWIS | 11 | 0 | THERESA STEWART |
| 04 | | SIR FRANK WHITTLE | 12 | | |
| 05 | MW | SISTER DORA | 13 | | ANTHONY NOLAN |
| 06 | | ALAN GARNER | 14 | | JIM EAMES |
| 07 | MW | BILLY WRIGHT | 15 | | AGENORIA |
| 08 | | JOSEPH CHAMBERLAIN | 16 | | GERWYN JOHN |

## CAF URBOS 3                    5-SECTION TRAMS

**Built:** 2013–14 by CAF, Zaragoza, Spain.
**Wheel Arrangement:** Bo-2-Bo.  **Traction Motors:** 8 x 65 kW.
**Dimensions:** 32.96 x 2.65 m.  **Seats:** 52.
**Doors:** Sliding plug.  **Couplers:** Albert.
**Weight:** 41.0 t.  **Maximum Speed:** 43 mph.
**Braking:** Regenerative, disc and magnetic track.

**Livery:** Network West Midlands tram livery (silver & pink).

| 17 | 21 | 25 | 29 | 33 |
|----|----|----|----|----|
| 18 | 22 | 26 | 30 | 34 |
| 19 | 23 | 27 | 31 | 35 |
| 20 | 24 | 28 | 32 | 36 |

# 6.9. SHEFFIELD SUPERTRAM

This system opened in 1994 and has three lines radiating from Sheffield City Centre. These run to Halfway in the south-east, with a spur from Gleadless Townend to Herdings Park, to Middlewood in the north with a spur from Hillsborough to Malin Bridge and to Meadowhall Interchange in the north east, adjacent to the large shopping complex. The total length is 18 miles. The system is a mixture of on-street and segregated running.

The cars are owned by South Yorkshire Light Rail Ltd, a subsidiary of South Yorkshire PTE. The operating company, South Yorkshire Supertram Ltd, is contracted to Stagecoach who operate the system as Stagecoach Supertram.

Because of severe gradients in Sheffield (up to 1 in 10) all axles are powered on the vehicles, which have low-floor outer sections.

**System:** 750 V DC overhead.          **Platform Height:** 450 mm.
**Depot & Workshops:** Nunnery.
**Standard livery:** Stagecoach (All over blue with red & orange ends).

**Non-standard/Advertising liveries:** 111 – East Midlands Trains (blue).
116 – Genting Club (black & red).
120 – Original Sheffield Corporation tram livery (cream & blue).

## SIEMENS                              3-SECTION TRAMS

**Built:** 1993–94 by Siemens, Krefeld, Germany.
**Wheel Arrangement:** B-B-B-B.
**Traction Motors:** 4 x monomotor drives of 250 kW.
**Dimensions:** 34.75 x 2.65 m.          **Seats:** 80 (6).
**Doors:** Sliding plug.                 **Couplers:** Not equipped.
**Weight:** 52 t.                        **Maximum Speed:** 50 mph.
**Braking:** Regenerative, disc and emergency track.

| | | | | | | | | | | |
|---|---|---|---|---|---|---|---|---|---|---|
| 101 | 106 | 110 | | 114 | | 118 | | 122 |
| 102 | 107 | 111 | AL | 115 | | 119 | | 123 |
| 103 | 108 | 112 | | 116 | AL | 120 | O | 124 |
| 104 | 109 | 113 | | 117 | | 121 | | 125 |
| 105 | | | | | | | | |

# 6.10. TYNE & WEAR METRO

The Tyne & Wear Metro system covers 48 route miles and can be described as the UK's first modern light rail system.

The initial network opened between 1980 and 1984, consisting of a line from South Shields via Gateshead and Newcastle Central to Bank Foot (extended to Newcastle Airport in 1991) and the North Tyneside loop (over former BR lines) serving Tynemouth and Whitley Bay with a terminus at St James. A more recent extension was from Pelaw to Sunderland and South Hylton in 2002, using existing heavy rail infrastructure between Heworth and Sunderland.

The system is owned by Nexus (the Tyne & Wear PTE) and operated by DB Regio.

**System:** 1500 V DC overhead.          **Depot & Workshops:** South Gosforth.

368          TYNE & WEAR METRO

# METRO-CAMMELL                    2-SECTION UNITS

**Built:** 1978–81 by Metropolitan Cammell, Birmingham (Prototype cars 4001 and 4002 were built by Metropolitan Cammell in 1975 and rebuilt 1984–87 by Hunslet TPL, Leeds).

A refurbishment is now taking place at Wabtec, Doncaster but this will only include 86 cars. The work commenced in 2010 and is due to be complete by late 2015. As part of this work the number of seats is reduced from 68 to 64. Refurbished cars are shown as **TW**.

**Wheel Arrangement:** B-2-B.
**Traction Motors:** 2 x Siemens of 187 kW each.
**Dimensions:** 27.80 x 2.65 m.        **Seats:** 68 (**TW** = 64).
**Doors:** Sliding plug.              **Couplers:** BSI.
**Weight:** 39.0 t.                   **Maximum Speed:** 50 mph.
**Braking:** Air/electro magnetic emergency track.

**Standard livery:** Red & yellow unless otherwise indicated.
**B** Blue & yellow.                        **G** Green & yellow.
**0 (4001)** Original 1975 Tyne & Wear Metro livery of yellow & cream.
**0 (4027)** Original North Eastern Railway style (red & white).
**TW** New Tyne & Wear Metro (grey, black & yellow).

**Advertising liveries:**

4002 – Tyne & Wear Metro (orange & black).
4038 and 4084 East Coast trains (silver).
4040 and 4083 – Emirates Airlines (red).
4045 – Newcastle International Airport – 75 years (purple).
4055 – European Regional Development Fund (blue & yellow).
4067 – Artist Alexander Millar (white & blue).
4080 – South Shields market (white).

| | | | | | | | | | | | |
|----|----|----|----|----|----|----|----|----|----|----|----|
| 4001 | O | 4016 | B | 4031 | TW | 4046 | TW | 4061 | TW | 4076 | TW |
| 4002 | AL | 4017 | TW | 4032 | | 4047 | B | 4062 | TW | 4077 | |
| 4003 | | 4018 | TW | 4033 | TW | 4048 | | 4063 | TW | 4078 | TW |
| 4004 | G | 4019 | | 4034 | TW | 4049 | TW | 4064 | | 4079 | TW |
| 4005 | | 4020 | TW | 4035 | B | 4050 | | 4065 | | 4080 | AL |
| 4006 | TW | 4021 | | 4036 | G | 4051 | G | 4066 | B | 4081 | TW |
| 4007 | | 4022 | TW | 4037 | | 4052 | TW | 4067 | AL | 4082 | TW |
| 4008 | TW | 4023 | TW | 4038 | AL | 4053 | TW | 4068 | | 4083 | AL |
| 4009 | | 4024 | B | 4039 | B | 4054 | TW | 4069 | | 4084 | AL |
| 4010 | TW | 4025 | | 4040 | AL | 4055 | AL | 4070 | | 4085 | |
| 4011 | TW | 4026 | | 4041 | TW | 4056 | | 4071 | | 4086 | |
| 4012 | | 4027 | O | 4042 | TW | 4057 | TW | 4072 | TW | 4087 | |
| 4013 | TW | 4028 | | 4043 | | 4058 | TW | 4073 | TW | 4088 | |
| 4014 | | 4029 | TW | 4044 | TW | 4059 | TW | 4074 | TW | 4089 | TW |
| 4015 | TW | 4030 | TW | 4045 | AL | 4060 | TW | 4075 | TW | 4090 | TW |

**Names (all to be removed on refurbishment):**

| | | | |
|----|----|----|----|
| 4026 | George Stephenson | 4065 | DAME Catherine Cookson |
| 4064 | Michael Campbell | 4077 | Robert Stephenson |

# 7. CODES

## 7.1. LIVERY CODES

Livery codes are used to denote the various liveries carried. It is impossible to list every livery variation which currently exists. In particular items ignored for this publication include:

- Minor colour variations.
- Omission of logos.
- All numbering, lettering and brandings.

Descriptions quoted are thus a general guide only. Logos as appropriate for each livery are normally deemed to be carried. The colour of the lower half of the bodyside is stated first.

*Code Description*

| | |
|---|---|
| **1** | "One" (metallic grey with a broad black bodyside stripe. White National Express/Greater Anglia "interim" stripe as branding). |
| **AB** | Arriva Trains Wales/Welsh Government sponsored dark blue. |
| **AG** | Arlington Fleet Services (green). |
| **AI** | Aggregate Industries (green, light grey & blue). |
| **AL** | Advertising/promotional livery (see class heading for details). |
| **AN** | Anglia Railways Class 170s (white & turquoise with blue vignette). |
| **AR** | Anglia Railways (turquoise blue with a white stripe). |
| **AV** | Arriva Trains (turquoise blue with white doors & a cream "swish"). |
| **AW** | Arriva Trains Wales/Welsh Government sponsored dark & light blue. |
| **AZ** | Advenza Freight (deep blue with green Advenza brandings). |
| **B** | BR blue. |
| **BG** | BR blue & grey lined out in white. |
| **BL** | BR Revised blue with yellow cabs, grey roof, large numbers & logo. |
| **BP** | Blue Pullman ("Nanking blue & white). |
| **CC** | BR Carmine & Cream. |
| **CD** | Cotswold Rail (silver with blue & red logo). |
| **CE** | BR Civil Engineers (yellow & grey with black cab doors & window surrounds). |
| **CH** | BR Western Region/GWR (chocolate & cream lined out in gold). |
| **CL** | Chiltern Railways Mainline Class 168 (white & silver). |
| **CM** | Chiltern Railways Mainline loco-hauled (two-tone grey & silver with blue stripes). |
| **CN** | Connex/Southeastern (white with black window surrounds & grey lower band). |
| **CR** | Chiltern Railways (blue & white with a red stripe). |
| **CS** | Colas Rail (yellow, orange & black). |
| **CU** | Corus (silver with red logos). |
| **CX** | Connex (white with yellow lower body & blue solebar). |
| **DB** | DB Schenker (Deutsche Bahn red with grey roof & solebar). |
| **DC** | Devon & Cornwall Railways (metallic silver). |
| **DG** | BR Departmental (dark grey with black cab doors & window surrounds). |
| **DR** | Direct Rail Services (dark blue with light blue or dark grey roof). |
| **DS** | Revised Direct Rail Services (dark blue, light blue & green. "Compass" logo). |

| | |
|---|---|
| **E** | English Welsh & Scottish Railway (maroon bodyside & roof with a broad gold bodyside band). |
| **EB** | Eurotunnel (two-tone grey with a broad blue stripe). |
| **EC** | East Coast (silver or grey with a purple stripe). |
| **ECR** | Euro Cargo Rail (light grey). |
| **EG** | "EWS grey" (as **F** but with large yellow & red EWS logo). |
| **EL** | Electric Traction Limited (silver & red). |
| **EP** | European Passenger Services (two-tone grey with dark blue roof). |
| **EM** | East Midlands Trains {Connect} (blue with red & orange swish at unit ends). |
| **ER** | Revised Eurostar (deep blue & two-tone grey). |
| **EU** | Eurostar (white with dark blue & yellow stripes). |
| **EX** | Europhoenix (silver, blue & red). |
| **F** | BR Trainload Freight (two-tone grey with black cab doors & window surrounds. Various logos). |
| **FA** | Fastline Freight (grey & black with white & orange stripes). |
| **FB** | First Group dark blue. |
| **FD** | First Great Western & First Hull Trains "Dynamic Lines" (dark blue with thin multi-coloured lines on the lower bodyside). |
| **FE** | Railfreight Distribution International (two tone-grey with black cab doors & dark blue roof). |
| **FER** | Fertis (light grey with a dark grey roof & solebar). |
| **FF** | Freightliner grey (two-tone grey with black cab doors & window surrounds. Freightliner logo). |
| **FG** | First Group InterCity (indigo blue with a white roof & gold, pink & white stripes). |
| **FH** | Revised Freightliner {PowerHaul} (dark green with yellow cab ends & grey stripe/buffer beam). |
| **FI** | First Great Western "Local Lines" DMU (varying blue with local visitor attractions applied to the lower bodyside). |
| **FL** | Freightliner (dark green with yellow cabs). |
| **FP** | Old First Great Western (green & ivory with thin green & gold stripes). |
| **FO** | BR Railfreight (grey bodysides, yellow cabs & red lower bodyside stripe, large BR logo). |
| **FR** | Fragonset Railways (black with silver roof & a red bodyside band lined out in white). |
| **FS** | First Group (indigo blue with pink & white stripes). |
| **FT** | First TransPennine Express "Dynamic Lines" (varying blue with thin multi-coloured lines on the lower bodyside). |
| **FU** | First Group "Urban Lights" (varying blue or uniform indigo blue with pink, white & blue markings on the lower bodyside). |
| **FY** | Foster Yeoman (blue & silver. Cast numberplates). |
| **G**[1] | BR Green (plain green, with white stripe on main line locomotives). |
| **G**[2] | BR Southern Region/SR or BR DMU green. |
| **GA** | Greater Anglia (white with red doors). |
| **GB** | GB Railfreight (blue with orange cantrail & solebar stripes, orange cabs). |
| **GC** | Grand Central (all over black with an orange stripe). |
| **GG** | BR two-tone green. |
| **GIF** | GIF (Spain) (light blue with a dark blue band). |
| **GL** | First Great Western locomotives (green with a gold stripe). |
| **GN** | Great North Eastern Railway {modified} (dark blue with a white stripe). |
| **GS** | Royal Scotsman maroon. |

**GV**   Gatwick Express EMU (red, white & indigo blue with mauve & blue doors).
**GW**   Great Western Railway (green, lined out in black & orange).
**GX**   Gatwick Express InterCity (dark grey/white/burgundy/white).
**GY**   Eurotunnel (grey & yellow).
**HA**   Hanson Quarry Products (dark blue/silver with oxide red roof).
**HB**   HSBC Rail (Oxford blue & white).
**HC**   Heathrow Connect (grey with a broad deep blue bodyside band & orange doors).
**HE**   Heathrow Express (silver with purple doors and black window surrounds).
**HN**   Harry Needle Railroad Company (orange with a black roof and solebar).
**IC**   BR InterCity (dark grey/white/red/white).
**K**   Black.
**LH**   BR Loadhaul (black with orange cabsides).
**LM**   London Midland (white/grey & green with broad black stripe around the windows).
**LN**   LNER Tourist (green & cream).
**LO**   London Overground (all over white with a blue solebar & black window surrounds).
**LT**   London Transport maroon & cream.
**M**   BR maroon (maroon lined out in straw & black).
**MA**   Maintrain/East Midlands Trains blue.
**ME**   Merseyrail (metallic silver with yellow doors).
**ML**   BR Mainline Freight (aircraft blue with a silver stripe).
**MN**   Midland Mainline (thin tangerine stripe on the lower bodyside, ocean blue, grey & white).
**MT**   GB Railfreight Metronet (blue with orange cabsides).
**N**   BR Network SouthEast (white & blue with red lower bodyside stripe, grey solebar & cab ends).
**NC**   National Express White (white with blue doors).
**NO**   Northern (deep blue, purple & white). Some units have area-specific promotional vinyls (see class headings for details).
**NR**   Network Rail (blue with a red stripe).
**NX**   National Express (white with grey ends).
**O**   Non-standard (see class heading for details).
**P**   Porterbrook Leasing Company (white or grey & purple).
**PB**   Porterbrook Leasing Company blue.
**PC**   Pullman Car Company (umber & cream with gold lettering lined out in gold).
**RG**   BR Parcels (dark grey & red).
**RK**   Railtrack (green & blue).
**RM**   Royal Mail (red with yellow stripes above solebar).
**RP**   Royal Train (claret, lined out in red & black).
**RR**   Regional Railways (dark blue & grey with light blue & white stripes, three narrow dark blue stripes at vehicle ends).
**RS**   RMS Locotec blue.
**RV**   Riviera Trains (Oxford blue & cream lined out in gold {blue only for locos}).
**RX**   Rail Express Systems (dark grey & red with or without blue markings).
**RZ**   Royal Train revised (plain claret, no lining).
**SB**   Southeastern High Speed (all over blue with black window surrounds).
**SC**   Strathclyde PTE (carmine & cream lined out in black & gold).
**SD**   South West Trains outer suburban {Class 450 style} (deep blue with red doors & orange & red cab sides).

| | |
|---|---|
| **SE** | Southeastern (all over white with black window surrounds, light blue doors and (on some units) dark blue lower bodyside stripe). |
| **SP** | Strathclyde PTE {revised} (carmine & cream, with a turquoise stripe). |
| **SN** | Southern (white & dark green with light green semi-circles at one end of each vehicle. Light grey band at solebar level). |
| **SR** | ScotRail – Scotland's Railways (dark blue with Scottish Saltire flag & white/light blue flashes). |
| **SS** | South West Trains inner suburban {Class 455 style} (red with blue & orange flashes at unit ends). |
| **ST** | Stagecoach {long-distance stock} (white & dark blue with dark blue window surrounds and red & orange swishes at unit ends). |
| **TL** | New Thameslink (light grey & white with bluee doors). |
| **TT** | Transmart Trains (all over green). |
| **U** | White or grey undercoat. |
| **V** | Virgin Trains (red with black doors extending into bodysides, three white lower bodysides stripes). |
| **VP** | Virgin Trains shunters (black with a large black & white chequered flag on the bodyside). |
| **VN** | Northern Belle (crimson lake & cream lined out in gold). |
| **VT** | Virgin Trains silver (silver, with black window surrounds, white cantrail stripe & red roof. Red swept down at unit ends). |
| **WA** | Wabtec Rail (black). |
| **WC** | West Coast Railway Company maroon. |
| **XC** | CrossCountry (two-tone silver with deep crimson ends & pink doors). |
| **Y** | Network Rail yellow. |
| **YR** | West Yorkshire PTE/Northern EMUs (red, lilac & grey). |

# 7.2. OWNER CODES

The following codes are used to define the ownership details of the locomotives or rolling stock listed in this book. Codes shown indicate either the legal owner or "responsible custodian" of each vehicle.

| | |
|---|---|
| 20 | Class 20189 |
| 40 | Class 40 Preservation Society |
| 47 | Stratford 47 Group |
| 50 | Class 50 Alliance |
| 56 | Class 56 Locomotives |
| 62 | The Princess Royal Class Locomotive Trust |
| 70 | 7029 Clun Castle |
| 71 | 71A Locomotives |
| 2L | Class 20 Locomotive Society |
| A | Angel Trains |
| AI | Aggregate Industries |
| AM | Alstom |
| AV | Arriva UK Trains |
| BA | British American Railway Services |
| BB | Balfour Beatty Rail Infrastructure Services |
| BK | The Scottish Railway Preservation Society |
| BN | Beacon Rail Leasing |
| BT | Bombardier Transportation UK |

| | |
|---|---|
| BY | Bridgeway Railcare |
| CR | The Chiltern Railway Company |
| CS | Colas Rail |
| DB | DB Schenker Rail (UK) |
| DP | Deltic Preservation Society |
| DR | Direct Rail Services |
| DT | The Diesel Traction Group |
| E | Eversholt Rail (UK) |
| EL | Electric Traction Limited |
| EM | East Midlands Trains |
| EP | Europhoenix |
| ET | Eurotunnel |
| EU | Eurostar (UK) |
| FC | First Capital Connect |
| FG | First Group |
| FL | Freightliner |
| FW | First Great Western (assets of the Greater Western franchise) |
| GB | GB Railfreight |
| GL | GE Capital |
| H1 | Network Rail (High Speed) |
| HA | Hanson Group |
| HB | HBOS |
| HD | Hastings Diesels |
| HE | British Airports Authority |
| HJ | Howard Johnston |
| HN | Harry Needle Railroad Company |
| JH | Jeremy Hosking Locomotive Services |
| LM | London Midland |
| MG | Mid Glamorgan County Council |
| MQ | Macquarie Group |
| MW | Beaver Sports (Yorkshire) |
| NM | National Museum of Science & Industry |
| NR | Network Rail |
| NS | Nemesis Rail |
| NY | North Yorkshire Moors Railway Enterprises |
| OE | Orient Express Hotels |
| P | Porterbrook Leasing Company |
| PO | Other owner |
| PP | Peter Pan Locomotive Company |
| QW | QW Rail Leasing |
| RA | Railfilms |
| RE | Railway Vehicle Engineering |
| RL | Rail Management Services (trading as RMS Locotec) |
| RM | Royal Mail |
| RP | Rampart Engineering |
| RV | Riviera Trains |
| SB | SNCB/NMBS (Société Nationale des Chemins de fer Belges/ Nationale Maatschappij der Belgische Spoorwegen) |
| SF | SNCF (Société Nationale des Chemins de fer Français) |
| SG | South Glamorgan County Council |
| SI | Speno International |

| | |
|---|---|
| SK | Swietelsky Babcock Rail |
| SM | Siemens Transportation |
| SR | ScotRail |
| SN | Southern |
| SW | South West Trains |
| TT | Transmart Trains |
| UR | UK Rail Leasing |
| VI | Virgin Trains |
| VL | Voyager Leasing (Lloyds Banking Group/Angel Trains) |
| VO | VolkerRail |
| VT | Vintage Trains |
| WA | Wabtec Rail Group |
| WC | West Coast Railway Company |
| X | Sold for scrap/further use and awaiting collection |

# 7.3. LOCOMOTIVE POOL CODES

Locomotives are split into operational groups ("pools") for diagramming and maintenance purposes. The official codes used to denote these pools are shown in this publication.

| | |
|---|---|
| ACAC | Electric Traction Limited locomotives. |
| ACXX | Electric Traction Limited locomotives for static depot use. |
| ATLO | Alstom Class 08. |
| AWCA | West Coast Railway Company operational locomotives. |
| AWCX | West Coast Railway Company stored locomotives. |
| CFOL | Class 50 Operations locomotives. |
| COFS | Colas Rail Class 56. |
| COLO | Colas Rail Class 47 and 66. |
| COLS | Colas Rail stored locomotives. |
| DFGC | Freightliner Intermodal Class 86/5. |
| DFGH | Freightliner Heavy Haul Class 70. |
| DFGI | Freightliner Intermodal Class 70. |
| DFGM | Freightliner Intermodal Class 66. |
| DFHG | Freightliner Heavy Haul low emission Class 66. |
| DFHH | Freightliner Heavy Haul Class 66. |
| DFIM | Freightliner Intermodal modified Class 66. |
| DFIN | Freightliner Intermodal low emission Class 66. |
| DFLC | Freightliner Intermodal Class 90. |
| DFLH | Freightliner Heavy Haul Class 47. |
| DFLS | Freightliner Class 08. |
| DFNC | Freightliner Intermodal Class 86/6. |
| DHLT | Freightliner locomotives awaiting maintenance/repair/disposal. |
| EFOO | First Great Western Class 57. |
| EFPC | First Great Western Class 43. |
| EFSH | First Great Western Class 08. |
| EHPC | CrossCountry Class 43. |
| EJLO | London Midland Class 08. |
| ELRD | East Lancashire Railway-based main line registered locomotives. |
| EMPC | East Midlands Trains Class 43. |
| EMSL | East Midlands Trains Class 08. |

| EPEX | Europhoenix locomotives for export. |
|------|-------------------------------------|
| EPUK | Europhoenix UK locomotives. |
| ETLO | Electric Traction Limited Class 87. |
| GBBR | GB Railfreight Class 73/9. |
| GBCM | GB Railfreight Class 66. General. |
| GBDR | GB Railfreight Class 66. Locomotives from Germany. |
| GBED | GB Railfreight Class 73. |
| GBEE | GB Railfreight Class 20. On hire from Harry Needle/Class 20189. |
| GBET | GB Railfreight Class 92. |
| GBFM | GB Railfreight Class 66. RETB fitted. |
| GBNL | GB Railfreight Class 66. Locomotives from the Netherlands. |
| GBRT | GB Railfreight Class 66. Network Rail duties. |
| GBSD | GB Railfreight Class 66. |
| GBWM | GB Railfreight Class 08/09. |
| GCHP | Grand Central Class 43. |
| GPSS | Eurostar (UK) Class 08. |
| HBSH | Wabtec hire shunting locomotives. |
| HNRL | Harry Needle Railroad Company hire locomotives. |
| HNRS | Harry Needle Railroad Company stored locomotives. |
| HTLX | British American Railway Services locomotives. |
| HWSU | Southern Class 09. |
| HYWD | South West Trains Class 73. |
| IANA | Greater Anglia Class 90. |
| IECA | East Coast Class 91. |
| IECP | East Coast Class 43. |
| MBDL | Non TOC-owned diesel locomotives. |
| MBED | Non TOC-owned electro-diesel locomotives. |
| MBEL | Non TOC-owned electric locomotives. |
| MRSO | RMS Locotec Class 08. |
| NRLO | Nemesis Rail locomotives. |
| PTXX | GB Railfreight Class 92 (stored). |
| QACL | Network Rail Class 86. |
| QADD | Network Rail diesel locomotives. |
| QCAR | Network Rail New Measurement Train Class 43. |
| QETS | Network Rail Class 37. |
| RFSH | Wabtec Rail locomotives. |
| RTLO | Riviera Trains Class 47. |
| RVLO | Rail Vehicle Engineering locomotives. |
| WAAC | DB Schenker Class 67. |
| WABC | DB Schenker Class 67. RETB fitted. |
| WACC | DB Schenker Class 67 for hire to Chiltern Railways. |
| WAWC | DB Schenker Class 67 for hire to Arriva Trains Wales. |
| WBAT | DB Schenker Class 66. |
| WBBT | DB Schenker Class 66. RETB fitted. |
| WBLT | DB Schenker Industrial Class 66. Dedicated locomotives for Lickey Incline banking duties. |
| WCAT | DB Schenker Class 60. |
| WCBT | DB Schenker Class 60. Extended-range fuel tanks. |
| WDAM | DB Schenker Class 59. |
| WEAC | DB Schenker Class 90. |
| WEDC | DB Schenker Class 90 for hire to DRS. |

| | |
|---|---|
| WFAC | DB Schenker Class 92. |
| WFBC | DB Schenker Class 92 with commissioned TVM430 cab signalling equipment for use on High Speed 1. |
| WFCC | DB Schenker Class 92 for hire to DRS. |
| WFDC | DB Schenker Class 92 for hire to DRS with commissioned TVM430 cab signalling equipment for use on High Speed 1. |
| WQAA | DB Schenker stored locomotives Group 1A (short-term maintenance). |
| WQAB | DB Schenker stored locomotives Group 1B. |
| WQBA | DB Schenker stored locomotives Group 2 (unserviceable). |
| WQCA | DB Schenker stored locomotives Group 3 (unserviceable). |
| WQDA | DB Schenker stored locomotives Group 4 (awaiting disposal). |
| WSGC | DB Schenker Class 08/09. GSMR fitted. |
| WSRC | DB Schenker Class 08/09. Remote control fitted. |
| WSXX | DB Schenker Class 08. Internal/depot use. |
| WSSC | DB Schenker Class 08/09. |
| XHAC | Direct Rail Services Classes 37/4 and 47. |
| XHCK | Direct Rail Services Class 57/0. |
| XHHP | Direct Rail Services locomotives – holding pool. |
| XHIM | Direct Rail Services locomotives – Intermodal traffic. |
| XHNB | Direct Rail Services Class 47 for use on the Northern Belle. |
| XHNC | Direct Rail Services locomotives – nuclear traffic/general. |
| XHSS | Direct Rail Services stored locomotives. |
| XHVE | Direct Rail Services Class 68. |
| XHVT | Direct Rail Services Class 57/3 for hire to Virgin Trains. |
| XYPA | Mendip Rail Class 59/1. |
| XYPO | Mendip Rail Class 59/0. |

## 7.4. OPERATOR CODES

Operator codes are used to denote the organisation that facilitates the use of that vehicle, and may not be the actual Train Operating Company which runs the train. Where no operator code is shown, vehicles are currently not in use.

| | |
|---|---|
| *62* | The Princess Royal Class Locomotive Trust |
| *AW* | Arriva Trains Wales |
| *BK* | The Scottish Railway Preservation Society |
| *BP* | British Pullman (Orient Express Hotels) |
| *C2* | c2c |
| *CR* | Chiltern Railways |
| *CS* | Colas Rail |
| *DB* | DB Schenker |
| *DR* | Direct Rail Services |
| *EC* | East Coast |
| *EM* | East Midlands Trains |
| *EU* | Eurostar (UK) |
| *FC* | First Capital Connect |
| *GA* | Greater Anglia |
| *GB* | GB Railfreight |
| *GC* | Grand Central |
| *GW* | First Great Western |
| *HC* | Heathrow Connect |
| *HD* | Hastings Diesels |
| *HE* | Heathrow Express |
| *HT* | First Hull Trains |
| *LO* | London Overground |
| *LM* | London Midland |
| *ME* | Merseyrail |
| *NB* | Northern Belle (Orient Express Hotels) |
| *NO* | Northern |
| *NY* | North Yorkshire Moors Railway |
| *RP* | Royal Train |
| *RS* | The Royal Scotsman (Orient Express Hotels) |
| *RV* | Riviera Trains |
| *SE* | Southeastern |
| *SN* | Southern |
| *SR* | ScotRail |
| *ST* | Statesman Rail |
| *SW* | South West Trains |
| *TP* | TransPennine Express |
| *VT* | Vintage Trains |
| *VW* | Virgin Trains |
| *WC* | West Coast Railway Company |
| *XC* | CrossCountry |

## 7.5. ALLOCATION & LOCATION CODES

Allocation codes are used in this publication to denote the normal maintenance base ("depots") of each operational locomotive, multiple unit or coach. However, maintenance may be carried out at other locations and may also be carried out by mobile maintenance teams.

Location codes are used to denote common storage locations whilst the full place name is used for other locations. The designation (S) denotes stored.

| Code | Depot | Operator |
|------|-------|----------|
| AD | Ashford (Kent) | Hitachi |
| AF | Ashford Chart Leacon Works (Kent) | Bombardier Transportation |
| AK | Ardwick (Manchester) | Siemens |
| AL | Aylesbury | Chiltern Railways |
| AN | Allerton (Liverpool) | Northern |
| BA | Basford Hall Yard (Crewe) | Freightliner |
| BD | Birkenhead North | Merseyrail |
| BF | Bedford Cauldwell Walk | First Capital Connect |
| BH | Barrow Hill (Chesterfield) | Barrow Hill Engine Shed Society |
| BI | Brighton Lovers Walk | Southern |
| BL* | Shackerstone, Battlefield Line | *Storage location only* |
| BM | Bournemouth | South West Trains |
| BN | Bounds Green (London) | East Coast |
| BO | Burton-upon-Trent | Nemesis Rail |
| BQ | Bury (Greater Manchester) | East Lancashire Rly/Riley & Son (Railways) |
| BS | Bescot (Walsall) | DB Schenker Rail (UK) |
| BT | Bo'ness (West Lothian) | The Bo'ness & Kinneil Railway |
| BY | Bletchley | London Midland |
| BZ | St Blazey (Par) | *Storage location only* |
| CD | Crewe Diesel/Down Holding Sdgs | DB Schenker Rail (UK)/Riviera Trains |
| CE | Crewe International | DB Schenker Rail (UK) |
| CF | Cardiff Canton | Arriva Trains Wales/Colas Rail |
| CH | Chester | Alstom |
| CK | Corkerhill (Glasgow) | ScotRail |
| CM | East Cranmore | Cranmore Traincare |
| CO | Coquelles (France) | Eurotunnel |
| CP | Crewe Carriage | LNWR (part of Arriva) |
| CQ | Crewe Heritage Centre | LNWR Heritage Company |
| CR | Crewe Gresty Bridge | Direct Rail Services |
| CS | Carnforth | West Coast Railway Company |
| CZ | Central Rivers (Barton-under-Needwood) | Bombardier Transportation |
| DR | Doncaster | DB Schenker Rail (UK) |
| DY | Derby Etches Park | East Midlands Trains |
| EC | Edinburgh Craigentinny | East Coast |
| EH | Eastleigh | LNWR (part of Arriva) |
| EM | East Ham (London) | c2c |
| EX | Exeter | First Great Western |
| FF | Forest (Brussels) | SNCB/NMBS |
| GW | Glasgow Shields Road | ScotRail |
| HA | Haymarket (Edinburgh) | ScotRail |

| HE | Hornsey (London) | First Capital Connect |
|----|------------------|----------------------|
| HT | Heaton (Newcastle) | Northern |
| IL | Ilford (London) | Greater Anglia |
| IS | Inverness | ScotRail |
| KM | Carlisle Kingmoor | Direct Rail Services |
| KR | Kidderminster | Severn Valley Railway |
| LA | Laira (Plymouth) | First Great Western |
| LB | Loughborough Works | Wabtec Rail |
| LD | Leeds Midland Road | Freightliner Engineering |
| LE | Landore (Swansea) | First Great Western |
| LG | Longsight (Manchester) | Northern |
| LM | Long Marston (Warwickshire) | Motorail Logistics |
| LR | Leicester | UK Rail Leasing |
| LY | Le Landy (Paris) | SNCF |
| MA | Alstom Longsight (Manchester) | Alstom |
| MD | Merehead | Mendip Rail |
| ME | Mossend Yard | DB Schenker Rail (UK) |
| MI* | Minehead | West Somerset Railway |
| MH | Millerhill (Edinburgh) | DB Schenker Rail (UK) |
| MN | Machynlleth | Arriva Trains Wales |
| NC | Norwich Crown Point | Greater Anglia |
| NG | New Cross Gate (London) | London Overground |
| NH | Newton Heath (Manchester) | Northern |
| NL | Neville Hill (Leeds) | East Midlands Trains/Northern |
| NM | Nottingham Eastcroft | East Midlands Trains |
| NN | Northampton King's Heath | Siemens |
| NT | Northam (Southampton) | Siemens |
| NY | Grosmont (North Yorkshire) | North Yorkshire Moors Railway |
| OH | Old Oak Common Heathrow | Heathrow Express |
| OO | Old Oak Common HST | First Great Western |
| PG | Peterborough | GB Railfreight |
| PM | St Philip's Marsh (Bristol) | First Great Western |
| PZ | Penzance Long Rock | First Great Western |
| RG | Reading | First Great Western |
| RM | Ramsgate | Southeastern |
| RU | Rugby | Colas Rail |
| RY | Ryde (Isle of Wight) | South West Trains |
| SA | Salisbury | South West Trains |
| SE | St Leonards (Hastings) | St Leonards Railway Engineering |
| SG | Slade Green (London) | Southeastern |
| SH | Southall (London) | Jeremy Hosking Locomotive Services |
| SJ* | Stourbridge Junction | Parry People Movers |
| SK | Swanwick Junction (Derbyshire) | Midland Railway-Butterley |
| SL | Stewarts Lane (London) | Southern/Orient Express Hotels |
| SO | Soho (Birmingham) | London Midland |
| SP | Spings Branch (Wigan) | DB Schenker Rail (UK) |
| SU | Selhurst (Croydon) | Southern |
| TI | Temple Mills (London) | Eurostar (UK) |
| TJ | Tavistock Junction Yard (Plymouth) | *Storage location only* |
| TM | Tyseley Locomotive Works | Birmingham Railway Museum |
| TN | Thornton (Fife) | John Cameron |

| TO | Toton (Nottinghamshire) | DB Schenker Rail (UK) |
| TS | Tyseley (Birmingham) | London Midland |
| TW* | Tonbridge West Yard | GB Railfreight |
| TY | Tyne Yard (Newcastle) | DB Schenker Rail (UK) |
| WB | Wembley (London) | Alstom |
| WD | Wimbledon (London) | South West Trains |
| WE | Willesden Brent sidings | *Storage location only* |
| WH* | Washwood Heath (Birmingham) | Boden Rail Engineering/RMS Locotec |
| WN | Willesden (London) | London Overground |
| WO* | Wolsingham, Weardale Railway | RMS Locotec |
| WR* | Willesden Railnet PRDC | Royal Mail |
| XW | Crofton (Wakefield) | Bombardier Transportation |
| YK | National Railway Museum (York) | National Museum of Science & Industry |
| ZA | RTC Business Park (Derby) | Railway Vehicle Engineering |
| ZB | Doncaster Works | Wabtec Rail |
| ZC | Crewe Works | Bombardier Transportation |
| ZD | Derby Works | Bombardier Transportation |
| ZG | Eastleigh Works | Arlington Fleet Services |
| ZH | Springburn Depot (Glasgow) | Knorr-Bremse Rail Systems UK |
| ZI | Ilford Works | Bombardier Transportation |
| ZJ | Stoke-on-Trent Works | Axiom Rail |
| ZK | Kilmarnock Works | Wabtec Rail Scotland |
| ZN | Wolverton Works | Knorr-Bremse Rail Systems UK |
| ZR | York (Holgate Works) | Network Rail |

* unofficial code.

# 7.6. ABBREVIATIONS

**The following general abbreviations are used in this book:**

| | |
|---|---|
| AC | Alternating Current (ie Overhead supply) |
| AFD | Air Force Department |
| BAA | British Airports Authority |
| BR | British Railways |
| BSI | Bergische Stahl Industrie |
| CRDC | Component Recovery & Disposal Centre |
| C&W | Carriage & Wagon |
| DC | Direct Current (ie Third Rail) |
| DEMU | Diesel Electric Multiple Unit |
| DERA | Defence Evaluation & Research Agency |
| DfT | Department for Transport |
| Dia | Diagram number |
| DMU | Diesel Multiple Unit (general term) |
| DSDC | Defence Storage & Distribution Centre |
| DRS | Direct Rail Services |
| EMU | Electric Multiple Unit (general term) |
| GWR | Great Western Railway |
| FLT | Freightliner Terminal |
| H-B | Hunslet-Barclay |
| hp | Horse power |
| HNRC | Harry Needle Railroad Company |
| Hz | Hertz |
| kN | Kilonewtons |
| km/h | Kilometres per hour |
| kW | Kilowatts |
| lbf | Pounds force |
| LT | London Transport |
| LUL | London Underground Limited |
| m | Metres |
| mm | Millimetres |
| mph | Miles per hour |
| NPCCS | Non Passenger Carrying Coaching Stock |
| PTE | Passenger Transport Executive |
| RCH | Railway Clearing House |
| rpm | Revolutions per minute |
| RR | Rolls Royce |
| RSL | Rolling Stock Library |
| SR | BR Southern Region and Southern Railway |
| t | Tonnes |
| T | Toilet |
| TD | Toilet suitable for disabled passengers |
| TDM | Time Division Multiplex |
| TOPS | Total Operations Processing System |
| V | Volts |
| W | Wheelchair space |

# 7.7 BUILDERS

These are shown in class headings. The workshops of British Railways and the pre-nationalisation and pre-grouping companies were first transferred to a wholly-owned subsidiary called "British Rail Engineering Ltd", abbreviated to BREL. These workshops were later privatised, BREL then becoming "BREL Ltd". Some of the works were then taken over by ABB, which was later merged with Daimler-Benz Transportation to become "Adtranz". This company has now been taken over by Bombardier Transportation, which had taken over Procor at Horbury previously. Bombardier also builds vehicles for the British market in Brugge, Belgium.

Other workshops were the subject of separate sales, Springburn, Glasgow and Wolverton becoming "Railcare" and Eastleigh becoming "Wessex Traincare". All three were sold to GEC-Alsthom (now Alstom) but Eastleigh Works closed in 2006, although the site is now used as a storage and refurbishment location.

Part of Doncaster works was sold to RFS Engineering, which became insolvent and was bought out and renamed RFS Industries. This is now part of Wabtec Rail Group.

The builder details in the class headings show the owner at the time of vehicle construction followed by the works as follows:

| | |
|---|---|
| Ashford | Ashford Works (now Ashford Rail Plant depot). This is not the same location as the current Bombardier Ashford depot (at Chart Leacon). |
| Birmingham | The former Metro-Cammell works at Saltley, Birmingham. |
| Cowlairs | Cowlairs Works, Glasgow. |
| Derby | Derby Carriage Works (also known as Litchurch Lane). |
| Doncaster | Doncaster Works. |
| Eastleigh | Eastleigh Works |
| Swindon | Swindon Works. |
| Wolverton | Wolverton Works. |
| York | York Carriage Works. |

Other builders are:

| | |
|---|---|
| Alexander | Walter Alexander, Falkirk. |
| Barclay | Andrew Barclay, Caledonia Works, Kilmarnock (now Wabtec Rail Scotland). |
| BRCW | Birmingham Railway Carriage & Wagon, Smethwick. |
| CAF | Construcciones y Auxiliar de Ferrocarriles, Zaragosa, Spain. |
| Cravens | Cravens, Sheffield. |
| Gloucester | Gloucester Railway Carriage & Wagon, Gloucester. |
| Hunslet-Barclay | Hunslet-Barclay, Caledonia Works, Kilmarnock (now Wabtec Rail Scotland). |
| Hunslet TPL | Hunslet Transportation Projects, Leeds. |
| Lancing | SR, Lancing Works. |
| Leyland Bus | Leyland Bus, Workington. |
| Metro-Cammell | Metropolitan-Cammell, Saltley, Birmingham |
| Pressed Steel | Pressed Steel, Linwood. |
| Charles Roberts | Charles Roberts, Horbury Junction, Wakefield. |
| SGP | Simmering-Graz-Pauker, Austria (now owned by Siemens). |
| Siemens | Siemens Transportation Systems (works in Germany (Krefeld), Austria (Vienna) and the Czech Republic (Prague). |
| SRP | Specialist Rail Products Ltd (A subsidiary of RFS). |